Nonverbal Communication
in Human Interaction FOURTH EDITION

Nonverbal Communication in Human Interaction FOURTH EDITION

Mark L. Knapp
University of Texas at Austin

Judith A. Hall
Northeastern University

Harcourt Brace College Publishers
Fort Worth Philadelphia San Diego New York Orlando Austin San Antonio
Toronto Montreal London Sydney Tokyo

Publisher	Christopher P. Klein
Senior Acquisitions Editor	Carol Wada
Developmental Editor	Cathlynn Richard
Project Editor	Kathryn Stewart
Production Manager	Lois F. West
Art Director	David A. Day

Cover Image   © The Image Bank/White/Packert

Literary Credits   "Something" (p. 30) by George Harrison, Copyright © 1969 HARRISONGS, LTD. International Copyright Secured. All rights reserved.

Supplements: Harcourt Brace & Company may provide complimentary instructional aids and supplements or supplement packages to those adopters qualified under our adoption policy. Please contact your sales representative for more information. If as an adopter or potential user you receive supplements you do not need, please return them to your sales representative or send them to: Attn: Returns Department, Troy Warehouse, 465 South Lincoln Drive, Troy, MO 63379.

Address for Editorial Correspondence: Harcourt Brace College Publishers, 301 Commerce Street, Suite 3700, Fort Worth, TX 76102

Address for Orders: Harcourt Brace College Publishers, 6277 Sea Harbor Drive, Orlando, FL 32887 1-800-782-4479 or 1-800-433-0001 (in Florida)

ISBN: 0-03-018023-6

Library of Congress Catalog Card Number: 96-78487

Printed in the United States of America

9 0 1 2 3 4 5   039   9 8 7 6 5

PREFACE

Normally, the last thing authors do in a preface is to thank those who have been instrumental in the development of their book. We'd like to depart from that tradition somewhat by starting with our heartfelt thanks to the thousands of students and instructors who have used and provided feedback during the past twenty-five years. More than anyone else, you are responsible for the longevity of this book. With this in mind, we undertook this fourth edition by putting what we believe to be instructor and student needs at the forefront of our writing. As with previous editions, we encourage you to let us know whether or not we have succeeded.

This edition, like the last, is coauthored. One of us represents the field of communication and the other social psychology. This collaboration, which requires the blending of two distinct perspectives, is symbolic of the nonverbal literature we report in this volume. The theory and research addressing nonverbal phenomena comes from scholars with a wide variety of academic backgrounds and perspectives—for example, communication, counseling, psychology, psychiatry, linguistics, sociology, management, speech, and others. Understanding the nature of nonverbal communication is truly an interdisciplinary enterprise.

In revising this book, we retained the features that students and instructors valued from the previous edition while changing other things that we expect will improve the book. Since the visual dimension is so crucial to much of our nonverbal understandings, we have increased the photographs and drawings used to illustrate nonverbal actions. And, as in every new edition, we have incorporated the most recent theory and research while retaining definitive studies from the past. As in past editions, extensive bibliographies follow each chapter, and we have tried to retain a writing style that is scientifically accurate as well as interesting to the reader. We are honored that our book serves as both a textbook and a reference work. With superb guidance from Rhonda Sprague, a revitalized Instructor's Manual provides the information and imagination necessary for effective classroom learning in nonverbal communication.

The book is divided into five parts. Part I introduces the reader to some *fundamental ideas* and addresses the following questions: What is nonverbal communication? How do verbal and nonverbal communication interrelate? What difference does a knowledge of nonverbal communication make to your everyday life? Are some people more skilled than others at communicating nonverbally? How did they get that way? With this general perspective in mind, Parts II, III, and IV take the reader through the nonverbal elements involved in any interaction: *the environment* within which the interaction occurs; *the physical features of the two interactants* themselves; and *their behavior* (gestures, touching, facial expressions, eye gazing, and vocal sounds). Part V concludes with a chapter focused on how all these separate parts of an interaction combine as we seek to accomplish very common goals in daily life—for example, communicating who we are, communicating closeness and distance, and communicating varying degrees of status and/or power; deceiving others; and effectively managing the back-and-forth flow of conversation itself. Throughout the book we repeatedly point out how all interactants involved are likely to play a role in whatever behavior is displayed by a single individual—even though this perspective is not always adequately developed in the research we review.

For twenty-five years, thousands of readers have been exposed to the last page of this book (the toilet paper photograph). Scores of students from all parts of the United States have written letters inquiring about it and commenting on it. Needless to say, their ideas were interesting. In an effort to clarify things, we published the story behind this picture in the last edition and we repeat it here. As the first edition of this book was going to the publisher, the first author was reminded of a photo that appeared at the end of another book. It was a picture of a fencelike barrier at the end of a road that was under construction, and it was used to communicate the end of the book, *Nonverbal Communication: Notes on the Visual Perception of Human Relations*—the first book to use the word "nonverbal" in its title. In an attempt to improve upon this same idea, the first author wanted to communicate to readers that even though this was the end of one learning experience (represented by the empty toilet roll), there were other experiences ahead if the learner would take the initiative (represented by the full roll of paper waiting to be placed on the wooden dowel). This photo has become one of (if not *the*) most talked about features of the book. Needless to say, not many readers interpreted the photo the way it was intended. Sometimes nonverbal messages are much clearer when accompanied by verbalizations. We hope the preceding explanation does that.

Each of us has our own special thank you's associated with the development of this edition of the book. Gratitude is extended to the following reviewers for their input during the development of this edition: Jean Civikly, University of New Mexico; Susan Collie, Winona State University; Ronna Liggett, University of Nevada at Reno; John W. Staas, Monroe County Community College; and Todd Thomas, Indiana University. Collaborating on a writing project is filled with potential difficulties, but in the view of the first author, Judy Hall is the dream-come-true coauthor. The influence on this project of her unflagging dedication, insightful observations, attention to detail, and her effectiveness as a communicator has been immense. The second author feels the same way about the first author and is extremely grateful for the opportunity to work with him and learn even more about nonverbal communication. Both of us would like to acknowledge Kathryn Stewart and Cathy Richard at Harcourt Brace whose ability to effectively produce a book is only exceeded by their ability to make uneasy authors feel at ease. Many thanks.

M. L. Knapp, Austin, Texas
J. A. H., Boston, Massachusetts

CONTENTS

committee was established to decide whether deceit tainted Hans's performances. Professors of psychology and physiology, the director of the Berlin Zoological Garden, a director of a circus, veterinarians, and cavalry officers were appointed to this commission. An experiment with Hans from which von Osten was absent demonstrated no change in the apparent intelligence of the horse. This was sufficient proof for the commission to announce that no trickery was involved.

The appointment of a second commission was the beginning of the end for Clever Hans. Von Osten was asked to whisper a number into the horse's left ear while another experimenter whispered a number into the horse's right ear. Hans was told to add the two numbers—an answer none of the onlookers, von Osten, nor the experimenter knew. Hans failed. And with further tests, he continued to fail. The experimenter, Pfungst, had discovered that Hans could answer a question only if someone in his visual field knew the answer and was attentive to the situation (Pfungst, 1911/1965).

When Hans was given the question, onlookers who knew the answer assumed an expectant posture, increased their body tension, and bent their heads slightly forward. When Hans reached the correct number of taps, the onlookers would relax and make a slight movement of their heads—which was Hans's signal to stop tapping. Evidence suggests that Hans could detect head movements as slight as one-fifth of a millimeter. Subsequent experiments found that Hans also would cease tapping as a knowledgeable onlooker raised his or her eyebrows or even showed a dilation of the nostrils.

The story of Clever Hans functions as a vivid introduction to the field of nonverbal communication (Sebeok & Rosenthal, 1981; Sebeok & Umiker-Sebeok, 1980). Hans's cleverness was not in his ability to verbalize or understand verbal commands but in his ability to respond to almost imperceptible and unconscious movements by those surrounding him. A French horse named Clever Bertrand may have developed his cleverness from entirely different, but equally subtle, signals—although he was not studied scientifically. It is reported that Bertrand could do everything that Hans could do, but Bertrand was blind! Indeed, some of the experiments with Hans had also shown that when auditory cues were added to the visual, Hans's accuracy increased. So Hans's cleverness was not limited to visual cues.

The story of Clever Hans makes two important points regarding the role of nonverbal behavior in human encounters:

1. While we are in the presence of another person, we are constantly giving signals about our attitudes, feelings, and personality.
2. Others may become particularly adept at sensing and interpreting these signals.

This ability is not unlike the perceptiveness or sensitivity to nonverbal cues exhibited by a Clever Carl, Christine, Frank, or Harriet when closing a business deal; presenting an intelligent and industrious image to a professor; knowing when to leave a party; and acting wisely in many other common situations. We also make interpretations about the *absence* of cues, as well as react to

Part One

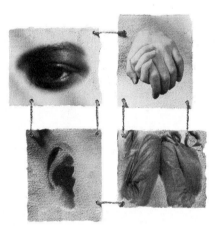

An Introduction to the Study of Nonverbal Communication

What is nonverbal communication? How does nonverbal behavior function in relation to verbal behavior? How does nonverbal communication affect our everyday lives? Do we learn how to perform body language or is it instinctive? Are some people more skilled at communicating with these face, voice, and body signals? The answers to these fundamental questions are the focus for Part One.

Nonverbal Commu

Basic Perspect

*Those of us who keep our eyes open can re
into what we see going on around*

—E. T. HALL

Herr von Osten purchased a horse in Berlin in
began training his horse, Hans, to count by tap
had no idea that Hans would soon become one of the
in history. Hans was a rapid learner and soon progr
adding, multiplying, dividing, subtracting, and even
involving factors and fractions. Even more startling, w
Hans to public audiences, he counted the size of th
wearing eyeglasses. Responding only with taps, Han
calendar, recall musical pitch, and perform numerous
tic feats. After von Osten taught Hans an alphabet tl
hoofbeats, the horse could answer virtually any quest
seemed that Hans, a common horse, had complete
German language, the ability to produce the equivalent
and an intelligence beyond that of many human bei

Even without promotion by the mass media, th
and Hans became known throughout the world. He w
Hans." Because of the profound implications for seve
because some skeptics thought a gimmick was inv

particular cues. For example, when a nephew does not get his usual greeting kiss from his favorite aunt, he wonders what is wrong. (Perhaps he never noticed the kiss nearly as much as he notices its absence.) As another example, when a doctor tries to act professionally neutral by being somewhat blank and unexpressive, the patient is likely to read the lack of cues as aloofness or disinterest, perhaps even suspecting the doctor of withholding important information. This is a good example of how what we *think* we are communicating may be very different from what we are actually communicating.

The purpose of this book is to expand your conscious awareness of the numerous nonverbal stimuli that you produce and confront in your everyday dialogue. Each chapter summarizes behavioral science research in a specific area of nonverbal communication. First, however, it is necessary to develop a few basic perspectives—a common frame of reference, a lens through which we can view the remaining chapters.

PERSPECTIVES on CONCEPTUALIZING and DEFINING NONVERBAL COMMUNICATION

To most people, the phrase *nonverbal communication* refers to *communication effected by means other than words* (assuming words are the verbal element). Like most definitions, this one is generally useful, but it does not adequately account for the complexity of this phenomenon. As long as we understand and appreciate the points listed below, this broad definition should serve us well.

First, we need to understand that separating verbal and nonverbal behavior into two separate and distinct categories is virtually impossible. Consider, for example, the hand movements that make up American Sign Language (a language of the deaf). These gesticulations are mostly linguistic (verbal), yet hand gestures are often considered behavior that is "other than words." McNeill (1992) has demonstrated the linguistic qualities of some gestures by noting that different kinds of gestures disappear with different kinds of aphasia, namely, those gestures with linguistic functions similar to the specific verbal loss. Conversely, not all spoken words are clearly or singularly verbal—as, for example, onomatopoeic words such as *buzz* or *murmur* and nonpropositional speech used by auctioneers and some aphasics.

We also need to understand that our definition does not adequately indicate whether the use of "means other than words" refers to the type of signal *produced* (encoded) or to the perceiver's code for *interpreting* (decoding) the signal. Generally, when people refer to nonverbal behavior, they are talking about the signals to which meaning will be attributed, not the process of attributing meaning. Furthermore, most people assume the cognitive process involved in interpreting nonverbal behavior is largely a verbal one. But let's examine each of these perspectives in more detail.

ENCODING

Ekman and Friesen (1969) have pointed out that verbal and nonverbal signals can be coded in many different ways. Their conceptualization follows a continuum like this:

INTRINSIC   ICONIC   ARBITRARY
CODING   CODING   CODING

Before these terms are explained, it is important to remember:

1. Behavior is a continuum, not discrete categories. A behavior may be identified that seems to fall between two of these points.
2. Although verbal behavior seems suited primarily for the right side of the continuum and nonverbal for the middle and left, there are exceptions.
3. The primary distinguishing feature among these three types of coding is the proximity of the code to its referent, that is, the thing it refers to.

Arbitrary coding puts the greatest distance between the code used and referents for the code. Resemblance to the referent is nonexistent. Most words, for instance, are arbitrarily coded with letters that show no resemblance to the things they refer to. Neither the word *cat* nor any of its letters looks like a cat. Onomatopoeic words, however, such as *buzz* and *murmur,* do take on aspects of the sounds they try to describe. Some nonverbal signals also may be arbitrarily coded; for example, the motions involved in hand-waving during the good-bye ritual do not seem to portray the activity of leaving with much fidelity.

Iconic coding preserves some aspects of the referent; that is, there is some resemblance between the code and the referent. Tracing an hourglass shape in the air to symbolize a shapely woman is an example of iconic coding, as is holding your hand to mimic a handgun, "slitting" your throat with your finger to indicate that you are "finished," or indicating with your hands how close to someone you would like to stand (with each hand representing a person).

Intrinsic coding puts the least distance between the code used and the referents for the code. At the extreme, it might be said that the manner of coding is the referent itself. Pointing, moving closer to someone, or actually hitting the person are examples of behaviors that do not resemble something else; they *are* the thing they represent.

DECODING

Currently, many brain researchers believe that the two hemispheres of the brain specialize in different information processing. It is believed that the left hemisphere processes mainly sequentially ordered, digital, verbal, or linguistic information; the right hemisphere processes mainly nonverbal, analogic, or

Gestalt information. The right hemisphere of the brain, then, is credited with processing visual/spatial relationships, which compose a large part of what is traditionally treated as nonverbal stimuli. The right hemisphere also seems to have primary responsibility for the vocal components that add emotion to our speech, for example, stress, pitch, and rhythm. Few argue that either side of the brain deals exclusively with a particular kind of information. In fact, the following case illustrates how adaptable the brain can be.

Bruce Lipstadt had the left hemisphere of his brain removed when he was five and one-half years old (Koutlak, 1976). Few doctors had hope for the development of his verbal ability, and most thought the operation would paralyze part of his body. Twenty-six years later, Bruce had an I.Q. of 126 (better than nine out of ten people), swam, rode bikes, and got an A in a statistics course. Since his speech was normal, it was assumed that the right side took over many of the functions formerly conducted mainly by the left side. Obviously, this does not always happen as a result of operations of this type, especially after puberty. It does suggest that although the right and left hemispheres seem to specialize in processing certain information, they are by no means limited to one type.

Even when information is being processed primarily by one hemisphere, it is unlikely that the other hemisphere is totally inactive. While reading a story, the right hemisphere may be playing a specialized role in understanding a metaphor or appreciating emotional content, while the left side simultaneously works harder at deriving meaning from the complex relations among word concepts and syntax. The different functions of the two brain hemispheres do not seem as clearly differentiated in women as in men, and some left-handed people are known to have hemispheric functions the opposite of those described (Andersen, Garrison, & Andersen, 1979; Iaccino, 1993).

Despite the apparent complexity demonstrated by the brain, much of what is processed by the right hemisphere seems to be what we call *nonverbal phenomena,* while much of what is processed by the brain's left hemisphere is what we categorize as *verbal phenomena.* Obviously, some nonverbal behavior is more closely aligned with verbal behavior than others (e.g., speech-independent gestures in Chapter 7), and we might expect more left hemispheric activity in such cases.

PERSPECTIVES on CLASSIFYING NONVERBAL BEHAVIOR

Another way of defining nonverbal communication is to look at the things people study. The theory and research associated with nonverbal communication focus on three primary units: the environmental structures and conditions within which communication takes place; the physical characteristics of the communicators themselves; and the various behaviors manifested by the communicators. A detailed breakdown of these three features follows.

I. THE COMMUNICATION ENVIRONMENT

A. PHYSICAL ENVIRONMENT   Although most of the emphasis in nonverbal research is on the appearance and behavior of the persons communicating, increasing attention is being given to the influence of nonhuman factors on human transactions. People change environments to help them accomplish their communicative goals; conversely, environments can affect our moods, choices of words, and actions. Thus, this category concerns those elements that impinge on the human relationship but are not directly a part of it. Environmental factors include the furniture, architectural style, interior decorating, lighting conditions, colors, temperature, additional noises or music, and the like, amid which the interaction occurs. Variations in arrangements, materials, shapes, or surfaces of objects in the interacting environment can be extremely influential on the outcome of an interpersonal relationship. This category also includes what might be called *traces of action*. For instance, as you observe cigarette butts, orange peels, and wastepaper left by the person you will soon interact with, you form an impression that will eventually influence your meeting. Perceptions of time and timing comprise another important part of the communicative environment. When something occurs, how frequently it occurs, and the tempo or rhythm of actions are clearly a part of the communicative world even though they are not a part of the physical environment per se.

B. SPATIAL ENVIRONMENT   Proxemics is the study of the use and perception of social and personal space. Under this heading is a body of work called *small group ecology*, which concerns itself with how people use and respond to spatial relationships in formal and informal group settings. Such studies deal with seating and spatial arrangements as related to leadership, communication flow, and the task at hand. On an even broader level, some attention has been given to spatial relationships in crowds and densely populated situations. Personal space orientation is sometimes studied in the context of conversation distance and how it varies according to sex, status, roles, cultural orientation, and so forth. The term *territoriality* is also used frequently in the study of proxemics to denote the human tendency to stake out personal territory (or untouchable space) much as wild animals and birds do.

II. THE COMMUNICATORS' PHYSICAL CHARACTERISTICS

The category of communicators' physical characteristics covers things that remain relatively unchanged during the period of interaction. They are influential nonverbal cues that are not visibly movement bound. Included are physique or body shape, general attractiveness, height, weight, hair, skin color or tone, and so forth. Odors (body or breath) associated with the person are normally considered part of a person's physical appearance. Further, objects associated with the interactants also may affect their physical appearance. These are called *artifacts* and include things such as clothes, lipstick, eyeglasses, wigs and other hairpieces, false eyelashes, jewelry, and accessories such as attaché cases.

III. Body Movement and Position

Body movement and position typically includes gestures, movements of the body (limbs, hands, head, feet, and legs), facial expressions (smiles), eye behavior (blinking, direction and length of gaze, and pupil dilation), and posture. The furrow of the brow, the slump of a shoulder, and the tilt of a head are all considered body movements and positions. Specifically, the major areas are gestures, posture, touching behavior, facial expressions, and eye behavior.

A. GESTURES   There are many different types of gestures (and variations of these types), but the most frequently studied are the following:

1. **Speech independent.** These gestures are not tied to speech, but they have a direct verbal translation or dictionary definition, usually consisting of a word or two or a phrase. There is high agreement among members of a culture or subculture on the verbal "translation" of these signals. The gestures used to represent "A-OK" or "Peace" (also known as the "V-for-Victory" sign) are examples of speech-independent gestures for large segments of the U.S. culture.
2. **Speech related.** These gestures are directly tied to, or accompany, speech—often serving to illustrate what is being said verbally. These movements may accent or emphasize a word or phrase, sketch a path of thought, point to present objects, depict a spatial relationship, depict the rhythm or pacing of an event, draw a picture of a referent, depict a bodily action, or serve as commentary on the regulation and organization of the interactive process.

B. POSTURE   Posture is normally studied in conjunction with other nonverbal signals to determine the degree of attention or involvement, the degree of status relative to the other interactive partner, or the degree of liking for the other interactant. A forward-leaning posture, for example, has been associated with higher involvement, more liking, and lower status in studies where the interactants did not know each other very well. Posture is also a key indicator of the intensity of some emotional states, for example, the drooping posture associated with sadness or the rigid, tense posture associated with anger. The extent to which the communicators mirror each other's posture may also reflect rapport or an attempt to build rapport.

C. TOUCHING BEHAVIOR   Touching may be self-focused or other focused. Self-focused manipulations, not usually made for purposes of communicating, may reflect a person's particular state or a habit. Many are commonly called *nervous mannerisms*. Some of these actions are relics from an earlier time in life—times when we first learn how to manage our emotions, develop social contacts, or perform some instructional task. Sometimes we perform these manipulations as we adapt to such learning experiences, and they stay with us when we face similar situations later in life, often as only part of the original movement. Ekman and Friesen (1969) call these types of self-focused manipulation *adaptors*. These adaptors may involve various manipulations of one's own body such as licking, picking, holding, pinching, and scratching. Object-adaptors are manipulations practiced in conjunction with an object, as when a reformed, male cigarette smoker reaches toward his breast pocket for the nonexistent package of cigarettes. Of course, not all behaviors that reflect habitual actions or an anxious disposition can be traced to earlier adaptations, but they do represent a part of the overall pattern of bodily action.

One of the most potent forms of nonverbal communication occurs when two people touch. Touch can be virtually electric, but it also can irritate, condescend, or comfort. Touch is a highly ambiguous form of behavior whose meaning often takes more from the context, the nature of the relationship, and the manner of execution than from the configuration of the touch per se. Some researchers are concerned with touching behavior as an important factor in the child's early development; some are concerned with adult touching behavior. Subcategories include stroking, hitting, greetings and farewells, holding, and guiding another's movements.

D. FACIAL EXPRESSIONS   Most studies of the face are concerned with the configurations that display various affective states, as the face is the primary source of affect. The six primary affects receiving the most study are anger, sadness, surprise, happiness, fear, and disgust. Facial expressions also can function as regulatory gestures, providing feedback and managing the flow of interaction.

E. EYE BEHAVIOR   Where one looks, when one looks, and how long one looks during interaction are the primary foci for studies of gazing. *Gaze* refers to the eye movement we make in the general direction of another's face. *Mutual gaze* occurs when interactants look into each other's eyes. The dilation and constriction of one's pupils also has interest to those who study nonverbal communication because it is sometimes an indicator of interest, attention, or involvement.

F. VOCAL BEHAVIOR   Vocal behavior deals with *how* something is said, not what is said. It deals with the range of nonverbal vocal cues surrounding common speech behavior. Generally, a distinction is made between two types of sounds:

Part One

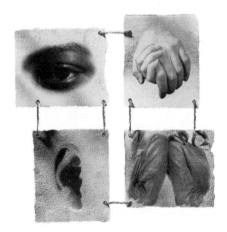

An Introduction to the Study of Nonverbal Communication

W hat is nonverbal communication? How does nonverbal behavior function in relation to verbal behavior? How does nonverbal communication affect our everyday lives? Do we learn how to perform body language or is it instinctive? Are some people more skilled at communicating with these face, voice, and body signals? The answers to these fundamental questions are the focus for Part One.

CHAPTER 1

Nonverbal Communication: Basic Perspectives

*Those of us who keep our eyes open can read volumes
into what we see going on around us.*

—E. T. HALL

Herr von Osten purchased a horse in Berlin in 1900. When von Osten began training his horse, Hans, to count by tapping his front hoof, he had no idea that Hans would soon become one of the most celebrated horses in history. Hans was a rapid learner and soon progressed from counting to adding, multiplying, dividing, subtracting, and eventually solving problems involving factors and fractions. Even more startling, when von Osten exhibited Hans to public audiences, he counted the size of the crowd or the number wearing eyeglasses. Responding only with taps, Hans could tell time, use a calendar, recall musical pitch, and perform numerous other seemingly fantastic feats. After von Osten taught Hans an alphabet that could be coded into hoofbeats, the horse could answer virtually any question—oral or written. It seemed that Hans, a common horse, had complete comprehension of the German language, the ability to produce the equivalent of words and numerals, and an intelligence beyond that of many human beings.

Even without promotion by the mass media, the word spread quickly, and Hans became known throughout the world. He was soon dubbed "Clever Hans." Because of the profound implications for several scientific fields and because some skeptics thought a gimmick was involved, an investigating committee was established to decide whether deceit tainted Hans's performances. Professors of psychology and physiology, the director of the Berlin Zoological Garden, a director of a circus, veterinarians, and cavalry officers were appointed to this commission. An experiment with Hans from which von Osten was absent demonstrated no change in the apparent intelligence of the horse. This was sufficient proof for the commission to announce that no trickery was involved.

The appointment of a second commission was the beginning of the end for Clever Hans. Von Osten was asked to whisper a number into the horse's left ear while another experimenter whispered a number into the horse's right ear. Hans was told to add the two numbers—an answer none of the onlookers, von Osten, nor the experimenter knew. Hans failed. And with further tests, he continued to fail. The experimenter, Pfungst, had discovered that Hans could answer a question only if someone in his visual field knew the answer and was attentive to the situation (Pfungst, 1911/1965).

When Hans was given the question, onlookers who knew the answer assumed an expectant posture, increased their body tension, and bent their heads slightly forward. When Hans reached the correct number of taps, the onlookers would relax and make a slight movement of their heads—which was Hans's signal to stop tapping. Evidence suggests that Hans could detect head movements as slight as one-fifth of a millimeter. Subsequent experiments found that Hans also would cease tapping as a knowledgeable onlooker raised his or her eyebrows or even showed a dilation of the nostrils.

The story of Clever Hans functions as a vivid introduction to the field of nonverbal communication (Sebeok & Rosenthal, 1981; Sebeok & Umiker-Sebeok, 1980). Hans's cleverness was not in his ability to verbalize or understand verbal commands but in his ability to respond to almost imperceptible and unconscious movements by those surrounding him. A French horse named Clever Bertrand may have developed his cleverness from entirely different, but equally subtle, signals—although he was not studied scientifically. It is reported that Bertrand could do everything that Hans could do, but Bertrand was blind! Indeed, some of the experiments with Hans had also shown that when auditory cues were added to the visual, Hans's accuracy increased. So Hans's cleverness was not limited to visual cues.

The story of Clever Hans makes two important points regarding the role of nonverbal behavior in human encounters:

1. While we are in the presence of another person, we are constantly giving signals about our attitudes, feelings, and personality.
2. Others may become particularly adept at sensing and interpreting these signals.

This ability is not unlike the perceptiveness or sensitivity to nonverbal cues exhibited by a Clever Carl, Christine, Frank, or Harriet when closing a business deal; presenting an intelligent and industrious image to a professor; knowing when to leave a party; and acting wisely in many other common situations. We also make interpretations about the *absence* of cues, as well as react to particular cues. For example, when a nephew does not get his usual greeting kiss from his favorite aunt, he wonders what is wrong. (Perhaps he never noticed the kiss nearly as much as he notices its absence.) As another example, when a doctor tries to act professionally neutral by being somewhat blank and unexpressive, the patient is likely to read the lack of cues as aloofness or disinterest, perhaps even suspecting the doctor of withholding important information. This is a good example of how what we *think* we are communicating may be very different from what we are actually communicating.

The purpose of this book is to expand your conscious awareness of the numerous nonverbal stimuli that you produce and confront in your everyday dialogue. Each chapter summarizes behavioral science research in a specific area of nonverbal communication. First, however, it is necessary to develop a few basic perspectives—a common frame of reference, a lens through which we can view the remaining chapters.

PERSPECTIVES on CONCEPTUALIZING and DEFINING NONVERBAL COMMUNICATION

To most people, the phrase *nonverbal communication* refers to *communication effected by means other than words* (assuming words are the verbal element). Like most definitions, this one is generally useful, but it does not adequately account for the complexity of this phenomenon. As long as we understand and appreciate the points listed below, this broad definition should serve us well.

First, we need to understand that separating verbal and nonverbal behavior into two separate and distinct categories is virtually impossible. Consider, for example, the hand movements that make up American Sign Language (a language of the deaf). These gesticulations are mostly linguistic (verbal), yet hand gestures are often considered behavior that is "other than words." McNeill (1992) has demonstrated the linguistic qualities of some gestures by noting that different kinds of gestures disappear with different kinds of aphasia, namely, those gestures with linguistic functions similar to the specific verbal loss. Conversely, not all spoken words are clearly or singularly verbal—as, for example, onomatopoeic words such as *buzz* or *murmur* and nonpropositional speech used by auctioneers and some aphasics.

We also need to understand that our definition does not adequately indicate whether the use of "means other than words" refers to the type of signal *produced* (encoded) or to the perceiver's code for *interpreting* (decoding) the signal. Generally, when people refer to nonverbal behavior, they are talking about the signals to which meaning will be attributed, not the process of attributing meaning. Furthermore, most people assume the cognitive process involved in interpreting nonverbal behavior is largely a verbal one. But let's examine each of these perspectives in more detail.

ENCODING

Ekman and Friesen (1969) have pointed out that verbal and nonverbal signals can be coded in many different ways. Their conceptualization follows a continuum like this:

INTRINSIC   ICONIC   ARBITRARY
CODING   CODING   CODING

Before these terms are explained, it is important to remember:

1. Behavior is a continuum, not discrete categories. A behavior may be identified that seems to fall between two of these points.
2. Although verbal behavior seems suited primarily for the right side of the continuum and nonverbal for the middle and left, there are exceptions.
3. The primary distinguishing feature among these three types of coding is the proximity of the code to its referent, that is, the thing it refers to.

Arbitrary coding puts the greatest distance between the code used and referents for the code. Resemblance to the referent is nonexistent. Most words, for instance, are arbitrarily coded with letters that show no resemblance to the things they refer to. Neither the word *cat* nor any of its letters looks like a cat. Onomatopoeic words, however, such as *buzz* and *murmur,* do take on aspects of the sounds they try to describe. Some nonverbal signals also may be arbitrarily coded; for example, the motions involved in hand-waving during the good-bye ritual do not seem to portray the activity of leaving with much fidelity.

Iconic coding preserves some aspects of the referent; that is, there is some resemblance between the code and the referent. Tracing an hourglass shape in the air to symbolize a shapely woman is an example of iconic coding, as is holding your hand to mimic a handgun, "slitting" your throat with your finger to indicate that you are "finished," or indicating with your hands how close to someone you would like to stand (with each hand representing a person).

Intrinsic coding puts the least distance between the code used and the referents for the code. At the extreme, it might be said that the manner of coding is the referent itself. Pointing, moving closer to someone, or actually hitting the person are examples of behaviors that do not resemble something else; they *are* the thing they represent.

DECODING

Currently, many brain researchers believe that the two hemispheres of the brain specialize in different information processing. It is believed that the left hemisphere processes mainly sequentially ordered, digital, verbal, or linguistic information; the right hemisphere processes mainly nonverbal, analogic, or

Gestalt information. The right hemisphere of the brain, then, is credited with processing visual/spatial relationships, which compose a large part of what is traditionally treated as nonverbal stimuli. The right hemisphere also seems to have primary responsibility for the vocal components that add emotion to our speech, for example, stress, pitch, and rhythm. Few argue that either side of the brain deals exclusively with a particular kind of information. In fact, the following case illustrates how adaptable the brain can be.

Bruce Lipstadt had the left hemisphere of his brain removed when he was five and one-half years old (Koutlak, 1976). Few doctors had hope for the development of his verbal ability, and most thought the operation would paralyze part of his body. Twenty-six years later, Bruce had an I.Q. of 126 (better than nine out of ten people), swam, rode bikes, and got an A in a statistics course. Since his speech was normal, it was assumed that the right side took over many of the functions formerly conducted mainly by the left side. Obviously, this does not always happen as a result of operations of this type, especially after puberty. It does suggest that although the right and left hemispheres seem to specialize in processing certain information, they are by no means limited to one type.

Even when information is being processed primarily by one hemisphere, it is unlikely that the other hemisphere is totally inactive. While reading a story, the right hemisphere may be playing a specialized role in understanding a metaphor or appreciating emotional content, while the left side simultaneously works harder at deriving meaning from the complex relations among word concepts and syntax. The different functions of the two brain hemispheres do not seem as clearly differentiated in women as in men, and some left-handed people are known to have hemispheric functions the opposite of those described (Andersen, Garrison, & Andersen, 1979; Iaccino, 1993).

Despite the apparent complexity demonstrated by the brain, much of what is processed by the right hemisphere seems to be what we call *nonverbal phenomena,* while much of what is processed by the brain's left hemisphere is what we categorize as *verbal phenomena.* Obviously, some nonverbal behavior is more closely aligned with verbal behavior than others (e.g., speech-independent gestures in Chapter 7), and we might expect more left hemispheric activity in such cases.

PERSPECTIVES on CLASSIFYING NONVERBAL BEHAVIOR

Another way of defining nonverbal communication is to look at the things people study. The theory and research associated with nonverbal communication focus on three primary units: the environmental structures and conditions within which communication takes place; the physical characteristics of the communicators themselves; and the various behaviors manifested by the communicators. A detailed breakdown of these three features follows.

I. THE COMMUNICATION ENVIRONMENT

A. PHYSICAL ENVIRONMENT   Although most of the emphasis in nonverbal research is on the appearance and behavior of the persons communicating, increasing attention is being given to the influence of nonhuman factors on human transactions. People change environments to help them accomplish their communicative goals; conversely, environments can affect our moods, choices of words, and actions. Thus, this category concerns those elements that impinge on the human relationship but are not directly a part of it. Environmental factors include the furniture, architectural style, interior decorating, lighting conditions, colors, temperature, additional noises or music, and the like, amid which the interaction occurs. Variations in arrangements, materials, shapes, or surfaces of objects in the interacting environment can be extremely influential on the outcome of an interpersonal relationship. This category also includes what might be called *traces of action.* For instance, as you observe cigarette butts, orange peels, and wastepaper left by the person you will soon interact with, you form an impression that will eventually influence your meeting. Perceptions of time and timing comprise another important part of the communicative environment. When something occurs, how frequently it occurs, and the tempo or rhythm of actions are clearly a part of the communicative world even though they are not a part of the physical environment per se.

B. SPATIAL ENVIRONMENT   Proxemics is the study of the use and perception of social and personal space. Under this heading is a body of work called *small group ecology,* which concerns itself with how people use and respond to spatial relationships in formal and informal group settings. Such studies deal with seating and spatial arrangements as related to leadership, communication flow, and the task at hand. On an even broader level, some attention has been given to spatial relationships in crowds and densely populated situations. Personal space orientation is sometimes studied in the context of conversation distance and how it varies according to sex, status, roles, cultural orientation, and so forth. The term *territoriality* is also used frequently in the study of proxemics to denote the human tendency to stake out personal territory (or untouchable space) much as wild animals and birds do.

II. THE COMMUNICATORS' PHYSICAL CHARACTERISTICS

The category of communicators' physical characteristics covers things that remain relatively unchanged during the period of interaction. They are influential nonverbal cues that are not visibly movement bound. Included are physique or body shape, general attractiveness, height, weight, hair, skin color or tone, and so forth. Odors (body or breath) associated with the person are normally considered part of a person's physical appearance. Further, objects associated with the interactants also may affect their physical appearance. These are called *artifacts* and include things such as clothes, lipstick, eyeglasses, wigs and other hairpieces, false eyelashes, jewelry, and accessories such as attaché cases.

III. Body Movement and Position

Body movement and position typically includes gestures, movements of the body (limbs, hands, head, feet, and legs), facial expressions (smiles), eye behavior (blinking, direction and length of gaze, and pupil dilation), and posture. The furrow of the brow, the slump of a shoulder, and the tilt of a head are all considered body movements and positions. Specifically, the major areas are gestures, posture, touching behavior, facial expressions, and eye behavior.

A. GESTURES   There are many different types of gestures (and variations of these types), but the most frequently studied are the following:

1. **Speech independent.** These gestures are not tied to speech, but they have a direct verbal translation or dictionary definition, usually consisting of a word or two or a phrase. There is high agreement among members of a culture or subculture on the verbal "translation" of these signals. The gestures used to represent "A-OK" or "Peace" (also known as the "V-for-Victory" sign) are examples of speech-independent gestures for large segments of the U.S. culture.
2. **Speech related.** These gestures are directly tied to, or accompany, speech—often serving to illustrate what is being said verbally. These movements may accent or emphasize a word or phrase, sketch a path of thought, point to present objects, depict a spatial relationship, depict the rhythm or pacing of an event, draw a picture of a referent, depict a bodily action, or serve as commentary on the regulation and organization of the interactive process.

B. POSTURE   Posture is normally studied in conjunction with other nonverbal signals to determine the degree of attention or involvement, the degree of status relative to the other interactive partner, or the degree of liking for the other interactant. A forward-leaning posture, for example, has been associated with higher involvement, more liking, and lower status in studies where the interactants did not know each other very well. Posture is also a key indicator of the intensity of some emotional states, for example, the drooping posture associated with sadness or the rigid, tense posture associated with anger. The extent to which the communicators mirror each other's posture may also reflect rapport or an attempt to build rapport.

C. TOUCHING BEHAVIOR   Touching may be self-focused or other focused. Self-focused manipulations, not usually made for purposes of communicating, may reflect a person's particular state or a habit. Many are commonly called *nervous mannerisms*. Some of these actions are relics from an earlier time in life—times when we first learn how to manage our emotions, develop social contacts, or perform some instructional task. Sometimes we perform these manipulations as we adapt to such learning experiences, and they stay with us when we face similar situations later in life, often as only part of the original movement. Ekman and Friesen (1969) call these types of self-focused manipulation *adaptors*. These adaptors may involve various manipulations of one's own body such as licking, picking, holding, pinching, and scratching. Object-adaptors are manipulations practiced in conjunction with an object, as when a reformed, male cigarette smoker reaches toward his breast pocket for the nonexistent package of cigarettes. Of course, not all behaviors that reflect habitual actions or an anxious disposition can be traced to earlier adaptations, but they do represent a part of the overall pattern of bodily action.

One of the most potent forms of nonverbal communication occurs when two people touch. Touch can be virtually electric, but it also can irritate, condescend, or comfort. Touch is a highly ambiguous form of behavior whose meaning often takes more from the context, the nature of the relationship, and the manner of execution than from the configuration of the touch per se. Some researchers are concerned with touching behavior as an important factor in the child's early development; some are concerned with adult touching behavior. Subcategories include stroking, hitting, greetings and farewells, holding, and guiding another's movements.

D. FACIAL EXPRESSIONS   Most studies of the face are concerned with the configurations that display various affective states, as the face is the primary source of affect. The six primary affects receiving the most study are anger, sadness, surprise, happiness, fear, and disgust. Facial expressions also can function as regulatory gestures, providing feedback and managing the flow of interaction.

E. EYE BEHAVIOR   Where one looks, when one looks, and how long one looks during interaction are the primary foci for studies of gazing. *Gaze* refers to the eye movement we make in the general direction of another's face. *Mutual gaze* occurs when interactants look into each other's eyes. The dilation and constriction of one's pupils also has interest to those who study nonverbal communication because it is sometimes an indicator of interest, attention, or involvement.

F. VOCAL BEHAVIOR   Vocal behavior deals with *how* something is said, not what is said. It deals with the range of nonverbal vocal cues surrounding common speech behavior. Generally, a distinction is made between two types of sounds:

1. The sound variations made with the vocal cords during talk that are a function of changes in pitch, duration, loudness, and silence
2. Sounds that result primarily from physiological mechanisms other than the vocal cords, for example, the pharyngeal, oral, or nasal cavities

Most of the research on vocal behavior and its effects on human interaction has focused on pitch level and variability; the duration of sounds (clipped or drawn out); pauses within the speech stream and the latency of response during turn exchanges; loudness level and variability; resonance; precise or slurred articulation; rate; rhythm; and intruding sound during speech such as "uh" or "um." The study of vocal signals encompasses a broad range of interests, from questions focusing on stereotypes associated with certain voices to questions about the effects of vocal behavior on comprehension and persuasion. Thus, even specialized sounds such as laughing, belching, yawning, swallowing, moaning, and the like may be of interest to the extent that they may affect the outcome of interaction.

PERSPECTIVES on NONVERBAL COMMUNICATION in the TOTAL COMMUNICATION PROCESS

Even though this book emphasizes nonverbal communication, the reader should not forget the inseparable nature of verbal and nonverbal signals. Ray Birdwhistell, a pioneer in nonverbal research, reportedly said that studying only *nonverbal* communication is like studying *noncardiac* physiology. His point is well taken. It is not easy to dissect human interaction and make one diagnosis that concerns only verbal behavior and another that concerns only nonverbal behavior. The verbal dimension is so intimately woven and subtly represented in so much of what has been previously labeled *non*verbal that the term does not always adequately describe the behavior under study. Some of the most noteworthy scholars associated with nonverbal study refuse to segregate words from gestures and hence work under the broader terms *communication* or *face-to-face interaction.* Kendon (1983, pp. 17, 20) puts it this way:

> It is a common observation that, when a person speaks, muscular systems besides those of the lips, tongue, and jaws often become active . . . gesticulation is organized as part of the same overall unit of action by which speech is also organized . . . gesture and speech are available as two separate modes of representation and are coordinated because both are being guided by the same overall aim. That aim is to produce a pattern of action that will accomplish the representation of a meaning.

Because verbal and nonverbal systems operate together as part of the larger communication process, efforts to clearly distinguish between the two have not been very successful. One common misconception, for example, assumes nonverbal behavior is used solely to communicate emotional messages, whereas verbal behavior is for conveying ideas. Although it is true that abstract concepts and descriptions of events are hard to express through nonverbal channels and that we often express emotion with our face, body, and voice tone, the concept-emotion distinction is not a good one for distinguishing verbal and nonverbal behavior. Words can carry much emotion—we can talk explicitly about emotions, and we also communicate emotion between the lines in verbal nuances. Conversely, nonverbal cues are often used for purposes other than showing emotion; as examples, people in conversation use eye movements to help tell each other when it is time to switch speaking turns, and people commonly use hand gestures while talking to help convey their ideas.

Argyle (1988) has identified the following primary functions of nonverbal behavior in human communication as:

1. Expressing emotion
2. Conveying interpersonal attitudes (like/dislike, dominance/submission, etc.)
3. Presenting one's personality to others
4. Accompanying speech for the purposes of managing turn taking, feedback, attention, etc.

Argyle also notes that nonverbal behaviors are important in many rituals, such as greeting. Notice that none of these functions of nonverbal behavior is limited to nonverbal behavior alone; that is, we can express emotions and attitudes, present ourselves in a particular light, and manage the interaction using verbal cues, too. This does not suggest, however, that in any given situation we might not rely more heavily on verbal behavior for some purposes and on nonverbal for others.

We also need to recognize that the ways we attribute meanings to verbal and nonverbal behavior are not all that different either. Nonverbal actions, like verbal ones, may communicate more than one message at a time—for example, the way you nonverbally make it clear to another person that you want to keep talking may simultaneously express your need for dominance over that person and, perhaps, your emotional state. When you grip a child's shoulder during a reprimand, you may increase comprehension and recall, but you may also elicit such a negative reaction that the child fails to obey. A smile can be a part of an emotional expression, an attitudinal message, part of a self-presentation, or a listener response to manage the interaction. And, like verbal behavior, the meanings attributed to nonverbal behavior may be stereotyped, idiomatic, or ambiguous. Furthermore, the same nonverbal behavior performed in different contexts may, like words, receive different attributions of meaning. For example, looking down at the floor may reflect sadness in one situation and submissiveness or lack of involvement in another. Finally, in an effort to identify the fundamental categories of meaning associated with nonverbal behavior, Mehrabian (1970, 1981) identified a threefold perspective resulting from his extensive testing:

1. **Immediacy.** Sometimes we react to things by evaluating them—positive or negative, good or bad, like or dislike.
2. **Status.** Sometimes we enact or perceive behaviors that indicate various aspects of status to us—strong or weak, superior or subordinate.
3. **Responsiveness.** This third category refers to our perceptions of activity—slow or fast, active or passive.

In various verbal and nonverbal studies over the past three decades, dimensions similar to Mehrabian's have been reported consistently by investigators from diverse fields studying diverse phenomena. It is reasonable to conclude, therefore, that these three dimensions are basic responses to our environment and are reflected in the way we assign meaning to both verbal and nonverbal behavior. Most of this work, however, is dependent on subjects translating their reactions to a nonverbal act into one identified by verbal descriptors. This issue has already been addressed in the discussion of the way the brain processes different pieces of information. In general, then, nonverbal signals, like words, can and do have multiple uses and meanings; like words, nonverbal signals have denotative and connotative meanings; and like words, nonverbal signals play an active role in communicating liking, power, and responsiveness. With these in mind, we can now examine some of the important ways verbal and nonverbal behavior interrelate during human interaction. Ekman (1965) identified the following: repeating, contradicting, complementing, substituting, accenting/moderating, and regulating.

REPEATING

Nonverbal communication can simply repeat what was said verbally. For instance, if you told a person he had to go north to find a newspaper stand and then pointed in the proper direction, this would be considered repetition.

CONTRADICTING

In this case, the term *contradicting* includes a variety of ways verbal and nonverbal signals can be at variance with one another. They may literally contradict one another, but, in other cases, one may simply perceive an incongruity. In both instances, though, two messages that do not appear to be consistent with one another are perceived. It is quite common (and probably functional) to have mixed feelings about some things. As a result, incongruous verbal and nonverbal messages may be more common than we realize. But it is the more dramatic contradictions we are more likely to notice. Perhaps it is the parent who yells to his or her child in an angry voice "Of course I love you!" Or the public speaker, who, with trembling hands and knees and beads of perspiration on the brow, says, "I'm not nervous." When you are trying to express disagreement with an idea, the linguistic choices also may reveal differences in directness; for example, "John has done good work" is less direct than "John does good work" (Wiener & Mehrabian, 1968).

Why do these contradictory messages occur? In some cases it is a natural response to a situation in which communicators perceive themselves in a bind. They do not want to tell the truth, and they do not want to lie. As a result, their ambivalence and frustration produce a discrepant message (Bavelas, 1990). Suppose you have just given a terrible presentation, and you ask me how you did. I may say you did fine, but my voice, face, and body may not support my words. In other situations, contradictory messages occur because people do an imperfect job of lying. On still other occasions, contradictory messages may be the result of an attempt to communicate sarcasm or irony, saying one thing with words and the opposite with vocal tone and/or facial expression. The term *coy* is used to describe the display of coexisting signals that invite friendly contact with those that signal rejection and withdrawal.

These displays of incongruous or contradictory signals may occur in a variety of ways. Sometimes two nonverbal signals may manifest the discord (e.g., vocal with visual), but verbal and nonverbal signals can combine in several ways: positive voice/negative words; negative voice/positive words; positive face/negative words; negative face/positive words.

Figure 1–1

a   b

(a) Contradictory verbal/nonverbal signals. (b) Is this an aggressive or playful situation? What observations influenced your decision?

When confronted with contradictory verbal and nonverbal messages, how do we react? Leathers (1979) has identified a common three-step process:

1. The first reaction is confusion and uncertainty.
2. Next, we search for additional information that will clarify the situation.
3. If clarification is not forthcoming, we will probably react with displeasure, hostility, or even withdrawal.

Responses to contradictory messages are often ambiguous themselves. Some believe a constant barrage of inconsistent messages can contribute to a psychopathology for the receiver. This may be particularly true when people have a close relationship, and the receiver has no other people he or she can turn to for discussion and possible clarification of the confusion. Some research finds that parents of disturbed children produce more messages with conflicting cues (Bugental, Love, Kaswan, & April, 1971). Other work suggests that the differences are not in conflicting cues but in negative messages; that is, parents with disturbed children send more negative messages (Beakel & Mehrabian, 1969). The combination of negativity, confusion, and punishment can be very harmful if it is a common style of communication directed toward children. Date rape is another situation where testimony often centers around the extent to which the signals of rejection were unequivocal.

We do not wish to give the impression that all forms of discrepancy are harmful. Our daily conversations are probably peppered with instances where gestures and speech do not exactly match one another—for example, a speaker telling a story about someone climbing up a pipe while simultaneously gesturing like he or she was climbing a ladder (McNeill, Cassell, & McCullough, 1994). Sometimes these discrepancies go unnoticed, and many are cognitively "resolved" without overtly discussing the mismatch. Even contradictions with more important implications for the conversants may not, in some situations, be considered very harmful. Moreover, as stated earlier, discrepancy is *required* for achieving certain effects: Sarcasm occurs when the words are pleasant and the voice quality is unpleasant; when the words are unpleasant but the tone of voice is pleasant, we are likely to communicate the message "just joking."

Finally, some discrepancies may be helpful in certain situations. In an experiment, teachers used mixed messages while teaching a lesson to sixth-grade pupils. When the teachers combined positive words with a negative nonverbal demeanor, pupils learned more than with any other combination (Woolfolk, 1978). Similarly, a study of doctors talking with patients found that the combination of positive words said in a negative voice tone was associated with the highest levels of patient satisfaction with the visit (Hall, Roter, & Rand, 1981). Possibly the positive verbal/negative nonverbal combination is perceived in classrooms and doctors' office as serious and concerned and, therefore, makes a better impression than a consistently positive communication style (the consistently positive style might seem flippant or unrealistically optimistic).

Some research has questioned whether we trust and believe nonverbal signals more than verbal when we are confronted with contradictory messages (Bugental, 1974; Mehrabian, 1972; Stiff, Hale, Garlick, & Rogan, 1990). Burgoon (1980, p. 184), after surveying numerous studies in this area, concluded that

> the nonverbal channels carry more information and are believed more than the verbal band, and that visual cues generally carry more weight than vocal ones.

Burgoon goes on to discuss some important reservations about this general conclusion. It is often assumed that nonverbal signals are more spontaneous, harder to fake, and less likely to be manipulated—hence, more believable. It is probably more accurate to say, however, that some nonverbal behaviors are more spontaneous and harder to fake than others and that some people are more proficient than others at nonverbal deception. With two contradictory cues (both of which are nonverbal) we predictably place our reliance on the cues we consider harder to fake. One research team found that people tended to rely primarily on visual cues in visual/auditory discrepancies, but when the discrepancy was great, people tended to rely on the audio signals (DePaulo, Rosenthal, Eisenstat, Rogers, & Finkelstein, 1978).

Credibility of the information presented is also an important factor in determining which cues to believe most in inconsistent messages. If the information being communicated in one channel lacks credibility, we are likely to discount it and look to other channels for the "real" message (Bugental, 1974). Sometimes we are faced with the difficult dilemma of perceiving the meaning communicated by hard-to-fake cues that do not seem credible. If a person says, "This is really great" with a sad tone of voice upon receiving a gift you know he had long wanted, you are likely to search for other explanations—for example, something else may be bothering the person.

Interestingly, young children seem to give less credence to certain nonverbal cues than adults do when confronted with conflicting verbal and nonverbal messages (Bugental, Kaswan, Love, & Fox, 1970; Bugental, Love, & Gianetto, 1971; Volkmar & Siegel, 1982). Conflicting messages in which the speaker smiled while making a critical statement were interpreted more negatively by children than adults, particularly when the speaker was a woman.

Other work casts a further shadow on the "reliance on nonverbal cues in contradictory situations" theory. Shapiro (1968) found that student judges differed as to whether they relied on linguistic or facial cues when asked to select the affect being communicated by incongruent sketched faces and written messages and to be consistent in their choices. Vande Creek and Watkins (1972) extended Shapiro's work by using real voices and moving pictures. The stimulus persons were portraying inconsistencies in the degree of stress in verbal and nonverbal channels. Again, they found some respondents tended to rely primarily on verbal cues; some tended to rely on nonverbal cues; and some responded to the degree of stress in general regardless of the channels manifesting it. The cross-cultural research of Solomon and Ali (1975) suggests that familiarity with the verbal language may affect one's reliance on verbal or nonverbal cues. They found, for instance, that persons who were not as familiar with the language used to construct the contradictory message relied on the content for judgments of affective meaning. Those who knew the language well were more apt to rely on the vocal intonation for the affective meaning. So it appears some people rely more heavily on the verbal message, while others rely on the nonverbal.

We do not know all the conditions that affect which signals people look to for valid information. As a general rule, people tend to rely on those signals they perceive harder to fake, but this will most likely vary with the situation; so the ultimate impact of verbal, visual, and vocal signals is best determined by a close examination of the people involved and the communication context.

Complementing

Nonverbal behavior can modify, or elaborate on, verbal messages. When the verbal and nonverbal channels are complementary, rather than contradictory, our messages are usually decoded more accurately. Some evidence suggests that complementary nonverbal signals also may be helpful in remembering the verbal message. A student who reflects an attitude of embarrassment when talking to a professor about a poor performance in class assignments is exhibiting nonverbal behavior that complements the verbal. When clarity is of utmost importance (as in a job interview or when making up with a loved one after a fight), one should be especially concerned with making verbal and nonverbal behavior complement one another.

Substituting

Nonverbal behavior can also substitute for verbal messages. It may indicate more permanent characteristics (sex, age), moderately long-lasting features (personality, attitudes, social group), and relatively short-term states. In the latter case, we may find a dejected and downtrodden executive (or janitor) walk into his or her house after work with a facial expression that substitutes for the statement "I've had a rotten day." With a little practice, people soon learn to identify a wide range of these substitute nonverbal displays—all the way from "It's been a fantastic, great day!" to "Oh, God, am I miserable!" We do not need to ask for verbal confirmation of our perception.

Sometimes, when substitute nonverbal behavior fails, the communicator resorts to the verbal level. Consider the woman who wants her date to stop trying to become physically intimate with her. She may stiffen, stare straight ahead, or act unresponsive and cool. If the suitor still does not stop, she might say something like "Look, Larry, please don't ruin a nice friendship."

ACCENTING/MODERATING

Nonverbal behavior may accent (amplify) or moderate (tone down) parts of the verbal message. Accenting is much like underlining or *italicizing* written words to emphasize them. Movements of the head and hands are frequently used to accent the verbal message. When a father scolds his son about staying out too late, he may accent a particular phrase with a firm grip on the son's shoulder and an accompanying frown. In some instances, one set of nonverbal cues can accent or moderate other nonverbal cues. The intensity of a facial expression of emotion, for example, may be revealed by observing other parts of the body.

REGULATING

Nonverbal behavior is also used to regulate verbal behavior. We do this in two ways:

1. Coordinating our own verbal and nonverbal behavior in the production of our messages
2. Coordinating our verbal and nonverbal message behavior with those of our interaction partner(s)

We regulate the production of our own messages in a variety of ways. Sometimes we use nonverbal signs to segment units of interaction. Posture changes may demarcate a topic change; a gesture may forecast the verbalization of a particular idea; pauses may help in organizing spoken information into units. When we speak of a series of things, we may communicate discreteness by linear, staccato movements of the arm and hand; for example, "We must consider A, B, and C." When we insert one of these chopping gestures after each letter, it may suggest a separate consideration of each letter; a single chop after C might indicate either a consideration of all three (as a group) or just C in particular.

We also regulate the flow of verbal and nonverbal behavior between ourself and an interactant. This may manifest itself in the type of behavior two interactants elicit from one another (e.g., every time one person gets mad and yells, the other behaves in a solicitous manner) or in less obvious ways (e.g., the signals of initiation, continuation, and termination of interaction). The way one person stops talking and another starts in a smooth, synchronized manner may be as important to a satisfactory interaction as the content. After all, we do make judgments about people based on their regulatory skills (for example, "Talking to him is like talking to a wall" or "You can't get a word in edgewise with her"). When another person frequently interrupts or is inattentive, we may feel this person is making a statement about the relationship, perhaps one of disrespect. There are rules for regulating conversations, but they are generally implicit. It is not written down, but we seem to know that two people should not talk at the same time, that each person should get an equal number of turns at talking if he or she desires, that a question should be answered, and so forth. Wiemann's (1977) research found that relatively minute changes in these regulatory behaviors (interruptions, pauses longer than three seconds, unilateral topic changes, etc.) resulted in sizeable variations in how competent a communicator was perceived to be. As listeners, we are apparently attending to and evaluating a host of fleeting, subtle, and habitual features of another's conversational behavior. There are probably differences in the actual behaviors used to manage conversational flow across cultures or within subcultural groups. As children are first learning these rules, they use less subtle cues, for example, tugging on clothing, raising a hand, and the like. Children are also less skilled in accomplishing smooth turn taking, as you will have noticed if you have conversed with a young child on the telephone.

Conversational regulators involve several kinds of nonverbal cues. When we want to indicate we are finished speaking and the other person can start, we may increase our eye contact with the other person. This is often accompanied by the vocal cues associated with ending declarative or interrogative statements. If the other person still does not figuratively pick up the conversational ball, we might extend silence or interject a "trailer," for example, "you know . . ." or "so, ah . . ." Keeping another from speaking in a conversation means we have to keep long pauses from occurring, decrease eye contact, and perhaps raise the volume if the other tries to speak. When we do not want to take a speaking turn, we might give the other some reinforcing head nods, maintain attentive eye contact, and, of course, refrain from speaking when the other begins to yield. When we do want the floor, we might raise our index finger or enact an audible inspiration of breath with a straightening of the posture as if ready to take over. Rapid nodding may signal the other to hurry up and finish, but, if we have trouble getting in, we may have to talk simultaneously for a few words or engage in stutter starts that, we hope, will be more easily observed cues to signal our desire.

Conversational beginnings and endings also act as regulatory points. When we are greeting others, eye contact indicates that the channels are open. A slight head movement and an *eyebrow flash* of recognition (a barely detectable but distinct up-and-down movement of the eyebrows) may be present. The hands are also used in greetings for salutes, waves, handshakes, handslaps, emblematic signals such as the peace or victory sign, a raised fist, or thumbs-up. Hands may also perform grooming activities (running fingers through one's hair) or be involved in various touching activities such as kissing, embracing, or hitting another on the arm. The mouth may form a smile or an oval shape, as if one were ready to start talking (Krivonos & Knapp, 1975).

Saying goodbye in semiformal interviews was shown, in one study, to elicit many nonverbal behaviors. The most common included the breaking of eye contact more often and for longer periods of time, positioning one's body toward an exit, and leaning forward and nodding. Less frequent, but very noticeable, were accenting behaviors that signaled, "This is the termination of our conversation, and I don't want you to miss it!" These accenters included explosive hand and foot movements such as raising the hands and/or feet and bringing them down with enough force to make an audible slap while simultaneously using the hands and feet as leverage to catapult the interactant out of his or her seat. A less direct manifestation was placing hands on thighs or knees in a leveraging position (as if one were preparing to catapult), hoping that the other person picked up the good-bye cue (Knapp, Hart, Friedrich, & Shulman, 1975).

HISTORICAL PERSPECTIVES

The scientific study of nonverbal communication is primarily a post–World War II activity. This does not mean we cannot find important early tributaries of knowledge; even ancient Greek and Roman scholars commented on what we today would call nonverbal behavior. Quintilian's *Institutio Oratoria,* for example, is an important source of information on gesture. It was written in the first century c.e. If we traced the history of fields including animal behavior, anthropology, dance, linguistics, philosophy, psychiatry, psychology, sociology, and speech, we would no doubt find important antecedents for today's work (Asendorpf & Wallbott, 1982; Davis, 1979). Nonverbal studies never have been the province of any one particular discipline. In the last half of the nineteenth century, Delsarte (among others) attempted to codify and set forth rules for managing both "voice culture" and body movements/gestures (Shawn, 1954). Although Delsarte's "science of applied esthetics" and the elocutionary movement gave way to a less formal, less stylized twentieth century, it represents one of several early attempts to identify various forms of bodily expression. One of the most influential pre–twentieth century works was Darwin's *Expression of the Emotions in Man and Animals* in 1872. This work spawned the modern study of facial expressions, and many of his observations and ideas have been validated by other researchers (Ekman, 1973).

During the first half of the twentieth century, there were isolated studies of the voice, physical appearance and dress, and the face. An unsystematic look at the publications during this period suggests that studies of proxemics, the environment, and body movement received even less attention, while the least attention was given to the investigation of eye behavior and touching. Two noteworthy, but very different, events occurred during this period. The first involved some controversial scholarship and a scandal; the second concerns a work of extraordinary influence in the study of nonverbal behavior.

In 1925, Kretschmer authored a book, *Physique and Character.* This was followed in 1940 by Sheldon's book *The Variations of Human Physique.* These works were based on the idea that if we precisely measure and analyze a person's body, we can learn much about his or her intelligence, temperament, moral worth, and future achievement. Sheldon's belief that certain characteristics are associated with certain body types (the thin ectomorph, the muscular mesomorph, and the fatty endomorph) is still debated (see Chapter 6). His work was featured on the cover of the popular magazine *Life* in 1951. To develop a catalogue of body types, Sheldon was permitted to photograph freshman students in the nude at Yale, Wellesley, Vassar, Princeton, Smith, Mt. Holyoke, and other colleges (Rosenbaum, 1995). The students were told it was a project involving posture, and thousands complied—including future president George Bush and future first lady Hilary Rodham Clinton. The photos have reportedly been destroyed, and Sheldon's personal notes have revealed him as drawing racial conclusions from his work. People continue to associate certain characteristics with different body types, but the validity of these perceptions was not proven by Sheldon nor any researchers since.

In contrast, Efron's book *Gesture and Environment* (1941) has become a classic because it made three important contributions. Efron's innovative and detailed methods of studying gesture and body language, along with his framework for classifying nonverbal behavior, influenced future generations of scholars. In addition, Efron's work documented the important role of culture in shaping our gestures and body movement—which, at the time, was contrary to the belief of many (including Adolf Hitler) that people's behavior is not subject to much modification by changing contexts and environments.

The 1950s showed a significant increase in the number of nonverbal research efforts. Some of the milestones of this decade include the following:

1. Birdwhistell's *Introduction to Kinesics* appeared in 1952 and Hall's *Silent Language* in 1959. These anthropologists were responsible for taking some of the principles of linguistics and applying them to nonverbal phenomena, providing new labels for the study of body movement (kinesics) and space (proxemics), and launching a program of research in each area.
2. Trager's 1958 delineation of the components of paralanguage greatly enhanced the precision with which we classify and study vocal cues.
3. Psychiatrist Jurgen Ruesch and photographer Weldon Kees combined their efforts to produce a popular book titled *Nonverbal Communication: Notes on the Visual Perception of Human Relations* in 1956. This was probably the first book to use the term *nonverbal communication* in its title. Therapists, including Freud, had been interested in nonverbal cues prior to the 1950s, but this work provided additional theoretical insights into the origins, usage, and coding of nonverbal behavior and provided extensive visual documentation for the communicative role of environments.
4. Also in 1956, Maslow's and Mintz's study of the environmental effects of a "beautiful" room and an "ugly" room was published. This oft-cited study is a highlight in the history of environmental forces impinging on human communication.

5. Frank's comprehensive article "Tactile Communication" appeared in 1957 and suggested a number of testable hypotheses about touching in human interaction.

If the 1950s produced an increase in the number of nonverbal studies, the 1960s must be classified as a nuclear explosion. Specific areas of the body were the subject of extensive programs of research: Exline's work on eye behavior; the Davitz work on vocal expressions of emotion, which culminated in *The Communication of Emotional Meaning* in 1964; Hess's work on pupil dilation; Sommer's continued exploration of personal space and design; Goldman-Eisler's study of pauses and hesitations in spontaneous speech; and the study of a wide range of body activity by Dittmann, Argyle, Kendon, Scheflen, and Mehrabian. During this time, psychologist Robert Rosenthal brought vividly to our attention the potential impact of nonverbal subtleties when he showed how experimenters can affect the outcome of experiments and teachers can affect the intellectual growth of their students through nonverbal behavior (*Experimenter Effects in Behavioral Research,* 1966, and *Pygmalion in the Classroom,* 1968). Perhaps the classic theoretical piece of the 1960s is Ekman's and Friesen's article on the origins, usage, and coding of nonverbal behavior. This article distinguished five areas of nonverbal study that comprise a major part of Ekman's and Friesen's research—emblems, illustrators, affect displays, regulators, and adaptors.

The 1970s began with a journalist's account of nonverbal study from the perspective of a handful of researchers (Fast's *Body Language,* 1970). This best-selling volume was followed by a steady stream of books that attempted to make nonverbal findings understandable and usable to the American public. These books, in the interest of simplification and readability, often misrepresented findings when recounting how to make a sale, detect deception, assert one's dominance, obtain a sex partner, and the like.

Although such books aroused the public's interest in nonverbal communication, they incurred some anticipated fallout (Koivumaki, 1975). Readers were too often left with the idea that reading nonverbal cues was *the* key to success in any human encounter; some of these books implied that single cues (legs apart) represent single meanings (sexual invitation). Not only is it important to look at nonverbal *clusters* of behavior but also to recognize that nonverbal cues, like verbal ones, rarely have a single denotative meaning. Some of these popularized accounts do not sufficiently remind us that the meaning of a particular behavior is often understood by looking at the context in which the behavior occurs; for example, looking into someone's eyes may reflect affection in one situation and aggression in another.

Another common reaction to such books was the concern that once the nonverbal code was broken we would be totally transparent; people would know everything about us because we could not control these nonverbal signals. As you will learn from this book, we do have varying degrees of control over our nonverbal behavior. Some behavior is very much under our control; other behavior is not (but may be once awareness is increased). Further, it may be that as soon as someone exhibits an understanding of your body language, you will modify it and make adaptations. We have been studying verbal behavior for more than two thousand years, and we know much about the impact of certain verbal strategies, but we are still a long way from understanding the totality of verbal behavior.

The 1970s were also a time of summarizing and synthesizing. Ekman's research on the human face (*Emotion in the Human Face,* 1972, with W. V. Friesen and P. Ellsworth); Mehrabian's research on the meaning of nonverbal cues of immediacy, status, and responsiveness (*Nonverbal Communication,* 1972); Scheflen's kinesic research in the framework of general systems theory (*Body Language and Social Order,* 1972); Hess's study of the pupil size (*The Tell-Tale Eye,* 1975); Argyle's study of body movement and eye behavior (*Bodily Communication,* 1975, rev. 1988, and *Gaze and Mutual Gaze,* with M. Cook, 1975); Montagu's *Touching* (1971); and Birdwhistell's *Kinesics and Context* (1970) were all attempts to bring together the growing literature or a particular research program in a single volume.

During the 1980s, some scholars continued to specialize, but others focused on identifying the ways a variety of nonverbal signals work together to accomplish common communicative goals, for example, getting someone to do something for you, showing affection, lying to someone, and so forth (Patterson, 1983). It became clear that we could not fully understand the role of nonverbal behavior in accomplishing these goals unless we also looked at the role of co-occurring verbal behavior and tried to develop theories about how various verbal and nonverbal cues interact in the process (Streeck & Knapp, 1992). Thus, we are gradually beginning to learn how to put the pieces back together after several decades of separating them to examine them microscopically. This trend is a manifestation of a larger movement to bring our research efforts more in line with the way we know human communication occurs in life's laboratory (Archer, Akert, & Costanzo, 1993; Knapp, 1984; Patterson, 1984). Therefore, nonverbal research continues to change in the following ways:

- From studying noninteractive situations to studying interactive ones
- From studying one person to studying both interactants
- From studying a single point in time to studying changes over time
- From studying single behaviors to studying multiple behaviors
- From the view that we perceive everything that occurs to acknowledging that we need to know more about how people perceive signals during interaction
- From single-meaning and single-intent perspectives to acknowledging that often multiple meanings occur and multiple goals exist
- From a measurement perspective focused almost exclusively on frequency and duration to one that also includes issues related to when and how a behavior occurs
- From attempting to control context by eliminating important and influential elements to attempting to account for such effects
- From studying only face-to-face interaction to examining the role of

nonverbal messages in mediated communication with the new technologies

- From an overemphasis on studying how strangers interact to one equally concerned about how intimates interact
- From studying only culture or only biology as possible explanations of behavior to examining the roles both play

Such a brief historical view inevitably leaves out many important contributions. The preceding discussion is simply our attempt to highlight some important developments and depict a general background for current perspectives.

APPLIED PERSPECTIVES: NONVERBAL COMMUNICATION in EVERYDAY LIFE

It should be clear by now that nonverbal signals are a critical part of all our communicative endeavors. Sometimes nonverbal signals are the most important part of our message. Understanding and effectively using nonverbal behavior is crucial in virtually every sector of our society.

Consider the role of nonverbal signals in therapeutic situations. Therapists use nonverbal behavior to build rapport with clients (Tickle-Degnen & Rosenthal, 1992). Their ability to read nonverbal signals associated with client problems surely assists in diagnosis and treatment. A slight change in tone of voice or a glance away from the patient at the wrong time and a physician may communicate a message very different from intended (Buller & Street, 1992). In situations where verbal communication is often constrained, as in nurse-physician interaction during an operation, effective nonverbal communication is literally the difference between life and death. The significance of nonverbal cues in the arts—dance, theatrical performances, music, films, photography, and so on—is obvious. The nonverbal symbolism of various ceremonies and rituals (for example, the trappings of the marriage ceremony, Christmas decorations, religious rituals, funerals, and so forth) creates important and necessary responses in the participants. Certainly, an understanding of nonverbal signals prepares us for communicating across cultures, classes, or age groups and with different ethnic groups within our culture (Lee, Matumoto, Kobayashi, Krupp, Maniatis, & Roberts, 1992). Nonverbal messages not only help determine how well you do in a job interview, but also play an integral part in your job performance—whether it involves public relations, customer service, marketing, advertising, supervision, or leadership (Hecker & Stewart, 1988; DePaulo, 1992). Diplomats often prefer implicit accommodation rather than explicit, thereby using and relying heavily on nonverbal signals.

A list of all the situations where nonverbal communication plays an important role would be interminable—especially if we included our everyday activities involving forming impressions of other people and building, maintaining, and ending relationships. Therefore, we will limit our discussion in this chapter to four areas that touch all our lives: crime and punishment, televised politics, classroom behavior, and courtship behavior. In Chapter 12 we return to our consideration of how nonverbal communication helps us accomplish some common goals: communicating intimacy, status, identity, and deception.

CRIME AND PUNISHMENT

The desire to identify criminal types has been a subject of study for centuries. Since it is unlikely that a person will tell you that he or she is a criminal or potential criminal, nonverbal indicators become especially important. At one time, some people thought criminals could be identified by their facial features or the pattern of bumps on their head. In recent years, scientists have used a knowledge of nonverbal behavior to examine both criminal acts and the arena for assessing guilt or innocence, the courtroom.

One study analyzed the appearance and movements of people who walked through one of the highest assault areas in New York City (Grayson & Stein, 1981). Then, prisoners who had knowledge of such matters were asked to view the films of the potential victims and indicate the likelihood of assault. In addition to finding that older people are a prime target, the researchers also found that potential victims tended to move differently. They tended to take long or short strides (not medium); and their body parts did not seem to move in synchrony, that is, they seemed less graceful and fluid in their movement. Other studies have tried to identify nonverbal characteristics rapists use to select their victims. Some rapists look for women who exhibit passivity, a lack of confidence, and vulnerability; others prefer the exact opposite, wishing to "put an uppity woman in her place." The conclusion seems to recommend a public nonverbal demeanor that is confident yet not aggressive (Myers, Templer, & Brown, 1984).

Another study that assessed potentially aggressive acts focused on mothers who abused their children (Givens, 1978). It was noted that even while playing with their children, these mothers communicated their dislike (turning away, not smiling, etc.) by their nonverbal behavior. Just as abusive and nonabusive mothers differ in their behavior, the children of abusive parents and nonabusive parents differ in their nonverbal behavior (Hecht, Foster, Dunn, Williams, Anderson, & Pulbratek, 1986). In a study reported in Chapter 9, it is shown that the facial expressions of children in response to violence on television may have some predictive value for identifying aggressive behavior (Ekman, Liebert, Friesen, Harrison, Zlatchin, Malmstrom, & Baron, 1972). In short, scientists are examining nonverbal signals of both potential perpetrators of violence and the potential victims of that violence.

Once a person has been charged with a crime and the trial process begins, we can see several important and influential sources of nonverbal cues (Peskin, 1980; Pryor & Buchanan, 1984). One of this text's authors received a letter from an attorney in Florida who was seeking information about nonverbal behavior in order to identify the possible effects of an appellate judge making a decision based on the written record of the trial, without any nonverbal signals. Because of the important implications of decisions made in courtrooms and the desire to maintain impartial communication, almost every facet of the courtroom process is being analyzed. Judges are cautioned to minimize possible signs of partiality in their voice and positioning. Research suggests that judges' attitudes and nonverbal cues may indeed influence the outcome of a trial (Blanck & Rosenthal, 1992). In Chapter 6, several studies are reported concerning the effects of physically attractive witnesses and defendants. In some cases, attorneys and witnesses have been videotaped in pretrial practice sessions to determine whether they are conveying nonverbally any messages they want to avoid. The study of nonverbal behavior also may be important in the process of jury selection. One attorney asks a potential juror to look at his client and then asks, "Tell me whether you could see him as innocent" while looking at the face of the potential juror for favorable or unfavorable reactions. Other attorneys look only at nervous hand movements during the pretrial jury selection process. Although this attention to nonverbal signals emanating from prospective jurors may indicate a degree of sensitivity that did not previously exist, we need not worry that attorneys or social scientists will become so skilled they can rig juries (Saks, 1976).

TELEVISED POLITICS

Politicians have long recognized the important role of nonverbal behavior. President Lyndon Johnson is said to have been very sensitive to what nonverbal cues can communicate. He reportedly cautioned his staff not to stand in front of the windows and look across the street at the White House the day after President John F. Kennedy's assassination for fear it would appear they were looking for power. But television, and specifically the televised presidential debates, has focused both candidates and voters on the role of nonverbal behavior as never before.

Tired, overweight, physically unappealing political bosses are being replaced by younger, good-looking, vigorous candidates who can capture the public's vote with an assist from their nonverbal attraction. The average American currently watches between thirty and forty hours of television each week. Television has certainly helped to structure some of our nonverbal perceptions, and more and more political candidates recognize the tremendous influence these perceptions may have on the eventual election outcome. Television seems especially well suited to nonverbal signals that express positive relationship messages (e.g., facial expressions that communicate sincerity, body positions that suggest immediacy, or vocal tones that are perceived as caring). Television requires what Jamieson (1988) calls "a new eloquence— a softer, warmer style of communication." This in no way minimizes the necessity of a candidate also displaying nonverbal signals that would help to communicate assertiveness and energy. How have our presidential candidates fared?

During the first of the 1960 television debates between presidential candidates Richard Nixon and John Kennedy, analysts often discussed Nixon's loss in terms of how he presented himself on television, that is, his five o'clock shadow showing through the stage makeup, lighting conditions that accentuated a tired face, a suit that blended into the background, and so forth. Nixon has been quoted as saying he spent too much time studying and not enough time on his physical appearance (Bryski & Frye, 1979–80; Tiemens, 1978). A movement analysis by Davis (1995) indicates Nixon's appearance was only one of his nonverbal drawbacks.

> Nixon sits with a tense, narrow posture, while Kennedy sits with legs crossed, hands resting easily, his weight centered. In the medium camera shots, Nixon can be seen gripping the lectern tightly and not gesticulating for long periods of time, although his head movements are clear and emphatic. And Nixon displays a disastrous pattern of hyper-blinking—not just abnormally frequent (more than one per second), but at times with such rapid flutters that his eyes momentarily close. . . . By comparison Kennedy clearly wins despite his rather ordinary and constricted showing. (p. 213)

It was widely reported and believed that radio listeners judged the debate a draw, while television viewers felt Kennedy was the winner. Even though the accuracy of this conclusion has been questioned, the belief that it was true may have been largely responsible for subsequent concern about the influence of nonverbal signals in political campaigns and debates (Vancil & Pendell, 1987). By 1968, though, candidate Nixon felt he knew a great deal more about the role of nonverbal signals and the use of television. Joe McGinniss's book *The Selling of the President 1968* presents a vivid, if not frightening, picture of the role nonverbal signals may play in televised politics:

> Television seems particularly useful to the politician who can be charming but lacks ideas. . . . On television it matters less that he does not have ideas. His personality is what the viewers want to share. He need be neither statesman nor crusader; he must only show up on time. Success and failure are easily measured: how often is he invited back? Often enough and he reaches his goal—to advance from "politician" to "celebrity," a status jump bestowed by grateful viewers who feel that finally they have been given a basis for making a choice.
>
> The TV candidate, then, is measured not against his predecessors—not against a standard of performance established by two centuries of democracy—but against Mike Douglas. How well does he handle himself? Does he mumble, does he twitch, does he make me laugh? Do I feel warm inside? (p. 29–30)

The words would be the same ones Nixon always used—the words of the acceptance speech. But they would all seem fresh and lively because a series of still pictures would flash on the screen while Nixon spoke. If it were done right, it would permit Treleaven to create a Nixon image that was entirely independent of the words. Nixon would say his same old tiresome things but no one would have to listen. The words would become Muzak. Something pleasant and lulling in the background. The flashing pictures would be carefully selected to create the impression that somehow Nixon represented competence, respect for tradition, serenity, faith that the American people were better people than people anywhere else, and that all these problems others shouted about meant nothing in a land blessed with the tallest building, strongest armies, biggest factories, cutest children, and rosiest sunsets in the world. Even better: through association with these pictures, Richard Nixon could become these very things. . . . (p. 85)

An analysis of the 1976 Carter-Ford presidential debates argues that Gerald Ford's "loss" was attributable to less eye gaze with the camera, grimmer facial expressions, and less favorable camera angles (Tiemens, 1978). Subsequently, Jimmy Carter's loss to Ronald Reagan in the 1980 debate was attributed to Carter's visible tension and his inability to "coordinate his nonverbal behavior with his verbal message" (Ritter & Henry, 1990). In 1984, Reagan's expressiveness and physical attractiveness were evident, whereas his opponent, Walter Mondale, was perceived as low in expressiveness and attractiveness (Patterson, Churchill, Burger, & Powell, 1992).

Fortunately, media experts do not control all the variables—not the least of which is the public's increasing knowledge of how political images can be molded through television. One of Richard Nixon's image-makers in 1968, Roger Ailes, offered the following perspective fifteen years later: "The TV public is very smart in the sense that somewhere, somehow, they make a judgment about the candidates they see. Anybody who claims he can figure out that process is full of it."

CLASSROOM BEHAVIOR

Whether it takes place in the classroom itself or not, the teaching/learning process is a gold mine for discovering the richness and importance of nonverbal behavior (Andersen & Andersen, 1982; Babad, 1992; Philpott, Feldman, & McGee, 1992; Woolfolk & Brooks, 1983).

Acceptance and understanding of ideas and feelings by both teacher and student, encouraging and criticizing, silence, and questioning all involve nonverbal elements. Consider the following instances as representative of the variety of classroom nonverbal cues:

1. The frantic hand-waver who is sure he or she has the correct answer
2. The student who is sure she or he does not know the answer and tries to avoid eye contact with the teacher

3. The effects of student dress, hair length, and adornment on teacher-student interaction
4. The glowering facial expressions, threatening gestures, and critical tone of voice frequently used for discipline in elementary schools
5. Teachers who request student questioning and criticism, but whose nonverbal actions make it clear they will not be receptive
6. The message conveyed by being absent from class
7. The way arrangement of seating and monitoring behavior during examinations reveal a teacher's degree of trust in students
8. The variety of techniques students use to make sleeping appear to be studying or listening
9. Professors who announce they have plenty of time for student conferences, but whose fidgeting and glancing at a watch suggest otherwise
10. Teachers who try to assess visual feedback to determine student comprehension
11. The ways different classroom designs (wall colors, space between seats, windows) influence student participation and learning
12. The nonverbal cues that signal student-teacher closeness

Subtle nonverbal influence in the classroom can sometimes have dramatic results, as Rosenthal and Jacobson (1968) found. Intelligence quotient (I.Q.) tests were given to elementary school pupils prior to their entering for the fall term. Randomly (that is, not according to scores), some students were labeled as high scorers on an "intellectual blooming test" indicating they would show unusual intellectual development in the following year. Teachers were given this information. These students showed a sharp rise on I.Q. tests given at the end of the year, which experimenters attributed to teacher expectations and to the way these students were treated.

> To summarize our speculations, we may say that by what she said, by how and when she said it, by her facial expressions, postures, and perhaps by her touch, the teacher may have communicated to the children of the experimental group that she expected improved intellectual performance. Such communications together with possible changes in teaching techniques may have helped the child learn by changing his self-concept, his expectations of his own behavior, and his motivation, as well as his cognitive style and skills. (p. 180)

In an effort to identify the cues associated with teacher expectancies, Chaikin, Sigler, and Derlega (1974) asked people to tutor a twelve-year-old boy. The boy was described as either bright or dull to some, while a third group was given no information about the boy's intelligence. A five-minute videotape of the tutoring was analyzed for behaviors indicating liking and approval. Tutors of the so-called bright boy smiled more, had more direct eye contact, leaned forward more, and nodded more than either of the other two groups. In general, then, people who expect others to do well (as compared to those who expect poor performance) seem to:

1. Create a warm socioemotional climate.
2. Provide more differentiated performance feedback.
3. Give more (and more difficult) material.
4. Give more opportunities for the performer to respond (Blanck, 1993; Rosenthal, 1985).

Do students perceive teacher biases even when the teachers believe they are controlling them? Not always, but certainly much more than teachers believe. Students are often keenly aware of subtle nonverbal signals that convey messages teachers believe they are effectively masking. Babad (1992) argues that teachers need to admit their biases to themselves and recognize they are likely to be perceived by others. Once that is done, more realistic goals for student-teacher communication can be developed.

> The main obstacle is teachers' complacency and (self) deceit. They prefer to see themselves as treating all students alike and to feel righteous about investing extra effort and trying hard to teach low-achievers more. At the same time, they believe they have their emotional transmissions under control and that students are not aware of their hidden feelings. (It is really interesting how most of us believe that we can control our nonverbal behavior and conceal anything we wish, concurrently being convinced that nobody could do that to us!) Thus, the absence of personal awareness and personal goal setting constitute the major obstacle to successful application. (p. 186–87)

Finally, it should be noted that the influence of nonverbal behavior rooted in expectancies is a two-way street. Although this has received less research, student expectations influence their own behavior as well as the behavior of their teachers.

COURTSHIP BEHAVIOR

One commentary on nonverbal courtship behavior is found in the following excerpts from the Beatles' song "Something":

> Something in the way she moves
> Attracts me like no other lover
> Something in the way she woos me . . .
>
> Something in her smile she knows
> That I don't need no other lover
> Something in her style that shows me . . .
>
> You're asking me will my love grow . . .
> You stick around, now
> It may show . . .

As the song suggests, we know there is "something" highly influential in our nonverbal courtship behavior. We are, however, at a very early stage in quantifying these patterns of behavior. On a purely intuitive level, we know that some men and some women can exude such messages as "I'm available," "I'm knowledgeable," or "I want you" without saying a word. These messages can be expressed by the thrust of one's hips, touch gestures, extra long eye contact, carefully looking at the other's body, showing excitement and desire in fleeting facial expressions, and gaining close proximity. When subtle enough, these moves will allow both parties to deny that either had committed themselves to a courtship ritual.

Studies involving flirtation behavior between men and women in bars (singles bars, hotel cocktail lounges, bars within restaurants, etc.) provide some observational data on the role of nonverbal signals in the courtship process (McCormick & Jones, 1989; Moore, 1985; Perper & Weis, 1987). Most of the early signaling seemed to be performed by women. The most frequently observed behaviors included three types of eye gaze (a room-encompassing glance; a short, darting glance at a specific person; and a fixed gaze of at least three seconds at a specific other); smiling at a specific other person; laughing and giggling in response to another's comments; tossing one's head, a movement sometimes accompanied by stroking of the hair; grooming, primping, and adjustment of clothes; caressing objects such as keys or a glass; a solitary dance (keeping time to the music with visible movements); and a wide variety of seemingly "accidental" touching of a specific other. The researchers did not specifically examine the type of clothing, nor did they examine the tone of voice used—both of which are likely to be influential flirtation behaviors. In an effort to determine whether these behaviors were more likely to occur in a context where signaling interest in and attraction to others was expected, the researchers observed the behavior of women and men in snack bars, meetings, and libraries. None of these contexts revealed anything close to the number of flirting behaviors found in bars. Scheflen (1965) identified four broad categories of what he called "quasi-courtship" behavior—meaning they could be used during courtship, but they could also be used to communicate affiliative interest of a nonromantic type (see Chapter 12). Scheflen's categories included courtship readiness, preening behavior, positional cues, and actions of appeal or invitation.

Does the courtship process proceed according to a sequence of steps? Perper (1985) describes courtship's "core sequence" like this: The *approach* involves getting the two people in the same general proximity; *acknowledging and turning toward the other* is the invitation to begin talking; during *talk,* there will be an increasing amount of fleeting, *nonintimate touching* and a *gradually increasing intensity* in *eye gaze;* finally, Perper says the two will exhibit *more and more synchrony in their movements.* Obviously, either person can short-circuit the sequence at any point.

Nielsen (1962), citing Birdwhistell, described the "courtship dance" of the American adolescent. He claimed to have identified twenty-four steps from the "initial contact between the young male and female and the coitional act." These steps, he maintained, occur in a particular sequence: When a boy begins holding a girl's hand, he must wait until she presses his hand (signaling a go-ahead) before he can take the next step of allowing his fingers to inter-twine with hers. Girls and boys are labeled "fast" or "slow" according to whether they follow the order of the steps. If a step is skipped or reversed, the person who does so is labeled "fast." If a person ignores the signal to move on to the next step or takes actions to prevent the next step, he or she is considered "slow."

Morris (1971) also believes that heterosexual couples in Western culture go through a sequence of steps, like courtship patterns of other animals, on the road to sexual intimacy. Notice the predominant nonverbal theme:

1. Eye to body
2. Eye to eye
3. Voice to voice
4. Hand to hand
5. Arm to shoulder
6. Arm to waist
7. Mouth to mouth
8. Hand to head
9. Hand to body
10. Mouth to breast
11. Hand to genitals
12. Genitals to genitals and/or mouth to genitals

Morris, like Nielson, believes these steps generally follow the same order although he admits there are variations. Skipping steps or moving to a level of intimacy beyond what would be expected is found in socially formalized types of bodily contact, for example, a good-night kiss or a hand-to-hand introduction.

Up to now, we have concentrated on the nonverbal courtship behavior of unmarried men and women. The use of specific types of gazing, touching, and other actions studied in heterosexual courtship patterns are also an important part of homosexual courtship (Delph, 1978). The complex ways in which intimates and nonintimates signal their ongoing closeness is further developed in Chapter 12.

SUMMARY

The term *nonverbal* is commonly used to describe all human communication events that transcend spoken or written words. At the same time, we should realize that these nonverbal events and behaviors can be interpreted through verbal symbols. We also found that any classification scheme that separates things into two discrete categories (e.g., verbal/nonverbal, left/right brain, vocal/nonvocal, etc.) will not be able to account for factors that do not seem to fit either category. We might more appropriately think of behaviors as existing on a continuum with some behaviors overlapping two continua.

Verbal and nonverbal signals can be coded in different ways. The signals produced can be coded on a continuum of coding behavior ranging from intrinsic (the referent) to iconic (some aspect of the referent preserved) to arbitrary (none or little of the referent preserved). The decoding of nonverbal signals is often done with the right hemisphere of the brain, but there is considerable overlapping of functions between right and left hemispheres—especially if one side has to compensate due to surgery on the other hemisphere.

The theoretical writings and research on nonverbal communication can be broken down into the following three areas:

1. The communication environment (physical and spatial)
2. The communicator's physical characteristics
3. Body movement and position (gestures, posture, touching, facial expressions, eye behavior, and vocal behavior

Nonverbal communication should not be studied as an isolated phenomenon but as an inseparable part of the total communication process. The interrelationships between verbal and nonverbal behavior were illustrated in our discussion of how nonverbal behavior functions in repeating, contradicting, substituting, complementing, accenting/moderating, and regulating verbal communication. Nonverbal communication is important because of its role in the total communication system, the tremendous quantity of informational cues it gives in any particular situation, and its use in fundamental areas of our daily life.

This chapter also reviewed some of the historical highlights, noting the current influence of the works of Darwin, Efron, Birdwhistell, Hall, Ruesch and Kees, Mehrabian, Rosenthal, Ekman and Friesen, and others. The important role and shortcomings of the popular literature were reviewed. The chapter concluded with an account of the prevalence and importance of nonverbal signals in selected areas of our daily life. We emphasized nonverbal manifestations in crime and punishment, televised politics, classroom behavior, and courtship behavior.

QUESTIONS for DISCUSSION

1. Identify a situation in which you believe verbal behavior was clearly more important to the outcome of an interaction than nonverbal behavior. Explain why.
2. Suppose you were hired to advise incoming college freshmen on what nonverbal behavior they should enact to impress their teachers. What advice would you give?
3. Discuss the most unusual or subtle nonverbal signal or signals you have observed in an interaction partner of yours. What helped you assess their meaning(s)?
4. What do teachers need to do nonverbally to show they are trying to treat all students fairly?

REFERENCES and SELECTED BIBLIOGRAPHY

Andersen, P. A., & Andersen, J. (1982). Nonverbal immediacy in instruction. In L. L. Barker (Ed.), *Communication in the classroom*. Englewood Cliffs, NJ: Prentice-Hall.

Andersen, P. A., Garrison, J. P., & Andersen, J. F. (1979). Implications of a neurophysiological approach for the study of nonverbal communication. *Human Communication Research, 6,* 74–89.

Archer, D., Akert, R., & Costanzo, M. (1993). The accurate perception of nonverbal behavior: Questions of theory and research design. In Blanck, P. D. (Ed.), *Interpersonal expectations: Theory, research, and applications.* Cambridge: Cambridge University Press.

Argyle, M. (1988). *Bodily communication* (2d ed.). London: Methuen.

Argyle, M., & Cook, M. (1976). *Gaze and mutual gaze.* New York: Cambridge University Press.

Asendorpf, J., & Wallbott, H. G. (1982). Contributions of the German 'Expression Psychology' to nonverbal communication research. *Journal of Nonverbal Behavior, 6,* 135–47, 199–219; and, *7,* 20–32.

Babad, E. (1992). Teacher expectancies and nonverbal behavior. In R. S. Feldman (Ed.), *Applications of nonverbal behavioral theories and research.* Hillsdale, NJ: Erlbaum.

Bavelas, J. B., Black, A., Chovil, N., & Mullett, J. (1990). *Equivocal communication.* Newbury Park, CA: Sage.

Beakel, N. G., & Mehrabian, A. (1969). Inconsistent communications and psychopathology. *Journal of Abnormal Psychology, 74,* 126–30.

Birdwhistell, R. L. (1952). *Introduction to kinesics: An annotation system for analysis of body motion and gesture.* Washington, DC: Foreign Service Institute, U.S. Department of State/Ann Arbor, Michigan: University Microfilms.

Birdwhistell, R. L. (1970). *Kinesics and context.* Philadelphia: University of Pennsylvania Press.

Blanck, P. D. (Ed.) (1993). *Interpersonal expectations: Theory, research, and applications.* New York: Cambridge University Press.

Blanck, P. D., & Rosenthal, R. (1992). Nonverbal behavior in the courtroom. In R. S. Feldman (Ed.), *Applications of nonverbal behavioral theories and research.* Hillsdale, NJ: Erlbaum.

Bryski, B. G., & Frye, J. K. (1979–80). Nonverbal communication in presidential debates. *Australian Scan, 7,* and *8,* 25–31.

Bugental, D. E. (1974). Interpretations of naturally occurring discrepancies between words and intonation: Modes of inconsistency resolution. *Journal of Personality and Social Psychology, 30,* 125–33.

Bugental, D. E., Kaswan, J. W., Love, L. R., & Fox, M. N. (1970). Child versus adult perception of evaluative messages in verbal, vocal, and visual channels. *Developmental Psychology, 2,* 367–75.

Bugental, D. E., Love, L. R., & Gianetto, R. M. (1971). Perfidious feminine faces. *Journal of Personality and Social Psychology, 17,* 314–18.

Bugental, D. E., Love, L. R., Kaswan, J. W., & April, C. (1971). Verbal-nonverbal conflict in parental messages to normal and disturbed children. *Journal of Abnormal Psychology, 77,* 6–10.

Buller, D. B., & Street, R. L., Jr. (1992). Physician-patient relationships. In R. S. Feldman (Ed.), *Applications of nonverbal behavioral theories and research.* Hillsdale, NJ: Erlbaum.

Burgoon, J. K. (1980). Nonverbal communication research in the 1970s: An overview. In D. Nimmo (Ed.), *Communication yearbook 4.* New Brunswick, NJ: Transaction.

Chaikin, A. L., Sigler, E., & Derlega, V. J. (1974). Nonverbal mediators of teacher expectancy effects. *Journal of Personality and Social Psychology, 30,* 144–49.

Darwin, C. (1872). *The expression of the emotions in man and animals.* London: John Murray.

Davis, M. (1979). The state of the art: Past and present trends in body movement research. In A. Wolfgang (Ed.), *Nonverbal behavior: Applications and cultural implications.* New York: Academic Press.

Davis, M. (1995). Presidential body politics: Movement analysis of debates and press conferences. *Semiotica, 106,* 205–44.

Davitz, J. R. (1964). *The communication of emotional meaning.* New York: McGraw-Hill.

Delph, E. W. (1978). *The silent community: Public homosexual encounters.* Beverly Hills, CA: Sage.

DePaulo, B. M., & Friedman, H. S. (1996). Nonverbal communication. In D. T. Gilbert, S. T. Fiske, & G. Lindzey (Eds.), *The handbook of social psychology* (4th ed.). New York: McGraw-Hill.

DePaulo, B. M., Rosenthal, R., Eisenstat, R., Rogers, P. L., & Finkelstein, S. (1978). Decoding discrepant nonverbal cues. *Journal of Personality and Social Psychology, 36,* 313–23.

DePaulo, P. J. (1992). Applications of nonverbal behavior research in marketing and management. In R. S. Feldman (Ed.), *Applications of nonverbal behavioral theories and research.* Hillsdale, NJ: Erlbaum.

Dittmann, A. T. (1977). The role of body movement in communication. In A. W. Siegman & S. Feldstein (Eds.), *Nonverbal behavior and communication.* Potomac, MD: Erlbaum.

Efron, D. (1941). *Gesture and environment.* New York: King's Crown Press (Republished as *Gesture, race and culture* in 1972).

Ekman, P. (1965). Communication through nonverbal behavior: A source of information about an interpersonal relationship. In S. S. Tomkins & C. E. Izard (Eds.), *Affect, cognition and personality.* New York: Springer.

Ekman, P. (Ed.). (1973). *Darwin and facial expression: A century of research in review.* New York: Academic Press.

Ekman, P., & Friesen, W. V. (1969). The repertoire of nonverbal behavior: Categories, origins, usage, and coding. *Semiotica, 1,* 49–98.

Ekman, P., Friesen, W. V., & Ellsworth, P. (1972). *Emotion in the human face.* Elmsford, NY: Pergamon Press.

Ekman, P., Liebert, R. M., Friesen, W. V., Harrison, R., Zlatchin, C., Malmstrom, E. J., & Baron, R. A. (Eds.). (1972). Facial expressions of emotion while watching televised violence as predictors of subsequent aggression. In G. A. Comstock, E. A. Rubinstein, & J. P. Murray, *Television and social behavior: Vol. 5*. Washington, DC: U. S. Government Printing Office.

Fast, J. (1970). *Body language*. New York: M. Evans.

Frank, L. K. (1957). Tactile communication. *Genetic Psychology Monographs, 56*, 209–55.

Givens, D. B. (1978). Contrasting nonverbal styles in mother-child interaction: Examples from a study of child abuse. *Semiotica, 24*, 33–47.

Goldman-Eisler, F. (1968). *Psycholinguistics: Experiments in spontaneous speech*. New York: Academic Press.

Grayson, B., & Stein, M. I. (1981). Attracting assault: Victims' nonverbal cues. *Journal of Communication, 31*, 68–75.

Hall, E. T. (1959). *The silent language*. Garden City, NY: Doubleday.

Hall, J. A., Roter, D. L., & Rand, C. S. (1981). Communication of affect between patient and physician. *Journal of Health and Social Behavior, 22*, 18–30.

Hecht, M., Foster, S. H., Dunn, D. J., Williams, J. K., Anderson, D. R., & Pulbratek, D. (1986). Nonverbal behavior of young abused and neglected children. *Communication Education, 35*, 134–42.

Hecker, S., & Stewart, D. W. (Eds.). *Nonverbal communication in advertising*. Lexington, MA: Lexington Books.

Hess, E. H. (1975). *The tell-tale eye*. New York: Van Nostrand Reinhold.

Iaccino, J. F. (1993). *Left brain–right brain differences*. Hillsdale, NJ: Erlbaum.

Jamieson, K. H. (1988). *Eloquence in an electronic age*. New York: Oxford University Press.

Kendon, A. (1977). *Studies in the behavior of social interaction*. Bloomington, IN: University of Indiana Press.

Kendon, A. (1983). Gesture and speech: How they interact. In J. M. Wiemann & R. P. Harrison (Eds.), *Nonverbal interaction*. Beverly Hills, CA: Sage.

Knapp, M. L. (1984). The study of nonverbal behavior vis-à-vis human communication theory. In A. Wolfgang (Ed.), *Nonverbal behavior: Perspectives, applications, and intercultural insights*. New York: Hogrefe.

Knapp, M. L., Hart, R. P., Friedrich, G. W., & Shulman, G. M. (1975). The rhetoric of goodbye: Verbal and nonverbal correlates of human leave-taking. *Speech Monographs, 40*, 182–98.

Koivumaki, J. H. (1975). 'Body language taught here.' *Journal of Communication, 25*, 26–30.

Koutlak, R. (1976, November 7). With half a brain, his IQ is 126, and doctors are dumbfounded [Section one]. *Chicago Tribune*, p. 6.

Kretschmer, E. (1925). *Physique and character*. New York: Harcourt Brace Jovanovich.

Krivonos, P. D., & Knapp, M. L. (1975). Initiating communication: What do you say when you say hello? *Central States Speech Journal, 26*, 115–25.

Leathers, D. G. (1979). The impact of multichannel message inconsistency on verbal and nonverbal decoding behaviors. *Communication Monographs, 46*, 88–100.

Lee, M. E., Matsumoto, D., Kobayashi, M., Krupp, D., Maniatis, E. F., & Roberts, W. (1992). Cultural influences on nonverbal behavior in applied settings. In R. S.

Feldman (Ed.), *Applications of nonverbal behavioral theories and research.* Hillsdale, NJ: Erlbaum.

Maslow, A. H., & Mintz, N. L. (1956). Effects of esthetic surroundings: I. Initial effects of three esthetic conditions upon perceiving "energy" and "well-being" in faces. *Journal of Psychology, 41,* 247–54.

McCormick, N. B., & Jones, A. J. (1989). Gender differences in nonverbal flirtation. *Journal of Sex Education & Therapy, 15,* 271–82.

McGinnis, J. (1969). *The selling of the president 1968.* New York: Simon & Schuster, Inc.

McNeill, D. (1992). *Hand and mind: What gestures reveal about thought.* Chicago: University of Chicago Press.

McNeill, D., Cassell, J., & McCullough, K.E. (1994). Communicative effects of speech-mismatched gestures. *Research on Language and Social Interaction, 27,* 223–37.

Mehrabian, A. (1970). A semantic space for nonverbal behavior. *Journal of Consulting and Clinical Psychology, 35,* 248–57.

Mehrabian, A. (1972). Inconsistent messages and sarcasm. In A. Mehrabian (Ed.), *Nonverbal communication.* Chicago: Aldine-Atherton.

Mehrabian, A. (Ed.) (1972). *Nonverbal communication.* Chicago: Aldine-Atherton.

Mehrabian, A. (1981). *Silent messages* (2d ed.). Belmont, CA: Wadsworth.

Montagu, M. F. A. (1971). *Touching: The human significance of the skin.* New York: Columbia University Press.

Moore, M. M. (1985). Nonverbal courtship patterns in women: Content and consequences. *Ethology and Sociobiology, 6,* 237–47.

Morris, D. (1971). *Intimate behavior.* New York: Random House.

Myers, M. B., Templer, D. I., & Brown, R. (1984). Coping ability of women who become victims of rape. *Journal of Consulting and Clinical Psychology, 52,* 73–78.

Nielsen, G. (1962). *Studies in self-confrontation.* Copenhagen: Munksgaard; Cleveland: Howard Allen.

Patterson, M. L. (1983). *Nonverbal behavior: A functional perspective.* New York: Springer-Verlag.

Patterson, M. L. (1984). Nonverbal exchange: Past, present, and future. *Journal of Nonverbal Behavior, 8,* 350–59.

Patterson, M. L., Churchill, M. E., Burger, G. K., & Powell, J. L. (1992). Verbal and nonverbal modality effects on impressions of political candidates: Analysis from the 1984 presidential debates. *Communication Monographs, 59,* 231–42.

Perper, T. (1985). *Sex signals: The biology of love.* Philadelphia: ISI Press.

Perper, T., & Weis, D. L. (1987). Proceptive and rejective strategies of U.S. and Canadian college women. *Journal of Sex Research, 23,* 455–80.

Peskin, S. H. (1980). Nonverbal communication in the courtroom. *Trial Diplomacy Journal, 3,* 8–9 (Spring); 6–7, 55 (Summer).

Pfungst, O. (1965). *Clever Hans (the horse of Mr. Von Osten): A contribution to experimental, animal and human psychology* (C. L. Rahn, Trans.). New York: Holt, Rinehart & Winston. (Original work published 1911)

Philippot, P., Feldman, R. S., & McGee, G. (1992). Nonverbal behavioral skills in an educational context: Typical and atypical populations. In R. S. Feldman (Ed.),

Applications of nonverbal behavioral theories and research. Hillsdale, NJ: Erlbaum.

Pryor, B., & Buchanan, R. W. (1984). The effects of a defendant's demeanor on juror perceptions of credibility and guilt. *Journal of Communication, 34,* 92–99.

Quintilian, M. F. (1922). *Quintiliani instituiones* (H. E. Butler, Trans.). London: Heinemann. (Original work published A.D. 100)

Ritter, K., & Henry, D. (1990). The 1980 Reagan-Carter presidential debate. In R. V. Friedenberg (Ed.), *Rhetorical studies of national political debates: 1960–1988.* New York: Praeger.

Rosenbaum, R. (1995, January 15) The posture photo scandal. *New York Times Magazine,* pp. 26–31, 40, 46, 55–56.

Rosenthal, R. (1966). *Experimenter effects in behavioral research.* New York: Appleton-Century-Crofts.

Rosenthal, R. (1985). Nonverbal cues in the mediation of interpersonal expectancy effects. In A. W. Siegman & S. Feldstein (Eds.), *Multichannel integration of nonverbal behavior* (pp. 105–28). Hillsdale, NJ: Erlbaum.

Rosenthal, R., & Jacobson, L. (1968). *Pygmalion in the classroom.* New York: Holt, Rinehart & Winston.

Ruesch, J., & Kees, W. (1956). *Nonverbal communication: Notes on the visual perception of human relations.* Los Angeles: University of California Press.

Saks, M. J. (1976). Social scientists can't rig juries. *Psychology Today, 9,* 48–50, 55–57.

Scheflen, A. E. (1965). Quasi-courtship behavior in psychotherapy. *Psychiatry, 28,* 245–57.

Scheflen, A. E. (1972). *Body language and the social order.* Englewood Cliffs, NJ: Prentice-Hall.

Sebeok, T. A., & Rosenthal, R. (Eds.). (1981). The Clever Hans phenomenon. *Annals of the New York Academy of Sciences, 364.*

Sebeok, T. A., & Umiker-Sebeok, J. (1980). *Speaking of apes: Critical anthology of two-way communication with man.* New York: Plenum.

Shapiro, J. G. (1968). Responsivity to facial and linguistic cues. *Journal of Communication, 18,* 11–17.

Shawn, T. (1954). *Every little movement: A book about Francois Delsarte.* Pittsfield, MA: Eagle Print & Binding Co.

Sheldon, W. H. (1940). *The varieties of human physique.* New York: Harper and Row.

Solomon, D., & Ali, F. A. (1975). Influence of verbal content and intonation on meaning attributions of first-and-second language speakers. *Journal of Social Psychology, 95,* 3–8.

Sommer, R. (1969). *Personal space.* Englewood Cliffs, NJ: Prentice-Hall.

Stiff, J. B., Hale, J. L., Garlick, R., & Rogan, R. G. (1990). Effect of cue incongruence and social normative influences on individual judgments of honesty and deceit. *Southern Communication Journal, 55,* 206–29.

Streeck, J., & Knapp, M. L. (1992). The interaction of visual and verbal features in human communication. In F. Poyatos (Ed.), *Advances in nonverbal communication.* Amsterdam: John Benjamins.

Tickle-Degnen, L., & Rosenthal, R. (1992). Nonverbal aspects of therapeutic rapport. In R. S. Feldman (Ed.), *Applications of nonverbal behavioral theories and research*. Hillsdale, NJ: Erlbaum.

Tiemens, R. K. (1978). Television's portrayal of the 1976 presidential debates: An analysis of visual content. *Communication Monographs, 45*, 362–70.

Trager, G. L. (1958). Paralanguage: A first approximation. *Studies in Linguistics, 13*, 1–12.

Vancil, D. L., & Pendell, S. D. (1987). The myth of viewer-listener disagreement in the first Kennedy-Nixon debate. *Central States Speech Journal, 38*, 16–27.

Vande Creek, L., & Watkins, J. T. (1972). Responses to incongruent verbal and nonverbal emotional cues. *Journal of Communication, 22*, 311–16.

Volkmar, F. R., & Siegel, A. E. (1982). Responses to consistent and discrepant social communications. In R. S. Feldman (Ed.), *Development of nonverbal behavior in children*. New York: Springer-Verlag.

Wiemann, J. M. (1977). Explication and test of a model of communicative competence. *Human Communication Research, 3*, 195–213.

Wiener, M., & Mehrabian, A. (1968). *Language within language*. New York: Appleton-Century-Crofts.

Woolfolk, A. (1978). Student learning and performance under varying conditions of teacher verbal and nonverbal evaluative communication. *Journal of Educational Psychology, 70*, 87–94.

Woolfolk, A. E., & Brooks, D. M. (1983). Nonverbal communication in teaching. In E. Gordon (Ed.), *Review of Research in Education, 10*. Washington, DC: American Educational Research Association.

ADDITIONAL READINGS

The following sources were selected using the same criteria as the material in Chapter 1: to provide an introductory, broad-based perspective for understanding nonverbal communication.

THEORIES, SUMMARIES, AND OVERVIEWS

Bavelas, J. B., & Chovil, N. (in press). Redefining language: An integrated message model of language in face-to-face dialogue. *Psychological Review*.

Benthall, J., & Polhemus, T. (Eds.). (1975). *The body as a medium of expression*. New York: E. P. Dutton.

Bosmajian, H. (Ed.). (1971). *The rhetoric of nonverbal communication*. Glenview, IL: Scott-Foresman.

Buck, R. (1984). *The communication of emotion*. New York: Guilford.

Bull, P. (1983). *Body movement and interpersonal communication*. New York: Wiley.

Burgoon, J. K. (1994). Nonverbal signals. In M. L. Knapp & G. R. Miller (Eds.), *Handbook of interpersonal communication*, Beverly Hills, CA: Sage.

Burgoon, J. K., Buller, D. B., & Woodall, W. G. (1996). *Nonverbal communication: The unspoken dialogue.* New York: Harper & Row.

Cappella, J. N. (1981). Mutual influence in expressive behavior: Adult-adult and infant-adult dyadic interaction. *Psychological Bulletin, 89,* 101–32.

Cappella, J. N., & Palmer, M. T. (Eds.). (1989). *Journal of Language and Social Psychology, 8,* 3–4.

Davis, F. (1971). *Inside intuition.* New York: McGraw-Hill.

DePaulo, B. M., & Friedman, H. S. (1996). Nonverbal communication. In D. T. Gilbert, S. T. Fiske, & G. Lindzey (Eds.), *The handbook of social psychology* (4th ed.). New York: McGraw-Hill.

Druckman, D., Rozelle, R. M., & Baxter, J. C. (1982). *Nonverbal communication: Survey, theory and research.* Beverly Hills, CA: Sage.

Duncan, S., Jr., & Fiske, D. W. (1977). *Face-to-face interaction: Research, methods, and theory.* Hillsdale, NJ: Erlbaum.

Ekman, P. (1977). What's in a name? *Journal of Communication, 27,* 237–39.

Ekman, P., & Friesen, W. V. (1969). The repertoire of nonverbal behavior: Categories, origins, usage, and coding. *Semiotica, 1,* 49–98.

Ellyson, S. L., & Dovidio, J. F. (Eds.). (1985). *Power, dominance, and nonverbal behavior.* New York: Springer-Verlag.

Feldman, R. S. (Ed.). (1992). *Applications of nonverbal behavioral theories and research.* Hillsdale, NJ: Erlbaum.

Feldman, R. S., & Rimé, B. (Eds.). (1991). *Fundamentals of nonverbal behavior.* New York: Cambridge University Press.

Goffman, E. (1971). *Relations in public.* New York: Basic Books.

Hall, J. A. (1984). *Nonverbal sex differences: Communication accuracy and expressive style.* Baltimore: Johns Hopkins University Press.

Harper, R. G., Wiens, A. N., & Matarazzo, J. D. (1978). *Nonverbal communication: The state of the art.* New York: John Wiley & Sons.

Harrison, R. P. (1973). Nonverbal communication. In I. deSola Pool, W. Schramm, F. W. Frey, N. Maccoby, & E. B. Parker (Eds.), *Handbook of communication.* Chicago: Rand McNally.

Harrison, R. P., & Knapp, M. L. (1972). Toward an understanding of nonverbal communication systems. *Journal of Communication, 22,* 339–52.

Hinde, R. A. (Ed.). (1972). *Non-verbal communication.* New York: Cambridge University Press.

Kendon, A. (1981). Introduction: Current issues in the study of 'nonverbal communication.' In A. Kendon (Ed.), *Nonverbal communication, interaction, and gesture.* The Hague: Mouton.

Kendon, A. (1989). Nonverbal communication. In E. Barnouw, G. Gerbner, W. Schramm, T. L. Worth, & L. Gross (Eds.). *International encyclopedia of communications* (Vol. 3.). New York: Oxford University Press.

Kendon, A., Harris, R. M., & Key, M. R. (Eds.). (1975). *Organization of behavior in face-to-face interaction.* The Hague: Mouton.

Key, M. R. (Ed.). (1980). *The relationship of verbal and nonverbal communication.* The Hague: Mouton.

Knapp, M. L., Wiemann, J. M., & Daly, J. A. (1978). Nonverbal communication: Issues and appraisal. *Human Communication Research, 4,* 271–80.

Koneya, M. (1977). Nonverbal movements or verbal surrogates? *Journal of Communication, 27,* 235–37.

Leathers, D. G. (1986). *Successful nonverbal communication.* New York: Macmillan.

Marsh, P. (1988). *Eye to eye: How people interact.* Topsfield, MA: Salem House.

Mehrabian, A. (1972). *Nonverbal communication.* Chicago: Aldine-Atherton.

Mehrabian, A. (1981). *Silent messages* (2d ed.). Belmont, CA: Wadsworth.

Melbin, M. (1974). Some issues in nonverbal communication. *Semiotica, 10,* 293–304.

Morris, D. (1977). *Manwatching: A field guide to human behavior.* New York: Harry N. Abrams.

Morris, D. (1985). *Bodywatching.* New York: Crown.

Patterson, M. L. (1983). *Nonverbal behavior: A functional perspective.* New York: Springer-Verlag.

Polhemus, T. (Ed.). (1978). *The body reader: Social aspects of the human body.* New York: Pantheon Books.

Poyatos, F. (1980). Interactive functions and limitations of verbal and nonverbal behaviors in natural conversation. *Semiotica, 30,* 211–44.

Poyatos, F. (Ed.). (1992). *Advances in nonverbal communication.* Amsterdam: John Benjamins.

Ruesch, J., & Kees, W. (1956). *Nonverbal communication: Notes on the visual perception of human relations.* Berkeley and Los Angeles: University of California Press.

Scherer, K. R., & Ekman, P. (Eds.). (1982). *Handbook of nonverbal behavior research.* New York: Cambridge University Press.

Sebeok, T. A., Hayes, A. S., & Bateson, M. C. (Eds.). (1964). *Approaches to semiotics.* The Hague: Mouton.

Siegman, A. W., & Feldstein, S. (Eds.). (1985). *Multichannel integrations of nonverbal behavior.* Hillsdale, NJ: Erlbaum.

Siegman, A. W., & Feldstein, S. (Eds.). (1987). *Nonverbal behavior and communication* (2d ed.). Hillsdale, NJ: Erlbaum.

Spiegel, J., & Machotka, P. (1974). *Messages of the body.* New York: Free Press.

Tickle-Degnen, L., Hall, J., & Rosenthal, R. (1994). Nonverbal behavior. In Ramachandran, V. S. (Ed.), *Encyclopedia of human behavior* (Vol. 3.). New York: Academic Press.

von Cranach, M., & Vine, I. (Eds.). (1973). *Social communication and movement.* New York: Academic Press.

Weitz, S. (Ed.). (1979). *Nonverbal communication: Readings with commentary* (2d ed.). New York: Oxford University Press.

Wertz, M. D. (1972). Toward a theory of nonverbal communication: A critical analysis of Albert Scheflen, Edward Hall, George Mahl and Paul Ekman. Unpublished doctoral dissertation, University of Michigan.

Wiemann, J. M., & Harrison, R. P. (Eds.). (1983). *Nonverbal interaction.* Beverly Hills, CA: Sage.

Wiener, M., Devoe, S., Rubinow, S., & Geller, J. (1972). Nonverbal behavior and nonverbal communication. *Psychological Review, 79,* 185–214.

Wolfgang, A. (Ed.). (1979). *Nonverbal behavior: Applications and cultural implications.* New York: Academic Press.

Wolfgang, A. (Ed.). (1984). *Nonverbal behavior: Perspectives, applications, intercultural insights.* New York: Hogrefe.

CHAPTER 2

The Roots of Nonverbal Behavior

There are no universal gestures. As far as we know, there is no single facial expression, stance or body position which conveys the same meaning in all societies.

—R. L. BIRDWHISTELL

As we look back on a long phylogenetic history, which has determined our present day anatomical, physiological, and biochemical status, it would be simply astounding if it were found not to affect our behavior also.

—T. K. PITCAIRN AND I. EIBL-EIBESFELDT

Children sometimes put parents on the spot by innocently asking, "Where did I come from?" When these same children reach adulthood, other questions of origin may be of interest, such as "Am I doing this because of the way I was raised, or because of my particular genes, or do all human beings do this?" The answers are often rapid, definite, and expressed with missionary zeal. On one side we hear scholars saying that behavior is innate, instinctive, inborn, or genetic; others argue that behavior is acquired, learned, culturally taught, imposed, imitated, or environmentally determined. It is the familiar nature/nurture dichotomy. The quotations at the beginning of this chapter aptly illustrate these differing points of view. In this chapter, we examine the origins of nonverbal behavior from two perspectives: *phylogeny* (the roots of nonverbal behavior in human evolutionary history) and *ontogeny* (the roots of nonverbal behavior in our current lifetime).

First, let us look at the dichotomy confronting us: innate versus learned. As in most dichotomies, each side's proponents lose some of their capacity to explain things by supporting a polarized and inflexible position—trying to squeeze all observations into a single point of view. Instead of looking for a single origin, then, we might more productively look at the contribution of each side to the manifestation of any given behavior. No doubt much of our nonverbal behavior has both innate and learned (including imitative) aspects. Ekman and Friesen (1969), whose work in this area is detailed later, outline three primary sources of our nonverbal behavior:

1. Inherited neurological programs
2. Experience common to all members of the species (for example, regardless of culture the hands are used to place food in the mouth)
3. Experience that varies with culture, class, family, or individual

Biological and cultural forces overlap in many important ways. Some common biological processes can be used to communicate—for example, breathing becomes a sigh of relief, grief, or boredom; a hiccup becomes an imitation of a drunk's behavior; audible blowing through one's nose may be interpreted as a snort of scorn; coughing becomes "ahem"; and so on. Later in this chapter, we discuss studies that suggest some aspects of our facial expressions of emotion are inherited and are common to other members of the human species. These studies, however, do not negate the importance of our cultural learning in these expressions. The neurological program for any given facial expression can be altered or modified by learned "display rules" that are specific to our culture, for example, that men should not cry. Different stimuli may trigger a given facial expression, again, depending on one's cultural training. A snake may evoke an expression of fear in one culture and bring out an expression of joy in another (perhaps to those who see it as an important food source). The society we grow up in is also largely responsible for the way we blend two or more emotional expressions, for example, showing some features of surprise and of anger at the same time.

Studies of birds show clearly the joint impact of biology and environment on behavior. The European male robin will attack strange robins that enter his territory during the breeding season. Research using stuffed models has shown that the red breast alone triggers this attack mechanism. The female robin who shares the nest, however, also has a red breast and is not attacked. Thus, this aggressive behavior, which is believed to be innate, is modified by certain conditions in the environment or by the situation that calls forth the response. As another example, some birds instinctively sing a song common to their own species without ever having heard another bird sing the song. These birds may, upon hearing the songs of their particular group, develop a variation on the melody that reflects a local dialect. It has also been noted that without exposure to mature songs, the young bird's song will remain rudimentary and imperfect. And even when a bird is born with its basic song, it may have to learn to whom the call should be addressed and under what circumstances, and how to recognize signals from other birds. Many of the inherited components of human behavior can be modified similarly. It is like our human predisposition for or capacity to learn verbal language (Lenneberg, 1969). Although we are born with the capacity to learn language, it is not learned without cultural training. Children isolated from human contact do not develop linguistic competence. Some nonverbal signals probably are dependent primarily on inherited neurological programs; others probably depend primarily on environmental learning; and, of course, many behaviors are influenced by both.

Finally, the answer to the nature/nurture issue concerning nonverbal behavior will vary with the behavior under consideration. As we shall see in Chapter 9, there may be multiple origins of facial expressions of emotion. Certain nervous mannerisms or self-touching gestures may be learned primarily as one is also learning to perform certain tasks and cope with various interpersonal experiences. Some behaviors may be primarily the product of imitating others. Some hand gestures, such as the thumbs-up gesture, are primarily culture specific, but certain patterns of eye gaze seem to have a strong genetic component. The stronger the learned component of nonverbal behavior, the more we would expect to find variations across cultural, class, and ethnic lines. It should be noted, however, that a behavior that varies from group to group may still have a common biological base after cultural teachings are stripped away. How can we *ever* know that a single behavior or a pattern of behavior has a common biological base?

THE DEVELOPMENT of NONVERBAL BEHAVIOR across EVOLUTIONARY TIME: PHYLOGENY

Human beings, like other species, have evolved through a process of adaptation to changing conditions. Which nonverbal behaviors have ancient roots in human history? On what basis do social scientists conclude that a behavior or behavioral pattern includes an inherited component? It is not an easy task. Some of our current behavioral displays are only fragments of larger patterns no longer enacted in their entirety; some behaviors now embedded in rituals have little to do with their original function; and some behavior that seems to serve one function may be associated with something completely different—for example, self-grooming may be the result of confusion or frustration in achieving a goal rather than being enacted for self-preservation, courtship, or cleanliness goals. And studying the fossil record is not much help in understanding the biological roots of behavior. Despite the difficulties inherent in any questions of phylogeny, researchers have made some important discoveries.

Inferences about whether any given behavior has been inherited and is genetically transmitted to every member of the human species have been made primarily from five research strategies:

1. Evidence from sensory deprivation, that is, noting the manifestation of a behavior in blind and/or deaf people who could not have learned it through visual or auditory channels
2. Evidence from neonates, that is, behaviors displayed within minutes or hours after birth
3. Evidence from identical twins reared in different environments, that is, identifying the behavioral similarities of people whose gene structure is known to be virtually identical and whose learning environment is known to be very different
4. Evidence from nonhuman primates, that is, showing an evolutionary continuity of a behavior up to and including our closest relatives, nonhuman primates
5. Evidence from multicultural studies, that is, observing the manifestation of similar behaviors used for similar purposes in other cultures around the world, both literate and preliterate

Obviously, if we can compile evidence in all five categories, our confidence in a phylogenetic dimension reaches the highest level. At present, no behaviors have been studied with such thoroughness; nor do we know much about how innate and learned factors combine and interact during infancy. Nevertheless, we can make some important inferences from studies in each area.

EVIDENCE FROM SENSORY DEPRIVATION

Many have observed the early appearance of nonverbal behavior in children. Perhaps the behaviors are just learned quickly. To verify such a hypothesis, we need to examine children who, because of being blind and deaf at birth, could not learn such behaviors from visual or auditory cues. Eibl-Eibesfeldt (1973, 1975; Pitcairn & Eibl-Eibesfeldt, 1976) filmed several blind/deaf children and reached conclusions similar to those of others who have systematically compared the behavior of blind/deaf children with sighted/hearing children. In short, the spontaneous expressions of sadness, crying, laughing, smiling, pouting, anger, surprise, and fear are not significantly different in blind/deaf children. Smiling and crying sequences filmed by Eibl-Eibesfeldt are shown in Figures 2-1, 2-2, and 2-3.

Some might argue that such expressions could be learned by touching or a slow reinforcement program. Eibl-Eibesfeldt points out, however, that even "thalidomide babies" (whose mothers were prescribed the drug thalidomide during pregnancy and who suffered severe birth defects as a

Figure 2–1

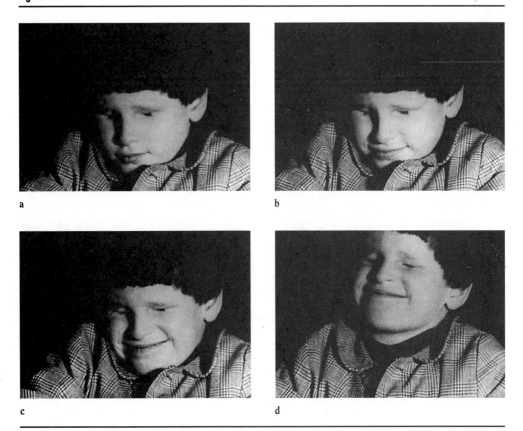

a   b

c   d

Eibl-Eibesfeldt's film of a blind/deaf smiling response. The head is lifted and tilted back as the intensity increases. (From I. Eibl-Eibesfeldt, "The Expressive Behavior of the Deaf-and-Blind Born," *in M. von Cranach and I. Vine [Eds.],* Social Communication and Movement. *New York: Academic Press, 1973)*

consequence) who had no arms, and children who could hardly be taught to raise a spoon to their mouths, showed similar expressions.

In addition to facial expressions, these deaf/blind children sought contact with others by stretching out one or both hands, wanted to be embraced and caressed when distressed, and, as the pictures in Figure 2-4 (page 50) reveal, showed a remarkably familiar sequence of refusal gestures.

Eibl-Eibesfeldt also reports some interesting eye patterns of blind children. When he complimented a ten-year-old girl on her piano playing, she looked at him, coyly looked down and away, and then looked at him again. A similar sequence was recorded for an eleven-year-old boy when asked about his girlfriend. This sequence of turning toward and away is also seen in sighted children under similar circumstances.

Figure 2–2

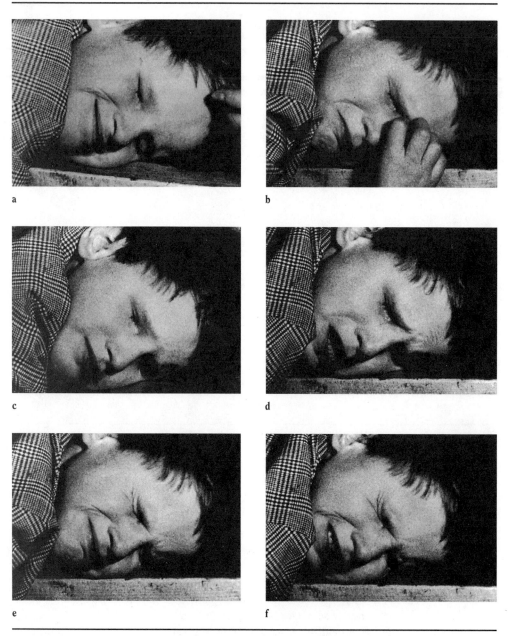

a

b

c

d

e

f

Blind/deaf crying response filmed by Eibl-Eibesfeldt. (From T. K. Pitcairn and I. Eibl-Eibesfeldt, "Concerning the Evolution of Nonverbal Communication in Man," in M. E. Hahn and E. C. Simmel [Eds.], Communicative Behavior and Evolution. *New York: Academic Press, 1976)*

Figure 2–3

Laughing response of blind/deaf children filmed by Eibl-Eibesfeldt. (From I. Eibl-Eibesfeldt, in M. von Cranach and I. Vine, 1973)

Naturally, blind/deaf children also show differences. The blind/deaf children do not show subtle gradations in expressions; for example, an expression may appear and suddenly disappear leaving the face blank. Some have noted that the expressions seem more restricted or restrained, for example, softer crying and laughing that resembles a giggle. Detailed studies of comparative facial structure would be most helpful in validating this observation. Blind/deaf children also appear to show fewer facial expressions generally with facial blends notably absent. Finally, when these blind/deaf children are asked to act out or mimic certain facial expressions, they show less ability than sighted/hearing children. All of these findings point to a joint role for innate predispositions and social learning.

Figure 2–4

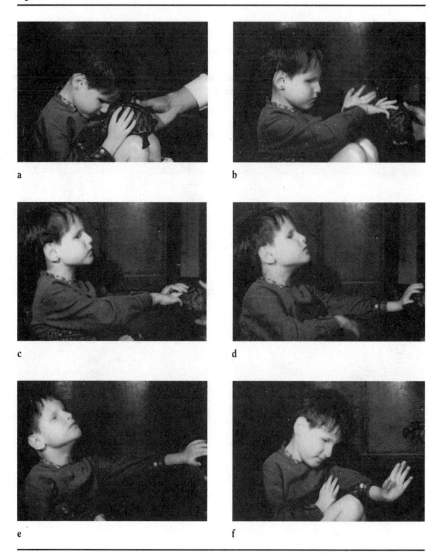

a   b

c   d

e   f

A blind/deaf child refusing an offer of a tortoise. The child sniffs at the object and pushes it back while simultaneously lifting her head in a movement of withdrawal. Finally, she puts out her hand in a gesture of warding off. (From I. Eibl-Eibesfeldt, in M. von Cranach and I. Vine, 1973)

EVIDENCE FROM INFANTS

Newborn babies (neonates) seem to have the facial muscle actions necessary to express virtually all basic affect displays of adults (Oster & Ekman, 1978). Do newborns show affect displays resembling those of adults, and if so do those displays convey the same emotions? Here the evidence is mixed, partly because of intrinsic difficulties in determining what emotion a baby is experiencing.

Researchers disagree: Does an infant's facial repertoire consist of undifferentiated expressions of arousal and distress, which are then shaped by experience, or is a baby instead born with a biologically based predisposition to display the whole repertoire of emotional expressions identified in adults? Much recent research has been inspired by the latter view, which is embodied in Differential Emotions Theory or DET (Izard, 1977; Izard & Malatesta, 1987). DET proposes that there is a strong genetic basis for facial expressions and that, because of this, emotions would produce the same distinctive facial patterns in both infants and adults.

Infants only a few months old do display some expressions consistent with prototypical emotional displays in adults—specifically expressions for joy, surprise, and interest (Oster, Hegley, & Nagel, 1992). These expressions are also easily recognizable by untrained observers as representing those emotions. This does not mean, of course, that the infants were actually experiencing those emotions, only that the facial configurations match the adult prototypes (Camras, 1994). For the negative emotions, however, there is evidence that discrete expressions corresponding to adults' for emotions such as fear, anger, disgust, and sadness do not exist in young infants (Camras, Sullivan, & Michel, 1993; Oster et al., 1992).

Thus, there is not complete support for the claim that infant data confirm the biological roots of discrete facial expressions of emotion. Moreover, it has been pointed out that too much emphasis on finding adults' expressions in infants might lead researchers to make several errors, including the following:

1. Reaching erroneous conclusions about what emotions are actually being felt (just because an infant and an adult show the same expression, we do not know they are feeling the same emotion)
2. Failing to observe distinctive infant emotional expressions that do not happen to match up with adult expressions (Barrett, 1993; Oster et al., 1992)

All researchers seem to agree, however, that infants' faces convey information about their states, that more research is needed to uncover exactly what is being conveyed and what regularities exist in the developmental unfolding of emotional expression, and that socialization still plays a crucial role.

The study of pain expression in infants and adults also yields information on the biological basis of expression and seems a less debatable topic than the expression of basic emotions. It is easy to argue that the adaptive advantage of being able to engage adult care from the earliest moments of life would lead to the evolution of an innate program for displaying pain (Prkachin & Craig, 1995). Expressions of pain in infants, even newborns, are highly similar to those observed in adults. The five most consistently seen facial movements are:

1. A lowered brow
2. Eyes squeezed tightly shut
3. Vertical wrinkles at the side of the nose (the nasolabial furrow)
4. Open lips and mouth
5. A taut cupped tongue (Grunau & Craig, 1990)

Adults routinely recognize these signs of pain, though there is also evidence that observers tend to underestimate the extent of pain in both infants and adults (Prkachin & Craig, 1995).

Research on imitation highlights the complex intertwining of biology and socialization in the development of expression. The early ability to imitate others' expressions may be inherited and may ultimately play a role in the development of various facial displays. Meltzoff and Moore (1977, 1983a, 1983b) demonstrated that twelve- to twenty-one-day-old infants imitated adults who performed four actions: tongue protrusion, mouth opening, lip protrusion, and sequential finger movement (see Figure 2-5). Subsequent research replicated the findings for tongue protrusion and mouth opening for neonates 0.7 to 71 hours old. Their experiments seem to negate explanations for such behavior based on innate releasing mechanisms similar to those found in many animals and the learning processes based on caregiver behavior. Instead, they argue that infants are born with the ability to use what they call "intermodal equivalencies," which means that the infant is able to use the "equivalence between the act seen and the act done as the fundamental basis for generating the behavioral match." Perception and production, then, are closely linked and mediated by a common representational system from birth.

Perhaps even more significant for understanding the early processes of learning and socialization is the finding that nine-month-old infants can imitate behavior from memory after a twenty-four-hour delay (Meltzoff, 1985; Meltzoff, 1988a; Meltzoff & Gopnik, 1989), and fourteen-month-olds can accurately imitate a sequence of acts after a week's delay (Meltzoff, 1988b). The early integration of cognitive, linguistic, and communicative development is also demonstrated by the infant's ability to visually process the connection between mouth shape and sound, for example, that the "ah" sound comes from a mouth with the lips wide open and the "ee" sound comes from a mouth where the corners are pulled back (Kuhl & Meltzoff, 1982).

This research is complemented by other studies (Field, Woodson, Greenberg, & Cohen, 1982) that examined the imitation of specific facial displays of emotion by two-day-old infants (see Figure 2-6). These findings support those of Meltzoff and Moore and indicate that the ability to discriminate and

Figure 2–5

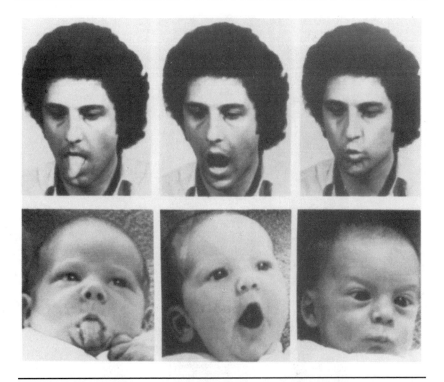

Sample photographs from videotape recordings of two- to three-week-old infants imitating (a) tongue protrusion, (b) mouth opening, and (c) lip protrusion demonstrated by an adult experimenter. (Photos © Meltzoff & Moore, 1977)

imitate happy, sad, and surprised facial expressions is one with which children enter their social environment.

EVIDENCE FROM TWIN STUDIES

Monozygotic (identical) twins are sometimes separated at birth and reared in very different environments. Since their genetic similarity is known, it is possible to compare and contrast their abilities and behavior in order to determine how much nature and nurture contribute.

Plomin (1989) provided an extensive review of the research using twins (identical and fraternal) as well as adopted children. This research shows a substantial (usually about 50 percent for identical twins) hereditary influence on such things as job satisfaction; religious interests, attitudes, and values; IQ; vocational interests; reading disability; mental retardation; extraversion;

Figure 2–6

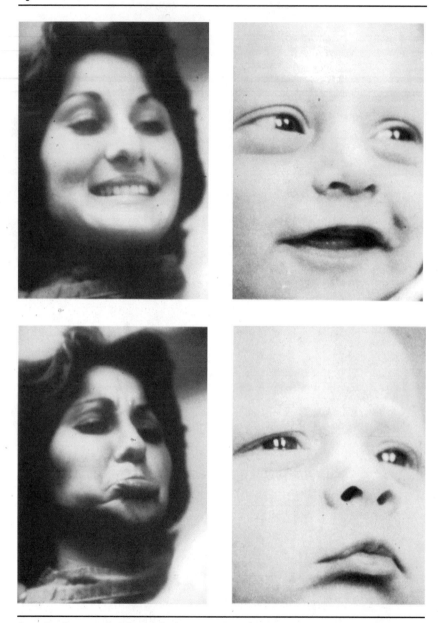

Sample photographs of model's happy, sad, and surprised (next page) expressions and infant's corresponding expressions. (Photos © Tiffany Field, Ph.D., 1982)

(Continued)

Figure 2–6 (Continued)

 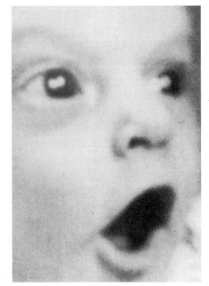

emotionality; sociability; alcoholism; and delinquency and criminal behavior. Thus, the genetic influence on behavioral factors is usually significant and often substantial, but nongenetic factors (family and nonfamily environment) are responsible for at least half of the variance in most complex behaviors. Even though genes may account for half of the variance associated with a particular behavior, it should be noted that this is almost never a highly deterministic, single-gene influence.

Despite the intriguing results from a variety of behavioral areas, we have almost no research that bears specifically on nonverbal behavior. Some anecdotal comments by researchers at the University of Minnesota Center for Twin and Adoption Research, however, portend some interesting findings (Bouchard, 1984, 1987). About identical twins reared apart, Bouchard says:

> We have also been especially impressed by similarities in a wide variety of expressive behaviors, such as body posture, gestures, tone of voice, impulsivity, and sense of humor, to name a few. (Bouchard, 1987, p. 427)

When asked to stand against a wall for a series of photographs, identical twins frequently assumed the same posture and hand positions; this happened only occasionally with fraternal twins reared apart. One pair of identical male twins reared apart had grown similar beards, had their hair cut similarly, and wore similar shirts and wire-rimmed glasses. Their photo shows them both with thumbs hooked into their pants tops. Another pair of female twins both started crying at the slightest provocation, and it was later learned that each had behaved in this manner since childhood. These unsystematic observations do not prove anything about heredity and nonverbal behavior; they only suggest intriguing avenues for research.

Most of the studies comparing twins reared apart have emphasized responses to paper-and-pencil tests. But it seems reasonable to assume detailed observational studies will indicate a hereditary influence associated with behavior as well. For example, studies of twins show an inherited component to the trait of extraversion (Pedersen, Plomin, McClearn, & Friberg, 1988; Viken, Rose, Kaprio, & Koskenvuo, 1994), and we know that certain nonverbal behaviors (for example, quicker and faster speech) are associated with the trait of extraversion. Therefore, it is not at all unlikely that these and other nonverbal cues related to extraversion will be found to be related between identical twins. Until more studies are done, though, we do not know what contribution twin studies will make to nature/nurture issues related to nonverbal behavior.

EVIDENCE FROM NONHUMAN PRIMATES

Human beings are primates, as are apes and monkeys. If we observe our nonhuman primate relatives manifesting behaviors similar to ours in similar situations, we are more confident that such behavior has phylogenetic origins.

For Charles Darwin, evidence of similarities in expressive behavior across different species constituted important support for his theory of evolution. For Darwin, the increasing use of the face, voice, and body for emotional and communicative purposes demonstrated the process of evolutionary advancement.

Darwin wrote:

> With mankind, some expressions, such as the bristling of the hair under the influence of extreme terror, or the uncovering of the teeth under that of furious rage, can hardly be understood, except on the belief that man once existed in much lower and animal-like condition. The community of certain expressions in distinct, though allied species, as in the movements of the same facial muscles during laughter by man and by various monkeys, is rendered somewhat more intelligible, if we believe in their descent from a common progenitor. (Darwin, 1872/1965, p. 12)

Among vertebrates, the functionality of a rich repertoire of expressive and signaling behaviors is clearly related to the complexity of a species' social organization. One need only compare the differing number of facial muscles possessed by a lizard to those of a monkey to understand why Darwin considered expression a critical link in the argument for evolution.

Before we begin emphasizing similarities, we should acknowledge some important differences in human and nonhuman primates. Human beings make little use of changes in body color, but we do have an extensive repertoire of gestures that attend our verbal language. We also seem to have a greater variety of facial blends. Our response repertoire is not nearly as limited to immediate and direct stimuli. And, although other animals are capable of complex acts, the level of complexity, control, and modification shown by the human animal may be hard to match.

Behavioral similarities are often linked to common biological and social problems that confront human and nonhuman primates, for example, mating, grooming, avoiding pain, expressing emotional states, rearing children, cooperating in groups, developing leadership hierarchies, defending, establishing contact, maintaining relationships, etc. Figure 2-7 shows some of these similarities in grooming and bodily contact. Of the many behaviors that might be explored for evolutionary roots (Altmann, 1968; Thorpe, 1972; van Hooff, 1973), we focus on two: facial expressions and eye behavior during greetings.

Studies comparing the facial displays of nonhuman primates and human beings find that the "tense-mouth display" of nonhuman primates (see Figure 2-8) shows social and morphological kinship to anger on human faces. When circumstances trigger a combination of anger and fear, nonhuman primates manifest a threat display (see Figures 2-9 and 2-10, pages 60–61). In human beings, this most closely resembles a blend of anger in the mouth (openmouthed anger expression) and fear in the eye area (Redican, 1982).

Table 2-1 (pages 62–63) provides both written and visual descriptions of probable evolutionary paths for facial displays of anger in four living primates. It shows evolutionary dead ends for some expressions and a continuity for others. Chevalier-Skolnikoff has proposed similar phylogenetic chains for expressions of happiness (smiling and laughter) and sadness (with and without crying; Chevalier-Skolnikoff, 1973; van Hooff, 1972).

Like human beings, nonhuman primates may accompany their emotional facial displays with complementary cues in other body regions, for example, raised hair, muscle tenseness, and the like. Varying degrees of intensity (and blending) can be produced by nonhuman primates as well (see Figure 2-10).

Extensive studies of different species of macaques also demonstrate wide variety in the social functions served by particular facial expressions (Preuschoft, 1995). Thus, even within these closely related monkey species, the same facial expression can be used with different overall frequencies and have different meanings. For example, there are "remarkable species differences with respect to the exact social meaning of the silent bare-teeth display" or fear grimace (Preuschoft, 1995, p. 201) shown in Figure 2-11 (page 64). This "grimace" usually signifies submissiveness and appeasement in species marked by rigid status hierarchies. However, in species in which status differences are weakly expressed, the expression has converged with other expressions (for example, the "play face" shown in Figure 2-11, page 64, and the "openmouthed bared-teeth display," a more extreme version of the grimace) to signify genuinely affiliative and reciprocal social interaction—for example, during greeting, grooming, embracing, or huddling—and also to reassure a lower-ranking partner. The likely relation to human smiling has long been noted by primate researchers (van Hooff, 1972). Thus, in species marked by

Figure 2–7

Upper left: A human couple. Upper right: An approximately four-year-old female with an older male chimpanzee. Middle left: Rhesus monkey mother with child. Middle right: Sonjo children clasping each other in fright. Lower left: Social grooming of vervet monkeys. Lower right: Social grooming among Bali women. All photographs except the two chimpanzees were taken by I. Eibl-Eibesfeldt. (From I. Eibl-Eibesfeldt, Ethology: The Biology of Behavior, 2d ed. New York: Holt, Rinehart & Winston, 1975) Photograph of the chimpanzees by Baron Hugo van Lawick, © National Geographic Society, 1967. Originally published in Jane Goodall, My Friends the Wild Chimpanzees, National Geographic Society, p. 86.

Figure 2–8

A tense-mouth display by an adult female rhesus monkey. Ears are flattened, brows raised, gaze fixed and staring, jaws close together, and lips compressed. Teeth are not prominently exposed, although this animal is highly disposed toward attack. Angry humans display a quite similar configuration. (Photo © William K. Redican, Ph.D., 1982, San Francisco, CA)

a reduction of power asymmetry and an increased overlap of interests among interactants, there has occurred an "evolutionary emancipation of silent bared-teeth display from its originally fearful motivation" (Preuschoft, 1995, p. 209). Such evidence that the same expression can have a diversity of meanings and functions among macaques should caution researchers of human expressions not to leap to simplistic conclusions about what human expressions mean based on the primate evidence.

Many of our facial expressions have evolved from noncommunicative behaviors such as attacking, moving toward or away from things, self-protective movements, and movements associated with respiration and vision. Chevalier-Skolnikoff argues, for instance, that

> threat postures of most primates contain elements derived from attack (mouth open and ready for biting) and locomotion toward (body musculature tense and ready to advance), while the submissive postures contain elements derived from protective responses (retraction of lips and ears) and locomotion away from the sender.

Thus, a behavior such as flight from an enemy, which was originally critical to survival, may eventually become associated with feelings of fear and/or

Figure 2–9

An adult female rhesus macaque (Macaca mulatta) *displaying a facial threat. Notice that the teeth are not prominently exposed. Ears are flattened against the head, the brow is raised, the gaze is fixed and staring, nostrils are flared, and the upper lip is rounded over the teeth. (Photo © William K. Redican, Ph.D., 1982, San Francisco, CA)*

anger. It is possible, then, that an expression of fear and/or anger may appear even if the original behavior (fleeing) is unnecessary, for example, a monkey that feels fearful when approaching a female to copulate. The facial display has, over time, become associated with a particular feeling state and appears when that feeling state is aroused. It is likely that those animals who substituted facial expressions of threat for actual attack and fighting probably had a higher survival rate and, in turn, passed on this tendency to succeeding generations. In like manner, our dependence on signals received visually (rather than through smell, for instance) may have been especially adaptive as our ancestors moved into open areas and increased in physical size.

To this point, our focus has been on our closest living relatives, nonhuman primates. Although these studies may seem most relevant to us, it is worth noting that nonprimates also show discriminable facial displays. The open-mouth display is seen in reptiles, and the flattening of the ears in situations evoking threat or startle is seen in most mammals. Some discriminable facial displays in greeting, grooming, submission, and threat have been identified in fur seals and walruses (Miller, 1975).

Figure 2–10

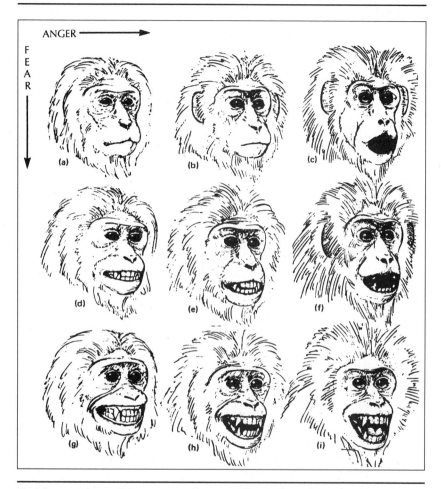

Facial expressions of Macacca arctoides *according to intensity and emotion. Note that on the anger axis (top row, left to right) as the monkey becomes increasingly angry, the stare intensifies, the ears are brought forward, the hair is raised over the head and neck, the lips are tightened and contracted, and the mouth is opened. On the fear axis (left column, top to bottom) as the animal's fear increases, the gaze is averted, the ears are drawn back against the head, where they do not show, and the lips are retracted horizontally and vertically, baring the teeth. (From Chevalier-Skolnikoff, 1973, p. 27. Drawn by Eric Stoelting)*

Reading left to right, and from top to bottom, these are the expressions: (a) Neutral face. (b) "Stare"; mild, confident threat. (c) "Round-mouthed stare"; intense, confident threat. (d) Slight "grimace"; slight fear. (e) No name; a mild fear-anger blend. (f) "Open-mouthed stare"; moderately confident, intense threat. (g) Extreme "grimace"; extreme fear. (h) Mild "bared-teeth stare"; extreme fear, blended with anger. (i) "Bared-teeth stare"; intense fear-anger blend.

Table 2–1

A BETWEEN-SPECIES ANALYSIS AND PROBABLE EVOLUTIONARY PATHS FOR FACIAL EXPRESSIONS OF ANGER

Lemurs	Macaques	Chimpanzees	Human Beings
	Confident Dominant ———▶ Threat; Anger Type I; "Stare" Eyes wide open; direct gaze, frequently with eye-to-eye contact. Brow often raised and lowered. Ears forward. Jaws closed; lips tightly closed.	Confident Dominant ———▶ Threat; Anger Type I; "Glare" Direct gaze. Jaws closed; lips closed.	Anger Type I; "Angry Face" Direct gaze, frequently with eye-to-eye contact; no sclera (white part of eye) showing above and below iris (colored part of eye); upper lids appearing lowered; upper lids sometimes tense and squared; lower lids raised and tensed, often producing a squint. Brows lowered and pulled together. Jaws clenched; lips contracted vertically and tightly pressed together.
	Confident Threat ———▶ Anger Type II; "Round-Mouthed Stare" Eyes wide open; direct gaze, frequently with eye-to-eye contact. Brow raised. Ears forward. Jaws open; lips contracted vertically and horizontally, covering the teeth and forming an "o" mouth opening. Often accompanied by a roar.	Confident Dominant Threat; Anger Type II; "Waa Bark" Direct gaze. Jaws half open; lips slightly extended and contracted, covering the teeth. Accompanied by a bark.	
Confident Threat ———▶ Anger Direct gaze. Jaws open; lips contracted, covering the teeth in some species. Invariably accompanied by a bark or coughing noise.	Moderately Confident Threat; Anger Type III; "Open-Mouthed Stare" Eyes wide open; direct gaze, frequently with eye-to-eye contact. Brow raised and then lowered. Ears forward. Jaws slightly to moderately open; lips moderately contracted vertically, covering the upper teeth, but often not the lower teeth. Often accompanied by hoarse roar.		

(Continued)

Lemurs	Macaques	Chimpanzees	Human Beings
Subordinate Threat ——→ Fear-Anger 　Alternation of jaws 　open and lips con- 　tracted, covering the 　teeth, and lips re- 　tracted horizontally 　producing a "grin." In- 　variably accompanied 　by shrieks.	Subordinate Threat ——→ Fear-Anger; "Bared-Teeth Stare" 　Eyes wide open; alterna- 　tion of direct gaze, of- 　ten with eye-to-eye 　contact, and gaze avoid- 　ance. Brow lowered; 　forehead retracted. Ears 　back. Jaws and teeth re- 　peatedly opened and 　closed; lips retracted 　vertically and horizon- 　tally, displaying the 　teeth. Often accompa- 　nied by high-pitched 　scream.	Subordinate Threat ——→ Fear-Anger; "Scream Calls" 　Jaws half or wide open; 　lips retracted vertically 　and horizontally, dis- 　playing the teeth. Often 　accompanied by 　screams.	Anger Type II; "Angry Face" 　Direct gaze, frequently 　with eye-to-eye contact; 　no sclera showing; up- 　per lids appearing low- 　ered; upper lids 　sometimes tense and 　squared; lower lids 　raised and tensed, often 　producing a squint. 　Brows lowered and 　pulled together. Jaws 　moderately open; lips 　moderately contracted 　vertically and horizon- 　tally and extended, form- 　ing a rectangular 　opening with teeth 　showing.

The information and drawings in Table 2-1 can be found in S. Chevalier-Skolnikoff, "Facial Expression of Emotion in Nonhuman Primates," in P. Ekman (Ed.), Darwin and Facial Expression *(New York: Academic Press, 1973). Drawn by Eric Stoelting.*

Figure 2–11

A grimace by an adult female rhesus macaque. Teeth receive a prominent frontal exposure in this and related compound displays. (Photo © William K. Redican, Ph.D., 1982, San Francisco, CA)

We also can look at entire sequences of behavior that may have some genetic components and evolutionary origins. For instance, many factors may affect the way greetings are handled: place, time, relationship between the greeters, and so forth. With so many sources of potential variation, then, it is noteworthy when we find seemingly invariant patterns. Pitcairn and Eibl-Eibesfeldt (1976) observed the eye behavior of adult human beings, human infants and children, blind persons, and nonhuman primates in greeting rituals and found some remarkable similarities (see Figure 2-13). They believe this behavior is a "stream of activity which, once started, must continue to the end" and that there is a strong possibility of a genetic or inherited program behind it.

Eibl-Eibesfeldt's studies of what he calls "basic interaction strategies" in several different cultures led him to conclude that rules related to dominance (and the fear of it) and bonding affiliation (and the fear of it) are at the root of human behavioral displays (nonverbal and verbal), whether in greeting, trying to block aggression, getting the focus of attention, or persuading a partner to give you something. But he acknowledges that cultural teachings and environmental factors may play an enormous role in making these strategies seem very different in one culture and another. Still, his observations of children in various cultures lead him to state: "We can assume there exists a system of universal rules that structure social interactions, verbal and nonverbal alike. These rules could be rooted in certain panhuman dispositions

Figure 2-12

A playful chimpanzee (Pan troglodytes) *displaying the primate equivalent to the human laugh and pleasurable smile. (Photo © Michael Lyster, London, 1982)*

that channel the acquisition of norms, and some norms may even be encoded in reference patterns given to us as phylogenetic adaptations" (Eibl-Eibesfeldt, 1987). Although Eibl-Eibesfeldt's view may be perceived as overstated or radically deterministic, given the evidence he provides for behavioral "universality," his observations do open the door for consideration of entire chains or sequences of behavior involved in relating to our fellow human beings that may be rooted in our biological makeup. Cappella (1991) also argues convincingly that there is a biological foundation for certain *patterns* (responses of both interactants) of interaction in humans.

EVIDENCE FROM MULTICULTURAL STUDIES

If we can observe human beings in different environments with different cultural guidelines similarly encoding and/or decoding certain nonverbal behaviors, we develop increasing confidence that inherited components of the species may be responsible. Even though multicultural similarities may be attributable to a common human inheritance, such observations are not absolute proof of innateness. It does mean that the cause of similarities across cultures is due to something we all have in common and makes a genetic explanation a possible one.

Figure 2–13

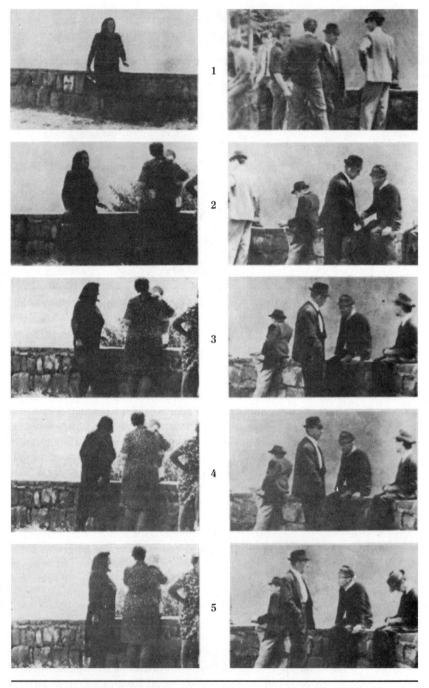

A comparative analysis of gazing patterns during greeting rituals (1 = looking during distant salutation; 2 = looking during close greeting; 3 = looking as interac-

(Continued)

Figure 2–13 (Continued)

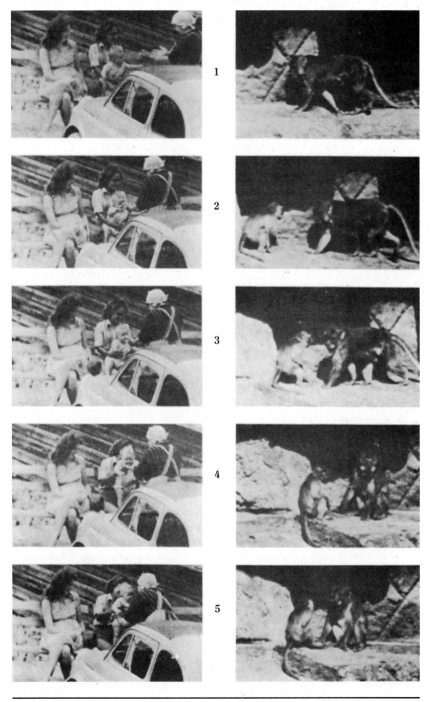

tion begins; 4 = looking away; 5 = looking as interaction continues). (Filmed by T. K. Pitcairn)

Because human beings around the world share certain biological and social functions, it should not be surprising to find areas of similarity. Eibl-Eibesfeldt suggests we might find entire sequences of behavior manifesting cross-cultural similarities, for example, coyness, flirting, embarrassment, open-handed greetings, a lowered posture for communicating submission, and so on. On the other hand, the role of one's culture surely will contribute significantly to differences in nonverbal behavior because the circumstances eliciting the behavior will vary and the cultural norms and rules that govern the management of behavior will differ. Here we detail two behaviors with widespread documentation in a variety of cultures—findings that urge us to look for the possibility of phylogenetic origins.

Eibl-Eibesfeldt (1972) has identified what he calls the "eyebrow-flash." He has observed this rapid raising of the eyebrows (maintained for about one-sixth of a second before lowering) among Europeans, Balinese, Papuans, Samoans, South American Indians, Bushmen, and others (see Figure 2-14). Although the eyebrow flash often can be seen in friendly greeting behavior, it has also been seen when people are giving approval or agreeing, seeking confirmation, flirting, thanking, and when beginning and/or emphasizing a statement. The common denominator seems to be a "yes" to social contact—requesting or approving such contact. Smiles and nods sometimes accompany this gesture. The Japanese, however, are reported to suppress it as an indecent behavior. There are, however, other instances of reported eyebrow raising that seem to indicate disapproval, indignation, or admonishment. These "no" eyebrow signals are often accompanied by a stare and/or head lift with lowering of the eyelids signaling a cutting off of contact. Because Eibl-Eibesfeldt observed eyebrow lifting in some Old World monkeys, he began speculating on the possible evolutionary development. He reasoned that in both the "yes" and "no" displays, a similar purpose was being served: calling attention to someone or letting someone know (for sure) they were being looked at. When we display the expression of surprise, for instance, we raise our eyebrows and call attention to the object of our surprise. It may be a friendly surprise or an annoyed surprise. The evolutionary chain hypothesized by Eibl-Eibesfeldt is presented in Figure 2-15.

Perhaps the most conclusive evidence supporting the universality of facial expressions is found in the work of Ekman and his colleagues (Fridlund, Ekman, & Oster, 1987). Photos of thirty faces expressing happiness, fear, surprise, sadness, anger, and disgust/contempt were presented to subjects in five literate cultures. Faces were selected on the basis of meeting specific criteria for facial musculature associated with such expressions. As Table 2-2 shows, there was generally high agreement among the respondents regarding which faces fit which emotions. Other studies have found results supporting the accuracy of decoding posed facial expressions of emotion. All in all, persons from Malaysia, countries of the former Soviet Union, and at least twelve other nations have been tested (Boucher & Carlson, 1980; Ekman, 1972; Izard, 1971; Niit & Valsiner, 1977; Shimoda, Argyle, & Bitti, 1978).

Figure 2—14

Eyebrow flash during friendly greetings. Filmed by I. Eibl-Eibesfeldt. (From I. Eibl-Eibesfeldt,
Ethology: The Biology of Behavior, *2d ed. New York: Holt, Rinehart and Winston)*

Because these people were exposed to the mass media and travelers, one
might argue that they learned to recognize aspects of faces in other cultures
from these sources. However, Ekman and Friesen's (1971) research with the
South Fore in Papua New Guinea and Heider's (1974) work with the Dani in
western Iran show that these isolated, nonliterate peoples who were not
exposed to the mass media decoded the posed expressions comparably to the
people from literate Eastern and Western cultures. In Ekman's work with the
South Fore, stories were told to the subjects who were then asked to select

Figure 2–15

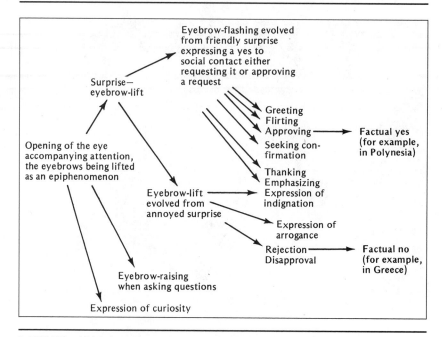

I. Eibl-Eibesfeldt's hypothesized evolution of eyebrow movements.

one of three facial photos that reflected the emotion of the story. Distinguishing fear from surprise was the most difficult discrimination to make. Perhaps, as Ekman says, fearful events in this culture are often surprising, too. Interestingly, when Ekman obtained photos of expressions made by these New Guineans and asked Americans to judge them, the Americans accurately decoded

Table 2–2
JUDGMENTS OF EMOTION IN FIVE LITERATE CULTURES

	Japan	Brazil	Chile	Argentina	United States
Happiness	87%	97%	90%	94%	97%
Fear	71	77	78	68	88
Surprise	87	82	88	93	91
Anger	63	82	76	72	69
Disgust/Contempt	82	86	85	79	82
Sadness	74	82	90	85	73
Number of Subjects	29	40	119	168	99

all the expressions with high levels of accuracy, with the exception of fear, which was often judged as surprise and vice versa.

Although Ekman's program of research is perhaps the most complete, other studies of other cultures support his findings. There does seem to be a universal association between particular facial muscular patterns and discrete emotions. It should be noted that this is only a specific element of universality and does not suggest that all aspects of facial affect displays are universal—as Ekman and Friesen (1969) testify:

> . . . we believe that, while the facial muscles which move when a particular affect is aroused are the same across cultures, the evoking stimuli, the linked effects, the display rules and the behavioral consequences all can vary enormously from one culture to another.

Do these cultural display rules follow a pattern too? Matsumoto (1991) believes there are two important dimensions of culture that will help us predict the display rules for facial expressions in any given culture:

1. Power distance, or the extent to which a culture maintains hierarchical, status, and/or power differences among its members
2. Individualism-collectivism, or the degree to which a culture encourages individual needs, wishes, desires, and values versus group and collective ones

Matsumoto hypothesizes that members of high power-distance cultures will display more emotions in public that preserve status differences. Cultures that stress individualism, according to this theory, will manifest greater differences in public emotional displays between ingroups and outgroups than in collective cultures.

Although the evidence points toward universal recognition of certain emotions from facial expressions (Ekman, 1994), it is important to acknowledge that recognition is nearly unanimous only for expressions of happiness, as indicated by Table 2-2 (also see Russell, 1994). The smile—surely the most salient feature of the happy expressions—may indeed have nearly universal meaning. But even here, one should note that judgment studies like Ekman's ask people to judge "pure" expressions out of context. The social and emotional context of a smile, and the exact combination of facial muscles used, can add many new and even contradictory meanings, as will be discussed in Chapter 9. The claim of universality is not, therefore, that all smiles will always be interpreted as happy, but that the prototypical happy expression, involving movements of certain facial muscles, will have a common meaning universally.

The possibility of great variation in the meanings attributed to facial expressions is made even clearer by the remaining emotions in Table 2-2, for which cross-cultural agreement was noticeably less than was the case for happiness. For these emotions, possibly the biological determinants are weaker or have been more overridden by cultural factors. Russell (1994) demonstrated that recognition scores for people from non-Western cultures are significantly lower than Western subjects for expressions of fear, disgust, and anger. Russell

(1994) describes the many problems with assessing universality in emotion recognition and cautions that we should not overlook the degree to which cultures do not agree.

These cross-cultural results suggest that, as with the bird songs mentioned earlier, emotional displays may have a "wired-in," neurologically determined basis that can be modified by local norms, values, and customs (see Chapter 9). This notion is consistent with the conclusions of studies, described in Chapter 3, showing that even though people may be generally accurate at interpreting others' nonverbal cues, they are *most* accurate when judging cues sent by people from their own culture.

As we will see in later chapters, there is also evidence that cultures can differ widely in the overall frequency with which specific gestures or expressions are used, as well as in the meanings attributed to those cues. Thus, again, the debate over universality versus cultural specificity cannot be viewed in an either-or light any more than the nature-versus-nurture debate can be. For illustration, two cultures might engage in different *amounts* of interpersonal touch, but the *meanings attributed to* various kinds of touches—sexual, friendly, dominant, aggressive, and so forth—may be the same in both. Thus, one would see cultural specificity in terms of usage but universality in terms of meaning. Or, different cultures might use the very same hand gesture (or emblem) with the same frequency, but use it to convey very different messages. In this case there would be universality on usage but cultural specificity on meaning.

We have ended this chapter by introducing the idea of differences among cultures in emotional displays and recognition. In the next chapter we expand upon the "difference" concept to examine differences among individuals in ability to send and understand nonverbal cues.

SUMMARY

In this chapter, we have examined five different ways researchers accumulate data relevant to questions of genetic and learned behavior. If we had data from each area for a particular behavior, the evidence would be strong. Instead, we have fragments and tantalizing possibilities. The evidence that facial expressions of emotion have an inherited component is, to date, the strongest data we have on any nonverbal behavior. Facial expressions of emotion seem to manifest themselves in children deprived of sight and hearing, in infants, in nonhuman primates, and in literate and preliterate cultures around the world. A genetic component passed on to members of the human species seems probable for this behavior. The innate capacity to perceive various kinds of behaviors and imitate them also has important implications for nonverbal study. And even though there is little detailed and systematic evidence available, the possibility that entire sequences of behavior may have a link to inheritance is most intriguing.

We take the point of view that neither nature nor nurture is sufficient to explain the origin of many nonverbal behaviors. In many instances, we inherit a neurological program that gives us the capacity to perform a particular act or sequence of acts; the fact that a particular behavior occurs at all may be genetically based. Our environment and cultural training, however, may be responsible for when the behavior appears, the frequency of its appearance, and the display rules accompanying it.

QUESTIONS for DISCUSSION

1. What do you think it means to say that nonverbal behavior is universal? State evidence supporting and not supporting such a claim. What exceptions can you think of?
2. Darwin thought there were many similarities between the expressions of humans and those of lower animals. Discuss communication in the animal world. Do you think animals send the same messages via nonverbal behavior that we do?
3. Why, in your opinion, do infants imitate adults' facial movements? Do you think they know what different expressions mean? Why do babies have such expressive faces and voices?
4. The "eyebrow flash" is seen in cultures around the world. Reflect on your own use of this gesture. Do you use it? If so, when do you use it and with what meanings? (You may have to observe your own behavior for a day or two to answer this question.)

REFERENCES and SELECTED BIBLIOGRAPHY

Additional references for Chapter 2 may be found on page 481.

Altmann, S. A. (1968). Primates. In T. A. Sebeok (Ed.), *Animal communication.* Bloomington: Indiana University Press.

Barrett, K. C. (1993). The development of nonverbal communication of emotion: A functionalist perspective. *Journal of Nonverbal Behavior, 17,* 145–69.

Cairns, R. B. (1976). The ontogeny and phylogeny of social interactions. In M. E. Hahn & E. C. Simmel (Eds.), *Communicative behavior and evolution.* New York: Academic Press.

Camras, L. A. (1994). Two aspects of emotional development: Expression and elicitation. In P. Ekman & R. J. Davidson (Eds.), *The nature of emotion: Fundamental questions.* New York: Oxford University Press.

Camras, L. A., Sullivan, J., & Michel, G. (1993). Do infants express discrete emotions? Adult judgments of facial, vocal, and body actions. *Journal of Nonverbal Behavior, 17,* 171–86.

Cappella, J. N. (1991). The biological origins of automated patterns of human interaction. *Communication Theory, 1,* 4–35.

Charlesworth, W. R., & Kreutzer, M. A. (1973). Facial expressions of infants and children. In P. Ekman (Ed.), *Darwin and facial expression.* New York: Academic Press.

Chevalier-Skolnikoff, S. (1973). Facial expression of emotion in nonhuman primates. In P. Ekman (Ed.), *Darwin and facial expression.* New York: Academic Press.

Darwin, C. (1965). *The expression of the emotions in man and animals.* Chicago: University of Chicago Press. (Original work published 1872)

Eibl-Eibesfeldt, I. (1972). Similarities and differences between cultures in expressive movements. In R. Hinde (Ed.), *Non-verbal communication.* Cambridge: Cambridge University Press.

Eibl-Eibesfeldt, I. (1973). The expressive behavior of the deaf-and-blind born. In M. von Cranach & I. Vine (Eds.), *Social communication and movement.* New York: Academic Press.

Eibl-Eibesfeldt, I. (1975). *Ethology: The biology of behavior* (2d ed). New York: Holt, Rinehart & Winston.

Eibl-Eibesfeldt, I. (1987). Social interactions in an ethological, cross-cultural perspective. In F. Poyatos (Ed.), *Cross-cultural perspectives in nonverbal communication.* Toronto: Hogrefe.

Ekman, P. (1972). Universals and cultural differences in facial expressions of emotion. In J. Cole (Ed.), *Nebraska symposium on motivation* (Vol. 19). Lincoln: University of Nebraska Press.

Ekman, P. (1973). Cross-cultural studies of facial expression. In P. Ekman (Ed.), *Darwin and facial expression.* New York: Academic Press.

Ekman, P. (1994). Strong evidence for universals in facial expressions: A reply to Russell's mistaken critique. *Psychological Bulletin, 115,* 268–87.

Grunau, R. V. E., & Craig, K. D. (1990). Facial activity as a measure of neonatal pain perception. In D. C. Tyler & E. J. Krane (Eds.), *Advances in pain research and therapy. Proceedings of the 1st International Symposium on Pediatric Pain.* New York: Raven.

Heider, K. (1974). *Affect display rules in the Dani.* Paper presented at the Annual Meeting of the American Anthropological Association, New Orleans.

Hinde, R. (Ed.). (1972). *Non-verbal communication.* Cambridge: Cambridge University Press.

Hinde, R. A. (1974). *Biological bases of human social behavior.* New York: McGraw-Hill.

Izard, C. E. (1971). *The face of emotion.* New York: Appleton-Century-Crofts.

Izard, C. E. (1977). *Human emotions.* New York: Plenum.

Izard, C. E., & Malatesta, C. (1987). Perspectives on emotional development I: Differential emotions theory of early emotional development. In J. Osofsky (Ed.), *Handbook of infant development.* New York: Wiley.

Matsumoto, D. (1991). Cultural influences on facial expressions of emotion. *Southern Communication Journal, 56,* 128–37.

Meltzoff, A. N. (1985). Immediate and deferred imitation in fourteen- and twenty-four-month-old infants. *Child Development, 56,* 62–72.

Meltzoff, A. N. (1988a). Infant imitation and memory: Nine-month-olds in immediate and deferred tests. *Child Development, 59,* 217–25.

Meltzoff, A. N. (1988b). Infant imitation after a 1-week delay: Long-term memory for novel acts and multiple stimuli. *Developmental Psychology, 24,* 470–76.

Meltzoff, A. N., & Gopnik, A. (1989). On linking nonverbal imitation, representation, and language learning in the first two years of life. In G. E. Speidel & K. E. Nelson (Eds.), *The many faces of imitation in language learning.* New York: Springer-Verlag.

Meltzoff, A. N., & Moore, M. K. (1977). Imitation of facial and manual gestures by human neonates. *Science, 198,* 75–78.

Meltzoff, A. N., & Moore, M. K. (1983a). Newborn infants imitate adult facial gestures. *Child Development, 54,* 702–9.

Meltzoff, A. N., & Moore, M. K. (1983b). The origins of imitation in infancy: Paradigm, phenomena, and theories. In L. P. Lipsitt (Ed.), *Advances in infancy research* (Vol. 2). Norwood, NJ: Ablex.

Meltzoff, A. N., & Moore, M. K. (1989). Imitation in newborn infants: Exploring the range of gestures imitated and the underlying mechanisms. *Developmental Psychology, 25,* 954–62.

Oster, H., Hegley, D., & Nagel, L. (1992). Adult judgments and fine-grained analysis of infant facial expressions: Testing the validity of a priori coding formulas. *Developmental Psychology, 28,* 1115–1131.

Pedersen, N. L., Plomin, R., McClearn, G. E., & Friberg, L. (1988). Neuroticism, extraversion, and related traits in adult twins reared apart and reared together. *Journal of Personality and Social Psychology, 55,* 950–57.

Preuschoft, S. (1995). *'Laughter' and 'smiling' in macaques: An evolutionary perspective.* Utrecht, Netherlands: University of Utrecht.

Prkachin, K. M., & Craig, K. D. (1995). Expressing pain: The communication and interpretation of facial pain signals. *Journal of Nonverbal Behavior, 19,* 191–205.

Redican, W. K. (1982). An evolutionary perspective on human facial displays. In P. Ekman (Ed.), *Emotion in the human face* (2d ed.). Cambridge: Cambridge University Press.

Russell, J. A. (1994). Is there universal recognition of emotion from facial expression? A review of the cross-cultural studies. *Psychological Bulletin, 115,* 102–41.

Scherer, K. R., & Wallbott, H. G. (1994). Evidence for universality and cultural variation of differential emotion response patterning. *Journal of Personality and Social Psychology, 66,* 329–40.

Shimoda, K., Argyle, M., & Ricci Bitti, P. (1978). The intercultural recognition of expressions by three national racial groups: English, Italian, and Japanese. *European Journal of Social Psychology, 8,* 169–79.

Smith, W. J. (1969). Displays and messages in intraspecific communication. *Semiotica, 1,* 357–69.

Spitz, R., & Wolf, K. (1946). The smiling response: A contribution to the ontogenesis of social relations. *Genetic Psychology Monographs, 34,* 57–125.

Viken, R. J., Rose, R. J., Kaprio, J., & Koskenvuo, M. (1994). A developmental genetic analysis of adult personality: Extraversion and neuroticism from 18 to 59 years of age. *Journal of Personality and Social Psychology, 66,* 722–30.

Wolff, P. H. (1963). Observations of the early development of smiling. In B. M. Foss (Ed.), *Determinants of infant behavior* (Vol. 2). London: Methuen.

CHAPTER 3

The Ability to Receive and Send Nonverbal Signals

The study of nonverbal communication as an interpersonal skill represents a significant shift in the investigation of human social behavior.

—H. S. Friedman

As we look around, we readily note that some people seem more socially wise than others. We have all known individuals who can "get along with anybody"; some people we call savvy, tactful, shrewd, or just "with it." In contrast, some people seem insensitive, awkward, or—to use one of our language's great phrases—"out to lunch." All of these qualities fit into the concept of *social competence*. Social competence is not easy to define, but it has long interested researchers, and *social intelligence* is now considered a basic intellectual capacity distinct from other cognitive abilities (Riggio, 1992; Rosenthal et al., 1979; Sternberg, 1984).

We definitely know that skill in nonverbal communication is part of social competence. Some people are comparatively more alert to nonverbal cues and better in tune with what these cues mean; some people are also more proficient at expressing their feelings and attitudes nonverbally. Some people will try, using nonverbal as well as verbal cues, to project an image of themselves as cool, reckless, intellectual, sincere, or competent, but they just can't pull it off convincingly—their performances seem fake or flawed. Others do an excellent job of projecting exactly the image they desire. The social competence that comprises such skills is essential in our daily life, whether in the office, the courtroom, the barroom, the bedroom, or in trying to bridge gaps in social class and/or culture. If we accept the premise that one's ability in nonverbal communication is important and that some people are more effective than others, we may legitimately ask how they became effective and whether the same ability can be developed in others.

In this chapter, we focus on the receiving and sending of nonverbal messages, which we refer to as nonverbal *skill* or *ability*. Although nonverbal communication skills are often talked about with reference to emotions, actually we are also called upon to read (decode) and send (encode) many other kinds of cues, such as:

- Interpersonal orientation, such as dominance/subordination and friend/stranger
- Attitudinal messages, such as "She likes me"
- Intentions or needs, such as "She wants to leave," "He wants to speak," and "She wants attention"

Other skills are also essential to adequate functioning. These include the ability to grasp verbal meanings (literal, metaphoric, and shades of innuendo); the ability to integrate verbal and nonverbal cues in order to understand how their meaning is jointly influenced (sarcasm and joking, for example, are expressed through particular combinations of verbal and nonverbal cues); and the ability to understand social contexts and roles (what's expected and unexpected in a given social situation and how people in particular roles, such as professor and student, are expected to behave; (Hall, 1979).

The ability to recognize a face seen before and to associate a name with a face are other skills required in daily life. Psychophysiologists now believe face-recognition ability is located in a particular region of the brain, because injury, such as a stroke, can selectively impair this capacity. Social factors also play an important role in this skill. For example, female faces are easier to recognize than male faces; females are somewhat more skilled at recognizing faces than males are; and it is harder to recognize the face of someone from a racial group different from one's own (Bruce, 1988; Hall, 1984; Shapiro & Penrod, 1986).

The notion of nonverbal skill can be used to gain new insight into other long-established concepts. Empathy, rapport, intuition, and charisma, as well as processes such as social comparison and impression formation, can all be construed in terms of accurate sending or receiving of nonverbal cues among people (Friedman, 1979; Rosenthal, 1979). Kurt Danziger (1976) has argued that social interaction is impossible without a subtle and unspoken negotiation over the respective roles to be played by the participants. Usually one person lays claim to a particular role or definition of the relationship (through nonverbal behavior), and the other has to go along or else counter with a different role definition. Until the two people agree, tacitly, on a common understanding, they cannot effectively interact—they simply *cannot be* "friends," "teacher-student," "salesperson-customer," "doctor-patient," or "mother-child." Because people generally know how to play these roles very well and do so unconsciously, their negotiating over roles usually slips by unnoticed until one person acts "out of role" or inappropriate to the other's unspoken expectations. Then people are likely to become conscious that the interaction has fallen apart, although they still may not know why. Clearly, the ability to read and send the subtle cues required for role negotiation is an important social skill.

Although the question of where nonverbal skill comes from and how it can be developed seems simple enough, many related questions add to the complexity of the issue and prohibit an easy answer. First, are we talking about sending ability or receiving ability? If you are proficient at sending, does this automatically mean you will also be a sensitive decoder of nonverbal cues? Immediately, then, we must ask if we are talking about a single skill or several. Second, are we talking about an ability that manifests itself in a particular channel (face, space, voice, touch) or an ability related to various combinations of channels (for example, facial plus vocal cues)? Third, are we talking about an ability that applies to all nonverbal messages or just specific types, for example, messages for specific emotions (angry, sad), messages for general affect (pleasant, unpleasant), or attitudinal messages (dominant, submissive)? Fourth, are we talking about an ability that has common standards for judging success? For instance, are we looking for similarities between the intended message sent and the message understood by the receiver? Are we comparing one's performance against norms developed from the performance of others? Or are we applying different standards for different age and cultural groups? Fifth, can we measure this ability by one or many methods—physiological, verbal, and paper-and-pencil methods, nonverbal response forms, self-reports, and the like? Sixth, are we talking about an ability that transcends specific situations or one that applies to many situations: Public versus private situations? Posed versus spontaneous situations? Meeting a course requirement versus defending yourself in court? And finally, are we talking about an ability that transcends different communication partners? Will we manifest a similar level of competence in interactions with superiors, subordinates, peers, intimates, and strangers?

METHODS for IMPROVING NONVERBAL SKILLS

Most of our ability to send and receive nonverbal signals is derived from "on-the-job training"—with the job being the process of daily living.

In short, we learn (not always consciously) our nonverbal skills by imitating and modeling ourselves after others and by adapting our responses to the coaching, feedback, and advice of others. This process starts in infancy with babies' mimicry of adult facial expressions. Even within the first few days of life, infants can imitate mouth opening and tongue protrusion; within the first few months imitation extends to lip protrusion, finger movements, brow movements, and even different emotional expressions on the face. By nine months, a mother's facial expressions not only are reciprocated but also have a clear influence on the baby's affect and play behavior (Field, 1982; Field et al., 1982; Meltzoff & Moore, 1983; Termine & Izard, 1988). Experts believe that an innate repertoire of facial expressions, innate imitative ability, and selective reinforcement by caretakers combine to produce in a child an understanding of the socially agreed on meanings of different nonverbal cues (Lewis & Rosenblum, 1978).

That nonverbal and other social skills are strongly rooted in learning seems apparent enough and gives insight into why individuals differ so much in these skills. Among many animals, social interaction is also essential to the development of appropriate social behavior later in life. Harlow's famous studies (Harlow & Mears, 1978) of rhesus macaque monkeys showed, for example, that monkeys who were raised in complete isolation for six months and then tested at 2 to 3½ years of age "displayed aggression even to 1-year-old infants, as no self-respecting socially raised rhesus would" (p. 272). Even specific communication skills in monkeys have been linked to social experience early in life. Miller and his colleagues found that rhesus monkeys reared in isolation were deficient in facial expression and judgment ability. In an experiment, two monkeys could each avoid an electric shock if one could communicate to the other through facial cues that the shock was imminent (indicated to the expressor monkey by a colored light), so that the other monkey could press a bar in time to cancel the shock for both of them. Monkeys reared in isolation were incapable of producing the necessary expressions and, when put in the role of receiver monkey, deficient at reading the fearful facial expressions of the other monkey (Miller, Caul, & Mirsky, 1967).

Feedback from others as we grow up does not have to mention our behavior explicitly; it can be a response *to* our behavior. Feedback, then, may be a person's saying, "Well, you don't look happy" or, even without making such a statement, your partner's responding to you as an unhappy person. Through feedback we increase our awareness of ourselves *and others*—for example, "Can't you see I don't like you!" We not only learn what behaviors to enact but also how they are performed, with whom, when, where, and with what consequences. Naturally, some of us have more and better helpers than others; some of us seek help more than others. You can practice nonverbal sending and receiving frequently, but, without regular, accurate feedback, you may not improve your ability.

Role playing is another popular method for teaching a social skill. Usually a situation is presented and the learner attempts to behave as he or she would if the situation actually occurred. In Stanislavsky's method of teaching acting, for instance, students may improvise various kinds of walks—walking impatiently, walking to pass time, walking to annoy people living in an apartment below them, and so on. Role playing and other exercises that make the learner an active participant are familiar fare in sensitivity groups and body-awareness workshops. Some contend that participants in such groups make great gains in their sensitivity to their own and others' nonverbal behavior. Objective data are difficult to obtain. Some people undoubtedly learn much from such experiences, though some may convince themselves they learned a lot partly to justify the time, money, and psychological effort expended.

In more rigorous studies using various media for nonverbal skill development, evidence does point to positive effects of training. Often studies take a cognitive approach, teaching the meanings of different cues using videotape playback, discussion, and feedback on correct answers. Ekman and Friesen (1975), in a relatively short six-hour training program, trained nurses to accurately identify micromomentary (extremely brief) facial expressions. Jecker, Maccoby, and Breitrose (1965) claimed success in improving, through short films, the accuracy with which teachers could judge student "understanding." The training consisted of four sessions of approximately two hours each, during which the attention of the trainees was focused on the gestures and facial expressions that accompanied "understanding." Teachers were tested on one set of films prior to the course, trained with another set of films, and posttested with still a third set of films. Control groups receiving no training did not improve in their recognition of these cues. Other research on adults (Costanzo, 1992; Davitz, 1964; Rosenthal et al., 1979), as well as on children (Beck & Feldman, 1989), support the use of this kind of skill training. Individuals from one culture have been successfully trained to understand and enact characteristic nonverbal behaviors of people from a different culture or subculture (Collett, 1971). Simply retaking a nonverbal decoding test can improve scores (especially on decoding of body cues), though it is not known how lasting or generalizable this effect is (Rosenthal et al., 1979).

The "social skills model" developed by Michael Argyle (1988) has stimulated a great deal of research and training. In this view, socially skilled behavior is seen as analogous to skilled motor behavior. In both kinds of skill, a person makes skilled moves, observes reactions to them (i.e., gets feedback), and takes corrective action, all with the purpose of obtaining a goal. The different elements of social behavior are seen as hierarchical. The finer, lower level elements are automatic and habitual; the higher level are more strategic in nature and therefore under more direct cognitive control. This kind of training involves more active role playing and practice than the research described previously. Social skills training based on this model has been used to train people of low social competence in the effective use of nonverbal cues to make friends; it is also aimed at helping distressed married couples, psychiatric patients, children with learning disabilities, and professionals who need social skills for their occupation (Argyle, Trower, & Bryant, 1974; Hargie, 1986a).

A major category of behavior emphasized in social skills training is *reinforcement*—the provision of encouragement and reward to others in the course of interaction. Reinforcers can be verbal and nonverbal. Verbal reinforcers include acknowledgement and agreement, praise, support, and compliments; nonverbal reinforcers include the positive or encouraging use of smiles, head nods, looking at the other, touching, body proximity, certain gestures (e.g., thumbs-up), and voice quality (Hargie, 1986b).

Finally, some educators and trainers argue in favor of lectures and reading assignments. Certainly any social skill is likely to profit somewhat from knowledge obtained in these ways. However, it is difficult to teach people about nonverbal behavior by words alone. Second, it is difficult to learn any social skill without practice in the skill itself. Ekman and Friesen's *Unmasking the Face* (1975) attempts to minimize these problems. The book contains many photographs of facial expressions that serve as models for various expressions of emotion, including blends. Test photos are provided for analyzing one's skill at decoding various expressions, and specific methods for analyzing one's encoding ability are also given as well as instructions for making visual records of one's own expressions, for obtaining reactions from people who view the photos, for interpreting these reactions from others, and for correcting any errors in encoding.

Students frequently ask whether all these attempts to learn about and develop skills in nonverbal communication will have negative consequences. They wonder whether we will know too much about others for their own good, whether those who have this information might use it to manipulate others for self-serving ends. Popular "how-to" books on nonverbal communication often make recommendations for manipulating others. For example, one book says if a man mimics the body positions of a woman to whom he is attracted, she is sure to fall for him. Another suggests that at a business lunch, the client will be put at an unconscious disadvantage if the host gradually moves his or her mat, plate, and silverware across the table, onto the client's side, thus invading the client's territory and weakening his or her defenses. However, many such "cookbook" recommendations are not based on reputable evidence. Even advice based on sound research would be far from a surefire scheme for success—people are not that predictable.

But assuming that knowledge of nonverbal cues *is* an asset in everyday life, should we be afraid of this knowledge? We think not. Consider the study of verbal persuasion. People have been studying the art of persuasion for over two thousand years, yet it does not appear that anyone has become so sophisticated that he or she invariably succeeds in persuading anyone in any situation. Furthermore, it is the nature of human adaptation to change behavior when it becomes unproductive. Whenever people who know more about nonverbal behavior are suspected of using it "against" others, we soon see attempts to expose or counteract the attempted influence. As a general rule, more knowledge is a good thing, for at least it may forewarn a person about others' tactics. We also believe that each person has the ethical responsibility not to use knowledge for harm.

However, people are less comfortable with the idea of skilled (conscious) use of nonverbal cues than with the idea of skilled use of words, as in persuasion. This is because people want to think that nonverbal communication is always a spontaneous (and therefore sincere) reflection of feelings or intentions. As long as people believe that all nonverbal cues are spontaneous expressions of feeling, they will be less on guard against nonverbal manipulation and, therefore, more vulnerable to it. But nonverbal communication is *much more* than a spontaneous "readout" of feelings. We use nonverbal cues for self-presentation and for a variety of strategic and communicative purposes.

The trial lawyer must act convinced of her client's innocence; the therapist must appear sincerely interested and accepting of a client's plight, whatever it might be; a manager manages a smile and a cheerful greeting for his subordinates even when his own mood is less than sunny; and a parent uses nonverbal communication constantly and deliberately to reinforce and direct a child's behavior in socially acceptable ways. Each of us has a multitude of roles to play in life, and a skilled understanding of the nonverbal cues that are relevant to each can only stand us in good stead.

ACCURACY of DECODING and ENCODING NONVERBAL CUES

Interest in measuring people's encoding and decoding skills goes back to the early decades of the twentieth century. Over the years, many researchers have measured these skills in order to answer a variety of scientific questions. Sometimes the purpose has been to study the encoding and decoding process itself. (Can emotions be recognized from nonverbal cues? What cues do people rely on most when making their judgments?) Sometimes the goal is to compare accuracy in different communication channels or among different emotions. (Is it easier to decode the face than the voice? Which are the hardest messages to send via nonverbal cues?) And sometimes the purpose is to compare the accuracy of individuals and groups. It is this last line of research that we will emphasize in this chapter.

Even though our working definition of social skill will be the accurate receiving (decoding) and sending (encoding) of nonverbal cues, there is still much latitude in how we might measure such skill. Many intriguing approaches have been taken. In one study, people rated as having high or low social competence interviewed a distressed student. The behavior that best distinguished these groups was that those rated as more competent knew to keep silent during sensitive parts of the student's account of her problems (Christensen, Farina, & Boudreau, 1980). The art of *not* talking is therefore a social skill, one that is recognized by medical educators who try to teach doctors to listen more and talk less. Another investigator saw accuracy of communication as inextricably connected to both the sender and receiver: Let us say that, after a period of interaction, you rated me on ten traits, and then I guessed how you rated me. Communication accuracy can be defined as the correlation between these two sets of ratings—with accurate communication occurring when my pattern of guesses over the ten traits matches the pattern of your actual ratings (Snodgrass, 1985). Using this method, one cannot separate the skills of encoder and decoder because high accuracy could result from an encoder (sender) who sends clear messages about what he or she thinks and feels, or from a decoder (receiver) who is extremely sensitive to the cues given off by the other person, or both. But most research has taken a more straightforward approach, one that allows a clearer separation of encoding skill from decoding skill.

For vocal encoding, senders may be asked to recite a standard sentence or the alphabet while expressing different emotional/attitudinal states or to describe a past emotional experience and thereby relive the emotion felt at the time. If, for example, the request is to "talk about a sad experience you have had," the tone of voice you use would be assumed to reflect your ability to communicate sadness through the voice. If the researcher wants to be sure that verbal cues are not a factor, methods can be applied to make the words unintelligible so that only nonverbal qualities remain (see Chapter 11).

For facial encoding, the person is asked to express a series of emotions or attitudes using his or her face or to relive an emotional experience while being videotaped. In the "slide-viewing paradigm" (Buck, Miller, & Caul, 1974), the researcher shows subjects a series of emotionally arousing slides categorized as scenic, sexual, unpleasant, or unusual. Facial reactions to the slides can then be assessed. Such facial expressions are much more spontaneous than in the previously described methods, for subjects do not know they are being videotaped while watching the slides (or films, as in some studies). The issue of posed versus spontaneous behavior is discussed later in this chapter.

The accuracy with which the encoders have nonverbally conveyed various emotions or messages is usually defined in terms of whether other people, who don't know what the original emotions or messages were, can accurately identify them. Thus, if encoder A was asked to pose a happy face and 85 percent of a group said "happy," while only 50 percent of the group judged encoder B's happy face correctly, one would conclude that encoder A did a better job of expressing the emotion than encoder B did.

Decoding or receiving ability is usually assessed by asking people to identify the emotional or attitudinal state expressed by another person either live or on film or videotape, in a photograph, or on an audio recording. A constant problem for this area of research centers on the question of *criterion:* It is easy to ask decoders to judge what the sender is feeling or communicating, but how do you know whether they are right? (Archer & Akert, 1984). If the communication is posed, the criterion is simply whatever the encoders were asked to pose. If the sender was asked to look happy, a judge would get a correct answer for saying the person looked happy. Using this system, a judge could get an error through no fault of his own if the encoder did a very poor job of showing the intended emotion. Other criteria have been used, but none is perfect. With the slide-viewing technique, a decoder's answer is typically scored as correct if he or she correctly identifies which slide the encoder was viewing when his or her face was filmed. This method assumes that encoders' faces show an appropriate response; sometimes they do not. Sometimes experts decide on what emotion is being expressed in a stimulus. Sometimes consensus is used, so that a correct answer is one that agrees with the majority of other judges.

Social psychologist Robert Rosenthal and his associates developed the most comprehensive method for testing nonverbal decoding ability, the Profile of Nonverbal Sensitivity (PONS). The PONS test is a forty-five-minute videotape that contains 220 numbered auditory and visual segments to which viewers are asked to respond. Each segment is a two-second excerpt from a scene portrayed by an American woman. Five scenes portray a positive-dominant affect or attitude (for example, "admiring a baby"); five scenes portray positive-submissive behavior (such as "expressing gratitude"); five scenes portray negative-dominant behavior (such as "criticizing someone for being late"); and five scenes portray negative-submissive behavior (for example, "asking forgiveness"). Each scene is presented to viewers in eleven different ways, representing the single or combined channels of face, body, and two different kinds of content-masked speech (see Chapter 11 for the description of the methods used to accomplish this). A receiver or viewer obtains a score for particular channels and combinations of channels in addition to a total score. The test has been administered to thousands of people of different ages, occupations, and nationalities.

Figure 3-1 shows three still photos taken from the PONS test. Each item has two choices, for example, "a. returning faulty item to a store, b. ordering food in a restaurant" or "a. talking about one's divorce, b. expressing motherly love."

In contrast to the PONS test's use of one expressor acting out a series of affective scenes, the Interpersonal Perception Task emphasizes more spontaneous behavior by many different expressors. Its developers reasoned that the best criterion is not a pure emotion or a decontextualized scenario but an actual event or relationship that is more like what people judge in "real life" (Archer & Akert, 1977; Costanzo & Archer, 1989). For example, a man and woman are interacting with two children—who is the child of the two adults? Two women discuss a racquetball game they have just played—which was the winner? A man tells his life story, then tells it again quite differently—which story is the truth? Two people are seen interacting—which has the higher status? In Figure 3-2 you can see some still frames from a preliminary version of the test.

For each item in the Interpersonal Perception task, there is an objectively correct answer. Archer believes that "ecologically valid" scenes like these will measure subtle and complex skills that people use in everyday life. There is, however, a trade-off in using more naturalistic scenes; for example, the test does not isolate cue channels, so one cannot separate accuracy for face, body, or voice. The quest for more "real-life" stimuli in nonverbal decoding tasks continues, with two of the most recently developed tests relying on cues generated in highly naturalistic circumstances (Magill-Evans, Koning, Cameron-Sadava, & Manyk, 1995; Trimboli & Walker, 1993).

Figure 3—1

Still photos from the PONS test.

CHARACTERISTICS of SKILLED NONVERBAL RECEIVERS

People are extremely sensitive to nonverbal cues. In Chapter 1 we showed that students react to very subtle positive and negative expectancy cues from their teachers. Recent research shows that first impressions of personality, based on superficial observation and no actual interaction, agree impressively among observers and with the targets' own self-descriptions. Thus, people

Figure 3–2

a

b

How's your interpersonal perception? In a, are the two people a couple married two years or strangers posing together? In b, which woman is the mother of the children? In c (on next page), is the woman waking her husband from a nap, watching an arm wrestling match, or playing with her baby daughter? Answers are given at the end of the chapter. (Photos a–c © Dane Archer, Ph.D., Santa Cruz, 1980)

(Continued)

Figure 3–2 (Continued)

c

agree on others' sociability or extraversion after the barest exposure to each other, and those ratings are more accurate than expected by chance (Albright, Kenny, & Malloy, 1988; Levesque & Kenny, 1993). Similarly, observers rating only a few seconds of silent video of teachers' classroom behavior agree remarkably on the teachers' qualities; and their ratings predict performance evaluations by the teachers' own students and principal (Ambady & Rosenthal, 1993). People may not be aware of how quickly, and accurately, they process a multitude of cues relating to physical appearance and nonverbal behavior.

Perhaps the most consistent correlate of nonverbal decoding scores is that females usually score higher than males. This is true from grade school up into adulthood. Although the difference is not great—there is only about a 2 percent difference in male and female PONS scores—it is extremely consistent. Females scored higher than males in 80 percent of 133 different groups given the PONS test, including a variety of non-U. S. samples (Hall, 1984; Rosenthal et al., 1979). Research using many other decoding tests has confirmed this sex difference, showing it across ages of subjects and regardless of whether the encoders are male or female (Hall, 1978); it also holds up, generally, whether the subjects are from the United States or not (Dickey & Knower, 1941; Izard, 1971). The Interpersonal Perception Task, which calls for a somewhat different kind of judgment than the PONS, also shows significantly higher accuracy for females (Costanzo & Archer, 1989). Research also finds that females are especially good at judging facial cues relative to other channels (Rosenthal & DePaulo, 1979). Recent research suggests, however, that in decoding of anger cues, males may have an advantage, particularly when the person being judged is male (Rotter & Rotter, 1988; Wagner, MacDonald, & Manstead, 1986). Females' decoding superiority also appears to be weaker for spontaneous than for posed emotion cues (Fujita, Harper, & Wiens, 1980).

Why are females better at nonverbal decoding? Many have pondered this question (Hall, 1984; Hall & Halberstadt, 1996; Henley, 1977; Noller, 1986). The most likely explanation comes from Noller (1986), who believes that females are better decoders (as well as encoders—see later) because they know:

1. The general social rules governing interpersonal relationships
2. The general display and decoding rules appropriate to various situations
3. The more specific rules governing the use of nonverbal cues in particular

It is society's expectation for females that they will be attuned to social interactions, indeed responsible for how they proceed.

We think it likely that females' greater skill as interpersonal decoders has been recognized throughout history and contributes to the notion of "female intuition." Intuition, of course, is a fuzzy term that can mean many things, from empathy to clairvoyance. But we think an important part of this concept is nonverbal sensitivity. The wide recognition that women are more sensitive to nonverbal cues is reflected in this excerpt from George Eliot's *Adam Bede* (1859), in which Seth talks to his mother Lisbeth about two young people, Adam and Sue:

> "She'd ne'er go away, I know, if Adam 'ud be fond on her an' marry her . . . ," said Lisbeth.
> Seth paused a moment, and looked up, with a slight blush, at his mother's face.
> "What! Has she said anything o' that sort to thee, mother?"
> "Said? Nay, she'll say nothin'. It's on'y the men as have to wait till folks say things afore they find 'em out."

Lisbeth goes on to explain that she recognized Sue's love for Adam in the girl's tendency to tremble in Adam's presence. Is it a coincidence, we wonder, that the author was a woman? (George Eliot was the pseudonym of the English novelist Mary Ann Evans.)

Researchers have also discovered, however, that females do not have an advantage on *all* kinds of nonverbal cue judging, for example, judging whether another person is lying (Zuckerman, DePaulo, & Rosenthal, 1981) or what another person was thinking and feeling at particular moments in a conversation, as measured by a later review of the videotape by both parties (Ickes, Stinson, Bissonnette, & Garcia, 1990; Marangoni, Garcia, Ickes, & Teng, 1995). Possibly, tasks that do not show a female advantage are those in which facial expression plays a weaker role. The face is, in fact, a very poor source of valid cues to deception (Zuckerman et al., 1981), and in the video-replay paradigm of Ickes the most important cues may be verbal or vocal rather than facial.

Age also has been studied in relation to decoding skill. Provocative research indicates that infants only a few months old have some ability to discriminate among facial and vocal expressions of emotion (Haviland & Lelwica, 1987; Walker-Andrews & Lennon, 1991). Of course, it is difficult to assess how much understanding of the cues' meaning a preverbal infant has; discrimination per se does not demonstrate this kind of understanding. But ingenious research found that seven-month-olds showed increased looking at a face that matched auditory tones on emotional quality; for example, they looked more at a "joy" face than a "sad" face when the associated tones were ascending, fast oscillating, high, and pulsing (Phillips, Wagner, Fells, & Lynch, 1990). Thus, by this age there seems to be some understanding of what facial expressions mean.

People generally show a gradually increasing skill from kindergarten until ages twenty to thirty (Dimitrovsky, 1964; Gates, 1925; Harrigan, 1984; Markham & Adams, 1992; Nowicki & Duke, 1992; Rosenthal et al., 1979). In a study that compared women averaging sixty-two years to women averaging twenty-two years, the PONS scores of the older were significantly lower, suggesting a role for age-related changes in attention, memory, and perception (Lieberman, Rigo, & Campain, 1988).

In two studies, the race of the receiver did not provide any advantage or disadvantage in accurately judging facial expressions (Eiland & Richardson, 1976; Gates, 1925). Indeed, in a review of the literature, Halberstadt (1985) concluded that there was no overall difference between blacks' and whites' nonverbal skill.

The results from several groups of high-school students who took the PONS test tend to refute the notion that intelligence or academic ability characterizes effective nonverbal receivers. IQ scores, SAT (Scholastic Aptitude Test) scores, class rank, and scores on vocabulary tests showed little relationship to this nonverbal ability. However, as seen later in this chapter, in children there does seem to be a relation between decoding skill and academic performance.

People who do well on the PONS and other decoding tests seem to have the following personality profile:

- Better adjusted
- Less hostile and manipulating
- More interpersonally democratic and encouraging
- Less dogmatic
- More extraverted

In addition, skilled nonverbal receivers are judged more popular and interpersonally sensitive by others, such as acquaintances, clients, spouses, and supervisors. Snyder (1974) would include what he calls "self-monitoring" as a characteristic of accurate decoders of nonverbal information in both face and voice. Self-monitors are sensitive to and exert strong control over their own behavior, but they are also sensitive to the behaviors of others and use these cues as guidelines for monitoring their own self-presentation. Results for the Interpersonal Perception Task support this finding: Higher scorers on this test also scored significantly higher on the Self-Monitoring Scale (Costanzo & Archer, 1989).

Using an extensive battery of nonverbal tests, Nowicki and Duke (1994) have determined that children in grades one through five who score higher at decoding face, posture, gesture, and voice tone are more popular and less emotionally disturbed. Further decrements in decoding ability have been found in boys referred to clinics for various kinds of childhood psychopathology (Russell, Stokes, Jones, Czogalik, & Rohleder, 1993). Interestingly, boys with problems of self-control and social incompetence made the majority of their decoding errors on PONS items requiring a judgment about the dominant-submissive dimension of behavior, consistent with previous findings that aggressive boys tend to see aggressiveness in neutral stimuli (Dodge & Newman, 1981).

Children scoring higher on Nowicki and Duke's battery of decoding tests were also higher scoring on academic achievement. After reviewing twenty-two other studies of cognitive ability and nonverbal decoding skill in children, Halberstadt and Hall (1980) concurred with this latter result and added the intriguing finding that children scoring higher on the PONS test are *perceived* by their teachers as smarter, even when the pupils' actual academic and IQ scores are controlled. Thus, it is possible that nonverbally sensitive youngsters create such a good impression that adults attribute more cognitive ability to them than they have, which may create a positive self-fulfilling prophecy in which these children are taught more and encouraged more, leading to actual gains in academic achievement. One study has found that decoding skill also seems to have a direct role in the learning process. Bernieri (1991) found that high-school students who scored higher on the PONS learned more from a peer in a brief teaching session than did students who scored lower.

Certain groups tend to have better scores on the PONS. The top three groups so far include actors, students studying nonverbal behavior, and students studying visual arts. Buck's (1976) research on the interpretation of facial expressions found that students who were fine arts or business majors were better receivers than science majors (students in biology, chemistry, math, and physics). Business executives who took the PONS test did not seem to show the same expertise that Buck's business majors did. Business executives and teachers showed significantly less ability than clinical psychologists and college students, who were significantly lower than the top three groups previously mentioned. (Do not forget that these are group scores. Individual teachers, foreign service officers, and clinicians who were rated excellent at their job also did well on the PONS instrument.) It also seems that parents (particularly mothers) of preverbal children have more nonverbal receiving sensitivity than married nonparents, suggesting that the parents acquired knowledge about nonverbal cues from living with young children.

Mental and alcoholic patients score considerably lower than a norm group on the PONS. Another group with interpersonal communication difficulties is autistic people (Philippot, Feldman, & McGee, 1992). Autism is a disorder largely defined in terms of deficient verbal, and especially nonverbal, communication and an extreme inability to relate to other human beings. The neurologist Oliver Sacks has written about Temple Grandin, an autistic academician whose insights greatly illuminate our understanding of the inner experience of autism. Grandin's understanding of others' feelings and intentions comes from "immense intellectual effort" as opposed to the unconscious, intuitive process used by nonautistic people. Commenting on her childhood experiences, Sacks writes:

> Something was going on between the other kids, something swift, subtle, constantly changing—an exchange of meanings, a negotiation, a swiftness of understanding so remarkable that sometimes she wondered if they were all telepathic. She is now aware of the existence of these social signals. She can infer them, she says, but she herself cannot perceive them, cannot participate in this magical communication directly . . . This is why she often feels excluded, an alien. (Sacks, 1993, p. 116)

Alcohol consumption, in its extreme form, can also be considered a psychopathology. An intriguing experiment using photographs of six emotions found that when normal subjects were given alcohol, their decoding accuracy was impaired, especially men's ability to identify anger, disgust, and contempt (Borrill, Rosen, & Summerfield, 1987). Perhaps some of the antisocial behavior of drinkers is linked to an impairment in their sensitivity to these cues.

The work of Robin DiMatteo and her colleagues (DiMatteo et al., 1980; DiMatteo, Hays, & Prince, 1986) on the nonverbal skills of physicians offers especially strong evidence that these skills truly matter in daily life. In this research, the PONS scores of physicians were related to the satisfaction and appointment-keeping records of actual patients. Patients were more satisfied when their physician was a good decoder of body cues; patients also showed up more often for scheduled appointments when their physician was a good decoder of tone-of-voice cues. Although more research needs to be done to document *how* physicians translate their decoding skill into effective behavior with their patients, one can imagine that they pick up on subtle cues of distress, dissatisfaction, or indecision and then address those issues with the patient.

The PONS has been administered to people from over twenty nations. People from countries most similar to the United States in language and culture (modernization, widespread use of communications media) scored highest. The PONS research therefore offers a synthesis of two opposed positions on the universality of emotional expressions: One states that these are universally used and recognized, the other that nonverbal communication is as culture-specific as verbal language itself. The universalist position is supported by the fact that all cultures were able to perform at higher than chance levels on the PONS; the specificity argument is supported by the fact that groups more culturally similar to that of the PONS sender were able to extract more accurate meaning from the cues. In a related venture, word-free voice samples of Cree Indians and white, English-speaking, Canadian residents were also judged along ethnic and cultural lines (Albas, McCluskey, & Albas, 1976). Each group was more accurate in perceiving the emotional content in the voice samples made by members of their own group. As stated in earlier chapters, some cultures use and pay more attention to certain types of nonverbal behavior and would naturally be expected to show more proficiency in those areas than a culture that de-emphasized a particular behavior or channel of communication.

A vast amount of research on the topic of attraction suggests that similarity in attitudes or background is a key to selecting and maintaining friends and romantic partners. The nonverbal realm offers supporting evidence. Friends are more similar to each other in their understanding of facial cues of emotion than people who are not friends (Brauer & DePaulo, 1980). When friends are more similar in this kind of skill (Brauer & DePaulo, 1980) or when both have high ability (Hodgins & Zuckerman, 1990), the relationship is marked by deeper emotional sharing.

OTHER FACTORS AFFECTING NONVERBAL RECEIVING ACCURACY

You may think the particular channels (face, voice, and the like) that are tested will make a difference in a person's nonverbal receiving accuracy. Indeed, several studies show that emotions and attitudes of liking or disliking are more accurately perceived in the face than in the voice. And, although you may be better able to recognize many emotions and attitudes if you get both audio and visual cues, some messages may be more effectively communicated in one mode than another; for example, vocal cues may be more effective for communicating anxiety and seductiveness than other individual communication channels (Burns & Beier, 1973). If you are accurate in recognizing facial signals, you will also be accurate in perceiving vocal ones (Zuckerman et al., 1975). This does not deny that some people may have a preference for, or rely more heavily on, a particular channel. Beldoch's (1964) work extended beyond the traditional facial/vocal dichotomy. He obtained word-free tape recordings of people vocally expressing twelve emotions, asked musicians to write and record short musical renditions of the same twelve emotions, and, finally, asked artists to create abstract art they felt captured the emotions under consideration. The results support the idea that one's ability to accurately decode feelings in one medium may carry over to other media. Similarly, accuracy may vary according to whether expressions are posed (usually higher) or spontaneous, but if you do well in decoding one, you'll probably do well in the other (Zuckerman et al., 1976). It is clear that some emotional and attitudinal states are more difficult to judge than others. Negative nonverbal messages, some argue, may be more readily conveyed than positive ones, although findings are inconsistent on this and also seem to vary with the nonverbal channel in which the cues are conveyed (Zuckerman et al., 1976).

We might also speculate, as did the PONS researchers, that the amount of time a receiver was exposed to a nonverbal signal would affect his or her accuracy in identification. The PONS materials were presented to people with the exposure time varied, for example, $\frac{1}{24}$ of a second, $\frac{3}{24}$ of a second, and so on. Although accuracy did increase as exposure time increased, these differences are probably minimal when exposure times reach higher levels. Some people, it seems, achieve high levels of accuracy with minimal exposure time. They perceive and process this nonverbal information quickly. It is even speculated that these persons may "see too much" and have less satisfying interpersonal relationships because of the acuity of their perceptions.

Now that we have examined decoding abilities, we can turn to encoding or sending ability.

CHARACTERISTICS of SKILLED NONVERBAL SENDERS

When broadly conceived, a definition of "nonverbal sending" is even more complex than a definition of nonverbal decoding ability. In a sense, nonverbal sending is everything we do of an interpersonal nature. Indeed, it is impossible *not* to send some sort of nonverbal cues that are perceived and interpreted by others—even if your intention is to appear neutral or unexpressive. At-tempts to control nonverbal cues by trying not to express them at all are likely to be interpreted as dullness, withdrawal, uneasiness, aloofness, or even deceptiveness (DePaulo, 1992).

A person's nonverbal sending is a mixture of spontaneous cues and more deliberate or intentional ones. The latter are used in daily life to convey a host of impressions of ourselves as nice, smart, youthful, honest, dominant, brave, and so forth. We also use nonverbal communication intentionally as part of our effort to act socially appropriate, for example, to be respectful to authorities, dignified in a fancy restaurant, or polite in the face of disap-pointment.

Children attain these more deliberate self-presentational skills through a long process that combines social experience with their own development of identity; numerous studies testify to developmental trends in these skills (DePaulo, 1992; Harrigan, 1984; Nowicki & Duke, 1989; Rosenthal et al., 1979), though one should not underestimate the skill of young children in simulating and masking expressions of emotion (Halberstadt, Grotjohn, Johnson, Furth, & Greig, 1992). According to DePaulo, success at regulating nonverbal behaviors to promote the public presentation of oneself depends on knowledge, skill, practice, experience, confidence, and motivation. The success of nonverbal self-presentation is also limited by the inherent controllability of different nonverbal channels and the intensity of the reality one might wish to mask (for example, the more angry you are, the harder it will be to act as if everything is fine), as well as individual differences among people.

One individual difference that definitely affects self-presentation is spontaneous expressiveness of the sort we have discussed in relation to the slide-viewing paradigm, for example, how much your face reflects the content of a grisly or romantic scene you watch on television. These differences are observable in infancy and are stable over the course of development. The spontaneously expressive person has many social advantages, as we will outline shortly, but may be handicapped whenever self-presentation calls for application of display rules or deception. It is often said, for example, that good poker players are not spontaneously expressive (DePaulo, 1992).

Another factor influencing nonverbal self-presentation involves enduring physical and expressive qualities that bestow a particular demeanor on a person. Thus, for example, the man with thick, bushy eyebrows may look threatening no matter how gentle he actually is. Research finds that some people's demeanors tend to make them look honest or dishonest or pleasant or unpleasant, no matter what they actually feel or say (Walbott & Scherer, 1986; Zuckerman et al., 1979). Demeanor can work for or against you, depending on your goals; the socially skilled person may learn to complement demeanor with other expressive cues to enhance self-presentation. For example, the person with a naturally babyish or frank face may develop a repertoire of "innocent" nonverbal cues to enhance the impression of sincerity. Children with high achievement in school seem to develop an "intelligent" demeanor—a look that gives the impression they understand what they are listening to, whether they do or not; the faces of children with low school achievement accurately reveal their level of understanding (Allen & Atkinson, 1978).

Most research on sending (encoding) accuracy involves emotions. The person who is spontaneously emotionally expressive tends to be female, experiences less internal physiological arousal (see Chapter 9), and reports less ability to control his or her emotions (Tucker & Riggio, 1988). Thus, people can have insight into their spontaneous expressiveness although research often finds very weak relations between self-reports of posed encoding skill and subjects' ability to act out emotions on purpose (Riggio, Widaman, & Friedman, 1985; Zuckerman & Larrance, 1979).

The seemingly elusive concept of *charisma* has now been operationally defined as expressiveness, including both spontaneous and more intentional sending. Using statements such as "I show that I like someone by hugging or touching that person," "I dislike being watched by a large group of people," "I usually have a neutral facial expression" (scored in reverse), and "I can easily express emotion over the telephone," Friedman and his colleagues have documented that the expressive person is socially influential (Friedman & Riggio, 1981; Friedman, Prince, Riggio, & DiMatteo, 1980; Friedman, Riggio,

& Casella, 1988). For example, high scorers were more likely to have given a lecture, to have been elected to office in a political organization, to influence others' moods, and to be perceived as more likeable while meeting new people; in a sample of physicians, they were likely to have more patients than their counterparts. High scorers were also more likely to have had acting experience, to have had a job in sales, to desire an occupation that uses social skills (such as counselor, minister, or diplomat), and to be extraverted, affiliative, and dominant. Comparable findings have emerged for a longer self-report instrument designed to measure seven dimensions of social skills (Riggio, 1986).

Studies that actually measure people's nonverbal sending abilities (rather than ask for self-reports) have also produced a variety of findings. Females manifest greater encoding skills than males, both in facial expressiveness and posed and spontaneous facial accuracy (Buck, Miller, & Caul, 1974; Friedman, Riggio, & Segall, 1980; Wagner, Buck, & Winterbotham, 1993; Zaidel & Mehrabian, 1969). Possibly contributing to these effects is that females, it was found, are more successful than males at mimicking facial expressions shown in photographs and on videotape (Berenbaum & Rotter, 1992). However, evidence is extremely mixed on whether there is a sex difference for vocal encoding of emotions. The sex-related difference in sending ability has not been found with children between four and six years old for spontaneous facial expressions (Buck, 1975). Buck actually found preschool boys to be more accurate senders of spontaneous facial cues than preschool girls, but boys' accuracy declined over the ages four through six, perhaps due to socialization pressure related to the male gender role (Buck, 1977).

Some personality characteristics also have been associated with accurate senders of nonverbal information. Like receivers, high "self-monitors" are better able to send emotional information through facial and vocal channels (Snyder, 1974). "Internalizers" are poorer stimuli for others to judge than "externalizers" (Buck, Savin, Miller, & Caul, 1972). Buck's personality profile for young children shows many of the same characteristics we reviewed earlier for decoders (Buck, 1975). Children who were effective senders were extraverted, outgoing, active, popular, and somewhat bossy and impulsive. Ineffective senders tended to play alone and were introverted, passive, shy, controlled, and rated as cooperative. Among adults, there are also personality correlates of posed nonverbal encoding: Highly accurate senders are more dominant and exhibitionistic (Friedman, Riggio, & Segall, 1980); better senders also make an impression of greater expressiveness, confidence, and likability and, among males, use more fluent speech, more fluent body movements, and more smiles (Riggio & Friedman, 1986). Spontaneous expressiveness seems to be a stronger correlate of posed encoding skill among females than among males (Friedman, Prince, Riggio, & DiMatteo, 1980). Physicians who are more skilled in expressing emotions through the voice also receive higher ratings of satisfaction from their patients (DiMatteo, 1979).

Noller (1980; Noller & Gallois, 1986) conducted ingenious experiments to test the accuracy of husbands' and wives' nonverbal communication to each other. Women were better encoders than men, both in terms of judges' accuracy scores and in terms of using the particular cues associated with a given message (e.g., smiling for a positive message, frowning for a negative message). Marital adjustment was related to encoding skill among men. Men in happier marriages sent clearer messages through the face. High-adjustment husbands were more likely to smile during positive messages than low-adjustment husbands (a correct cue for a positive message), while low-adjustment husbands used more eyebrow flashes (a cue not associated with a positive message). This research clearly suggests that marital unhappiness might be partly due to the husband's inadequacy in nonverbal communication. Unhappy husbands were, in fact, more accurate in decoding the nonverbal behavior of an unknown married woman than of their own spouse. Low marital adjustment was also characterized by more gazing at one's partner on negative messages, more gazing while smiling, and less similarity in gazing patterns than the high-adjustment couples.

When both spontaneous and posed expressions are obtained from the same people, these two abilities are positively related. That is, if a person's spontaneous facial expression to pleasant stimuli (such as a television comedy scene) and unpleasant stimuli (such as a gory accident scene) was easy to "read," the same person would show skill in performing posed expressions.

Now we are ready to address the final question for this chapter: Are skilled encoders also skilled decoders?

The RELATIONSHIP between SENDING and RECEIVING SKILLS

As far back as 1945, Knower reported evidence suggesting that effective senders of facial and vocal expressions of emotions were also effective receivers. Since then, some other studies have reported a similar conclusion. Levy (1964), for instance, found a strong relationship among one's ability to send vocal emotional signals, to interpret vocal signals of others, and to interpret one's own vocal cues. These and other researchers, then, hypothesize a "general communication ability" (Zuckerman et al., 1976). This theory means that, although there are separate skills involved in sending and receiving, there also seems to be a general ability that overlaps these separate skills: Effective senders are often effective receivers and vice versa.

But other researchers have found no, or even a *negative*, relationship between sending and receiving ability. The study by Lanzetta and Kleck (1970) is frequently cited as support for this position because a negative relationship between sending and receiving ability was found; that is, people who were accurate senders were poor receivers and vice versa. College-aged males were videotaped as they responded to a series of red and green lights. The red signaled the advent of a shock. These subjects and others were then asked to

discriminate between shock and no-shock trials by viewing the videotaped reactions.

Across all the available studies, there is only a weak positive association
between encoding and decoding accuracy (DePaulo & Rosenthal, 1979). Researchers do not know what accounts for such variation in results. Zuckerman
and his associates (1976) suggested one resolution: In a study that used several
emotions, overall encoding and decoding were positively related, but for the
same emotion, they were negatively related (Zuckerman et al., 1975)! Thus,
if you sent anger relatively well, you decoded anger relatively poorly. A negative
sending-receiving relationship may also be more likely with spontaneous than
posed expressions.

This negative relation of encoding and decoding skill, when it occurs,
could stem from one's childhood socialization experience, in particular, the
communication environment within the family (Izard, 1971; Zuckerman
et al., 1975). The reasoning goes like this: In a highly expressive family,
expression skills will be well developed; but because emotional cues are so
clearly sent by other family members, one never needs to fine-tune one's
decoding skill, and, therefore, decoding ability is relatively undeveloped. However, in unexpressive homes, a child's expression skills may be poorly developed, but his or her decoding skill is sharpened because the child is forced
to read minimal or ambiguous cues coming from other family members.

Using the Family Expressiveness Questionnaire to measure the communication environment in the family, Halberstadt (1983, 1986) found support
for the predictions stemming from this theory: Encoding skill would be
positively related to greater freedom of emotional expression in the family,
and, second, decoding skill would be negatively related to freedom of emotional expression.

Although we have discussed nonverbal encoding and decoding as separate
skills that can be compared, in real interpersonal interaction they are not, of
course, separate. A person is required to encode and decode simultaneously—
to act out or display feelings, reactions, intentions, and attitudes, while at
the same time noticing the other's cues, forming impressions, interpreting
the meanings of expressions, and evaluating feedback from his or her own
behavior. This "parallel processing" aspect of interpersonal communication
puts many demands on the cognitive system, insofar as it is difficult to allocate
attention or effort to all of these tasks at the same time (Patterson, 1995).
The process is made somewhat easier by the fact that a certain amount of
nonverbal processing is overlearned and therefore automatic, requiring fewer
cognitive resources. The complex sending and receiving of turn-taking cues
in conversation is a good example. However, when individuals engage in
strategic behavior (as in deliberately trying to persuade someone) or suffer
from social anxiety, considerable expenditure of cognitive resources is required
which can selectively affect either the encoding or decoding process. For
example, social anxiety tends to bring a self-focus that would likely detract
from one's processing of the other person's cues (Patterson, 1995).

ON BEING an OBSERVER of NONVERBAL COMMUNICATION

The observation of Expression is by no means easy.

—CHARLES DARWIN

As you set out to read the remaining chapters of this book, now seems a good time to reflect on how you can best use the knowledge contained in it. You will learn quite a lot about the meanings and functions of nonverbal behaviors conveyed in all cue channels. You will learn that nonverbal cues are major indicators of emotion and play a crucial role in making social impressions and influencing others. People differ markedly in their skills in judging and using nonverbal cues. Although certain groups such as actors and mental patients fall at the extremes of skill, even in the middle, "normal" range there is a great deal of variation from person to person.

The research indicates that there may not be strong general skills; instead, there appear to be distinctive skills in different domains. A person may be skilled at judging emotions in the face but not in the voice; another may have the opposite pattern. Sarah may be good at identifying nonverbal deceptions, whereas Jim specializes in recognizing faces, and Martha can tell who stands where in the pecking order simply from hearing their tone of voice. In short, there are many ways to be accurate in nonverbal communication (Boice, 1983).

Underlying the various nonverbal abilities are *outlooks* and *attitudes* that profoundly influence what we "see" in the world and what we make of it. At this point we would like to focus on you as an observer of nonverbal communication in everyday life. How can you do the best possible job of understanding what is going on around you? As the sociologist Erving Goffman (1974, p. 9) said, "To speak of something happening before the eyes of observers is to be on firmer ground than usual in the social sciences; but the ground is still shaky." Goffman is saying that one's perspective, expectations, assumptions, and values—the way we *frame* our experiences—matter greatly in determining the meaning we extract from them.

When we look back at especially good observers of human behavior, Aristotle and Darwin inevitably come up. It is not clear why some people seem to make more insightful observations than others, but we can offer a few ideas based on our own experience. The effective observer should be able to maintain a delicate balance between assuming a knowledgeable role as an expert in his or her field and the ignorance and wide-eyed naïveté of a child. When you are feeling very confident about your understanding of what is taking place around you, it is time to shift your perspective to that of the child; when you feel a great deal of chaos and disorder in your observation field, it is time to shift to that of the expert. Just as effective speakers are highly motivated to have their audience understand their ideas, an effective observer probably has a strong interest and drive to understand the behavior of the observed. This does not mean, however, that the observer cannot achieve a sense of detachment from those being observed when necessary.

Effective observers probably have had a variety of educational and personal experiences. This experience assists the observer in processing complex and fleeting ongoing stimuli and in putting isolated observations in their proper perspective later. Put another way, the observer should have skills necessary for slow, careful, detailed work *and* the skills necessary to see unifying threads of broad concepts that tie the many isolated observations together. Both suggest a need for patience and perseverance. Finally, if people are going to be effective observers of others, it seems reasonable that they also will show some skill at self-insight—seeing and accepting both positive and negative qualities in themselves. Not everyone will agree with this last point. It is true that we do not know whether those who are best at understanding themselves are also the best at understanding others or whether those who are skilled at observing and interpreting the behavior of friends are equally proficient at similar processes with strangers.

Another way to view successful observers is to look at the information they seek and obtain. The following list can be useful to observers of any human transaction. At times some of the following information will contribute to observer bias, but the information may be necessary at some point to interpret the observations fully:

1. Find out about the *participants*—age, sex, position or status, relationship to each other, previous history, and the like.
2. Find out about the *setting* of the interaction—kind of environment, relationship of the participants to the environment, and expected behavior in that environment.
3. Find out about the *purposes* of the interaction—hidden goals, compatibility of goals, and so on.
4. Find out about the *social behavior*—who does what to or with whom, form of the behavior, its intensity, what initiates it, apparent objective of the behavior, effect on the other interactants, and so forth.
5. Find out about the *frequency* and *duration* of such behavior—when it occurs, how long it lasts, whether it recurs, frequency of recurrence, and how typical such behavior is in this situation.

You will also have to decide whether the cues you see are intentional or unintentional. The term *unintentional* may itself have a range of meaning; a behavior may be truly accidental, or it may have significance that is not recognized by its enactor. Two behaviors may be unintentional but in somewhat different ways. Attributions of intention also may vary depending on the nature of the behavior in question. Some people feel spoken words are generally designed with some goal in mind, but what about situations where you "didn't mean to say that" or ritualistic verbal exchanges such as the following?

"Hi."

"Hi."

"How ya doin'?"

"Fine."

"How 'bout you?"

"Fine."

How much conscious intent is represented here? Even emblems such as the A-OK hand gesture are generally planned, but habitual use can almost extinguish a sender's awareness of doing it—even though a receiver might think it consciously enacted. Some people feel that the more easily observed behaviors are subject to greater control and, therefore, are more likely to be intentional. In other instances, we alter our expectations about intentionality based on whom we are communicating with: "We've known each other for ten years, Schultz. Don't tell me you didn't know what you were doing." Of course, we are more confident in attributing intentionality to someone if we perceive the same message in several channels, for example, face, voice, words, and so forth.

In some situations, it is important to know why a person is judging another's degree of intention. Is it an experimenter whose subjects have behaved contrary to the hypotheses? Is it a person who must attribute a certain intent to you in order to justify his or her own behavior? Finally, certain environments will cause us to focus or attend to the issue of intention more than others. Take the act of being bumped by another person: At a crowded football stadium, the question of the person's intent may not even be considered; being bumped while walking down an uncrowded hallway may be another matter entirely. A full understanding of the nuances of intentionality poses many difficult barriers (Stamp & Knapp, 1990). However, we know the issues facing us are important enough not to be dismissed or ignored. Knowing the extent to which a person's behavior is consciously planned to elicit certain desired responses is important information for any practicing communicator.

THE FALLIBILITY OF HUMAN PERCEPTION

It is not unusual for several observers of the same event to see very different things; nor is it unusual for one observer to see very different things in the same event at two different times. Sometimes an observer will perceive a sequence of action as one perceptual unit; another observer may see the same sequence as several units or only part of a unit. The following are some of the factors that may contribute to differences in perception and that successful observers must take into account.

First, we must recognize that our perceptions are structured by our own cultural conditioning, education, and personal experiences. Adults teach children what they think are critical dimensions of others by what they choose to talk about and make note of. Thus, we form associations that inevitably enter into our observations. For instance, we may be unable to see what we consider to be contradictory traits or behaviors in others; that is, can you conceive of a person who is both quiet and active? Wealthy and accessible? Short and romantic? Another aspect of this internally consistent worldview that may affect our observations concerns preconceptions about what we will see. For example, "My observations will take place in a nursing home. Therefore, the people I will observe will be old, noncommunicative, sick, inactive, and so on." Social psychological experimentation has produced many demonstrations that people see what they expect or wish to see, often without any awareness or intention to distort their perceptions. Such expectations and stereotypes can sometimes be helpful, but sometimes they prevent accurate observations.

We should also be aware that we will sometimes project our own qualities onto the object of our attention—after all, we think, if these qualities are a part of us, they must be true of others. Sometimes such projection stems less from the desire to flatter ourselves than from a distorted worldview, as in bullies who see others as hostile and threatening. We do reverse the process sometimes when we want to see ourselves as unique; for example, "I am a rational person, but most people aren't." This interaction between our own needs, desires, or even temporary emotional states and what we see in others sometimes causes us to see only what we want to see or miss what may be obvious to others. This process is known as *selective perception*. To show the various mental gyrations we can perform in the pursuit of selective perception, let us observe a mother slapping her child—a mother previously perceived as incapable of such an act. We can ignore the act altogether: "She's a wonderful mother, so she couldn't have been slapping her child." We can reduce the importance of the contradictory information: "Kids can be exasperating, and it's understandable that parents have to 'get tough' sometimes—besides, it wasn't a hard slap." We can change the meaning of the inconsistency: "It couldn't have been slapping because the child would have recoiled more and cried harder—it must have been a 'love tap'." We can reinterpret previously observed traits to fit the contradictory information: "I think she is an energetic, committed, and generous person, but she may be quick-tempered and overly punitive." Thus, it is not uncommon for people to twist observations that contradict what they believe to be true so that they "make sense." When adults observe animals or infants, it is difficult to resist analyses deeply rooted in adult human activity. Because of these perceptual biases, it is important that observers check their observations against the independent reports of others—or check the consistency of their own observations at several different points over an extended period of time.

We must also recognize that our perceptions will be influenced by which people we choose to observe. We probably do not use the same criteria for observing our friends, our parents, and strangers. To see our own children or our spouse as others do is about as difficult as hearing a tape recording of ourselves as others do. We attribute more positively perceived behaviors to our friend's personality and negatively perceived behaviors to situational constraints. Familiarity can either assist observation or create observational "noise," but it does affect our perceptions. Furthermore, some phenomena will cause us to zero in on one particular kind of behavior, observing it very closely but missing simultaneous behaviors occurring elsewhere. It may be that the behavior receiving the scrutiny is bigger, more active, or just more interesting. It might be that we monitor deviant behavior more closely than normative or expected behavior. When observing a conversation, we cannot possibly attend to everything as it happens. Sometimes we will look for, see, respond to, and interpret a particular set of cues, and at other times the same cues will go unnoticed or disregarded. Sometimes observers will fall prey to the natural tendency to follow the conversational speaking turns, viewing the speaker and missing other nonverbal events associated with the nonspeaker. And, of course, some phenomena are so complex, so minute, or so frequent that observer fatigue becomes a major concern.

Even if two people observe the same event and attach similar meanings to it, they may express their observations differently. Others may suspect, then, that the two observers saw two different things. It is the difference among describing a facial expression as happiness, joy, delight, pleasure, or amusement. Or it might be the difference between saying "She struck him" versus "She pushed him" or between describing a girl as "aggressive" but a boy as "exhibitionistic" when they are engaging in the same behavior. Hence, the language we use to express our perceptions can be an important variable in judging the accuracy of those perceptions.

Observers also must be sensitive to the possible influence of order effects. Sometimes we will observe some feature of another's behavior that will influence our perceptions of what follows. Sometimes a person's last act causes us to reanalyze and reinterpret all the behavior preceding it.

Finally, we must be concerned about factual, nonevaluative descriptions of behavior and the interpretations we give to these descriptions. At the most basic level, we can say that a successful observer is careful not to confuse pure description with inferences or interpretations about the behavior. Failure at the inference stage is aptly illustrated by the familiar story of the scientist who told his frog to jump and, after a few minutes, the frog jumped. The scientist then amputated one of the frog's hind legs. Again he told the frog to jump. He repeated his instruction several times, and, in time, the frog made a feeble attempt to jump with one hind leg. Then the scientist cut off the other hind leg and repeatedly ordered the frog to jump. When no jumping occurred, the scientist recorded in his log: "Upon amputation of one of the frog's hind legs, it begins to lose its hearing; upon severing both hind legs, the frog becomes totally deaf." Clearly, such "evidence" can lead to a highly flawed conclusion.

When one is judging the meanings of the highly complex behaviors that comprise nonverbal communication, it is quite possible to perceive the behaviors accurately but not know what they mean. Although most people (as well as popular "how-to" books on nonverbal communication) associate certain cues with certain meanings, there is no sure fire dictionary of nonverbal cue meanings. For example, it is tempting to infer that when someone seems to avoid eye contact with you, he or she is hiding something or is ashamed. Many observers of the O. J. Simpson homicide trial interpreted the jury's lack of eye contact with the defendant just before the verdict was announced as a sure sign that they had found him guilty and did not want to face him. It was soon discovered that, whatever the evasion of eye contact meant, it did not mean a guilty verdict. Thus, we should constantly be on guard against simple cause-effect explanations of observed behavior. Only after considering the total context of the event can we even begin to make inferences about why such behavior occurred. Even then, we only speak with varying degrees of probability, never with complete certainty.

When observers do wish to make interpretations of observed behaviors, considerable caution must be exercised. For instance, let's suppose you observed someone from a distance and you saw that person using what you thought was an inordinate number of hand movements. Whether this was just the person's usual communicative style or the result of the situation (for example, talking to a person who didn't speak the language very well) would not be clear until you obtained further information. Sometimes we are faced with the question of whether a behavior is attributable to a person's personality or to something in the immediate situation. We might look for a situational cause for some undesirable behavior, but if we do not find a plausible explanation, we may attribute the behavior to the person's personality with even more confidence. We should, however, recognize that we could have missed the situational cause, being unable to view the situation as the participant does. If we err in any direction, we are more apt to attribute actions to enduring dispositions of others and minimize the situational demands. Obviously, if a behavior is a part of a person's personality and is carried from place to place, our predictions about this person are made considerably easier.

These perceptual tendencies are only some of the issues that a successful observer must be aware of, adapt to, and account for.

SUMMARY

This chapter dealt with nonverbal skills, how to develop them, and the characteristics of people who have such skills. In the first part of the chapter, we reviewed different definitions of communication skill, as well as the major methodologies for measuring sending and receiving skills. We also presented findings on the training of nonverbal skills, using methods such as feedback, observation, and role playing. It appears that nonverbal skill development will accrue with a strong desire or motivation to improve, with positive and productive attitudes toward the learning situation, with an adequate understanding of the knowledge related to nonverbal behavior, and with guided experience and practice in a variety of situations.

The second half of this chapter examined traits and conditions associated with effectiveness in nonverbal sending and receiving. Most research in this area has focused on questions of decoding or receiving ability. The most comprehensive and widely used instrument, developed by Robert Rosenthal and his colleagues at Harvard University, is called the Profile of Nonverbal Sensitivity (PONS). The results of this eleven-channel test and other measures provided the following information about nonverbal receiving skills:

1. As a group, females are generally better decoders than males.
2. Decoding skills seem to exist in infants and increase up to the mid-twenties.
3. There seems to be a minimal relationship between intelligence and nonverbal decoding ability, though in children there is a relation to academic achievement.
4. The personalities of effective decoders seem to reflect extraversion, self-monitoring, overall adjustment, popularity, and interpersonal effectiveness as judged by others.
5. Actors, students of nonverbal behavior, and students in visual arts tend to score well on tests of nonverbal decoding ability, and persons in certain occupational groups who are rated excellent on their job can be expected to do well at nonverbal decoding.
6. The facial, body, and vocal stimuli of a person from the United States tend to elicit the highest scores from cultures most similar to the United States, but accuracy scores do suggest the possibility of a pancultural component in decoding nonverbal behavior.

We also discussed how one's accuracy in decoding may vary due to the channel in which the information was presented, whether the expressions were posed or spontaneous, what characteristics the stimulus person had, and how long the behavior was seen or heard. In spite of these possible variations, some evidence suggests that if you are proficient at decoding one channel, you will be proficient in others; and if you are proficient at decoding posed expressions, you will be proficient at decoding spontaneous ones.

Problems associated with simultaneously encoding and decoding cues (as we routinely do in conversation) were presented. Our discussion of sending or encoding skills found that females are more skilled senders; and skilled senders are extraverted, dominant, exhibitionistic, and popular and show decreased physiological arousal. Again, if you can send accurate spontaneous expressions, it is likely that you will also accurately send posed expressions—and vice versa.

Evidence is extremely mixed on whether being a good decoder implies being a good encoder. It does not necessarily follow that proficiency in one skill (encoding or decoding) makes one proficient in the other, although sometimes this is the case. Sometimes skill in one area detracts from proficiency in another. A theory relating this phenomenon to norms of emotional expression in the family was presented.

Finally, we talked about what is entailed in being a good observer of nonverbal behavior. Knowing the most likely meanings of particular cues and cue combinations is important, but so are other factors relating to one's attitudes and the context in which observation is taking place.

Answers to Figure 3-2: *a.* strangers posing together, *b.* woman on the left, *c.* playing with her baby daughter.

QUESTIONS for DISCUSSION

1. Women exceed men in ability to understand nonverbal cues in nearly all countries and cultures where the skill has been measured. Why?
2. It has been argued that abilities to send and receive nonverbal expressions may be inversely related, in part due to the expression norms within families. Is your own family high or low on expressiveness? How might your family's expression norms have influenced your encoding and decoding skills?
3. Ability to decode other people's nonverbal emotional expressions is only one definition of nonverbal sensitivity. Think of some other definitions of nonverbal sensitivity and analyze why and when they are useful.
4. Are there any moral or ethical issues related to the decoding and encoding of nonverbal cues?

REFERENCES and SELECTED BIBLIOGRAPHY

Albas, D. C., McCluskey, K. W., & Albas, C. A. (1976). Perception of the emotional content of speech: A comparison of two Canadian groups. *Journal of Cross Cultural Psychology, 7,* 481–90.

Albright, L., Kenny, D. A., & Malloy, T. E. (1988). Consensus in personality judgments at zero acquaintance. *Journal of Personality and Social Psychology, 55,* 387–95.

Allen, V. L. (1981). The role of nonverbal behavior in children's communication. In W. P. Dickson (Ed.), *Children's oral communication skills.* New York: Academic Press.

Allen, V. L., & Atkinson, M. L. (1978). Encoding of nonverbal behavior by high-achieving and low-achieving children. *Journal of Educational Psychology, 70,* 298–305.

Ambady, N., & Rosenthal, R. (1993). Half a minute: Predicting teacher evaluations from thin slices of nonverbal behavior and physical attractiveness. *Journal of Personality and Social Psychology, 64,* 431–41.

Archer, D., & Akert, R. (1977). Words and everything else: Verbal and nonverbal cues in social interaction. *Journal of Personality and Social Psychology, 35,* 443–49.

Archer, D., & Akert, R. M. (1984). Problems of context and criterion in nonverbal communication: A new look at the accuracy issue. In M. Cook (Ed.), *Issues in person perception*. New York: Methuen.

Argyle, M. (1988). *Bodily communication* (2nd ed.). London: Methuen.

Argyle, M., Trower, P., & Bryant, B. (1974). Explorations in the treatment of personality disorders and neuroses by social skills training. *British Journal of Medical Psychology, 47*, 63–72.

Beck, L., & Feldman, R. S. (1989). Enhancing children's decoding of facial expression. *Journal of Nonverbal Behavior, 13*, 269–78.

Beldoch, M. (1964). Sensitivity to expression of emotional meaning in three modes of communication. In J. R. Davitz (Ed.), *The communication of emotional meaning*. New York: McGraw-Hill.

Berenbaum, H., & Rotter, A. (1992). The relationship between spontaneous facial expressions of emotion and voluntary control of facial muscles. *Journal of Nonverbal Behavior, 16*, 179–90.

Bernieri, F. J. (1991). Interpersonal sensitivity in teaching interactions. *Personality and Social Psychology Bulletin, 17*, 98–103.

Boice, R. (1983). Observational skills. *Psychological Bulletin, 93*, 3–29.

Borrill, J., Rosen, B. K., & Summerfield, A. B. (1987). The influence of alcohol on judgment of facial expressions of emotion. *British Journal of Medical Psychology, 60*, 71–77.

Boyatzis, C. J., & Satyaprasad, C. (1994). Children's facial and gestural decoding and encoding: Relations between skills and with popularity. *Journal of Nonverbal Behavior, 18*, 37–55.

Brauer, D. V., & DePaulo, B. M. (1980). Similarities between friends in their understanding of nonverbal cues. *Journal of Nonverbal Behavior, 5*, 64–68.

Bruce, V. (1988). *Recognising faces*. Hillsdale, NJ: Erlbaum.

Buck, R. (1975). Nonverbal communication of affect in children. *Journal of Personality and Social Psychology, 31*, 644–53.

Buck, R. (1976). A test of nonverbal receiving ability: Preliminary studies. *Human Communication Research, 2*, 162–71.

Buck, R. (1977). Nonverbal communication of affect in preschool children: Relationships with personality and skin conductance. *Journal of Personality and Social Psychology, 35*, 225–36.

Buck, R., Miller, R.E., & Caul, W.F. (1974). Sex, personality and physiological variables in the communication of affect via facial expression. *Journal of Personality and Social Psychology, 30*, 587–96.

Buck, R., Savin, V., Miller, R., & Caul, W. (1972). Communication of affect through facial expressions in humans. *Journal of Personality and Social Psychology, 23*, 362–71.

Burns, K. L., & Beier, E. G. (1973). Significance of vocal and visual channels in the decoding of emotional meaning. *Journal of Communication, 23*, 118–30.

Camras, L. A., Ribordy, S., Hill, J., Martino, S., Spaccarelli, S., & Stefani, R. (1988). Recognition and posing of emotional expressions by abused children and their mothers. *Developmental Psychology, 24*, 776–81.

Christensen, D., Farina, A., & Boudreau, L. (1980). Sensitivity to nonverbal cues as a function of social competence. *Journal of Nonverbal Behavior, 4,* 146–56.

Collett, P. (1971). On training Englishmen in the non-verbal behaviour of Arabs: An experiment in intercultural communication. *International Journal of Psychology, 6,* 209–15.

Costanzo, M. (1992). Training students to decode verbal and nonverbal cues: Effects on confidence and performance. *Journal of Educational Psychology, 84,* 308–13.

Costanzo, M., & Archer, D. (1989). Interpreting the expressive behavior of others: The Interpersonal Perception Task. *Journal of Nonverbal Behavior, 13,* 225–45.

Danziger, K. (1976). *Interpersonal communication.* New York: Pergamon.

Davitz, J. R. (1964). *The communication of emotional meaning.* New York: McGraw-Hill.

DePaulo, B. M. (1991). Nonverbal behavior and self-presentation: A developmental perspective. In R. S. Feldman & B. Rimé (Eds.), *Fundamentals of nonverbal behavior.* Cambridge: Cambridge University Press.

DePaulo, B. M. (1992). Nonverbal behavior and self-presentation. *Psychological Bulletin, 111,* 203–43.

DePaulo, B. M., & Rosenthal, R. (1979). Ambivalence, discrepancy, and deception in nonverbal communication. In R. Rosenthal (Ed.), *Skill in nonverbal communication: Individual differences.* Cambridge, MA: Oelgeschlager, Gunn & Hain.

Dickey, E. C., & Knower, F. H. (1941). A note on some ethnological differences in recognition of simulated expressions of emotions. *American Journal of Sociology, 47,* 190–93.

DiMatteo, M. R. (1979). Nonverbal skill and the physician-patient relationship. In R. Rosenthal (Ed.), *Skill in nonverbal communication: Individual differences.* Cambridge, MA: Oelgeschlager, Gunn & Hain.

DiMatteo, M. R., Hays, R. D., & Prince, L. M. (1986). Relationship of physicians' nonverbal communication skill to patient satisfaction, appointment noncompliance, and physician workload. *Health Psychology, 5,* 581–94.

DiMatteo, M. R., Taranta, A., Friedman, H. S., & Prince, L. M. (1980). Predicting patient satisfaction from physicians' nonverbal communication skills. *Medical Care, 18,* 376–87.

Dimitrovsky, L. (1964). The ability to identify the emotional meaning of vocal expressions at successive age levels. In J. R. Davitz (Ed.), *The communication of emotional meaning.* New York: McGraw-Hill.

Dodge, K. A., & Newman, J. P. (1981). Biased decision-making process in aggressive boys. *Journal of Abnormal Psychology, 60,* 375–79.

Eiland, R., & Richardson, D. (1976). The influence of race, sex and age on judgments of emotion portrayed in photographs. *Communication Monographs, 3,* 167–75.

Ekman, P., & Friesen, W. V. (1975). *Unmasking the face.* Englewood Cliffs, NJ: Prentice-Hall.

Eliot, G. (1859). *Adam Bede.* New York: Harper & Brothers.

Field, T. (1982). Individual differences in the expressivity of neonates and young infants. In R. S. Feldman (Ed.), *Development of nonverbal behavior in children.* New York: Springer-Verlag.

Field, T. M., Woodson, R., Greenberg, R., & Cohen, D. (1982). Discrimination and imitation of facial expressions of neonates. *Science, 218*, 179–81.

Friedman, H. S. (1979). The concept of skill in nonverbal communication: Implications for understanding social interaction. In R. Rosenthal (Ed.), *Skill in nonverbal communication: Individual differences*. Cambridge, MA: Oelgeschlager, Gunn & Hain.

Friedman, H. S., Prince, L. M., Riggio, R. E., & DiMatteo, M. R. (1980). Understanding and assessing nonverbal expressiveness: The Affective Communication Test. *Journal of Personality and Social Psychology, 39*, 333–51.

Friedman, H. S., & Riggio, R. E. (1981). Effect of individual differences in nonverbal expressiveness on transmission of emotion. *Journal of Nonverbal Behavior, 6*, 96–104.

Friedman, H. S., Riggio, R. E., & Cassella, D. F. (1988). Nonverbal skills, personal charisma, and initial attraction. *Personality and Social Psychology Bulletin, 14*, 203–11.

Friedman, H. S., Riggio, R. E., & Segall, D. O. (1980). Personality and the enactment of emotion. *Journal of Nonverbal Behavior, 5*, 35–48.

Fujita, B. N., Harper, R. G., & Wiens, A. N. (1980). Encoding-decoding of nonverbal emotional messages: Sex differences in spontaneous and enacted expressions. *Journal of Nonverbal Behavior, 4*, 131–45.

Funder, D. C., & Harris, M. J. (1986). On the several facets of personality assessment: The case of social acuity. *Journal of Personality, 54*, 528–50.

Gates, G. S. (1925). A test for ability to interpret facial expressions. *Psychological Bulletin, 22*, 120.

Gitter, G., Mostofsky, D., & Quincy, A. (1971). Race and sex differences in the child's perception of emotion. *Child Development, 42*, 2071–75.

Goffman, E. (1974). *Frame analysis: An essay on the organization of experience.* Cambridge, MA: Harvard University Press.

Guilford, J. P. (1929). An experiment in learning to read facial expressions. *Journal of Abnormal and Social Psychology, 24*, 191–202.

Halberstadt, A. G. (1983). Family expressiveness styles and nonverbal communication skills. *Journal of Nonverbal Behavior, 8*, 14–26.

Halberstadt, A. G. (1985). Race, socioeconomic status, and nonverbal behavior. In A. W. Siegman and S. Feldstein (Eds.), *Multichannel integrations of nonverbal behavior*. Hillsdale, NJ: Erlbaum.

Halberstadt, A. G. (1986). Family socialization of emotional expression and nonverbal communication styles and skills. *Journal of Personality and Social Psychology, 51*, 827–36.

Halberstadt, A. G., Grotjohn, D. K., Johnson, C. A., Furth, M. S., & Greig, M. M. (1992). Children's abilities and strategies in managing the facial display of affect. *Journal of Nonverbal Behavior, 16*, 215–30.

Halberstadt, A. G., & Hall, J. A. (1980). Who's getting the message? Children's nonverbal skill and their evaluation by teachers. *Developmental Psychology, 16*, 564–73.

Hall, J. A. (1978). Gender effects in decoding nonverbal cues. *Psychological Bulletin, 85*, 845–57.

Hall, J. A. (1979). Gender, gender roles, and nonverbal communication skills. In R. Rosenthal (Ed.), *Skill in nonverbal communication: Individual differences*. Cambridge, MA: Oelgeschlager, Gunn & Hain.

Hall, J. A. (1984). *Nonverbal sex differences: Communication accuracy and expressive style*. Baltimore: Johns Hopkins University Press.

Hall, J. A., & Halberstadt, A. G. (1981). Sex roles and nonverbal communication skills. *Sex Roles, 7*, 273–87.

Hall, J. A., & Halberstadt, A. G. (1996). Subordination and nonverbal sensitivity: A hypothesis in search of support. In M. R. Walsh (Ed.), *Women, men, and gender: Ongoing debates*. New Haven: Yale University Press.

Hamilton, M. L. (1973). Imitative behavior and expressive ability in facial expressions of emotions. *Developmental Psychology, 8*, 138.

Hargie, O. (Ed.). (1986a). *A handbook of communication skills*. New York: New York University Press.

Hargie, O. (1986b). Communication as skilled behaviour. In O. Hargie (Ed.), *A handbook of communication skills*. New York: New York University Press.

Harlow, H. F., & Mears, C. (1978). The nature of complex, unlearned responses. In M. Lewis & L. A. Rosenblum (Eds.), *The development of affect*. New York: Plenum.

Harrigan, J. A. (1984). The effects of task order on children's identification of facial expressions. *Motivation and Emotion, 8*, 157–69.

Haviland, J. M., & Lelwica, M. (1987). The induced affect response: 10-week-old infants' responses to three emotion expressions. *Developmental Psychology, 23*, 97–104.

Henley, N. M. (1977). *Body politics: Power, sex, and nonverbal communication*. Englewood Cliffs, NJ: Prentice-Hall.

Hodgins, H., & Zuckerman, M. (1990). The effect of nonverbal sensitivity on social interaction. *Journal of Nonverbal Behavior, 14*, 155–70.

Ickes, W., Stinson, L., Bissonnette, V., & Garcia, S. (1990). Naturalistic social cognition: Empathic accuracy in mixed-sex dyads. *Journal of Personality and Social Psychology, 59*, 730–42.

Izard, C. E. (1971). *The face of emotion*. New York: Appleton-Century-Crofts.

Jecker, J.D., Maccoby, N., & Breitrose, H. S. (1965). Improving accuracy in interpreting nonverbal cues of comprehension. *Psychology in the Schools, 2*, 239–44.

Keeley-Dyreson, M., Burgoon, J. K., & Bailey, W. (1991). The effects of stress and gender on nonverbal decoding accuracy in kinesic and vocalic channels. *Human Communication Research, 17*, 584–605.

Kellogg, W. N., & Eagleson, B. M. (1931). The growth of social perception in different racial groups. *Journal of Educational Psychology, 22*, 374–75.

Knower, F. H. (1945). Studies in the symbolism of voice and action: V. The use of behavioral and tonal symbols as tests of speaking achievement. *Journal of Applied Psychology, 29*, 229–35.

Lanzetta, J.T., & Kleck, R. E. (1970). Encoding and decoding nonverbal affect in humans. *Journal of Personality and Social Psychology, 16*, 12–19.

Levesque, M. J., & Kenny, D. A. (1993). Accuracy of behavioral predictions at zero acquaintance. A Social Relations Analysis. *Journal of Personality and Social Psychology, 65*, 1178–87.

Levy, P. K. (1964). The ability to express and perceive vocal communication of feelings. In J. R. Davitz (Ed.), *The communication of emotional meaning*. New York: McGraw-Hill.

Lewis, M., & Rosenblum, L. A. (Eds.). (1978). *The development of affect*. New York: Plenum.

Lieberman, D. A., Rigo, T. G., & Campain, R. F. (1988). Age-related differences in nonverbal decoding ability. *Communication Quarterly, 36*, 290–97.

Magill-Evans, J., Koning, C., Cameron-Sadava, A., & Manyk, K. (1995). The Child and Adolescent Social Perception Measure. *Journal of Nonverbal Behavior, 19*, 151–69.

Marangoni, C., Garcia, S., Ickes, W., & Teng, G. (1995). Empathic accuracy in a clinically relevant setting. *Journal of Personality and Social Psychology, 68*, 854–69.

Markham, R., & Adams, K. (1992). The effect of type of task on children's identification of facial expressions. *Journal of Nonverbal Behavior, 16*, 21–39.

Meltzoff, A. N., & Moore, M.K. (1983). Newborn infants imitate adult facial gestures. *Child Development, 54*, 702–9.

Miller, R. E., Caul, W. F., & Mirsky, I. A. (1967). Communication of affects between feral and socially isolated monkeys. *Journal of Personality and Social Psychology, 7*, 231–39.

Noller, P. (1980). Misunderstandings in marital communication: A study of couples' nonverbal communication. *Journal of Personality and Social Psychology, 39*, 1135–48.

Noller, P. (1986). Sex differences in nonverbal communication: Advantage lost or supremacy regained? *Australian Journal of Psychology, 38*, 23–32.

Noller, P., & Gallois, C. (1986). Sending emotional messages in marriage: Non-verbal behaviour, sex and communication clarity. *British Journal of Social Psychology, 25*, 287–97.

Nowicki, S., Jr., & Duke, M. P. (1994). Individual differences in the nonverbal communication of affect: The Diagnostic Analysis of Nonverbal Accuracy Scale. *Journal of Nonverbal Behavior, 18*, 9–35.

Odom, R. D., & Lemond, C. M. (1972). Developmental differences in the perception and production of facial expressions. *Child Development, 43*, 359–69.

Patterson, M. L. (1995). A parallel process model of nonverbal communication. *Journal of Nonverbal Behavior, 19*, 3–29.

Philippot, P., Feldman, R. S., & McGee, G. (1992). Nonverbal behavioral skills in an educational context: Typical and atypical populations. In R. S. Feldman (Ed.), *Applications of nonverbal behavioral theories and research*. Hillsdale, NJ: Erlbaum.

Phillips, R. D., Wagner, S. H., Fells, C. A., & Lynch, M. (1990). Do infants recognize emotion in facial expressions?: Categorical and "metaphorical" evidence. *Infant Behavior and Development, 13*, 71–84.

Riggio, R. E. (1986). Assessment of basic social skills. *Journal of Personality and Social Psychology, 51*, 649–60.

Riggio, R. E. (1992). Social interaction skills and nonverbal behavior. In R. S. Feldman (Ed.), *Applications of nonverbal behavioral theories and research*. Hillsdale, NJ: Erlbaum.

Riggio, R. E., & Friedman, H. S. (1986). Impression formation: The role of expressive behavior. *Journal of Personality and Social Psychology, 50*, 421–27.

Riggio, R. E., Widaman, K. F., & Friedman, H. S. (1985). Actual and perceived emotional sending and personality correlates. *Journal of Nonverbal Behavior, 9*, 69–83.

Rosenthal, R. (Ed.). (1979). *Skill in nonverbal communication: Individual differences.* Cambridge, MA: Oelgeschlager, Gunn & Hain.

Rosenthal, R., & DePaulo, B. M. (1979). Sex differences in accommodation in nonverbal communication. In R. Rosenthal (Ed.), *Skill in nonverbal communication: Individual differences.* Cambridge, MA: Oelgeschlager, Gunn & Hain.

Rosenthal, R., Hall, J. A., DiMatteo, M. R., Rogers, P. L., & Archer, D. (1979). *Sensitivity to nonverbal communication: The PONS test.* Baltimore: Johns Hopkins University Press.

Rotter, N. G., & Rotter, G. S. (1988). Sex differences in the encoding and decoding of negative facial emotions. *Journal of Nonverbal Behavior, 12*, 139–48.

Russell, R. L., Stokes, J., Jones, M. E., Czogalik, D., & Rohleder, L. (1993). The role of nonverbal sensitivity in childhood psychopathology. *Journal of Nonverbal Behavior, 17*, 69–83.

Sacks, O. (1993, December 27/1994, January 3). An anthropologist on Mars. *The New Yorker*, 106–25.

Shapiro, P. N., & Penrod, S. (1986). Meta-analysis of facial identification studies. *Psychological Bulletin, 100*, 139–56.

Snodgrass, S. (1985). Women's intuition: The effect of subordinate role on interpersonal sensitivity. *Journal of Personality and Social Psychology, 49*, 146–55.

Snyder, M. (1974). Self-monitoring of expressive behavior. *Journal of Personality and Social Psychology, 30*, 526–37.

Stamp, G., & Knapp, M. L. (1990). The construct of intent in interpersonal communication. *Quarterly Journal of Speech, 76*, 282–99.

Sternberg, R. (1984). *Beyond I.Q.: A triarchic theory of human intelligence.* Cambridge: Cambridge University Press.

Termine, N. T., & Izard, C. E. (1988). Infants' responses to their mothers' expressions of joy and sadness. *Developmental Psychology, 24*, 223–29.

Thompson, D. F., & Meltzer, L. (1964). Communication of emotional intent by facial expression. *Journal of Abnormal and Social Psychology, 68*, 129–35.

Trimboli, A., & Walker, M. (1993). The CAST test of nonverbal sensitivity. *Journal of Language and Social Psychology, 12*, 49–65.

Tucker, J. S., & Riggio, R. E. (1988). The role of social skills in encoding posed and spontaneous facial expressions. *Journal of Nonverbal Behavior, 12*, 87–97.

Wagner, H. L. (1993). On measuring performance in category judgment studies of nonverbal behavior. *Journal of Nonverbal Behavior, 17*, 3–28.

Wagner, H. L., Buck, R., & Winterbotham, M. (1993). Communication of specific emotions: Gender differences in sending accuracy and communication measures. *Journal of Nonverbal Behavior, 17*, 29–53.

Wagner, H. L., MacDonald, C. J., & Manstead, A. S. R. (1986). Communication of individual emotions by spontaneous facial expressions. *Journal of Personality and Social Psychology, 50*, 737–43.

Walker-Andrews, A. S., & Lennon, E. (1991). Infants' discrimination of vocal expressions: Contributions of auditory and visual information. *Infant Behavior and Development, 14,* 131–42.

Wallbott, H. G., & Scherer, K. R. (1986). Cues and channels in emotion recognition. *Journal of Personality and Social Psychology, 51,* 690–99.

Zaidel, S., & Mehrabian, A. (1969). The ability to communicate and infer positive and negative attitudes facially and vocally. *Journal of Experimental Research in Personality, 3,* 233–41.

Zuckerman, M., DeFrank, R. S., Hall. J. A., Larrance, D. T., & Rosenthal, R. (1979). Facial and vocal cues of deception and honesty. *Journal of Experimental Social Psychology, 15,* 378–96.

Zuckerman, M., DePaulo, B. M., & Rosenthal, R. (1981). Verbal and nonverbal communication of deception. In L. Berkowitz (Ed.), *Advances in experimental social psychology* (Vol. 14). New York: Academic Press.

Zuckerman, M., Hall, J. A., DeFrank, R. S., & Rosenthal, R. (1976). Encoding and decoding of spontaneous and posed facial expressions. *Journal of Personality and Social Psychology, 34,* 966–77.

Zuckerman, M., & Larrance, D. T. (1979). Individual differences in perceived encoding and decoding abilities. In R. Rosenthal (Ed.), *Skill in nonverbal communication: Individual differences.* Cambridge, MA: Oelgeschlager, Gunn & Hain.

Zuckerman, M., Lipets, M. S., Koivumaki, J. H., & Rosenthal, R. (1975). Encoding and decoding nonverbal cues of emotion. *Journal of Personality and Social Psychology, 32,* 1068–76.

Part Two

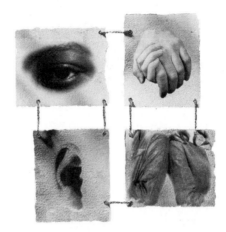

The Communication Environment

The features of the environment within which our interactions take place can exert a powerful influence on human interaction. Lighting, color schemes, furniture, and architecture, among other features, affect what we say and even how often we say it; sometimes we deliberately structure these same features in order to obtain certain responses from others. The way we affect and are affected by interaction distance and territorial claims to these environments are then explored as a preface to discussing the people who do the communicating and their behavior.

CHAPTER 4

The Effects of the Environment on Human Communication

Every interior betrays the nonverbal skills of its inhabitants. The choice of materials, the distribution of space, the kind of objects that command attention or demand to be touched—as compared to those that intimidate or repel—have much to say about the preferred sensory modalities of their owners.

—RUESCH & KEES

When people communicate with one another, there are always features of the surrounding environment that exert an influence on their interaction. What are these environmental features, and how do they affect us?

First, let's look at a familiar communication environment—the classroom. Most often, it is a rectangular room with straight rows of chairs for student seating. A row of windows along one side of the room may determine the direction students face (and, consequently, the "front" of the room). Many classroom seats are permanently attached to the floor for ease of maintenance and tidiness. Most classrooms have some type of partition (usually a desk) separating the teacher from students. Most students and teachers can provide a long list of problems encountered in environments designed for learning: poor lighting and acoustics; inadequate climate control; external construction noises; banging radiators; inoperative electrical outlets; immovable seats;

gloomy, dull, or distracting color schemes; unpleasant odors, and so forth. Both students and teachers recognize that such problems impede the purpose for gathering in these rectangular rooms—to increase knowledge through effective student/teacher communication. The influence of the classroom environment on student and teacher behavior remained relatively unexplored until Sommer (1967, 1969, 1974) took a closer look. Sommer focused his attention on the influence of classroom design on student participation.

First, Sommer selected six different types kinds of classrooms for his study. He wanted to compare the amount of student participation in these classrooms and to analyze aspects of participatory behavior in each type. He selected seminar rooms with movable chairs, usually arranged in a horseshoe shape; laboratories (complete with Bunsen burners, bottles, and gas valves), which represented an extreme in straight-row seating; a windowless room; and one with an entire wall of windows. Distaste for the laboratory rooms and the windowless room caused instructors and students to attempt to change rooms or hold classes outside. There were no differences between open and windowless rooms with respect to participation behavior. Comparisons among room types showed that in seminar rooms fewer people participated, but those who did participated for longer periods of time. In addition, the average amount of student participation varied between large and small classes: 2.5 minutes during one class period for the large lecture classes and 5.8 minutes for classes of twenty and fewer. Thus, the odds of a student participating in class discussion are slightly greater in small classes. One important content-related aspect Sommer hints at is a potentially significant difference in the *type* of participation. Student participation in the large classes seemed to be questions of clarification or requests for repeating an idea—a type of participation that differs radically from the intellectual give and take between two people seeking to understand, to refine, to see ramifications and related ideas.

When seminar rooms were analyzed separately, Sommer noted, most participation came from students seated directly opposite the instructor. Students generally avoided the two chairs on either side of the instructor, even when all other seats were filled. When students did occupy these seats, they generally were silent throughout the period. In straight-row rooms, the following observations were made:

1. Students within eye contact range of the instructor participated more.
2. More participation occurred in the center sections.
3. There was a general decrease from the front rows to the back. This tendency, however, was not evident when interested students sat in locations other than those providing maximum visual contact with the instructor.
4. Participation decreased as class size increased.

A related research project offers additional support for Sommer's observations on participation in straight-row classrooms. Adams and Biddle (1970) noted a remarkably consistent pattern of interaction in grades 1, 6, and 11 that indicated most student participation comes from students sitting in the center of the room. Sixty-three percent of the 1,176 behaviors observed came from students located in three positions, one behind the other, down the center of the room. Almost all pupil-initiated comments came from the shadowed area in Figure 4-1. In no instance did teachers select special students for placement in these locations. The authors claim, "It is now possible to discriminate an area of the classroom that seems to be literally and figuratively the center of the activity."

Koneya (1973) felt there were still some questions Sommer and Adams and Biddle had not explored sufficiently. Do high participators choose certain seats, or does seat location itself bring about high participation? High- and low-participating students were given the chance to choose a seat from a classroom diagram. High verbalizers tended to select seats in the zone of participation more often than low or moderate verbalizers. Koneya then put students who were previously identified as high, moderate, or low participators in different seats and observed their participation over seven class periods. Both the high and moderate participators talked more in the zone of participation than their counterparts in noncentral areas. Those who were low participators were consistently low, whether in or out of the central areas. In a study conducted at five colleges, ethnic, racial, and religious minorities tended to select peripheral seating even when they were a majority at a particular college (Haber, 1982). From these studies, we can conclude that classroom seating is not random, that certain types of people gravitate to central and

Figure 4–1

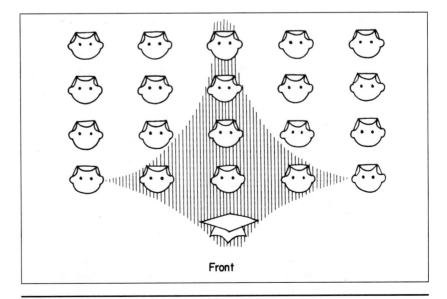

Front

The zone of class participation.

noncentral areas, and that the zone of participation (heavily influenced by teacher/student visibility) will promote participation for everyone except initially low participators. Even then, we might find increased participation at some point after the seventh class period if a teacher rewards and supports participation. Participation is important because it may help clarify difficult ideas to be learned, and it may link teacher and student in a social bond that can create a better learning environment. And, to no student's surprise, "getting to know your instructor" also may influence grades.

The preceding discussion of the classroom is an example of a specific context in which spatial relationships, architecture, and objects surrounding the participants influence the amount and type of interaction that occur. We will examine other environmental factors that impinge on human communication behavior, but we should remember that the environment is only one element in structuring such behavior. If students, administrators, teachers, secretaries, and custodians want to run a school or university like a prison or a dehumanized bureaucracy, changes in the classroom structure may have very little impact.

Throughout this chapter, we discuss a number of characteristics of environments, but let us initiate our exploration of environments by examining the way we perceive our surroundings.

PERCEPTIONS of OUR SURROUNDINGS

The number of places in which we communicate with others is limitless— buses, homes, apartments, restaurants, offices, parks, hotels, sports arenas, factories, libraries, movie theaters, museums. Despite their diversity, these environments probably are evaluated along similar dimensions. Once we perceive our environment in a certain way, we may incorporate such perceptions in the development of the messages we send. And, once these messages have been sent, the environmental perceptions of the other person have been altered. Thus, we influence and are influenced by our environments.

How do we see our environments? We believe the following six dimensions are central to our perceptions and consequently to how we send and receive messages.

PERCEPTIONS OF FORMALITY

One familiar dimension along which environments can be classified is a formal/informal continuum. Reactions may be based on the objects present, the people present, the functions performed, or any number of other variables. Individual offices may be more formal than a lounge in the same building; a year-end banquet takes on more formality than a "come as you are" party;

an evening at home with one other couple may be more informal than an evening with ten other couples. The greater the formality, the greater the chances that the communication behavior will be less relaxed and more superficial, hesitant, and stylized.

PERCEPTIONS OF WARMTH

Environments that make us feel psychologically warm encourage us to linger, to relax and feel comfortable. It may be some combination of the color of the drapes or walls, paneling, carpeting, texture of the furniture, softness of the chairs, soundproofing, and so on. Fast-food chains try to exhibit enough warmth in their decor to seem inviting but enough coldness to encourage rapid turnover. Interestingly, environments that make us feel psychologically warm may also make us feel physically warmer. Students were asked to spend two hours studying or reading in a room with a neutral decor, similar to that of a classroom. Then they were asked to read or study in a room that resembled a walk-in meat cooler. Nearly all the students felt the second room was cooler, even though the temperature was actually the same in both rooms. Then the meat cooler room was paneled, carpeted, and equipped with subdued lighting and other appointments. Another group of students was asked to read or study in each room. This time, the redesigned meat cooler room was judged to have a higher temperature than the classroom. Again, actual temperatures were the same (Rohles, 1980).

PERCEPTIONS OF PRIVACY

Enclosed environments usually suggest greater privacy, particularly if they accommodate only a few people. If the possibility of other people's entering and/or overhearing our conversation is small (even if we are outdoors), there is a greater feeling of privacy. Sometimes objects in the setting add to the perceptions of privacy, for example, toilet articles and other personal items. With greater privacy, we will probably find close speaking distances and more personal messages, designed and adapted for the specific other person rather than people in general.

PERCEPTIONS OF FAMILIARITY

When we meet a new person or encounter an unfamiliar environment, our responses typically are cautious, deliberate, and conventional. Unfamiliar environments are laden with ritual and norms we do not yet know, so we are hesitant to move too quickly. We will probably go slowly until we can associate this unfamiliar environment with one we know. One interpretation for the stereotyped structures of quick-food stops is that they allow us (a mobile society) to readily find a familiar and predictable place that will guarantee minimal demands for active contact with strangers. In unfamiliar environments, the most likely initial topic of conversation will be the environment itself—for example, "Have you ever been here before? What is it like? Who comes here?"

PERCEPTIONS OF CONSTRAINT

Part of our total reaction to our environment is based on our perception of whether (and how easily) we can leave it. Some students feel confined in their own homes during the school Christmas break. But consider the differences between this two-week constraint and a permanent live-at-home arrangement. The intensity of these perceptions of constraint is closely related to the space available to us (and the privacy of this space) during the time we will be in the environment. Some environments seem to be only temporarily confining, such as a long trip in an automobile; other environments seem more permanently confining, such as prisons, spacecrafts, or nursing homes.

PERCEPTIONS OF DISTANCE

Sometimes our responses within a given environment are influenced by how close or far away we must conduct our communication with another. This may reflect actual physical distance (an office on a different floor, a house in another part of the city), or it may reflect psychological distance (barriers clearly separating people who are fairly close physically). You may be seated close to someone and still not perceive it as a close environment, for example, interlocking chairs facing the same direction in an airport. When the setting forces us into close quarters (elevators, crowded buses) with other people not well known to us, we try to increase distance psychologically to reduce threatening feelings of intimacy. We can do this through less eye contact, body tenseness and immobility, cold silence, nervous laughter, jokes about the intimacy, and public conversation directed at all present.

The foregoing perceptions represent only some of the dimensions along which communication settings can be viewed. Generally, more intimate communication is associated with informal, unconstrained, private, familiar, close, and warm environments. In everyday situations, however, these dimensions combine in complex ways. The mixture of intimate and nonintimate factors can be seen in an elevator if it is perceived as close, familiar, and temporarily confining but also public, formal, and cold.

Once these perceptions are made, how do they affect our reactions? Mehrabian (1976) argued that we react emotionally to our surroundings. These emotional reactions can be accounted for in terms of how *aroused* the environment makes us feel, how *pleasurable* we feel, and how *dominant* we feel. *Arousal* refers to how active, stimulated, frenzied, or alert we are. Novel, surprising, and complex environments will probably produce higher arousal. Those people less able to screen out unwanted information from the environment will inevitably have to respond to more stimuli and, in turn, become more aroused. Although we all probably respond as "screeners" and "nonscreeners" on occasions, some people tend to respond habitually as either screeners or nonscreeners. *Pleasure* refers to feelings of joy, satisfaction, or happiness. And *dominance* suggests that we feel in control, important, and free to act in a variety of ways.

PERCEPTIONS of TIME

Time is also a part of the communicative environment. At first, it may seem strange to include something as seemingly intangible as time in the same environmental package as chairs, walls, noise, or even weather conditions. However, people in the United States do treat time as something tangible, a commodity that can be divided up, saved, spent, and made. Furthermore, we often project temporal qualities onto objects within our environment, for example, a chair that looks like it has been there "forever" or an elevator that "never seems to be on time."

Time is important to us. It governs when we eat and sleep; it often determines how much we get paid at work; and it sets limits on how much material students can learn in a given class period. Time plays a key role in social interaction as well. It influences our perceptions of people; for example, responsible people are "on time," boring people talk "too long," inconsiderate people let the beepers on their watches go off when we are talking to them, or a good romantic partner gives us some "time to ourself" (Leonard, 1978; Werner & Baxter, 1994). A course in "time management" is a staple for anyone expecting to climb the corporate ladder in U. S. organizations. Time plays such an important role in our lives that we often carry the date and time around with us on our wrist. Most cars have clocks, and some of them even have devices for computing the time it will take to drive from one location to another. We are very much aware of the stress time can create in our lives. We think of a vacation as a retreat to a place where time matters less. Ironically, though, vacations themselves are usually thought of as a set period of time.

Time is perceived very differently in other cultures (Hall, 1959). These varying orientations to time are often a central factor in misunderstandings among members of different cultures. Psychology professor Robert Levine gives this account of his teaching experience in Brazil:

As I left home for my first day of class, I asked someone the time. It was 9:05 A.M., which allowed me time to relax and look around the campus before my 10 o'clock lecture. After what I judged to be half an hour, I glanced at the clock I was passing. It said 10:20! In panic, I broke for the classroom, followed by gentle calls of "Hola, professor" and "Tudo bem, professor?" from unhurried students, many of whom, I later realized, were my own. I arrived breathless to find an empty room. Frantically, I asked a passerby the time. "Nine forty-five" was the answer. No, that couldn't be. I asked someone else. "Nine fifty-five." Another said: "Exactly 9:43." The clock in a nearby office read 3:15. I had learned my first lesson about Brazilians: Their timepieces are consistently inaccurate. And nobody minds. My class was scheduled from 10 until noon. Many students came late, some very late . . . none seemed terribly concerned about lateness. . . . The real surprise came at noon . . . only a few students left immediately. Others drifted out during the next fifteen minutes, and some continued asking me questions long after that. (Levine & Wolff, 1985, p. 30)

To understand cultural variations in perceiving time, it is important first to understand our own culture. We know that our responses are influenced by our experiences with time at several different levels (Cottle, 1976; Doob, 1964; Hall, 1983; McGrath & Kelly, 1986). Biologically, our bodies seem to be programmed so that "internal clocks" regulate our physical, emotional, and intellectual functioning (Luce, 1971). We also know that people have differing psychological orientations to time. There are important differences among people within this culture regarding their orientations to the past, present, and future. These orientations may represent a long-term style or be subject to change; for example, a person who "lives for the moment" at one point in his or her life might later adapt to a future-oriented style that involves evaluating today's "moments" in terms of the "long-range picture" (Gonzalez & Zimbardo, 1985). When we assess our social encounters, there are four fundamental ways we view time:

1. As the location of events
2. As the duration of events
3. As the interval between events
4. As the patterning of intervals

As we understand more about the environmental stimuli and conditions that trigger the following perceptions, we can use this knowledge to construct environments that give off the temporal messages we desire.

TIME AS LOCATION

Some of our perceptions of time have to do with when something happens, the timing of an event. The onsets of some events are evaluated as well timed, for example, "You hugged me at the exact moment I needed it most"; some are viewed as ill timed, for example, "I don't like eating dinner at 10 P.M." Sometimes our perceptions of when something happens are precise, and sometimes they represent a general time frame. For some, the time to eat lunch is precisely noon; for others it can be anytime between 11 A.M. and 2 P.M. Just as we attribute many different meanings to the timing of events in our lives, we also can communicate multiple meanings as we set deadlines for the occurrence of events in the future. For example, if something is due much sooner than expected, it may mean it is a form of punishment, a reward, very important, or very unimportant.

TIME AS DURATION

Our temporal perceptions also include how long some event lasts. We develop expectations for the proper and improper length of events, but perceptions of duration are not always a reflection of actual duration. An environment with little activity can be perceived as so boring that we perceive we have been there "forever."

TIME AS INTERVALS

The periods between events also constitute a way of perceiving time. The rate at which something happens is really a perception of the time since it last occurred. The perceived tempo of our lives is likely to be a reflection of how much or how little time separates each of our activities. We learn to expect certain intervals with certain activities. The phrase "It's been too long since I've seen you" suggests a contact-interval norm associated with close relationships that has been exceeded for this person. Similarly, we may not object to a person's using obscene language, but we may object to the brevity of the intervals between usage.

TIME AS PATTERNS OF INTERVALS

As we observe recurrent sequences of intervals, we begin to sense social rhythm—the regularity/irregularity, order/disorder comprising the cycles of our behavior and routines. Of all our time-bound perceptions, the pattern of intervals is the most complex and the most difficult to articulate to others. Understanding the patterning of intervals is, however, crucial to understanding ourselves as well as understanding our interaction with another person. When we feel in tune with another person, we are focusing on a pleasing perception of interactional synchrony, and when we feel awkward with someone, it may be because their patterning of nonverbal gestures or pauses is very different from ours. The understanding of patterns of intervals in our environment, whether it is a talk/silence pattern or a sunny/cloudy atmospheric pattern, is fundamental to making daily predictions about our lives.

The remainder of this chapter is devoted to the characteristics of environments that form the bases of the perceptions just outlined (perceptions of our surroundings and perceptions of time). Each environment has three major components:

1. The natural environment—geography, location, atmospheric conditions
2. The presence or absence of other people
3. Architectural and design features, including movable objects

THE NATURAL ENVIRONMENT

Some of us live in densely populated urban areas, some in smaller towns, some in suburban areas on the outskirts of these cities and towns, and others in rural areas. Within these broad areas, we find other environmental features that affect the nature of human interaction, for example, apartment complexes, neighborhoods, high-rise buildings, and so forth. The places we live, play, and work are bound to have an impact on our behavior. The number of people we communicate with can influence our interaction style, but perhaps more important is the number of different people for whom we have to adapt our messages. Some environments are very homogeneous and provide inhabitants with fewer experiences and examples of diverse styles, behavior, and values. The pace of life and the time devoted to developing social and personal relationships may also vary as a function of where we live. In slums or ghettos in urban areas, we often find a social climate that encourages or fosters unconventional and deviant behavior—or at least tolerates it. Thus, slum areas show a high incidence of juvenile delinquency, prostitution, alcohol and drug addiction, physical and mental disability, and crimes of violence (Krupat, 1985).

According to Lee, geographical location also may affect behavior, in particular, more mental and physical lethargy in tropical climates:

> Some loss of mental initiative is probably the most important single direct result of exposure to tropical environment. . . . Certainly, the usual pattern of life in tropical countries is more leisurely and less productive of material goods than that which is found in most temperate latitudes, and a case can be made for at least some influence of climate in this respect. Man in the temperate zones has built up his civilization around the important demands created by cold weather for securing food and shelter in advance. In so doing,

he has developed a culture in which activity and making provisions for the future have high social values.

In tropical populations, on the other hand, climate provides neither the social nor the psychological drive for activity and saving beyond the needs of the more or less immediate future. This difference in "spontaneous" activity marks one of the most important conflicts at the personal level between temperate and tropical modes of behavior. (Lee, 1957, pp. 99, 100)

The preceding speculation is based on the premise that climate and weather conditions affect behavior and that some parts of the world have very different conditions than others. There is no shortage of interest and speculation among behavioral scientists in the United States today concerning the effects of various weather conditions on human behavior. For example, high or rising barometric pressure has been associated with feelings of good health; low or falling barometric pressure is more likely to be linked to feelings of pain or depression. Optimum student behavior and performance have been observed when the barometer was high or rising and on cool days with little wind and precipitation. Increase in positive air ions also seems to increase a person's irritability and tension.

The changing seasons also seem to have an impact on behavior. Even in areas of the United States with minimal seasonal variations in temperature, national routines associated with changing seasons are still followed, for example, taking summer vacations and starting school in the fall. Some of the ways in which our behavior varies with the seasons include:

1. Suicide rates and admissions to public mental hospitals rise dramatically in the spring and peak in the summer.
2. College students tend to break up with their dating partners at the beginnings and endings of semesters (May/June, September, or December/January).
3. During the summer, people tend to see their friends more often.
4. During the summer, crimes of assault and rape increase.
5. From July to November, people tend to report less happiness but more activity and less boredom.
6. One study found people using the phone less in the summer than winter.
7. Some believe we do our best mental work in late winter, early spring, and fall (Moos, 1976; Rubin, 1979).

Temperature and the way it affects human responses is the climatic factor that has received the most scientific attention. McClelland, in his analysis of folk stories in primitive societies, found that achievement motivation was highest in areas where the mean annual temperature ranged between 40 and 60 degrees Fahrenheit (McClelland, 1961). He also concluded that temperature variation was important in determining achievement motivation, with at least fifteen degrees daily or seasonal variation needed for high achievement motivation. In the early twentieth century, Huntington advanced the theory that for mental vigor, an average outdoor temperature of 50 to 60 degrees was better than one above 70 degrees Fahrenheit (Huntington, 1915). Others have suggested the ideal temperature should average about 64 degrees Fahrenheit. Lengthy periods of extreme heat are often associated with discomfort, irritability, reduced work output, and unfavorable evaluations of strangers.

The issue of extreme heat acting as a stimulus for aggressive behavior has been the subject of several studies. Researchers have noted that the right combination of atmospheric pressure and high temperatures may lead to restlessness, irritability, temper tantrums, and even aggressive acts. An analysis of riots in India over a twenty-two-year period found that most took place during the months when the temperature was between 80 and 90 degrees Fahrenheit (Berke & Wilson, 1951). The National Advisory Commission on Civil Disorders, reporting on riots in the United States, said that hot summer nights added to an already explosive situation that eventually resulted in widespread rioting in ghetto areas: "In most instances, the temperature during the day on which the violence erupted was quite high" (Goranson & King, 1970; National Advisory Commission on Civil Disorders, 1968). An analysis of 102 riots in the United States between 1967 and 1971 concluded that the most likely temperature/riot sequence was one in which the temperature rose to between 81 and 85 degrees Fahrenheit and remained within that range for about seven days preceding the riot. Riots tended not to occur as temperatures rose into the high 80s and 90s. If extremely hot temperatures tend to minimize rioting, this effect is not likely to occur until mid-90 degree temperatures and above (Baron & Ransberger, 1978; Carlsmith & Anderson, 1979).

Obviously, the relationship between temperature and aggression is not simple. Probably, a number of factors interact with the temperature to increase the chance of aggression; for example, prior provocation, the presence of aggressive models, negative affect experienced from sources other than temperature, perceived ability to leave the environment, and so on. A thorough review of the literature, however, concludes:

> Clearly, hot temperatures produce increases in aggressive motives and tendencies. Hotter regions of the world yield more aggression; this is especially apparent when analyses are done within countries. Hotter years, quarters of years, seasons, months, and days all yield relatively more aggressive behaviors such as murders, rapes, assaults, riots, and wife beatings, among others. Finally, those concomitant temperature-aggression studies done in the field also yielded clear evidence that uncomfortably hot temperatures produce increases in aggressive motives and behaviors. (Anderson, 1989, p. 93)

The heat-aggression relationship seems to carry over to our sporting activities as well. An analysis of all major-league baseball games between 1986 and 1988 showed a strong correlation between higher temperatures and the number of batters hit by pitched balls (Reifman, Larrick, & Fein, 1991).

Griffitt varied heat and humidity under controlled laboratory conditions for students and confirmed a relationship to interpersonal responses. As temperature and humidity increased, evaluative responses for interpersonal attraction to another student decreased (Griffitt, 1970; Griffitt & Veitch, 1971).

There may be more truth than fiction in the familiar explanation for a particularly unpleasant encounter, "Oh, he was just hot and irritable." It should be noted, however, that sometimes unpleasant environmental factors such as heat or noise can increase attraction for others. In such cases, the aversive stimulus may function as "something we both have in common" (Kenrick & Johnson, 1979; Schneider, Lesko, & Garrett, 1980). The extent to which heat and other environmental variables increase or decrease attraction for others depends on how these interact with many other factors—the interactants' personalities and the presence or absence of simultaneously occurring rewarding stimuli, for example.

The effects of the moon and sunspots on human behavior also have been studied scientifically. Psychiatrist Arnold Lieber reasoned that human beings, like the earth, are subject to gravitational forces created by different positions of the moon. (Human beings are, like the planet itself, about 80 percent water and 20 percent solids.) He then plotted the number of murders in relation to the position of the moon and concluded a strong relationship between the two (Lieber, 1978). There is considerable skepticism towards Lieber's theory and similar work because research of this type shows how two things vary together, *not* that a particular moon position actually *causes* certain behaviors. Several other factors likely are interacting and affecting the two. Two separate analyses of over thirty-seven studies that purportedly linked moon positions and the frequency of psychiatric hospital admissions, suicides, homicides, traffic accidents, and changes in the stock market concluded that there is a spurious relationship between moon phases and these acts of human behavior (Campbell & Beets, 1978; Rotton & Kelly, 1985).

These reports on geography, climate, and celestial bodies provide us with little reliable and valid information. That our behavior is influenced by such factors seems a reasonable assumption, but the exact nature of this influence, the specific conditions under which this influence occurs, and the degree of the influence are still unknown. Most people seem to believe that the weather has less impact on their own behavior than it does on others'; that it has less impact on behavior than it does on emotional states; and that it has more impact on positive states than negative ones (Jorgenson, 1981). Kraut and Johnston (1979) found that people walking on the sidewalk smiled more when the weather was sunny and pleasant than when it was rainy and overcast. This difference was much smaller than the effect of being with others; people smiled much more when in interaction than when alone. Thus, compared to more social factors, climatic and other environmental variables may have weak influences on our behavior.

OTHER PEOPLE in the ENVIRONMENT

Chapter 5 examines the reactions of people to overpopulated environments. For now, we will point out that people can be perceived as part of the environment and will have an effect on the behavior of others. These people may be perceived as active or passive participants, depending on the degree to which they are perceived as "involved" (speaking or listening) in conversations. In many situations, these people will be seen as active, especially if they are able to overhear what is being said. In some situations, we grant another person or persons the dubious status of "nonperson" and behave accordingly. This may occur in high-density situations, but it is also common with just one other person. Cab drivers, janitors, and children achieve nonperson status with regularity. The presence of nonpersons, of course, allows the uninhibited flow of interaction because, as far as the active participants are concerned, they are the only human interactants present. Parents sometimes talk to others about very personal aspects of their child while the child is playing nearby. For the interactants, the child is perceived as "not here." Any relevant verbal or nonverbal responses on the part of the nonperson that are picked up by the interactants immediately strip the person of the nonperson role.

When others are perceived as an active ingredient in the environment, certain kinds of communication may be facilitated or inhibited. The chief difference in communication with active others is that messages must be adapted to multiple audiences rather than to a single one. Even telephone conversations in which the third party can hear only one of the interactants are altered to account for the uninvited listener. Sometimes the existence of these additional audiences presents such a strain or threat that one or both communicators leave the scene. On the other hand, the appearance of a third party can provide an opportunity to ease out of a conversation with an undesirable other by "dumping" the focus of the interaction onto this third party and making a polite exit.

The presence of others may increase our motivation to look good in what we say and do, which may be either detrimental (distorting information) or beneficial. The benefits of looking good in the presence of others is exemplified by constructive approaches to conflict. For instance, the presence of others may prohibit overt fighting, albeit temporarily. Others in the environment have ensured a delay, which may act as a cooling-off period or may further frustrate and/or aggravate the person who had to repress such feelings. If the people present are not highly interdependent, the communication probably will be less personal, more conventional, and more stereotyped—a form of communication designed for broader, less specific audiences.

When it was observed that the home team was usually the winner in sporting events (53 percent of the time in professional baseball, 58 percent in professional football, 60 percent in college football, 67 percent in professional basketball, and 64 percent in professional hockey), it was attributed primarily to the home team's familiarity with the home field or to the visiting team's travel fatigue. Further analysis showed, however, that the primary factor contributing to the home team's victories was the spectators, who seemed to provide psychological support that improved performance. On the other hand, unfriendly home crowds may increase performance errors (Schwartz & Barsky,

1977; Thirer & Rampey, 1979). Some analyses of home team performances before supportive fans suggested there was a tendency for the home team to "choke" in championship games, but recent studies do not show this to be true for baseball or basketball (Schlenker, Phillips, Boniecki, & Schlenker, 1995). Within the framework of these generalizations, we also may observe that sometimes friendly support is taken for granted and performance lags, or performers may excel in response to negative feedback from others. The point to remember, though, is that friendly or unfriendly "home town" supporters in the communication environment, just as in sporting events, are likely to affect performance.

The ways in which groups influence individual performance are too numerous and too large a topic to discuss here. Two examples will illustrate the subtlety of some of these effects:

1. In one of social psychology's first experiments, it was found that boys wound line on fishing reels faster when others were present performing the same activity, even though there was no competition and no emphasis on speed. Many studies have since found this "social facilitation" effect whereby performance (on simple and well-learned tasks, at least) is enhanced by the mere presence of others.
2. If people feel others are working with them on a joint task, they often slack off without realizing it. "Social loafing" is strongest when people feel their own contributions cannot be tallied or evaluated (Harkins & Szymanski, 1987).

ARCHITECTURAL DESIGN and MOVABLE OBJECTS

Hall (1966) has labeled the architecture and objects in our environment as either fixed-feature space or semifixed-feature space. *Fixed-feature* refers to space organized by unmoving boundaries (rooms of houses); *semifixed-feature* refers to the arrangement of movable objects such as tables or chairs. Both can have a profound impact on our communication behavior.

At one time in U. S. history, banks were deliberately designed to project an image of strength and security. The design frequently featured large marble pillars, an abundance of metal bars and doors, uncovered floors, and bare walls. This style generally projected a cold, impersonal image to visitors. Later bankers perceived the need to change their environment, to create a friendly, warm, "homey" place where people would enjoy sitting down and discussing their financial needs and problems. Bank interiors began to change. Carpeting was added; wood replaced metal; cushioned chairs were added; potted plants and art were brought in for additional warmth. This is only one example of the recognition that many times the interior in which interaction occurs can significantly influence the nature of the interaction. Nightclub owners and restaurateurs are aware that dim lighting and sound-absorbing surfaces such as carpets, drapes, and padded ceilings provide greater intimacy and cause patrons to linger longer than they would in an interior with high illumination and no soundproofing.

The way people decorate their rooms may also forecast future behavior. In one study, photographs were taken of eighty-three incoming-freshman students' rooms. When the photos of the rooms of students who had dropped out of school a year and a half later were analyzed, it was noted that the dropouts had more decorations reflecting high school and home and fewer related to the university community. Dropouts also seemed to have fewer ways to protect their privacy. Their favorite way to combat unwanted noise was to override it with more noise of their own (Vinsel, Brown, Altman, & Foss, 1980).

Sometimes we get very definite person or couple-related messages from home environments. The designation of places in the home for certain activities (and not for others); the symbolism attached to various objects in the home; and ways of decorating the home may tell us a lot about the nature of a couple's relationship (Altman, Brown, Staples, & Werner, 1992). Sometimes we perceive a home environment before we meet the inhabitants (e.g., as a prospective buyer being shown a home by a real-estate agent). In such cases, we may reflect on whether they decorated their home for themselves, for others, for conformity, for comfort, and so on (Sandalla, 1987). We may be influenced by the mood created by the wallpaper, by the symmetry and/ or orderliness of objects displayed, by pictures on the walls, and by the quality and apparent cost of items placed around the house. Most of us have experienced being ushered into a living room that we perceive as an "unliving" room. We hesitate to sit down or touch anything because the room seems to say, "This room is for show purposes only; sit, walk, and touch carefully. It takes a lot of time and effort to keep this room neat, clean, and tidy; we don't want to clean it after you leave." The arrangement of other living rooms seems to say, "Sit down, make yourself comfortable, feel free to talk informally, and don't worry about spilling things." Interior decorators and product promotion experts often make experimental and intuitive judgments about the influence of certain colors, objects, shapes, arrangements, and so forth, but few empirical attempts have been made to validate these feelings.

One of the earliest empirical studies to focus on the influence of interior decoration on human responses was conducted by Maslow and Mintz (1956) and Mintz (1956). Maslow and Mintz selected three rooms for study: One was an "ugly" room (designed to give the impression of a janitor's storeroom in disheveled condition); one was a "beautiful" room (complete with carpeting, drapes, and the like); and one was an "average" room (a professor's office). Subjects sitting in these rooms were asked to rate a series of negative print photographs (to control for color, shading, and so forth) of faces. The experimenters tried to keep all factors, such as time of day, odor, noise, type of seating, and experimenter, constant from room to room so that results could

Figure 4–2

Environmental Perception Test: (a) Describe the person or persons who live here. (b) Tell why you would or would not like to meet the person(s) who lives here. (c) How much communication takes place here? (d) What topics are most likely discussed? (e) Which dimensions listed on pp. 118–20 influenced your perceptions most? (f) Compare your answers with others. (Photo © John T. Hill, Bethany, Connecticut)

be attributed to the type of room. Results showed that subjects in the beautiful room gave significantly higher ratings on "energy" and "well-being" to the faces than did participants in the ugly room. Experimenters and subjects alike engaged in various escape behaviors to avoid the ugly room. The ugly room was variously described as producing monotony, fatigue, headache, discontent, sleep, irritability, and hostility. The beautiful room, however, produced feelings of pleasure, comfort, enjoyment, importance, energy, and desire to continue the activity. In this instance, we have a well-controlled study that offers some evidence of the impact of visual-aesthetic surroundings on the nature of human interaction. Similar studies found that students do better on tests, rate teachers higher, and solve problems more effectively in "beautiful" rooms than in "ugly" ones (Campbell, 1979; Wollin & Montagre, 1981). Because at least one study did not find mood or evaluations of others to change with drastic changes in appointments and decor (Kasmar, Grifin, & Mauritzen, 1968), we are reminded that the impact of the environment is only one source of influence on our perceptions. Sometimes it is a powerful force, but sometimes the close relationship between the two parties, an understanding of or tolerance for clutter, positive behavior on the part of the other person, and other factors will offset any negative effects emanating from an "ugly" environment.

COLOR

People believe colors can affect behavior. In fact, some believe "prisoner mischief" will vary as a function of the colors surrounding them. For example, the walls of the San Diego city jail were at one time reportedly painted pink, baby blue, and peach on the assumption that pastel colors would have a calming effect on the inmates. In Salem, Oregon, the cell bars of Oregon's Correctional Institution were painted soft greens, blues, and buffs; some cell doors were painted bright yellow, orange, green, and blue. In addition, the superintendent of the institution said that the color schemes would be continually changed to keep it "an exciting place to work and live in." Following a research study that concluded that looking at pink would make people weaker (Pelligrini & Schauss, 1980), the San Jose, California, county jail reportedly painted two holding cells "shocking pink" in the belief that prisoner hostility would be reduced. Prisoners seemed less hostile for about fifteen minutes, but soon the hostility reached a peak, and after three hours some prisoners were tearing the paint off the wall. A few years later, researchers again tested pink. This time pink was found to be arousing rather than weakening (Smith, Bell, & Fusco, 1986)! More effective results seemed to come from the program that allowed prisoners to paint their cells with colors they chose. These are a few examples of organizations that have tried to use findings from environmental research suggesting that colors, in conjunction with other factors, do influence moods and behavior.

A group of researchers in Munich, Germany, studied the impact of colors on mental growth and social relations ("Blue Is Beautiful," 1973). Children who were tested in rooms they thought beautiful scored about twelve points higher on an IQ test than those in rooms they thought ugly. Blue, yellow, yellow-green, and orange were considered beautiful; white, black, and brown were considered ugly. The beautifully colored rooms also seemed to stimulate alertness and creativity. In the orange room, these psychologists found that positive social reactions (friendly words, smiles) increased 53 percent, while negative reactions (irritability, hostility) decreased 12 percent.

Mehrabian says the *most pleasant* hues are, in order, blue, green, purple, red, and yellow (Mehrabian, 1976). He suggests that the *most arousing* hue is red, followed by orange, yellow, violet, blue, and green. Although Mehrabian's proposals are not completely comparable with the following paper-and-pencil research on colors and mood-tones, there are a number of similarities. Wexner presented eight colors and eleven mood-tones to ninety-four subjects. The results (see Table 4-1) show that for some mood-tones a single color is significantly related; for others there may be two or more colors (Murray & Deabler, 1957; Wexner, 1954).

The problem in interpreting such research concerns determining whether people choose colors actually associated with particular moods or whether they respond using learned verbal stereotypes. Another problem with some of the color preference research concerns the lack of association between color and objects. Pink may be your favorite color, but you may still dislike pink hair. A third problem concerns the failure to separate the effects of changing the colors of an environment from the effects of the color per se. Nevertheless, we cannot ignore the educational and design literature that suggests that carefully planned color schemes seem to have *some* influence on improving scholastic achievement. We cannot make any final judgments about the impact of color on human interaction until behavioral studies link different colored environments with different types of verbal behavior or communication patterns.

A series of studies on the color of uniforms worn by football and hockey players pinpointed the complex ways colors may affect behavior. Frank and Gilovich (1988) began by demonstrating that students rated black uniforms as connoting meanness and aggression more than other colors. Then they

Table 4–1
COLORS ASSOCIATED WITH MOODS

Mood-Tone	Color	Frequency of Times Chosen
Exciting/Stimulating	Red	61
Secure/Comfortable	Blue	41
Distressed/Disturbed/Upset	Orange	34
Tender/Soothing	Blue	41
Protective/Defending	Red	21
	Brown	17
	Blue	15
	Black	15
	Purple	14
Despondent/Dejected/Unhappy/Melancholy	Black	25
	Brown	25
Calm/Peaceful/Serene	Blue	38
	Green	31
Dignified/Stately	Purple	45
Cheerful/Jovial/Joyful	Yellow	40
Defiant/Contrary/Hostile	Red	23
	Orange	21
	Black	18
Powerful/Strong/Masterful	Black	48

examined statistics from actual professional games and found that football and hockey teams wearing black uniforms were penalized more than teams wearing other colors. And when a team changed its color to black from some other color, it began getting more penalties! The researchers then asked whether the effect was caused by the players themselves (maybe they acted meaner and rougher wearing black) or by the stereotyped perceptions of referees. The researchers made experimental films in which they varied the uniforms of players engaging in identical moves and then showed these to subjects acting as "referees." These "referees" did find more instances of penalizable behavior among those suited in black, even though there actually were no differences. However, when the researchers put black uniforms on students, they found evidence that wearing a black uniform produced more aggressive behavior in the wearer. Thus, both processes seem to be at work: Players wearing black may be rougher, but people also *perceive* the play of those in black uniforms as rougher. This perception could, of course, make black-suited players even rougher, because of the ways people treat them.

SOUND

Types of sounds and their intensity also seem to affect interpersonal behavior. We may have very different reactions to the drone of several people's voices, the overpowering sound of a nearby jackhammer, or the soothing or stimulating sounds of music. "Music," says Mehrabian (1976, p. 50), "can have a stronger and more immediate effect on arousal level and pleasure than, say, several cups of coffee." That often unpleasant, arousing, and powerful sound of the morning alarm clock may have a good deal to do with some people's irritability on rising. Generally, the more pleasant the music, the more likely we are to engage in "approaching" rather than "avoiding" behavior. Slow, simple, soft, and familiar music is likely to lower arousal levels while maintaining pleasure, eliciting an easygoing and satisfying feeling.

Glass and Singer (1972) conducted a series of studies on the impact of noise on performance. People were asked to perform a variety of tasks, varying in complexity, while noises were manipulated by the experimenters. Noise levels were varied; some noise was predictable (following a pattern) and some was not. Various noise sources were tested (for example, typewriters, machinery, people speaking a foreign language). Although noise alone did not seem to have a substantial effect on performance, deterioration was observed when noise interacted with other factors. For instance, performance decreased when the workload was high and the noise uncontrollable and unpredictable. Other factors determining whether noise is a problem or a pleasure include the type of noise (e.g., music versus people talking), the volume, the length of time it lasts, and whether the listener is accustomed to it or not. Obviously, some individuals may be more influenced by noise than others. Noise-sensitive incoming freshmen perceived more noise than other students, and these perceptions increased after seven months into the school year. The noise-sensitive students also received lower grades, felt less secure in their social interactions, and had a greater desire for privacy than did their peers who were less sensitive to noise (Weinstein, 1978).

In some environments, we want to change the sound to change behavior, for example, raising the volume of supermarket music to stimulate more purchases in a shorter time. In other instances, we may try to reduce unproductive noise through structural changes. In one mental institution, floor tiles were replaced with carpeting, which was felt to make patients less irritable and the hospital warmer and more like a home. This, in turn, encouraged the patients to spend more time taking care of their environment (Cheek, Maxwell, & Weisman, 1971). Another study tested the effects of rooms of different sizes (150 cubic feet versus 1,600 cubic feet), different shapes (circular versus rectangular), and different reverberation times (.8 to 1.0 seconds versus .2 to .3 seconds) upon a speaker's rate and intensity in reading aloud (Black, 1950). Generally, the data suggest that the rate and intensity of reading were affected by the size of the room and the reverberation time, but not by the shape. The rate seemed to be slower in the larger and less reverberant rooms; vocal intensity was greater in smaller and less reverberant rooms; and intensity consistently increased as the subject read through the twelve phrases provided in the less reverberant rooms.

LIGHTING

Lighting also helps to structure our perceptions of an environment, and these perceptions also may influence the type of messages we send. If we enter a dimly lit or candlelit room, we may talk more softly, sit closer together, and presume that more personal communication will take place (Meer, 1985). When the dim lights are brightened, however, the environment tends to invite less intimate interaction. When dimly lit nightclubs flash on bright lights, it is often a signal that closing time is near and allows patrons some time to make the transition from one mood to another. Carr and Dabbs found that the communication of intimate questions in dim lighting with nonintimates caused a significant hesitancy in responding, a significant decrease in eye gaze, and a decrease in the average length of gaze (Carr & Dabbs, 1974). All of these nonverbal behaviors appear to be efforts to create more psychological distance and decrease the perceived inappropriateness of the intimacy created by the lighting and the questions.

The absence of light seems to be a central problem for people who suffer from "seasonal affective disorder," a form of depression particularly acute in winter months. Therapists have successfully treated these people by exposing them to extremely bright lighting for several hours each morning. Artificial lighting that provides a full-range light spectrum like that of the sun is most effective in this therapy (Lewry, Sack, Miller, & Hoban, 1987). In view of this need for sunlight, some researchers wondered whether cities that had the lowest amount of annual sunlight also had the highest suicide rates. Their findings do not provide support for this hypothesis (Lester, 1988).

MOVABLE OBJECTS

If we know that the arrangement of certain objects in our environment can help structure communication, it is not surprising that we often try to manipulate objects to elicit certain types of response. Special, intimate evenings are often highlighted by candlelight, soft music, favorite drinks, fluffed pillows on the couch, and the absence of dirty dishes, trash, and other impersonal material associated with daily living.

Employees often use objects to personalize their offices. These signs of personal identity make the employee feel more satisfied with his or her work life and provide visitors with information to initiate a conversation. Since the company also wants to communicate its identity, the amount and kind of personal objects employees display must also be consistent with the image the company wants to display. Objects in our work environment also can be arranged to reflect certain role relationships—to demarcate boundaries or to encourage greater affiliation. The interior of an executive suite clearly may indicate the perceived status of the inhabitant, for example, expensive paintings, large desk, plush sofa and chairs, drapes, and so forth (Monk, 1994). Such an atmosphere may be inappropriate for a personal counseling situation, but it can be rearranged to make it more conducive to such a purpose. Of course, we sometimes are able to communicate well in seemingly inappropriate settings, as when lovers say good-bye in relatively cold and public airport terminals.

Desks seem to be important objects in the conduct of interpersonal communication. An experiment set in a doctor's office suggests that the presence or absence of a desk may significantly alter the patient's "at ease" state (White, 1953). With the desk separating doctor and patient, only 10 percent of the patients were perceived "at ease," whereas removal of the desk increased the percentage of "at ease" patients to 55 percent. Student/teacher relationships also seem to be affected by desk placement (Zweigenhaft, 1976). (See Figure 4-3.) Faculty members were asked to sketch the furniture arrangement of their offices. These sketches were collected and analyzed with other information obtained from the professors and a schoolwide teacher evaluation. Twenty-four of thirty-three senior faculty members (full professors and associate professors) put their desks between themselves and their students, but only fourteen of thirty junior faculty members (assistant professors and lecturers) did so. Furthermore, students rated the "unbarricaded" professors as more willing to "encourage the development of different viewpoints by students," ready to give "individual attention to students who need it," and less likely to show "undue favoritism." Because another study did not find the desk barrier related to undesirable experiences in student/professor interactions, we

Figure 4–3

A classroom design that discourages student-to-student interaction.

are reminded that other factors may neutralize or override the potentially troublesome effects of the desk barrier (Campbell & Herren, 1978). For example, students expect greater formality in student/teacher relationships in some situations than others, or the basis for an effective working relationship may have been established outside the professor's office, so the "barrier" is not perceived as a barrier. The podium separating the president's press secretary from the press during White House press briefings also has been perceived both as appropriate and as a barrier to effective communication. During the Nixon administration, press briefings were formal, and the press secretary stood behind a podium. Ron Nessen, President Ford's press secretary, felt the podium contributed to an unproductive "us and them" feeling, which prompted him to conduct briefings without the obstacle.

Less obvious barriers also exist. For instance, if you find a delicate *objet d'art* placed in front of some books in a bookcase, you likely will feel hesitant about using the books. Keep in mind that desks and other "barriers" are not inherently good or bad. Should you want to keep a distant, formal relationship, the desk can help to create that feeling.

The arrangement of other items of furniture can facilitate or inhibit communication. The location of the television set in a room very likely will affect the placement of chairs and, in turn, the pattern of conversations in that room. Sommer and Ross found that some residents in a geriatric ward were "apathetic" and had few friends, in spite of a generally cheerful and bright environment. Rearranging the furniture to encourage interaction doubled the frequency of resident conversations (Sommer & Ross, 1958). Even when conversational possibilities have been maximized, not everyone will talk to everyone else. Consider the arrangement in Figure 4-4. We would predict exchanges marked by the arrows to be most frequent, but the four people seated on the couch as well as persons F and G will probably talk to each other infrequently. The four people on one end are not likely to communicate very often with the four people on the other end. If the participants are periodically rearranged, the conversational groupings can be altered. Finally, notice that there are no empty chairs in this arrangement, which poses the question of where one goes when "bored stiff" with the current conversational grouping.

In at least one case, a furniture designer deliberately designed a chair to exert disagreeable pressure on a person's spine when the chair was occupied for more than a few minutes. The Larsen Chair was originally designed to keep patrons from becoming too comfortable and remaining in seats that could be occupied by other customers (Sommer, 1969, p. 121). Hotel owners and airport designers apparently are already aware of the "too comfortable" phenomenon. You may have noticed the slightly uncomfortable nature of the 10 degree forward angle of chairs in some fast-food restaurants. Thus, seating arrangements deliberately are made uncomfortable for long seating and conversations, so patrons will move along and perhaps drift into nearby shops, where they can spend money. The Port Authority Bus Terminal in New York replaced its old wooden seats with folding plastic seats, only eight inches deep, that "require so much concentration to balance that sleeping or even sitting for long is impossible." This was done to keep homeless people from sleeping in the terminal ("For Homeless," 1989).

Some environments seem to have an unwritten code that virtually prohibits interaction. Lone men entering, sitting through, and leaving XXX-rated movies without uttering a word are a case in point.

Figure 4–4

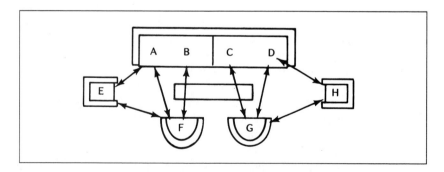

Conversation flow and furniture arrangement (from A. Mehrabian, Public Places and Private Spaces: The Psychology of Work, Play, and Living Environm, © *1976 by Basic Books, Inc. Reprinted by permission of Basic Books, a division of Harper Collins Publishers, Inc.*

STRUCTURE AND DESIGN

We spend much of our time in buildings. Most of us spend the day in a dwelling supposedly designed for effective performance of our work; in the evening, we enter another structure supposedly designed for the effective conduct of our personal and family life. The architecture of these buildings can go a long way toward determining who shall meet whom, where, and perhaps for how long.

The life of domestic animals is controlled through, among other things, the erection of fences, flap doors, or the placement of food and water in particular locations. Although verbal and nonverbal actions help control human situations, manipulation of barriers, openings, and other physical arrangements is also helpful. Meeting places can be appropriately arranged to regulate human traffic and, to a certain extent, the network of communication.

U. S. office buildings often are constructed from a standard plan that reflects a pyramidal organization. A large number of people are supervised by a few executives at the upper levels. These executives generally have the most space, the most privacy, and the most desirable office locations, namely, on the highest floor of the structure. Achieving a height above the "masses" and occupying a significant amount of space are only two indications of power. Corner offices, large picture windows, and private elevators also are associated with status and power (Monk, 1994). An office next to an important executive also may be a formidable power base. A similar pattern seems to exist in academic settings as well, with the higher ranking professors normally having more space, windows, privacy, and choice of office location (Farrenkopf & Roth, 1980). The offices of top-level executives are often hard to reach, the assumption being that the more complicated the path to get to the executive, the more powerful he or she seems. Figure 4-5 is a hypothetical, but not far-fetched, example of the long and circuitous route to a president's office. To get to the office, the visitor must be screened by a receptionist and a private secretary and in either or both places may be asked to sit and wait. So, although the status and power of an executive may be related to his or her inaccessibility, secretaries and receptionists may value open views that allow them to act as lookouts and defenders against unwanted intrusions. It is common for people on the lowest rungs of the organizational ladder to find themselves in a large open "pit." These "offices" (desks) have little or no privacy, and complaints are common. Although privacy is minimal, communication opportunities are plentiful.

Some dormitories are built from floor plans that resemble many office buildings and old hotels. It has been speculated that these corridor-type dorms tend to encourage bureaucratic management, which seems to fit the orderly and uniform structure. Rigid rules are easier to enforce in these structures, and interaction among the residents is discouraged. Compared with suite-type dorms, corridor types are perceived by residents as being more crowded, less private, and conducive to avoiding others (Baum & Vallins, 1979). The

Figure 4–5

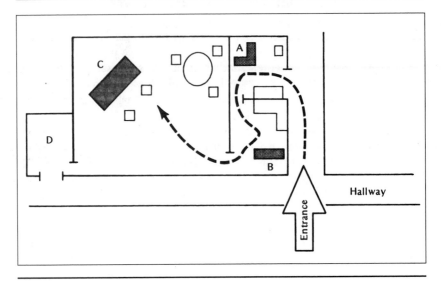

Getting to the president's office. A = Receptionist. B = Private secretary. C = President. D = Private room with rear exit.

sense of community and the resulting responsibility for the living space are difficult to achieve. Lounges are sometimes intended to facilitate such interaction, but their usefulness has been questioned by architects and behavioral scientists. Lounges, like other design features, must be integrated into the entire architectural plan developed from an analysis of *human needs*— not inserted in places where they fit nicely or look good for parents and visitors.

If you look carefully, you can see many environmental structures that inhibit or prohibit communication. Fences separating yards create obvious barriers, even if they are only waist high; locating laundry rooms in dark, isolated areas of apartment buildings and public housing discourages their use, particularly at night; providing access to patios only through a bedroom will probably discourage use; and so on.

Other environmental situations seem to facilitate interaction. Homes located in the middle of a block seem to draw more interpersonal exchanges than those located in other positions. Houses with adjacent driveways seem to have a built-in structure, drawing the neighbors together and inviting communication. Cavan (1966) reports that the likelihood of interaction between strangers at a bar varies directly with the distance between them. As a rule, a span of three bar stools is the maximum distance over which patrons will attempt to initiate an encounter. Two men conversing but separated by an empty bar stool are likely to remain in that position since they would be too close if they sat next to each other. However, if a man is talking to a woman and there is an empty stool between them, he will likely move onto it—to prevent someone else from coming between them. Most bars, however, are not designed for optimum interaction. Note that the three bar designs in Figure 4-6 provide very different opportunities for facing an interaction partner, for mutual eye gaze, and for getting physically close. Most bars are similar to type B, which seems to discourage interaction the most.

Some recent designs for housing elderly people have taken into consideration the need for social contact. In these apartment dwellings, the doors of the apartments on each floor open onto a common entranceway. This greatly increases the probabilities for social exchange as compared to buildings in which apartment doors are staggered on either side of a long hallway with no facing doorways. If you want a structure that encourages social interaction, you must have human paths crossing; but if you want people to interact, there must be something that will encourage them to linger. Differences in interaction frequency are often related to the distances people must travel between activities. For example, a comparison was made between two high schools: One was "centralized" with classrooms in one or two buildings; one was "campus style" with classrooms spread among several buildings. The campus design prompted 5 to 10 percent more interactions in the halls, stairs, and lobbies but 7 to 10 percent fewer in the classrooms than the centralized design. There were 20 percent fewer interactions between students and teachers before and after class in the campus-style high school (Myrick & Marx, 1968).

Fast-food restaurants also seem to vary with regard to how much they contribute to the interactive involvement of their customers. In one study, for example, the behavior of customers at McDonald's showed more involvement than those at Burger King (Eaves & Leathers, 1991). The shorter distance across the tables and the generally less comfortable surroundings seemed to be factors in the greater involvement of the patrons at McDonald's.

Architects and social scientists have even been experimenting with new prison designs. The older structures, which had linear tiers of steel cages, are being replaced with modular units that have fewer inmates and fewer barriers between them and their guards. These new designs, coupled with

Figure 4–6

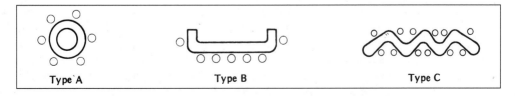

Designs for drinking. (from Public Places and Private Spaces: The Psychology of Work, Play, and Living Environm *by Albert Mehrabian. © 1976 by Basic Books, Inc. Reprinted by permission of Basic Books, a division of Harper Collins Publishers, Inc.*

new ways of managing the prisoners, seem to result in more positive behavior on the part of both guards and prisoners, reduced costs, and more opportunities for rehabilitation (Cronin, 1992).

Furthermore, the nature of the design may encourage or discourage certain *types* of communication—that is, the structure may determine how much interaction takes place and what the general content of that interaction will be. Drew (1971) reports a study of three different designs for nursing stations within a mental hospital. In one, interaction had to take place by opening a door; in another, interaction was conducted through a glass-enclosed counter; and in the third, interaction took place over an open counter. Although substantially more patients entered the nursing station with the door, interactions occurred less frequently than in the other two stations. An average of only 1 interaction per each fifteen-minute observation period occurred with the door; 5.3 interactions per period occurred in the glass-enclosed counter; and 8.7 occurred with the open counter. Although interaction was higher for the open counter, the author noted a preponderance of social conversation here; the door design seemed to encourage more item requests and permission interactions. In short, the more inaccessible setting decreased interaction frequency and increased task-oriented messages; the more accessible setting increased interaction frequency and increased the amount of "small talk."

A more complete analysis of physical proximity and spatial distance appears in Chapter 5, but it is clearly relevant to this discussion on the environment as well. As Stouffer put it:

> Whether one is seeking to explain why persons go to a particular place to get jobs, why they go to trade at a particular store, why they go to a particular neighborhood to commit a crime, or why they marry a particular spouse they choose, the factor of spatial distance is of obvious significance. (Stouffer, 1940, p. 845)

Many studies have confirmed Stouffer's remark. Students tend to develop stronger friendships with students who share their classes, dormitory, or apartment building, or who sit near them, than with others who are geographically distant. Workers tend to develop closer friendships with those who work close to them. The effect of proximity seems to be stronger for employees with less status in the organization. Managers are more likely to choose their business friends according to their status rather than their proximity (Schutte & Light, 1978). Some believe that increased proximity of white and black persons will assist in reducing prejudice. Although close proximity may bring about positive attitude changes, caution should be exercised in the generalization of such an idea. If the two groups are extremely polarized, or perceive no mutual problems or projects requiring cooperation, proximity may only magnify the hostilities.

Several studies show an inverse relationship between the distance separating potential marriage partners and the number of marriages. Proximity allows us to obtain more information about the other person. The inescapable conclusion is that as proximity increases, attraction is likely to increase. One might also posit that as attraction increases, proximity will tend to increase.

A number of studies have shown how friendships are influenced by proximity. In one study conducted in a townhouse development, most friendships occurred between people who lived within 100 feet of each other. Next-door neighbors became close friends 46 percent of the time; neighbors who lived two or three doors away became close friends 24 percent of the time; and people who lived three or four doors away became friends 13 percent of the time (Athanasiou & Yoshioka, 1973). Perhaps the most famous study of proximity, friendship choice, and interpersonal contact was conducted by Festinger, Schachter, and Back (1950) in a housing development for married students. Concern for what the authors called "functional distance" led to data clearly demonstrating that architects can have a tremendous influence on the social life of residents in these housing projects. Functional distance is determined by the number of contacts that position and design encourage, for example, factors such as which way apartments face, where exits and entranceways are located, and location of stairways, mailboxes, and the like. Figure 4-7 shows the basic design of one type of building studied.

The researchers asked the residents of seventeen buildings (with the design of Figure 4-7) which people they saw most often socially and what friendship choices they made. Among the findings from this study, the following are noteworthy:

1. There seemed to be a greater number of friendship choices for those physically close to one another (on the same floor or in the same building). It was rare to find a friendship between people separated by more than four or five houses.
2. People living in apartments 1 and 5 gave and received from the upper-floor residents more friendship choices than the people living in any other apartments on the lower floor.
3. Apartments 1 and 6 exchanged more choices than apartments 2 and 7. Similarly, apartments 5 and 10 exchanged more choices than apartments 4 and 9. Although this represents the same physical distance, functional distance differed.

Figure 4–7

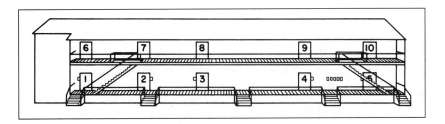

4. Apartment 7 chose 6 more than it chose 8; apartment 9 chose 10 more than it chose 8. This relationship did not hold true for corresponding first-floor apartments.
5. Because of the mailboxes, apartment 5 chose more upper-level friends, more of those choices being apartments 9 and 10.

There are many ways of making friends, but functional distance seems to be highly influential, and functional distance is sometimes the result of architectural design.

SUMMARY

The environment in which people communicate frequently contributes to the overall outcome of their encounters. We have seen that both the frequency and the content of our messages are influenced by various aspects of the setting in which we communicate. We have seen how the environment influences our behavior, but we also know that we can alter environments in order to elicit certain types of responses. As our knowledge of environments increases, we may deliberately use them to help us obtain desired responses. In many respects, we are products of our environment, and if we want to change behavior, we need to learn to control the environment in which we interact.

Throughout this chapter, we referred to a number of different types of environments—the classroom, dormitories, offices, prisons, fast-food restaurants, homes, and bars. We suggested that there were several different ways of looking at environments. Mehrabian, following research in other areas of human perception, suggested that all environments could profitably be examined by looking at emotional reactions to them. These emotions, or feelings, says Mehrabian, can be plotted on three dimensions: arousing/nonarousing, pleasant/unpleasant, and dominant/submissive. We suggested six perceptual bases for examining environments: formal/informal, warm/cold, private/public, familiar/unfamiliar, constraining/free, and distant/close. We also pointed out that people perceive temporal aspects of their environments: when things happen, how long they last, how much time exists between events, and the pattern or rhythm of events.

Each environment seems to have three major characteristics:

1. The natural environment
2. The presence of or absence of other people
3. Architectural design and movable objects, including lighting, sound, color, and general visual-aesthetic appeal

The quantity and quality of the research in each of these areas vary considerably, but it is clear that any analysis of human behavior must account for the influence of environmental features.

QUESTIONS for DISCUSSION

1. Select a familiar environment that effectively encourages or discourages human interaction. Now indicate all the changes you would make so this environment would have the exact opposite effect.
2. Assume the role of a stranger entering your own apartment or your family's home. What messages does the environment communicate?
3. Identify an environment that is clearly designed to accomplish certain goals or effects—but does not. What explanation helps us understand this situation?
4. How do people communicate time-related messages by their behavior?

REFERENCES and SELECTED BIBLIOGRAPHY

Adams, R. S. (1969). Location as a feature of instructional interaction. *Merrill-Palmer Quarterly, 15,* 309–21.

Adams, R. S., & Biddle, B. (1970). *Realities of teaching: Explorations with video tape.* New York: Holt, Rinehart & Winston.

Altman, I., Brown, B.B., Staples, B., & Werner, C.M. (1992). A transactional approach to close relationships: Courtship, weddings and placemaking. In B. Walsh, K. Craik, & R. Price (Eds.), *Person-environment psychology: Contemporary models and perspectives*. Hillsdale, NJ: Erlbaum.

Altman, I., & Chemers, M. M. (1988). *Culture and environment*. New York: Cambridge University Press.

Altman, I., & Gauvain, M. (1981). A cross-cultural and dialectic analysis of homes. In L.S. Liben, A.H. Patterson, & N. Newcombe (Eds.), *Special representation and behavior across the life span*. New York: Academic Press.

Altman, I., & Low, S.M. (Eds.). (1992). *Place attachment. Human behavior and environment: Advances in theory and research* (Vol 12). New York: Plenum.

Anderson, C. A. (1989). Temperature and aggression: Ubiquitous effects of heat on occurrence of human violence. *Psychological Bulletin, 106,* 74–96.

Anderson, C. A., & Anderson, D. C. (1984). Ambient temperature and violent crime: Tests of the linear and curvilinear hypotheses. *Journal of Personality and Social Psychology, 46,* 91–97.

Athanasiou, R., & Yoshioka, G. A. (1973). The spatial character of friendship formation. *Environment and Behavior, 5,* 43–65.

Barker, R. (1968). *Ecological psychology*. Palo Alto, CA: Stanford University Press.

Barker, R., & Wright, H. (1957). *Midwest and its children*. Lawrence, KS: University of Kansas Press.

Baron, R. A. (1972). Aggression as a function of ambient temperature and prior anger arousal. *Journal of Personality and Social Psychology, 21,* 183–89.

Baron, R. A., & Bell, P. A. (1975). Aggression and heat: Mediating effects of prior provocation and exposure to an aggressive model. *Journal of Personality and Social Psychology, 31,* 825–32.

Baron, R. A., & Bell, P. A. (1976). Aggression and heat: The influence of ambient temperature, negative affect, and a cooling drink on physical aggression. *Journal of Personality and Social Psychology, 33,* 245–55.

Baron, R. A., & Lawton, S. F. (1972). Environmental influences on aggression: The facilitation of modeling effects by high ambient temperatures. *Psychonomic Science, 26,* 80–82.

Baron, R. A., & Ransberger, V. M. (1978). Ambient temperature and the occurrence of collective violence: The 'long hot summer' revisited. *Journal of Personality and Social Psychology, 36,* 351–60.

Baum, A., & Davis, G. E. (1980). Reducing the stress of high density living: An architectural intervention. *Journal of Personality and Social Psychology, 38,* 471–81.

Baum, A., & Valins, S. (1979). Architectural mediation of residential density and control: Crowding and regulation of social contact. In L. Berkowitz (Ed.), *Advances in experimental social psychology* (Vol. 12). New York: Academic Press.

Baumeister, R.F. (1995). Disputing the effects of championship pressures and home audiences. *Journal of Personality and Social Psychology, 68,* 649–52.

Berke, J., & Wilson, V. (1951). *Watch out for the weather.* New York: Viking.

Birren, F. (1969). *Light, color and environment.* New York: Van Nostrand Reinhold.

Black, J. W. (1950). The effect of room characteristics upon vocal intensity and rate. *Journal of the Acoustical Society of America, 22,* 174–76.

Blake, R. R., Rhead, C. C., Wedge, B., & Mouton, J. S. (1956). Housing architecture and social interaction. *Sociometry, 19,* 133–39.

Blue is beautiful. (1973, September 17). *Time,* p. 66.

Breed, G., & Colaiuta, V. (1974). Looking, blinking, and sitting: Nonverbal dynamics in the classroom. *Journal of Communication, 24,* 75–81.

Byrne, D. (1961). The influence of propinquity and opportunities for interaction on classroom relationships. *Human Relations, 14,* 63–70.

Campbell, D. E. (1979). Interior office design and visitor response. *Journal of Applied Psychology, 64,* 648–53.

Campbell, D. E., & Beets, J. L. (1978). Lunacy and the moon. *Psychological Bulletin, 85,* 1123–29.

Campbell, D. E., & Herren, K. A. (1978). Interior arrangement of the faculty office. *Psychological Reports, 43,* 234.

Canter, D. (1977). *The psychology of place.* London: Architectural Press.

Carlsmith, J. M., & Anderson, C. A. (1979). Ambient temperature and the occurrence of collective violence: A new analysis. *Journal of Personality and Social Psychology, 37,* 337–44.

Carr, S. J., & Dabbs, J. M. (1974). The effect of lighting, distance and intimacy of topic on verbal and visual behavior. *Sociometry, 37,* 592–600.

Cavan, S. (1966). *Liquor license.* Chicago: Aldine Publishing.

Cheek, F. E., Maxwell, R., & Weisman, R. (1971). Carpeting the ward: An exploratory study in environmental psychiatry. *Mental Hygiene, 55,* 109–18.

Child, I. L. (1968). Esthetics. In G. Lindsey & E. Aronson (Eds.), *Handbook of Social Psychology* (Vol. 3). Reading, MA: Addison-Wesley.

Cottle, T. J. (1976). *Perceiving time.* New York: John Wiley and Sons.

Craik, K. (1981). Environmental assessment and situational analysis. In D. Magnusson (Ed.), *Toward a psychology of situations: An interactional perspective.* New York: Erlbaum.

Cronin, M. (May 1992). Gilded cages. *Time,* pp. 52–54.

Deutsch, M., & Collins, M. (1951). *Interracial housing: A psychological evaluation of a social experiment.* Minneapolis, MN: University of Minnesota Press.

Doob, L. (1964). *Patterning of time.* New Haven, CT: Yale University Press.

Drew, C. J. (1971). Research on the psychological-behavioral effects of the physical environment. *Review of Educational Research, 41,* 447–63.

Duncan, F. (1981). Dormitory architecture influences patterns of student social relations over time. *Environment and Behavior, 13,* 23–41.

Eaves, M. H., & Leathers, D. G. (1991). Context as communication: McDonald's vs. Burger King. *Journal of Applied Communication Research, 19,* 263–89.

Falender, C. A., & Mehrabian, A. (1978). Environmental effects on parent-infant interaction. *Genetic Psychology Monographs, 97,* Pt. 1, 3–41.

Farrenkopf, T., & Roth, V. (1980). The university faculty office as an environment. *Environment and Behavior, 12,* 467–77.

Festinger, L. (1951). Architecture and group membership. *Journal of Social Issues, 1,* 152–63.

Festinger, L., Schachter, S., & Back, K. (1950). *Social pressures in informal groups: A study of human factors in housing.* New York: Harper & Row.

Ford, C. S., Rothro, E. T., & Child, I. L. (1966). Some transcultural comparisons of esthetic judgment. *Journal of Social Psychology, 68,* 19–26.

Fraisse, Paul. (1963). *The psychology of time.* New York: Harper and Row.

Frank, M. S., & Gilovich, T. (1988). The dark side of self- and social perception: Black uniforms and aggression in professional sports. *Journal of Personality and Social Psychology, 54,* 74–85.

Fraser, J. T. (1981). A report on the literature of time, 1900–1980. In J. T. Fraser, N. Lawrence, & D. Park (Eds.), *The study of time IV.* New York: Springer-Verlag.

Gans, H. J. (1961). Planning and social life: Friendship and neighbor relations in suburban communities. *Journal of the American Institute of Planners, 27,* 134–40.

Glass, D., & Singer, J. E. (1973). Experimental studies of uncontrollable and unpredictable noise. *Representative Research in Social Psychology, 4,* 165.

Gonzalez, A., & Zimbardo, P. G. (1985). Time in perspective. *Psychology Today, 19,* 21–26.

Goranson, R. E., & King, D. (1970). *Rioting and daily temperature: Analysis of the U. S. riots in 1967.* Unpublished manuscript, York University, Ontario, Canada.

Griffin, W. V., Mauritzen, J. H., & Kasmar, J. V. (1969). The psychological aspects of the architectural environment: A review. *American Journal of Psychiatry, 125,* 1057–62.

Griffith, W. (1970). Environmental effects of interpersonal affective behavior. Ambient effective temperature and attraction. *Journal of Personality and Social Psychology, 15,* 240–44.

Griffith, W., & Veitch, R. (1971). Hot and crowded: Influence of population density and temperature on interpersonal affective behavior. *Journal of Personality and Social Psychology, 17,* 92–98.

Haber, G. M. (1982). Spatial relations between dominants and marginals. *Social Psychology Quarterly, 45,* 221–28.

Hall, E. T. (1959). *The silent language.* Garden City, NY: Doubleday.

Hall, E. T. (1966). *The hidden dimension.* Garden City, NY: Doubleday.

Hall, E. T. (1983). *The dance of life.* Garden City, NY: Anchor Books.

Hambrick-Dixon, P. J. (1986). Effects of experimentally imposed noise on task performance of black children attending day care centers near elevated subway trains. *Developmental Psychology, 22,* 259–64.

Harkins, S., & Szymanksi, K. (1987). Social facilitation and social loafing: New wine in old bottles. In C. Hendrick (Ed.), *Review of personality and social psychology* (Vol 9). Beverly Hills, CA: Sage.

Hazard, J. N. (1962). Furniture arrangement as a symbol of judicial roles. *ETC, 19,* 181–88.

Heilweil, M. (Ed.). (1973). Student housing, architecture, and social behavior. *Environment and Behavior, 5,* entire issue.

Holahan, C. J. (1972). Seating patterns and patient behavior in an experimental dayroom. *Journal of Abnormal Psychology, 80,* 115–24.

Holahan, C. J., Wilcox, B. L., Burnam, M. A., & Culler, R. E. (1978). Social satisfaction and friendship formation as a function of floor level in high-rise student housing. *Journal of Applied Psychology, 63,* 527–29.

For homeless, no welcome in public places. (1989, November 18). *New York Times.*

Huntington, E. (1915). *Civilization and climate.* New Haven, CT: Yale University Press.

Hutte, H. (1972). Door-knocks in terms of authority and urgency. *European Journal of Social Psychology, 2,* 98–99.

Infante, D. A., & Berg, C. M. (1979). The impact of music modality on the perception of communication situations in video sequences. *Communication Monographs, 46,* 135–41.

Jackson, P. W. (1968). *Life in classrooms.* New York: Holt, Rinehart & Winston.

Johnson, J. D. (1987). Development of the communication and physical environment scale. *Central States Speech Journal, 38,* 35–43.

Jorgenson, D. O. (1981). Perceived causal influence of weather: Rating the weather's influence on affective states and behaviors. *Environment and Behavior, 13,* 239–56.

Kasmar, J. V., Griffin, W. V., & Mauritzen, J. H. (1968). The effect of environmental surroundings on outpatients' mood and perception of psychiatrists. *Journal of Consulting and Clinical Psychology, 32,* 223–26.

Katz, A. M., & Hill, R. (1958). Residential propinquity and marital selection: A review of theory, method, and fact. *Marriage and Family Living, 20,* 327–35.

Kennedy, R. (1943). Premarital residential propinquity. *American Journal of Sociology, 48,* 580–84.

Kenrick, D. T., & Johnson, G. A. (1979). Interpersonal attraction in aversive environments: A problem for the classical conditioning paradigm? *Journal of Personality and Social Psychology, 37,* 572–79.

Koneya, M. (1973). *The relationship between verbal interaction and seat location of members of large groups.* Unpublished doctoral dissertation, Denver University.

Korda, M. (1975, January 13). Office power—You are where you sit. *New York Times,* pp. 36–44.

Kraut, R. E., & Johnston, R. E. (1979). Social and emotional messages of smiling: An ethological approach. *Journal of Personality and Social Psychology, 37,* 1539–53.

Krupat, E. (1985). *People in cities: The urban environment and its effects.* New York: Cambridge University Press.

Krupat, E., & Kubzansky, P. E. (1987). Designing to deter crime. *Psychology Today, 21,* 58–61.

Lawton, M. P., & Cohen, J. (1974). Environments and the well-being of elderly inner-city residents. *Environment and Behavior, 6,* 194–211.

Lee, D. (1957). *Climate and economic development in the tropics.* New York: Harper & Row.

Leonard, G. (1978). The rhythms of relationships. In G. Leonard (Ed.), *The silent pulse.* New York: Elsevier-Dutton.

Lester, D. (1988). Geographical variables and behavior: XLVIII. Climate and personal violence (suicide and homicide): A cross cultural study. *Perceptual and Motor Skills, 66,* 602.

Levine, D. W., O'Neal, E. C., Garwood, S. G., & McDonald, P. J. (1980). Classroom ecology: The effects of seating position on grades and participation. *Personality and Social Psychology Bulletin, 6,* 409–12.

Levine, R., & Wolff, E. (1985). Social time: The heartbeat of culture. *Psychology Today, 19,* 30.

Lewry, A. J., Sack, R. L., Miller, L. S., & Hoban, T. M. (1987). Anti-depressant and circadian phase shifting effects of light. *Science, 235,* 352–53.

Lieber, A. L. (1978). *The lunar effect: Biological tides and human emotions.* New York: Anchor/Doubleday.

Lipman, A. (1968). Building design and social interaction. *The Architect's Journal, 147,* 23–30.

Luce, G. G. (1971). *Biological rhythms in human and animal physiology.* New York: Dover.

Macey, Samuel L. (1991). *Time: A bibliographic guide.* New York and London: Garland.

Maines, David R. (1987). The significance of temporality for the development of sociological theory. *The Sociological Quarterly, 28/3,* 303–11 (special issue on temporality in sociological theory).

Maslow, A. H., & Mintz, N. L. (1956). Effects of esthetic surroundings: I. Initial effects of three esthetic conditions upon perceiving 'energy' and 'well-being' in faces. *Journal of Psychology, 41,* 247–54.

McClanahan, L. E., & Risly, T. R. (1975). Design of living environments for nursing home residents: Increasing participation in recreation activities. *Journal of Applied Behavior Analysis, 8,* 261–68.

McClelland, D. (1961). *The achieving society.* New York: Van Nostrand Reinhold.

McCroskey, J. C., & McVetta, W. R. (1978). Classroom seating arrangements: Instructional communication theory versus student preferences. *Communication Education, 27,* 99–110.

McGrath, J. E., & Kelly, J. R. (1986). *Time and human interaction.* New York: Guilford Press.

McLuhan, M. (1976). Inside on the outside or the spaced-out American. *Journal of Communication, 26,* 46–53.

Meer, J. (1985, September). The light touch. *Psychology Today, 19,* 60–67.

Mehrabian, A. (1976). *Public places and private spaces.* New York: Basic Books.

Mehrabian, A., & Diamond, S. G. (1971). The effects of furniture arrangement, props, and personality on social interaction. *Journal of Personality and Social Psychology, 20,* 18–30.

Mehrabian, A., & Russell, J. A. (1974). The basic emotional impact of environments. *Perceptual and Motor Skills, 38,* 283–301.

Mehrabian, A., & Russell, J. A. (1975). Environmental effects on affiliation among strangers. *Humanitas, 11,* 219–30.

Merton, R. (1948). The social psychology of housing. In W. Dennis (Ed.), *Current trends in social psychology.* Pittsburgh: University of Pittsburgh Press.

Michael, R. P., & Zumpe, D. (1983). Sexual violence in the United States and the role of season. *American Journal of Psychiatry, 140,* 883–86.

Michelson, W. (1971). Some like it hot: Social participation and environmental use as functions of the season. *American Journal of Sociology, 76,* 1072–83.

Mintz, N. L. (1956). Effects of esthetic surroundings: II. Prolonged and repeated experience in a 'beautiful' and 'ugly' room. *Journal of Psychology, 41,* 459–66.

Monk, R. (1994). *The employment of corporate non-verbal status communicators in western organisations.* Unpublished doctoral dissertation, The Fielding Institute, Santa Barbara, CA.

Moos, R. H. (1976). *The human context: Environmental determinants of behavior.* New York: John Wiley and Sons.

Moos, R. H., Harris, R., & Schonborn, K. (1969). Psychiatric patients and staff reaction to their physical environment. *Journal of Clinical Psychology, 25,* 322–24.

Moriarty, B. M. (1974). Socioeconomic status and residential location choice. *Environment and Behavior, 6,* 448–69.

Murray, D. C., & Deabler, H. L. (1957). Colors and mood-tones. *Journal of Applied Psychology, 41,* 279–83.

Myrick, R., & Marx, B. S. (1968). An exploratory study of the relationship between high school building design and student learning. U. S. Department of Health, Education and Welfare, Office of Education, Bureau of Research, Washington, DC.

National Advisory Commission on Civil Disorders (1968). Report from the U. S. Government Printing Office, Washington, DC.

Newman, O. (1973). *Defensible space.* New York: Macmillan.

Norman, R. D., & Scott, W. A. (1952). Color and affect: A review and semantic evaluation. *Journal of General Psychology, 46,* 185–223.

Osmond, H. (1957). Function as the basis of psychiatric ward design. *Mental Hospitals, 8,* 23–29.

Pellegrini, R. F., & Schauss, A. G. (1980). Muscle strength as a function of exposure to hue differences in visual stimuli: An experiential test of Kinesoid theory. *Journal of Orthomolecular Psychiatry, 2,* 144–47.

Proshansky, H. M., Ittelson, W. H., & Rivlin, L. G. (Eds.). (1970). *Environmental psychology: Man and his physical setting.* New York: Holt, Rinehart & Winston.

Rapoport, A. (1982). *The meaning of the built environment.* Beverly Hills, CA: Sage.

Reifman, A. S., Larrick, R. P., & Fein, S. (1991). Temper & temperature on the diamond: The heat-aggression relationship in major league baseball. *Personality and Social Psychology Bulletin, 17,* 580–85.

Rice, A. H. (1953). Color: What research knows about the classroom. *Nation's Schools, 52,* 1–8, 64.

Rieber, M. (1965). The effect of music on the activity level of children. *Psychonomic Science, 3,* 325–26.

Roethlisberger, F. J., & Dickson, W. J. (1939). *Management and the worker.* Cambridge, MA: Harvard University Press.

Rohles, F. H. (1967). Environmental psychology: A bucket of worms. *Psychology Today, 1,* 54–62.

Rohles, F. H., Jr. (1980). Temperature or temperament: A psychologist looks at thermal comfort. *ASHRAE Transactions, 86,* (I) 541–51.

Rosenfield, P., Lambert, N. M., & Black, A. (1985). Desk arrangement effects on pupil classroom behavior. *Journal of Educational Psychology, 77,* 101–8.

Rotton, J., & Kelly, I. W. (1985). Much ado about the full moon: A meta-analysis of lunar-lunacy research. *Psychological Bulletin, 97,* 286–306.

Rubin, Z. (1979). Seasonal rhythms in behavior. *Psychology Today, 12,* 12–16.

Ruesch, J., & Kees, W. (1956). *Nonverbal communication.* Berkeley and Los Angeles: University of California Press.

Russell, J. A., & Mehrabian, A. (1976). Environmental variables in consumer research. *Journal of Consumer Research, 3,* 62–63.

Sandalla, E. (1987). Identity symbolism in housing. *Environment and Behavior, 19,* 569–87.

Schlenker, B. R., Phillips, S. T., Boniecki, K. A., and Schlenker, D. R. (1995). Championship pressures: Choking or triumphing in one's own territory? *Journal of Personality and Social Psychology, 68,* 632–43.

Schneider, F. W., Lesko, W. A., & Garrett, W. A. (1980). Helping behavior in hot, comfortable, and cold-temperatures: A field study. *Environment and Behavior, 12,* 231–40.

Schutte, J. G., & Light, N. M. (1978). The relative importance of proximity and status for friendship choices in social hierarchies. *Social Psychology, 41,* 260–64.

Schwartz, B., & Barsky, S. (1977). The home advantage. *Social Forces, 55,* 641–61.

Schwebel, A. I., & Cherlin, D. L. (1972). Physical and social distancing in teacher-pupil relationships. *Journal of Educational Psychology, 63,* 543–50.

Smith, E., Bell, P. A., & Fusco, M. E. (1986). The influence of color and demand characteristics on muscle strength and affective ratings of the environment. *Journal of General Psychology, 113,* 289–97.

Smith, R. H., Downer, D. B., Lynch, M. T., & Winter, M. (1969). Privacy and interaction within the family as related to dwelling space. *Journal of Marriage and the Family, 31,* 559–66.

Solomon, P., Leiderman, P. H., Mendelsohn, J., & Wexler, D. (1957). Sensory deprivation: A review. *American Journal of Psychiatry, 114,* 357–63.

Sommer, R. (1967). Classroom ecology. *Journal of Applied Behavioral Science, 3,* 487–503.

Sommer, R. (1969). *Personal space.* Englewood Cliffs, NJ: Prentice-Hall.

Sommer, R. (1972). *Design awareness.* San Francisco: Rinehart Press.

Sommer, R. (1974). *Tight spaces: Hard architecture and how to humanize it.* Englewood Cliffs, NJ: Prentice-Hall.

Sommer, R., & Gilliland, G. W. (1961). Design for friendship. *Canadian Architect, 6,* 59–61.

Sommer, R., & Ross, H. (1958). Social interaction in a geriatric ward. *International Journal of Social Psychiatry, 4,* 128–33.

Stires, L. (1980). Classroom seating location, student grades, and attitudes: Environment or self selection? *Environment and Behavior, 12,* 241–54.

Stokois, D. (1981). Group × place transactions: Some neglected issues in psychological research on settings. In D. Magnusson (Ed.), *Toward a psychology of situations: An interactional perspective.* New York: Erlbaum.

Stouffer, S. A. (1940). Intervening opportunities: A theory relating mobility and distance. *American Sociological Review, 5,* 845–67.

Sundstrom, E. (1986). *Workplaces: The psychology of the physical environment in offices and factories.* New York: Cambridge University Press.

Tars, S., & Appleby, L. (1974). The same child in home and institution. *Environment and Behavior, 5,* 3.

Thirer, J., & Rampey, M. S. (1979). Effects of abusive spectators' behavior on performance of home and visiting intercollegiate basketball teams. *Perceptual and Motor Skills, 48,* 1047–53.

Todd-Mancillas, W. R. (1982). Classroom environments and nonverbal behavior. In L. L. Barker (Ed.), *Communication in the classroom.* Englewood Cliffs, NJ: Prentice-Hall.

Vinsel, A., Brown, B. B., Altman, I., & Foss, C. (1980). Privacy regulation, territorial displays, and effectiveness of individual functioning. *Journal of Personality and Social Psychology, 39,* 1104–15.

Weinstein, C. S. (1979). The physical environment of the school: A review of research. *Review of Educational Research, 49,* 577–610.

Weinstein, N. D. (1978). Individual differences in reactions to noise: A longitudinal study in a college dormitory. *Journal of Applied Psychology, 63,* 458–66.

Wells, B. W. P. (1965). The psycho-social influence of building environment: Sociometric findings in large and small office spaces. *Building Spaces, 1,* 153–65.

Werner, C. M., & Baxter, L. A. (1994). Temporal qualities of relationships: Organismic, transactional, and dialectical views. In M. L. Knapp & J. R. Miller (Eds.), *Handbook of interpersonal communication* (2d ed.). Thousand Oaks, CA: Sage.

Werner, C. M., Irwin, A., & Brown, B. B. (1992). A transactional approach to interpersonal relations: Physical environment, social context and temporal qualities. *Journal of Social and Personal Relationships, 9,* 297–323.

Wexner, L. B. (1954). The degree to which colors (hues) are associated with moodtones. *Journal of Applied Psychology, 38,* 432–35.

White, A. G. (1953). The patient sits down: A clinical note. *Psychosomatic Medicine, 15,* 256–57.

Whyte, W. (1949). The social structure of a restaurant. *American Journal of Sociology, 54,* 302–10.

Wilner, D., Walkley, R. P., & Cook, S. W. (1952). Residential proximity and intergroup relations in public housing projects. *Journal of Social Issues, 8,* 45–69.

Wollin, D. D., & Montagre, M. (1981). College classroom environment: Effects of sterility versus amiability on student and teacher performance. *Environment and Behavior, 13,* 707–16.

Wong, H., & Brown, W. (1923). Effects of surroundings upon mental work as measured by Yerkes' multiple choice method. *Journal of Comparative Psychology, 3,* 319–31.

Zerubavel, E. (1981). *Hidden rhythms: Schedules and calendars in social life.* Chicago: University of Chicago Press.

Zweigenhaft, R. (1976). Personal space in the faculty office: Desk placement and the student-faculty interaction. *Journal of Applied Psychology, 61,* 529–32.

CHAPTER 5

The Effects of Territory and Personal Space on Human Communication

Spatial changes give a tone to a communication, accent it, and at times even override the spoken word.

—E. T. HALL

"If you can read this, you're too close," announces a familiar automobile bumper sticker. It is an attempt to regulate the amount of space between vehicles for traffic safety. Signs reading "Keep Out" and "Authorized Personnel Only" are also attempts to regulate the amount of space among human beings. We do not put up signs in daily conversation, but we use other signals to avoid uncomfortable crowding and other perceived invasions of our personal space. Our use of space (our own and others') can affect dramatically our ability to achieve certain desired communication goals, whether they involve romance, diplomacy, or aggression. A fundamental concept in any discussion of human spatial behavior is the notion of territoriality. An understanding of this concept provides a useful perspective for our later examination of conversational space.

THE CONCEPT of TERRITORIALITY

The term *territoriality* has been used for years in the study of animal and bird behavior. Generally, it means behavior characterized by identification with a geographic area in a way that indicates ownership and defense of this territory against "invaders." Some territorial indicators around the home are particularly strong—Dad's chair, Mom's study, Billy's stereo, or Barbara's phone. There are many kinds of territorial behavior, and, frequently, they perform useful functions for a given species. For instance, territorial behaviors may help coordinate activities, regulate density, ensure propagation of the species, hold the group together, and provide hiding places and staging areas for courtship, nesting, or feeding.

Most behavioral scientists agree that territoriality exists in human behavior, too. It helps to regulate social interaction, but it also can be the source of social conflict. Like animals, the more powerful, dominant humans seem to have control over more territory—as long as the group or societal structure is stable.

Altman (1975) has identified three types of territories: primary, secondary, and public. *Primary territories* are clearly the exclusive domain of the owner. Central to the daily functioning of the owner, they are guarded carefully against uninvited intruders. Homes or bedrooms often qualify as primary territory. Goffman's (1971) description of possessional territories also seems to fit the requirements of primary territory. Possessional territories include personal effects such as jackets, purses, and even dependent children. In this same category, Goffman discusses objects that can be claimed temporarily by people, for example, a magazine, a television set, or eating utensils. These, however, seem to be more representative of what Altman calls *secondary territories,* which are not as central to the daily life of the owner, nor are they perceived as clearly exclusive to the owner. The neighborhood bar or the objects cited above are examples of secondary territories. More frequent conflicts are apt to develop over these territories because the public/private boundary is blurred—for example, "Let me watch my program on TV. You don't own it." *Public territories* are available to almost anyone for temporary ownership, for example, parks, beaches, streets, seats on public transportation, telephone booths, a place in line, or an unobstructed line of vision to see a particular object of interest. The words *temporary occupancy* are important. Most of us would not consider it a territorial violation if a cleaning person entered our office to clean without our permission. It would be a different story, however, if this person occupied the office all day or used it for noncleaning activities such as eating lunch.

While territorial behavior seems to be a standard part of our daily contact with others, it also is evident when sufficient social contact is denied. Altman and Haythorn (1967) analyzed the territorial behavior of socially isolated and nonisolated pairs of men. For ten days, two individuals lived in a small room with no outside contact, while a matched group received outside contacts.

The men in the isolated groups showed a gradual increase in territorial behavior and a general pattern of social withdrawal. They desired more time alone. Their territorial behavior first evidenced itself with fixed objects (areas of the room) and personal objects (beds). Later they began to claim more mobile and less personal objects. Incompatibility of the two men living together with respect to dominance and affiliation resulted in high territoriality.

TERRITORIALITY: INVASION and DEFENSE

Instructions to police interrogators sometimes suggest sitting close to the suspect without the intervention of a desk that might provide protection or comfort. This theory of interrogation assumes that invasion of the suspect's personal territory (with no chance for defense) will give the officer a psychological advantage. We noted in Chapter 4 that a desk or similar office barrier can inhibit friendly interaction and perceptions of closeness. On a larger scale, adolescent gangs and ethnic groups stake out territory in urban areas and defend it against intruders. Preserving national boundaries often underlies international disputes. What happens when somebody invades your territory? For instance, how do you feel when the car behind you is tailgating? When you have to stand in a crowded theater lobby or bus? When somebody sits in "your" seat? What do you do? Researchers have asked similar questions, and their answers help us understand further how we use the space around us.

Obviously, not all territorial encroachments are the same. Lyman and Scott (1967) identify three types:

1. *Violation* involves the unwarranted use of another's territory. This may be done with the eyes (staring at somebody eating in a public restaurant); with the voice or other sounds (construction noise next to a classroom); or with the body (taking up two subway seats).
2. *Invasion* is more all-encompassing and permanent. It is an attempt to take over another's territory. This may be an armed invasion of another country or the act of a wife who has turned her husband's den into a computer room.
3. *Contamination* is defiling another's territory, not by our presence but by what we leave behind. When we take temporary occupancy of a hotel room, for instance, we do not want to find the previous "owner's" toilet articles and soiled sheets. Similarly, we are frequently upset by someone else's dog leaving feces in our yard or by food particles on "our" silverware in restaurants.

Encroachments on our territory do not always produce defensive maneuvers. The intensity of our reaction to territorial encroachment will vary depending on a number of factors including:

1. Who violated our territory? We may have very different reactions to friends as opposed to strangers; males as opposed to females; high-status individuals as opposed to low-status ones; objects as opposed to people; and peers as opposed to people of very different ages.
2. Why did they violate our territory? If we feel that the violator "knew better," we might react more strongly than if we felt he or she "couldn't help it" or was naive.
3. What type of territory was it? We may perceive a violation of our primary territory as far more serious than a violation of a public territory.
4. How was the violation accomplished? If our body was touched, we may be more aroused than if someone walked across our grass.
5. How long did the encroachment last? If the violation is perceived as temporary, reactions may be less severe.
6. Do we expect further violations in the future? If so, the initial territorial defense may be more intense.
7. Where did the violation occur? The population density and opportunities for negotiating new territorial boundaries will surely affect our reaction.

Later in this chapter, we discuss high-density situations and the way people react.

The two primary methods for territorial defense are *prevention* and *reaction*. Prevention is a means of staking out our territory so that others recognize it as ours and go elsewhere. A person's mere presence in a place can keep others from entering it. If we stay in a place long enough or often enough, others think we "own" it, for example, a seat in a classroom. (See Figure 5-1.) Sometimes we ask others to assist us in staking out and defending territory—for example, "Would you hold my seat while I go get some popcorn?" Neighbors' help will vary, of course, depending on how urgently their aid is requested, for how long, how important the territory appears, and so on. Objects are also used as territorial *markers* to designate "your" spatial area. In places with relatively low density, markers such as umbrellas, coats, notebooks, and so on are often effective; indeed, sometimes these markers will reserve not only a seat in a public area but also an entire table. Markers that appear more personal probably are more effective in preventing violations. If the marked territory is highly desirable to many others in the immediate area, markers probably will maintain their effectiveness for shorter periods of time. In public territories, it may be more effective to leave several markers, as these areas are open to nearly everyone. Sometimes uniforms help identify the territory that can be legitimately used by a particular person. Often we construct fences and grow hedges to demarcate territory. And sometimes we stake out territory simply by the way we conduct our verbal interaction; for example, special jargon or dialects can warn others that a particular space is reserved for those who "know the language."

Figure 5–1

Marking public territory. (Photo © 1991 Psychotex/Kevin E. White, P. O. Box 470701, Fort Worth, Texas 76147.)

If the prevention of territorial violations does not work, how do people react? When people come close to us in face-to-face encounters, we are physiologically aroused; heart rate and galvanic skin responses increase (Finando, 1973; McBride, King, & James, 1965). Arousal varies with eye gaze and touch as well as distance. Once aroused, we need to label our state as "positive" (liking, love, relief) or "negative" (dislike, embarrassment, stress, anxiety). If the aroused state is labeled positively, Patterson (1976) predicts, we will reciprocate the behavior; if it is labeled negatively, we will take measures to compensate. If someone is aroused by another person's approach and identifies it as undesirable, we would predict behavior designed to restore the "proper" distance between the interactants: looking away, changing the topic to a less personal one, crossing one's arms to form a frontal barrier to the invasion, covering body parts, rubbing one's neck (making the elbow protrude sharply toward the invader), and so on.

Russo conducted a two-year study of invading the territory of female college students seated in a college library (Sommer, 1969, pp. 35, 46–48, 64). The study compared the responses of those invaded and a similar group that was not invaded. Several different invasion techniques were used—sitting next to subjects, across from them, and so on. The quickest departure or flight was triggered when the researcher sat next to a subject and moved her chair closer (approximately one foot). Other researchers have suggested that when strangers are involved, males feel more stress from frontal invasions, while women react more unfavorably to adjacent invasions (Fisher & Byrne, 1975; Hall, 1984). After approximately thirty minutes, about 70 percent of the people Russo approached at the one-foot distance moved. From Russo's study, a whole vocabulary of defense was developed. For instance, defensive and offensive displays included the use of position, posture, and gesture. *Position* refers to location in the room; a newcomer to the room will interpret the situation differently if the other person has selected a corner position rather than one in the middle of the room. *Posture* refers to such indicators as whether a person has materials spread out "like he or she owned the place" or whether they are tightly organized. *Gestures* can be used to indicate receptivity or rejection of communication, for example, hostile glances, turning or leaning away, blocking with hands or arms, and so on. Finally, although under some circumstances verbal defense is less likely to occur, verbal defenses such as profanity (or generally obnoxious behavior) can be effectively used. Russo's work is summarized by Sommer (1969):

> There were wide individual differences in the ways victims reacted—there is no single reaction to someone's sitting too close; there are defensive gestures, shifts in posture, and attempts to move away. If these fail or are ignored by the invader, or he shifts position too, the victim eventually takes to flight. . . . There was a dearth of direct verbal responses to the invasions. . . . Only one of the eighty students asked the invader to move over. (pp. 35–36)

It is interesting that the norm of politeness is too strong to permit such direct verbal response. This demonstrates one important feature of nonverbal communication: It is "off the record" and can convey messages subtly, without provoking confrontation. The person who glares, shuffles papers, or leans away does not have to acknowledge publicly his or her irritation. Verbal statements are on the public record much more than nonverbal gestures, and this is ironic because the nonverbal messages are often much richer in emotional meaning. Barash (1973) conducted a study similar to Russo's, but the library invaders' status was manipulated. Students fled more quickly from the more formally dressed, "high-status" invaders. Knowles (1973) also experimented with a familiar type of invasion—talking to somebody in a hallway while other people decide whether to walk through the conversants or around them. Only 25 percent of the people in this study walked through, but when the conversants were replaced with barrels, 75 percent of the passersby walked through. The fewest intrusions occurred with four-person groups (rather than a dyad) and "high-status" conversants (older and more formally dressed). This study illustrates that, besides not wanting others to violate our territory, we generally do not want to violate their territory either—as the mumbled apologies and bowed heads of some of Knowles's invaders testified.

Increasing the density of a species also will result in territorial violations. What happens when the population becomes so dense that one cannot exercise usual territorial behavior? The possibility of human overpopulation makes this a particularly important concern.

DENSITY and CROWDING

To begin, let us examine some examples of animal behavior under conditions of high density or overpopulation. For years, scientists were intrigued by the large-scale suicides of lemmings, rabbits, and rats. Their interest was increased by the fact that at the time of the suicides, there was plenty of food, predators were not in evidence, and infection was not present. An ethologist with training in medical pathology hypothesized that such suicides were triggered by an endocrine reaction that resulted from stress built up during an increase of population (Christian & Davis, 1964). This hypothesis was confirmed in a study of the deer population on James Island, one mile off the coast of Maryland in the Chesapeake Bay. Careful histological studies over a period of years showed that the deer on James Island died from overactive adrenal glands resulting from stress. The adrenal glands play an important part in the regulation of growth, reproduction, and the level of the body's defenses. Thus, overpopulation caused death not by starvation, infection, or aggression from others but by a physiological reaction to the stress created.

Calhoun's (1962) experiments go even further to suggest peculiar modes of behavior under conditions of overpopulation. Calhoun noted that with plenty of food and no danger from predators, Norway rats in a quarter-acre outdoor pen stabilized their population at about 150. His observations, covering twenty-eight months, indicated that spatial relationships were extremely important. He then designed an experiment in which he could maintain a stressful situation through overpopulation while three generations of rats were reared. He labeled this experiment a *behavioral sink,* an area or receptacle where most of the rats exhibited gross distortions of behavior. Some of Calhoun's observations are worth noting:

1. Some rats withdrew from social and sexual intercourse completely; others began to mount anything in sight; courtship patterns were totally disrupted, and females were frequently pursued by several males.
2. Nest-building patterns, ordinarily neat, became sloppy or nonexistent.
3. Litters of young rats became mixed; newborn and young rats were stepped on or eaten by invading hyperactive males.
4. Unable to establish spatial territories, dominant males fought over positions near the eating bins; classes of rats shared territories and exhibited similar behaviors; the hyperactive males violated all territorial rights by running around in packs and disregarding any boundaries except those backed by force.
5. Pregnant rats frequently had miscarriages; disorders of the sex organs were numerous; only a fourth of the 558 newborns in the sink survived to be weaned.
6. Aggressive behavior increased significantly.

Can we generalize from rats to people? Some early studies that found moderate correlations between various socially undesirable outcomes, such as crime, delinquency, and mental and physical disorders, and high population seemed to say yes. Others facetiously contend that the only generalization we can make from Calhoun's work is "Don't crowd a rat!" In light of additional studies using rats and other animals, even this injunction may need qualification. It seems that nonhuman animals do not always respond to high density in negative or aggressive ways (Freedman, 1979; Weiss, 1994). In one study, the number of aggressive acts performed by monkeys living in environments of differing densities (from cages to free-ranging activity on an island) were compared (Weiss, 1994). Aggression was not significantly more prevalent in high-density environments, but coping behavior was. As density increased, the following types of coping behavior also increased: mutual grooming, rapid reconciliation after a fight, and the use of specific facial expressions to indicate the desire to avoid trouble. This tendency to develop ways to cope with high-density life in ways other than aggression is much like the human adaptations reported in the next two sections. Behavioral sinks are not a natural result of unchecked population growth, and physiological changes may be as much a result of the number of animals present as the amount of space available. In other words, the widely publicized results of Calhoun's work, which suggested unequivocally harmful consequences of increasing density, are incorrect. Based on the human density and crowding research conducted thus far, the results are also complex and do not lend themselves to a simple "crowding is good or bad" answer.

To understand the effects of population density on human beings, it is first necessary to distinguish between the terms *density* and *crowding*. *Density* refers to the number of people per unit of space; *crowding* is a feeling state that may develop in high- or low-density situations. What factors determine whether we are likely to feel crowded? Perceptions of being crowded may be influenced by the following:

1. *Environmental factors,* such as reduced space, unwanted noise, the lack of needed resources or the ability to obtain them, and the absence of territorial markers such as screens and partitions
2. *Personal factors,* such as gender (males tend to feel the effects of density more acutely than females); personality characteristics reflecting low self-esteem, dominance, control, and desire for social contact; and prior unpleasant experiences with high density
3. *Social factors,* such as a high frequency of unwanted social contact from many people at close quarters (and the inability to change such patterns), interactions with people from a different group membership, and unpleasant interactions (hostile or competitive)
4. *Goal-related factors,* such as the inability to accomplish what is desired

The central theme characterizing most of the research in this area is that perceptions of crowding tend to increase as we perceive a decrease in our ability to control and influence our physical and social surroundings. While the factors in the preceding list may contribute to perceptions of crowding, most high-density situations are characterized by some factors that decrease control and some that do not. Given these conditions, what can we say about the effects of high density and human reactions to it?

THE EFFECTS OF HIGH DENSITY

Definitions of density are complex and varied. Correlational studies have used number of people per city, per census tract, per dwelling unit; number of rooms per dwelling unit; number of buildings per neighborhood; and so on. Experimental studies sometimes put the same-sized group into different-sized rooms; others vary the number of people in the same room. Laboratory studies that vary density in order to analyze its effects on perceptions of crowding may have relevance only to those situations where high density is a temporary condition, for example, elevators, buses, and so forth. Few studies have considered the rate at which high density evolves or whether participants feel they had any control over the development of a high-density situation. In order to sort through these variations in measurement, the following conclusions seem warranted.

First, it seems clear that increased density does not automatically increase stress or antisocial behavior for human beings. Sometimes we even seek the pleasures of density. Football games and rock concerts are familiar examples. If we take responsibility for our presence in a highly populated situation, and if we know the condition will terminate in a matter of hours, the chances of negative effects seem to be minimal. Although some studies have found results that might fit well into a "behavioral sink" theory (for example, aggression, stress, criminal activity, hostility toward others, and a deterioration of mental and physical health), in most every case, we find other studies that do not confirm these effects. Usually, the difference lies in the fact that one of the factors mentioned earlier (environmental, personal, social, goal-oriented) provided a form of control that was influential in offsetting undesirable influences. For example, Altman (1975, pp. 157, 165, 182) cites a study by Rohe and Patterson (1974), which found that if children were provided with enough of the toys they wanted, increased density would not produce the withdrawal and aggression suggested by previous studies. Some high-density neighborhoods that are highly cohesive actually have a lower incidence of mental and physical health problems.

Second, we sometimes blame high density for undesirable effects either because it is an obvious feature of the situation and has a reputation for causing problems or because the real causes are things we do not wish to face. Students who took a long time to complete their college registration tended to perceive the large number of students trying to register as the cause for their delays. They did not attribute their delays to forgetting needed forms, filling out forms incorrectly, and not preparing alternative course selections prior to registration (Gochman & Keating, 1980). High density *can* produce a host of problems, but human beings do not stand by passively in situations that demand a long-term commitment to high density. Instead, they try various methods to cope with or offset potentially harmful effects. What are some of the methods of coping?

COPING WITH HIGH DENSITY

Milgram (1970) felt city dwellers are exposed to an overload of information, people, things, problems, and so forth. As a result, city dwellers engage in behavior designed to reduce this overload, which sometimes causes outsiders to see them as distant and emotionally detached from others. Some of these methods for coping in populated cities include:

1. Spending less time with each input, for example, having shorter conversations with people
2. Disregarding low-priority inputs, for example, ignoring the drunk on the sidewalk or not talking to people seen on a commuter train every day
3. Shifting the responsibility for some transactions to others, for example, relieving bus drivers of the responsibility for making change
4. Blocking inputs, for example, using attendants to guard apartment buildings

How do people in densely populated areas in other cultures cope? A summary of these studies can be found in Aiello and Thompson (1980) and Altman and Chemers (1988). Coping strategies include such things as clearly specified interaction rules for high/low-status interactants, men and women, children and adults, and so forth; taking pride in the perfection of smaller things; and constructing homes with movable partitions.

Munroe and Munroe (1972) studied three East African societies that varied in population density from 250 to 1,400 persons per square mile. The higher-density groups seemed to develop practices that involved avoidance of close contact with others, a devaluation of others, and less desire for affiliative activities. Like Milgrim's residents in urban areas, these people were developing ways of controlling the unwanted inputs resulting from high density. The !Kung of Namibia (formerly South-West Africa) also have been of interest to those studying reactions to high density (Draper, 1973). Here is a society with one of the lowest population densities in the world (about 1 person per 10 square miles) that deliberately builds camps creating very close living conditions: The design of their huts produces a situation that approximates 30 people living in one room! There is close contact and extensive social interaction, but there seem to be no adverse effects. Several other facts may explain the coping methods of the !Kung. First, individuals or families are permitted to leave one camp and join another, typically 15 or more miles away. Thus, each person feels he or she can "escape" if the situation warrants it—and, perhaps more important, can escape to a friendly place, a camp with the same lifestyles and values. A new environment can be found, but it is not staffed with inhospitable strangers. The fact that camps are widely separated also may be beneficial.

Now let us shift our attention from spatial relationships in overpopulated conditions to those involved in a two-person conversation.

CONVERSATIONAL DISTANCE

As children, we are exposed to gradually increasing distances for various communication situations. The first few years of life provide a familiarity with what is known as *intimate distance;* the child then learns appropriate conversational distances for an increasing number of acquaintances obtained from family, neighborhood, and school; and by about age seven the child may have incorporated the concept of *public distance* into his or her behavioral repertoire. So, by the time children reach about the third grade, their behavior has stabilized and tends to more closely reflect adult norms. (See Figure 5-2.) What are these adult norms? What are comfortable conversational distances?

To answer these questions, we need to first acknowledge the astute observations of human spatial behavior made by anthropologist Edward T. Hall as published in his books *The Silent Language* (1954) and *The Hidden Dimension* (1966). Hall identified several types of space, but our concern here is with what he called "informal space." Others have referred to this as "personal space," but since the space between people is the result of negotiating their personal preferences, it is more appropriately labeled *interpersonal space.* The informal space for each individual expands and contracts under varying circumstances, depending on the type of encounter, the relationship of the communicating persons, their personalities, and many other factors. Hall further classified informal space into four subcategories: intimate, casual-personal, social-consultative, and public. According to Hall, *intimate* distances range from actual physical contact to about eighteen inches; *casual-personal* extends from one and one-half feet to four feet; *social-consultative* (for impersonal business) ranges from four to twelve feet; *public* distance covers the area from twelve feet to the limits of visibility or hearing. Hall was quick to note that these distances are based on his observations of a particular sample of adults from business and professional occupations, primarily white, middle-class males native to the northeastern United States, and that any generalization to other ethnic and racial groups in this country should be made with considerable caution.

Robert Sommer (1961) also sought answers to questions about comfortable conversational distance. He studied people who were brought into a room and told to discuss various impersonal topics. Two sofas were placed in this room at various distances, and subjects were observed to see whether they sat opposite or beside one another. It was hypothesized that when they began to sit side by side, it would mean the conversational distance was too far to

Figure 5–2

a

b

Variations in conversational distance and position. (Photos © Lawrence B. Rosenfeld)

sit opposite one another on the two couches. From one to three feet, the subjects sat on different couches facing one another. After three and one-half feet, people sat side by side. If one measures distance "nose to nose," this would make the participants five and one-half feet apart when they started to sit side by side. In a follow-up study, Sommer used chairs and, hence, was able to vary side-by-side distance as well as distance across. Here he found that people chose to sit across from one another until the distance across exceeded the side-by-side distance; they then sat side by side.

How generalizable are these findings? A critical look at this study immediately leads us to question what other variables may affect the distance relationship. For instance, this study was conducted with people who knew each other slightly, were discussing impersonal topics, and were in a large lounge. How would other factors affect the distance relationship? Argyle and Dean (1965) have theorized that distance is based on the balance of approach and avoidance forces. What are some of these forces? Burgoon and Jones (1976) say that the expected distance in a given conversation is a function of the social norms combined with idiosyncratic patterns of the interactants. What are some of these norms and idiosyncratic patterns? What factors modify the distances we choose?

Answering these questions is the focus of the remainder of this chapter. Again, however, we must sort through conflicting results due to variations in research methodology and conceptualization of personal space. Logically, we know that conversational distance is the product of both interactants' negotiations. But some research is based on the behavior of a single person; some research does not distinguish between actual physical distance and perceptions of distance; some research measures distance by floor tiles or space between chair legs and totally ignores the ability of the communicators to vary the "psychological distance" by changes in topic, eye gaze, and body lean; and most research does not distinguish between initial distance and changes that take place over the course of a conversation. Since the methods of measuring personal space vary, we even have to be cautious about results that agree with other studies. Sometimes people complete questionnaires about preferred distances; sometimes they are asked to approach nonhuman objects, for example, coat racks and life-sized photographs; sometimes people are unknowingly approached at various distances by others; and sometimes they are asked to arrange miniature dolls, photographs, or silhouettes as if they were in various communication situations. With these factors in mind, the following nine sources of variation in conversational distance are presented:

1. Sex
2. Age
3. Cultural and ethnic background
4. Topic or subject matter
5. Setting for the interaction
6. Physical characteristics

7. Attitudinal and emotional orientation
8. Characteristics of the interpersonal relationship
9. Personality characteristics

SEX

Many studies have looked at sex differences in interpersonal space, using all the methodologies listed earlier. Judith Hall (1984) has summarized this research. In naturalistic interaction—that is, settings where people are interacting more or less naturally and are not aware of being observed—females predominantly choose to interact with others (of either sex) more closely than males do. This tendency is apparent among toddlers and older children, as well as among adults, although the toddler data may have limited generality since the other person in the interaction was usually the child's mother. One study of young children showed an interesting exception. DiPietro (1981) put children together in same-sex groups of three and found a strong tendency for girls to keep the greater distances. However, such a situation probably invites the kind of rough-and-tumble play that young boys are known for, which would naturally involve high levels of proximity and contact.

Not all ways of measuring distance preferences find such compelling evidence for females' closer distances. For example, in some studies, subjects are asked outright by the experimenter to stand at a comfortable distance from a confederate; in others, they manipulate or position stick figures or cutouts of people. Research using these nonnaturalistic methods finds very weak evidence that females prefer closer distances. Why should this be? Hall (1984) suggests that the answer may be in the emotional tone of the encounters being studied. In naturalistic studies, the encounters are almost always friendly, or at least neutral, in emotional tone. In the more artificial studies, the experimeter often varies who the other person is—for example, a threatening or angry other as opposed to a liked or friendly other. When this is done, the sex differences tend to diverge, with females now establishing smaller distances than males with the friendly others (which is consistent with the naturalistic studies) but *larger* distances with the alienating others. This divergence could make the overall sex difference for these kinds of studies disappear. Thus, it appears, females prefer closer distances as long as they are neutral or friendly interactions.

Another way of understanding sex differences in interpersonal distance is to examine how the *other person's sex* influences the distance one sets. (The preceding discussion applies only to the influence of one's own sex on that distance.) The research shows very convincingly that people approach females closer than they approach males, and that this remains true no matter what kind of methodology is used. When the effects for one's own sex and those for the other's sex are combined, they yield a pattern of interaction such that female-female pairs interact most closely and male-male pairs interact most distantly, with mixed-sex pairs setting intermediate distances. This pattern shows up frequently in the research, especially in Anglo-American samples.

Based on this evidence, predictions can be made on what will happen when someone (male or female) invades personal space by sitting or standing very close: People depart more hastily from a male invader. Is this because men connote threat, especially when they are positioned very close, or because people are simply upset when others do not behave as they are "supposed to"? That is, people *expect* men to keep larger distances, and when they do not, it may be disturbing.

This raises a more general question: How can we explain the sex differences in preferred distances? Some believe we need to look at the early childhood experiences of boys and girls. It has been noted, for example, that the same stimuli may cause parents to put male infants on the floor or in a playpen but to hug the females or put them in a nearby high chair. Boys are frequently given toys that seem to encourage activities demanding more space, often away from the confines of the home itself—for example, footballs, cars, trains, and so forth. Girls, on the other hand, may receive dolls, doll houses, and other domestic toys that require less space and encourage activity directed toward the home environment (Rheingold & Cook, 1975). Observations of children at play tend to confirm the notion that many males learn the need for and use of greater territory at early ages. Boys spent more time outside, entered more areas than the girls, and maintained between 1.2 and 1.6 times the amount of space females did (Harper & Sanders, 1975).

Other authors argue that we needn't rely on early childhood experiences to explain sex differences in conversational distancing. Instead, they see the smaller distances set by, and toward, women as a reflection of women's lower status in this society. As Henley (1977) puts it, women do not command respect, and this is reflected in people's tendency to violate their personal space. Whether this interpretation is correct cannot be ascertained, since it is notoriously hard to test explanations of sex differences. One issue involves the validation of closer distances in general as an "invasion"; just being closer does not necessarily mean one is invading or being invaded, since "invasion" implies psychological discomfort. Also, some published findings do not support the "low-status" interpretation for the sex differences. For example, irrespective of sex, people tend to approach equal-status others the closest, not lower-status others (Gifford, 1982; Latta, 1978). And two studies that specifically connote invasion (they noted who displaced whom from a narrow sidewalk when people had to pass each other) found that women were displaced *less* often than men, not more, as one would predict if women were of lower status and likely to be spatially invaded (Sobel & Lillith, 1975; Willis, Gier, & Smith, 1979).

Alternative explanations for the prevailing sex differences regarding personal space often focus on different personalities and social orientations of males versus females. For example, if women are more socially oriented and are more comfortable and affiliative in interaction, they should prefer closer distances, which usually connote warmth, trust, and friendship (as is discussed later). One promising perspective is provided by social role theory, which says that sex differences in social behavior are determined by the present or future roles that people play in society (Eagly, 1987). Women, traditionally, play more person-oriented and prosocial roles, and therefore their repertoire of social behaviors (including nonverbal communication) can be expected to reflect that orientation.

AGE

If distance reflects our general comfort with a person, it seems reasonable to predict that we would interact closer to people in our own general age range. The exceptions, of course, are the very old and very young who, for various reasons, often elicit interaction at closer quarters. Generally, interaction distance seems to expand gradually from about age six to early adolescence, when adult norms seem to be reflected (Aiello & Aiello, 1974). Adults are more likely to hold older children responsible for an understanding of adult norms, too. When five-year-olds invaded the personal space of people waiting in line to see a movie, they were received positively, but when ten-year-olds were the invaders they were met with negative responses (Fry & Willis, 1971). Obviously, these reactions will be modified by the communicative context, but these studies do suggest that adults expect the norms for conversational distance to be learned before the child is ten. Children are able to decode proxemic meanings before they encode them in their daily interactions, as is true of many behaviors.

In terms of interpersonal distance, an interesting parallel between young people and older people is that between shorter people and taller people. Irrespective of one's sex, shorter individuals seem to invite smaller interpersonal distances than do taller individuals (Caplan & Goldman, 1981; Hartnett, Bailey, & Hartley, 1974).

CULTURAL AND ETHNIC BACKGROUND

Volumes of folklore and isolated personal observations suggest that spatial relationships in other cultures with different needs and norms may produce very different distances for interacting.

Infants reared in different cultures learn different proxemic patterns. Japanese mothers tend to spend more time than a comparable group of mothers in the United States in close contact with their infants. Mother, father, and infant in Japan usually sleep in the same room. In the Nyansongo culture of Kenya, infants are always in close proximity to a family member, and the infant sleeps in the mother's arms at night (Caudill & Weinstein,

1972). It is not hard to see how such patterns provide a different sense of distance when compared to those of children who are put into a separate room to sleep several times during the day as well as at night.

Watson (1970) reported numerous observations on individuals representing "contact" and "noncontact" cultures. *Contact* refers to interactants who face one another more directly, interact closer to one another, touch one another more, look one another in the eye more, and speak in a louder voice. Contact groups in Watson's study were Arabs, Latin Americans, and southern Europeans. Noncontact groups were Asians, Indians and Pakistanis, northern Europeans, and Americans (U. S. citizens). Watson and Graves (1966) found substantial and consistent differences between pairs of Arab students and pairs of American students in conversational settings. These differences included such things as:

1. Arabs confronted one another more directly.
2. Arabs moved closer together.
3. Arabs used more touch behavior.
4. Arabs were likely to look each other squarely in the eye, an event that occurred less frequently with American pairs.

A number of studies comparing interactants from contact and noncontact cultures confirm predicted differences. However, some do not (Remland, Jones, & Brinkman, 1991). The effects of the relationship between the interactants, the topic they are discussing, the emotions involved, and other factors may offset broad cultural distance norms.

Shuter's (1976, 1977) systematic field observations suggest we may be too imprecise when we talk about broad cultural groups being contact or noncontact. He found, for instance, that there were significant differences within the so-called Latin American cultural group. Costa Ricans interacted more closely than did Panamanians or Colombians. And, contrary to predictions, he found no significant differences in interaction distance and touching for women in Milwaukee, Wisconsin and Venice, Italy. Italian men did not manifest closer interaction positions or face their interaction partners more directly than did German men, but they did engage in more touching. This seems to suggest that within the general tendencies of a culture, we can expect to find subcultural differences.

Variations in proxemic patterns in the United States have been the subject of several research projects. Because of Edward Hall's comment that "Negroes have a much higher involvement ratio," the question of whether blacks interact at closer distances than whites has been studied. Developmental studies show that when entering elementary school, black children may indeed exhibit closer interaction distances than white children, but by the fifth grade these differences are minimized, and by age sixteen black Americans tend to maintain greater conversational distances (Aiello & Thompson, 1980; Halberstadt, 1985). Most studies reveal that interactions involving black and white communicators occur at greater distances than those involving persons of the same race. Another large subcultural group in the United States, Hispanic-Americans, has also been observed. These studies generally support the prediction that Hispanic-Americans interact at closer distances than do Anglo-Americans.

Scherer (1974) contended that any differences between blacks and whites (and presumably Hispanic-Americans) may be confounded by socioeconomic factors not attributable to ethnic background. This study found middle-class children maintained greater conversational distance than lower-class children, but there were no differences between middle-class blacks and whites nor lower-class blacks and whites. Finally, an intriguing aside offered by Connolly (1975) begs for further research. He said he observed black interactants moving around and altering the proxemic distances during the conversation more than white interactants. This observation may be of particular interest in light of Erickson's observation, reported next.

TOPIC OR SUBJECT MATTER

Erickson (1975) wanted to find out if proxemic shifts (forward or backward) were associated with any other events in a conversation. By coding co-occurring behavior, he determined that proxemic shifts may mark important segments of the encounter (for example, beginnings, endings, and topic changes).

Earlier we noted that Sommer, in his efforts to examine the limits of conversational distance, tried to use impersonal topics that would not obviously influence the distances chosen. Personal topics, for intimates, may demand less conversational distance unless other factors, such as an impersonal setting, neutralize such inclinations.

Leipold's (1963) work demonstrates how anticipated treatment of the same general topic can influence conversational distance. Students entered a room and were given either a negative comment ("Your grade is poor, and you have not done your best"), praise ("You are doing very well, and Mr. Leipold wants to talk to you further"), or a neutral comment ("Mr. Leipold is interested in your feelings about the introductory course"). Students given the negative comment sat furthest from the experimenter, while those who were praised sat closest. Following insults, people may want to assume a greater distance than they normally would with that person, particularly if the person giving the insult was perceived as a higher-status person (O'Neal et al., 1980). Regardless of topic, close distances may result in less talking generally (Schulz & Barefoot, 1974).

SETTING FOR THE INTERACTION

Obviously, the social setting makes a great deal of difference in how far we stand from others in conversation. A crowded cocktail party demands a different distance than a comfortable evening in the living room with one's spouse. Lighting, temperature, noise, and available space will affect interaction distance. Some authors have hypothesized that as room size increases, people tend to sit closer together. If the setting is perceived as a formal and/or unfamiliar one, we would predict greater distances from unknown others and closer distances to known others. Little (1965) had people arrange actresses in certain settings to determine the interpersonal distances perceived as necessary in various situations. Each student was a director and was to place the interactants in a street-corner setting, an office waiting room, the lobby of a public building, and a campus location. The maximum placement distance was in the office, while the closest placement was in the street scene.

Physical Characteristics

As we mentioned when we described age differences, a person's height may call for changes in interaction distance, perhaps to avoid overpowering or being overpowered or simply to achieve a better angle of gaze. There is also evidence that obese people are accorded greater interaction distances (Lerner, Venning, & Knapp, 1975). A series of studies conducted by Kleck (1969; Kleck & Strenta, 1985) shows that persons interacting with stigmatized individuals (a left-leg amputation was simulated with a special wheelchair) choose greater initial speaking distances than with nonstigmatized, or "normal," persons, but that this distance decreases as the length of the interaction increases. Similar results have been found for perceived epileptics and people with facial disfigurations (scars and port-wine stains). Kleck points out that when people with physical disabilities expect others to behave in a distant manner, they may prepare themselves for such reactions and thereby increase the chances that it will happen.

Attitudinal and Emotional Orientation

Kleck's work also included situations in which the subject was told the other person was either "warm and friendly" or "unfriendly." Not surprisingly, the subjects chose greater distances when interacting with a person perceived to be unfriendly. Similarly, when told to enter into conversation with another person and to behave in a friendly way, subjects chose closer distances than when told to "let him know you aren't friendly." This friendly/unfriendly relationship to distance seems to manifest itself even with preschool children (King, 1966). The number of unfriendly acts was directly related to the distance maintained by the recipient of such acts during free-play situations. The distance could be reduced, however, by putting a prized toy near the aggressive child. In some instances, our anger will cause us to withdraw from others, but if we seek retaliation, we may of course reduce our distance (Meisels & Dosey, 1971). Changes in our emotional state can sometimes make vast differences in how close or far away we want to be from others, for example, states of depression or fatigue versus states of extreme excitement or joy.

A study reported by Patterson (1968) reveals we may make a whole host of interpersonal judgments about another person based on distance. Subjects were told to interview others and secretly rate them on traits of friendliness, aggressiveness, dominance, extraversion, and intelligence. The interviewees were actually confederates who approached the interviewers at different distances and gave standard answers to the questions asked. The mean ratings for all the traits at four different distances were tabulated and revealed that the most distant position yielded significantly lower (less favorable) ratings. So, barring any contradictory information, people choosing closer distances are often seen as warmer, liking one another more, more empathic, and more understanding.

When we seek to win another's approval, we will reduce conversational distance as opposed to instances when we are deliberately trying to avoid approval. Rosenfeld's (1965, 1966) female subjects seeking approval maintained a mean distance of fifty-seven inches; those trying to avoid approval averaged ninety-four inches. When the distance was held constant at five feet, approval seekers compensated by smiling more and engaging in gestural activity. Mehrabian (1969) concluded his review of attitude/distance research by saying:

> . . . the findings from a large number of studies corroborate one another and indicate that communicator-addressee distance is correlated with the degree of negative attitude communicated to and inferred by the addressee. In addition, studies carried out by sociologists and anthropologists indicate that distances which are too close, that is, inappropriate for a given interpersonal situation, can elicit negative attitudes when the communicator-addressee relationship is not an intimate one. (p. 363)

Characteristics of the Interpersonal Relationship

Willis (1966) also found that strangers seemed to begin conversations further away than did acquaintances; women stood closer to close friends than did men but further away from "just friends" (the author suggests this may be due to a more cautious approach used in making friends); and parents were found to be as distant from each other as strangers! The range of distances measured in Willis's study was from 17.75 inches (close friends speaking to women) to 28 inches (white to black). Little (1968), in a cross-cultural study, also found friends were perceived as interacting closer together than acquaintances and acquaintances closer than strangers were. In a study of 108 married couples, husbands were asked to walk toward their wives and stop when they got to a comfortable conversation distance. The more dissatisfied the husbands were with their marriage, the greater the distance they chose (Crane et al., 1987). Preschoolers seem to be able to use distance as a criterion for determining liking and disliking. Like adults, children seem to maintain greater distances with unknown adults, unfriendly and/or threatening persons, teachers, and endomorphs.

These and other studies suggest that closer relationships are likely to be associated with closer interaction distance. Obviously, there is a point at which we would not expect interactants to get any closer, no matter how close their relationship. And even people who are very close will not always interact at close distances due to the ebb and flow of their relationship as well as the influence of other distance-altering factors.

PERSONALITY CHARACTERISTICS

Much has been written about the influence of introversion and extraversion on spatial relationships. It is difficult to draw any firm conclusions, but the bulk of the evidence seems to indicate that introverts tend to stand further away than extraverts and to generally prefer greater interpersonal distances. Other studies suggest that anxiety-prone individuals will maintain greater distances, but closer distances are seen when people have a high self-concept, have affiliative needs, are low on authoritarianism, and are "self-directed." People with various personality abnormalities can probably be counted on to show greater nonnormative spatial behavior, both too far away and too close.

The preceding are some of the many factors that will influence conversational distance. Greater conversational distances between white male strangers also have been found to be associated with prior social isolation, longer conversations about personal topics, conversations observed by others, and conversations occurring in small, rectangular rooms rather than large or square rooms (Worchel, 1986). The list of variables affecting personal space seems to be a lengthy one.

In addition to studying human spatial behavior in overcrowded situations and in conversation, some researchers have examined such questions in the context of the small group, particularly in regard to seating patterns.

SEATING BEHAVIOR and SPATIAL ARRANGEMENTS in SMALL GROUPS

The body of work on seating behavior and spatial arrangements in small groups is known as *small-group ecology*. Results of these studies show that our seating behavior is not generally accidental or random. There are explanations for much of it, whether we are fully conscious of them or not. The particular position chosen in relation to the other person or persons varies with the task at hand, the degree of relationship between the interactants, the personalities of the two parties, and the amount and kind of available space. The findings about seating behavior and spatial positioning can be summarized under the following categories:

- Leadership
- Dominance
- Task
- Sex and acquaintance
- Motivation
- Introversion-extraversion

LEADERSHIP

It seems to be a norm, in the United States at least, that leaders are expected to be found at the head or foot of the table. At a family gathering, we generally find the head of the household sitting at the head of the table. Elected group leaders generally put themselves in the head positions at rectangular tables, and the other group members try to position themselves so they can see the leader. Strodtbeck and Hook (1961) set up experimental jury deliberations revealing that a man sitting at the head position was chosen significantly more often as the leader, particularly if he was perceived as a person from a high economic class. If the choice was between two people at each end, the one perceived to be of higher economic status was chosen. The reaction to women who are positioned at the head of the table is not as consistently linked to the leadership role (Porter & Geis, 1981). As long as the group consists of all women, the one at the head of the table is perceived as the leader. In groups consisting of men and women, however, a woman at the head position is much less likely to be perceived in a leadership role than a man who occupies the end position.

Howells and Becker (1962) add further support to the idea that one's position in a group is an important factor in leadership emergence. They reasoned that spatial position determines the flow of communication, which, in turn, determines leadership emergence. Five-person decision-making groups were examined. Three people sat on one side of a rectangular table and two sat on the other side. Since previous work suggested that communication usually flows across the table rather than around it, the researchers predicted that the side with two people would be able to influence the most people (or at least talk more) and therefore emerge more often as group leaders. This hypothesis was confirmed.

An experiment by Ward (1968) helps to unravel how seating position can create leaders. College males were assigned at random to sit in particular seats at a round table. The experimenters arranged it so that more people were seated in one half of the table than in the other; only two people sat at the less-populated end, and these two seats were considered visually central, since their occupants would receive more undivided gaze from people at the other, more densely occupied, end. As predicted, occupants of these visually central seats received higher ratings of leadership after discussions had taken place. But were they really leaders or just perceived to be? While other research (Taylor & Fiske, 1975) does indicate that the person on whom attention is centered will appear to be an initiator (causally responsible for the course of the conversation), in Ward's study there was evidence that those who were visually central actually behaved differently: They talked more. It would be interesting to unravel further the complex routes by which seating position might affect leadership. For example, does the visually central person think, "I'm in a central position; I'd better start acting like a leader"? Or do the attention and subtle cues of the other members of the group trigger leader-like behavior, perhaps without the visually central person even realizing it?

People seem well aware of these different perceptions and communicative potential associated with different seating positions. When people were asked to select seats to convey different impressions, they chose end positions to convey leadership or dominance, positions that furnished the closest distances to convey interpersonal attraction, and seats that afforded the greatest interpersonal distance and least visual accessibility vis-à-vis the end positions to indicate they did not wish to participate (Reiss & Rosenfeld, 1980).

DOMINANCE

The end positions also seem to carry a status or dominance factor. Russo (1967) found that people rating various seating arrangements on an "equality" dimension stated that one person seated at the head and one on the side indicated more unequal status than if they were seated side by side or both on the ends. In an analysis of talking frequency in small groups, Hare and Bales (1963) noted that people in positions 1, 3, and 5 (at left) were frequent talkers. Subsequent studies revealed that these people were likely to be dominant personalities, while those who avoided the central or focal positions (by choosing seats 2 and 4) were more anxious and actually stated they wanted to stay out of the discussion. These self-selection effects demonstrate the importance of conducting randomized studies such as Ward's, mentioned earlier. Would the communication of nondominant persons placed in focal positions radically change? We don't know. This research has not been done.

Positions 1, 3, and 5 also were considered to be positions of leadership but leadership of a different type, depending on the position. The two end positions (1 and 5) attracted the task-oriented leader, while the middle position attracted a socioemotional leader—one concerned about group relationships, getting everyone to participate, and so forth. Lott and Sommer (1967) wanted to find out how others located themselves vis-à-vis higher- and lower-status people. Generally, the results suggest that people (in this case, students) will sit further away from both higher-status (professor) and lower-status (failing freshman) persons than from peers.

TASK

Sommer's observations of seating behavior in student cafeterias and libraries led him to study how students would sit in different task situations. The same study was conducted by Cook in the United Kingdom with Oxford University students and a sample of nonstudents—civil servants, schoolteachers, and secretaries. In each case, persons were asked to imagine themselves sitting at a table with a friend of the same sex in each of the following four situations:

1. **Conversation.** Sitting and chatting for a few minutes before class ("before work" for nonstudents)
2. **Cooperation.** Sitting and studying together for the same exam ("sitting doing a crossword or the like together" for nonstudents)
3. **Coaction.** Sitting studying for different exams ("sitting at the same table reading" for nonstudents)
4. **Competition.** Competing to see who will be the first to solve a series of puzzles

Each subject was shown a round table and a rectangular table. Each had six chairs. The results of these two studies are presented in Table 5-1 for rectangular tables and Table 5-2 for circular tables.

There are many similarities between the different groups concerning order of preference, but there are also some differences worth noting. For instance, the U. K. nonuniversity sample differs less from the U. S. student sample than does the Oxford University group. Conversations before class (or work) involved primarily corner or "short" opposite seating at rectangular tables and side-by-side seating at round tables. Oxford students seemed to be more favorable toward distant seating for conversation than other groups, but the value of closeness and visibility for this task seems to prevail. Cooperation seems to elicit a preponderance of side-by-side choices from everyone except the Oxford group. The author suggests that since Oxford students are encouraged to do most of their work alone, they may not have realized the question meant cooperating with another person. More doubt is cast on the validity of the Oxford responses to this question since their responses to the coaction question were similar. Coaction, studying for different exams or

Table 5–1

SEATING PREFERENCES AT RECTANGULAR TABLES

	x▭x	x▭ (x below)	xx▭	x▭x (sides)	▭ (x top/bottom)	▭x (x ends)
Conversation						
U. S. sample (151 responses)	42%	46%	11%	0%	1%	0%
U. K. (univ.) sample (102 responses)	51	21	15	0	6	7
U. K. (nonuniv.) sample (42 responses)	42	42	9	2	5	0
Cooperation						
U. S. sample	19	25	51	0	5	0
U. K. (univ.) sample	11	11	23	20	22	13
U. K. (nonuniv.) sample	40	2	50	5	2	0
Coaction						
U. S. sample	3	3	7	13	43	33
U. K. (univ.) sample	9	8	10	31	28	14
U. K. (nonuniv.) sample	12	14	12	19	31	12
Competition						
U. S. sample	7	41	8	18	20	5
U. K. (univ.) sample	7	10	10	50	16	7
U. K. (nonuniv.) sample	4	13	3	53	20	7

reading at the same table as another, necessitated plenty of room between the participants, and the most distant seating positions were generally selected. The slightly different instructions for the nonuniversity sample may explain the greater variety of responses to the coaction question. Most persons wanted to compete in an opposite seating arrangement. However, the U. S. students wanted to establish a closer opposite relationship. Apparently this would afford them an opportunity not only to see how the other person was progressing but would also allow them to use various gestures, body movements, and eye contact to upset their opponents. The more distant opposite position chosen by the United Kingdom samples would, on the other hand, prevent spying.

SEX AND ACQUAINTANCE

The nature of the relationship may make a difference in spatial orientation and, hence, in seating selection. Cook (1970) conducted a questionnaire study

Table 5–2
SEATING PREFERENCES AT ROUND TABLES

	side-by-side adjacent	around corner	opposite
Conversation			
U. S. sample (116 responses)	63%	17%	20%
U. K. (univ.) sample (102 responses)	58	37	5
U. K. (nonuniv.) sample (42 responses)	58	27	15
Cooperation			
U. S. sample	83	7	10
U. K. (univ.) sample	25	31	44
U. K. (nonuniv.) sample	97	0	3
Coaction			
U. S. sample	13	36	51
U. K. (univ.) sample	16	34	50
U. K. (nonuniv.) sample	24	26	50
Competition			
U. S. sample	2	25	63
U. K. (univ.) sample	15	22	63
U. K. (nonuniv.) sample	9	21	70

and obtained some observational data of persons interacting in a restaurant and several bars. Subjects in the questionnaire study were asked to select seating arrangements when:

- Sitting with a casual friend of the same sex
- Sitting with a casual friend of the opposite sex
- Sitting with a boyfriend or girlfriend

The results for the "public house" or bar are found in Table 5-3 and results for the restaurant in Table 5-4.

The predominant seating pattern, as stated by questionnaire respondents using a bar as a referent, was corner seating for the same-sex friends and casual friends of the opposite sex. Intimate friends appear to desire side-by-side seating, however. In a restaurant, all variations of sex and acquaintance seem to select opposite seating, with more side-by-side seating occurring between intimate friends. There may be some very practical reasons for opposite seating in restaurants. For instance, other patrons will not have to sit

Table 5–3
SEATING PREFERENCES FOR A BAR OR "PUBLIC HOUSE"

	Corner	Opposite	Side-by-side	Other
Same-sex friend	70	25	45	2
Casual friend of opposite sex	63	37	29	7
Intimate friend of opposite sex	43	11	82	4

Table 5–4
SEATING PREFERENCES FOR A RESTAURANT

	Corner	Opposite	Side-by-side	Other
Same-sex friend	30	73	34	4
Casual friend of opposite sex	43	64	28	4
Intimate friend of opposite sex	40	53	46	2

opposite you, which might create some uncomfortable situations with respect to eye contact and overheard conversation. In addition, you will not poke the other person with your elbow while eating. The actual observations of seating in a restaurant, presented in Table 5-5, seem to validate the questionnaire responses. Most people do select opposite seating in restaurants. However, the observations of people sitting in bars do not agree with the questionnaire study of seating preferences in bars (see Table 5-6). Although questionnaire preferences favored corner seating, observations show a marked preference for side-by-side seating. Cook suggests this may have been because the bars

Table 5–5
OBSERVATIONS OF SEATING BEHAVIOR IN A RESTAURANT

	Opposite	Side-by-side	Diagonal
Two males	6	0	0
Two females	6	0	1
Male with female	36	7	1
Total	48	7	2

Table 5-6
OBSERVATIONS OF SEATING BEHAVIOR IN THREE BARS

	X X □, X □	X □, X	X X □
Bar A			
Two males	7	8	13
Male with female	6	4	21
Total	13	12	34
Bar B			
Two males	1	0	9
Male with female	4	3	20
Total	5	3	29
Bar C			
Two males	0	11	7
Male with female	1	4	10
Total	1	15	17
Overall			
Two males	8	19	29
Male with female	11	11	51
Total	19	30	80

were equipped with many seats located against the wall. Supposedly this allowed persons to sit side by side, not have their backs to anyone, and have a good view of the other patrons. Thus, paper-and-pencil preferences were overruled by environmental factors. From this study, we must conclude that sex and acquaintance with the other person do have an effect on one's actual and preferred seating positions. These findings are consistent with a great deal of work that suggests we will try to reduce the distance between ourselves and those we feel have attitudes similar to ours. And similarly, we seem to develop positive relationships more frequently with those in close proximity to us, at home or in a classroom.

MOTIVATION

Earlier we mentioned the idea that one may regulate intimacy with another through either increasing eye contact or decreasing distance. Of course, we may do both. Prior to another study by Cook (1970), we did not know what conditions prompt the use of distance and what conditions prompt the use of eye contact. Again respondents made seating selections based on different types (positive and negative) and different levels (high, medium, and low) of motivation. For example, high-positive motivation was "sitting with your boy- or girlfriend," and low-negative motivation was "sitting with someone you do not like very much and do not wish to talk to." He found that as motivation increased, persons wanted to sit closer or to have more eye contact. When the motivation was affiliative, the choice was to sit closer, and when the motivation was competitive, the choice was one that would allow more eye contact. It seems, then, that the choice of eye contact or proximity depends on the motives of the interacting pair. It is quite permissible to sit close to another when there is high-affiliative motivation, but when there are high levels of nonaffiliative motivation, such proximity is not as permissible, so eye contact is used.

INTROVERSION-EXTRAVERSION

We have already discussed the possible influence of introversion and extraversion on conversational distance. Cook (1970) found some relation between this personality variable and seating preference. Extraverts chose to sit opposite (either across the table or down the length of it) and disregarded positions that would put them at an angle. Many extraverts also chose positions that would put them in close physical proximity to the other person. Introverts generally chose positions that would keep them more at a distance, visually and physically.

A discussion of the shape of the negotiating table at the 1968 Paris peace talks (attempting to end the Vietnam War) is a most appropriate way to conclude this chapter. It incorporates elements of territoriality and seating arrangements that are influenced by culture, attitudes, leadership perceptions, and the type of task undertaken. It took negotiators eight months just to reach an agreement on the shape of the table! The diagrams in Figure 5-3 mark the chronology of the seating proposals.

> The United States (U. S.) and South Vietnam (S. V.) wanted a seating arrangement in which only two sides were identified. They did not want to recognize the National Liberation Front (NLF) as an equal party in the negotiations. North Vietnam (N. V.) and the NLF wanted equal status given to all parties, represented by a four-sided table. The final arrangement was such that both parties could claim "victory." The round table minus the dividing lines allowed North Vietnam and NLF to claim all four delegations were equal. The existence of the two secretarial tables (interpreted as dividers), the lack of identifying symbols on the table, and an AA, BB speaking rotation permitted the United States and South Vietnam to claim victory for the two-sided approach. Considering the lives lost during the eight months needed to arrive at the seating arrangement, we must certainly conclude that proximity and territoriality are far from trivial concerns in some human encounters. (McCroskey, Larson, & Knapp, 1971, p. 98)

Figure 5-3

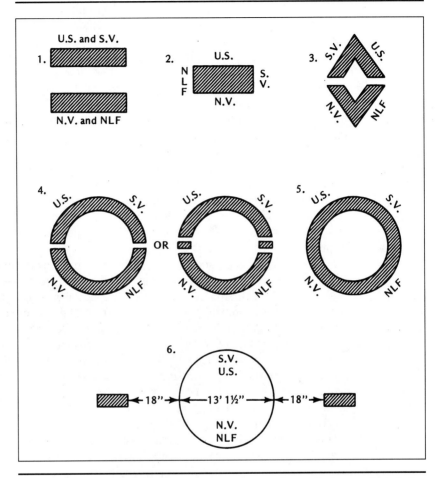

Proposals for a table to be used at the Paris peace talks, 1968. (Drawn from J. C. McCroskey, C. E. Larson, and M. L. Knapp, An Introduction to Interpersonal Communication. *Englewood Cliffs, NJ: Prentice-Hall, 1971, p. 9.)*

SUMMARY

Our perceptions and use of space contribute extensively to various communication outcomes we seek. Some of our spatial behavior is related to a need to stake out and maintain territory. Our territorial behavior can be helpful in regulating social interaction and controlling density; it also can be the source of conflict when territory is disputed or encroached upon. We identified three different types of territories (primary, secondary, and public) and several different levels at which territorial behavior exists (individual, group, community, and nation). Although we often think people vigorously defend their territory, the type of defense is highly dependent on who the intruder is, why the intrusion is taking place, what type of territory is being encroached upon, what type of encroachment is used (violation, invasion, or contamination), how long the encroachment takes, and where it occurs. We often try to prevent people from moving into our territory by marking it as "ours." This can be done by our physical presence or the presence of a friend who agrees to "watch" our territory. Territorial invasion also can be prevented by using markers (fences, coats, and the like) or a special kind of language. When someone does invade another's territory, we sometimes find the "owner's" physiological arousal increased. In addition, various defensive maneuvers are used, for example, flight, hostile looks, turning or leaning away, blocking advances with objects or hands and arms, or even verbal defenses. Just as people do not like others to invade their territory, we also find that they are reluctant to invade the territory of others, often apologizing when it cannot be prevented.

We examined density and crowding in both animal and human interaction. Animal studies showed numerous undesirable effects from overpopulation. High-density human situations, however, are not always disruptive. Sometimes we want the company of many people. The best predictor of individually stressful and socially undesirable outcomes seems to be the number of people per room rather than other density measures. When people do feel the stress of a crowded situation, they will seek ways to cope with it, much like the !Kung or urban dwellers. We also distinguished between density (number of people per unit of space) and crowding (a feeling brought on by the environment, personal, or social factors).

Our examination of spatial behavior in conversations revealed that there are many ways of conceptualizing and measuring this behavior. As a result, firm conclusions are difficult to reach. We do know that each of us seeks a comfortable conversational distance that will vary depending on age, sex, cultural and ethnic background, setting, attitudes, emotions, topics, physical characteristics, personality, and our relationship with the other person. We also know conversational distance changes during the course of a conversation.

Finally, we discussed seating arrangements in small groups. Distances and seats chosen do not seem to be accidental. Leaders and dominant personalities tend to choose specific seats, but seating position also can determine one's role in a group. Seating also will vary with the topic at hand, the nature of the relationships among the parties, and certain personality variables.

QUESTIONS for DISCUSSION

1. Identify a *secondary* territory you have experienced. Discuss what happened.

2. What cultural differences within the United States would you expect to find in comfortable conversational distances?
3. When is a woman's purse a *primary* territory? When can it become a *secondary* territory?
4. Think of a time when you did not experience a comfortable conversational distance with someone. What were the major factors influencing this situation? How did you deal with it?

REFERENCES and SELECTED BIBLIOGRAPHY

Aiello, J. R., & Aiello, T. C. (1974). The development of personal space: Proxemic behavior of children 6 through 16. *Human Ecology, 2,* 177–89.

Aiello, J. R., & Jones, S. E. (1971). Field study of the proxemic behavior of young school children in three subcultural groups. *Journal of Personality and Social Psychology, 19,* 351–56.

Aiello, J. R., & Thompson, D. E. (1980). Personal space, crowding, and spatial behavior in a cultural context. In I. Altman, A. Rapoport, & J. F. Wohlwill (Eds.), *Human behavior and environment* (Vol. 4). New York: Plenum.

Albert, S., & Dabbs, J. M., Jr. (1970). Physical distance and persuasion. *Journal of Personality and Social Psychology, 15,* 265–70.

Allekian, C. I. (1973). Intrusions of territory and personal space: An anxiety-inducing factor for hospitalized persons. *Nursing Research, 22,* 236–41.

Allgeier, A. R., & Byrne, D. (1973). Attraction toward the opposite sex as a determinant of physical proximity. *Journal of Social Psychology, 90,* 213–19.

Altman, I. (1975). *The environment and social behavior.* Monterey, CA: Brooks/Cole.

Altman, I., & Chemers, M. M. (1988). *Culture and environment.* New York: Cambridge University Press.

Altman, I., & Haythorn, W. W. (1967). The ecology of isolated groups. *Behavioral Science, 12,* 169–82.

Ardrey, R. (1966). *The territorial imperative.* New York: Atheneum Press.

Argyle, M., & Dean, J. (1965). Eye contact, distance and affiliation. *Sociometry, 28,* 289–304.

Barash, D. P. (1973). Human ethology: Personal space reiterated. *Environment and Behavior, 5,* 67–73.

Bass, B. M., & Klubeck, S. (1952). Effects of seating arrangements on leaderless group discussions. *Journal of Abnormal and Social Psychology, 47,* 724–27.

Baum, A., & Greenberg, C. I. (1975). Waiting for a crowd: The behavioral and perceptual effects of anticipated crowding. *Journal of Personality and Social Psychology, 32,* 671–79.

Baum, A., Riess, M., & O'Hara, J. (1974). Architectural variants of reaction to spatial invasion. *Environment and Behavior, 6,* 91–100.

Baxter, J. C. (1970). Interpersonal spacing in natural settings. *Sociometry, 33,* 444–56.

Becker, F. D. (1973). Study of spatial markers. *Journal of Personality and Social Psychology, 26,* 439–45.

Bull, R. (1985). The general public's reactions to facial disfigurement. In J. A. Graham & A. M. Kligman (Eds.), *The psychology of cosmetic treatments*. New York: Praeger.

Buller, D. B. (1987). Communication apprehension and reactions to proxemic violations. *Journal of Nonverbal Behavior, 11,* 13–25.

Burgoon, J. K. (1982). Privacy and communication. In M. Burgoon (Ed.), *Communication yearbook 6*. Beverly Hills, CA: Sage.

Burgoon, J. K. (1983). Nonverbal violations of expectations. In J. M. Wiemann & R. P. Harrison (Eds.), *Nonverbal interaction*. Beverly Hills, CA: Sage.

Burgoon, J. K., & Jones, S. B. (1976). Toward a theory of personal space expectations and their violations. *Human Communication Research, 2,* 131–46.

Byrne, D., & Buehler, J. A. (1955). A note on the influence of propinquity upon acquaintanceships. *Journal of Abnormal and Social Psychology, 51,* 147–48.

Calhoun, J. B. (1962). Population density and social pathology. *Scientific American, 206,* 139–48.

Caplan, M. E., & Goldman, M. (1981). Personal space violations as a function of height. *Journal of Social Psychology, 114,* 167–71.

Cappella, J. N. (1986). Violations of distance norms: Reciprocal and compensatory reactions for high and low self-monitors. In M. L. McLaughlin (Ed.), *Communication yearbook 9*. Beverly Hills, CA: Sage.

Carpenter, C. R. (1958). Territoriality: A review of concepts and problems. In A. Roe & G. G. Simpson (Eds.), *Behavior and evolution*. New Haven: Yale University Press.

Caudill, W., & Weinstein, H. (1972). Maternal care and infant behavior in Japan and America. In C. Lavatelli & F. Stendler (Eds.), *Readings in child behavior and development*. New York: Harcourt.

Christian, J. J., & Davis, D. E. (1964). Social and endocrine factors are integrated in the regulation of mammalian populations. *Science, 146,* 1550–60.

Ciolek, T. M., & Kendon, A. (1980). Environment and the spatial arrangement of conversational encounters. *Sociological Inquiry, 50,* 237–76.

Connolly, P. R. (1975). The perception of personal space among black and white Americans. *Central States Speech Journal, 26,* 21–28.

Cook, M. (1970). Experiments on orientation and proxemics. *Human Relations, 23,* 61–76.

Crane, D. R., Dollahite, D. C., Griffin, W., & Taylor, V. L. (1987). Diagnosing relationships with spatial distance: An empirical test of a clinical principle. *Journal of Marital and Family Therapy, 13,* 307–10.

DeLong, A. J. (1970). Dominance-territorial relations in a small group. *Environment and Behavior, 2,* 190–91.

DiPietro, J. A. (1981). Rough and tumble play: A function of gender. *Developmental Psychology, 17,* 50–58.

Draper, P. (1973). Crowding among hunter-gatherers: The !Kung bushmen. *Science, 182,* 301–3.

Drucker, S. J., & Gumpert, G. (1991). Public space and communication: The zoning of public interaction. *Communication Theory, 1,* 294–310.

Eagly, A. H. (1987). *Sex differences in social behavior: A social-role interpretation*. Hillsdale, NJ: Erlbaum.

Edney, J. J. (1974). Human territoriality. *Psychological Bulletin, 31,* 959–75.

Efran, M. G., & Cheyne, J. A. (1974). Affective concomitants of the invasion of shared space: Behavioral, physiological and verbal indicators. *Journal of Personality and Social Psychology, 29,* 219–26.

Erickson, F. (1975). One function of proxemic shifts in face-to-face interaction. In A. Kendon, R. M. Harris, & M. R. Key (Eds.), *Organization of behavior in face-to-face interaction.* Chicago: Aldine.

Esser, A. H. (1971). *Environment and behavior: The use of space by animals and men.* New York: Plenum.

Evans, G. W. (1979). Behavioral and physiological consequences of crowding in humans. *Journal of Applied Social Psychology, 9,* 27–46.

Evans, G. W., & Howard, R. B. (1973). Personal space. *Psychological Bulletin, 80,* 334–44.

Felipe, N. J., & Sommer, R. (1966). Invasions of personal space. *Social Problems, 14,* 206–14.

Finando, S. J. (1973). *The effects of distance norm violation on heart rate and length of verbal response.* Unpublished doctoral dissertation, Florida State University.

Fisher, J. D., & Byrne, D. (1975). Too close for comfort: Sex differences in response to invasions of personal space. *Journal of Personality and Social Psychology, 32,* 15–21.

Freedman, J. L. (1975). *Crowding and behavior.* New York: Viking.

Freedman, J. L. (1979). Reconciling apparent differences between the responses of humans and other animals to crowding. *Psychological Review, 86,* 80–85.

Fry, A. M., & Willis, F. N. (1971). Invasion of personal space as a function of the age of the invader. *Psychological Record, 21,* 385–89.

Galle, O. R., Gove, W. R., & McPherson, J. M. (1972). Population density and pathology: What are the relationships for man? *Science, 176,* 23–30.

Gifford, R. (1982). Projected interpersonal distance and orientation choices: Personality, sex, and social situation. *Social Psychology Quarterly, 45,* 145–52.

Gifford, R., & O'Connor, B. (1986). Nonverbal intimacy: Clarifying the role of seating distance and orientation. *Journal of Nonverbal Behavior, 10,* 207–14.

Gochman, I. R., & Keating, J. P. (1980). Misattributions to crowding: Blaming crowding for non-density caused events. *Journal of Nonverbal Behavior, 4,* 157–75.

Goffman, E. (1971). *Relations in public.* New York: Basic Books.

Greenberg, C. I., & Firestone, I. J. (1977). Compensatory responses to crowding: Effects of personal space intrusion and privacy reduction. *Journal of Personality and Social Psychology, 35,* 637–44.

Guardo, C. J., & Meisels, M. (1971). Child-parent spatial patterns under praise and reproof. *Developmental Psychology, 5,* 365.

Halberstadt, A. G. (1985). Race, socioeconomic status and nonverbal behavior. In A. W. Siegman & S. Feldstein (Eds.), *Multichannel integrations of nonverbal behavior* (pp. 227–66). Hillsdale, NJ: Erlbaum.

Hall, E. T. (1959). *The silent language.* Garden City, NY: Doubleday.

Hall, E. T. (1963). A system for the notation of proxemic behavior. *American Anthropologist, 65,* 1003–26.

Hall, E. T. (1966). *The hidden dimension.* Garden City, NY: Doubleday.

Hall, J. A. (1984). *Nonverbal sex differences: Communication accuracy and expressive style.* Baltimore: Johns Hopkins University Press.

Hansen, J. F. (1976). Proxemics and the interpretive processes in human communication. *Semiotica, 17,* 165–79.

Hare, A., & Bales, R. (1963). Seating position and small group interaction. *Sociometry, 26,* 480–86.

Harper, L., & Sanders, K. M. (1975). Preschool children's use of space: Sex differences in outdoor play. *Developmental Psychology, 11,* 119.

Hartnett, J. J., Bailey, K. G., & Hartley, C. S. (1974). Body height, position, and sex as determinants of personal space. *Journal of Psychology, 87,* 129–36.

Hayduk, L. A. (1978). Personal space: An evaluative and orienting overview. *Psychological Bulletin, 85,* 117–34.

Hayduk, L. A. (1994). Personal space: Understanding the simplex model. *Journal of Nonverbal Behavior, 18,* 245–60.

Hearn, G. (1957). Leadership and the spatial factor in small groups. *Journal of Abnormal and Social Psychology, 104,* 269–72.

Hediger, H. P. (1961). The evolution of territorial behavior. In S. L. Washburn (Ed.), *Social life of early man* (pp. 34–57). Chicago: Aldine.

Henley, N. M. (1977). *Body politics: Power, sex, and nonverbal communication.* Englewood Cliffs, NJ: Prentice-Hall.

Hildreth, A. M., Derogatis, L. R., & McCusker, K. (1971). Body buffer zone and violence: A reassessment and confirmation. *American Journal of Psychiatry, 127,* 1641–45.

Hoppe, R. A., Greene, M. S., & Kenney, J. W. (1972). Territorial markers: Additional findings. *Journal of Social Psychology, 88,* 305–6.

Horowitz, M. J. (1965). Human spatial behavior. *American Journal of Psychotherapy, 19,* 20–28.

Horowitz, M. J. (1968). Spatial behavior and psychopathology. *The Journal of Nervous and Mental Disease, 146,* 24–35.

Howells, L. T., & Becker, S. W. (1962). Seating arrangement and leadership emergence. *Journal of Abnormal and Social Psychology, 64,* 148–50.

Hutt, C., & Vaizey, M. J. (1966). Differential effects of group density on social behavior. *Nature, 209,* 1371–72.

Jones, S. E., & Aiello, J. R. (1973). Proxemic behavior of black and white first, third, and fifth grade children. *Journal of Personality and Social Psychology, 25,* 21–27.

King, M. J. (1966). Interpersonal relations in preschool children and average approach distance. *Journal of Genetic Psychology, 109,* 109–16.

Kinzel, A. S. (1970). Body buffer zone in violent prisoners. *American Journal of Psychiatry, 127,* 59–64.

Kleck, R. E. (1969). Physical stigma and task oriented interaction. *Human Relations, 22,* 51–60.

Kleck, R., Buck, P. L., Goller, W. L., London, R. S., Pfeiffer, J. R., & Vukcevic, D. P. (1968). The effect of stigmatizing conditions on the use of personal space. *Psychological Reports, 23,* 111–18.

Kleck, R. E., & Strenta, A. C. (1985). Physical deviance and the perception of social outcomes. In J. A. Graham & A. M. Kligman (Eds.), *The psychology of cosmetic treatments*. New York: Praeger.

Klopfer, P. M. (1968). From Ardrey to altruism: A discourse on the biological basis of human behavior. *Behavioral Science, 13,* 399–401.

Klopfer, P. M. (1969). *Habitats and territories: A study of the use of space by animals*. New York: Basic Books.

Knowles, E. S. (1973). Boundaries around group interaction: The effect of group size and member status on boundary permeability. *Journal of Personality and Social Psychology, 26,* 327–32.

Knowles, E. S. (1979). An affiliative conflict theory of personal and group spatial behavior. In P. B. Paulus (Ed.), *Psychology of group influence*. Hillsdale, NJ: Erlbaum.

Latta, R. M. (1978). Relation of status incongruence to personal space. *Personality and Social Psychology Bulletin, 4,* 143–46.

Leibman, M. (1970). The effects of sex and race norms on personal space. *Environment and Behavior, 2,* 208–46.

Leipold, W. E. (1963). *Psychological distance in a dyadic interview*. Unpublished doctoral dissertation, University of North Dakota.

LePoire, B. A., Burgoon, J. K., & Parrott, R. (1992). Status and privacy restoring communication in the workplace. *Journal of Applied Communication Research, 20,* 419–36.

Lerner, R. M., Venning, J., & Knapp, J. R. (1975). Age and sex effects on personal space schemata toward body build in late childhood. *Developmental Psychology, 11,* 855–56.

Little, K. B. (1965). Personal space. *Journal of Experimental Social Psychology, 1,* 237–47.

Little, K. B. (1968). Cultural variations in social schemata. *Journal of Personality and Social Psychology, 10,* 1–7.

Loo, C. M. (1973). The effect of spatial density on the social behavior of children. *Journal of Applied Social Psychology, 2,* 372–81.

Lott, D. F., & Sommer, R. (1967). Seating arrangements and status. *Journal of Personality and Social Psychology, 7,* 90–94.

Lyman, S. M., & Scott, M. B. (1967). Territoriality: A neglected sociological dimension. *Social Problems, 15,* 236–49.

Malmberg, T. (1980). *Human territoriality*. Mouton: The Hague.

McBride, G., King, M. G., & James, J. W. (1965). Social proximity effects on galvanic skin responses in adult humans. *Journal of Psychology, 61,* 153–57.

McCallum, R., Rusbult, C. E., Hong, G. K., Walden, T. A., & Schopler, J. (1979). Effects of resource availability and importance of behavior on the experience of crowding. *Journal of Personality and Social Psychology, 37,* 1304–13.

McCroskey, J. C., Larson, C. E., & Knapp, M. L. (1971). *An introduction to interpersonal communication.* Englewood Cliffs, NJ: Prentice-Hall.

McDowell, K. V. (1972). Violations of personal space. *Canadian Journal of Behavioral Science, 4,* 210–17.

Mehrabian, A. (1969). Significance of posture and position in the communication of attitude and status relationships. *Psychological Bulletin, 71,* 363.

Mehrabian, A., & Diamond, S. G. (1971). Seating arrangement and conversation. *Sociometry, 34,* 281–89.

Meisels, M., & Dosey, M. (1971). Personal space, anger arousal, and psychological defense. *Journal of Personality, 39,* 333–34.

Meisels, M., & Guardo, C. (1969). Development of personal space schemata. *Child Development, 40,* 1167–78.

Milgram, S. (1970). The experience of living in cities. *Science, 167,* 1461–68.

Mitchell, R. (1971). Some social implications of higher density housing. *American Sociological Review, 36,* 18–29.

Moos, R. H., & Kulik, J. (1976). Population density, crowding and the use of space. In R. H. Moos (Ed.), *The human context.* New York: Wiley.

Munroe, R. L., & Munroe, R. H. (1972). Population density and affective relationships in three East African societies. *Journal of Social Psychology, 88,* 15–20.

Newman, O. (1972). *Defensible space.* New York: Macmillan.

O'Neal, E. C., Brunalt, M. A., Carifio, M. S., Troutwine, R., & Epstein, J. (1980). Effect of insult upon personal space preferences. *Journal of Nonverbal Behavior, 5,* 56–62.

Pagan, G., & Aiello, J. R. (1982). Development of personal space among Puerto Ricans. *Journal of Nonverbal Behavior, 7,* 59–68.

Pastalan, L., & Carson, D. H. (Eds.). (1970). *Spatial behavior of older people.* Ann Arbor: University of Michigan/Wayne State University Press.

Patterson, M. L. (1968). Spatial factors in social interaction. *Human Relations, 21,* 351–61.

Patterson, M. L. (1975). Personal space—Time to burst the bubble? *Man-Environment Systems, 5,* 67.

Patterson, M. L. (1976). An arousal model of interpersonal intimacy. *Psychological Review, 83,* 235–45.

Patterson, M. L. (1978). The role of space in social interaction. In A. W. Siegman & S. Feldstein (Eds.), *Nonverbal behavior and communication.* Hillsdale, NJ: Erlbaum.

Patterson, M. L., & Edinger, J. A. (1987). A functional analysis of space in social interaction. In A. W. Siegman & S. Feldstein (Eds.), *Nonverbal behavior and communication* (2d ed.). Hillsdale, NJ: Erlbaum.

Patterson, M. L., Mullens, S., & Romano, J. (1971). Compensatory reactions to spatial intrusion. *Sociometry, 34,* 114–21.

Pedersen, D. M., & Shears, L. M. (1973). A review of personal space research in the framework of general system theory. *Psychological Bulletin, 80,* 367–88.

Porter, E., Argyle, M., & Salter, V. (1970). What is signalled by proximity? *Perceptual and Motor Skills, 30,* 39–42.

Porter, N., & Geis, F. (1981). Women and nonverbal leadership cues: When seeing is not believing. In C. Mayo & N. M. Henley (Eds.), *Gender and nonverbal behavior*. New York: Springer-Verlag.

Priest, R. F., & Sawyer, J. (1967). Proximity and peership: Bases of balance in interpersonal attraction. *American Journal of Sociology, 72,* 633–49.

Reiss, M., & Rosenfeld, P. (1980). Seating preferences as nonverbal communication: A self-presentational analysis. *Journal of Applied Communication Research, 8,* 22–30.

Remland, M. S., Jones, T. S., and Brinkman, H. (1991). Proxemic and haptic behavior in three European countries. *Journal of Nonverbal Behavior, 15,* 215–32.

Rheingold, H. L., & Cook, K. V. (1975). The contents of boys' and girls' rooms as an index of parents' behavior. *Child Development, 46,* 459–63.

Rohe, W., & Patterson, A. H. (1974). *The effects of varied levels of resources and density on behavior in a day care center.* Paper presented at Environmental Design and Research Association, Milwaukee, WI.

Rosenfeld, H. (1965). Effect of approval-seeking induction on interpersonal proximity. *Psychological Reports, 17,* 120–22.

Rosenfeld, H. (1966). Instrumental and affiliative functions of facial and gestural expressions. *Journal of Personality and Social Psychology, 4,* 65–72.

Russo, N. (1967). Connotation of seating arrangement. *Cornell Journal of Social Relations, 2,* 37–44.

Scheflen, A. E. (1975). Micro-territories in human interaction. In A. Kendon, R. M. Harris, & M. R. Key (Eds.), *Organization of behavior in face-to-face interaction* (pp. 159–73). Chicago: Aldine.

Scheflen, A. E., & Ashcraft, N. (1976). *Human territories: How we behave in space-time.* Englewood Cliffs, NJ: Prentice-Hall.

Scherer, S. E. (1974). Proxemic behavior of primary school children as a function of their socioeconomic class and subculture. *Journal of Personality and Social Psychology, 29,* 800–805.

Schmidt, D. E., & Keating, J. P. (1979). Human crowding and personal control: An integration of the research. *Psychological Bulletin, 86,* 680–700.

Schulz, R., & Barefoot, J. (1974). Non-verbal responses and affiliative conflict theory. *British Journal of Social and Clinical Psychology, 13,* 237–43.

Shuter, R. (1976). Proxemics and tactility in Latin America. *Journal of Communication, 26,* 46–52.

Shuter, R. (1977). A field study of non-verbal communication in Germany, Italy and the United States. *Communication Monographs, 44,* 298–305.

Smith, D. E. (1986). The influence of contextual variables on interpersonal spacing. *Journal of Communication, 29* (Autumn), 34–39.

Smith, M. J., Reinheimer, R. E., & Gabbard-Alley, A. (1981). Crowding, task performance, and communicative interaction in youth and old age. *Human Communication Research, 7,* 259–72.

Sobel, R. S., & Lillith, N. (1975). Determinants of nonstationary personal space invasion. *Journal of Social Psychology, 97,* 39–45.

Sommer, R. (1959). Studies in personal space. *Sociometry, 22,* 247–60.

Sommer, R. (1961). Leadership and group geography. *Sociometry, 24,* 99–110.

Sommer, R. (1962). The distance for comfortable conversation: A further study. *Sociometry, 25,* 111–16.

Sommer, R. (1965). Further studies of small group ecology. *Sociometry, 28,* 337–48.

Sommer, R. (1967). Small group ecology. *Psychological Bulletin, 67,* 145–52.

Sommer, R. (1969). *Personal space.* Englewood Cliffs, NJ: Prentice-Hall.

Sommer, R., & Becker, F. D. (1969). Territorial defense and the good neighbor. *Journal of Personality and Social Psychology, 11,* 85–92.

Sommer, R., & Ross, H. (1958). Social interaction on a geriatrics ward. *International Journal of Social Psychiatry, 4,* 128–33.

Steinzor, B. (1950). The spatial factor in face to face discussion groups. *Journal of Abnormal and Social Psychology, 45,* 552–55.

Stockdale, J. E. (1978). Crowding: Determinants and effects. In L. Berkowitz (Ed.), *Advances in experimental social psychology* (Vol. 11). New York: Academic Press.

Stokols, D. (1972). On the distinction between density and crowding: Some implications for future research. *Psychological Review, 79,* 275–78.

Stokols, D., Rall, M., Pinner, B., & Schopler, J. (1973). Physical, social, and personal determinants of the perception of crowding. *Environment and Behavior, 5,* 87–117.

Stratton, L. O., Tekippe, D. J., & Flick, G. L. (1973). Personal space and self concept. *Sociometry, 36,* 424–29.

Strodtbeck, F., & Hook, L. (1961). The social dimensions of a twelve man jury table. *Sociometry, 24,* 397–415.

Strube, M. J., & Werner, C. (1984). Personal space claims as a function of interpersonal threat: The mediating role of need for control. *Journal of Nonverbal Behavior, 8,* 195–209.

Sundstrom, E. (1978). Crowding as a sequential process: Review of research on the effects of population density on humans. In A. Baum & Y. M. Epstein (Eds.), *Human responses to crowding.* Hillsdale, NJ: Erlbaum.

Sundstrom, E., & Altman, I. (1976). Interpersonal relationships and personal space: Research review and theoretical model. *Human Ecology, 4,* 47–67.

Sundstrom, E., & Sundstrom, M. G. (1977). Personal space invasions: What happens when the invader asks permission? *Environmental Psychology and Nonverbal Behavior, 2,* 76–82.

Sussman, N. M., & Rosenfeld, H. M. (1982). Influence of culture, language, and sex on conversational distance. *Journal of Personality and Social Psychology, 42,* 66–74.

Taylor, R. B. (1988). *Human territorial functioning.* New York: Cambridge University Press.

Taylor, S. E., & Fiske, S. T. (1975). Point of view and perceptions of causality. *Journal of Personality and Social Psychology, 32,* 429–45.

Vine, I. (1975). Territoriality and the spatial regulation of interaction. In A. Kendon, R. M. Harris, & M. R. Key (Eds.), *Organization of behavior in face to face interaction.* Chicago: Aldine.

Ward, C. (1968). Seating arrangement and leadership emergence in small discussion groups. *Journal of Social Psychology, 74,* 83–90.

Watson, O. M. (1970). *Proxemic behavior: A cross-cultural study.* The Hague: Mouton.

Watson, O. M. (1972). Symbolic and expressive uses of space: An introduction to proxemic behavior. Module No. 20. Reading, MA: Addison-Wesley.

Watson, O. M. (1973). Proxemics. In T. A. Sebeok (Ed.), *Current trends in linguistics.* The Hague: Mouton Press.

Watson, O. M., & Graves, T. D. (1966). Quantitative research in proxemic behavior. *American Anthropologist, 68,* 971–85.

Weiss, R. (1994). Studies on crowding-aggression conflict. *Austin American-Statesman,* July 24, F5.

Williams, J. L. (1971). Personal space and its relation to extroversion-introversion. *Canadian Journal of Behavioral Science, 3,* 156–60.

Willis, F. N. (1966). Initial speaking distance as a function of the speaker's relationship. *Psychonomic Science, 5,* 221–22.

Willis, F. N., Jr., Gier, J. A., & Smith, D. E. (1979). Stepping aside: Correlates of displacement in pedestrians. *Journal of Communication, 29* (Autumn), 34–39.

Worchel, S. (1986). The influence of contextual variables on interpersonal spacing. *Journal of Nonverbal Behavior, 10,* 230–54.

Part Three

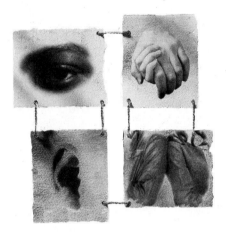

The Communicators

M uch of our nonverbal behavior is characterized by change and move-ment during a conversation. But some of the nonverbal signals we bring to each interaction remain relatively unchanging during the course of the interaction. These are the individual features of each communica-tor—skin color, hairstyle, facial features, height, weight, clothes, and so forth. These features affect how others perceive us and how they communicate with us.

CHAPTER 6

The Effects of Physical Characteristics on Human Communication

By a man's finger-nails, by his coat-sleeve, by his boots, by his trouser-knees, by the callosities of his forefinger and thumb, by his expression, by his shirt-cuffs— by each of these things a man's calling is plainly revealed. That all united should fail to enlighten the competent inquirer in any case is almost unconceivable.

—SHERLOCK HOLMES

Picture the following scene: Mr. and Mrs. American wake and prepare to start the day. Mrs. American takes off her nighttime bra and replaces it with a "slightly padded uplift" bra. After removing her chin strap, she further pulls herself together with her girdle. Then she begins to "put on her face." This may involve eye shadow, eye liner, mascara, false eyelashes, lipstick, and blush. She has removed the hair under her arms and on her legs. She places a hairpiece on her head. False fingernails, nail polish, and tinted contact lenses precede the deodorant, perfume, and endless decisions concerning clothes. Mr. American shaves the hair on his face and puts a toupee on his head. He removes his false teeth from a solution used to whiten them, gargles with a breath sweetener, selects his aftershave lotion, puts on his elevator shoes, and begins making his clothing decisions. This hypothetical example represents an extreme, but there is no doubt that people do go to great lengths, even surgery, to make themselves attractive. Surgery may reconstruct a nose; change breast size; eliminate bags, wrinkles, or birthmarks; flatten ears; "tuck" thighs or tummies; vacuum fat from the body (liposuction) or insert fat (lipofilling); or even remove the upper layer of skin if it is perceived as too blotchy or rough (a "chemical peel"). In 1992 over 350,000 Americans had cosmetic surgery and 13 percent of these were men. Why do men and women expend so much effort and invest so much money trying to improve their physical attractiveness? Does it influence our interpersonal contacts?

OUR BODY: ITS GENERAL ATTRACTIVENESS

People care a great deal about each other's appearance. Have you noticed that if a friend tells you about someone you have not met, you are likely to ask what the person looks like—you want a face to associate with the information you are receiving. Why? Novelists present intricately detailed descriptions of their characters' appearance. Publishers put photos of book authors on book jackets and in book ads. Why? Even the austere *Wall Street Journal,* which does not print news photos, includes line drawings of the faces of the main persons featured in its front-page stories. Why must readers *see* the person being discussed in an article on airline deregulation, stock fraud, or the manufacture of computer chips? Because people think they learn things from appearance. Looks are taken as indicators of a person's background, character, personality, talents, and likely future behavior.

While it is not uncommon to hear people muse about inner beauty being the only thing that really counts, research suggests that outer beauty, or physical attractiveness, plays an influential role in determining responses for a broad range of interpersonal encounters. The evidence from this culture overwhelmingly supports the notion that *initially* we respond much more favorably to those we perceive as physically attractive than to those we see as unattractive. Numerous studies reveal that physically attractive persons exceed unattractive ones on a wide range of socially desirable evaluations, such as success, personality, popularity, sociability, sexuality, persuasiveness, and often happiness (Hatfield & Sprecher, 1986; Herman, Zanna, & Higgins, 1986). Even when positive personality traits are not attributed to physically attractive people, such people still seem to have a positive appeal (Timmerman & Hewitt, 1980). On the other hand, our behavior toward unattractive people seems to be largely negative. For example, unattractive patients in hospitals are reportedly visited less, remain hospitalized longer, are judged less pleasant, and are less involved with others (Farina, Fischer, Sherman, Smith, Groh, & Mermin, 1977).

Judgments linked to a person's attractiveness begin early in life. One study found children as young as two to three months looking significantly longer at an attractive face (as judged by adults) than at an unattractive one. This tendency occurred regardless of whether the infant's mother was considered attractive or unattractive (Langlois, Roggman, Casey, Ritter, Rieser-Danner, & Jenkins, 1987). Cultural guidelines for physical attractiveness are well established by age six (Cavior & Lombardi, 1973; Dion & Berscheid, 1972). It is not surprising, then, to find peer popularity and physical attractiveness highly correlated in a number of elementary and secondary schools. The perceptions of attractiveness in a child's world are not limited to his or her peers. Teachers tend to see attractive children as more intelligent, more socially adept, higher in educational potential, and more positive in their attitudes toward school—even when the unattractive children had similar academic performance records. As children develop, they are exposed to these attitudes and evaluations made by teachers and parents. Teachers interact less (and less positively) with the so-called unattractive elementary school child. There are many occasions in a child's life when adults ask, "Who dunnit?" If there is an unattractive child available, the chances are stronger that he or she will be pointed out as the culprit. As the unattractive child grows older, he or she probably will not be discriminated against if his or her task performance is impressive; but as soon as performance declines, the less attractive person will receive more sanctions than unattractive ones. Antisocial behavior, such as throwing a brick through a window, was seen differently for attractive and unattractive children (Dion, 1972). The transgression was seen as an enduring trait of the unattractive child but only a temporary problem for the attractive one. The act was evaluated more negatively for the unattractive child, too. It does not surprise us, then, to find that juvenile delinquents were also rated as lower on attractiveness. In a study of nine- to fourteen-year-old boys, differences in perceived physical attractiveness were systematically related to social acceptance (Kleck, Richardson, & Ronald, 1974).

Although much evidence testifies to the existence of a norm that says, "what is beautiful is good," physical attractiveness also may be associated with undesirable traits, for example, vanity, egotism, snobbishness, unsympathetic attitudes toward oppressed people, and a greater likelihood to have marital problems (Dermer & Thiel, 1975). These negative attributions and the knowledge that beautiful people sometimes experience appearance-related problems suggest all is not perfect for these people. The research to date, however, still suggests it is far better to be attractive than unattractive. In fact, women who were average in looks were rated higher when viewed in a photograph in which they were posed alongside other women who were attractive. Subsequently, these average-looking women were viewed with other average-looking women and perceived as more attractive by those who had seen them with the attractive women. So it appears that women can boost their attractiveness ratings by being seen with more attractive women, and this linkage does not seem to decrease the attractive women's ratings (Geiselman, Haight, & Kimata, 1984).

While there are those who would like us to believe that "everything is beautiful in its own way," some people are beautiful in much the same way to large segments of the population. The stereotypes of American male and female beauty found on television and in popular magazines and movies seem to be influential in setting cultural norms. To some, these standards of beauty promoted through the mass media are oppressive and create an undesirable yearning for often unreasonable goals (Wolf, 1991). Nevertheless, the standards for what is beautiful permeate the culture, so it was not surprising when over four thousand judges, differing in age, sex, occupation, and geographical location, exhibited high levels of agreement concerning prettiness in young women's faces (Iliffe, 1960). Such consistency among people who judge attractiveness lies behind the important role physical attractiveness seems to play in several facets of daily life: selecting dating and marriage partners; getting and succeeding in a job; persuading others; maintaining high self-esteem; and dealing with antisocial behavior of others.

DATING AND MARRIAGE

Physical attractiveness is probably more important to dating partners than it is to friends or married couples, although perceptions of physical attractiveness still may play an important role in such relationships (Stroebe, Insko, Thompson, & Layton, 1971). Physical attraction may be most important when dating involves short-term goals and more public, rather than private, activities. Certainly there is no shortage of testimony from unmarried men and women that physical attractiveness also is a valued feature in mate selection. One early study asked students if they would marry a person who ranked low in such qualities as economic status, good looks, disposition, family religion, morals, health, education, intelligence, or age (Baber, 1939). Men most frequently rejected women who were deficient in good looks, disposition, morals, and health. Women did not seem to worry as much about marrying a man who was deficient in good looks. Based on the responses of twenty-eight thousand readers of *Psychology Today*, Table 6-1 also shows an emphasis on female attractiveness primarily by men, but generally supported by women. The percentages indicate the number of respondents who said attractiveness was "essential" or "very important" to the ideal man or woman (Tavris, 1977).

Such disproportionate concern for physical attractiveness prompted Susan Sontag (1972) to argue against the social convention that aging enhances

Table 6–1

IS ATTRACTIVENESS A CRUCIAL QUALITY IN THE IDEAL MAN OR WOMAN?

	Male Respondents	Female Respondents
In the Ideal Man	26%	29%
In the Ideal Woman	47	32

a man's appearance but progressively diminishes a woman's. She points out that women are taught from childhood to care in a "pathologically exaggerated way" about their appearance. Men, she says, need only have a clean face, but a woman's face is a "canvas upon which she paints a revised, corrected portrait of herself." "Ruggedly attractive men" is a familiar concept, but is there a similar form of attractiveness for women who do not conform to the ideal? In many quarters, masculinity means, among other things, not caring for one's looks; femininity, on the other hand, means caring a great deal. We have heard much about discrimination against women, but when men apply for jobs that traditionally have been held by women, they often feel discriminated against. Could it be that a secretary, for instance, is perceived by some male employers as a "decoration" as well as a worker?

In recent years males have become increasingly concerned about their own physical appearance. Another survey of the *Psychology Today* readership indicated a heightened concern on the part of males regarding the impact of their physical appearance. Men, in fact, thought physical appearance was more influential in women's preferences for them than women openly indicated. One group of women did, however, place a high value on male physical appearance—those women who were attractive and financially independent (Pertschuk, Trisdorfer, & Allison, 1994).

Gender seemed to make little difference in a study that asked persons to evaluate strangers of the same or opposite sex who had previously been rated as either physically attractive or unattractive (Byrne, London, & Reeves, 1968). Interpersonal attraction was greatest toward the physically attractive strangers, regardless of sex. In this phase of the study, subjects had no other information about the stranger; through subsequent study, the same researchers found that physical attractiveness was still an important determinant of attraction when subjects had additional information about the strangers, their attitudes, for example. Such findings do not seem limited to the United States. A study conducted in India found that men wanted wives who were more physically beautiful than themselves, and women wanted husbands who were equal to them in physical beauty (Singh, 1964).

We might suspect that actual dating patterns would reflect the preference for a physically attractive partner. This hypothesis was confirmed by a series of "computer dance" studies at the Universities of Texas, Illinois, and Minnesota, in which physical attractiveness superseded a host of other variables in determining liking for one's partner and desire to date in the future. For example, Walster and her colleagues randomly paired 752 college students for a freshman dance (Walster, Aronson, Abrahams, & Rottmann, 1966). A great deal of information was gathered from each student, including self-reports about popularity, religious preference, height, race, expectations for the date, self-esteem, high school academic percentile rank, scholastic aptitude score, and personality test scores. In addition, each student was rated by several judges for attractiveness. Physical attractiveness was by far the most important determinant of how much a date would be liked by his or her partner. It appears that physical attractiveness was just as important an asset for a man as for a woman, since it was a reliable predictor for both groups. Brislin and Lewis replicated this study with fifty-eight unacquainted men and women and again found a strong correlation (.89) between "desire to date again" and "physical attractiveness" (Brislin & Lewis, 1968). In addition, this study asked each person whether he or she would like to date anyone else at the dance. Of the thirteen other people named, all had previously, and independently, been rated as very attractive. In light of the many findings that seem to favor the physically attractive, it may be of some comfort to note that women who had more variable attractiveness ratings (not uniformly judged as very attractive or unattractive) were the group most satisfied with their socializing in general with both men and women (Reis, Nezlek, & Wheeler, 1980; Reis, Wheeler, Spiegel, Kernis, Nezlek, & Perri, 1982).

In many situations, everyone prefers the most attractive date possible regardless of his or her own attractiveness and regardless of the possibility of being rejected by the most attractive date. There are obvious exceptions. Some men believe that if they approach a somewhat less attractive woman who is in the company of very attractive women, the likelihood of these women being seen as an attractive choice for a new relationship increases. Some attractive persons have more dating opportunities than they desire; others, however, are almost untouched in the mainstream of dating behavior. Why? Walster and her colleagues proposed the "matching hypothesis." Since this hypothesis was presented, other studies have confirmed its validity, including a study of middle-aged, married couples. Essentially, the matching hypothesis argues that each person may be attracted to only the best-looking partners, but reality sets in when actual dates are made. You may face an unwanted rejection if you select only the best-looking person available, so the tendency is to select a person similar to yourself in physical attractiveness (Hinsz, 1989). Or, alternatively, the least good-looking people must settle for each other after all the most good-looking people choose each other (Kalick & Hamilton, 1986). In fact, one study found evidence to suggest that the greater the match on physical attractiveness for romantic couples at low levels of intimacy, the greater the chances that this couple would develop a more intimate relationship (White, 1980). Even same-sex friends have been rated similarly on physical attractiveness (Cash & Derlega, 1978). Thus, we seem to try to maximize the attractiveness of our choice while simultaneously minimizing the possibilities of rejection. If you have high self-esteem, you might seek out highly attractive partners in spite of a considerable gap between your looks and theirs (Berscheid & Walster, 1969). Self-esteem, in this case, will affect the perception of and possible reaction to rejection.

Sometimes we observe couples whose physical attractiveness seems to be "mismatched." One study suggests that evaluations of males may change dramatically if they are viewed as "married" to someone very different in general attractiveness (Bar-Tal & Saxe, 1976). Unattractive men who were seen with attractive women were judged, among other things, as making more money, as being more successful in their occupations, and as being more intelligent than attractive men with attractive partners. Judges must have reasoned that for an unattractive man to marry an attractive women, he must have to offset this imbalance by succeeding in other areas, such as making money. Unattractive women seen with attractive men, however, did not receive compensating attributions. This study raises the question of what "other resources" unattractive women are perceived to have to offset deficits in physical attractiveness.

The whole question of what is sex appeal seems relevant at this point. The answer is far from clear-cut because so many aspects vary with the situation, the time (both in a person's life and in history), and the experiences and preferences of individuals. For instance, one may make different evaluations of another's sex appeal depending on whether the person is known or a stranger. A student attending a university in a rural area may consider another person particularly sexy—only to find his or her judgment changed when returning to the city, where there is a greater variety of potential partners to choose from. Others may label sexy those with whom they feel they have some chance of success in a sexual encounter. They may react to cues suggesting readiness or openness. Still others may identify sex appeal with pleasant early love experiences (with parents and relatives) and select people with the same pleasantness, the same interests, or the same values. Possibly the most familiar reaction to the question of what constitutes sex appeal involves judgments about physical features, for example. "I'm a breast man," or "He's got muscles that ripple." Frequently, these responses to physical characteristics are defined by one's reference group or the mass media (for example, movie idols) and have relatively little to do with sexual expertise. In one study, male college students said they were interested in different characteristics in a woman depending on whether it was a purely sexual relationship or one expected to be long term. A wide range of features associated with physical attractiveness were chosen for the sexual partner, but such features played a far less important role for long-term partners. Female students wanted virtually the same things in a long-term relationship as the men (honesty, fidelity, sensitivity, warmth, personality, kindness, character, tenderness, patience, and gentleness), but, unlike the men, they also wanted more than mere physical attractiveness for the sexual relationship (Nevid, 1984).

Another effort to determine more precisely what women like in a man's body surveyed seventy women from age eighteen to thirty. The favorite male physique had a medium-wide trunk, a medium-thin lower trunk, and thin legs ("V" look). The most disliked physique had either a thin upper trunk or a wide lower trunk (pear-shaped look). Women who saw themselves as traditionally feminine and conservative in their lifestyle favored "muscle men"; more "liberated" women liked thinner, more linear bodies; big women went for big men. The best clue to a woman's favorite male physique, however, was the type of physique belonging to the man who was "most important to her" at the time of the survey (Beck, Ward-Hull, & McLear, 1976; Lavrakas, 1975; Pertschuk, Trisdorfer, & Allison, 1994; Wiggins & Wiggins, 1969). Perceptions of ideal physical characteristics change over time. Beauty is in the era of the beholder as well as the eye.

On the Job

Several studies suggest that physical attractiveness may be an advantage in obtaining a job, obtaining a more prestigious job, and being hired at a higher salary (Cash, Gillen, & Burns, 1977; Dipboye, Arvey, & Terpstra, 1977; Hamermesh & Biddle, 1994). Unless the job is deemed inappropriate or irrelevant to the applicant's level of attractiveness, the more attractive applicants are more likely to get the job, assuming that all other qualifications are equal. Sometimes attractiveness will provide an edge even when the less attractive competitor is more qualified for the position. Once a position has been obtained, less attractive workers may be discriminated against on performance appraisals unless they maintain a consistently high level of productivity.

Attractiveness is not always beneficial in the workplace, though. Attractiveness seems to be a factor in the likely advancement of women, but not so much for men. Women who are neither very attractive nor very unattractive are the most likely to succeed in most corporate environments today. Extreme attractiveness can be a barrier to rapid and high-level achievement. It may be that success at higher levels is too often associated with masculine skills, and an attractive woman is presumed to be too feminine for such positions (Heilman & Saruwatari, 1979). It also may be that it is hard for an attractive woman to be viewed in a task, rather than social, role, thereby making supervision and management of men more difficult. In such cases, however, it may be possible for women to dress so that their physical beauty is not the immediate focus of attention.

Persuading Others

Getting others to agree with you or do something for you is often based on the extent to which you can demonstrate your knowledge or expertise as well as your ability to marshal effective supporting arguments (Maddux & Rogers, 1980). But, as several research projects show, being physically attractive also may help (Chaiken, 1986). This is especially true when the persuader seeks compliance on relatively low ego-involving topics; when the persuasion involves a relatively short, perhaps one-time, request; and when the effects of initial impressions are crucial to achieving influence. Although most of this research has been done with college students, the association of persuasive effectiveness with physical attractiveness has been documented in the behavior of ten- and eleven-year-old children (Dion & Stein, 1978).

The following research on persuasiveness focused on the attractiveness of female communicators (Mills & Aronson, 1965). Actually, one woman was made up to look different under two conditions. In the unattractive condition, she was rated "repulsive" by independent observers; she wore loose-fitting clothing, her hair was messy, makeup was conspicuously absent, a trace of a mustache was etched on her upper lip, and her complexion was oily and "unwholesome looking." The experimenter suggested to a group of students that they would complete some questionnaires more quickly if a volunteer would read the questions aloud and indicate what they meant. The "volunteer" was either the attractive or unattractive woman. The attractive woman, especially when she stated her desire to influence the audience, was far more effective in modifying the opinions of college students toward issues dealing with higher education. Other studies also support the influence of attractiveness in persuasive situations (Horai, Naccari, & Faloultah, 1974; Widgery, 1974).

While the preceding research focused primarily on female communicators, attractiveness also seems to help male persuaders. Independent assessments of their verbal performance as well as their ability to obtain signatures on a campus petition showed attractive men and women outperforming those who were rated as unattractive. Is the persuasiveness of attractive communicators due solely to their looks, or do they actually have persuasive skills? An examination of previous tests showed attractive students to have higher grades, SAT scores, self-concepts, and communication skills (Chaiken, 1979). In summary, then, physically attractive persuaders (as compared with unattractive ones) initially elicit higher credibility and expectations for a skilled performance. There is some evidence that physically attractive people seem to have these skills. The advantages derived from one's physical attractiveness is probably strongest during the initial stages of a persuasive effort.

SELF-ESTEEM

Does physical attractiveness increase self-esteem? The answer seems to be yes, particularly for women. Women who perceive themselves as physically attractive seem also to perceive greater happiness, self-esteem, and less neuroticism than those who perceive themselves as unattractive (Mathes & Kahn, 1975). As noted earlier, physical attractiveness is playing a more important role in a man's life today, so men, too, probably think better of themselves when they feel more attractive. Women aged eighteen to sixty who used cosmetics to improve their appearance also reported psychological benefits from doing so. Greater attractiveness for those between the ages of forty and sixty was perceived as most beneficial for masking the aging process and improving one's physical and mental health (Graham & Jouhar, 1982). Training in the use of cosmetics for elderly women has reportedly had a positive effect on self-image, too.

Since physical attractiveness seems to have its greatest impact during the initial stages of a relationship, it is reasonable to assume that attractive men and women whose occupational demands or lifestyles necessitate meeting people in short-term encounters may obtain more self-esteem from their physical attractiveness than an equally attractive person who has a few, long-term relationships. Although the self-esteem derived from appearance is important, it is only one factor that makes people feel good about themselves. Sometimes looking good is very important; sometimes it isn't. But the knowledge that we can achieve attractiveness when we want to should make us feel much better than the person who isn't sure he or she can. Hatfield and Sprecher (1986) point out that there are people who are more likely to give us a boost in self-esteem by positively evaluating our looks, for example, people who have a great deal of self-esteem themselves, people who are sexually aroused, people who look like us, people who know us, and people who are not likely to compare our looks with media idols.

ANTISOCIAL BEHAVIOR

What happens when attractive and unattractive people are charged with committing a criminal act? Are judges and juries influenced by a person's looks? As expected, a number of studies show that attractive defendants are less likely to be judged guilty and, if convicted, more likely to receive a shorter sentence (Downs & Lyons, 1991; Efran, 1974; Kulka & Kessler, 1978; Weiten, 1980). The evidence for attractive defendants receiving lighter sentences is stronger than the evidence linking attractiveness to guilt or innocence. Although much of the research is based on the results of simulated juries and cases, Stewart (1980) had the attractiveness of sixty-seven actual defendants rated. The less attractive defendants were charged with more serious crimes and given longer sentences, but attractiveness did not significantly affect judgments of conviction or acquittal.

Obviously, a defendant's attractiveness is rarely assessed in isolation in the courtroom, and other factors interact with attractiveness, for example, the extent to which the defendant expresses repentance, the degree of commitment jurors have toward impartiality, the extent to which jurors discuss the case, the perceived similarity of jurors and defendant, defendant verbalizations, and the nature of the crime being examined. For some crimes, attractiveness may be a liability for the defendant, as when it is used to commit a crime such as a swindle. For the crime of rape, the relative attractiveness of the victim and the defendant may influence the jury. Attractive rape victims may be perceived as more likely to have provoked the attack (Jacobson, 1981; Seligman, Brickman & Koulack, 1977).

Once a person has been convicted and sent to prison, some feel that antisocial behavior can sometimes be reduced by radical changes in appearance. It is reported, for instance, that a nineteen-year-old woman with a face "so deformed that little kids ran away crying" threw a brick through a bank window and waited for police to arrest her. "I was willing to die to get a better face," she said. The judge ordered extensive plastic surgery ("Deformed Brick-Thrower," 1975). The same reasoning launched a massive plastic-surgery program for reshaping noses, removing tattoos, tightening sagging skin, disguising ugly scars, reducing extensive ear protrusion, and removing other deformities of convicts at the Kentucky State Reformatory (Watson, 1975). Authorities at this institution reasoned that everyday social ridicule and potential discrimination in hiring may lead to a feeling of rejection and frustration that can manifest itself in antisocial behavior. Similar programs by doctors at the University of Virginia and Johns Hopkins have not shown significant changes in postinstitutionalized behavior for convicts with changes in their appearance. Obviously, appearance is only one factor that might contribute to antisocial behavior. For some, however, it may be the most important one.

Throughout this section we have pointed out some important qualifications to the dictum that "what is beautiful is good." Here are three other observations that should be noted (Knapp, 1985).

1. INTERACTION EFFECTS   Methodological issues may provide some comfort to those who perceive themselves as unattractive. Although it is not true of all studies of physical attractiveness, most use frontal facial photographs that, prior to the study, are judged by a panel of "experts" to fall into the "beautiful" or "ugly" category. Hence, in most cases, we are not reporting results from living, moving, talking human beings in a particular environment, nor are we generally dealing with subtle differences in physical attractiveness that lie between the extremes of beautiful and ugly.

When future studies begin to examine actual interactive situations, we may learn how talking and other behaviors affect perceptions of attractiveness. We know that talking can change our judgments. The normally strong effects of attraction to attitudinally similar others have been completely changed by letting the research subjects talk to each other for five minutes. Attitudinally dissimilar interactants were more attracted to their partners than attitudinally dissimilar *non*interactants (Sunnafrank & Miller, 1981). The particular attitudes involved, the strength with which they are held, and their salience to the interaction are all important factors in determining the influence of interaction on attitudes (Cappella & Palmer, 1990). We know very little about the appearance perceptions of a socially skilled, but homely, person; we know very little about what constitutes communicative beauty. We do know that as we talk to others, we become a part of the object we are evaluating. This involvement has the potential to change the way we see the appearance of our partner.

2. EFFECT OF OTHER FACTORS   Judgments of one's appearance in everyday life interact with other factors. Our judgments of appearance may be relative to the context in which it is judged; for example, we may perceive a popular singer on stage or television as sexy, but the same person in our living room may seem much less glamorous. Men who rated the attractiveness of middle-aged women tended to give lower ratings when they were in the presence of other men and their rating was made public than they did when in the company of women or when their ratings were kept private (Berman, O'Nan, & Floyd, 1981). Sometimes judgments are affected by what the other person says as much as by their physical appearance. This may be especially true for people we have known longer. Attraction ratings also may vary as a function of the rater's gender. Often the highest evaluations of attractiveness come from the opposite sex. In short, many factors provide a basis for any person's being perceived as attractive or unattractive by another, even though that person may not be rated the same way when all other situational factors are removed.

3. CHANGING STANDARDS OVER TIME   It should also be noted that judgments of attractiveness may change over time or may be altered at any point in time. While ratings of facial attractiveness (not body) appear to be fairly stable from about ages sixteen to fifty, the overall ratings of attractiveness for both men and women tend to decline as one reaches middle and old age. The decline is more severe for women.

In one study of the effects of time on attractiveness, the high school pictures of one thousand three hundred males and females were rated for attractiveness. The lives of these people were examined fifteen years later. Attractive females in high school had husbands with more education and higher salaries, but their own occupational status and income were not significantly different from their less attractive counterparts. The least-attractive males in high school had more prestigious occupations and more education, and they married women with more education than the men who were judged to be attractive in high school. Income levels did not differ. The authors speculate that the social ostracism of the less attractive men in high school may have turned their attention to educational achievements that paid off later in life (Udry & Eckland, 1982). Aging also may reveal changes associated with self-esteem and attractiveness. Middle-aged women who had been identified as attractive college students seemed to be less happy, less satisfied with their lives, and less well adjusted than their plainer counterparts (Berscheid & Walster, 1974, pp. 200–201).

Because appearance can be changed, people who are judged unattractive are not necessarily doomed to a long list of pitfalls or problems. Changes in makeup and hairstyle have been shown to increase ratings of general attractiveness as well as ratings of desired personality characteristics (Graham & Jouhar, 1981). Cosmetics have even been used to aid recovery and adjustment of people recuperating from illnesses.

Now that we have examined the global concept of attractiveness, we can ask: What *specific* aspects of another's appearance do we respond to? Does it make any difference how we perceive our own body and appearance? The answers to these questions are the focus of the remainder of this chapter.

OUR BODY: ITS SPECIFIC FEATURES

THE FACE

Even though the face has long been the specific body feature most commonly examined in studies of physical attractiveness, a basic question remained unanswered. What is facial beauty? Most researchers believed this question could not be answered by measuring facial features and depended instead on people's judgments of general attractiveness. The research by Langlois and Roggman (1990), however, not only pointed the way toward a measure of facial attractiveness but also made a surprising discovery. Contrary to popular belief, Langlois and Roggman found that physically attractive faces approximate the mathematical average of all faces in a particular population. For example, this research would predict that the most attractive man in a school is one who comes closest to the school average for male facial features.

Langlois and Roggman took photographs of ninety-six college males and ninety-six college females. These photos were scanned by a video lens connected to a computer that converted each picture into a matrix of tiny digital units with numerical values. The authors divided the male and female faces into three subsets of thirty-two faces each. From each subset, the computer randomly chose two faces and mathematically averaged their digitized values. It then transformed this information into a composite face of the two individuals. Composite faces then were generated for four, eight, sixteen, and thirty-two members of each set. Ratings by students showed that composite faces were more attractive than virtually any of the individual faces, and the most attractive faces were composites of sixteen and thirty-two faces. The authors also acknowledge that in some cases people are perceived as attractive by large numbers of people even though their features obviously are not the population average. In the case of the singer and film actress Cher, for example, factors other than facial features account for the perceptions of her attractiveness.

Another promising approach for identifying facial attractiveness is based on the principle of symmetry (Grammer & Thornhill, 1994). Photographs of male and female students are precisely measured at numerous points to determine whether features on one side of the face are equidistant to a midpoint as the same features on the other side of the face. For example, to what extent does the midpoint between the corners of your mouth match up to the midpoint between the corners of your eyes? On perfectly symmetrical faces, all the midpoints meet and roughly form a vertical line. Horizontal symmetry is also calculated. The most symmetrical faces were also those chosen as the most attractive. The researchers believe these preliminary results are consistent with findings that show symmetry is also a powerful attractant for other animal and insect species.

Because the face is so central in judgments of attractiveness, it is no surprise that it is the source of stereotyping. People long have believed that the face reveals important information about character and personality. Aristotle described features he believed were associated with strength versus weakness, genius versus stupidity, and so forth. The most famous promoter of the idea that facial features indicate personality was J. C. Lavater, the Swiss physiognomist born in 1741. Lavater's book (1783) promoting his so-called science was extremely popular, going through over a dozen editions in many languages. Although today we look skeptically on the idea that one's brows, nose, or shape of mouth reveal whether one is mean, smart, or benevolent, Lavater was a sincere believer who saw his work as scientific.

Much as a behavioral scientist would today, Lavater advocated developing one's powers of observation by constantly studying people in one's environment. He took pride that his system was based on objective reality. Just as we judge physical nature by its appearance (we look at the sky, for example, for clues to the weather), so should we look at the exterior of the body for clues to the temperament of the person. Lavater believed facial features were more reliable than facial expressions because people could dissimulate with their expressions but not with their physical features. (Lavater felt that women were particularly hard to judge from expressions because they could assume expressions they thought would please men!) Lavater tried to reduce his observations "to a rule," that is, to systematic principles, which would give them more credibility than mere idiosyncratic opinions of one person.

Lavater's book is filled with drawings of faces with such descriptions as brutal, unheroic, calm, fiendlike, passionate, and enterprising. He believed that those who looked somewhat like an animal would have traits associated with that animal—clever if the resemblance were to a monkey, dull if the resemblance were to an ox, and so on.

We should credit Lavater with his attempts to be scientific. However, Lavater confused facial *stereotypes* with *actual* associations between features and behavior; he chronicled what he (and others, no doubt) believed were these associations, without recognizing the need to test the validity of this initial premise. Apparently his many readers, as well as readers of similar books published in the next century, also failed to make this distinction. Even in the 1970s, such books were still being written: *Face Reading* by Timothy T. Mar was published by a major U. S. paperback company in 1974. Among the innumerable claims in this book are:

- In a round face, the jawbones suggest affection, generosity, and self-control.
- A dark mole just above the eyebrows is an obstacle to official promotion and a sign of repeated career changing.
- Three vertical lines below the eyes predict an unhappy marriage ending in divorce or death.
- Full, firm, large ears indicate nobility and prosperity while ears with the middle overgrown signify an inability to save money.

We do not report these claims simply to amuse our readers. Students of human behavior find two serious lessons here. First, people's willingness over the centuries to believe in physiognomy tells us something important about human nature: People latch onto such bogus principles because they help to reduce uncertainty in their own minds and provide a sense of control and understanding in daily life. And, once the stereotype is planted in the mind, every confirmation is remembered and serves to strengthen the stereotype ("That man who held me up had thick, bushy eyebrows just like a criminal!"), while every disconfirmation (the handsome serial killer Ted Bundy) is conveniently forgotten.

The other lesson is that, in spite of their falseness, facial stereotypes surely influence the behavior of the stereotype holder. If people believe a drooping nose is a sign of treachery (another gem from Mar), then an unfortunate neighbor with such a nose is at a considerable disadvantage in interpersonal relations. Moreover, the way people are treated can bring about self-fulfilling prophecies, so that facial stereotypes can, conceivably, have potent effects on the subsequent behavior of the target.

Behavioral scientists have long been interested in facial stereotypes and their possible effects on behavior (Keating, Mazur, & Segall, 1977; Keating, Mazur, & Segall, 1981; Secord, Dukes, & Bevan, 1954). Laser and Mathie (1982), for example, engaged an artist to prepare nine charcoal drawings of a male face, varying thickness of the eyebrows and lips and the shape of the face. Subjects rated these faces with adjectives. The features had marked effects on these ratings: The face with thick eyebrows was seen as less warm, more angry, more stern, less cheerful, and less at ease than those with thin or normal brows; thicker lips connoted warmth and less tension than thinner lips; and narrow faces were seen as more tense and suspicious than the others.

McArthur and her colleagues have gone beyond simply describing facial stereotypes to develop a theory for why they exist. Their work focuses on facial features associated with age and the kinds of interpretations people make of faces that have more or less "youthful" features; in particular, they focus on the adult with "baby-faced" features such as large forehead, short chin, and big eyes. McArthur and Baron (1983) proposed that people correctly differentiate traits that accompany younger age but then incorrectly ascribe these traits (overgeneralize them) to people with younger-looking faces, even though they are not necessarily young. McArthur and her colleagues found, in support of this, that people rated babyish adult faces as weaker, more submissive, and more intellectually naive than mature-looking faces (Berry & McArthur, 1986).

These investigators also simulated a courtroom trial in which a defendant was charged with an offense that was marked either by negligence or by deliberate deception; the defendant's appearance was manipulated to be either baby faced or mature faced. Subjects, acting as jurors, more often convicted the baby-faced man for crimes of negligence and the mature-faced man for intentional crimes. This result was predicted based on the earlier finding that adults with babyish features were perceived as more naive and more honest.

Facial babyishness has also been found to affect judgments of attractiveness (Berry, 1991). Facially attractive people are rated higher on characteristics such as honesty, warmth, and sincerity when facial babyishness is high—and lower on those same traits when facial babyishness is low. Since all the faces were perceived as attractive, this suggests the possibility that there are different types of facial attractiveness.

In sum, there is no doubt that the way one's face is structured and contoured creates strong impressions on others. Facial endowment may harm or benefit a person, depending on the stereotypes associated with the features. Future research may be able to tell us to what extent actual personality and ways of expressing oneself will override initial impressions based on facial stereotype; we suspect such initial impressions are easily overturned by behavioral evidence.

BODY SHAPE

To add a personal dimension to some of the theory and research in this section, a short Self-Description Test follows. By taking this test, you can gather some data on yourself, which can be compared with that of others who have taken it.

> **Instructions:** Fill in each blank with a word from the suggested list following each statement. For each blank, three in each statement, you may select any word from the list of twelve immediately below. An exact word to fit you may not be in the list, but select the words that seem to fit *most closely* the way you are.

1. I feel most of the time _____, _____, and _____.

calm	relaxed	complacent
anxious	confident	reticent
cheerful	tense	energetic
contented	impetuous	self-conscious

2. When I study or work, I seem to be _____, _____, and _____.

efficient	sluggish	precise
enthusiastic	competitive	determined
reflective	leisurely	thoughtful
placid	meticulous	cooperative

3. Socially, I am _____, _____, and _____.

outgoing	considerate	argumentative
affable	awkward	shy
tolerant	affected	talkative
gentle-tempered	soft-tempered	hot-tempered

4. I am rather _____, _____, and _____.

active	forgiving	sympathetic
warm	courageous	serious
domineering	suspicious	soft-hearted
introspective	cool	enterprising

5. Other people consider me rather _____, _____, and _____.

generous	optimistic	sensitive
adventurous	affectionate	kind
withdrawn	reckless	cautious
dominant	detached	dependent

6. Underline *one* word out of the three in each of the following lines which most closely describes the way you are:

   (a) assertive, relaxed, tense

   (b) hot-tempered, cool, warm

   (c) withdrawn, sociable, active

   (d) confident, tactful, kind

   (e) dependent, dominant, detached

   (f) enterprising, affable, anxious

This test has been given to numerous individuals in studies on the relationship between certain personality and temperament characteristics and certain body types or builds (Cortes & Gatti, 1965). Generally, these studies are concerned with a person's physical similarity to three extreme varieties of human physique, shown in Figure 6-1.

Because most people do not fit these extremes exactly, a system has been developed for specifying body type based on the assumption that they may have some features of all three types. Sheldon's work helps explain this system (Sheldon, 1940; Sheldon, 1954). A person's physical characteristics are rated on a scale from 1 to 7, with 7 representing the highest correspondence with one of the three body types. The first number refers to the degree of endomorphy, the second to the degree of mesomorphy, and the third to the degree of ectomorphy. A grossly fat person would be 7/1/1; a broad shouldered, athletic person would be 1/7/1; and a very skinny person would be a 1/1/7. Reportedly, Jackie Gleason was roughly 6/4/1, Muhammad Ali 2/7/1 (in his prime), and Abraham Lincoln 1/5/6. Although there has been scientific criticism of Sheldon's work, it has been the basis for many studies investigating the same general question. In spite of critical errors in Sheldon's methodology, many later studies using more precise measurements and research designs have confirmed some of his early conclusions.

Now look at the test you took earlier. When this test was used to measure temperament, it showed a high correspondence with measures of physique. On the basis of this work, we would expect to have a fairly good idea of your body build by the answers you gave on the Self-Description Test. To calculate your score on the test, simply add the number of adjectives you chose from each of the endomorph, mesomorph, and ectomorph categories listed in Table 6-2.

If you chose six adjectives from the endomorph list, twelve from the mesomorph, and three from the ectomorph, your temperament score would be 6/12/3. If we assume a high correlation with body features, we would assume you are primarily mesomorphic with a leaning toward endomorphism. The first author of this text was 5/11/5 in 1978, 8/10/3 in 1982, 8/9/4 in 1988, and 10/7/4 in 1996. This test and the body-personality research allow us to make some predictions based on probabilities, but, of course, there may be individual exceptions. Several reports suggest that the relationship between body build and temperament also holds for young children (Parnell, 1958; Walker, 1963). For example, thin ectomorph boys and girls were more anxious, more conscientious, and more meticulous than children with other body builds.

Figure 6–1

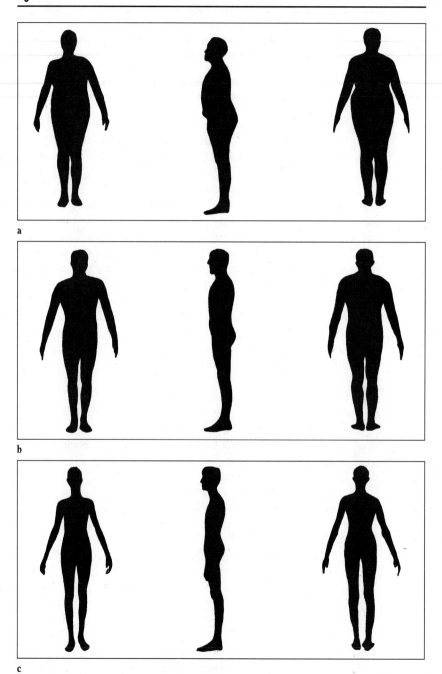

a

b

c

(a) The endomorph: soft, round, fat. (b) The mesomorph: bony, muscular, athletic.
(c) The ectomorph: tall, thin, fragile.

Table 6–2

THREE PHYSIQUE CATEGORIES AND TEMPERAMENT STEREOTYPES

Endomorphic	Mesomorphic	Ectomorphic
dependent	dominant	detached
calm	cheerful	tense
relaxed	confident	anxious
complacent	energetic	reticent
contented	impetuous	self-conscious
sluggish	efficient	meticulous
placid	enthusiastic	reflective
leisurely	competitive	precise
cooperative	determined	thoughtful
affable	outgoing	considerate
tolerant	argumentative	shy
affected	talkative	awkward
warm	active	cool
forgiving	domineering	suspicious
sympathetic	courageous	introspective
soft-hearted	enterprising	serious
generous	adventurous	cautious
affectionate	reckless	tactful
kind	assertive	sensitive
sociable	optimistic	withdrawn
soft-tempered	hot-tempered	gentle-tempered

We should not assume from this work that the body causes temperament traits. The high correspondence between certain temperament traits and body builds may be due to life experiences, environmental factors, self-concept, and a host of other variables, including other people's expectations. If there are clearly defined and generally accepted physique-temperament stereotypes, we can reason that they will have much to do with the way people are perceived and responded to by others and with the personality traits expected of people by others. Wells and Siegel (1961) uncovered some data supporting the existence of such stereotypes. One hundred twenty adult subjects were shown silhouette drawings of the endomorph, ectomorph, and mesomorph and asked to rate them on a set of twenty-four bipolar adjective scales such as lazy/energetic, fat/thin, intelligent/unintelligent, dependent/self-reliant, and so forth. The investigators deliberately chose people who had not attended college, assuming these people would not be contaminated with information from previous studies that might structure their answers. Their results show that

1. The *endomorph* was rated fatter, older, shorter (silhouettes were the same height), more old-fashioned, less strong physically, less

good-looking, more talkative, more warmhearted and sympathetic, more good-natured and agreeable, more dependent on others, and more trusting of others.

2. The *mesomorph* was rated stronger, more masculine, better-looking, more adventurous, younger, taller, more mature in behavior, and more self-reliant.

3. The *ectomorph* was rated thinner, younger, more ambitious, taller, more suspicious of others, more tense and nervous, less masculine, more stubborn and inclined to be difficult, more pessimistic, and quieter.

Another study, using a written description of body extremes, asked personality questions about the written descriptions and found similar results (Strongman & Hart, 1968).

We have been trained for so long to believe that stereotypes are harmful distortions of the truth that we often fail to consider another plausible explanation—that a particular stereotype may be the result of the distillation of ages of social experience. In other words, a stereotype may be more accurate than we wish to admit; there may be some reason for the stereotype other than prejudicial whims. Clearly, the evidence shows we do associate certain personality and temperament traits with certain body builds. These expectations may or may not be accurate, but they do exist; they are a part of the psychological mortar in interpersonal communication. We must recognize these stereotypes as potential stimuli for communication responses so we can deal with them effectively.

As early as kindergarten, children seem to prefer the more muscular mesomorphs to either the thin or fat body types (Johnson & Staffieri, 1971; Lerner & Gellert, 1969; Lerner & Korn, 1972; Lerner & Schroeder, 1971; Staffieri, 1972). Youngsters seem to have a particular aversion to the fat physiques. Older children who select descriptive adjectives for these body types tend to see the mesomorph as "all things good," with ectomorphs and endomorphs attracting a host of unfavorable descriptors. In fact, ten- and eleven-year-olds seemed to consider body build as a more important characteristic in judging physical appearance than such things as deformities, disfigurements, and handicaps (Richardson et al., 1961). The psychological aversion to chubby figures results in children maintaining a greater physical distance from them (Lerner, Karabenick, & Meisels, 1975; Lerner, Venning, & Knapp, 1975). In turn, we find that chubby children often tend to have a negative perception of their own bodies, which may later generalize to a negative self-image (Walker, 1963). Even the elderly rate the endomorph as a less desirable communication partner—both socially as well as for working on tasks together (Portney, 1993).

Negative reactions to overweight individuals are frequently reported. Such individuals report being discriminated against when seeking to obtain life insurance, adopt children, get jobs, and gain entrance to college (Channing & Mayer, 1966). While only a small amount of empirical evidence supports the bases of these claims (DeJong & Kleck, 1986), it is safe to say that being excessively overweight in our culture is often a handicap. Researchers who followed ten thousand people between the ages of sixteen and twenty-four for seven years found obesity meant you were less likely to marry, more likely to have a lower income, and more likely to receive less schooling (Gortmaker et al., 1993). People often believe that the inability to lose weight reflects a character flaw. During the past three decades, the cultural ideal for U. S. women has tended toward thinness. As a result, women have tended to be more conscious of their weight than have men. In recent years, though, there seem to be more media portrayals (and a generally greater acceptance) of female bodies that are not extremely slender. And men are increasingly concerned about their weight. Another trend in recent years has been toward the development of healthy bodies—"eating right," exercising, and developing muscle strength. These body standards apply to both men and women and will probably constitute some of the features comprising the next cultural standard for the ideal body shape. But whatever the desired body shape, it will inevitably interact with other body features. This means, for example, that the perfect body may not be nearly as attractive without a pleasing smile.

HEIGHT

Another dimension of body build that may influence interpersonal responses in this culture is height. People seem to know height can be important to their social and work lives. Pediatricians report that parents are often concerned that their child is not as tall as he or she should be at a certain age. Children themselves are asked to focus on height when their teachers tell them to line up by height. Adults seem to overestimate their height. Advertisements for romantic partners often give height as one critical piece of information (Cameron, Oskamp, & Sparks, 1978; Harrison & Saeed, 1977). In some areas of the country, police officers and firefighters are required to meet minimum height requirements. Some applicants, according to newspaper accounts, have actually bludgeoned their heads in the hope that the swelling would make up the difference between their height and the required height!

Height derives its importance from a widespread belief that major deviations from median heights (about five feet, four inches for women and five feet, nine inches for men) will incur negative judgments from others. While it is possible to be "too tall," most negative judgments are thought to be associated with shortness. As Stabler and his colleagues (1980) noted: "There is a pervasive social attitude which associates tallness with positive characteristics and assigns negative attributes to shortness." Is there any truth to this? The anecdotal evidence is far more plentiful than the empirical research. In addition, most of the research focuses on men only (Roberts & Herman, 1986). Still, it seems we tend to favor tallness in this culture. The research examines three dominant perceptions associated with height: status, attractiveness, and competence.

HEIGHT AND STATUS   Height has long been a metaphor for power and prestige. The taller of the two U. S. presidential candidates has usually won since 1900, with five-foot, nine-inch Jimmy Carter a notable exception in 1976. When Carter debated President Ford, his campaign advisors did not want him to be seen standing next to the six-foot, one-inch president. Consequently, they asked that the debates be conducted from a sitting position. Ford's advisors refused. The compromise involved placing the lecterns far apart. Further testimony to the stigma associated with shorter people and power is that behavior labeled "competitive" for a taller man is labeled a "Napoleonic complex" for a shorter one. If status and power inhere in taller people, are they also more persuasive? One study indicates they are not (Baker & Redding, 1962). Photographs were taken of the same person (a male) from two different angles: one designed to make him look short, one to make him look tall. These pictures, plus a tape-recorded persuasive speech, were the stimuli for various student groups. Attitude measures indicated there was no statistically significant difference between the "tall" and "short" speakers.

It is more likely that tallness interacts with other factors, such as general body size, girth, and facial features. In your own experience, you probably can recall some tall individuals who seemed almost frighteningly "overpowering," while others of the same height did not have this quality. Science has not yet established a clear-cut relationship between a person's actual height and his or her social status. Nevertheless, the connection is often made when, without any other information, people are asked to make a judgment about height and status. We know of a woman who earned her doctoral degree under a famous psychologist and believed, while she was his student, that he was a tall, imposing figure. Later, she was genuinely surprised to realize that he was actually a short man! He had merely *seemed* tall to her.

HEIGHT AND ATTRACTIVENESS   Taller men are frequently perceived as more attractive than shorter men. The ideal male lover is not described as "short, dark, and handsome." Male romantic leads in movies are usually either tall or made to look tall by photographic techniques. Numerous sources attest to the important role of height in perceptions of attractiveness, but obviously we do not make judgments of another's attractiveness based on height alone. Therefore, we can conclude that height is one important feature involved in judgments of attractiveness, but we cannot say that tallness is always associated with the highest judgments of attractiveness. We do know that moviegoers are often taken aback when they learn that a male icon of physical attractiveness is much shorter than he is portrayed in his movies.

HEIGHT AND COMPETENCE   Several reports indicate tall males are perceived as more competent on the job and rewarded with higher salaries. Although actual performance records showed few differences between shorter and taller policemen, their supervisors felt shorter policemen were more aggressive law enforcers and more likely to be a source of discontent in the police department (Lester & Sheehan, 1980). Another study indicated that men who were selected to advance in corporate training programs were significantly taller than average (Farb, 1978). Further evidence of discrimination against the short man comes from a study of 140 sales recruiters who were asked to choose between two men just by reading their applications for employment. The applications were exactly the same except that one listed a height of six feet, one inch and the other five feet, five inches. Only 1 percent favored the short man (Kurtz, 1969).

BODY IMAGE

So far we have discussed our perceptions of others. An equally important dimension of interpersonal communication is what we think of ourselves— our self-image. The self-image is the root system from which our overt communication behavior grows. Our overt communication behavior is an extension of the accumulated experiences that have made up our understanding of self. In short, what you are, or think you are, organizes what you say and do. An important part of your self-image is body image, perhaps the first part formed in very young children (Gorman, 1969; Shontz, 1969;). Jourard and Secord (1955) found adult males most satisfied with their bodies when they were somewhat larger than normal; females were most satisfied when their bodies were smaller than normal but when their busts were larger than average. In an effort to test the belief that larger bust sizes were more desirable to others, photographs were taken of three women who artificially altered their bust size. The smallest (about thirty-four inches) received the highest ratings on competence, ambition, intelligence, morality, and modesty (Kleinke & Staneski, 1980). Sex researchers have frequently noted emotional problems in males stemming from a perceived incongruence between their genital size and the supposed masculine ideal perpetuated by our literary and folklore heritage. More than 71 percent of the women in a 1994 survey agreed or strongly agreed that "men seem too concerned with the size and shape of their genitals" (Pertschuk, Trisdorfer, & Allison, 1994). As we develop, we learn the cultural ideal of what the body should be like. This results in varying degrees of satisfaction with the body, particularly during adolescence.

A national survey of several thousand adults indicated that between 1972 and 1986 both men and women's dissatisfaction with their bodies rose sharply. Weight was a major factor contributing to dissatisfaction for both men and women (Cash, Winstead, & Janda, 1986). A number of studies show, however, that we are notoriously inaccurate in our perceptions of our own body size and weight. One study indicates that the presentation of ideal body images in television advertising and programming has a significant effect in altering the perceptions of young women's body shape and size (Meyers & Biocca, 1992). We not only misjudge our own body size and weight, but we also seem to misjudge the body type that is most appealing to the opposite sex. Women seem to think men prefer a thinner person than men actually report; men seem to think women want a heavier man than women actually report. Men thought that having an attractive face and body build was more important to women than women said it was (Fallon & Rozin, 1985; Pertschuk, Trisdorfer, & Allison, 1994).

Body Color

In many respects, skin color has been the most potent body stimulus for determining interpersonal responses in this culture. There is no need to review the abuses heaped upon black persons in America on the basis of skin color alone. The words of a white man who changed his skin pigmentation and experienced the dramatic and unforgettable life of a black man in America will be sufficient reminder:

> When all the talk, all the propaganda has been cut away, the criterion is nothing but the color of skin. My experience proved that. They judged me by no other quality. My skin was dark. That was sufficient reason for them to deny me those rights and freedoms without which life loses its significance and becomes a matter of little more than animal survival.
>
> I searched for some other answer and found none. I had spent a day without food and water and for no other reason than that my skin was black. I was sitting on a tub in the swamp for no other reason. (Griffin, 1960, pp. 121–22)

As U.S. demographics change, the variety of skin colors manifested by the people in our work and leisure activities will continue to increase, and sharp distinctions among peoples' skin colors will become increasingly difficult to make. Still, there will always be those who want a simple method of classifying their social world, and skin color is easily observed. We can only hope that the number of people who believe skin color is an accurate gauge for identifying friend and foe will continue to decrease.

There are, of course, other judgments made about the less permanent colors that show up on bodies. A pale color, for example, may indicate a person is ill. A rosy flush may indicate embarrassment. A red neck can appear with anger.

Body Smell

While it is obvious that vision and hearing are the most important sensors for social situations in Western societies, the sense of smell also may influence responses. The scientific study of the human olfactory system is in its infancy, but we know other animals obtain a great deal of information from their sense of smell: the presence of an enemy, territorial markers, finding members of the same species or herd, sexual stimulation, and emotional states. Dogs are well known for their ability to sense fear, hate, or friendship in human beings and to track them by only the scent from clothing. The difficulty dogs seem to have in distinguishing between the smells of identical twins prompted Davis (1971) to suggest that we each have an "olfactory signature."

Americans do not seem to consciously rely on their sense of smell for much interpersonal information unless perspiration odor, breath, or some other smell is unusually strong or inappropriate to the situation. It is believed that all of us could enhance our olfactory sensitivity if we learned the words needed to differentiate among various odors. We have a rather limited vocabulary for discussing subtle differences in smells, which, in turn, may hinder their identification. If it is true that we tend to neglect our olfactory skills, it seems ironic that we spend so much time and money on artificial scents. Each year American men and women spend millions of dollars on deodorant containers and soaps, mouthwashes, breath mints, perfumes, aftershave lotions, and other products used to add to or cover up natural body scents. Publicly, the so-called natural scent seems to have a low priority in our cultural development, but we are not at all reluctant to buy a commercial product that will purportedly make us smell "*natural* and sexy."

Artificial scents are not always designed for pleasant reactions. During World War II, scientists developed a noxious-smelling compound they called "Who Me?" This product was put into collapsible plastic tubes and distributed to Chinese children in cities occupied by the Japanese. The children squirted "Who Me?" onto the trouser seats of Japanese officers. The foul-smelling result was more than just a temporary irritant—it was nearly impossible to wash out (Russell, 1981).

What is the role of human odors in daily interaction? Our reactions may be consciously or unconsciously processed, but the message can be quite strong. During heightened emotional arousal, chemical-olfactory signals may even assume an importance that rivals the normally dominant visual/auditory channels. Human odors are primarily emitted through glands found in the anal/genital region and secretory glands in the face, hands, feet, and sometimes across the chest. Odors collect in the mouth and regions of the body with hair. Several experiments attest to the fact that people are usually able to identify the odors of specific other human beings. These "dirty T-shirt" studies instructed people to wear a cotton T-shirt for periods ranging from one day to one week and to avoid using any perfumes and deodorants. Seventy-five percent of the people tested were able to sniff out their own T-shirt and those of a male and female stranger; 50 percent of the spouses were able to identify their mate's T-shirt. Parents can identify their children (some only two hours old) with accuracy rates sometimes over 90 percent; and children are generally able to identify their siblings (Lord & Kasprzak, 1989; Porter, Cernoch, & Balogh, 1985; Porter, Cernoch, & McLaughlin, 1983; Porter & Moore, 1981; Russell, 1976). By the age of six weeks, infants respond to the odor on a breast pad from their mother and not from a stranger. One study even found people able to identify gender from hand odors. An important qualification is in order: Although we do seem to be able to identify others by smell, the accuracy rate depends a great deal on how many competing stimuli we have to judge from. It may be much easier to choose a spouse's T-shirt from one other than from twenty.

Odor also seems to play a role in synchronizing female menstrual cycles. It was discovered that friends and college roommates moved from an average of 8.5 days apart in their menstrual cycle to less than 5 during the school year. Another experimenter attempted to explain why, by taking odor samples from the underarm of a female colleague, which was called "Essence of Genevieve." This odor was dabbed on the upper lips of female volunteers three times a week for four months. Another group of women were dabbed with alcohol. The alcohol group showed no change, but the group receiving "Essence of Genevieve" tended to synchronize their cycle with Genevieve's. This group went from an average of 9.3 days apart in their cycle to 3.4, with four women moving to within one day of Genevieve's cycle. Subsequent work has examined the role of a man's perspiration odor on women's menstrual cycles. The procedures used in the "Essence of Genevieve" study were replicated using women whose cycles were longer than normal and shorter than normal. Those whose upper lips were dabbed with the male odor developed cycles that were closer to normal, while the control group did not (Cutler, Preti, Krieger, Huggins, Garcia, & Lawley, 1986; McClintock, 1971; Russell, 1976). Of special significance from this research is its reminder of the link between physiological processes and odor. Physicians long have known that people with certain illnesses tend to give off certain odors, but now we are finding that certain physiological processes can be modified by odor. It does not surprise us that such effects take place in the animal or insect worlds, but until recently we have not thought of human behavior in this way. Now there are people who practice aroma therapy, using odors to alleviate anxiety, headaches, and hypertension, for example.

Another source of odor is flatulent air, generally adding a negative or insulting aura to an interpersonal encounter in this culture (Lippman, 1980). In fact, anticipation of expelling flatus may lead to rapid termination of an interpersonal contact. Under certain conditions, however, emission of flatulent air may be used deliberately to draw attention to oneself. The extent to which odors attributed to flatus or unpleasant body odors are evaluated negatively is probably related to the extent to which others believe people are aware of it and whether it is controllable.

The role of odors in human interaction varies considerably from culture to culture. Asians are reported to manifest underarm odor only rarely. But odor seems to play a prominent role in some Arab countries:

> Olfaction occupies a prominent place in Arab life. Not only is it one of the distance-setting mechanisms, but it is a vital part of a complex system of

behavior. Arabs consistently breathe on people when they talk. However, this habit is more than a matter of different manners. To the Arab good smells are pleasing and a way of being involved with each other. To smell one's friend is not only nice but desirable, for to deny him your breath is to act ashamed. Americans, on the other hand, trained as they are not to breathe in people's faces, automatically communicate shame in trying to be polite. (Hall, 1966, pp. 159–60)

In addition to human odors, environmental odors also may affect human encounters by setting the mood or bringing back memories associated with the smell. For the first author of this book, there is a distinct smell associated with high schools; each time he enters one it triggers a chain of memories from his own history.

Body Hair

The length of a person's hair can dramatically affect perceptions and human interaction. In 1902, the U. S. Commissioner of Indian Affairs sent out an order to forcibly, if necessary, cut all male Indians' hair so they would look "civilized." Similar behavior has occurred from the 1960s to the present.

During the 1960s, males who allowed the hair on their head to grow over their ears and foreheads and sometimes to their shoulders found that they frequently attracted abuse similar to that leveled at black-skinned individuals. Cases of discrimination in housing, school admittance, jobs, and commercial establishments, to mention a few, were numerous.

In late 1971, the U. S. Army dropped an advertising campaign using the slogan "We care more about how you think than how you cut your hair"—apparently because too many servicemen believed it! The army later stated it did not condone long hair and that the youth featured in the ad campaign did not meet army regulations. Visitors to Taiwan in the early 1970s were greeted with cards saying, "Welcome to the Republic of China. No long hair or long beards, please." In fact, the mania against long hair may even be fatal. United Press International ran a story in April 1970 that reported a father had shot his son to death in a row over long hair and his "negative attitude toward society." The term *longhair,* which once referred to the revered and accomplished musicians and writers of the past, has become a label that may designate young (and old) "undesirables."

The media regularly report stories involving reactions to, or regulations directed toward, human hair, mostly male hair. A sampling from the last twenty-five years follows.

WEST GERMANY (1972)   Fifteen months before, a defense minister said members of the German Army could have beards and long hair as long as they were clean and well groomed. The hoopla created by this order—including complaints by longtime soldiers that long hair interfered with discipline and troop readiness—caused the defense minister to revise his order so that no soldier's hair falls below his collar.

AUSTIN, TEXAS (1973)   Long hair on boys and men is the sign of a sissy and should be banned from American athletic fields, according to the lead article in the May issue of the Texas High School Coaches Association's magazine. A head football coach at a junior high school in Houston said God made man to dominate woman and, therefore, meant for man to wear short hair. Simpson told his fellow coaches in the article that "a good hair code will get abnormals out of athletics before they become coaches and bring their 'losers' standards into the coaching profession."

NEW JERSEY (1973)   The headmaster of a well-known preparatory school (who sports a beard and a mustache) said about sixty seniors will be suspended if they don't cut their hair to meet regulations on hair grooming. One student reported he was told by the headmaster, "I hold your diploma. Either you get a haircut or don't get your diploma."

BERLIN (1974)   One officer and six enlisted men faced courts-martial on charges of disobeying an order to trim their hair or beards. Regulations said mustaches must be neatly trimmed, beards are not allowed (although they were in the navy), and hair on the head may not come over the ears or eyebrows or touch the collar except for closely cut hair at the back of the neck.

CONNECTICUT (1975)   A woman was fired from her waitress job because she refused to shave her legs.

FRANKFURT (1975)   The army dropped charges against a lieutenant for violating hair regulations because he agreed to leave the army with an honorable discharge. Other servicemen, however, were serving terms in army jails for such violations.

SCOTTSDALE, ARIZONA (1977)   An outfielder in a well-known major league baseball team said he was asked by his general manager to cut his hair. The outfielder pointed out that the length of his Afro haircut had been the same for the past five years.

SEOUL, KOREA (1980)   The national police were ordered to refrain from arresting males because of their long hair. During the first eight months of the year 14,911 men were arrested on such a charge.

HOUSTON, TEXAS (1989)   Two brothers who refused to cut their shoulder-length hair vowed to spend a second year out of class unless their school district changed a policy barring their long locks. "I want to go back, but I want to go back like I am," one brother said.

LOS ANGELES (1989)   The First Officer of the Queen Mary had his mustache for forty-two years. He was ordered to shave it or be fired. The company that owns the Queen Mary instituted a policy barring beards, mustaches, and long hair on men. The policy has been in effect for thirty-five years.

LUBBOCK, TEXAS (1990)   A mother in Texas did not see how the rat-tail hairdo her eleven-year-old son had been wearing for three years was suddenly in violation of the Lubbock Independent School District's dress code. LISD officials were enforcing a policy that prohibits boys from having longer than shoulder length hair, ponytails, rat tails, patterns shaved into their hair, and braids. Her son, a Boy Scout and honor student before his withdrawal, was being tutored at home because he refused to conform to the new policy.

BASTROP, TEXAS (1990)   An eight-year-old boy had to cut off his ponytail if he wanted to return to his regular classroom, a district judge ruled, but the child's mother said she would teach him at home before she would snip his hair. The third-grader was sequestered in a twelve-by-fifteen-foot room inside his school. The windows that looked out into the school's hallways were covered with paper and the boy was not allowed to eat lunch with his classmates, attend recess, sing in the choir, or take part in physical education or music.

DALLAS (1991)   A fifth-grader's haircut was too close for comfort as far as school officials were concerned, so they suspended him from class. The principal, saying the haircut violated the "startling and unusual" clause of the school district's code of conduct, suspended the boy from class for three days. The boy's parents said if there were more black students, or if there were any black teachers at the school, the boy's haircut would have been recognized as ordinary. "We're trying to encourage this child to use everything at his disposal to fit into society," a school district spokeswoman said.

WASHINGTON, D.C. (1994)   A woman with a mustache alleged that her facial hair was the reason she was fired.

COLUMBIA, S.C. (1995)   Prisoners at a correctional institution stabbed five guards and took three hostages to protest a policy that would require them to cut their hair.

BASTROP, TEXAS (1996)   A state appeals court ruled school officials were out of bounds when they sent a ponytailed eight-year-old to the equivalent of solitary confinement. The school district's claims that its hair rule was needed to prevent gangs, teach gender identity, and maintain discipline were

Figure 6–2

How do hair length and style influence your perceptions?

sheer nonsense, the Third Court of Appeals said. "[The boy] wore the same hairstyle during the previous school year without causing any disruption," the court said. The school district's lawyer said he would recommend the district take the case to the Texas Supreme Court.

Most of the negative reactions against long hair are directed at males; negative reactions against hair that is too short ("microbuzzes") are more likely to be directed against females. But men who go to the extreme of shaving off all their hair also risk social condemnation. Men are often concerned about baldness as detracting from their attractiveness. Just as often, women report male baldness does not significantly detract from a male's attractiveness. The motivation for negative responses to these extreme hairstyles by some members of our culture is an interesting question but not our major concern here. The fact that body hair, in and of itself, elicits feelings either of appreciation or repugnance is the important point. Other body hair also seems to be important in judgments of attractiveness, illustrated by the comment, "I like him, but he's *so* hairy." For years, *Playboy* magazine neatly airbrushed or did not display pubic hair on its models. Even magazines depicting figures in nudist colonies were so well known for such alterations of pubic hair that many subsequently advertised their magazines as "unretouched." But when nude photographs of the pop singer Madonna appeared in two national magazines, many people commented more about the hair under her arms than about her lack of clothing. Some liked it; some did not. It is reported that the Cacobo Indians of the Amazon rain forest carefully trim and groom their head hair but feel that other body hair is not attractive; they methodically eliminate eyebrows by plucking them. The lack of eyebrows on the Mona Lisa is some evidence that at one time it may have been desirable to pluck them for beauty's sake.

Obviously, there are many other body features we have not covered, such as freckles, moles, acne, and so-called beauty marks, all of which may be very important in a given situation. The numerous individuals who have had "nose jobs" must have felt their nose created an undesirable impression in face-to-face interaction. However, our responses to body shape, color, smell, and hair seem to be the major factors affecting human communication along with clothing and artifacts such as cosmetics, eyeglasses, jewelry, and so forth.

OUR BODY: CLOTHES and OTHER ARTIFACTS

Examine the clothing types shown in Figure 6-3. What are your first impressions?

On the following list are twenty characteristics that may be associated with one or more of these clothing types. Check the spaces you think apply to specific clothing types, and compare your impressions with those of your friends, family, or associates:

	Males				Females			
1	**2**	**3**	**4**	**1**	**2**	**3**	**4**	
—	—	—	—	—	—	—	—	1. Has smoked marijuana.
—	—	—	—	—	—	—	—	2. Is shy, doesn't talk much.
—	—	—	—	—	—	—	—	3. Is a fraternity or sorority member.
—	—	—	—	—	—	—	—	4. Is a Democrat.
—	—	—	—	—	—	—	—	5. Is involved in athletics.
—	—	—	—	—	—	—	—	6. Is married.
—	—	—	—	—	—	—	—	7. Is generous.
—	—	—	—	—	—	—	—	8. Drives a sports car.
—	—	—	—	—	—	—	—	9. Is a Republican.
—	—	—	—	—	—	—	—	10. Is vocationally oriented.
—	—	—	—	—	—	—	—	11. Is active politically.
—	—	—	—	—	—	—	—	12. Is dependable.
—	—	—	—	—	—	—	—	13. Listens most to classical music.
—	—	—	—	—	—	—	—	14. Lives with parents.
—	—	—	—	—	—	—	—	15. Has long hair.
—	—	—	—	—	—	—	—	16. Has many friends.
—	—	—	—	—	—	—	—	17. Is intelligent.
—	—	—	—	—	—	—	—	18. Is religious.
—	—	—	—	—	—	—	—	19. Is open-minded.
—	—	—	—	—	—	—	—	20. Is older.

Did you find any similarities in your responses and those of your peers? Were there any major differences between your responses and the responses of people with distinctly different backgrounds? Later in this chapter we will focus on what impressions clothes communicate, but first we need to answer an even more basic question: *"Do clothes communicate?"* Anecdotal evidence that they do is plentiful. For instance, the Associated Press once reported that the Lutheran Church felt the attire worn by clergy in the pulpit was responsible for some churchgoers' switching denominations. Many tailors, manufacturers, and sellers of clothes claim to be "wardrobe engineers"— engineering their clients' outward appearance to increase their sales, assert their authority, or win more court cases. In a survey of 415 personnel executives in the Chicago area, 91 percent claimed that a job applicant's dress and grooming showed his or her attitude toward the company; 95 percent said appropriate dress was a definite aid in career advancement. Thirty-one percent said they had a formalized dress code. In another study, women identified as "clothing conscious" from responses to a paper-and-pencil test were also more likely to dress conservatively on the job and be more satisfied with their jobs

Figure 6–3

Males: 1   2   3   4

Females: 1   2   3   4

Four clothing styles.

(Gorden, Tengler, & Infante, 1982). Clothes also seem to be important to first impressions. Males and females were asked what things they noticed about persons when they first met them. They were given ten characteristics of appearance from which to choose. Females noticed clothes first for both same- and opposite-sexed partners; males also looked at clothes first for same-sexed partners, but for members of the opposite sex, clothes took third place behind figure and face ("First Impressions," August/September 1983). The Associated Press reported in 1994 that several Houston-area school districts outlawed what they called the "grunge look." Students were prohibited from wearing baggy pants; untucked shirts; pierced rings in the lips, nose, or eyebrows; torn or ripped clothing; duster-type coats; or trench coats. Earrings were prohibited for boys, and girls could not wear miniskirts, tank tops, cutoffs, halter tops, strapless garments, casual pants, dress slacks, or skirts worn on hips. Administrators reportedly wanted to ban clothing that could hide weapons, ban clothing that might convey gang-related messages, and encourage clothing that would convey dignity and respect.

All of the aforementioned incidents suggest clothing is believed to play an important role in interpersonal relations. They also suggest that, in general, clothing decisions should be adapted to one's role and the surroundings. This principle was clearly demonstrated when people who were dressed well (as opposed to sloppily) asked others for a dime to make a phone call. When well dressed, those requesting aid received more cooperation in a clean, neatly appointed airport where most of the people were also well dressed; when they were poorly dressed, the greatest cooperation was obtained from those in a bus station where the people and surroundings more closely resembled their poorly dressed outfits (Hensley, 1981). We seem to know when attire is and is not appropriate to the situation. It should not be surprising, then, to learn that the business outfits of working women on television are "sexier" and more provocative than those of actual businesswomen (White, 1995).

You may have had the experience in a restaurant of responding only to the uniform of the waiter or waitress and later, when you were ready to leave, not knowing who waited on your table. It is reasonable to assume that, in most instances, our perception of others is influenced by clothes and partly by other factors. To determine whether our judgments of others are ever made on the basis of clothes alone, it is necessary to measure the effects of changing the type of clothing while keeping everything else the same. Experiments by Hoult (1954) were designed on this basis. First, forty-six students rated thirteen male classmates on such things as "best-looking," "most likely to succeed," "most intelligent," "most like to date or double date with," "best personality," and "most likely to have as class president." The four men with the highest ratings were told to "dress down," while the four with the lowest ratings were told to "dress up." Others were told to dress the same. Two weeks later, ratings were again obtained. Hoult found no evidence that clothes had been influential in changing the ratings, even though the independent ratings of the clothes showed they did, indeed, indicate "dressing up" or "dressing down" from the previous outfits. A high correlation between the social closeness of the raters and models and the social ratings prompted Hoult to conduct another study using models who were complete strangers to the raters. In this study, he used photos of male strangers who were rated by 254 students from two colleges. Having obtained independent ratings of clothes and the models' heads, Hoult was able to place high-ranked outfits on models with low-ranked heads. Lower-ranked clothing was placed on models with higher-ranked heads. He found that higher-ranked clothing was associated with an increase in rank, while lower-ranked clothing was associated with loss of rank. Clothing, then, did seem to be a significant factor affecting judgments students made about these strangers.

While Hoult's work is helpful in demonstrating the communicative value of clothes, an equally important conclusion can be derived from the failure of his first experiment. This first experiment demonstrates one of the conditions under which clothing may not be a highly influential factor in interpersonal perception of others: when the observer is well acquainted with the person being observed. Changes in the clothing of a family member or close friend may indicate a temporary change of mood, but it is likely that we will not perceive any basic change in values, attitudes, or personality traits unless the clothing change becomes permanent for that individual. In addition to social closeness to the person being observed, other factors may modify responses to clothes, such as the psychological-social orientation and background of the observer and the particular task or situation within which the observation is made. We should also remember that any given item of clothing can convey several different meanings. For instance, the tie a person wears may reflect sophistication or high status, but the way the tie is worn (tightly knotted, loosened, thrown over one's shoulder) may provide additional information about the wearer and evoke different reactions.

To understand the relationship between clothes and communication, we should be familiar with the various functions clothes may fulfill: decoration, protection (both physical and psychological), sexual attraction, self-assertion, self-denial, concealment, group identification, and display of status or role. Since there are some widely accepted cultural rules for combining certain colors and styles of dress, clothes also may function to inform the observer of one's knowledge of such rules. There seems to be a current trend in which mass-produced, inexpensive copies of high-status items give nearly everyone a chance to display status on occasions, for example, Cartier look-alike watches, knockoffs of designer jeans, and so forth. Once these items saturate the marketplace, however, they lose much of their status value.

An interesting study by Lefkowitz, Blake, and Mouton (1955) shows not only how clothes fulfill a particular function but also how they affect the behavior of others. They found pedestrians will violate the instructions given by a traffic signal light more often when another person violates it ahead of them. More important, significantly more violations occurred when the original violator was dressed to represent a high-status person. Additional studies of this type find that a variety of requests (making change, accepting leaflets, giving detailed street directions, returning a dime left in a phone booth, and so on) are more easily granted if one is dressed to fit the situation or is dressed in what would be considered higher-status clothing (Fortenberry, MacLean, Morris, & O'Connell, 1978). Bickman (1974a, 1974b), for example, had four men stop 153 adults on the streets of Brooklyn and make various requests. The men's clothing varied and included civilian (sports jacket and tie), milkman (uniform, white pants, milk bottles), and guard (uniform, badge, insignia, no gun). The men asked pedestrians to pick up a bag, to put a dime in a parking meter for someone else, or to stand on the opposite side of a bus-stop sign. In each case, when dressed in the guard uniform, the men received greater compliance. In fact, 83 percent of those who were asked to put a dime in the parking meter obeyed even after the person in the guard uniform had left the scene.

Uniforms do help people identify the wearer's probable areas of expertise. And this knowledge may affect behavior. In public-service announcements, the same woman dressed as a nurse and a businesswoman and asked for contributions to fight leukemia. The nurse was judged to be more knowledgeable and received more pledged contributions (Lawrence & Watson, 1991). The issue of wearing uniforms to school gained a great deal of notoriety when President Clinton declared in his 1995 State of the Union address: "If it means that teenagers will stop killing each other over designer jackets, then our public schools should be able to require students to wear school uniforms." For some students, uniforms would provide a needed form of structure and control, but it is not realistic to expect uniforms will eliminate most of the offensive behaviors manifested by troubled teens.

Lawyers have long known that their client's manner of dress may have an impact on the judgments made by the judge and/or jury. Some defendants have even been encouraged to put on a simulated wedding ring to offset any prejudice against single persons. This brings us to the question of what specific things clothing communicates.

To make a list of the things invariably communicated by clothes would be impossible; such a list would vary with the demand of each particular situation, ethnic group, time (of day and era), region of the country, and so forth. If the fashion industry could devise such a list, it would need to spend far less on advertising designed to persuade men and women that a particular cosmetic or dress actually communicates "beauty." Some of the potential personal attributes that may be communicated by dress include sex, age, nationality, relation to opposite sex (a function, sometimes, of matched sweaters), socioeconomic status, identification with a specific group, occupational or official status, mood, personality, attitudes, interests, and values. Clothes also set our expectations for the behavior of the wearer, especially if it is a uniform of some type. Obviously, the accuracy of such judgments varies considerably; *the more concrete items such as age, sex, nationality, and socioeconomic status are signaled with greater accuracy than more abstract qualities such as attitudes, values, and personality.* In recent years, the "message" T-shirt has become a vehicle for communicating some attitudes that might otherwise be more difficult to assess.

Up to this point, we have established that clothing communicates a variety of messages and that the people we interact with respond in various ways to those messages. But what about the effect of clothing on the self-image of the wearer? Some authors feel clothes help satisfy a personal image of one's ideal self. Gibbins, in his work with fifteen- and sixteen-year-old girls, for instance, found a definite relationship between clothes that were liked and ratings of ideal self. Clothing was a means of communicating messages about the wearer, and liking for a particular outfit was "related to the extent to which this message is similar to the subject's ideal self image" (Gibbins, 1969). In another fascinating discovery, we see a potential link between clothing and self-concept. High-school boys who had higher achievement test scores but who wore clothing deemed "unacceptable" by their peers were found to have lower grade point averages than those who wore "acceptable" clothing (Hamilton & Warden, 1966). This latter group also found themselves in less conflict and in more school activities. Clothes, then, may encourage or discourage certain patterns of communication. A new outfit may promote feelings of gaiety and happiness; people may feel less efficient in shoes that hurt; self-consciousness may result from wearing an "inappropriate" outfit—a common feeling for adolescents trying to understand their own self-image. Some graduate teaching assistants wear suits to class to distinguish themselves from their students who frequently are almost age-mates. Some report that such attire gives them added confidence or assurance in dealing with their students.

Rosenfeld and Plax (1977) wanted to determine whether attitudes toward clothing were related to certain personality characteristics. This study obtained responses from both males and females on a questionnaire about clothing attitudes. A massive battery of personality tests also was given to this group of 371 men and women. The results of these personality tests were then matched with the scores on four dimensions of the clothing questionnaire. These results are listed as follows according to the males and females who scored high or low on each dimension.

1. **Clothing Consciousness** ("The people I know always notice what I wear.")
   - High males were deliberate; guarded; deferential to authority, custom, and tradition. They did not value beauty, form, and unity very highly, and they believed people were easily manipulated.
   - High females were inhibited, anxious, compliant before authority, kind, sympathetic, loyal to friends.
   - Low males were aggressive, independent, and did not believe people could be easily manipulated.
   - Low females were forceful, independent, dominant, clear thinking, and had low motivation for heterosexual relationships or for manipulating others.
2. **Exhibitionism** ("I approve of skimpy bathing suits and wouldn't mind wearing one myself.")
   - High males were aggressive, confident, outgoing, unsympathetic, unaffectionate, moody, impulsive, and had a low self-concept regarding their familial interactions.
   - High females were radical, detached from interpersonal relationships, and had a high opinion of their own self-worth and moral/ethical beliefs.

- Low males were guarded about self-revelations. They had a low self-concept regarding their familial interactions, and they believed people could be easily manipulated.
- Low females were timid, sincere, accepting of others, patient, and had a low motivation for heterosexual relationships. They also had feelings of inferiority.

3. **Practicality** ("When buying clothes, I am more interested in practicality than beauty.")
   - High males were inhibited, cautious, rebellious, dissatisfied, and had a low motivation to make friends, sustain relationships, or gain recognition from authorities.
   - High females were clever, enthusiastic, confident, outgoing, and guarded about personal self-revelations. They had feelings of superiority but did not wish to lead.
   - Low males were success oriented, mature, forceful, serious, and analytical and tried to predict responses of others in various situations.
   - Low females were self-centered, independent, detached.

4. **Designer** ("I should love to be a clothes designer.")
   - High males were cooperative, sympathetic, warm, helpful, impulsive, irritable, demanding, and conforming. They worried about their behavior and sought encouragement from others.
   - High females were irrational, uncritical, stereotyped in thinking, quick, expressive, and ebullient.
   - Low males were adventurous, egotistic, dissatisfied, and anxious. They had feelings of superiority and were not highly motivated to form friendships.
   - Low females were efficient, clear thinking, resourceful, persistent, and easily disorganized under pressure. They believed people were easily manipulated, and they were pessimistic about their occupational future.

The mutual effects of clothing on wearer and on perceiver were amply demonstrated in a study of the uniforms worn by teams in the National Hockey League and National Football League. In this study, teams with black uniforms ranked near the top of their leagues in penalties, and those teams who switched from nonblack to black uniforms incurred more penalties after the switch. The authors suggest that wearers of the black uniforms perceive themselves as more aggressive and that this, coupled with similar perceptions by referees, leads to more penalties (Frank & Gilovich, 1988).

People adorn themselves with a number of other *artifacts* such as badges, tattoos, masks, earrings, and jewelry. Any discussion of clothing must take these artifacts into consideration because they are also potential communicative stimuli. A ring worn on a particular finger, a fraternity or sorority pin worn in a particular configuration, and a single earring worn on a particular ear all may communicate something about the nature of one's relationships and self-image. There is a dearth of research on such artifacts.

We do know that people around the world choose to decorate and alter their bodies in a variety of ways. Sometimes the body is scarred, mutilated, or painted. In the case of binding infant feet, bone structure is reshaped. In this society, we circumcise many male children, and the piercing of various body parts with rings has become increasingly popular with young adults in recent years. The use of tattoos to decorate the body is also widely practiced (Sanders, 1989).

In addition, we know people will sometimes react strongly to a particular artifact or decoration—for example, eyeglasses or lipstick. And while the initial effect of such features may be strong, cooccurring features and verbal behavior soon blend together to form an overall impression—thereby minimizing the effect of any single feature.

SUMMARY

Appearance and dress are part of the total nonverbal stimuli that influence interpersonal responses, and under some conditions they are the primary determinants of such responses. Physical attractiveness may be influential in determining whether a person is sought out; it may have a bearing on whether a person is able to persuade or manipulate others. It is often an important factor in the selection of dates and marriage partners; it may determine whether a defendant is deemed guilty or innocent; it may even have an effect on whether the prisoner is able to decrease the antisocial behavior responsible for his or her imprisonment. It may be a major factor contributing to how others judge personality, sexuality, popularity, success, and often happiness. Fortunately for some and unfortunately for others, such judgments begin early in life. Not all children are conventionally beautiful. There are indications that teachers not only make attractiveness judgments about young children but also treat the unattractive ones with fewer and less-positive communications. A sizeable proportion of the American public still thinks of the ideal man or woman in terms of physical attractiveness.

In spite of the overwhelming evidence that physical attractiveness is a highly desirable quality in interpersonal situations, other factors temper these general findings. For instance, all positive findings for attractiveness are based on probabilities, not certainty. Many unattractive persons will not be evaluated unfavorably. For example, judgments can be tempered by the persons they are seen with, the environment in which they are judged, other communicative behavior they engage in, and/or the time of life at which they are evaluated. In addition, many of the attractiveness studies have used photographs rather than live, interacting human beings.

In addition to the importance of general physical attractiveness in influencing the responses of others, we have some information on stereotyped responses to specific features—general body build, skin color, odor, hair, and clothes. These specific features may have a profound influence on one's self-image and, hence, on patterns of communication with others. Future work in this area will have to consider such basic questions as:

- Under what conditions do physical appearance and dress make a critical difference in the total communication event?
- What is the relative impact of physical appearance and dress when combined with other verbal and nonverbal cues?
- Are there any specific features of physical appearance that consistently act as primary sources of information for the perceiver?
- If not, which features act as primary sources of information under certain circumstances?
- How valid are the various stereotypes associated with physical appearance and dress?
- What effect does one's self-image concerning one's own appearance and dress have on interpersonal communication behavior?

QUESTIONS for DISCUSSION

1. Can our verbal behavior affect the way people perceive our physical attractiveness? What verbal behavior might cause people to perceive us as less physically attractive? What verbal behavior might make us appear more physically attractive?
2. Throughout this chapter you have read about a number of stereotypes people have about physical appearance. In your opinion, is there any truth to any of these stereotypes? Which ones?
3. If you wanted to change stereotypes about physical appearance, how would you do it? Take one stereotype as an example, and show what you would do to change it.
4. People have been refused employment or fired from their job because of perceived problems with their height, weight, odor, skin color, clothing, hairstyle, or general attractiveness. Under what conditions (if any) do you think such characteristics are legitimate reasons for not hiring a person or for firing them?

REFERENCES and SELECTED BIBLIOGRAPHY

Additional references for Chapter 6 may be found on page 482.

Adams, G. R. (1977). Physical attractiveness research: Toward a developmental social psychology of beauty. *Human Development, 20,* 217–39.

Addison, W. E. (1989). Beardedness as a factor in perceived masculinity. *Perceptual and Motor Skills, 68,* 921–22.

Aiken, L. (1963). Relationship of dress to selected measures of personality in undergraduate women. *Journal of Social Psychology, 59,* 119–28.

Anderson, R., & Nida, S. (1978). Effects of physical attractiveness on opposite and same sex evaluations. *Journal of Personality, 46,* 401–13.

Aronson, E., & Golden, B. W. (1962). The effect of relevant and irrelevant aspects of communicator credibility on opinion change. *Journal of Personality, 30,* 135–46.

Baber, R. E. (1939). *Marriage and family.* New York: McGraw-Hill.

Baker, E. E., & Redding, W. C. (1962). The effects of perceived tallness in persuasive speaking: An experiment. *Journal of Communication, 12,* 51–53.

Banner, I. (1986). *American beauty.* Chicago: University of Chicago Press.

Bar-Tal, D., & Saxe, L. (1976). Perceptions of similarly and dissimilarly attractive couples and individuals. *Journal of Personality and Social Psychology, 33,* 772–81.

Bassett, R. E. (1979). Effects of source attire on judgments of credibility. *Central States Speech Journal, 30,* 282–85.

Beck, S. B., Ward–Hull, C. I., & McLear, P. M. (1976). Variables related to women's somatic preferences of the male and female body. *Journal of Personality and Social Psychology, 34,* 1200–1210.

Berman, P. W., O'Nan, B. A., & Floyd, W. (1981). The double standard of aging and the social situation: Judgments of attractiveness of the middle-aged woman. *Sex Roles, 7,* 87–96.

Berry, D. S. (1991). Attractive faces are not all created equal: Joint effects of facial babyishness and attractiveness on social perception. *Personality and Social Psychology Bulletin, 17,* 523–31.

Berry, D. S., & McArthur, L. Z. (1986). Perceiving character in faces: The impact of age-related craniofacial changes on social perception. *Psychological Bulletin, 100,* 3–18.

Berscheid, E., & Walster, E. H. (1969). *Interpersonal attraction.* Reading, MA: Addison-Wesley.

Berscheid, E., & Walster, E. H. (1974). Physical attractiveness. In L. Berkowitz (Ed.), *Advances in experimental social psychology* (Vol. 7). New York: Academic Press.

Bickman, L. (1971). The effects of social status on the honesty of others. *Journal of Social Psychology, 85,* 87–92.

Bickman, L. (1974a). The social power of a uniform. *Journal of Applied Social Psychology, 4,* 47–61.

Bickman, L. (1974b). Social roles and uniforms: Clothes make the person. *Psychology Today, 7,* 48–51.

Brain, R. (1979). *The decorated body.* New York: Harper & Row.

Brislin, R. W., & Lewis, S. A. (1968). Dating and physical attractiveness: Replication. *Psychological Reports, 22,* 976.

Byrne, D., Ervin, C. R., & Lamberth, J. (1970). Contiguity between the experimental study of attraction and real-life computer dating. *Journal of Personality and Social Psychology, 16,* 157–65.

Byrne, D., London, O., & Reeves, K. (1968). The effects of physical attractiveness, sex, and attitude similarity on interpersonal attraction. *Journal of Personality, 36,* 259–72.

Cahnman, W. J. (1968). The stigma of obesity. *Sociological Quarterly, 9,* 283–99.

Cameron, C., Oskamp, S., & Sparks, W. (1978). Courtship American style: Newspaper advertisements. *The Family Coordinator, 26,* 27–30.

Cappella, J. N., & Palmer, M. T. (1990). Attitude similarity, relational history, and attraction: The mediating effects of kinesic and vocal behaviors. *Communication Monographs, 57,* 161–83.

Cash, T. F., & Derlega, V. J. (1978). The matching hypothesis: Physical attractiveness among same-sexed friends. *Personality and Social Psychology Bulletin, 4,* 240–43.

Cash, T. F., Gillen, B., & Burns, S. (1977). Sexism and 'beautism' in personnel consultant decision making. *Journal of Applied Psychology, 62,* 301–10.

Cash, T. F., & Pruzinsky, T. (1990). *Body images: Development, deviance, and change.* New York: Guilford.

Cash, T. F., Winstead, B. A., & Janda, L. H. (1986). The great American shape-up. *Psychology Today, 20,* 30–37.

Cavior, N., & Lombardi, D. H. (1973). Developmental aspects of judgment of physical attractiveness in children. *Developmental Psychology, 8,* 67–71.

Chaikin, A. L., Derlega, V. J., Yoder, J., & Phillips, D. (1974). The effects of appearance on compliance. *Journal of Social Psychology, 92,* 199–200.

Chaiken, S. (1979). Communicator physical attractiveness and persuasion. *Journal of Personality and Social Psychology, 37,* 1387–97.

Chaiken, S. (1986). Physical appearance and social influence. In C. P. Herman, M. P. Zanna, & E. T. Higgins (Eds.), *Physical appearance, stigma, and social behavior: The Ontario Symposium* (Vol. 3). Hillsdale, NJ: Erlbaum.

Channing, H., & Mayer, J. (1966). Obesity—Its possible effect on college acceptance. *New England Journal of Medicine, 275,* 1172–74.

Cortes, J. B., & Gatti, F. M. (1965). Physique and self-description of temperament. *Journal of Consulting Psychology, 29,* 432–39.

Cortes, J. B., & Gatti, F. M. (1966). Physique and motivation. *Journal of Consulting Psychology, 30,* 408–14.

Cunningham, M. R., Roberts, A. R., Barbee, A. P., Druen, P. B., & Wu, C. H. (1995). 'Their ideas of beauty are, on the whole, the same as ours': Consistency and variability in the cross-cultural perception of female physical attractiveness. *Journal of Personality and Social Psychology, 68,* 261–79.

Curran, J. P. (1973). Correlates of physical attractiveness and interpersonal attraction in the dating situation. *Social Behavior and Personality, 1,* 153–57.

Curran, J. P., & Lippold, S. (1975). The effects of physical attraction and attitude similarity on dating dyads. *Journal of Personality, 43,* 528–39.

Cutler, W. B., Preti, G., Krieger, A., Huggins, G. R., Garcia, C. R., & Lawley, H. J. (1986). Human axillary secretions influence women's menstrual cycles: The role of donor extract from men. *Hormones and Behavior, 20,* 463–73.

Dannenmaier, W., & Thumin, F. (1964). Authority status as a factor in perceptual distortion of size. *Journal of Social Psychology, 63,* 361–65.

Darden, E. (1972). Masculinity-femininity body rankings by males and females. *Journal of Psychology, 80,* 205–12.

Darley, J. M., & Cooper, J. (1972). The 'Clean Gene' phenomenon: The effect of students' appearance on political campaigning. *Journal of Applied Social Psychology, 2,* 24–33.

Davis, F. (1971). *Inside intuition.* New York: McGraw-Hill.

Davis, F. (1992). *Fashion, culture, and identity.* Chicago: University of Chicago Press.

Deformed brick-thrower eyes future with new face. (1975, December 15). *Lafayette Journal and Courier,* p. A-6.

DeJong, W., & Kleck, R. E. (1986). The social psychological effects of overweight. In C. P. Herman, M. P. Zanna, & E. T. Higgins (Eds.), *Physical appearance, stigma, and social behavior: The Ontario Symposium* (Vol. 3). Hillsdale, NJ: Erlbaum.

DeLong, R. R. (1978). Dimensions of visual perceptions of clothing. *Perceptual and Motor Skills, 47,* 907–10.

Dermer, M., & Thiel, D. L. (1975). When beauty may fail. *Journal of Personality and Social Psychology, 31,* 1168–76.

Dion, K. K. (1972). Physical attractiveness and evaluation of children's transgressions. *Journal of Personality and Social Psychology, 24,* 207–13.

Dion, K. K. (1973). Young children's stereotyping of facial attractiveness. *Developmental Psychology, 9,* 183–88.

Dion, K. K., Berscheid, E. (1972). Physical attractiveness and peer perception among children. *Sociometry, 37,* 1–12.

Dion, K. K., Berscheid, E., & Walster, E. (1972). What is beautiful is good. *Journal of Personality and Social Psychology, 24,* 285–90.

Dion, K. K., & Stein, S. (1978). Physical attractiveness and interpersonal influence. *Journal of Experimental Social Psychology, 14,* 97–108.

Dipboye, R. L., Arvey, R. D., & Terpstra, D. E. (1977). Sex and physical attractiveness of raters and applicants as determinants of resume evaluations. *Journal of Applied Psychology, 62,* 288–94.

Doty, R. L. (1981). Olfactory communication in humans. *Chemical Senses, 6,* 351–76.

Doty, R. L., Orndorff, M. M., Leyden, J., & Kligman, A. (1978). Communication of gender from human axillary odors: Relationship to perceived intensity and dedonicity. *Behavioral Biology, 23,* 373–80.

Douty, H. I. (1963). Influence of clothing on perception of persons. *Journal of Home Economics, 55,* 197–202.

Downs, A. C., & Lyons, P. M. (1991). Natural observations of the links between attractiveness and initial legal judgments. *Personality and Social Psychology Bulletin, 17,* 541–47.

Efran, M. G. (1974). The effect of physical appearance on the judgment of guilt, interpersonal attraction and severity of recommended punishment in a simulated jury task. *Journal of Experimental Research in Personality, 8,* 45–54.

Fallon, A., & Rozin, P. (1985). Sex differences in perceptions of desirable body shape. *Journal of Abnormal Psychology, 94,* 102–5.

Farb, B. (1978). *Humankind.* Boston: Houghton-Mifflin.

Farina, A., Fischer, E., Sherman, S., Smith, W., Groh, T., & Mermin, P. (1977). Physical attractiveness and mental illness. *Journal of Abnormal Psychology, 86,* 510–17.

First impressions. *Public Opinion, 6* (August/September 1983).

Fisher, S. (1964). Sex differences in body perception. *Psychological Monographs, 78,* No. 14 (Whole No. 591).

Flugel, J. (1930). *The psychology of clothes.* London: Hogarth Press.

Fortenberry, J. H., MacLean, J., Morris, P., & O'Connell, M. (1978). Modes of dress as a perceptual cue to deference. *Journal of Personality and Social Psychology, 104,* 139–40.

Freedman, R. (1986). *Beauty bound.* Lexington, MA: Lexington Books.

Friend, R. M., & Vinson, M. (1974). Leaning over backwards: Jurors' responses to defendants' attractiveness. *Journal of Communication, 24,* 124–29.

Garner, D. M., Garfinkel, P. E., Schwartz, D., & Thompson, M. (1980). Cultural expectations of thinness in women. *Psychological Reports, 47,* 483–91.

Gascaly, S. A., & Borges, C. A. (1979). The male physique and behavioral expectancies. *Journal of Psychology, 101,* 97–102.

Geiselman, R. E., Haight, N., & Kimata, L. (1984). Context effects of the perceived physical attractiveness of faces. *Journal of Experimental Social Psychology, 20,* 409–24.

Gibbins, K. (1969). Communication aspects of women's clothes and their relation to fashionability. *British Journal of Social and Clinical Psychology, 8,* 301–12.

Giles, H., & Chavasse, W. (1975). Communication length as a function of dress style and social status. *Perceptual and Motor Skills, 40,* 961–62.

Gillis, J. S., & Avis. W. E. (1980). The male-taller norm in mate selection. *Personality and Social Psychology Bulletin, 6,* 396–401.

Goffman, E. (1959). *The presentation of self in everyday life.* Garden City, NY: Doubleday.

Goldberg, P. A., Gottesdiener, N., & Abramson, P. R. (1975). Another put-down of women?: Perceived attractiveness as a function of support for the feminist movement. *Journal of Personality and Social Psychology, 32,* 113–15.

Gorden, W. I., Tengler, C. D., & Infante, D. A. (1982). Women's clothing predispositions as predictors of dress at work, job satisfaction, and career advancement. *Southern Speech Communication Journal, 17,* 422–34.

Gorman, W. (1969). *Body image and the image of the brain.* St. Louis: W. H. Green.

Gortmaker, S. L., Must, A., Perrin, J. N., Sobol, A. M., & Dietz, W. H. (1993). Social and economic consequences of overweight in adolescence and young adulthood. *New England Journal of Medicine, 329,* 1008–12.

Graham, J. A., & Jouhar, A. J. (1980). Cosmetics considered in the context of physical attractiveness: A review. *International Journal of Cosmetic Science, 2,* 77–101.

Graham, J. A., & Jouhar, A. J. (1981). The effects of cosmetics on person perception. *International Journal of Cosmetic Science, 3,* 199–210.

Graham, J. A., & Jouhar, A. J. (1982). The effects of cosmetics on self perception: How we see ourselves. Unpublished manuscript, University of Pennsylvania.

Graham, J. A., & Kligman, A. M. (Eds.). (1985). *The psychology of cosmetic treatments.* New York: Praeger.

Grammer, K., & Thornhill, R. (1994). Human (homo sapiens) facial attractiveness and sexual selection: The role of symmetry and averageness. *Journal of Comparative Psychology, 108,* 233–42.

Graziano, W. G., Jensen-Campbell, L. A., Shebilske, L. J., & Lundgren, S. R. (1993). Social influence, sex differences, and judgments of beauty: Putting the *interper-*

sonal back into interpersonal attraction. *Journal of Personality and Social Psychology, 65,* 522–31.

Griffin, J. H. (1960). *Black like me.* Boston: Houghton Mifflin.

Gurel, L., Wilbur, J. C., & Gurel, L. (1972). Personality correlates of adolescent clothing styles. *Journal of Home Economics, 64,* 42–47.

Hall, E. T. (1966). *The hidden dimension.* Garden City, NY: Doubleday.

Hallpike, C. R. (1969). Social hair. *Man, 4,* 256–64.

Hamermesh, D. S., & Biddle, J. E. (1994). Beauty and the labor market. *American Economic Review, 84,* 1174–94.

Hamid, P. (1972). Some effects of dress cues on observational accuracy: A perceptual estimate, and impression formation. *Journal of Social Psychology, 86,* 279–89.

Hamilton, J., & Warden, J. (1966). Student's role in a high school community and his clothing behavior. *Journal of Home Economics, 58,* 789–91.

Harrison, A. A., & Saeed, L. (1977). Let's make a deal: An analysis of revelations and stipulations in Lonely Hearts advertisements. *Journal of Personality and Social Psychology, 35,* 257–74.

Hartmann, G. W. (1949). Clothing: Personal problem and social issue. *Journal of Home Economics, 41,* 295–98.

Hatfield, E., & Sprecher, S. (1986). *Mirror, mirror . . . : The importance of looks in everyday life.* Albany, NY: SUNY Press.

Heilman, M. E., & Saruwatari, L. F. (1979). When beauty is beastly: The effects of appearance and sex on evaluations of job applicants for managerial and nonmanagerial jobs. *Organizational Behavior and Human Performance, 22,* 360–72.

Hendricks, S. H., Kelley, E. A., & Eicher, J. B. (1968). Senior girls' appearance and social acceptance. *Journal of Home Economics, 60,* 167–72.

Hensley, W. E. (1981). The effects of attire, location, and sex on aiding behavior: A similarity explanation. *Journal of Nonverbal Behavior, 6,* 3–11.

Herman, C. P., Zanna, M. P., & Higgins, E. T. (Eds.). (1986). *Physical appearance, stigma, and social behavior: The Ontario Symposium* (Vol. 3). Hillsdale, NJ: Erlbaum.

Hinsz, V. B. (1989). Facial resemblance in engaged and married couples. *Journal of Social and Personal Relationships, 6,* 223–29.

Holman, R. H. (1980). A transcription and analysis system for the study of women's clothing. *Semiotica, 32,* 11–34.

Hopson, J. L. (1979). *Scent signals.* New York: William Morrow.

Horai, J., Naccari, N., & Faloultah, E. (1974). The effects of expertise and physical attractiveness upon opinion agreement and liking. *Sociometry, 37,* 601–6.

Hoult, R. (1954). Experimental measurement of clothing as a factor in some social ratings of selected American men. *American Sociological Review, 19,* 324–28.

Hubble, M. A., & Gelso, C. J. (1978). Effect of counselor attire in an initial interview. *Journal of Counseling Psychology, 25,* 581–84.

Iliffe, A. M. (1960). A study of preferences in feminine beauty. *British Journal of Psychology, 51,* 267–73.

Izzett, R. R., & Leginski, W. (1974). Group discussion and the influence of defendant characteristics in a simulated jury setting. *Journal of Social Psychology, 93,* 271–79.

Jackson, L. A. (1992). *Physical appearance and gender: Sociobiological and sociocultural perspectives.* Albany: SUNY Press.

Jacobson, M. B. (1981). Effects of victim's and defendant's physical attractiveness on subjects' judgments in a rape case. *Sex Roles, 7,* 247–55.

Jacobson, S. K., & Berger, C. R. (1974). Communication and justice: Defendant attributes and their effects on the severity of his sentence. *Speech Monographs, 41,* 282–86.

Jensen-Campbell, L. A., Graziano, W. G., & West, S. G. (1995). Dominance, prosocial orientation, and female preferences: Do nice guys really finish last? *Journal of Personality and Social Psychology, 68,* 427–40.

Johnson, B. H., Nagasawa, R. H., & Peters, K. (1977). Clothing style differences: Their effect on the impression of sociability. *Home Economics Research Journal, 6,* 58–63.

Johnson, P. A., & Staffieri, J. R. (1971). Stereotypic affective properties of personal names and somatypes in children. *Developmental Psychology, 5,* 176.

Joseph, N., & Alex, N. (1972). The uniform: A sociological perspective. *American Journal of Sociology, 77,* 719–30.

Joseph, W. B. (1982). The credibility of physically attractive communicators: A review. *Journal of Advertising, 11,* 15–24.

Jourard, S. M., & Secord, P. F. (1955). Body-cathexis and personality. *British Journal of Psychology, 46,* 130–38.

Jourard, S. M., & Secord, P. F. (1955). Body-cathexis and the ideal female figure. *Journal of Abnormal and Social Psychology, 50,* 243–46.

Kaiser, S. B. (1985). *The social psychology of clothing.* New York: Macmillan.

Kalick, S. M., & Hamilton, T. E. (1986). The matching hypothesis reexamined. *Journal of Personality and Social Psychology, 51,* 673–82.

Keating, C. F. (1985). Gender and the physiognomy of dominance and attractiveness. *Social Psychology Quarterly, 48,* 61–70.

Keating, C. F., Mazur, A., & Segall, M. H. (1977). Facial features which influence the perception of status. *Sociometry, 40,* 374–78.

Keating, C. F, Mazur, A., & Segall, M. H. (1981). A cross-cultural exploration of physiognomic traits of dominance and happiness. *Ethology and Sociobiology, 2,* 41–48.

Kenny, C., & Fletcher, D. (1973). Effects of beardedness on person perception. *Perceptual and Motor Skills, 37,* 413–14.

Kenrick, D. T., & Gutierres, S. E. (1980). Contrast effects and judgments of physical attractiveness: When beauty becomes a social problem. *Journal of Personality and Social Psychology, 38,* 131–40.

Keyes, R. (1980). *The height of your life.* New York: Warner Books.

Kiesler, S. B., & Baral, R. L. (1970). The search for a romantic partner: The effects of self-esteem and physical attractiveness on romantic behavior. In K. J. Gergen & D. Marlowe (Eds.), *Personality and social behavior.* Reading, MA: Addison-Wesley.

Kitson, H. D. (1922). Height and weight as factors in salesmanship. *Journal of Personnel Research, 1.*

Kleck, R. E., Richardson, S. A., & Ronald, L. (1974). Physical appearance cues and interpersonal attraction in children. *Child Development, 45,* 305–10.

Kleinke, C. L., & Staneski, R. A. (1980). First impression of female bust size. *Journal of Social Psychology, 110,* 123–24.

Knapp, M. L. (1985). The study of physical appearance and cosmetics in Western culture. In J. A. Graham & A. M. Kligman (Eds.), *The psychology of cosmetic treatments.* New York: Praeger.

Krebs, D., & Adinolfi, A. A. (1975). Physical attractiveness, social relations and personality style. *Journal of Personality and Social Psychology, 31,* 107–14.

Kretschmer, E. (1925). *Physique and character.* New York: Harcourt Brace.

Kulka, R. A., & Kessler, J. B. (1978). Is justice really blind?—The influence of litigant physical attractiveness on juridical judgment. *Journal of Applied Social Psychology, 8,* 366–81.

Kurtz, D. L. (1969, December). Physical appearance and stature: Important variables in sales recruiting. *Personnel Journal,* 981–83.

Lakoff, R. T., & Scherr, R. L. (1985). *Face value: The politics of beauty.* London: Routledge & Kegan Paul.

Lambert, S. (1972). Reactions to a stranger as a function of style of dress. *Perceptual and Motor Skills, 35,* 711–12.

Landy, D., & Sigall, H. (1974). Beauty is talent: Task evaluation as a function of the performer's physical attractiveness. *Journal of Personality and Social Psychology, 29,* 299–304.

Langlois, J. H., & Downs, A. C. (1979). Peer relations as a function of physical attractiveness: The eye of the beholder or behavioral reality? *Child Development, 50,* 409–18.

Langlois, J. H., & Roggman, L. A. (1990). Attractive faces are only average. *Psychological Science, 1,* 115–21.

Langlois, J. H., Roggman, L. A., Casey, R. J., Ritter, J. M., Rieser-Danner, L. A., & Jenkins, V. Y. (1987). Infant preferences for attractive faces: Rudiments of a stereotype? *Developmental Psychology, 23,* 363–69.

Langlois, J. H., Roggman, L. A., & Musselman, L. (1994). What is average and what is not average about attractive faces? *Psychological Science, 5,* 214–20.

Largey, G. P., & Watson, D. R. (1972). The sociology of odors. *American Journal of Sociology, 77,* 1021–34.

Laser, P. S., & Mathie, V. A. (1982). Face facts: An unbidden role for features in communication. *Journal of Nonverbal Behavior, 7,* 3–19.

Lavater, J. C. (1783). *Essays on physiognomy.* London: Ward, Lock.

Lavrakas, P. J. (1975). Female preferences for male physiques. *Journal of Research in Personality, 9,* 324–34.

Lefkowitz, M., Blake, R., & Mouton, J. (1955). Status factors in pedestrian violation of traffic signals. *Journal of Abnormal and Social Psychology, 51,* 704–6.

Lerner, R. M., & Gellert, E. (1969). Body build identification, preference and aversion in children. *Developmental Psychology, 1,* 456–62.

Lerner, R. M., Karabenick, S. A., & Meisels, M. (1975). Effects of age and sex on the development of personal space schemata toward body build. *Journal of Genetic Psychology, 127,* 91–101.

Lerner, R. M., Karabenick, S. A., & Stuart, J. L. (1973). Relations among physical attractiveness, body attitudes, and self-concept in male and female college students. *Journal of Psychology, 85,* 119–29.

Lerner, R. M., & Korn, S. J. (1972). The development of body build stereotypes in males. *Child Development, 43,* 908–20.

Lerner, R. M., & Schroeder, C. (1971). Physique identification, preference and aversion in kindergarten children. *Developmental Psychology, 5,* 538.

Lerner, R. M., Venning, J., & Knapp, J. R. (1975). Age and sex effects on personal space schemata toward body build in late childhood. *Developmental Psychology, 11,* 855–56.

Lester, D., & Sheehan, D. (1980). Attitudes of supervisors toward short police officers. *Psychological Reports, 47,* 462.

Levine, J. M., & McBurney, D. H. (1977). Causes and consequences of effluvia: Body odor awareness and controllability as determinants of interpersonal evaluation. *Personality and Social Psychology Bulletin, 3,* 442–45.

Lippman, L. G. (1980). Toward a social psychology of flatulence: The interpersonal regulation of natural gas. *Psychology: A Quarterly Journal of Human Behavior, 17,* 41–50.

Long, T. J. (1978). Influence of uniform and religious status on interviewees. *Journal of Counseling Psychology, 25,* 405–9.

Lord, T., & Kasprzak, M. (1989). Identification of self through olfaction. *Perceptual and Motor Skills, 69,* 219–24.

Lurie, A. (1981). *The language of clothes.* New York: Random House.

Maddux, J. E., & Rogers, R. W. (1980). Effects of source expertness, physical attractiveness, and supporting arguments on persuasion: A case of brains over beauty. *Journal of Personality and Social Psychology, 39,* 235–44.

Malloy, J. T. (1975). *Dress for success.* New York: P. H. Wyden.

Malloy, J. T. (1977). *The women's dress for success book.* Chicago: Follet.

Mar, T. T. (1974). *Face reading.* New York: New American Library (Signet Book).

Marks, G., Miller, N., & Maruyama, G. (1981). Effect of targets' physical attractiveness on assumptions of similarity. *Journal of Personality and Social Psychology, 41,* 198–206.

Martin, J. G. (1964). Racial ethnocentrism and judgment of beauty. *Journal of Social Psychology, 63,* 59–63.

Mathes, E. W., & Kahn, A. (1975). Physical attractiveness, happiness, neuroticism and self esteem. *Journal of Psychology, 90,* 27–30.

McArthur, L. Z., & Baron, R. M. (1983). Toward an ecological theory of social perception. *Psychological Review, 90,* 215–38.

McBurney, D. H., Levine, J. N., & Cavanaugh, P. H. (1977). Psychophysical and social ratings of human body odor. *Personality and Social Psychology Bulletin, 3,* 135–38.

McClintock, M. K. (1971). Menstrual synchrony and suppression. *Nature, 229,* 244–45.

Mills, J., & Aronson, E. (1965). Opinion change as a function of the communicators' attractiveness and desire to influence. *Journal of Personality and Social Psychology, 1,* 173–77.

Monetmayor, R. (1978). Men and their bodies: The relationship between body type and behavior. *Journal of Social Issues, 34,* 48–64.

Morris, T. L., Gorham, J., Cohen, S. H., & Huffman, D. (1996). Fashion in the classroom: Effects of attire on student perceptions of instructors in college classes. *Communication Education, 45,* 135–48.

Moss, M. K., Miller, R., & Page, R. A. (1975). The effects of racial context on the perception of physical attractiveness. *Sociometry, 38,* 525–35.

Murstein, B. I. (1972). Physical attractiveness and marital choice. *Journal of Personality and Social Psychology, 23,* 8–12.

Murstein, B. I., & Christy, P. (1976). Physical attractiveness and marriage adjustment in middle-aged couples. *Journal of Personality and Social Psychology, 34,* 537–42.

Murstein, B. I., Gadpaille, W. J., & Byrne, D. (1971). What makes people sexually appealing? *Sexual Behavior, 1,* 75–77.

Myers, P. N., Jr., & Biocca, F. A. (1992). The elastic body image: The effect of television advertising and programming on body image distortions in young women. *Journal of Communication, 42,* 108–33.

Nemmeth, C., & Hyland, R. (1973). A simulated jury study: Characteristics of the defendant and the jurors. *Journal of Social Psychology, 90,* 223–29.

Nevid, J. S. (1984). Sex differences in factors of romantic attraction. *Sex Roles, 2,* 401–411.

Parnell, R. W. (1958). *Behavior and physique: An introduction to practical and applied somatometry.* London: Edward Arnold.

Pellegrini, R. J. (1973). The virtue of hairiness. *Psychology Today, 6,* 14.

Pellegrini, R. J. (1989). Beardedness as a stimulus variable: Note on methodology and meta-analysis of impression-formation data. *Perceptual and Motor Skills, 69,* 161–62.

Pennebaker, J. W., Dyer, M. A., Caulkins, R. S., Litowitz, D. L., Ackerman, P. L., Anderson, D. B., & McGraw, K. M. (1979). Don't the girls get prettier at closing time: A country and western application to psychology. *Personality and Social Psychology Bulletin, 5,* 122–25.

Pertschuk, M., Trisdorfer, A., & Allison, P. D. (1994). Men's bodies—The survey. *Psychology Today* (November/December) 35–36, 39, 72.

Polhemus, T., & Proctor, L. (1978). *Fashion and anti-fashion: An anthropology of clothing and adornment.* London: Thames & Hudson.

Polivy, J., Garner, D. M., & Garfinkel, P. E. (1986). Causes and consequences of the current preference for thin female physiques. In C. P. Herman, M. P. Zanna, & E. T. Higgins (Eds.), *Physical appearance, stigma, and social behavior: The Ontario Symposium* (Vol. 3, pp. 89–112). Hillsdale, NJ: Erlbaum.

Porter, R. H., Cernoch, J. M., & Balogh, R. D. (1985). Odor signatures and kin recognition. *Physiology and Behavior, 34,* 445–48.

Porter, R. H., Cernoch, J. M., & McLaughlin, F. J. (1983). Maternal recognition of neonates through olfactory cues. *Physiology and Behavior, 30,* 151–54.

Porter, R. H., & Moore, J. D. (1981). Human kin recognition by olfactory cues. *Physiology and Behavior, 27,* 493–95.

Portnoy, E. J. (1993). The impact of body type on perceptions of attractiveness by older individuals. *Communication Reports, 6,* 101–8.

Ray, W. S. (1958). Judgments of intelligence based on brief observation of physiognomy. *Psychological Reports, 13,* 478.

Raymond, B., & Unger, R. (1972). The apparel oft proclaims the man. *Journal of Social Psychology, 87,* 75–82.

Reed, J. A. P. (1973). *Clothing: A symbolic indicator of the self.* Unpublished doctoral dissertation, Purdue University.

Reis, H. T., Nezlek, J., & Wheeler, L. (1980). Physical attractiveness in social interaction. *Journal of Personality and Social Psychology, 38,* 604–17.

Reis, H. T., Wheeler, L., Spiegel, N., Kernis, M. H., Nezlek, J., & Perri, M. (1982). Physical attractiveness in social interaction: II. Why does appearance affect social experience? *Journal of Personality and Social Psychology, 43,* 979–96.

Richardson, S. A., Goodman, N., Hastorf, A., & Dornbusch, S. (1961). Cultural uniformities in relation to physical disabilities. *American Sociological Review, 26,* 241–47.

Roach, M. E., & Eicher, J. B. (Eds.). (1965). *Dress, adornment, and the social order.* New York: John Wiley and Sons.

Roberts, J. V., & Herman, C. P. (1986). The psychology of height: An empirical review. In C. P. Herman, M. P. Zanna, & E. T. Higgins (Eds.), *Physical appearance, stigma, and social behavior: The Ontario Symposium* (Vol. 3, pp. 113–40). Hillsdale, NJ: Erlbaum.

Robinson, D. E. (1975). Style changes: Cyclical, inexorable, and foreseeable. *Harvard Business Review, 53,* 121–31.

Rosencranz, M. L. (1962). Clothing symbolism. *Journal of Home Economics, 54,* 18–22.

Rosenfeld, L. B., & Plax, T. G. (1977). Clothing as communication. *Journal of Communication, 27,* 24–31.

Rosenthal, T. L., & White, G. M. (1972). On the importance of hair in students' clinical inferences. *Journal of Clinical Psychology, 28,* 43–47.

Rudofsky, B. (1971). *The unfashionable human body.* Garden City, NY: Doubleday.

Rump, E. E., & Delin, P. S. (1973). Differential accuracy in the status-height phenomenon and an experimenter effect. *Journal of Personality and Social Psychology, 28,* 343–47.

Russell, F. (1981). *The secret war.* Chicago: Time Life Books.

Russell, M. J. (1976). Human olfactory communication. *Nature, 260,* 520–22.

Ryan, M. S. (1966). *Clothing: A study in human behavior.* New York: Holt, Rinehart & Winston.

Ryckman, R. M., Robbins, M. A., Thornton, B., Kaczor, L. M., Gayton, S. L., & Anderson, C. V. (1991). Public self-consciousness and physique stereotyping. *Personality and Social Psychology Bulletin, 17,* 400–405.

Secord, P. F., Dukes, W. F., & Bevan, W. W. (1954). Personalities in faces: I. An experiment in social perceiving. *Genetic Psychology Monographs, 49,* 231–79.

Seligman, C., Brickman, J., & Koulack, D. (1977). Rape and physical attractiveness: Assigning responsibility to victims. *Journal of Personality, 45,* 554–63.

Sheldon, W. H. (1940). *The varieties of human physique.* New York: Harper & Row.

Sheldon, W. H. (1942). *The varieties of temperament.* New York: Harper & Row.

Sheldon, W. H. (1954). *Atlas of man: A guide for somatyping the adult male at all ages.* New York: Harper & Row.

Shontz, F. C. (1969). *Perceptual and cognitive aspects of body experience.* New York: Academic Press.

Sigall, H., & Landy, D. (1973). Radiating beauty: Effects of having a physically attractive partner on person perception. *Journal of Personality and Social Psychology, 26,* 218–23.

Sigall, H., & Ostrove, N. (1975). Beautiful but dangerous: Effects of offender attractiveness and nature of the crime of juridic judgment. *Journal of Personality and Social Psychology, 31,* 410–14.

Singer, J. E. (1964). The use of manipulative strategies: Machiavellianism and attractiveness. *Sociometry, 27,* 128–51.

Singh, B. N. (1964). A study of certain personal qualities as preferred by college students in their marital partners. *Journal of Psychological Researches, 8,* 37–48.

Singh, D. (1993). Adaptive significance of female physical attractiveness: Role of waist-to-hip ratio. *Journal of Personality and Social Psychology, 65,* 293–307.

Smith, K., & Sines, J. O. (1960). Demonstration of a peculiar odor in the sweat of schizophrenic patients. *Archives of General Psychiatry, 2,* 184–88.

Solénder, E. K., & Solender, E. (1976). Minimizing the effect of the unattractive client on the jury: A study of the interaction of physical appearance with assertions and self-experience references. *Human Rights, 5,* 201–14.

Solomon, M. R. (Ed.). (1985). *The psychology of fashion.* New York: Lexington Books.

Sontag, S. (1972, September 23). The double standard of aging. *Saturday Review,* 29–38.

Stabler, B., Whitt, K., Moreault, D., D'Ercole, A., & Underwood, L. (1980). Social judgments by children of short stature. *Psychological Reports, 46,* 743–46.

Staffieri, J. R. (1972). Body build and behavioral expectancies in young females. *Developmental Psychology, 6,* 125–27.

Stewart, J. E. (1980). Defendant's attractiveness as a factor in the outcome of criminal trials: An observational study. *Journal of Applied Social Psychology, 10,* 348–61.

Stewart, R. A., Tufton, S. J., & Steel, R. E. (1973). Stereotyping and personality: Sex differences in perception of female physiques. *Perceptual and Motor Skills, 36,* 811–14.

Stroebe, W., Insko, C. A., Thompson, V. D., & Layton, B. D. (1971). Effects of physical attractiveness, attitudes similarity and sex on various aspects of interpersonal attraction. *Journal of Personality and Social Psychology, 79,* 79–91.

Strongman, K. T., & Hart, C. J. (1968). Stereotyped reactions to body build. *Psychological Reports, 23,* 1175–78.

Suedfeld, P., Bochner, S., & Matas, C. (1971). Petitioner's attire and petition signing by peace demonstrators: A field experiment. *Journal of Applied Social Psychology, 1,* 278–83.

Sunnafrank, M. J., & Miller, G. R. (1981). The role of initial conversations in determining attraction to similar and dissimilar strangers. *Human Communication Research, 8,* 16–25.

Sybers, R., & Roach, M. E. (1962). Clothing and human behavior. *Journal of Home Economics, 54,* 184–87.

Tavris, C. (1977). Men and women report their views on masculinity. *Psychology Today, 10,* 34–42, 82.

Timmerman, K., & Hewitt, J. (1980). Examining the halo effect of physical attractiveness. *Perceptual and Motor Skills, 51,* 607–12.

Udry, J. R., & Eckland, B. K. (1982, September). *The benefits of being attractive: Differential payoffs for men and women.* Paper presented at the meeting of the American Sociological Association.

Walker, R. N. (1963). Body build and behavior in young children. *Child Development, 34,* 1–23.

Walker, R. N. (1963). Body build and behavior in young children: II. Body build and parents' ratings. *Child Development, 34,* 1–23.

Wallace, P. (1977). Individual discrimination of human by odor. *Physiology and Behavior, 19,* 577–79.

Walster, E., Aronson, V., Abrahams, D., & Rottmann, L. (1966). Importance of physical attractiveness in dating behavior. *Journal of Personality and Social Psychology, 4,* 508–16.

Warr, P. B., & Knapper, C. (1968). *The perception of people and events.* New York: John Wiley and Sons.

Watson, B. (1975, May 16). Cons get cosmetic surgery. *Lafayette Journal and Courier,* p. A-8.

Weiten, W. (1980). The attraction-leniency effect in jury research: An examination of external validity. *Journal of Applied Social Psychology, 10,* 340–47.

Wells, W., & Siegel, B. (1961). Stereotyped somatypes. *Psychological Reports, 8,* 77–78.

White, G. L. (1980). Physical attractiveness and courtship progress. *Journal of Personality and Social Psychology, 39,* 660–68.

White, S. E. (1995). A content analytic technique for measuring the sexiness of women's business attire in media presentations. *Communication Research Reports, 12,* 178–85.

Widgery, R. N. (1974). Sex of receiver and physical attractiveness of source as determinants of initial credibility perceptions. *Western Speech, 38,* 13–17.

Widgery, R. N., & Ruch, R. S. (1981). Beauty and the Machiavellian. *Communication Quarterly, 29,* 297–301.

Wiener, H. (1966). External chemical messengers: I. Emission and reception in man. *New York State Journal of Medicine, 66,* 3153.

Wiggins, J. S., Wiggins, N., & Conger, J. C. (1968). Correlates of heterosexual somatic preference. *Journal of Personality and Social Psychology, 10,* 82–90.

Wiggins, N., & Wiggins, J. S. (1969). A topological analysis of male preferences for female body types. *Multivariate Behavioral Research, 4,* 89–102.

Wilson, P. R. (1968). Perceptual distortion of height as a function of ascribed academic status. *Journal of Social Psychology, 10,* 97–102.

Wolf, N. (1991). *The beauty myth.* New York: Morrow.

Yates, J., & Taylor, J. (1978). Stereotypes for somatypes: Shared beliefs about Sheldon's physiques. *Psychological Reports, 43,* 777–78.

Part Four

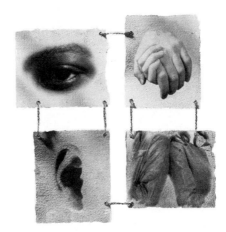

The Communicators' Behavior

M ost of our nonverbal behavior involves change or movement. We exhibit different gestures and postures during an encounter; sometimes we touch others and sometimes we do not; our face, eyes, and voice also are displayed in various patterns. Part Four examines these behaviors individually; but in everyday conversation, the combination of such signals working in concert characterizes our communication behavior. In Part Five, Chapter 12 shows how these nonverbal signals combine to accomplish our communicative goals.

CHAPTER 7

The Effects of Gesture and Posture on Human Communication

We respond to gestures with an extreme alertness and, one might say, in accordance with an elaborate and secret code that is written nowhere, known by none, and understood by all.

—EDWARD SAPIR

Sapir's view (quoted above) aptly characterized the prevailing view of gestures during the *first* part of the twentieth century. If he were alive today, his assessment would no doubt be somewhat different. Spoken language and gestures are commonly acknowledged as building blocks of human interaction (informal conversation as well as more formal public discourse), but, unlike language, gestures have received relatively little scholarly attention until recently. Kendon (1981a) identified only six scholarly books on gesture published between 1900 and 1979 in the English language. Now, however, we are beginning to understand and write down the complex nature of gestures that are coded. We also are learning how people come to understand gestures that are not highly coded.

What exactly is a gesture? Gestures are movements of the body (or some part of it) used to communicate an idea, intention, or feeling. Many of these actions are made with the arms/hands, but the face/head area is also used in gesturing. Some actions *not* normally considered gestures include self-touchings, grooming, clothing adjustments, and nervous mannerisms. Many body-focused movements reflect or regulate states of arousal (Barroso et al., 1978). Others may be task oriented. Actions used in performing a task such as smoking, eating, or picking up a book also are normally considered outside the realm of gestures. If, however, these instrumental actions are perceived as performed in an affected manner (with "style") or if they are performed in coordination with speech, they would qualify as an intended gesture. In at least one case, people have tried to perform an easily recognized gesture, the forearm jerk (meaning "fuck you"), so that it does not look like a gesture but still communicates the gesture's meaning (see Figure 7-1). Because performing the forearm jerk was illegal in Malta, some residents acted as if they simply were rubbing the upper part of a straightened and extended arm. The rubbed arm also had a fist.

Actions that we perceive to be the unplanned result of a felt emotion are not part of a planned message and also are excluded from the category of gesticulations. In short, actions that are not part of a person's "given" performance normally are not considered gestures. As we observe others, we seem able to easily identify movements that are part of a person's communicative effort and those that are not.

Gestures perform many functions. They may replace speech (during dialogue or when speech is not used at all), regulate the flow and rhythm of

Figure 7–1

a   b

(a) The forearm jerk. (b) The upper-arm rub used as an insulting gesture. (Photo © 1991 Psychotex/Kevin E. White, P.O. Box 470701, Fort Worth, Texas 76147. All rights reserved.)

interaction, maintain attention, add emphasis and/or clarity to speech, help characterize and make memorable the content of speech, and act as forecasters of forthcoming speech.

What types of gestures are commonly employed in everyday interaction? Gestures may be categorized in many ways (Morris, 1977, 1994), but the two primary types are *speech-independent* and *speech-related* gestures.

SPEECH-INDEPENDENT GESTURES

Speech-independent gestures are also known as *emblems* (Ekman, 1976, 1977) or *autonomous gestures* (Kendon, 1984, 1989). They are nonverbal acts that have a direct verbal translation or dictionary definition, usually consisting of a word or two or a phrase. There is high agreement among members of a culture or subculture on the verbal "translation" of these signals. These gestures are the least dependent on speech for their meaning and most commonly occur as a single gesture. The "ring gesture" in Figure 7-2 is an example of a speech-independent gesture found in several cultures.

Figure 7–2

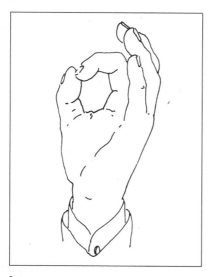

a   b

The ring gesture signifies "A-OK" or "Good" in the United States as a speech independent gesture. It may stand for "zero" or "worthless" in certain conversational contexts. (Photo © 1991 Psychotex/Kevin E. White, P.O. Box 470701, Fort Worth, Texas 76147. All rights reserved.)

Children are able to decode some of these speech-independent gestures by the time they are three years old, and this ability increases dramatically by age five (Kumin & Lazar, 1974; Michael & Willis, 1968, 1969). In one study, four-year-olds of both sexes accurately decoded the emblems for "yes," "no," "come here," "quiet," "good-bye," "two," "I won't listen," "blowing a kiss," "I'm going to sleep," and "I won't do it." None of the four-year-olds was able to accurately decode "crazy." Generally, children at this age understand and decode accurately more speech-independent gestures than they actually use in their own interactions.

Adult awareness of speech-independent gestures is about the same as of word choice. It is a behavior we are usually very conscious of enacting. Gestures often are produced with the hand, but not exclusively. A nose-wrinkle may say "I'm disgusted!" or "Phew! It stinks!" To say "I don't know" or "I'm helpless" or "I'm uncertain" one might turn both palms up, shrug the shoulders, or do both simultaneously. Ekman believes that facial emblems differ from facial expressions of emotion by being more stylized and presented for longer or shorter duration. Facial emblems also may emphasize particular parts of the face, for example, smiling to indicate happiness or mechanically dropping the jaw or dramatically raising the eyebrows to indicate surprise.

In some cultures, speech-independent gestures are strung together to form a sequential message, but this is unusual in the United States. Although it could happen if you were on the phone when a visitor enters your office and you need to indicate "wait a minute," "come in," and "sit down" in succession. Sometimes an entire system of speech-independent gestures develops as with underwater divers, umpires, and television directors. Even though these gestures form a system of signals related to performing a specific task, such systems can grow beyond the boundaries of those tasks. In the sawmills of British Columbia, for example, the noise level made spoken communication very difficult. A system of task-related gestures developed but eventually came to include messages not associated with the tasks of the sawmill (Meissner & Philpott, 1975). Gesture systems that are not limited to a specific task are known as *sign languages*. Sign language is commonly thought of as a form of communication for the hearing impaired, but sign languages also develop in other contexts. Examples are in religious orders where vows of silence are taken and in social situations where some participants are forbidden to speak, as has been reported for Armenian wives in the presence of their husbands (Kendon, 1983).

Speech-independent gestures may be used when verbal channels are blocked or fail, but they also are used during verbal interaction. A person may be telling the story of another person's strange behavior and may conclude by making a gesture that communicates "He's crazy." In this case, the circular gesture at the side of the head substitutes for the entire sentence. This gesture also could be used to complete an utterance: "If you ask me, I think . . . " In this case, the verbalizations are redundant and unnecessary for understanding the message being communicated. In this example, the speech-independent gesture occurred at the end of a speaker's turn, but others may occur at the beginning. Ekman's study of the "shrug" emblem finds it occurs most often at the beginning of a speaker's turn (see Figure 7-3).

In an interview observed by Ekman, he noted an emblem that was used for a long time during the interaction and served as the interviewee's commentary on the episode. This "emblematic slip" (analogous to a slip of the tongue) occurred when a woman was subjected to a stressful interview by a person whose status forbade free expressions of dislike. The woman, unknown to herself or the interviewer, displayed "the finger" for several minutes during the interview. Listeners also may use speech-independent gestures to comment on or qualify what the speaker is saying. "Yes" and "no" gestures are common listener responses during another's speech.

Thus, even though speech-independent gestures can communicate messages without attendant speech, their meanings are still influenced by context. Giving someone "the finger" can be humorous or insulting, depending on who is performing it, who is the target, and what other behaviors accompany

Figure 7–3

The shrug gesture. (Photo Researchers, Inc. NYC © Richard Hutchings)

it. Facial expressions and eye movement accompanying speech-independent gestures are likely to expand the range of possible meanings associated with a hand gesture. And it is always possible that the meaning associated with a gesture in the absence of speech will be modified if it is accompanied by speech, including those occasions when the accompanying speech is seemingly redundant. Some of these emblematic gestures are specifically adapted to particular subgroups within a given culture. In the United States, for example, the finger-wag gesture indicating "no-no" is used primarily when adults are addressing children; the "shame on you" gesture seems limited to usage by children (see Figure 7-4).

Sherzer's (1974, 1982) detailed work of the pointed-lip gesture used by the San Blas Cuna of Panama and the thumbs-up gesture used by urban Brazilians illustrates how gestures may have a general meaning that is modified by context. For example, the thumbs-up gesture has a general meaning of "good" or "positive" (see Figure 7-5). Context, however, expands the range of meanings. It can be used to indicate understanding the point of what someone said or did; to acknowledge a favor granted; to greet someone; to indicate knowledge of the next move in an interactional sequence and who is going to perform it; and to request permission to carry out an action as when a customer signals a waiter about the availability of a table.

Sometimes the context does not affect the meaning so much as the slight changes in the way the gesture is performed. When the forefinger extended (with the rest of the hand in a fist) is held motionless about twelve inches

Figure 7–4

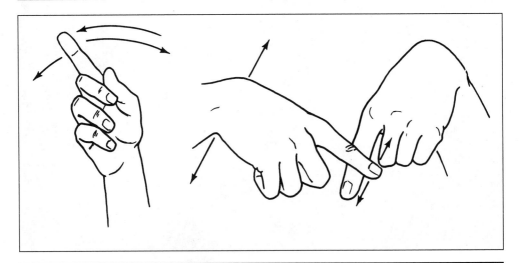

Finger emblems (United States) for "no" (left) and "shame on you" (right).

Figure 7–5

The thumbs-up gesture. (Photo © AP/Wide World Photos)

in front of one's chest, the meaning is "wait a minute"; when the finger repeatedly moves up and down, the meaning shifts to one of emphasis or reprimand; when the same finger and hand are put perpendicularly in front of the lips, it means "be quiet."

There are published lists of emblematic gestures for cultures around the world (Axtell, 1991; Barakat, 1973; Creider, 1977; Johnson, Ekman, & Friesen, 1975; Morris, Collett, Marsh, & O'Shaughnessy, 1979; Saitz & Cervenka, 1972; Sparhawk, 1978; Trupin, 1976; Wylie, 1977). Kendon's (1981b) analysis of over 800 emblematic gestures contained in these lists revealed three broad categories of meaning that accounted for 80 percent of the speech-independent gestures observed in the United States, Colombia, France, southern Italy, and Kenya and 66 percent of those found in Iran. These categories were interpersonal control, announcement of one's current state or condition, and an evaluative response to the actions or appearance of another. Ekman's studies of five cultures indicate each had emblematic gestures for greeting and departing, replying, directing locomotion (all forms of interpersonal control); for insults as evaluation of another's actions or appearance; and for referring to one's physical and affective state or announcing one's current condition or state. Some cultures have many emblems in a particular category (e.g., evaluations of another's behavior), while the emblems in another culture may emphasize other messages (e.g., interpersonal control).

As yet, no speech-independent gestures have been found that are made the same and have the same meaning in every culture studied. Future research may identify some, however. The most likely candidates are gestures having to do with affirmation, negation, stop, don't know, and sleeping, eating, and drinking (functions all human beings share).

Far more common are examples of gestures of similar form that differ in meaning from culture to culture. In 1877–78, Bulgaria and Russia combined forces to fight Turkey. The alliance discovered a real problem in that the Russian way of saying "no" was to shake the head from side to side, and a very similar Bulgarian gesture (a head sway) meant "yes" (Jacobson, 1972). The ring gesture (thumb and forefinger in a circle) pictured in Figure 7-2 indicates "you're worth zero" in France and Belgium; "money" in Japan; and "asshole" in parts of southern Italy; and in Greece and Turkey it is an insulting or vulgar sexual invitation. Of course, to many U. S. residents it is simply "A-OK." Things certainly would not be "A-OK" if the ring gesture were used in cultures that attached other meanings to it. The thumbs-up gesture pictured in Figure 7-5 is usually decoded as "good," "positive," or "OK" in the United States, but in the Middle East it is an obscene gesture. The thumb inserted between the index and third finger (fig gesture) is an invitation to have sex in Germany, Holland, and Denmark but is a wish for good luck or protection in Portugal and Brazil (see Figure 7-6). The "V" gesture with the palm toward the performer is a sexual insult in Great Britain but means "victory" if the palm is facing away from the body. During World War II, Winston Churchill made the "V for victory" gesture world famous. In the United States, there does not seem to be the British meaning of sexual insult associated with the "V" sign, nor is there any distinction in the form of the "V" for victory and the "V" for peace—a meaning that gained popularity in the anti-Vietnam War protests of the 1960s (see Figure 7-7). The vertical horn sign pictured in Figure 7-8 (page 262)is normally decoded "cuckold" in Portugal, Spain, Italy, and places in Central and South America. Students from cultures in which this gesture indicates that "your wife has been unfaithful to you, and you are either too stupid to know it or not man enough to satisfy her" would indeed be surprised if they were to attend the University of Texas. Here, and throughout Texas, the horns hand is used to show identification with the university and represents school spirit. It is modeled after longhorn cattle and literally represents the University of Texas Longhorns. Consider the reaction of people who associate the horns hand with "cuckold" viewing a University of Texas football game with 75,000 fans making the sign vigorously, repeatedly, and in unison. In addition, another sign that is similar, but has the thumb thrust out instead of tucked in, is decoded by many people around the world as "I love you." The origin of this sign is in the finger spelling of deaf communicators.

Many autonomous gestures have no equivalent in other cultures. In France, for example, one can signal "drunk" by making a fist around the nose and twisting. Some messages have different gestural forms from culture to

Figure 7–6

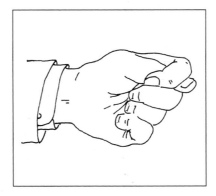

The fig gesture.

culture. Notice how the gestures for suicide in Figure 7-9 (page 264) reflect the most common methods of suicide in each culture. The number of speech-independent gestures used within a given culture may vary considerably, from fewer than 100 in the United States to more than 250 identified with Israeli students.

One of the problems in comparing studies of speech-independent gestures across cultures is the lack of a uniform method for identifying them. Johnson, Ekman, and Friesen's study (1975) of American emblematic gestures proposes a systematic procedure that future studies may want to use. The authors ask members of a particular group or culture to produce emblems associated with a list of verbal statements and phrases. They report that after about ten or fifteen informants have been tested, a great majority of the emblems have been identified. To qualify as a "verified" emblem, at least 70 percent of the encoders must perform the action in a similar way. The emblems that are similarly encoded are then presented to a group of decoders who are asked to identify the meaning of the gestures and the extent to which they reflect natural usage in everyday situations. Gestures used primarily for games like charades normally are not considered "natural." Inventions and performances that require speech are also eliminated. At least 70 percent of the decoders also have to match the encoder's meaning and judge the gesture to be used naturally in everyday communication situations. The index finger pointed at the head can mean "smart" or "stupid" depending on context, but if 70 percent of those in a given community say it means "stupid," then this is considered a verified emblem for "stupid" among this group. It does not prevent context from changing the meaning, however. The authors do not claim to have identified a complete list of American emblems, but the ones they verified are listed in Table 7-1.

Figure 7–7

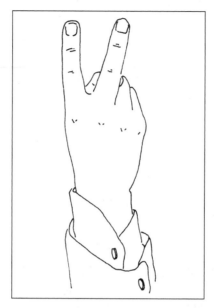

a

b

(a) "V" gesture used to insult. (b) Richard Nixon makes the "V for victory" gesture at the 1968 Republican Convention in Miami. (Photo credit: UPI/Bettmann Newsphotos)

(Continued)

Figure 7–7 (Continued)

c

d

(c) Former Texas governor Ann Richards makes the "V for victory" gesture during her political campaign in 1990. (Photo © Daennrich/The Image Works) (d) People at an anti-Persian Gulf War demonstration in Washington, DC, use the "V" gesture to signify "peace." (Photo © 1991 Misha Erwitt/Magnum Photos, Inc.)

Figure 7–8

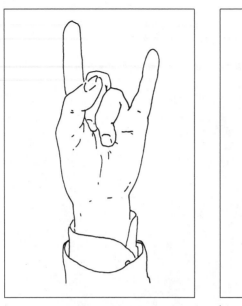

a

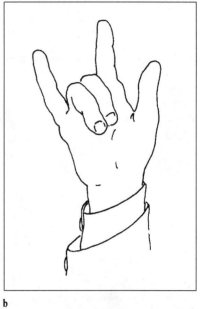

b

c

(a) The vertical horn gesture. (b) The "I love you" sign. (c) The University of Texas baseball team making the "Hook 'em, Horns" gesture during their victory celebration at a College World Series. (Photo © Daennrich/The Image Works)

(Continued)

Figure 7–8 (Continued)

d   e

(d) Former president George Bush makes the "Hook 'em, Horns" gesture at the 1990 University of Texas commencement. (Photo © Ralph Barrera/Austin American Statesman, 1990) (e) The double horn gesture in Naples meaning "cuckolded." (Photo © 1991 Psychotex/Kevin E. White, P.O. Box 470701, Fort Worth, Texas 76147. All rights reserved.)

SPEECH-RELATED GESTURES

Speech-related gestures, sometimes called *illustrators,* are directly tied to, or accompany, speech. The meanings and functions of these gestures are revealed as we examine how they relate to the attendant spoken language. Attempts to classify the various types of speech-related gestures have used different terminology (Efron, 1941; Ekman, 1977; Kendon, 1989; McNeill 1992; Streeck, 1992;) but four common types emerge:

1. Gestures related to the speaker's referent—concrete or abstract
2. Gestures indicating the speaker's relationship to the referent
3. Gestures that act as visual punctuation for the speaker's discourse
4. Gestures that assist in the regulation and organization of the spoken dialogue between two interactants

REFERENT-RELATED GESTURES

As we talk, we use gestures to characterize the content of our speech. Sometimes these will be movements depicting fairly concrete referents; sometimes vague, abstract ideas will be the referent for gestural depiction.

Figure 7-9

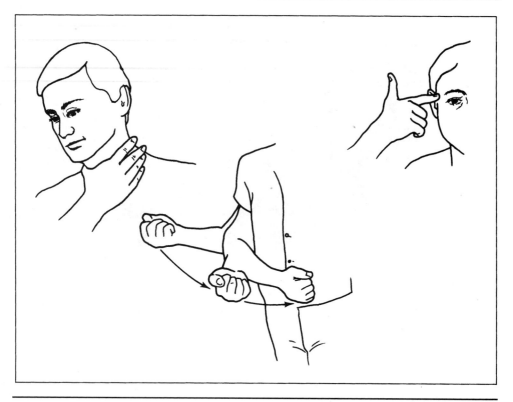

Cultural variations in suicide gestures. Top left: the South Fore, Papua New Guinea; bottom: Japan; top right: the United States.

Pointing movements, for instance, can help indicate a specific person, place, or thing being discussed. The referent may be in the immediate conversational environment or something more distant, as is the case when you say, "And where did you come from before that?" while pointing your finger in the direction of the referred-to place. Gestures that draw the referent's shape or movement, and gestures that depict spatial relationships, can be used to help a listener visualize features associated with concrete referents. When you say, "I had to bend the branch way back," while illustrating how you did this, the gesture bears a close relationship to the concrete semantic content of your speech. When referent-related gestures outline the referent by drawing a picture in space (e.g., an hourglass figure signifying "shapely woman"), it may be asked whether this is truly speech related. The test for determining whether such a picture may be speech independent is if 70 percent of the members of the usage community respond with the "shapely woman" meaning when confronted with the gestural portrayal without any speech context.

Table 7–1
VERIFIED AMERICAN EMBLEMS

Message Type	Encoded Message Meaning	Decoded Message Meaning	% Decoded Correctly	% Considered Natural Usage
Interpersonal Directions (Commands)	Sit down beside me	Sit down beside me	100	100
	Be silent, hush	Be silent, hush	100	100
	Come here	Come here	100	100
	I can't hear you	I can't hear you	100	100
	Wait—hold it	Wait—hold it	100	100
	I warn you	I warn you	100	94
	Get lost	*Get lost or get out or go away	100	93
	Be calm	Be calm	100	93
	Follow me	*Follow me or this way	100	88
	†Time to go	*Time to go or what time is it?	100	87
	Stop	*Stop or halt	100	81
	Go the other way	*Go the other way or no, not that way	96	96
	‡I want to smoke and got a cigarette?	*I want to smoke or got a cigarette?	96	74
	Look!	*Look or I see something or look over there	91	100
	Go away	Go away or rejection or get out of here	91	96
	Take it away	*Take it away or go away or get out of here	90	87
	Go this way	*Go this way or over there or that way	89	86
	Go ahead	*Go ahead or go on by	87	83
	‡Hurry and quickly	*Quickly or hurry or come here quickly	85	100
	†What time is it?	*What time is it? or time to go	77	100
	Stay here	*Stay here or down here	77	100
Own Physical State	‡I'm hot and it's hot	*I'm hot or hard work or a close shave	100	88
	‡Hard work	*Hard work or I'm hot or a close shave	81	100
	‡A close shave	*A close shave or I'm hot or hard work	81	100
	‡It's cold and I'm cold	*It's cold or I'm cold	100	70
	I'm full of food	I'm full of food	93	93
	I've got a headache	I've got a headache	93	93
	I've got a toothache	I've got a toothache	87	87
	I've got an earache	I've got an earache	70	81
	Tastes good	Tastes good	93	70
	I am smart	I am smart	93	73
	How could I be so dumb?	How could I be so dumb?	100	95
Insults	§Fuck you (finger)	*Screw you or up yours or fuck you	100	100
	§Fuck you (arm)	*Fuck you or up yours or screw you	100	81

(Continued)

Table 7–1 (Continued)

Message Type	Encoded Message Meaning	Decoded Message Meaning	% Decoded Correctly	% Considered Natural Usage
Insults *(continued)*	‡The hell with you and rejection	*The hell with you or rejection	100	94
	‡He's crazy and he's stupid	*He's crazy or he's stupid	100	75
	Shame on you	Shame on you	100	70
Replies	OK (fingers)	OK	100	100
	‡No (head) and I disagree	*No or I disagree	100	100
	I don't know	I don't know	100	100
	‡Yes and I agree and I like it	*Yes or I agree or I like it	100	100
	Absolutely no	*Absolutely no or no way	100	95
	I dislike it	*I dislike it or no way	100	93
	I promise	*I promise or cross my heart	100	74
	Absolutely yes	Absolutely yes	93	81
	‡Hard to think about this and thinking	*Hard to think about this or puzzlement or thinking	89	100
	I doubt it	I doubt it	70	81
Own Affect	I'm angry	I'm angry	100	94
	‡I'm disgusted and something stinks	*Something stinks	100	81
	I'm sad	*I'm sad or I'm ashamed	95	72
	I'm surprised	I'm surprised	95	88
	Whoopee!	*Whoopee! or hooray!	88	74
Greetings and Departures	Good-bye	Good-bye	94	100
	Hello	Hello	80	100
Physical Appearance	‡Woman and nice figure	*Woman or nice figure	100	100
Unclassified	You (finger point)	You	100	100
	Me (own chest)	Me	100	100
	Hitchhiking	Hitchhiking	100	94
	Counting	Counting	100	70
	Gossip	*Gossip or talk-talk-talk	96	91
	Fighting	Fighting	96	73
	‡Peace and victory	*Peace or victory	94	87
	Good luck	Good luck	92	100
	Money	Money	92	79
	It's far away	*It's far away or over there	87	96
	Suicide (gun)	*Suicide or shoot myself	83	73
	Finished	*It's finished or that's enough	78	83

*Either decoded message was accepted, although the first message was given more often than the second.
†Two subtly different actions were performed for two subtly different messages.
‡The same action was performed for each encoded message.
§Two different actions were performed as alternatives for the same message.
Source: From H. G. Johnson, P. Ekman, and W. V. Friesen, "Communicative Body Movements: American Emblems," Semiotica 15 (1975): 335–53.

More abstract referents are characterized when we sketch the path or direction of an idea in the air; when we make a series of circular movements with the hand and/or arm suggesting, "I mean more than the specific words I've used"; and when we use expansion and contraction gestures, like those of an accordion player, to indicate the breadth of the subject being discussed. Sometimes we represent abstract content via gestural metaphors. For example, cup-shaped gestures in the following sample of discourse (McNeill, 1985) represent containers of what could be supposed. When they spread apart, they seem to convey the idea that "anything is possible," and their sudden disappearance suggests that what might have been did not happen:

> "Even though one might *(both hands form cups and spread wide apart)* have supposed *(cups vanish abruptly)* . . ."

SPEAKER'S-RELATIONSHIP-TO-THE-REFERENT GESTURES

These gestures, rather than characterizing the nature of the thing being talked about, comment on the speaker's orientation to the referent. The positioning of the palms can show very different orientations toward one's own message (see Figure 7-10). For example, palms up for more uncertainty ("I think" or "I'm not sure"); palms down for certainty ("clearly" or "absolutely"); palms out and facing the listener for assertions ("Let me say this . . ." or "Calm down"); and palms facing the speaker for embracing a concept ("I've got this great idea . . . "). Palm positions can have other speech-related associations, such as a speaker's palms up when pleading, begging, or even anticipating closeness in greetings.

There are also oscillating hand movements that suggest a speaker "isn't sure" or "could go either way." Charles DeGaulle, former president of France,

Figure 7–10

Palm gestures.

Figure 7–11

1950   1964

General Charles DeGaulle's characteristic gesture, perceived by many as "grasping for control of an idea." (Photos © AP/Wide World Photos)

was noted for his grasping gesture, which many felt signified his desire to control the subject under discussion (see Figure 7-11).

PUNCTUATION GESTURES

Punctuation gestures accent, emphasize, and organize important segments of the discourse. Such a segment may be a single word or a larger utterance unit (e.g., a summary or a new theme). When these gestures are used to emphasize a particular word or phrase, they often coincide with the primary voice stress. Punctuation gestures can also organize the stream of speech into units. When we speak of a series of things, we may communicate discreteness by rhythmic chopping hand gestures, for example, "We must consider A (gesture), B (gesture), and C (gesture)." Sometimes a single chopping hand gesture after C indicates C will be considered separately, or A, B, and C will be considered as a group. A slight downward movement of the head may accompany the hand gestures. Pounding the hand or fist in the air or on another object also acts as a device for adding emphasis and visually "underlining" a particular point being made (see Figure 7-12).

Punctuation can, of course, be accomplished with body movements other than the hands. The "eye flash" (not the "eye*brow* flash" discussed in Chapters 2 and 12) is one such display (Bull & Connelly, 1985; Walker & Trimboli, 1983). The momentary widening of a speaker's eyelids, without involving the

Figure 7–12

Punctuation gestures.

eyebrows, has been found to occur most often in conjunction with spoken adjectives and used for emphasis.

INTERACTIVE GESTURES

Thus far, the gesture categories have focused on the content of the speaker's monologue. *Interactive gestures* acknowledge the other interactant relative to the speaker and help to regulate and organize the dialogue itself. Because they are directed at the ongoing involvement and shared roles of the interactants, these gestures occur only in the presence of others. The main function of interactive gestures, then, is to include your interaction partner in the dialogue. This is usually done through some form of pointing gesture in the partner's direction. Such gestures probably constitute about 10 to 20 percent of the gestures observed in conversation.

Bavelas (1994) and her colleagues (1992, 1995) have identified four primary functions served by these gestures:

1. Delivering information
2. Citing a previous contribution by your partner
3. Seeking to solicit a specific response from your partner
4. Referring to issues associated with the exchange of speaking turns

These functions and certain variations associated with them are identified in Table 7-2 and illustrated in Figure 7-13. Others have found that the "thinking face" facial gesture also elicits audience coparticipation in word searches and thereby serves the overall inclusion function. The Goodwins (1986) have

Table 7-2
FUNCTIONS OF INTERACTIVE GESTURES

1. **Delivery Gestures**   As a group, these gestures refer to the delivery of information by the speaker to the addressee.

   General delivery gestures mark the standard relation of speaker to addressee; the speaker "hands over" to the addressee new information relevant to his or her main point. A verbal paraphrase is often "Here's my point."

   Shared information gestures mark material that the addressee probably already knows—information that is part of their common ground (Clark & Brennan, 1991). They mean, essentially, "As you know."

   Digression gestures mark information that should be treated by the addressee as an aside from the main point. Analogues to "By the way" or "Back to the main point."

   Elliptical gestures mark information that the addressee should elaborate for himself or herself; the speaker will not provide further details. Analogous to "or whatever."

2. **Citing Gestures**   As a group, these gestures refer to a previous contribution by the addressee.

   General citing indicates "as you said earlier," that is, that the point the speaker is now making had been contributed by the addressee.

   Acknowledgment of the addressee's response indicates that the speaker saw or heard that the addressee understood what had been said. Paraphrased, "I see that you understood me."

3. **Seeking Gestures**   As a group, these gestures aim to elicit a specific response from the addressee.

   Seeking help requests a word or phrase that the speaker cannot find at the moment. A verbal paraphrase would be "Can you give me the word for . . . ?"

   Seeking agreement asks whether the addressee agrees or disagrees with the point being made. Analogous to "Do you agree?"

   Seeking following asks whether the addressee understands what is being said. Verbal equivalents include "you know?" or "eh?" at the end of a phrase.

4. **Turn Gestures**   As a group, these gestures refer to issues around the speaking turn.

   Giving turn hands it over to the other person. As if to say, "Your turn."

   Taking turn accepts the turn from the other person. Paraphrased as "OK, I'll take over."

   Turn open indicates that it is anyone's turn, as if to say "Who's going to talk next?"

---

pointed out that self-touching contributes to a state of conversational disengagement, the opposite of inclusion.

While the preceding fourfold classification of speech-related gestures is useful for understanding how gestures and speech work together, some gestures may not be limited to a single function. For example, a speaker's

Figure 7–13

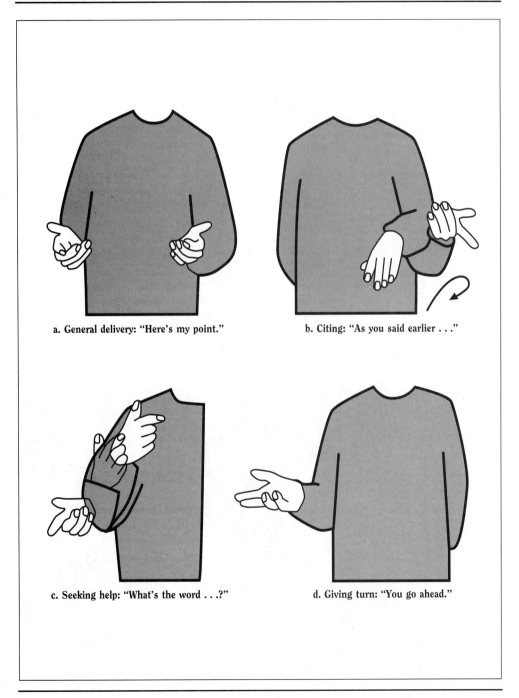

a. General delivery: "Here's my point."

b. Citing: "As you said earlier . . ."

c. Seeking help: "What's the word . . .?"

d. Giving turn: "You go ahead."

Interactive gestures.

relationship with the referent may be highly intense. Some of the gestural displays illuminating this relationship, however, may also emphasize (punctuate) certain specific message units. Nevertheless, it is important to recognize that there are different types of speech-related gestures and that they may serve different functions for the parties involved. Efron's (1941) cross-cultural comparison shows how helpful gestural distinctions can be. He found that as southern Italians talked, they made extensive use of gestures that had a close resemblance to their referent (e.g., pictorial), whereas Eastern European Jews made very little use of such gestures. It seems reasonable to expect that different cultures will value different kinds of information, and gestures will vary accordingly. Even the number of gestures in all categories may vary from culture to culture.

The frequency of gesturing can be influenced by several key factors. First, we would expect to find more speech-related gestures in face-to-face communication than over an intercom (Cohen, 1977; Cohen & Harrison, 1973). We do, of course, use some gestures when our listeners cannot see us, for example, when talking on the telephone (see Figure 7-14). Continued communication without visible contact will, however, reduce the number of gestures used. It is curious why we use any gestures when our audience cannot see them. It may be habit, but since gestures are knowingly used to help communicate ideas, we may continue to use them in order to maximize

Figure 7–14

Gesture made while speaking on the telephone. (Photo © 1987 Hazel Hankin, 40 7th Avenue, Brooklyn, NY 11217/Stock Boston)

the effectiveness of the only channel being used—the voice. In this sense, gestures act as a priming mechanism that activates the entire communicative system and thereby gets the most out of the vocal signals. Speech-related gestures are also likely to increase when a speaker is enthusiastic and involved in the topic being discussed. Similarly, the speaker's familiarity with the topic will affect the gestures used. We would expect speakers who are concerned about their listener's comprehension of their message to use more speech-related gestures, especially in difficult or complex communicative situations, as when the listener either isn't paying attention or isn't comprehending, or the speaker can't find the right words to express an idea. Speakers trying to dominate conversations also would be expected to use more speech-related gestures.

As noted in the next section, speech and gesture are intimately linked, and it would be hard for anyone to completely abstain from gesturing while speaking for very long. Even if it were possible, it would be ill-advised because gestures play an important role in communicating. An experiment reported in a 1931 Soviet publication asked subjects to talk while inhibiting all gestures of the head, hands, face, and body. It is reported that no one was able to carry out the instructions completely, and "the speech . . . lost its intonation, stress and expressiveness; even the very selection of words needed for the expression of content became labored; there was a jerkiness to the speech, and a reduction of the number of words used" (Dobrogaev, 1931). Without gestures, speakers also would have to increase the number of phrases and words used to describe spatial relations and would probably pause more often (Graham & Heywood, 1976). By far, the most important loss would be to the listeners. Gestures facilitate comprehension and help listeners access linguistic cues in their memory (Berger & Popelka, 1971; Rogers, 1978; Woodall & Folger, 1981). Actually, a more accurate statement is that gestures that are synchronized with the vocal/verbal stream increase comprehension. This is accomplished through the functions we've outlined: by vivifying ideas, by intensifying points, by maintaining listener attention and focus, and by marking the organizational structure of the discourse. Gestures that are out of synchrony with the vocal/verbal stream are distracting and interfere with listener comprehension (Woodall & Burgoon, 1981).

THE COORDINATION of GESTURE, POSTURE, and SPEECH

Earlier we said that speech-related gestures are tied to, or accompany, speech. That they are connected to speech is easily understood, but the exact nature of that connection is more difficult to understand. Most scholars agree that body movements and gestures are not randomly produced during the stream of speech; they are inextricably linked as parts of the same system. The disagreements among scholars in this area focus on how to define coordination or synchrony of speech and movement. Must two things happen at exactly the same time to be in sync? For the same length of time? If speech and gesture are closely coordinated, does the same part of the brain control both systems? Is there a synchrony of speech and movement between two speakers as well as within the behavior of a single speaker? This section focuses on the research on these issues. The first part addresses the coordination of a single speaker's speech and movement; the second examines the coordination of two speakers' behavior.

SELF-SYNCHRONY

In the early 1960s, William S. Condon began a microscopic analysis of the coordination between movement and speech. By examining individual frames of a 16 mm film, he was able to match body movements with a speech transcript. This allowed him to observe speech-body orientation accurate to one-twenty-fourth of a second. Condon (1976; Condon & Ogston, 1966) showed that even at the most microscopic levels (e.g., spoken syllables and smaller), speech and movement are rhythmically coordinated. This means that a change in one behavior (a body part, for instance) will coincide or be coordinated with the onset of change in another behavior (phonological segment or some other body part). Just as speech units can be grouped together to form larger units, so can movement units. A sweep of the arm or a turn of the head may occur over an entire phrase of several words, but we may see movements of the face and fingers coordinated with smaller units of speech. At every level, however, the phrases of speech production and the phrases of movement seem closely coordinated.

The smallest idea unit in spoken language is called the *phonemic clause.* This group of words, averaging about five in length, has only one primary stress, which is indicated by changes in pitch, rhythm, or loudness, and it is terminated by a juncture. This unit commonly has shown systematic relationships to body movements. Slight jerks of the head or hand often accompany the primary stress points in the speech of American English speakers. Gestures also seem to peak at the most salient part of the idea unit as well. At the junctures or boundaries, we also find movements of the head or hands indicating completion or initiation.

Birdwhistell's (1966) analysis of nonverbal activity that accompanies verbal behavior led him to postulate what he calls *kinesic markers.* These nonverbal behaviors mark a specific oral language behavior. Markers seem to operate at several different levels. For instance, we might see an eye blink at the beginning and end of some words; a microlateral head sweep may be seen during the expression of a compound word we would hyphenate in the written form. Figure 7-15 shows head, hand, and eyelid markers occurring at the end of statements and questions. Similarly, after making a point, the speaker may turn his or her head to one side, or tilt, or flex or extend the neck, signaling the transition to another point.

Another level of markers is characterized by gross shifts in postural behavior (involving half the body) indicating or marking a sequence of points or point of view expressed by the speaker. One marker on this level is simply the shift from leaning back when listening to leaning forward when talking. The observation that postural shifts mark new stages of interaction or topic shifts, particularly at the beginning or ending of speech segments, has been made by several researchers (Bull & Brown, 1977; Erickson, 1975; Scheflen, 1973). Markers on the next level are frequently complete changes in location, following the presentation of one's total position during an interaction.

Figure 7–15

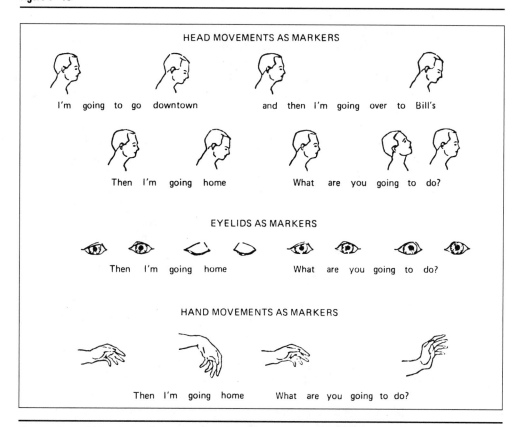

Some postural-kinesic markers of syntactic sentences in the United States (From A. E. Scheflen, "The Significance of Posture in Communication Systems," Psychiatry 27 (1964): 321. Used by permission of publisher.)

Kendon's (1972b, 1980, 1987, 1988) detailed analyses of speech and body movement confirm the notion of self-synchrony. He also supports the idea of a hierarchy of body movements that acts in conjunction with our speech behavior. Kendon found that the wrist and fingers tended to change positions most often, followed by the forearm, then the upper arm; elements of the face generally changed more often than the head; trunk and lower limb movements were rare. The larger units of body movement were related to the larger units of speech; the smaller body units were related to the smaller verbal units.

Kendon also made some important observations of when movements occur in relation to the speech stream. Some movements accompany speech, but many precede speech units. The time between the speech preparatory body movement and the onset of speech is apparently related to the size of the impending speech unit, with earlier and more extensive behavior (more body parts involved) for larger speech units. A change in body posture, for instance, may precede a long utterance and be held for the duration of the utterance. Like other researchers in this area, Kendon believes that the hierarchically structured body movements probably convey information about verbal structure and communicative involvement. The positions of the head, limb, and body sometimes will forecast information to a listener, such as length of utterance, change in argument strategy or viewpoint, and the like. The act of forecasting upcoming components of talk through gesture is a crucial function in social interaction. Speakers often shift their gaze to their hands during the production of iconic gestures, thereby calling them to the attention of the listener. Speaker gaze returns to the listener as the speech unit projected by the gesture is completed. In this process, gaze acts like a pointer (Streeck, 1993; Streeck & Knapp, 1992).

The linkage of gestures to speech has also been demonstrated in studies that show how gestures help speakers access and retrieve words from their mental lexicon (Hadar, 1989; Krauss, 1991; Morrel-Samuels & Krauss, 1992). Dittmann (1972) and his colleague (1967, 1968, 1969) based their research on the premise that some movements are so closely tied to the speech encoding process they are virtually motor manifestations of that process. You can probably recall instances when you were trying to communicate an exciting idea, an idea that was difficult to conceptualize, or an idea that you felt was very important. In such cases, you can get a "general feel" for the connections between the flow of your thoughts and the flow of your body movements. Dittmann's work also provides us with some data regarding timing and location of body movements in the speech stream. He finds that movements tend to occur early in phonemic clauses and at points following hesitations in speech.

The preceding research leads us to conclude that speech and gesture are coordinated. But why? Most likely because they are two components used in the expression of a single unit of content. Both systems are being guided by the same overall purpose, and both systems seem to be under the governance of the same parts of the brain (Cicone, Wapner, Foldi, Zurif, & Gardner, 1979; Kimura, 1976). It is not unreasonable, then, to assume a pathological state for people manifesting out-of-sync behavior (Condon, 1980). Nor should it surprise us that gestures and speech both break down in aphasia (McNeill, 1992).

Gesture and speech also appear to grow up together. In one remarkable study, Petitto and Marentette (1991) argue that *manual* infant babbling (rather than oral) may serve as a precursor to language learning. Several other studies indicate that children use more gestures as they develop, just as they use more words, and that the nature of that gesticulation varies with the changing nature of the speech production (McNeill, 1992). Kendon (1983, p. 25) put it this way:

> There appears to be a shift away from elaborate enactments or pantomimes, which serve instead of speech, toward a more precise coordination, as if gesture is coming to be used more selectively. Gesture is used much less to depict whole scenes. It is brought in only at certain points along the way. There is also an increasing use of abstract, discourse-making gesture; iconic gesture becomes more symbolic and more restricted in the aspects of meaning it is called upon to display.

INTERACTION SYNCHRONY

The preceding section revealed a speech-body movement coordination within the actions of a single speaker. This section provides information about a speech-body movement coordination between two speakers—a kind of social rhythm (Bernieri & Rosenthal, 1991). This behavior has been studied in two ways, which we will call *matching* and *meshing*.

MATCHING   Matching the behavior of our fellow interactant may occur in several different ways. Sometimes a speaker's behavior is followed in kind by the listener when he or she becomes the speaker (Cappella, 1981). Here the matched behavior occurs not simultaneously but in sequence. Chapter 11 reports research that shows how we tend to match our partner's utterance duration, loudness, precision of articulation, latency of response, silence duration, and speech rate. In some instances, the speaker's behavior elicits an offsetting or compensatory behavior from the other interaction partner. For example, if a speaker is leaning toward a listener and the listener perceives the interaction distance to be too close, the listener is likely to lean back or in other ways increase the interaction distance (see Chapter 5).

In Chapter 12 we examine two theories that have tried to explain why some behaviors are matched and some are offset with opposite behaviors. One of these theories (Patterson, 1982) says we exchange similar behavior (reciprocate) when we label the arousal caused by our partner's behavior as positive (like, relief, love) and exhibit offsetting behavior (compensatory) when the arousal caused by our partner's behavior is labeled negative (dislike, embarrassment, anxiety). To account for rapid exchanges of behavior, instances where we have little time to determine positive or negative aspects of our arousal, another theory argues, we engage in matching (reciprocated) behavior when our partner's behavior is perceived as moderately congruent with our expectations and involvement preferences. When our partner's behavior is sizeably discrepant from our expectations and involvement preferences, we are more likely to exhibit compensatory behavior (Cappella & Greene, 1982). Whether the interactants exhibit reciprocal exchanges or compensatory ones, these reactions are testimony to the existence of a mutual coordination of behavior.

Other researchers have been interested in those occasions when both interaction partners exhibit the same behavior at the same time. Postural congruence is one of those frequently matched behaviors. It may involve crossing the legs and/or arms, leaning, head propping, or any number of other positions. Notice the variety of postural congruence in Figures 7-16, 7-17, and 7-18. When the listener's behavior is a mirror image of the speaker's, this form of matching is called *mirroring.*

Postural congruence has been observed to occur during periods of more positive speech; rated by observers as an indicator of rapport and cooperation; and established as an act that is influential in creating rapport (Charney, 1966; LaFrance, 1979, 1985; LaFrance & Broadbent, 1976; Trout & Rosenfeld, 1980). In one study, a trained actor selectively mimicked postures and gestures of only some students in an interview situation. In a post-interview assessment of their partner (the actor), students who had been mimicked evaluated their partner significantly more favorably and indicated they "identified" with him or that he "thought like me" (Dabbs, 1969). None of the students reported an awareness of the mimicry. Noncongruent postures are more likely to be perceived as competitive or uninvolved.

Bavelas and her colleagues repeatedly tried to replicate the studies that indicated postural mimicry was a sign of rapport or cooperation—and failed. They did observe this behavior, however, and concluded it occurred during periods of conversational involvement rather than during cooperation or periods of rapport. Bavelas maintains it is a signal that the participants are talking *with* each other rather than *at* each other—performing symmetrical roles rather than complementary ones. Thus, from this perspective, the matching of an interaction partner's nonverbal behavior reflects the moment-to-moment aspects of conversational involvement.

Bavelas has also studied a related phenomenon she calls *motor mimicry.* A common example of motor mimicry is when a person you are near drops a heavy weight on his or her foot. As the injured party reacts in pain, your wincing facial expression seems to register an empathic response (see Figure 7-19b, page 282). Sometimes we lean in the direction of another person's efforts; sometimes we smile to another's joy. For many years, scholars believed this was a purely empathic reaction based on a vicarious experience. The

Figure 7–16

Postural congruence. The pair facing each other in the foreground are showing matching postures; the pair facing each other in the background are showing mirror-image postures.

work of Bavelas et al. does not deny this inner experience, but their research also shows motor mimicry is primarily a communicative phenomenon. Wincing to another's injury, for example, was strongly dependent on the visual accessibility of the injured party in Bavelas's experiments. Furthermore, the pattern and timing of the wincer's reaction was determined by eye contact with the victim (Bavelas, Black, Chovil, Lemery, & Mullett, 1988; Bavelas, Black, Lemery, & Mullett, 1986).

This tendency to match and mimic the behavior of others (posturally, facially, vocally, and so forth) sometimes leads to a condition known as *emotional contagion.* Emotional contagion occurs when an emotional experience is triggered as a result of mimicking someone else's behavior. Two of the essential conditions for this process to occur include strongly felt emotions and communicators who are skilled encoders and decoders (Hatfield, Caccioppo, & Rapson, 1994).

Figure 7–17

Examples of postural congruence through head-propping and leaning. (Photo credits: Top photo © 1981 Alex Webb/distributed by Magnum Photos, Inc.; Bottom photo Stock Boston/Charles Gupton.)

MESHING Another way of examining the phenomenon of interaction synchrony has been to observe the ongoing co-occurrence of changes in movement and speech by each of the two interactants. Changes, in this type of research, refer to the initiation, termination, speed, and/or direction of the behaviors under study.

Figure 7–18

Notice the postural congruence exhibited by cabinet official Joseph Califano and former president Carter, 1977. (Photo credit: AP/Wide World Photos)

Figure 7–19

a

b

(a) Former President Reagan and former defense secretary Weinberger exchange similar facial expressions. (Photo credit: AP/Wide World Photos) (b) An onlooker winces in pain as another experiences it. (Photo © 1991 Psychotex/Kevin E. White, P.O. Box 470701, Fort Worth, Texas 76147. All rights reserved.)

This type of work arose out of Condon's earlier work on self-synchrony. He observed how both interactants seemed to coordinate their actions. One person (Davis, 1971) who viewed his films reported:

> The third film clip Condon showed me was an example of heightened synchrony. A man and a woman—employer and job applicant—sat facing each other in a sequence that at normal speed seemed merely to involve rather a lot of shifting around, as the man first uncrossed and then recrossed his legs and the woman stirred in her chair. But when the film was run through a few frames at a time, their synchrony became clear. In the same frame, the two began to lean toward each other. They stopped at the same split second, both raised their heads, and then they swept backwards together into their chairs, stopping in the same frame. It was very like the elaborate courtship dances of some birds, or—in Condon's favorite analogy—they were like puppets moved by the same set of strings. Condon told me that this kind of heightened synchrony happens often between male and female. During courtship, it's one of the ways in which vast statements can be made between a man and a woman without a word being said. (p. 103)

As Condon suggests, this kind of interaction synchrony may reflect the nature of the ongoing relationship, whether it is the extent of involvement, rapport, or the degree of intimate, interpersonal knowledge about the other. In some instances, this relationship will be dramatically visible by the kind of synchrony taking place; at other times, the coordination may only be seen in the microscopic analysis of individual film frames. Out-of-sync partners are not likely to value the experience. The fact that out-of-sync experiences tend to stand out for us reminds us how often we operate in synchrony with others. Out-of-sync behavior may reflect decreased listening, a lack of knowledge of one's partner, and so forth. Interaction synchrony may also be a precursor of language learning. Condon and Sander (1974) found babies twelve hours old whose head, hands, elbows, hips, and leg movements tended to correspond to the rhythms of human speech. When the babies were exposed to disconnected speech or to plain tapping sounds, however, the rhythmic pattern was not observed. If this finding is validated by other researchers, it may mean that an infant has participated in and laid the groundwork for various linguistic forms and structures long before formal language learning begins (see Bernieri, Reznick, & Rosenthal, 1988).

Sometimes our responses as listeners and the feedback we provide in the form of facial expressions or head movements will appear at specific junctures in the speech of our partner. Vocalizations ("mmm-hmm," "I see," and the like), head nods, and movements of hands and feet tend to occur at the ends of rhythmical units of the talker's speech, that is, at pauses within phonemic clauses but mainly at junctures between these clauses. Vocally stressed words also tend to be accompanied by movements. Listener gestures and movements are often indications that the listener understands, appreciates, or anticipates speaker behavior.

Dittmann (1972) noticed that adults sometimes believe children are not listening to them and badger them with questions like "Did you hear me?"

Dittmann reasoned that this common adult-child perception may be associated with what he calls "listener responses," for example, head nods, some eyebrow raises, some types of smiles, "yeah," "I see," and so on. His study of children in grades one, three, and five found these listener responses were nearly absent except under "the strongest social pull" by the other interactant. Subsequent studies indicated the major deficiencies were in "mm-hm" and head-nod responses. By eighth grade, a dramatic increase in these listener responses is found. Now the early adolescent's peers are beginning to lengthen their response duration (providing more opportunity for such listener responses); the "response pull" from adult interactants is increasing; and there is a continuing movement away from a purely self-orientation and toward imagining what others are experiencing.

The detailed observations of researchers like Condon, Dittmann, and Kendon offer clear evidence that human interactants do exhibit a speech-body movement interaction synchrony. It is also clear that this synchrony may take place on very microscopic levels. Still, there are questions. How much of this synchrony is due to an ordered relationship between speech and body movements, and how much is due to coincidence? Are there social contexts that intensify the degree of synchrony? How much synchrony is desirable? At least one study suggests that *moderately* rhythmic social interactions are evaluated most positively (Warner, Malloy, Schneider, Knoth, & Wilder, 1987). Is it possible to predict which behaviors will synchronize with which other behaviors at which times? What is the best method of measuring these minute behavioral changes (Gatewood & Rosenwein, 1981; McDowall, 1978a, 1978b; Rosenfeld, 1981)?

SUMMARY

Although gestures are difficult to define, we seem to know what movements a person is using to communicate and what movements are merely nervous mannerisms, expressions associated with emotion, and task-related movements. Gestures help us communicate in many ways: They replace speech when we cannot or do not want to talk, help us regulate the back-and-forth flow of interaction, establish and maintain attention, add emphasis to our speech, and assist in making memorable the content of our speech. Although we do gesture when interaction partners are not visible (over the telephone), gestures are much more frequent when both interactants are visible to one another. We seem to use more gestures when we are knowledgeable about the topic being discussed, highly motivated to have our listener(s) understand our message, trying to dominate a conversation, and excited and enthusiastic about the topic being discussed. The absence of gestures affects our speech as well as listener comprehension.

Two major types of gestures were discussed: speech independent and speech related. Speech-independent gestures are operationally defined as gestures that 70 percent of the usage community decodes in a similar way. They have an almost direct verbal definition. We are normally very aware of using this type of gesture. Culture affects the number, frequency, and meanings associated with speech-independent gestures. While no universal gestures of this type have been found (that is, having the same meaning and form in every culture studied), the most likely candidates would be "affirmation," "negation," "stop," "don't know," "sleeping," "eating," and "drinking." Some speech-independent gestures are culture specific (not found in the same form in other cultures), but many gestures have basically the same form but different meanings from culture to culture. These different meanings are often the source of cross-cultural misunderstandings.

The other major category of gestures is called speech-related gestures. Some of these gestures characterize the content of speech; some show the speaker's relationship to the referent by indicating whether the speaker is certain or uncertain, embracing an idea or distancing himself from it, and the like; some are used to accent or emphasize speech units. Interactive gestures, unlike the other speech-related gestures, focus on the dialogue rather than the speaker's monologue. Interactive gestures focus on the ongoing involvement of the interactants and their shared roles.

The last part of this chapter examined the coordination and synchrony of speech and body movements. This synchrony between the larger and smaller units of speech and body is called self-synchrony. Gesture and speech, then, seem to be different outward manifestations of a process that is controlled and guided by the same part of the brain. Gesture and speech both play a role in communicating the same content. In addition to a self-synchrony, interactants also seem to display coordinated exchanges of behavior in many ways that suggest the existence of an interaction synchrony as well. Interaction synchrony can manifest itself through matching behavior—similar behavior occurring at the same time (postural congruence or motor mimicry) or similar behavior occurring in sequence (one speaker raises his or her voice, followed by the next speaker raising his or her voice). Interaction synchrony can also manifest itself in the moment-to-moment coordination of changes in the direction and timing of speech and movement—even though we do not yet know exactly what behaviors will change and how they will change.

QUESTIONS for DISCUSSION

1. Spend some time during the day interacting without using hand gestures. What does your experience tell you about the relationship of gestures and speech?

2. Some researchers have found matching behavior to be associated with rapport between the interactants. Can you think of a situation in which rapport would not involve matching behavior?
3. Can you think of any instance in which gestures might pose a challenge to the doctrine of freedom of speech?
4. Select a speech-independent gesture. Discuss the meaning of this gesture when accompanied by different facial expressions and speech.

REFERENCES and SELECTED BIBLIOGRAPHY

Allport, G. W., & Vernon, P. E. (1933). *Studies in expressive movement.* Boston: Houghton Mifflin.

Axtell, R. (1991). *Gestures.* New York: Wiley.

Barakat, R. (1973). Arabic gestures. *Journal of Popular Culture, 6,* 749–92.

Barroso, F., Freedman, N., Grand, S., & van Meel, J. (1978). Evocation of two types of hand movements in information processing. *Journal of Experimental Psychology: Human Perception and Performance, 4,* 321–29.

Barten, S. S. (1979). Development of gesture. In N. R. Smith & M. Franklin (Eds.), *Symbolic functioning in childhood.* Hillsdale, NJ: Erlbaum.

Bavelas, J. B. (1994). Gestures as part of speech: Methodological implications. *Research on Language and Social Interaction, 27,* 201–21.

Bavelas, J. B., Black, A., Chovil, N., Lemery, C. R., & Mullett, J. (1988). Form and function in motor mimicry: Topographic evidence that the primary function is communicative. *Human Communication Research, 14,* 275–99.

Bavelas, J. B., Black, A., Lemery, C. R., & Mullett, J. (1986). 'I show you how I feel': Motor mimicry as a communicative act. *Journal of Personality and Social Psychology, 50,* 322–29.

Bavelas, J. B., Chovil, N., Coates, L., & Roe, L. (1995). Gestures specialized for dialogue. *Personality and Social Psychology Bulletin, 21,* 394–405.

Bavelas, J. B., Chovil, N., Lawrie, D. A., & Wade, A. (1992). Interactive gestures. *Discourse Processes, 15,* 469–89.

Baxter, J. C., Winters, E. P., & Hammer, R. E. (1968). Gestural behavior during a brief interview as a function of cognitive variables. *Journal of Personality and Social Psychology, 8,* 303–7.

Beattie, G. W., & Beattie, C. A. (1981). Postural congruence in a naturalistic setting. *Semiotica, 35,* 41–55.

Benthall, J., & Polhemus, T. (1975). *The body as a medium of expression.* New York: E. P. Dutton.

Berger, K. W., & Popelka, G. R. (1971). Extra-facial gestures in relation to speech reading. *Journal of Communication Disorders, 3,* 302–8.

Bernieri, F. J., Reznick, J. S., & Rosenthal, R. (1988). Synchrony, pseudosynchrony, and dissynchrony: Measuring the entrainment process in mother-infant interactions. *Journal of Personality and Social Psychology, 54,* 243–53.

Bernieri, F. J., & Rosenthal, R. (1991). Interpersonal coordination: Behavior matching and interactional synchrony. In R.S Feldman, & B. Rimé, B. (Eds.), *Fundamentals of nonverbal behavior* (pp. 401–32). New York: Cambridge University Press.

Birdwhistell, R. L. (1952). *Introduction to kinesics.* Louisville: University of Louisville Press. (Now available on microfilm only. Ann Arbor, MI: University Microfilms.)

Birdwhistell, R. L. (1955). Background to kinesics. *ETC, 13,* 10–18.

Birdwhistell, R. L. (1960). Kinesics and communication. In E. Carpenter & M. McLuhan (Eds.), *Explorations in communication.* New York: Beacon.

Birdwhistell, R. L. (1963). Kinesic analysis in the investigation of emotions. In P. Knapp (Ed.), *Expression of the emotions in man.* New York: International Universities Press.

Birdwhistell, R. L. (1966). Some relations between American kinesics and spoken American English. In A. G. Smith (Ed.), *Communication and culture.* New York: Holt, Rinehart & Winston.

Birdwhistell, R. L. (1967). Some body motion elements accompanying spoken American English. In L. Thayer (Ed.), *Communication: Concepts and perspectives* (pp. 53–76). Washington, DC: Spartan Books.

Birdwhistell, R. L. (1970). *Kinesics and context.* Philadelphia: University of Pennsylvania Press.

Blake, J., & Dolgoy, S. J. (1993). Gestural development and its relation to cognition during the transition to language. *Journal of Nonverbal Behavior, 17,* 87–102.

Blass, T., Freedman, N., & Steingart, I. (1974). Body movement and verbal encoding in the congenitally blind. *Perceptual and Motor Skills, 39,* 279–93.

Boomer, D. S. (1978). The phonemic clause: Speech unit in human communication. In A. W. Siegman & S. Feldstein (Eds.), *Nonverbal behavior and communication* (pp. 245–62). Hillsdale, NJ: Erlbaum.

Bremmer, J., & Roodenburg, H. (Eds.). (1991). *A cultural history of gesture.* Ithaca, NY: Cornell University Press.

Brewer, W. D. (1951). Patterns of gesture among the Levantine Arabs. *American Anthropologist, 53,* 232–37.

Bull, P., & Connelly, G. (1985). Body movements and emphasis in speech. *Journal of Nonverbal Behavior, 9,* 169–87.

Bull, P. E. (1987a). *Posture and gesture.* New York: Pergamon Press.

Bull, P. E. (1987b). The interpretation of posture through an alternative methodology to role play. *British Journal of Social and Clinical Psychology, 17,* 1–6.

Bull, P. E., & Brown, R. (1977). The role of postural change in dyadic conversation. *British Journal of Social and Clinical Psychology, 16,* 29–33.

Burgoon, J., Olney, C. A., & Coker, R. A. (1987). The effects of communicator characteristics on patterns of reciprocity and compensation. *Journal of Nonverbal Behavior, 11,* 146–65.

Butterworth, B., & Beattie, G. W. (1978). Gesture and silence as indicators of planning in speech. In R. Campbell & P. Smith (Eds.), *Recent advances in psychology of language: Formal and experimental approaches.* New York: Plenum.

Butterworth, B., & Hadar, U. (1989). Gesture, speech and computational stage: A reply to McNeill. *Psychological Review, 96,* 168–74.

Cappella, J. N. (1981). Mutual influence in expressive behavior: Adult-adult and infant-adult dyadic interaction. *Psychological Bulletin, 89,* 101–32.

Cappella, J. N., & Greene, J. O. (1982). A discrepancy-arousal explanation of mutual influence in expressive behavior for adult and infant-adult interaction. *Communication Monographs, 49,* 89–114.

Carmichael, L., Roberts, S., & Wessell, N. (1937). A study of the judgment of manual expression as presented in still and motion pictures. *Journal of Social Psychology, 8,* 115–42.

Charney, E. J. (1966). Postural configurations in psychotherapy. *Psychosomatic Medicine, 28,* 305–15.

Cicone, M., Wapner, W., Foldi, N., Zurif, E., & Gardner, H. (1979). The relation between gesture and language in aphasic communication. *Brain and Language, 8,* 324–49.

Clark, H. H. & Brennan, S. A. (1991). Grounding in communication. In L. B. Resnick, J. M. Levine, & S. D. Teasely (Eds.), *Perspectives on socially shared cognition.* Washington: APA Books.

Cohen, A. A. (1977). The communicative functions of hand illustrators. *Journal of Communication, 27,* 54–63.

Cohen, A. A., & Harrison, R. P. (1973). Intentionality in the use of hand illustrators in face-to-face communication situations. *Journal of Personality and Social Psychology, 28,* 276–79.

Condon, W. S. (1976). An analysis of behavioral organization. *Sign Language Studies, 13,* 285–318.

Condon, W. S. (1980). The relation of interaction synchrony to cognitive and emotional processes. In M. R. Key (Ed.), *The relationship of verbal and nonverbal communication.* The Hague: Mouton.

Condon, W. S., & Ogston, W. D. (1966). Soundfilm analysis of normal and pathological behavior patterns. *Journal of Nervous and Mental Disease, 143,* 338–47.

Condon, W. S., & Ogston, W. D. (1967). A segmentation of behavior. *Journal of Psychiatric Research, 5,* 221–35.

Condon, W. S., & Ogston, W. D. (1971). Speech and body motion synchrony of the speaker-hearer. In D. L. Horton & J. J. Jenkins (Eds.), *Perception of language.* Columbus, OH: Merrill.

Condon, W. S., & Sander, L. W. (1974). Neonate movement is synchronized with adult speech: Interaction participation in language acquisition. *Science, 183,* 99–101.

Creider, C. (1977). Toward a description of East African gestures. *Sign Language Studies, 14,* 1–20.

Critchley, M. (1939). *The language of gesture.* London: Arnold.

Dabbs, J. M. (1969). Similarity of gestures and interpersonal influence. *Proceedings of the 77th annual convention of the American Psychological Association, 4,* 337–38.

Davis, F. (1971). *Inside intuition.* New York: McGraw-Hill.

Delis, D., Foldi, N. S., Hamby, S., Gardner, H., & Zurif, E. A. (1979). Note on temporal relations between language and gestures. *Brain and Language, 8,* 350–54.

Deutsch, F. (1947). Analysis of postural behavior. *Psychoanalytic Quarterly, 16,* 195–213.

Dittmann, A. T. (1962). The relationship between body movements and moods in interviews. *Journal of Consulting Psychology, 26,* 480.

Dittmann, A. T. (1971). Review of kinesics in context. *Psychiatry, 34,* 334–42.

Dittmann, A. T. (1972). The body movement-speech rhythm relationship as a cue to speech encoding. In A. W. Siegman & B. Pope (Eds.), *Studies in dyadic communication.* New York: Pergamon Press.

Dittmann, A. T. (1987). The role of body movement in communication. In A. W. Siegman & S. Feldstein (Eds.), *Nonverbal behavior and communication* (2d ed.). Hillsdale, NJ: Erlbaum.

Dittmann, A. T., & Llewellyn, L. G. (1967). The phonemic clause as a unit of speech decoding. *Journal of Personality and Social Psychology, 6,* 341–49.

Dittmann, A. T., & Llewellyn, L. G. (1968). Relationships between vocalizations and head nods as listener responses. *Journal of Personality and Social Psychology, 11,* 98–106.

Dittmann, A. T., & Llewellyn, L. G. (1969). Body movement and speech rhythm in social conversation. *Journal of Personality and Social Psychology, 11,* 98–106.

Dobrogaev, S. M. (1931). The study of reflex in problems of linguistics (M. Kendon, Trans.). In E. A. Marr (Ed.), *Lazykovedenie i Materializm* (Vol. II). Moscow and Leningrad: State Social Economic Publishing House.

Duffy, R. J., & Duffy, J. R. (1981). Three studies of deficits in pantomimic expression and pantomimic recognition in aphasia. *Journal of Speech and Hearing Research, 46,* 70–84.

Efron, D. (1941). Gesture and environment. New York: Kings Crown Press. (Republished as *Gesture, race and culture,* 1972, The Hague: Mouton.)

Ekman, P. (1964). Body position, facial expression, and verbal behavior during interviews. *Journal of Abnormal and Social Psychology, 48,* 295–301.

Ekman, P. (1976). Movements with precise meanings. *Journal of Communication, 26,* 14–26.

Ekman, P. (1977). Biological and cultural contribution to bodily and facial movement. In J. Blacking (Ed.), *The anthropology of the body.* London: Academic.

Ekman, P. (1979). About brows. In M. von Cranach, K. Foppa, W. Lepenier & D. Ploog (Eds.), *Human ethology: Claims and limits of a new discipline.* Cambridge: Cambridge University Press.

Ekman, P., & Friesen, W. (1969). The repertoire of non-verbal behavior: Categories, origins, usage, and coding. *Semiotica, 1,* 49–98.

Ekman, P., & Friesen, W. V. (1972). Hand movements. *Journal of Communication, 22,* 353–74.

Erickson, F. (1975). One function of proxemic shifts in face-to-face interaction. In A. Kendon, R. M. Harris, & M. R. Key (Eds.), *Organization of behavior in face-to-face interaction.* The Hague: Mouton.

Evans, M. A., & Rubin, K. H. (1979). Hand gestures as a communicative mode in school-aged children. *Journal of Genetic Psychology, 135,* 189–96.

Feyereisen, P. (1987). Gestures and speech, interactions and separations: A reply to McNeill. *Psychological Review, 94,* 493–98.

Feyereisen, P., & Lannoy, J. D. (1991). *Gestures and speech: Psychological investigations.* New York: Cambridge University Press.

Freedman, N. (1972). The analysis of movement behavior during clinical interviews. In A. Siegman & B. Pope (Eds.), *Studies in dyadic communication.* New York: Pergamon.

Freedman, N., Blass, T., Rifkin, A., & Quitkin, F. (1973). Body movements and the verbal encoding of aggressive affect. *Journal of Personality and Social Psychology, 26,* 72–85.

Fretz, B. R. (1966). Postural movements in a counseling dyad. *Journal of Counseling Psychology, 13,* 335–43.

Frey, S. (1975). Tonic aspects of behavior in interaction. In A. Kendon, R. M. Harris, & M. R. Key (Eds.), *Organization of behavior in face-to-face interaction.* Chicago: Aldine.

Gatewood, J. B., & Rosenwein, R. (1981). Interactional synchrony: Genuine or spurious? A critique of recent research. *Journal of Nonverbal Behavior, 6,* 12–29.

Givens, D. B. (1977). Shoulder shrugging: A densely communicative expressive behavior. *Semiotica, 19,* 13–28.

Goffman, E. (1979). Footing. *Semiotica, 25,* 1–29.

Goodglass, H., & Kaplan, E. (1963). Disturbance of gesture and pantomime in aphasia. *Brain, 86,* 702–12.

Goodwin, C. (1981). *Conversational organization.* New York: Academic Press.

Goodwin, C. (1986). Gestures as a resource for the organization of mutual orientation. *Semiotica, 62,* 29–49.

Goodwin, C., & Goodwin, M. H. (1986). Gesture and coparticipation in the activity of searching for a word. *Semiotica, 62,* 51–75.

Graham, J. A., & Argyle, M. A. (1975). A cross-cultural study of the communication of extra verbal meaning by gestures. *International Journal of Psychology, 10,* 56–67.

Graham, J. A., & Heywood, S. (1976). The effects of elimination of hand gestures and of verbal codability on speech performance. *European Journal of Social Psychology, 5,* 189–95.

Hadar, U. (1989). Two types of gesture and their role in speech production. *Journal of Language and Social Psychology, 8,* 221–28.

Hamalian, L. (1965). Communication by gesture in the Middle East. *ETC, 22,* 43–49.

Hatfield, E., Cacioppo, J. T., & Rapson, R. L. (1994). *Emotional contagion.* New York: Cambridge University Press.

Hayes, F. C. (1957). Gestures: A working bibliography. *Southern Folklore Quarterly, 21,* 218–317.

Hewes, G. W. (1957). The anthropology of posture. *Scientific American, 196,* 123–32.

Hewes, G. W. (1973). Primate communication and the gestural origin of language. *Current Anthropology, 14,* 1–2, 5–12.

Hewes, G. W. (1974). Gesture language in culture contact. *Sign Language Studies, 4,* 1–34.

Hewes, G. W. (1976). The current status of the gestural theory of language origin. *Annals of the New York Academy of Sciences, 280,* 482–504.

Hinsz, V. B., & Tomhave, J. A. (1991). Smile and (half) the world smiles with you, frown and you frown alone. *Personality and Social Psychology Bulletin, 17,* 586–92.

Jacobson, R. (1972). Motor signs for yes and no. *Language in Society, 1,* 91–96.

Jaffe, J., & Feldstein, S. (1970). *Rhythms of dialogue.* New York: Academic Press.

James, W. (1932). A study of the expression of bodily posture. *Journal of General Psychology, 7,* 405–36.

Jancovic, M. A., Devoe, S., & Wiener, M. (1975). Age related changes in hand and arm movements as non-verbal communication: Some conceptualizations and an empirical exploration. *Child Development, 46,* 922–28.

Johnson, D. R. (1972). Black kinesics: Some nonverbal communication patterns in the black culture. In L. A. Samovar & R. E. Porter (Eds.), *Intercultural communication: A reader.* Belmont, CA: Wadsworth.

Johnson, H. G., Ekman, P., & Friesen, W. V. (1975). Communicative body movements: American emblems. *Semiotica, 15,* 335–53.

Kempton, W. (1980). The rhythmic basis of interactional micro-synchrony. In M. R. Key (Ed.), *The relationship of verbal and nonverbal communication.* The Hague: Mouton.

Kendon, A. (1970). Movement coordination in social interaction: Some examples described. *Acta Psychologica, 32,* 101–25.

Kendon, A. (1972a). [Review of Birdwhistell's book *Kinesics and context*]. American Journal of Psychology, 85, 441–56.

Kendon, A. (1972b). Some relationships between body motion and speech: An analysis of an example. In A. Siegman & B. Pope (Eds.), *Studies in dyadic communication.* New York: Pergamon.

Kendon, A. (1975). Gesticulation, speech, and the gesture theory of language origins. *Sign Language Studies, 9,* 349–73.

Kendon, A. (1980). Gesticulation and speech: Two aspects of the process of utterance. In M. R. Key (Ed.), *The relationship of verbal and nonverbal communication.* The Hague: Mouton.

Kendon, A. (1981a). Current issues in 'nonverbal communication.' In A. Kendon (Ed.), *Nonverbal communication, interaction and gesture.* The Hague: Mouton.

Kendon, A. (1981b). Geography of gesture. *Semiotica, 37,* 129–63.

Kendon, A. (1983). Gesture and speech: How they interact. In J. M. Wiemann & R. P. Harrison (Eds.), *Nonverbal interaction.* Beverly Hills, CA: Sage.

Kendon, A. (1984). Did gesture have the happiness to escape the curse at the confusion of Babel? In A. Wolfgang (Ed.), *Nonverbal behavior: Perspectives, applications, intercultural insights.* Toronto: Hogrefe.

Kendon, A. (1987). On gesture: Its complementary relationship with speech. In A. W. Siegman & S. Feldstein (Eds.), *Nonverbal behavior and communication* (2d ed.). Hillsdale, NJ: Erlbaum.

Kendon, A. (1988). How gestures can become like words. In F. Poyatos (Ed.), *Cross-cultural perspectives in nonverbal communication.* Toronto: Hogrefe.

Kendon, A. (1989). Gesture. *International encyclopedia of communications* (Vol. 2). New York: Oxford University Press.

Kendon, A. (1992). Some recent work from Italy on quotable gestures ('emblems'). *Journal of Linguistic Anthropology, 2,* 72–93.

Kendon, A. (1993). Human gesture. In K. R. Gibson & T. Ingold (Eds.), *Tools, language and cognition in human evolution.* New York: Cambridge University Press.

Kendon, A. (1994). Do gestures communicate?: A review. *Research on Language and Social Interaction, 27,* 175–200.

Kendon, A., & Sigman, S. J. (in press). Ray L. Birdwhistell 1918–1994. *Semiotica.*

Kimura, D. (1976). The neural basis of language via gesture. In H. Whitaker & H. A. Whitaker (Eds.), *Studies in neurolinguistics.* (Vol. 2). New York: Academic Press.

Kirk, L., & Burton, M. (1976). Physical versus semantic classification of nonverbal forms: A cross cultural experiment. *Semiotica, 17,* 315–38.

Knapp, R. H. (1965). The language of postural interpretation. *Journal of Social Psychology, 67,* 371–77.

Krauss, R. M., Morrel-Samuels, P., & Colasante, C. (1991). Do conversational gestures communicate? *Journal of Personality and Social Psychology, 61,* 743–54.

Krout, M. (1954a). An experimental attempt to determine the significance of unconscious manual symbolic movements. *Journal of General Psychology, 51,* 296–308.

Krout, M. (1954b). An experimental attempt to produce unconscious manual symbolic movements. *Journal of General Psychology, 51,* 121–52.

Kumin, L., & Lazar, M. (1974). Gestural communication in preschool children. *Perceptual and Motor Skills, 38,* 708–10.

LaBarre, W. (1964). Paralinguistics, kinesics, and cultural anthropology. In T. A. Sebeok, A. S. Hayes, & M. C. Bateson (Eds.), *Approaches to semiotics.* The Hague: Mouton.

LaFrance, M. (1979). Non-verbal synchrony and rapport: Analysis by the cross-lag panel technique. *Social Psychology Quarterly, 42,* 66–70.

LaFrance, M. (1985). Postural mirroring and intergroup relations. *Personality and Social Psychology Bulletin, 11,* 207–17.

LaFrance, M., & Broadbent, M. (1976). Group rapport: Posture sharing as a non-verbal indicator. *Group and Organization Studies, 1,* 328–33.

LaFrance, M., & Ickes, W. (1981). Posture mirroring and interactional involvement: Sex and sex typing effects. *Journal of Nonverbal Behavior, 5,* 139–54.

Lindenfeld, J. (1971). Verbal and non-verbal elements in discourse. *Semiotica, 3,* 223–33.

Mahl, G. F. (1987). *Explorations in nonverbal and vocal behavior.* Hillsdale, NJ: Erlbaum.

Mallery, G. (1972). Sign language among North American Indians. *First annual report of the Bureau of American Ethnology.* Washington: U.S. Government Printing Office, 1881. (Republished by Mouton Press, The Hague.)

Markel, N. N. (1975). Coverbal behavior associated with conversation turns. In A. Kendon, R. M. Harris, & M. R. Key (Eds.), *Organization of behavior in face-to-face interaction.* Chicago: Aldine.

Matsumoto, D., & Kudoh, T. (1987). Cultural similarities and differences in the semantic dimensions of body postures. *Journal of Nonverbal Behavior, 11,* 166–79.

Maurer, R. E., & Tindall, J. H. (1983). Effect of postural congruence on client's perception of counselor empathy. *Journal of Counseling Psychology, 30,* 158–63.

McDowall, J. J. (1978a). Interactional synchrony: A reappraisal. *Journal of Personality and Social Psychology, 36,* 963–75.

McDowall, J. J. (1978b). Microanalysis of filmed movement: The reliability of boundary detection by observers. *Environmental Psychology and Nonverbal Behavior, 3,* 77–88.

McNeill, D. (1985). So you think gestures are nonverbal? *Psychological Review, 92,* 350–71.

McNeill, D. (1986). Iconic gestures of children and adults. *Semiotica, 62,* 107–28.

McNeill, D. (1992). *Hand and mind.* Chicago: Chicago University Press.

McNeill, D., Cassell, J., & McCullough, K. (1994). Communicative effects of speech-mismatched gestures. *Research on Language and Social Interaction, 27,* 223–37.

McNeill, D., & Levy, E. (1982). Conceptual representations in language activity and gesture. In R. J. Jarvella & W. Klein (Eds.), *Speech, place and action: Studies in deixis and related topics.* Chichester: Wiley.

Meissner, M., & Philpott, S. B. (1975). The sign language of sawmill workers in British Columbia. *Sign Language Studies, 9,* 291–308.

Meltzoff, A. N., & Moore, M. K. (1989). Imitation in newborn infants: Exploring the range of gestures imitated and the underlying mechanisms. *Developmental Psychology, 25,* 954–62.

Michael, G., & Willis, F. N. (1968). The development of gestures as a function of social class, education and sex. *Psychological Record, 18,* 515–9.

Michael, G., & Willis, F. N. (1969). The development of gestures in three subcultural groups. *Journal of Social Psychology, 79,* 35–41.

Morrel-Samuels, P., & Krauss, R. M. (1992). Word familiarity predicts temporal asynchrony of hand gestures and speech. *Journal of Experimental Psychology: Learning, Memory and Cognition, 18,* 615–62.

Morris, D. (1977). *Manwatching: A field guide to human behavior.* New York: Abrams.

Morris, D. (1994). *Bodytalk: The meaning of human gestures.* New York: Crown.

Morris, D., Collett, P., Marsh, P., & O'Shaughnessy, M. (1979). *Gestures: Their origins and distribution.* London: Jonathon Cape.

Morsbach, H. (1988). Nonverbal communication and hierarchical relationships: The case of bowing in Japan. In F. Poyatos (Ed.), *Cross-cultural perspectives in nonverbal communication.* Toronto: Hogrefe.

Patterson, M. L. (1982). A sequential functional model of nonverbal exchange. *Psychological Review, 89,* 231–49.

Pelose, G. C. (1987). The functions of behavioral synchrony and speech rhythm in conversation. In S. J. Sigman (Ed.), *Research on language and social interaction* (Vol. 20). Edmonton, Alberta: Boreal.

Peterson, L. N., & Kirshner, H. S. (1981). Gestural impairment and gestural ability in aphasia: A review. *Brain and Language, 14,* 333–48.

Petitto, L. A., & Marentette, P. F. (1991, March 22). Babbling in the manual mode: Evidence for the ontogeny of language. *Science, 251,* 1493–96.

Pickett, L. (1974). An assessment of gestural and pantomimic deficit in aphasic patients. *Acta Symbolica, 65,* 69–86.

Poyatos, F. (1975). Gesture inventories: Fieldwork methodology and problems. *Semiotica, 13,* 199–227.

Rimé, B., & Schiaratura, L. (1991). Gesture and speech. In R. Feldman & B. Rimé (Eds.), *Fundamentals of nonverbal behavior*. New York: Cambridge University Press.

Riseborough, M. G. (1985). Physiographic gestures as decoding facilitators: Three experiments exploring a neglected facet of communication. *Journal of Nonverbal Behavior, 5,* 172–83.

Rogers, W. T. (1978). The contribution of kinesic illustrators toward the comprehension of verbal behavior within utterances. *Human Communication Research, 5,* 54–62.

Rosenberg, B. G., & Langer, J. (1965). A study of postural-gestural communication. *Journal of Personality and Social Psychology, 2,* 593–97.

Rosenfeld, H. M. (1967). Nonverbal reciprocation of approval: An experimental analysis. *Journal of Experimental Social Psychology, 3,* 102–11.

Rosenfeld, H. M. (1981). Whither interactional synchrony? In K. Bloom (Ed.), *Prospective issues in infant research*. Hillsdale, NJ: Erlbaum.

Rosenfeld, H. M. (1987). Conversational control functions of nonverbal behavior. In A. W. Siegman & S. Feldstein (Eds.), *Nonverbal behavior and communication* (2d ed.). Hillsdale, NJ: Erlbaum.

Rosenfeld, H. M., & Hancks, M. (1980). The nonverbal context of verbal listener responses. In M. R. Key (Ed.), *The relationship of verbal and nonverbal communication*. The Hague: Mouton.

Saitz, R. L., & Cervenka, E. J. (1972). *Handbook of gestures: Colombia and the United States*. The Hague: Mouton.

Sapir, E. (1949). The unconscious patterning of behavior in society. In D. G. Mandelbaum (Ed.), *Selected writings of Edward Sapir in language, culture and personality*. Berkeley: University of California Press.

Scheflen, A. (1973). *Communicational structure: Analysis of a psychotherapy transaction*. Bloomington, IN: University of Indiana Press.

Scheflen, A. E. (1964). The significance of posture in communication systems. *Psychiatry, 27,* 316–31.

Scheflen, A. E., & Scheflen, A. (1972). *Body language and the social order*. Englewood Cliffs, NJ: Prentice-Hall.

Schegloff, E. A. (1984). On some gestures' relation to talk. In J. M. Anderson & J. Heritage (Eds.), *Structures of social action: Studies in conversational analyses*. Cambridge: Cambridge University Press.

Sherzer, J. (1974). Verbal and nonverbal deixis: The pointed lip gesture among the San Blas Cuna. *Language in Society, 2,* 117–31.

Sherzer, J. (1982). *Levels of analysis in sociolinguistics and discourse analysis: Two illustrative examples*. Paper read before the American Sociological Association, Los Angeles.

Slama-Cazacu, T. (1976). Nonverbal components in message sequence: 'Mixed syntax.' In W. C. McCormack & S. A. Wurm (Eds.), *Language and man: Anthropological issues*. The Hague: Mouton.

Sousa-Poza, J. F., Rohrberg, R., & Mercure, A. (1979). Effects of type of information (abstract-concrete) and field dependence on asymmetry of hand movements during speech. *Perceptual and Motor Skills, 48,* 1323–30.

Sparhawk, C. M. (1978). Contrastive identificational features of Persian gesture. *Semiotica, 24,* 49–86.

Stokoe, W. C. (1980). Sign language and sign languages. *Annual Review of Anthropology, 9,* 365–90.

Streeck, J. (1988). The significance of gesture: How it is established. *Papers in Pragmatics, 2,* 25–59.

Streeck, J. (1993). Gesture as communication I: Its coordination with gaze and speech. *Communication Monographs, 60,* 275–99.

Streeck, J. (1994). Gesture as communication II: The audience as co-author. *Research on Language and Social Interaction, 27,* 239–67.

Streeck, J., & Knapp, M. L. (1992). The interaction of visual and verbal features in human communication. In F. Poyatos (Ed.), *Advances in Nonverbal Communication.* Amsterdam: Benjamins.

Taylor, A. (1975). Nonverbal communication systems in native North America. *Semiotica, 13,* 329–74.

Teodorrson, S. T. (1980). Autonomy and linguistic status of non-speech language forms. *Journal of Psycholinguistic Research, 9,* 121–45.

Trout, D. L., & Rosenfeld, H. M. (1980). The effect of postural lean and body congruence on the judgment of psychotherapeutic rapport. *Journal of Nonverbal Behavior, 4,* 176–90.

Trupin, C. M. (1976). *Linguistics and gesture: An application of linguistic theory to the study of emblems.* Unpublished doctoral dissertation, University of Michigan.

van de Koppel, J. M. H., de Bok-Huurman, J. F. H., & Moezelaar, M. J. M. (1988). Understanding gestures in another culture: A study with children from the Dutch Antilles and the Netherlands. In F. Poyatos (Ed.), *Cross-cultural perspectives in nonverbal communication.* Toronto: Hogrefe.

Varney, N. R. (1978). Linguistic correlates of pantomime recognition in asphasic patients. *Journal of Neurology, Neurosurgery and Psychiatry, 41,* 546–68.

Walker, M. B., & Trimboli, C. (1983). The expressive functions of the eye flash. *Journal of Nonverbal Behavior, 8,* 3–13.

Warner, R. M., Malloy, D., Schneider, K., Knoth, R., & Wilder, B. (1987). Rhythmic organization of social interaction and observer ratings of positive affect and involvement. *Journal of Nonverbal Behavior, 11,* 57–74.

Washabaugh, W., Woodward, J., & DeSantis, S. (1978). Providence Island sign language: A context dependent language. *Anthropological Linguistics, 20,* 95–109.

Webb, J. T. (1972). Interview synchrony: An investigation of two speech rate measures. In A. W. Siegman & B. Pope (Eds.), *Studies in dyadic communication.* New York: Pergamon Press.

Wilkinson, L. C., & Rembold, K. L. (1981). The form and function of children gestures accompanying verbal directives. In P. S. Dale & D. Ingram (Eds.), *Child language: An international perspective.* Baltimore: University Park Press.

Wolff, C. (1945). *A psychology of gesture.* London: Methuen.

Wolff, P., & Gustein, J. (1972). Effects of induced motor gestures on vocal output. *Journal of Communication, 22,* 277–88.

Woodall, W. G,. & Burgoon, J. K. (1981). The effects of nonverbal synchrony on message comprehension and persuasiveness. *Journal of Nonverbal Behavior, 5*, 207–23.

Woodall, W. G., & Folger, J. P. (1981). Encoding specificity and nonverbal cue content: An expansion of episodic memory research. *Communication Monographs, 48*, 39–53.

Wundt, W. (1900/1973). *The language of gestures.* The Hague: Mouton.

Wylie, L. (1977). *Beaux gestes: A guide to French body talk.* Cambridge, MA: The Undergraduate Press.

CHAPTER 8

The Effects of Touch on Human Communication

We often talk about the way we talk, and we frequently try to see the way we see,
but for some reason we have rarely touched on the way we touch.

—D. MORRIS

The scene is a university library, but it could just as easily be the local supermarket, bank, or restaurant. What happens takes about half a second, and it is not noticed by those experiencing it. Remarkably, however, this event affects their evaluation of their experience in the library. What could be so mysterious and so powerful?

The answer begins with researchers at Purdue University (Fisher, Rytting, & Heslin, 1976) who wanted to investigate systematically the effects of a brief, seemingly accidental touch in a nonintimate context. They had male and female clerks return library cards to some students by placing their hand directly over the student's palm, making physical contact; other students were not touched. Outside the library, the students were approached by a researcher and asked questions about their feelings toward the library clerk and the library in general. Students who were touched, especially the females, evaluated the clerk and the library significantly more favorably than those not touched. This was true for both students who were aware of being touched and those who were not. One might suggest that the clerks may have inadvertently behaved differently in other ways when they touched (for example, smiling), even though they were trained to maintain consistent behaviors for all students. Nevertheless, other studies of fleeting and seemingly insignificant touches find similar results. Waitresses who touched diners got bigger tips (Crusco & Wetzel, 1984), and psychologists who touched students on the shoulder when requesting help found greater compliance (Patterson, Powell, & Lenihan, 1986). Maybe this is why politicians are so eager to shake hands ("press the flesh") with as many voters as possible. Thus, we know brief touch can be functionally influential; now we must find out how touch works in conjunction with other aspects of the setting, the relationship to the other, past experiences with touch, other behaviors, and so on.

Touching behavior is sometimes an important part of health care. Many studies support positive effects of massage on infants with a variety of problems including premature birth, failure-to-thrive syndrome, and cocaine exposure. Massage reduces anxiety, lowers stress hormones, and is associated with improved clinical outcomes (Field, 1995). Studies also support the positive effects of touching by physicians and nurses to hospitalized patients, although (as reported later in this chapter) the physiological, behavioral, and attitudinal effects are not *always* positive. Counselors use touch to reassure clients and to develop a relationship in which their clients trust them and feel free to talk. However, it is the type, timing, and location of the touch, as well as the counselor's comfort in giving the touch, that are the keys to success, not the act of touching by itself.

Touch is a crucial aspect of most human relationships. It plays a part in giving encouragement, expressing tenderness, showing emotional support, and many other things. Body-awareness and personal-growth workshops en-roll many Americans who feel a need to rediscover communication through touch. These workshops encourage physical contact as a way to break through some psychological barriers. People try to become more aware of themselves, other people, and the world around them through physical experiences rather than through words or sight. Some say it reflects a yearning for human contact and a desire to restore some unfilled tactile needs. As Montagu (1971) said:

> When affection and involvement are conveyed through touch, it is those meanings as well as the security-giving satisfactions, with which touch will become associated. Inadequate tactile experience will result in a lack of such associations and a consequent inability to relate to others in many fundamental human ways. (p. 292)

Perhaps the most dramatic testimony to the communicative potential of touch comes from the blind. Helen Keller's diary tells of an incident when she was touching her dog: "He was rolling on the grass . . . his fat body revolved, stiffened and solidified into an upright position, and his tongue gave my hand a lick . . . if he could speak, I believe he would say with me that paradise is attained by touch."

The act of touching is like any other message we communicate—it may elicit negative reactions as well as positive ones depending on the configuration of people and circumstances. We know that sometimes people get tense, anxious, and/or uncomfortable when touched; we know that touching perceived as inappropriate for the relationship can be met with aggressive reactions—touching back in the form of slapping or hitting. Some people seem to evaluate almost all touching negatively. In some cases, this dislike for touching may be related to early experiences with touch. What do we know about touching as it occurs throughout the life span?

TOUCHING and HUMAN DEVELOPMENT

Tactile communication is probably the most basic or primitive form of communication. In fact, tactile sensitivity may be the first sensory process to become functional. In fetal life, the child begins to respond to vibrations of the mother's pulsating heartbeat, which impinge on the child's entire body and are magnified by the amniotic fluid. Researchers have documented that a living fetus aborted during the third month of gestation, when only three inches long, will respond reflexively to the touch of a hair around its mouth (Maurer & Maurer, 1988). In one sense, our first input about what life itself will be like comes from the sense of touch.

Newborns continue to gain knowledge of themselves and the world around them through tactile explorations. Some common touch experiences include the obstetrician's hands and the parental (or caregiver) hands that change diapers, feed, bathe, rock, and give comfort. During early childhood, words accompany touch until the child associates the two; then words may replace touch entirely. For example, a mother may gently stroke or pat an infant to console him or her. As the child grows older, she strokes and pats while murmuring encouraging words. Eventually, the mother may call from another room, "It's all right, dear—Mommy's here." As words replace touch, an intimate closeness is replaced by distance.

There have been several efforts to examine parental touching of infants and children. Mothers tend to touch infants more than fathers do. The amount of touching behavior may vary. Mothers will touch children more who respond positively to touch, for example, a "cuddler"; later-born children may receive less touching; planned children may receive more touching than unplanned.

It seems reasonable to assume that the newborn and infant receive more tactile stimulation than children aged fourteen months to two years. In view of infant needs, this would seem both needed and predictable. However, Clay's (1966) results indicate children begin to receive *more* touching behavior between fourteen months and two years of age than as infants. This study also indicates that girl babies tend to receive more of these physical acts of affection than boy babies. Lewis (1972), however, summarizing several research projects, reported that for the first six months of life, boys receive more physical contact than girls. After six months of age, girls are not only allowed but also encouraged to spend more time touching and staying near their parents than boys.

Harrison-Speake and Willis (1995) gathered adults' views on the appropriateness of different kinds of parental touch with children of different ages. Rather clear norms were evident. Touch was seen as increasingly inappropriate as children grew from toddlers to young teenagers, especially for fathers and for boys. White respondents were more approving of parental touch than were black respondents, regardless of the kind of touch, the child's age, or the gender of the child or parent. However, because the interviewer was always white in this study, it is necessary to replicate the ethnic group differences using black interviewers.

Several observations of touching behavior have been made in the context of the developing child's school experiences. In one study, preschool boys tended to touch their male teachers more than their female teachers, while preschool girls touched teachers of both sexes about equally. The teachers themselves usually touched children of their own sex more (Perdue & Connor, 1978). Willis and his colleagues (Willis & Hoffman, 1975; Willis & Reeves, 1976) observed children in elementary school and junior high school. From kindergarten through sixth grade the amount of touching steadily declines but still surpasses most reports of adult touching. This same trend occurs in junior high, with about half as much touching as in the primary grades. Some other interesting findings emerged from these studies. The most touching occurred between same-sex dyads. Black children, especially black females, tended to exhibit more touching behavior. Although touching in the primary grades is more often initiated with the hands, the junior-high students showed much more shoulder to shoulder and elbow to elbow touching. Junior-high females began to show more aggressive touching, and junior-high boys were touched in more places, primarily because of the play-fighting so common at that age.

Following childhood, the American child goes through a latency period, in which tactile communication plays only a small role. Then, during adolescence, tactile experiences with members of the same, and then opposite, sex become increasingly important.

The use of touch to communicate emotional and relational messages to the elderly may be crucial, particularly as the reliance on verbal/cognitive message wanes. Although we seem to give the aged in this country a greater license to touch others, it is not clear how much others touch them. No doubt the infirmities of age require more touching, but it may make a big difference whether this increased touching is merely functional and professional or expresses affection. Observations of touching in four homes for the elderly reveal that this is another context in which females tend to initiate more touching than do males. And, as in childhood, same-sex touch is more likely than touch between members of the opposite sex (Rinck, Willis, & Dean, 1980).

Early tactile experiences seem crucial to later mental and emotional adjustment. Youngsters who have little physical contact during infancy may be slower to learn to walk and talk; many schizophrenic children are reported to have been deprived of handling and mothering as infants; some instances of difficulties and retardation in reading and speech are also associated with early deprivation of, and confusion in, tactile communication. Physical violence in adults may also be related to deprivation of touch during infancy. There are reports of infants crying less when given extra tactile stimulation, although this effect is contingent on the extent to which the infant perceives the touching as a reward for crying.

Ashley Montagu (1971) cites vast numbers of animal and human studies to support the theory that tactile satisfaction during infancy and childhood is of fundamental importance to subsequent healthy behavioral development. He maintains that we cannot handle a child too much, as "there is every reason to believe that, just as the salamander's brain and nervous system develops more fully in response to peripheral stimulation, so does the brain and nervous system of the human being" (p. 188). Harlow's (1958) famous "surrogate mother" experiments offer some supporting evidence from the animal world for the importance of touch to infants. Harlow constructed a monkey mother figure out of wire that could provide milk and protection; then he constructed another one out of sponge rubber and terry cloth that did not provide milk. Since infant monkeys consistently chose the terry cloth mother, Harlow concluded that contact comfort was a more important part of the mother-child relationship for monkeys than was sustenance per se. Nursing was less important as a food source and more a source of reassuring touch.

WHO TOUCHES WHOM, WHERE, and HOW MUCH?

The amount and kind of contact in adulthood vary considerably with the age, sex, situation, and relationship of the parties involved. There are reports of married couples who either have so little to say to each other, or who find it so difficult to establish closeness through verbal contact, that physical contact during sexual encounters becomes a primary mode of communication for establishing closeness. In fact, the sex researchers Masters and Johnson have claimed that they try to help people achieve more effective communication: "We believe that effective sexual intercourse is the ultimate in communication." Many factors in the development of American society have led to a common expectation that touching is conducted only in extremely personal and intimate relationships, which leads to the belief that all touching is somehow sensuous in nature. The irony is that long-term intimates probably touch each other less, and less intimately, than those who are either working to establish a romantic relationship or working to restore one that is losing intimacy (Guerrero & Andersen, 1991). For intimates in long-established romantic relationships, the quality of touch has likely replaced the quantity needed to initially establish the relationship as an intimate one. In married relations also, people are more likely to *reciprocate* touch than in dating relationships (Guerrero & Andersen, 1994).

For some individuals, the contact occurring in a crowded commuter train or theater lobby is very discomforting, especially opposite-sex contacts for women and same-sex contacts for men. Explanations for such feelings are numerous. Some children grow up learning not to touch a multitude of animate and inanimate objects. They are told not to touch their own body and later not to touch the body of their dating partner. Care is taken so children do not see their parents touch one another intimately; some parents demonstrate a noncontact norm through the use of twin beds. Touching is associated with admonitions of "not nice" or "bad," and is punished accordingly, and frequent touching between father and son is thought to be something less than masculine. Because of such experiences, some people become nontouchers in any situation. Several studies have tried to identify the personality characteristics of people who enjoy touching and those who do not (Andersen, Andersen, & Lustig, 1987; Deethardt & Hines, 1984). Nontouchers, when compared with touchers, report more anxiety and tension in their lives, less satisfaction with their bodies, and more suspicion of others; they are also more socially withdrawn and more likely to be rigid or authoritarian in their beliefs.

In North American society, men are less likely to touch others than women are. They are particularly averse to touching other men, except in certain prescribed settings such as team sports (both as part of the game and as expressions of team spirit). Both self-report and observational data indicate that same-sex touching is avoided by men but is quite welcome by women. One hypothesis for the men's avoidance is homophobic attitudes and the fear that touching will be seen as homosexual. Indeed, research by Roese, Olson, Borenstein, Martin, and Shores (1992) found that, among men, those with the least stated liking for same-sex touching had the highest scores on a so-called homophobia scale (which had items such as "Homosexuality is a sin and just plain wrong," and "Homosexual behavior disgusts me"). In a second study, college students who were observed to engage in less same-sex touching in a cafeteria had stronger homophobic attitudes when surveyed by the researchers; this was the case for both sexes, not just men (Roese et al., 1992).

Certain situations have a facilitating or inhibiting effect on touching behavior, too. Several studies have demonstrated that in public places where most observational research is done, at least in the "noncontact" cultures, touching can be quite infrequent. As an example, Hall and Veccia (1990) observed 4,500 pairs of people in public places and found that only 15 percent were already touching or touched during the observation period. Similarly, Remland, Jones, and Brinkman (1991) observed dyads in public places in several European locations and found that people touched in only 9 percent of the interactions that were observed. Some researchers, frustrated at the infrequency of touches in many settings, have designed clever ways to increase the likelihood that a touch will occur. Juni and Brannon (1981) disguised a confederate as a blind person, who then went out on the street and asked directions from passersby. The investigators reasoned that people would be less inhibited about touching a blind person while giving directions than about touching a sighted person.

Henley's (1977) research suggests that people may be more likely to touch when:

1. Giving information or advice rather than asking for it
2. Giving an order rather than responding to it
3. Asking a favor rather than agreeing to do one
4. Trying to persuade rather than being persuaded
5. The conversation is deep rather than casual
6. At a party rather than at work
7. Communicating excitement rather than receiving it from another
8. Receiving messages of worry from another rather than sending such messages

Greetings and departures at airport terminals are communicative situations that reflect a higher incidence of touching than would normally be expected. In one study, 60 percent of the people observed in greetings touched, while another study reports 83 percent of the participants touching (Greenbaum & Rosenfeld, 1980; Heslin & Boss, 1980). Heslin and Boss (1980) found that extended embraces and greater intimacy of touch were more likely to attend departures than greetings. The greater the emotion (as reflected in facial expressions) and the closer the perceived relationship, the greater the chances of increased touching. Another situation likely to show a higher incidence of touch than normally found in public settings involves team sports. In one study, the touching behavior of bowlers during league play was observed and found to be far more frequent than observations during normal social interaction (Smith, Willis, & Gier, 1980). High rates of touching following a successful performance were more characteristic of blacks than whites (winning usually begets more touching than losing).

The subject of male and female touching behavior has been of great interest because some believe it is closely linked to status, with the toucher said to have a higher status than the person touched. The issue was articulated by Henley (1973b, 1977) after research suggested that young men tended to initiate touch with young women more than the reverse. Henley asks us to consider who we would expect to initiate touching behavior in dyads such as the following: teacher-student; police-accused; doctor-patient; master-slave; supervisor-worker; advisor-advisee; and so on. Most people tend to see the person of higher status initiating the touch. For a subordinate (when the status roles are clearly defined) to initiate (or even reciprocate, sometimes) touching is perceived as out of line, presumptuous, or an affront. Thus, Henley argued that the predominantly male-initiated touch is just as likely (if not more so) to be an indication of power as a reflection of affection. When women initiate touch with men, it is frequently associated with sexual intent, since, as Henley concludes, "the implication of power is unacceptable."

Studies published subsequent to Henley's have been inconsistent on the question of which sex touches the other sex more, overall (Stier & Hall, 1984). But there is some concurrence that when the individuals are young adults and the touch is with the hand or the arm is put around the other person, males do take the touching initiative. However, the woman is more likely to touch the man than vice versa when the couple is in their forties or older, when the touch is either brief or involves linking her arm through the man's or initiating hand holding (Hall & Veccia, 1990), and when the couple is married rather than dating (Guerrero & Andersen, 1994; Willis & Briggs, 1992). Furthermore, observations of couples in flirtation sequences suggest that the woman often initiates touch that escalates intimacy when it is reciprocated by the man (Perper, 1989). Considering these complexities, it is probably too simplistic to view male-female touching as reflecting only (or mainly) status differences (Hall & Veccia, 1990; Lockard & Adams, 1980; Major, Schmidlin, & Williams, 1990; McCormick & Jones, 1989).

No matter who initiates the touch, observers seem to *perceive* the initiator as the person with greater power. Several studies support this conclusion. In one, ratings of dominance/power were obtained for people pictured in magazine ads. The pictures portrayed all male-female pairs that involved either no touching or nonreciprocated touching. Status (as exemplified by differences in age and dress) was varied so that males and females were portrayed as having both high and low status. Generally, results showed that regardless of initial status, the dominance/power ratings of the person being touched dropped significantly, although the power ratings of the toucher did not rise appreciably (Summerhayes & Suchner, 1978). A similar study, using silhouettes of people standing side by side, found the ratings of people who were touching their partner on the shoulder to increase significantly in not only dominance but also in assertiveness and warmth/expressiveness. The recipients of touch in this study were rated lower on these dimensions than the silhouettes that did not involve any touching (Major & Heslin, 1982; see also Goldberg & Katz, 1990). Taken together, these studies suggest that acts of nonreciprocated touching may indeed reflect the balance of relationship power to outside observers, enhancing the perceptions of power for the toucher and lessening perceptions of power for the nonreciprocating recipient. This perception seems to occur regardless of the gender, status, and age of the participants. Of course, perceptions of the interactants themselves may be quite different. In fact, perception of observers also may change, depending on the type of relationship they perceive, co-occurring behavior, and context.

As mentioned earlier, Henley argued that status is an important determinant of who touches whom. According to her analysis, the higher-status person has a privilege to touch; the lower person does not. Although numerous anecdotes (as well as some strong opinions) uphold this point of view, actual observational research on this important issue has been limited and inconsistent (Stier & Hall, 1984). Goldstein and Jeffords (1981), observing state legislators from the visitors' gallery, actually found a tendency for lower-status legislators to touch the higher-status ones *more* than vice versa. The findings just reviewed on what happens to people's perceived dominance/status after a touch has occurred should help us to recognize that there may be no simple pattern of touching as a function of status. If touching the other raises one's relative status, as the research shows, then the lower-status person in an encounter might consider it to his or her advantage to touch the other, as a way of redressing the status imbalance. As Goldstein and Jeffords commented concerning their observations of legislators, the governor was touched by many, but he touched no one himself. If both higher- and lower-status individuals stand to gain from touching others, one can expect observational studies to show complex patterns.

Research similar to Goldstein and Jeffords', conducted at professional academic meetings, found no overall effect of participants' professional status but did find that higher-status and lower-status academics touched in different ways (Hall, 1996). The higher-status person's touch was more likely to be hand-to-arm or hand-to-shoulder and to be rated as affectionate. The lower-status touches were much more likely to be handshakes and to be rated as more formal. Other research finds that handshakes are perceived as less affectionate, less dominant, and less status-equal than a variety of other touches (Burgoon, 1991). Thus, lower-status people may engage in more subservient forms of touch, while higher-status people have a greater license to show their friendly feelings through touch.

Jourard (1966) wanted to know what parts of the body people think are touched most often. He administered a questionnaire to students, who indicated which of twenty-four body parts they had seen or touched on others or that others had seen or touched on them within the past twelve months. The other persons were specified as mother, father, same-sex friend, and opposite-sex friend. Among other findings, Jourard's study found females were perceived to be considerably more accessible to touch by all persons than males were. Opposite-sex friends and mothers were reported as doing the most touching. Many fathers were recalled as touching not much more than the hands of the subjects. The likelihood of opposite-sex touching of course depends greatly on the relationship between the parties; this kind of touch is more likely when intimacy and familiarity are high (Stier & Hall, 1984).

Jourard's data for Figure 8-1 were gathered in 1963–64. A replication of this study more than a decade later revealed about the same results—with one exception (Rosenfeld, Kartus, & Ray, 1976). It seems that both males and females are perceived as even more accessible to opposite-sex friends than they were in the preceding decade, with increased touching reported for body parts normally considered more intimate, such as chest, stomach, hips, and thigh.[1] When people are asked to recall where they are touched and/or how often, there is always the possibility that these recollections will not be accurate. Jones (1991), using Jourard's methods, found that the number of

---

[1]A third study using Jourard's method was conducted in the 1980s, but the respondents were students attending a small, Catholic, liberal arts college. Although the results show less touch reported by these students, it is not clear how much of this finding is attributable to cultural changes associated with the 1980s and how much is related to the nature of the respondents. See K. L. Hutchinson, and C. A. Davidson, (1990), Body accessibility re-visited: The 60s, 70s, and 80s, *Journal of Social Behavior and Personality, 5,* 341–52.

body parts actually contacted was consistently lower than those anticipated or recalled by students filling out a questionnaire. In the area of touching, expectations about which touches *should* occur seem to exert an important influence on questionnaire responses.

Although our primary interest is in everyday social communication, the study of touch also has important implications for institutionalized persons. Watson (1975) found that there was more touching of residents in a home for the elderly if the following conditions were present:

Figure 8-1

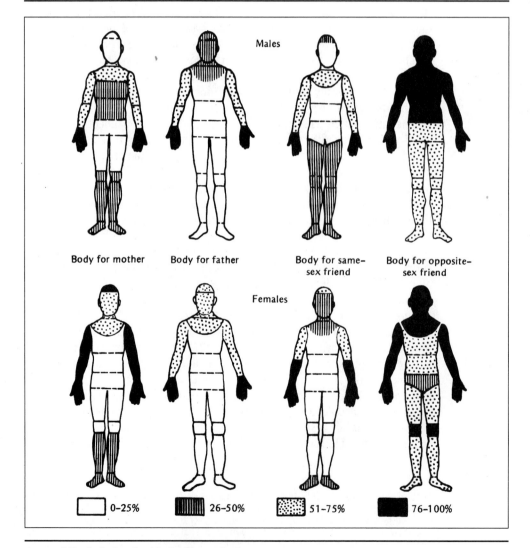

Areas of the body involved in bodily contact.

1. The area of touch was far from the genital region.
2. Staff and residents were of the same sex.
3. The touch initiator was perceived to have high status.
4. The resident was relatively free of stigmatizing physical impairments.

Watson goes on to point out that severely impaired residents and males (because the staff is largely female) will probably receive relatively little touching.

DIFFERENT TYPES of TOUCHING BEHAVIOR

Argyle (1975) listed the following kinds of bodily contact as most common in Western culture*:

Type of Touch	Bodily Areas Typically Involved
Patting	Head, back
Slapping	Face, hand, buttocks
Punching	Face, chest
Pinching	Cheek
Stroking	Hair, face, upper body, knee, genitals
Shaking	Hands, shoulders
Kissing	Mouth, cheek, breasts, hand, foot, genitals
Licking	Face, genitals
Holding	Hand, arm, knee, genitals
Guiding	Hand, arm
Embracing	Shoulder, body
Linking	Arms
Laying-on	Hands
Kicking	Legs, buttocks
Grooming	Hair, face
Tickling	Almost anywhere

*We made the following alterations to the original list:
  1. Changed *bottom* to *buttocks*
  2. Added *genitals* to four categories
  3. Added *shoulders* to the "shaking" category

Desmond Morris (1977) distinguished between touching others and touching oneself. He reported that field observations have led to the naming of 457 types of body contact falling into 14 major types of public body contact occurring between two people. These are called *tie signs* because they signal that some type of relationship exists between the two participants. Sometimes the specific nature of that relationship can be deduced by observing the way the touching is enacted. Morris's major categories of touching include the following:

1. **The Handshake.** The strength of the tie or desired tie between the participants can often be observed by watching the nonshaking hand.
2. **The Body-Guide.** Here, touching is a substitute for pointing. The person guiding the other's body is frequently the person in charge during that encounter.
3. **The Pat.** Morris says when adults pat other adults it is often a condescending gesture or a sexual one. The well-known exception is the congratulatory pat (often on the buttocks) following a successful performance in men's team sports.
4. **The Arm-Link.** This may be used for support when one person is infirm, but it is also frequently used to indicate a close relationship. The person in charge, says Morris, is less likely to be the person grasping the other's arm.
5. **The Shoulder Embrace.** This half-embrace is used in male-female romantic relationships as well as to signify "buddies" in male-male relationships.
6. **The Full Embrace.** This gesture, sometimes called a hug, frequently occurs during moments of intense emotion, sporting events, romance, greetings, farewells. It is also used ritualistically to show a relationship closer than a handshake would indicate.
7. **The Hand-in-Hand.** When adults hold hands with children it is designed for support, to keep the child close, or to protect the child. As adults, hand holding (because both parties are performing the same act) suggests an equality within the relationship. It is often thought of in opposite-sex relationships, but same-sex hand holding is not uncommon, particularly in groups.
8. **The Waist Embrace.** This, according to Morris, is frequently substituted for the full embrace when the participants wish to signal more intimacy than hand holding or a shoulder embrace yet still remain mobile.
9. **The Kiss.** The location, pressure, duration, and openness of a kiss help to signal the closeness or desired closeness of a particular moment.
10. **The Hand-to-Head.** Given the highly vulnerable nature of the head area, letting someone touch you on the head shows a trusting, often intimate, relationship.
11. **The Head-to-Head.** Two people touching heads renders them incapable of regarding other ongoing activities in a normal manner, so this is usually thought of as an agreement by both parties to shut out the rest of the world—a condition common to young lovers especially.
12. **The Caress.** This is a signal associated with romantic feelings for

one's partner although, like any signal, it can be used by nonintimates who are trying to deceive others about the depth of their relationship.

13. **The Body Support.** Parents often support children by carrying, lifting, or letting them sit in their laps. Such support may be sought among adults in playful situations or when one person feels physically helpless.

14. **The Mock-Attack.** These are aggressive-looking behaviors performed in a nonaggressive manner, for example, arm punches, hair rufflings, pushes, pinches, ear nibbles, and so forth. We sometimes allow or even encourage such gestures with friends to show the range of behavioral understanding between us. And sometimes these mock-attack touches are substitutes for more loving touches that, in the case of some fathers wishing to show love for their sons, may be too embarrassing.

Some of these forms of touch can be seen in Figure 8-2.

Another method of categorizing the various types of touching was undertaken by Heslin (Heslin & Alpert, 1983). This taxonomy is based on the types of messages communicated and ranges from less personal to more personal types of touch. Accidental touches and aggressive touches (hurting another through touch) seem to be a part of the intimacy continuum but are not presented in this list.

1. **Functional/Professional.** The communicative intent of this impersonal, often cold and businesslike, touching is to accomplish some task or to perform some service. The other person is considered as an object or nonperson to keep any intimate or sexual messages from interfering with the task at hand. Examples of such situations may include a golf pro with his or her student, a tailor with a customer, or a physician with a patient.

2. **Social/Polite.** This type of touching affirms the other person's identity as a member of the same species, operating by essentially the same rules of conduct. Although the other is treated as a person, there is still very little perceived involvement between the interactants. The handshake is the best example of this type of touching. Although the handshake is only about 150 years old, it was preceded by a handclasp, which goes back at least as far as ancient Rome.

3. **Friendship/Warmth.** This kind of touching behavior begins to recognize more of the other person's uniqueness and expresses a liking for that person. It is oriented toward the other person as a friend. However, this type of touch engenders uneasiness associated with it because it can be misunderstood as intimate or sexual touching. Private situations may exacerbate this problem, so it probably will take place in public if the toucher anticipates the possibility of misinterpretation.

4. **Love/Intimacy.** When you lay your hand on the cheek of a person or when you fully embrace another person, you are probably expressing an emotional attachment or attraction through touch. The other person is the object of feelings of intimacy or love. The various kinds of

Figure 8–2

a

b

c

Some common forms of touch. (a) Full embrace. (b) Shoulder embrace. (c) Arm-link. (Photo credits: top left Photo © Paul Rosenfeld; top right Photo © Lawrence Rosenfeld; bottom Photo © Paul Rosenfeld)

(Continued)

Figure 8–2 (Continued)

d   e

Some common forms of touch. (d) Kiss. (e) Head-to-head. (Photo credit: left Photo © Stock Boston)

touching at this point will probably be the least stereotyped and the most adapted to the specific other person.

5. **Sexual Arousal.** Although sexual arousal is sometimes an integral part of love and intimacy, it also may have characteristics distinct from that category. Here we are primarily looking at touch as an experience of physical attraction only. The other person is, in common parlance, a sex object.

Morris (1971) proposed that heterosexual couples in Western culture normally go through a sequence of steps (like courtship patterns in other animal species) on the road to sexual intimacy. Notice that each step, aside from the first three, involves some kind of touching.

1. Eye to body
2. Eye to eye
3. Voice to voice
4. Hand to hand
5. Arm to shoulder
6. Arm to waist
7. Mouth to mouth
8. Hand to head
9. Hand to body
10. Mouth to breast
11. Hand to genitals
12. Genitals to genitals (and/or mouth to genitals)

According to Morris, these steps generally follow the same order, although with variations. One form of skipping steps or moving to a level of intimacy beyond what would be expected is found in socially formalized types of bodily contact, for example, a good-night kiss or hand-to-hand introduction. Although mouth-to-mouth touching frequently may reflect an advancing stage of intimacy, it also may occur in the most nonintimate settings with the most nonintimate meaning attached to it, for example, when a host of a television quiz show dutifully "pecks" the contestants as they are greeted or as they depart.

THE MEANINGS of INTERPERSONAL TOUCH

The meanings of touch have been assessed in several different ways. One approach simply tries to determine whether touching is perceived as a positive or negative experience. However, without further knowledge of the participants and how, when, where, and why the touch was performed, statements about the positive or negative reactions to touch are of questionable value.

Data gathered by Jones and Yarbrough (1985) indicate a wide range of meanings associated with touch. They had thirty-nine male and female university students record the details of each touch experience over a three-day period. Over 1,500 acts of social touching were analyzed. The following meanings incorporate their findings.

TOUCH AS POSITIVE AFFECT

The touching in this category is very similar to what Heslin called warmth/intimacy and sexual arousal. It may involve support, reassurance, appreciation, affection, sexual attraction, or, if the touch is sustained, it may indicate inclusion ("we're together"). Touching behavior from nurses, which is perceived as comforting and relaxing, would probably fit in this category. Back rubs and massages may also express a positive affect from a friend but be perceived as task related when performed by a professional masseur. Therapists, too, recognize the importance of performing touch in such a way that it communicates positive regard but not too much intimacy. If touch is perceived as an indication of interpersonal warmth, it may bring forth other related behaviors, for example, increased verbal output of patients and improved patient attitudes toward nurses (Aguilera, 1967; Pattison, 1973). The enhanced positive affect that can be produced by even fleeting and innocuous touches may generalize to the entire local environment, as found in the library study described at the beginning of this chapter and in the consumer studies of Hornik (1991, 1992). Shoppers touched by student greeters spent more time shopping, bought more, and evaluated the store more favorably.

TOUCH AS NEGATIVE AFFECT

The students in Jones and Yarbrough's study did not report very many touches in this category, but we clearly perceive some touches as an expression of negative attitudes and emotions. It may be an expression of anger or frustration suggested by hitting, slapping, or tightly squeezing another's arm so they cannot escape. Generally, negative touch is much more likely among young children than among adults.

TOUCH AS PLAY

Sometimes we interpret the touching we give and receive as attempts to reduce the seriousness of a message—whether it is affection or aggression. When one person goes through the motions of landing a knockout punch on the other person, then stops the forward movement of the fist just as it makes contact with the skin, the message is "I'm not fighting; I'm playing." An accompanying smile or laugh may further reinforce this message.

TOUCH AS INFLUENCE

When the goal of the touch is to persuade the other to do something, touch is associated with influence. Jones and Yarbrough called these *compliance touches.* Several independent studies show how touch aided in getting signatures on petitions, increased the chances people would return money found in a phone booth, and helped in obtaining favors. In one study, people who were touched after agreeing to fill out a survey answered a significantly greater number of items than people who agreed but were not touched (Nannberg & Hansen, 1994).

TOUCH AS INTERACTION MANAGEMENT

We try to structure or control conversations or elements of conversations in many ways. These *management touches* may guide someone without interrupting verbal conversation; get someone's attention by touching or tugging at that person's arm or tapping him or her on the shoulder; indicate or mark the beginning (greeting) or end (good-bye) of a conversation; or fulfill some ritualistic function such as touching a baby's head at a baptism.

TOUCH AS INTERPERSONAL RESPONSIVENESS

Sometimes the meanings attributed to touch concern the level of involvement, responsiveness, or activity of the communicator(s). Sometimes touch simply means that the intensity of the interaction is high or that the interactant's level of involvement in the conversation is high. Interpersonal responsiveness may be perceived as positive affect when it is mutually felt or when one person feels he or she contributed to the other's behavior. Touch can also be perceived as a move to control someone—for example, "He's just trying to get me as excited about this thing as he is."

Touch as Accidental

Sometimes we perceive touch as unintentional. Normally, this occurs when someone brushes or bumps into us.

Touch as Task Related

There are times when we need to help someone get out of a car or our hands touch as the result of passing something back and forth. These touches, associated with the performance of the task, are similar to what Heslin called functional/professional touch. As with any other message, the two communicators may not have a similar meaning for the touch—or one person may deliberately try to mislead another. A not unfamiliar example of the latter deception is when one person touches another in a joking context but intends the touch to be a step toward intimacy.

Touch as Healing

A miraculous cure is one that cannot be explained by recognized medical or physiological therapy. Throughout recorded history, wondrous healings of the sick and infirm by religious workers, royalty, and other charismatic persons have had interpersonal touch as a major ingredient. The French and English kings were widely believed to be able to accomplish healing by the laying on of hands. Edward I of England is documented to have touched 938 of his subjects suffering from scrofula in the twenty-eighth year of his reign and over 1,000 four years later (Older, 1982). In later centuries, including our own, healing touch became the province of ministers and others who attribute the healing touch to the power of God. Currently, the medical and nursing professions have renewed interest in touching as a form of therapy (Borelli & Heidt, 1981; Krieger, 1987).

The healing power of touch has not been studied in a controlled way that could establish its effectiveness and the mechanisms by which it may work. While it may be difficult to rule out God's love or unknown physical forces, Older (1982) attributes the inexplicable cures to psychological factors:

- The patient feels a great need for improvement.
- The patient has profound trust in the healer's powers.
- The patient is part of a group that increases pressure and adds encouragement.
- There is a shared, irrational belief system, usually of a religious nature.
- Emotions are at a high pitch in the patient and any onlookers.

TOUCH AS SYMBOLISM

Perhaps because touch outside of intimate relationships is so infrequent, it is highly salient when it occurs. Touch can be so fraught with meaning that the act of touch itself comes to represent the significance of the relationship or occasion. Touch by heroes, religious leaders, and royalty can have this quality, as can certain ritual touches. The touch shown in Figure 8-3 between Israeli leader Yitzhak Rabin and Palestinian leader Yasir Arafat on the day they announced an Israeli-Palestinian reconciliation says more than words could. Ironically, that same handshake apparently sparked Rabin's assassin to plan the prime minister's death ("With a handshake, Rabin's fate was sealed," *New York Times,* November 19, 1995).

SUMMARY OF MEANINGS OF INTERPERSONAL TOUCH

The meanings of touch depend on many environmental, personal, and contextual variables. For example, the relationship between the interactants often provides a context for interpreting the meaning of touch. A touch on the arm, which might be interpreted as a social/polite or friendship gesture, may acquire sexual overtones if a friendly relationship did not exist prior to the touch, if the touch is not accompanied by other signals indicating that it should be interpreted as a friendly touch, if the other person is a possible sexual partner, if the touch is held an instant too long, if the environment is private, and so forth. As noted earlier, friendship/warmth touching may be more likely to occur in public settings because the same kind of contact in private is more likely to take on connotations of love or sexual intimacy. Certain parts of the body connote greater intimacy than other parts, but intimacy is also linked to the manner of touch. For instance, a touch and release on any part of the body is likely to be perceived as less intimate than a touch and hold. Both of the preceding ways of touching are likely to be perceived as less intimate than a touch and stroke. Touch meaning also may vary as a result of the sequencing. Jones and Yarbrough found a number of

Figure 8–3

Rabin and Arafat shaking hands. (Photo © AP/Wide World)

instances in which positive affect touching was repeated, either by one person or in a reciprocal pattern. They speculate that this increases the intensity of the feeling being expressed. Other sequences begin with one type of touch and then change to another, for example, affectionate touching that precedes influence touching.

Like other forms of nonverbal behavior, touching may support or contradict information communicated by other systems. A doctor may explain that you need not worry about your pending operation, and his or her touch may add confirmation; but it may contradict the verbalization if the doctor is nervous, still, and abrupt. Men and women may also attribute different meanings to similar types of touch. In one study, nurses touched patients during the explanation of procedures prior to surgery. Females reacted positively, showing lower anxiety, more positive preoperative behavior, and more favorable postoperative physiological responses. But men touched in the same way reacted less positively. A similar result was obtained by Lewis, Derlega, Nichols, Shankar, Drury, & Hawkins (1995), who obtained ratings of photographic representations of nurses touching or not touching patients at the bedside. Male subjects rated the nurses (both male and female) as more supportive if they did not touch the patient, while female subjects thought the nurses were more supportive if they did touch the patient.

Recognizing the many variables that can affect the meaning people attribute to touch, Heslin and his colleagues (1983; 1975; 1976) undertook a series of studies that examined the combined effects of type and location of touch, the gender of the communicators, and their relationship. In the first two studies, the researchers asked married and unmarried people to examine the body parts diagrammed in Figure 8-4.

Each person was asked to indicate what it meant to them to be touched in each of the eleven areas—that is, patted, squeezed, stroked, or brushed. To focus reactions, subjects were asked to respond only in the context of touching by an opposite-sex friend (not parents, siblings, or relatives). The method of responding was limited to scales representing various degrees of playfulness, warmth/love, friendship/fellowship, pleasantness, and sexual desire.

Generally, married persons reported a more positive reaction toward touch and tended to associate it with sex more often than did unmarried respondents. Unless the touch was in the genital region, sexual desire was not a common response for the unmarrieds. Although unmarried women did not perceive sexual touching to be as pleasant and as warm as unmarried men, married women did. Married men attributed less warmth/love and pleasantness to sexual touching than either single men or married women.

Figure 8–4

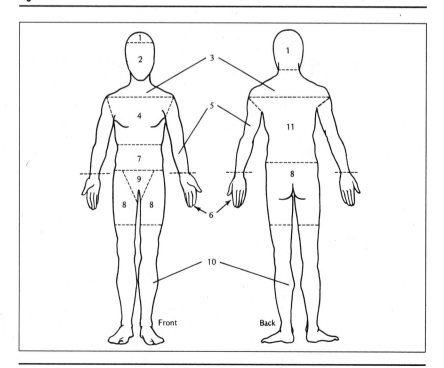

The human body diagrammed into eleven areas.

The type of touch seemed to be closely linked to one's judgments of playfulness and warmth/love; for example, patting was associated with play, but stroking was associated with warmth/love and sexual desire. On the other hand (no pun intended), friendliness and sexuality seemed most closely linked to the location of the touch. For example, hands, no matter how they were touched, were seen as pleasant, warm, and friendly; the genital area was not seen as playful regardless of what kind of touching was being evaluated.

Heslin's third study used the same methodology and focused on same-sex touching and touching from strangers. Overall, the touches from opposite-sex friends were perceived as more pleasant and less of an invasion of privacy than the same touching from same-sex friends or strangers of either sex. This was true for both men and women. However, men and women revealed important differences regarding the persons from whom touching would be the greatest invasion of privacy. Women indicated that touch from a stranger would be the greatest invasion of privacy; men felt that touch from a same-sex person would be the greatest invasion of privacy. Men reported themselves to be as comfortable with touch from women strangers as they were with touch from women friends! Both men and women agreed that the most pleasant type of touch was stroking in sexual areas by an opposite-sex friend. But the second most pleasant type of touch reported by women was for a male friend to stroke nonsexual areas, while the second most pleasant type of touch by men was for a female stranger to stroke sexual areas.

CULTURAL DIFFERENCES in TOUCHING BEHAVIOR

To anyone who travels widely, there seem to be vast differences in the amount of touching behavior in some countries compared with our own. Jourard (1966) counted the frequency of contact between couples in cafes in various cities and reported the following contacts per hour: San Juan, Puerto Rico, 180; Paris, 110; Gainesville, Florida, 2; London, 0. In the early 1970s, Barnlund (1975) conducted a comparative study of Japanese and U. S. touching patterns using 120 college students in each culture (60 males and 60 females). Figure 8-5 indicates that in almost every category, the amount of physical contact reported in the United States is twice that reported by Japanese. From these data, it is clear that U. S. respondents perceive themselves as both more accessible to, and more physically expressive toward, others in regard to touch. Future observational studies may confirm these perceptions that the Japanese tend to touch one another in public less than U. S. residents do.

Observations of differences in touching behavior around the world have led to the idea of *contact* and *noncontact* cultures; that is, some cultures encourage more touching of various kinds. The United States has traditionally been labeled a noncontact culture, but we are probably touching more now than at any time in our history (see Willis & Rawdon, 1984). In some ethnic groups, people probably touch a great deal.

Figure 8–5

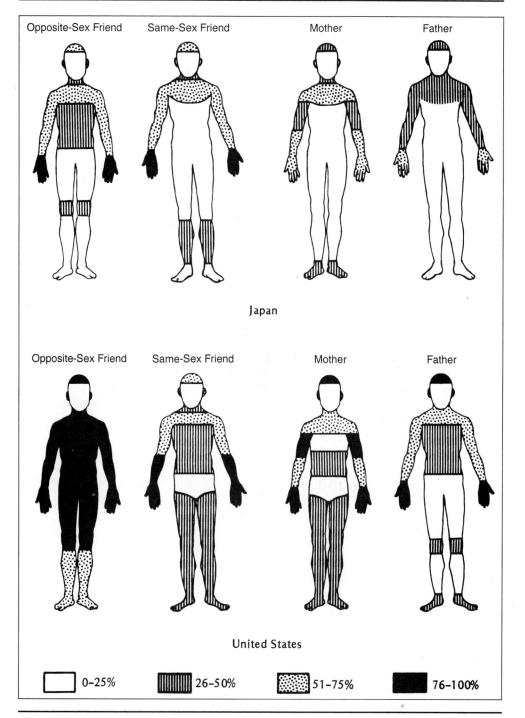

Physical contact patterns in Japan (above) and the United States (below).

Just as there are many differences within this so-called noncontact culture based on one's ancestry, social status, and living conditions, Shuter's observations led him to conclude that there may be significant differences among what we have traditionally called contact cultures (Shuter, 1976). Shuter systematically observed people interacting in natural settings in Costa Rica, Panama, and Colombia. His data seem to show that as one moves southward from Central America, the amount of public touching and holding decreases. Further evidence that *contact* and *noncontact* may be oversimplified labels comes from Halberstadt's (1985) review of race differences in nonverbal behavior. Among adults, blacks establish larger interpersonal distances than whites do but engage in *more* interpersonal touch.

Aside from a rich store of anecdotal material, we do not know much about the specifics of cultural differences in touching. We do know that there seem to be enormous differences; for example, two males interacting in some countries may hold hands or intertwine their legs, whereas this would be a surprising sight in other countries.

SELF-TOUCHING

We also engage in self-touching. Self-touches include nervous mannerisms such as nail chewing, picking on one's skin, twirling one's hair, wringing one's hands, and stroking oneself. This category of behavior has not been well studied. It is not clear whether all kinds of self-touching can be called self-adaptors, nor how such a distinction could be made. Various kinds of self-touching, or self-touching used in different circumstances, may serve different functions.

Desmond Morris (1971) offered a list of different kinds of self-touching:

1. **Shielding Actions.** These behaviors usually involve reducing input or output, for example, putting one's hand over one's mouth or ears.
2. **Cleaning Actions.** Sometimes we bring our hands up to our head to scratch, rub, pick, wipe—for literal cleaning. But sometimes similar self-touching is used for attending to one's appearance, for example, hair-grooming, clothes straightening, and other types of preening. Observations and subsequent interviews with people in public restrooms found women engaging in more of this behavior than men. People in the process of building an intimate relationship did more preening than those whose intimate relationship had been established for some time (Daly, Hogg, Sacks, Smith, & Zimring, 1983).
3. **Specialized Signals.** These gestures are used to communicate specific messages such as cupping the ear with one's hand to signal the inability to hear or holding a hand under one's chin to signal "I'm fed up to here."

4. Self-Intimacies. Self-intimacies, according to Morris, are comforting actions that represent unconsciously mimed acts of being touched by someone else. They may involve holding one's own hands, arm folding, leg crossing, masturbation, and so on. Some, he maintains, are more likely to be performed by women than men, for example, the head-lowered-on-to-the-shoulder posture and leg hugging. Thus, self-touching can be a substitute for comfort that might otherwise be provided by others.

Some of these self-touching behaviors are what Ekman and Friesen called *adaptors.* As the term implies, they are behavioral adaptations we make in response to certain learning situations, for example, performing some bodily or instrumental action, managing our emotions, satisfying our needs, or getting along with other people. These behaviors (or some residue of them) seem to appear in situations that we feel approximate the conditions of the early learning experiences. Generally, we are not aware of performing these behaviors, but frequent feedback may heighten our sensitivity—for example, "Stop picking your nose!" Although the research on adaptors is not extensive, there seems to be some consensus that adaptors are generally associated with negative feelings for oneself or another person. There are also some useful classifications of different types of adaptors, which include both the probable referent for the behavior (self, other, object) and the type of behavior (scratching, rubbing). Some attempts are now being made to link various adaptors to specific emotional or mood states. Most of the research has focused on self-adaptors.

Research on psychiatric patients has found that self-adaptors increase as a person's psychological discomfort, anxiety, or depression increase (Ekman & Friesen, 1972; Freedman, 1972; Freedman, Blass, Rifkin, & Quitkin, 1973; Freedman & Hoffmann, 1967; Waxer, 1977). If, however, the anxiety level is too high, a person may "freeze," engaging in little movement at all. The finding that self-adaptors also were associated with guilt feelings in the patients studied illuminates one aspect of the deception research reviewed in Chapter 12. Ekman and Friesen also discovered picking and scratching self-adaptors to be related to a person's hostility and suspiciousness. Theoretically, this picking and scratching is a manifestation of aggression against oneself or aggression felt for another person, which is projected on oneself. Other speculations and hypotheses about self-adaptors include the possibility that rubbing is used to give self-assurance, that covering one's eyes is associated with shame and/or guilt, and that self-grooming shows concern for one's self-presentation.

A number of studies have indicated that self-touching is associated with situational anxiety or stress. As an example, Ekman and Friesen (1974) asked people to watch one of two films, one highly stressful and the other quite pleasant. Viewers were then instructed to describe the film as pleasant to an interviewer; thus, those watching the stressful film were trying to deceive, which in itself can be considered stressful. Subjects in this group engaged in

Figure 8–6

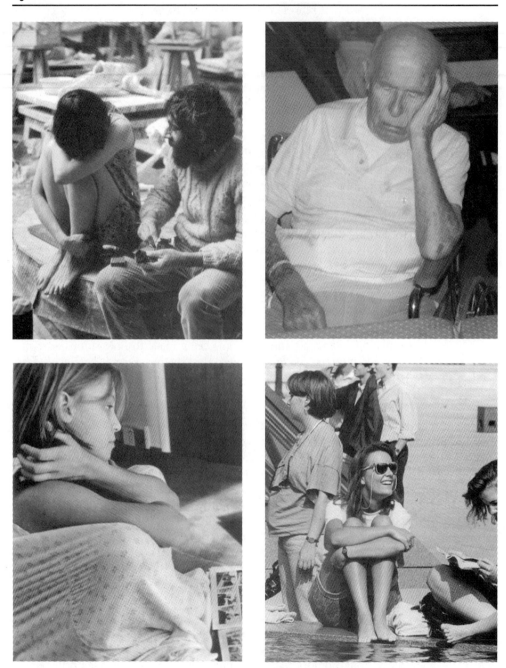

Self-touching. (Photo credits: top left Henri Cartier-Bresson/© distributed by Magnum; top right © Paul E. Rosenfeld; bottom left © Maureen Fenneill, 1979 Comstock; bottom right © Stuart Cohen, 1989 Comstock)

more self-adaptors than those simply describing the pleasant film as pleasant. Self-touching also may be greater in people who are chronically more anxious, for example, in some psychiatric patients. In a study of physician-patient communication, patients were more likely to touch their bodies when talking about their more conflictual hidden agendas than when talking about the primary complaint (Shreve, Harrigan, Kues, & Kagas, 1988). An interesting question is whether the self-touching associated with anxiety is simply a sign or indicator that anxiety is occurring or whether touching oneself actually relieves stress.

Another source of body-focused movements is cognitive (information-processing) demand. When engaged in a monologue, people touched themselves more than when simply sitting still. Similarly, when they are asked to read the names of colors that are printed in contradictory colors (e.g., the word *red* printed in blue), people touch themselves more than if they read color-consistent color names (Kenner, 1993).

Other adaptors are learned in conjunction with our early experiences with interpersonal relations: giving and taking from another, attacking or protecting, establishing closeness or withdrawing, and so forth. Leg movements may be adaptors showing residues of kicking aggression, sexual invitation, or flight. Ekman believes that many of the restless movements of the hands and feet, which have typically been considered indicators of anxiety, may be residues of adaptors necessary for flight from the interaction. An example from the interaction behavior of baboons will help illustrate the nature of these other-adaptors. When a young baboon is learning the fundamentals of attack and aggression, the mother baboon is watching from close by. The young baboon will enact aggressive behavior but also will turn its head laterally to check whether its mother is still there. As an adult, the baboon may still perform this lateral head movement in threatening conditions even though the mother is no longer there and the movement seems to serve no functional purpose.

Object adaptors involve the manipulation of objects and may be derived from the performance of some instrumental task (for example, smoking, writing with a pencil). Although we are typically unaware of performing adaptor behaviors, we are probably most aware of the object adaptors. They are often learned later in life, and there seem to be fewer social taboos associated with them.

Since there seem to be social constraints on displaying some adaptive behaviors, they are more often seen when a person is alone. At least, we would expect to see the full act rather than just a fragment of it. Alone you might pick your nose without inhibition; with other people, you may just touch your nose or rub it casually. Adaptors are not intended for use in communication, but they may be triggered by verbal behavior in a situation associated with conditions occurring when the adaptive habit was first learned.

Individual and group differences in self-touching have been noted. In a study of children in four countries, those speaking English (England and Australia) engaged in significantly less self-touching during experimental tasks than did Italian children and French-speaking children in Belgium. Also in those samples, significant individual variation was revealed, meaning that some children were consistently more likely to touch themselves across a variety of experimental tasks (Kenner, 1993). Some evidence suggests that females touch themselves in interpersonal interaction more than males do (Hall, 1984). It is not clear to what extent this may reflect greater social anxiety or arousal on the part of females, or whether it mainly reflects a heightened self-consciousness about appearance. Indeed, women's clothes and hairstyles seem to demand constant readjustment; a woman has to keep track of whether her panty hose are wrinkled, skirt is riding up, hair is in order, and so forth. It would be no surprise if women touch themselves more for these reasons alone.

SUMMARY

Our first information about ourselves, others, and our environment probably comes from touching. The act of touching or being touched can have a powerful impact on our response to a situation, even if that touch was unintentional. In some cases, touching is the most effective method for communicating; in others, it can elicit negative or hostile reactions. The meanings we attach to touching behavior vary according to what body part is touched, how long the touch lasts, the strength of the touch, the method of the touch (for example, open or closed fist), and the frequency of the touch. Touch also means different things in different environments (institutions, airports, and so on) and varies with communicators' age, sex, and stage of relationship. This chapter reported studies that explored different reactions to touch by married and unmarried people and by males and females. In our culture, women perceive touching by a stranger to be the greatest invasion of their privacy; men report the greatest invasion of their privacy to be touching by other men.

Although some believe societal power/status is represented by a preponderance of male-initiated touching of females, other studies suggest the issue is more complex. Moreover, whoever initiates the touch will be perceived by observers as gaining in relative status and power.

The common types of interpersonal touching and self-touching may communicate a variety of messages, including influence, positive affect, negative affect, play, interpersonal responsiveness, unintentional contact, interaction management, and task requirements. Heslin classified the various types of touching behavior on an intimacy continuum:

1. Functional/professional
2. Social/polite
3. Friendship/warmth
4. Love/intimacy
5. Sexual arousal

Although anecdotal reports and a few isolated studies would suggest that the United States represents a noncontact culture, there are several indications that this may be changing. At the least, it seems clear that there are significant variations in the amount of contact within this culture, regardless of what we choose to label the entire culture. There are indications that children in this culture touch more than adults; there seems to be a decreasing amount of touch from kindergarten through junior high. Some research reports that boys and girls get differential early experiences with touch from parents, but most agree that early experiences with touch are crucial for later adjustment.

QUESTIONS for DISCUSSION

1. Consider touch between people who differ in rank or status. To what extent may such touch reflect privileges, duties, or strategies on the part of both participants?
2. Research suggests that men in our society are more aversive to same-sex touch than women. Why? Does it represent a "problem" that should be solved?
3. Touch norms and practices seem to vary across cultures and subcultures. If possible, think of one or two cultures with which you are personally familiar and describe their touching behavior. Does it differ from, or agree with, findings you read about in this chapter?
4. Most studies find that touch is a rather infrequent event. Do you think this is correct? Discuss exceptions to this generalization. Why do you think touch might seem to be not very common?

REFERENCES and SELECTED BIBLIOGRAPHY

Aguilera, D. C. (1967). Relationships between physical contact and verbal interaction between nurses and patients. *Journal of Psychiatric Nursing, 5,* 5–21.

Alagna, F. J., Whitcher, S. J., Fisher, J. D., & Wicas, E. A. (1969). Evaluative reaction to interpersonal touch in a counseling interview. *Journal of Counseling Psychology, 26,* 465–72.

Andersen, J. F., Andersen, P. A., & Lustig, M. W. (1987). Opposite sex touch avoidance: A national replication and extension. *Journal of Nonverbal Behavior, 11,* 89–109.

Andersen, P. A., & Leibowitz, K. (1978). The development and nature of the construct touch avoidance. *Environmental Psychology and Nonverbal Behavior, 3,* 89–106.

Argyle, M. (1975). *Bodily communication.* New York: International Universities Press.

Barnlund, D. C. (1975). Communicative styles in two cultures: Japan and the United States. In A. Kendon, R. M. Harris, & M. R. Key (Eds.), *Organization of behavior in face-to-face interaction.* The Hague: Mouton.

Barroso, F., & Feld, J. K. (1986). Self-touching and attentional processes: The role of task difficulty, selection stage, and sex differences. *Journal of Nonverbal Behavior, 10,* 51–64.

Blondis, M., & Barbara, J. (1982). *Nonverbal communication in nursing: Back to the human touch.* New York: Wiley-Medical.

Borelli, M., & Heidt, P. (1981). *Therapeutic touch: A book of readings.* New York: Springer.

Brownlee, J., & Bakeman, R. (1981). Hitting in toddler-peer interaction. *Child Development, 52,* 1076–79.

Burgoon, J. K. (1991). Relational message interpretations of touch, conversational distance, and posture. *Journal of Nonverbal Behavior, 15,* 233–59.

Casher, L., & Dixson, B. K. (1967). The therapeutic use of touch. *Journal of Psychiatric Nursing and Mental Health Service, 5,* 442–51.

Casler, L. (1965). The effects of extra tactile stimulation on a group of institutionalized infants. *Genetic Psychology Monographs, 71,* 137–75.

Clay, V. S. (1966). *The effect of culture on mother-child tactile communication.* Unpublished doctoral dissertation, Columbia University.

Cooper, C. L., & Bowles, D. (1973). Physical encounter and self-disclosure. *Psychological Reports, 33,* 451–54.

Cooper, V. W. (1987). The tactile communication system: State of the art and research perspectives. In B. Dervin & M. J. Voigt (Eds.), *Progress in communication sciences* (Vol. 8). Norwood, NJ: Ablex.

Crusco, A. H., & Wetzel, C. G. (1984). The Midas touch: The effects of interpersonal touch on restaurant tipping. *Personality and Social Psychology Bulletin, 10,* 512–17.

Daly, J. A., Hogg, E., Sacks, D., Smith, M., & Zimring, L. (1983). Sex and relationship affect social self-grooming. *Journal of Nonverbal Behavior, 7,* 183–89.

Deethardt, J. F., & Hines, D. G. (1983). Tactile communication and personality differences. *Journal of Nonverbal Behavior, 8,* 143–56.

Dresslar, F. B. (1984). Studies in the psychology of touch. *American Journal of Psychology, 6,* 313–68.

Ekman, P., & Friesen, W. V. (1972). Hand movements. *Journal of Communication, 22,* 353–74.

Ekman, P., & Friesen, W. V. (1974). Detecting deception from the body or face. *Journal of Personality and Social Psychology, 29,* 288–98.

Field, T. (1995). Massage therapy for infants and children. *Developmental and Behavioral Pediatrics, 16,* 105–11.

Fisher, J. D., Rytting, M., & Heslin, R. (1976). Hands touching hands: Affective and evaluative effects of an interpersonal touch. *Sociometry, 39,* 416–21.

Forden, C. (1981). The influence of sex-role expectations on the perception of touch. *Sex Roles, 7,* 889–94.

Frank, L. K. (1957). Tactile communication. *Genetic Psychology Monographs, 56,* 209–55.

Freedman, N. (1972). The analysis of movement behavior during the clinical interview. In A. W. Siegman & B. Pope (Eds.), *Studies in dyadic communication.* New York: Pergamon.

Freedman, N., Blass, T., Rifkin, A., & Quitkin, F. (1973). Body movements and the verbal encoding of aggressive affect. *Journal of Personality and Social Psychology, 26,* 72–85.

Freedman, N., & Hoffman, S. P. (1967). Kinetic behavior in altered clinical states: Approach to objective analysis of motor behavior during clinical interviews. *Perceptual and Motor Skills, 24,* 527–39.

Goldberg, M. A., & Katz, B. (1990). The effect of nonreciprocated and reciprocated touch on power/dominance perception. *Journal of Social Behavior and Personality, 5,* 379–86.

Goldberg, S., & Rosenthal, R. (1986). Self-touching behavior in the job interview: Antecedents and consequences. *Journal of Nonverbal Behavior, 10,* 65–80.

Goldstein, A. G., & Jeffords, J. (1981). Status and touching behavior. *Bulletin of the Psychonomic Society, 17,* 79–81.

Greenbaum, P. E., & Rosenfeld, H. M. (1980). Varieties of touching in greetings: Sequential structure and sex-related differences. *Journal of Nonverbal Behavior, 5,* 13–25.

Guerrero, L. K., & Andersen, P. A. (1991). The waxing and waning of relational intimacy: Touch as a function of relational stage, gender and touch avoidance. *Journal of Social and Personal Relationships, 8,* 147–65.

Guerrero, L. K., & Andersen, P. A. (1994). Patterns of matching and initiation: Touch behavior and touch avoidance across romantic relationship stages. *Journal of Nonverbal Behavior, 18,* 137–53.

Halberstadt, A. G. (1985). Race, socioeconomic status, and nonverbal behavior. In A. W. Siegman and S. Feldstein (Eds.), *Multichannel integrations of nonverbal behavior.* Hillsdale, NJ: Erlbaum.

Hall, J. A. (1984). *Nonverbal sex differences: Communication accuracy and expressive style.* Baltimore: Johns Hopkins University Press.

Hall, J. A. (1996). Touch, status, and gender at professional meetings. *Journal of Nonverbal Behavior, 20,* 23–44.

Hall, J. A., & Veccia, E. M. (1991). More 'touching' observations: New insights on men, women, and interpersonal touch. *Journal of Personality and Social Psychology, 59,* 1155–62.

Harlow, H. F. (1958). The nature of love. *American Psychologist, 13,* 678–85.

Harrigan, J. A., Lucic, K. S., Kay, D., McLaney, A., et al. (1991). Effect of expressor role and type of self-touching on observers' perceptions. *Journal of Applied Social Psychology, 21,* 585–609.

Harrison-Speake, K., & Willis, F. N. (1995). Ratings of the appropriateness of touch among family members. *Journal of Nonverbal Behavior, 19,* 85–100.

Henley, N. (1973a). Status and sex: Some touching observations. *Bulletin of the Psychonomic Society, 2,* 91–93.

Henley, N. (1973b). The politics of touch. In P. Brown (Ed.), *Radical psychology.* New York: Harper & Row.

Henley, N. (1973–1974). Power, sex and non-verbal communication. *Berkeley Journal of Sociology, 18,* 1–26.

Henley, N. (1977). *Body politics: Power, sex, and nonverbal communication.* Englewood Cliffs, NJ: Prentice-Hall.

Heslin, R., & Alper, T. (1983). Touch: A bonding gesture. In J. M. Wiemann & R. P. Harrison (Eds.), *Nonverbal interaction*. Beverly Hills, CA: Sage.

Heslin, R., & Boss, D. (1980). Nonverbal intimacy in airport arrival and departure. *Personality and Social Psychology Bulletin, 6,* 248–52.

Heslin, R., Nguyen, T. D., & Nguyen, M. L. (1983). Meaning of touch: The case of touch from a stranger or same sex person. *Journal of Nonverbal Behavior, 7,* 147–57.

Hollender, M. H. (1970). The need or wish to be held. *Archives of General Psychiatry, 22,* 445–53.

Hollender, M. H., & Mercer, A. J. (1976). Wish to be held and wish to hold in men and women. *Archives of General Psychiatry, 33,* 49–51.

Hornik, J. (1991). Shopping time and purchasing behavior as a result of in-store tactile stimulation. *Perceptual and Motor Skills, 73,* 969–70.

Hornik, J. (1992). Tactile stimulation and consumer response. *Journal of Consumer Research, 19,* 449–58.

Hubble, M. A., Noble, F. C., & Robinson, S. E. (1981). The effects of counselor touch in an initial counseling session. *Journal of Counseling Psychology, 28,* 533–35.

Hunton, V. D., & Summer, F. C. (1948). The affective tone of tactual impressions. *Journal of Psychology, 26,* 235–42.

Hutchinson, K. L., & Davidson, C. A. (1990). Body accessibility re-revisited: The 60s, 70s, and 80s. *Journal of Social Behavior and Personality, 5,* 341–52.

Jones, S. (1991). Problems of validity in questionnaire studies of nonverbal behavior: Jourard's tactile body-accessibility scale. *Southern Communication Journal, 56,* 83–95.

Jones, S. E. (1986). Sex differences in touch communication. *Western Journal of Speech Communication, 50,* 227–41.

Jones, S. E. (1994). *The right touch: Understanding and using the language of physical contact.* Cresskill, NJ: Hampton Press.

Jones, S. E., & Yarbrough, A. E. (1985). A naturalistic study of the meanings of touch. *Communication Monographs, 52,* 19–56.

Jourard, S. M. (1966). An exploratory study of body-accessibility. *British Journal of Social and Clinical Psychology, 26,* 235–42.

Jourard, S. M. (1968). *Disclosing man to himself.* New York: Van Nostrand Reinhold.

Jourard, S. M., & Rubin, J. E. (1968). Self-disclosure and touching: A study of two modes of interpersonal encounter and their interrelation. *Journal of Humanistic Psychology, 8,* 39–48.

Juni, S., & Brannon, R. (1981). Interpersonal touching as a function of status and sex. *Journal of Social Psychology, 114,* 135–36.

Kauffman, L. E. (1971). Tacesics, the study of touch: A model for proxemic analysis. *Semiotica, 14,* 149–61.

Kenner, A. N. (1984). The effect of task differences, attention and personality on the frequency of body-focused hand movements. *Journal of Nonverbal Behavior, 8,* 159–71.

Kenner, A. N. (1993). A cross-cultural study of body-focused hand movement. *Journal of Nonverbal Behavior, 17,* 263–79.

Kirman, J. H. (1973). Tactile communication of speech: A review and an analysis. *Psychological Bulletin, 80,* 54–74.

Krieger, D. (1987). *Living the therapeutic touch: Healing as a lifestyle.* New York: Dodd, Mead.

Krout, M. (1954a). An experimental attempt to determine the significance of unconscious manual symbolic movements. *Journal of General Psychology, 51,* 296–308.

Krout, M. (1954b). An experimental attempt to produce unconscious manual symbolic movements. *Journal of General Psychology, 51,* 121–52.

Levine, S. (1972). Stimulation and infancy. *Scientific American, 202,* 80–86.

Lewis, M. (1972). Culture and gender: There is no unisex in the nursery. *Psychology Today, 5,* 54–57.

Lewis, R. J., Derlega, V. J., Nichols, B., Shankar, A., Drury, K. K., & Hawkins, L. (1995). Sex differences in observers' reactions to a nurse's use of touch. *Journal of Nonverbal Behavior, 19,* 101–13.

Lockard, J. S., & Adams, R. M. (1980). Courtship behaviors in public: Different age/ sex roles. *Ethology and Sociobiology, 1,* 245–53.

Lomranz, J., & Shapira, A. (1974). Communicative patterns of self-disclosure and touching behavior. *Journal of Psychology, 88,* 223–27.

Maier, R. A., & Ernest, R. C. (1978). Sex differences in the perception of touching. *Perceptual and Motor Skills, 46,* 577–78.

Maines, D. R. (1977). Tactile relationships in the subway as affected by racial, sexual, and crowded seating situations. *Environmental Psychology and Nonverbal Behavior, 2,* 100–108.

Major, B. (1981). Gender patterns in touching behavior. In C. Mayo & N. M. Henley (Eds.), *Gender and nonverbal behavior.* New York: Springer-Verlag.

Major, B., & Heslin, R. (1982). Perceptions of same-sex and cross-sex touching: It's better to give than to receive. *Journal of Nonverbal Behavior, 6,* 148–62.

Major, B., Schmidlin, A. M., & Williams, L. (1990). Gender patterns in touch: The impact of age and setting. *Journal of Personality and Social Psychology, 58,* 634–43.

Maurer, D., & Maurer, C. (1988). *The world of the newborn.* New York: Basic Books.

McCorkle, R. (1974). Effects of touch on seriously ill patients. *Nursing Research, 23,* 125–32.

McCormick, N. B., & Jones, A. J. (1989). Gender differences in nonverbal flirtation. *Journal of Sex Education & Therapy, 15,* 271–82.

Montagu, M. F. A. (1971). *Touching: The human significance of the skin.* New York: Columbia University Press.

Morris, D. (1971). *Intimate behaviour.* New York: Random House.

Morris, D. (1977). *Manwatching.* New York: Abrams.

Morry, M. M., & Enzle, M. E. (1994). Effect of gender dominance expectancies for knowledge on self-touching during conversations. *Social Behavior and Personality, 22,* 123–29.

Murphy, A. J. (1972). Effect of body contact on performance of a simple cognitive task. *British Journal of Social and Clinical Psychology, 11,* 402–8.

Nannberg, J. C., & Hansen, C. H. (1994). Post-compliance touch: An incentive for task performance. *Journal of Social Psychology, 134,* 301–7.

Nguyen, M. L., Heslin, R., & Nguyen, T. (1976). The meaning of touch: Sex and marital status differences. *Representative Research in Social Psychology, 7,* 13–18.

Nguyen, T., Heslin, R., & Nguyen, M. L. (1975). The meanings of touch: Sex differences. *Journal of Communication, 25,* 92–103.

Older, J. (1982). *Touching is healing: A revolutionary breakthrough in medicine.* New York: Stein and Day.

Patterson, M. L., Powell, J. L., & Lenihan, M. G. (1986). Touch, compliance, and interpersonal affect. *Journal of Nonverbal Behavior, 10,* 41–50.

Pattison, J. E. (1973). Effects of touch on self-exploration and the therapeutic relationship. *Journal of Consulting and Clinical Psychology, 40,* 170–75.

Perdue, V. P., & Connor, J. M. (1978). Patterns of touching between preschool children and male and female teachers. *Child Development, 49,* 1258–62.

Perper, T. (1989). Theories and observations on sexual selection and female choice in human beings. *Medical Anthropology, 11,* 409–54.

Pisano, M. D., Wall, S. M., & Foster, A. (1986). Perceptions of nonreciprocal touch in romantic relationships. *Journal of Nonverbal Behavior, 10,* 29–40.

Remland, M. S., Jones, T. S., & Brinkman, H. (1991). Proxemic and haptic behavior in three European countries. *Journal of Nonverbal Behavior, 15,* 215–32.

Rinck, C. M., Willis, F. N., & Dean, L. M. (1980). Interpersonal touch among residents of homes for the elderly. *Journal of Communication, 30,* 44–47.

Roese, N. J., Olson, J. M., Borenstein, M. N., Martin, A., & Shores, A. L. (1992). Same-sex touching behavior: The moderating role of homophobic attitudes. *Journal of Nonverbal Behavior, 16,* 249–59.

Rosenfeld, L. B., Kartus, S., & Ray, C. (1976). Body accessibility revisited. *Journal of Communication, 26,* 27–30.

Schaffer, H., & Emerson, E. (1964). Patterns of response to physical contact in early human development. *Journal of Child Psychology and Psychiatry, 5,* 1–13.

Shreve, E. G., Harrigan, J. A., Kues, J. R., & Kagas, D. K. (1988). Nonverbal expressions of anxiety in physician-patient interactions. *Psychiatry, 51,* 378–84.

Shuter, R. (1976). Proxemics and tactility in Latin America. *Journal of Communication, 26,* 46–52.

Sigelman, C. K., & Adams, R. M. (1990). Family interactions in public: Parent-child distance and touch. *Journal of Nonverbal Behavior, 14,* 63–75.

Silverman, A. F., Pressman, M. E., & Bartel, H. W. (1973). Self-esteem and tactile communication. *Journal of Humanistic Psychology, 13,* 73–77.

Silverthorne, C., Micklewright, J., O'Donnell, M., & Gibson, R. (1976). Attribution of personal characteristics as a function of the degree of touch on initial contact and sex. *Sex Roles, 2,* 185–93.

Smith, D. E., Willis, F. N., & Gier, J. A. (1980). Success and interpersonal touch in a competitive setting. *Journal of Nonverbal Behavior, 5,* 26–34.

Sokoloff, N., Yaffe, S., Weintraub, D., & Blase, B. (1969). Effects of handling on the subsequent development of premature infants. *Developmental Psychology, 1,* 765–68.

Spitz, R. (1945). Hospitalism: Genesis of psychiatric conditions in early childhood. *Psychoanalytic Study of the Child, 1,* 53–74.

Stier, D. S., & Hall, J. A. (1984). Gender differences in touch: An empirical and theoretical review. *Journal of Personality and Social Psychology, 47,* 440–59.

Summerhayes, D., & Suchner, R. (1978). Power implications of touch in male-female relationships. *Sex Roles, 4,* 103–10.

Sussman, N. M., & Rosenfeld, H. M. (1978). Touch, justification, and sex: Influences on the aversiveness of spatial violations. *Journal of Social Psychology, 106,* 215–22.

Thayer, S. (1982). Social touching. In W. Schiff & E. Foulke (Eds.), *Tactual perception: A sourcebook.* New York: Cambridge University Press.

Thayer, S. (1986). History and strategies of research on social touch. *Journal of Nonverbal Behavior, 10,* 12–28.

Watson, W. H. (1975). The meanings of touch: Geriatric nursing. *Journal of Communication, 25,* 104–12.

Waxer, P. H. (1977). Nonverbal cues for anxiety: An examination of emotional leakage. *Journal of Abnormal Psychology, 86,* 306–14.

Whitcher, S. J., & Fisher, J. D. (1979). Multidimensional reaction to therapeutic touch in a hospital setting. *Journal of Personality and Social Psychology, 37,* 87–96.

Williams, S. J., & Willis, F. N. (1978). Interpersonal touch among preschool children at play. *Psychological Record, 28,* 501–8.

Williams, T. (1966). Cultural structuring of tactile experience in a Borneo society. *The American Anthropologist, 68,* 27–39.

Willis, F. N., Jr., & Briggs, L. F. (1992). Relationship and touch in public settings. *Journal of Nonverbal Behavior, 16,* 55–63.

Willis, F. N., & Hamm, H. K. (1980). The use of interpersonal touch in securing compliance. *Journal of Nonverbal Behavior, 5,* 49–55.

Willis, F. N., & Hoffman, G. E. (1975). Development of tactile patterns in relation to age, sex, and race. *Developmental Psychology, 11,* 866.

Willis, F. N., & Rawdon, V. A. (1994). Gender and national differences in attitudes toward same-gender touch. *Perceptual and Motor Skills, 78,* 1027–34.

Willis, F. N., & Reeves, D. L. (1976). Touch interactions in junior high students in relation to sex and race. *Developmental Psychology, 12,* 91–92.

Willis, F. N., Reeves, D. L., & Buchanan, D. R. (1976). Interpersonal touch in high school relative to sex and race. *Perceptual and Motor Skills, 43,* 843–47.

CHAPTER 9

The Effects of the Face on Human Communication

Your face, my thane, is a book where men
May read strange matters.

—SHAKESPEARE, MACBETH, ACT 1

The face is rich in communicative potential. It is a primary site for communication of emotional states; it reflects interpersonal attitudes; it provides nonverbal feedback on the comments of others; and some scholars say it is the primary source of information next to human speech. For these reasons, and because of the face's visibility, we pay a great deal of attention to the messages we receive from the faces of others. Frequently, we rely heavily on facial cues when making important interpersonal judgments. This begins when, as infants, we take special interest in the huge face peering over our crib and tending to our needs. Most of the research on facial expressions (and various components of the face) has focused on the display and interpretation of emotional signals. While this is the major focus of this chapter, we also want to emphasize that the face may be the basis for judging another person's personality and that it can (and does) provide information other than one's emotional state.

THE FACE and PERSONALITY JUDGMENTS

The human face comes in many sizes and shapes. Faces may be triangular, square, or round; foreheads may be high and wide, high and narrow, low and wide, or protruding; complexions may be light, dark, smooth, wrinkled, or blemished; eyes may be close or far apart, or bulging; noses may be short, long, flat, crooked, "humpbacked," or a "ski slope"; mouths may be large or small with thin or thick lips; and cheeks can bulge or appear sunken. Besides the many facial features that we can respond to, the face in general receives much attention. "Facial primacy," or the tendency to give more weight to the face than to other communication channels, is well documented. Facial primacy may result from our belief that the face reveals a great deal about a person's personality or character. This belief goes back hundreds (perhaps thousands) of years. Facial stereotypes have been the topic of some scientific scrutiny. Secord and his colleagues (1959) explored the relationship of facial features and personality judgments and found some consistent associations, for example, high foreheads and intelligence, thin lips and conscientiousness, thick lips on females and "sexiness," and so on. Undesirable persons were portrayed by Secord's subjects as having more extreme features, that is, features that extended beyond the perceived normative boundaries. More recent research reveals many stereotypes associated with having a youthful-looking face (see Chapter 6).

This chapter focuses on the *dynamic* nature of the face—its ability to make practically an infinite number of expressions. At least twenty different muscles are used routinely in making facial expressions (Rinn, 1984)! The look a person's face has is due in part to the genetic blueprint that endows it with certain physical features, in part to transient moods that stimulate the muscles to move in distinctive ways, and in part to the lingering imprint of chronically held expressions that seem to "set in" and become virtually permanent over the years.

People undoubtedly make personality attributions based on dynamic facial behavior (and long-frozen expressions). For example, the person who smiles at us warmly upon introduction is immediately perceived to be nice (a personality attribution); likewise, we think that the sour-faced old man next door is a mean so-and-so. Little research exists on the validity of such stereotypes; certainly the person with the warm smile might be a cutthroat manipulator, and the "mean" neighbor may be a tenderhearted soul. Studies that support the validity of facial stereotypes showed that depressed individuals (whom we naturally expect to look sad) have sadder and less expressive faces than others (Fridlund, Ekman, & Oster, 1987). Another study found that college students believed that facially expressive individuals were more confident and likeable, and, indeed, in a sample of college women, those with more expressive faces were more extraverted according to several different self-report scales (Riggio & Friedman, 1986).

THE FACE and INTERACTION MANAGEMENT

Our faces also are used to facilitate and inhibit responses in daily interaction. Parts of the face are used to

1. Open and close channels of communication
2. Complement or qualify verbal and/or nonverbal responses
3. Replace speech

Behaviors can, of course, serve several functions simultaneously. For example, a yawn may replace the spoken message "I'm bored" and serve to shut down the channels of communication at the same time.

CHANNEL CONTROL

When we want a speaking turn, we sometimes open our mouths in readiness to talk—often accompanied by an inspiration of breath. As noted in Chapter 2, the eyebrow flash (frequently accompanied by a smile) is found in greeting rituals and signals a desire to interact. Interestingly, smiles also are found in situations where there is a desire to close the channels of communication, for example, a smile of appeasement as a person backs away from someone threatening physical harm. Smiling and winking also are used to flirt with others—an invitation that not only opens the channels of communication but also suggests the type of communication desired. Facial behaviors associated with flirtation seem to have very similar form across different cultures (Eibl-Eibesfeldt, 1974).

Although we usually think of smiles as showing emotion or attitudes, they actually have many complex functions. Brunner (1979) discovered that smiles serve as "listener responses" or "back channels" in conversation; they signal attentiveness and involvement just as head nods, "uh-huh," and "yeah" do. These smiles do not indicate joy or happiness in the sender but are meant to facilitate and encourage the other's speech.

COMPLEMENTING OR QUALIFYING OTHER BEHAVIOR

In normal conversational give and take, there are instances when we wish to underline, magnify, minimize, or contradict messages. These signals may be given by the speaker or listener. A sad verbal message may acquire added emphasis with the eyebrows' movements that normally accompany the expression of sadness. A smile may temper a message otherwise interpreted as negative. The hand emblem for "A-OK" may be accompanied by a wink, leaving little doubt that approval is being communicated.

REPLACING SPOKEN MESSAGES

Ekman and Friesen (1975) have identified what they call *facial emblems.* Like hand emblems, these displays have a fairly consistent verbal translation. Facial emblems are different from the actual emotional expressions in that the sender is trying to talk *about* an emotion while indicating he or she is not actually feeling it. These facial emblems usually will occur in contexts not likely to trigger the actual emotion; they are usually held for a longer or shorter time than the actual expression; and they are usually performed by using only a part of the face. When you drop your jaw and hold your mouth open without displaying other features of the surprise expression, you may be saying that the other person's comment is surprising or that you were dumbfounded by what was said. Widened eyes (without other features of the surprise and fear expressions) may serve the same purpose as a verbal "Wow!" If you want to comment nonverbally on your disgust for a situation, a nose wrinkle or raising your upper lip or raising one side of your upper lip should get your message across. Sometimes one or both eyebrows will communicate "I'm puzzled" or "I doubt that." Other facial messages that have common verbal translations but are not associated with expressions of emotion include the "You know what I mean" wink and sticking your tongue out to convey insult or disapproval (Smith, Chase, & Lieblich, 1974).

Chovil (1991/1992) identified four ways the face is used in the management of conversation. The most frequent function is *syntactic display.* Syntactic facial displays act as markers for words and clauses; they are directed toward the organizational structure of the conversation, marking beginnings, endings, restarts, continuations, and emphasis. Raising and lowering the eyebrows is a central activity in syntactic displays. Facial actions made by the speaker that are directly connected with the content of what is being said are called *semantic displays.* These may be redundant with the verbal behavior, or they may involve additional commentary (e.g., personal reactions) on the spoken words. The face also provides *listener responses,* as mentioned earlier. These are primarily facial displays that facilitate the flow of interaction but also include those that give personal reactions and seemingly empathic displays in the form of mimicry. Chovil also noticed facial *adaptors,* that is, biting one's lip or a twitch resulting from physiological activity.

Although the preceding discussion provides an overview of how the face is used in managing the interaction, it does not sufficiently reflect the complexity a thorough analysis requires. For instance, we did not deal with concomitant gaze behavior and other subtle movements such as head tilts. We talked about smiles as if there were only one variety. Brannigan and Humphries (1972) have identified nine smiles (representing various types and degrees of intensity), many of which seem to occur in distinctly separate situations. Ekman and Friesen, using an anatomically based coding system we shall describe shortly, have concluded that there are over 100 distinctly different human smiles!

THE FACE and EXPRESSIONS of EMOTION

The intellectual roots of our modern interest in facial expression stem from the mid–nineteenth century. Charles Darwin's *Expression of the Emotions in Man and Animals* (1872), though not as famous as his other writings on natural selection, was a major work of theory and empirical observation that was largely focused on the face (Ekman & Oster, 1982). To Darwin, the study of emotional expression was closely tied to his case for evolution, for he held that the capacity to communicate through nonverbal signals had evolved just as the brain and skeleton had. The face becomes increasingly mobile as one moves "up" the phylogenetic ladder. In most animals, the face is a fixed mask, but in primates we see a great variety of expressions (Redican, 1982). Because it would support his theory of evolution, Darwin considered it extremely important to document similarities in the nature of emotional expression across species and across human cultures.

Several strands of contemporary facial research can be traced to Darwin's insights, including conducting judgment studies to find out what meanings observers will ascribe to different expressions, conducting cross-cultural studies, studying the movements of particular facial muscles, and testing the hypothesis that facial expressions can intensify the experience of emotion. We will review each of these topics.

THE FACE—A COMPLEX STIMULUS

Consider the following situations:

1. A student who feels sure he is doing "C" work is told by his instructor that he is doing "A" work. His immediate reaction is total surprise (probably followed by glee), but how does he react? His face shows mild surprise, and he comments that he thought he was doing pretty good work in the course.
2. A poker player draws his fourth ace in a game with no wild cards. His face would lead the other players to believe he was unmoved.
3. A woman receives a Christmas present that she is pleasantly surprised about and happy to receive, but it is nothing spectacular. Her facial expression and comments, however, lead the giver (sitting nearby) to believe it was the only thing she ever wanted in her entire life.
4. The wife of a fledgling executive is forced to attend the boss's party and is told explicitly her behavior will have a profound impact on the promotion of her husband. She is nervous and upset. According to those who describe the party later, however, Mrs. Fledgling was the life of the party, happy and gay and carefree and content.

These four examples illustrate certain *display rules* we tend to follow (Ekman & Friesen, 1969). The student illustrated a *deintensified affect;* strong surprise was made to look like mild surprise. The poker player was trying to *neutralize an affect*—make it appear there was no affect at all. The person reacting to the Christmas present tried to make mild happiness appear to be strong happiness—an *overintensification of the affect.* Mrs. Fledgling was trying to *mask an affect* of tension or despondency with happiness and confidence. These display rules are learned, but we do not always use them at a conscious level of awareness. We learn that there are culturally prescribed display rules; we also develop personal display rules based on our needs or perhaps the demands of our occupation, for example, politicians or salespersons. We learn that some affect displays are appropriate in some places and not others, for some status and role positions and not others, for one sex and not another; and we may use different expressions responding to the same event at a different time and with different people.

The attempt to use display rules can lead to communication mishaps. After seeing former president Bush smiling while telling about the number of babies born with drug addiction and about other sad statistics on his first television address from the Oval Office, one of his advisers said in amazement, "What's with the grin?" The answer: Bush is emotional, hates to show it, and overcompensates by lightening his expression too much ("Why is this man smiling?" *Time,* September 18, 1989, p. 34).

The existence of display rules helps explain why some anthropologists have believed that emotions are expressed in sharply different ways from culture to culture. In one society, people may weep and moan at a funeral; in another they may celebrate with feast and dance. However, the underlying emotion, grief, *is* expressed similarly (as we shall see later). The difference is that in the second (hypothetical) society, the norm or display rule said "don't show grief at the funeral" or "show hope for the future."

The way we experience emotions can be quite complex. Sometimes we move rapidly from one emotion to another. For example, people reporting the feeling of jealousy indicate that the "jealous flash may move from shock and numbness to desolate pain to rage and anger to moral outrage in a very brief time" (Ellis & Weinstein, 1986). Sometimes we are not sure what emotion we are feeling, and at other times we seem to feel many emotions at once, as was the case with a woman who discovered her partner had a sexual fling with another woman: She felt a "sexual turn-on, excitement, anger, and a sense of loss" virtually simultaneously. Simultaneously felt emotions may even be contradictory, as in the case of a woman who described her experience with sadomasochism: "I felt repulsed and attracted at the same time. Indeed, that is what made S & M so attractive." When we experience more than one emotion, we sometimes try to control one while we deal with the other. These are only some of the many ways we experience emotions (Ellis, 1991). As we learn more about how we experience emotions, we will understand better how we express these emotions through the face.

Ekman and Friesen (1975) have developed a classification system for various styles of facial expressions. The styles are heavily based on personal display rules and represent extremes. A style may be displayed in a less extreme fashion in some situations or at a certain time in the person's life, but some people manifest a given style with consistency. These styles include the following:

1. **The Withholder.** The face inhibits expressions of actual feeling states. There is little facial movement.
2. **The Revealer.** This is the opposite of the Withholder. The face leaves little doubt how the person feels—continually.
3. **The Unwitting Expressor.** This pattern usually pertains to a limited number of expressions that a person may feel have been masked, that is, "How did you know I was angry?"
4. **The Blanked Expressor.** In this style, the person is convinced an emotion is being portrayed, but others see only a blank face!
5. **The Substitute Expressor.** Here the facial expression shows an emotion other than the one the person thinks is being displayed.
6. **The Frozen-Affect Expressor.** This style manifests at least a part of an emotional display at all times. Some people are born with a facial configuration that, in a relaxed, neutral state, shows the downturned mouth of sadness; others habitually experience an emotion (like sadness) enough so traces of the emotional display are permanently etched into the face. (This is an idea that Darwin proposed.)

Self-presentational desires can also produce distinctive styles of facial expression. President Clinton often uses a smile that we call his "brave smile" (Figure 9-1). It is not a pure expression of happiness, as our discussion of blends and "felt" smiles later in this chapter will make clear. Rather, we think Clinton is trying to convey a complex mixture of pride, determination, concern, and modesty with the combination of the paradoxically downturned mouth, the set chin, and the "smile wrinkles" around the eyes.

The preceding discussion of display rules and styles of emotional facial expression demonstrates that we have considerable control over our facial expressions, and this control is manifested in a variety of ways. Although we can present facial messages that we don't feel, sometimes we lie imperfectly by enacting an expression at the wrong time, enacting it too often or for too long (as when we insincerely display a smile too long), or using inappropriately various facial muscles. These factors may help us separate genuine from pseudoexpressions of emotion on the face. We undeniably are aware of the communicative potential of our face, and we tend to monitor it carefully by inhibiting or exhibiting when desired. With the constant feedback we receive about our facial expressions, we become rather proficient at controlling them. As Ekman and Friesen (1969) put it:

> Although we usually are aware of our facial affect displays, they may occur with or without a deliberate intention to communicate. Similarly, inhibition

Figure 9–1

The president smiles. (Photo credits: Reuters/Corbis-Bettman.)

of facial display, control of facial display, or dissimulation of an affect (looking cool even when tense), may or may not be intentional. Because we have such good feedback about our facial behavior, we usually are aware of what happens the moment we change facial movements. (p. 76)

As these comments imply, the distinction between spontaneous (i.e., unintentional) facial displays of emotion and deliberate (posed) displays may be quite difficult to make in practice, in part because the concept of intentionality is an extremely slippery one. Moreover, evidence is accumulating to suggest that a purely spontaneous "readout" of emotional states may be a rarer event than previously thought, and that, instead, facial expressions often reflect social circumstances and social goals.

Many studies support this claim. Kraut and Johnston (1979) found that after a good roll, bowlers smiled much more when turning to their friends than while still facing the pins. Research also has found that facial "motor mimicry"—displaying what another person is feeling, as when one person winces after a friend stubs his toe or when one grimaces upon hearing a friend tell about a "close call" she's had—decreases when there is no one to see the facial display (Bavelas, Black, Lemery, & Mullett, 1986; Chovil, 1991). Infants' smiles appear to be stimulated by expectations of eye contact with the mother and are greatly suppressed when the infants do not expect their mother to be watching (Jones, Collins, & Hong, 1991). College students watching emotionally provoking slides were more facially expressive when they watched them with a friend as opposed to a stranger (Wagner & Smith, 1991). Finally, at the Olympic Games, gold-medal winners were filmed while standing behind the podium away from public view, standing on the podium interacting with authorities and the public, and standing on the podium facing the flagpoles and listening to their national anthem (Fernández-Dols & Ruiz-Belda, 1995). Although their feelings of happiness probably did not vary across these three closely spaced periods, the winners smiled the most during the middle, interactive-public period, suggesting again that facial expression is not due solely to the emotion currently being experienced.

"Audience effects" such as these studies suggest may even occur when one is ostensibly alone and behaving "spontaneously," for even then one may respond to fantasies of social interaction. In support of this notion, Fridlund (1991) found that subjects watching pleasant films smiled more when watching with a friend than when watching alone, but subjects watching the same pleasant films in a different room from their friend (but aware that the friend was watching) also smiled more than subjects in the simple alone condition. Thus, the imagined presence or experience of others may serve to stimulate or facilitate facial displays.

Fridlund's behavioral ecology theory of facial expression asserts that facial expressions are virtually never simply emotional and are, instead, always enacted for social purposes (Fridlund, 1994). In Fridlund's view, spontaneous expression of emotion would not have been a selected trait during evolution because it would too often serve others' (possibly rivals') interests rather than the expressor's (for example, it would deprive the expressor of the ability to deceive). Fridlund's argument that facial expressions are meant to *communicate* rather than simply *reveal* is consistent with many examples of functional expressive behavior in the animal kingdom as well as with everyday observation of human interaction. However, most authors appear not to accept the extreme position that expressions are hardly ever purely emotional. The fact that audience presence effects can sometimes work in reverse, with people showing *less* facial expression with others present rather than more, suggests that people have spontaneous emotional reactions that they sometimes prefer to hide (Buck, 1984, 1991). According to Buck (1988, 1994), there is an important role for both spontaneous and symbolic (more deliberate) expressions.

Another important aspect of our facial expressions is that we do not always portray "pure" or single emotional states in which, for example, all the parts of our face show anger. Instead, the face conveys multiple emotions. These are called *affect blends*. These facial blends of several emotions may appear on the face in numerous ways:

1. One emotion is shown in one facial area and another is shown in another area; for example, brows are raised as in surprise, and lips are pressed as in anger.
2. Two different emotions are shown in one part of the face; for example, one brow is raised as in surprise, and the other is lowered as in anger.
3. A facial display is produced by muscle action associated with two emotions but containing specific elements of neither.

Figure 9-2 shows two examples of facial blends. One photograph shows a blend of happiness (mouth area) and surprise (eyebrows/forehead, eyes/lids, and a slight dropping of the jaw). Such an expression could occur if you thought you were going to get an *F* on an exam, but you received an "*A*." In the other photograph, the brows/forehead area and the eyes/lids area show anger while the mouth shows sadness. This combination might occur, for example, if your instructor told you that your grade on an exam you considered unfair was an "*F*." You feel sad about the low grade and angry at the instructor.

A final note about the complexity of our face concerns what Haggard and Isaacs (1966) have called "micromomentary facial expressions." While searching for indications of nonverbal communication between therapist and patient, they ran some film at slow motion and noticed that the expression on the patient's face would sometimes change dramatically—from a smile to a grimace to a smile, for example—within a few frames of the film. Further analysis revealed that when they ran their films at four frames per second instead of the normal twenty-four frames, there were 2.5 times as many changes of expression. At normal speed, expressions lasting about one-fifth second escaped notice; expressions that took about two-fifths second were seen as changes, but the kind of change could not be identified; expressions lasting longer than two-fifths second were usually identified, but not always the same way. It is thought these micromomentary expressions reveal actual

Figure 9–2

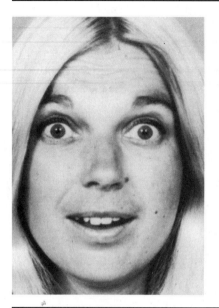

Facial blends. (Figure from P. Ekman and W. V. Friesen, Unmasking the Face: A Guide to Recognizing Emotions from Facial Clues, *1975. Reprinted by permission of Prentice-Hall, Inc., Englewood Cliffs, New Jersey)*

emotional states but are condensed in time because of repressive processes. They are often incompatible with both the apparent expression and the patient's words. One patient, saying nice things about a friend, had a seemingly pleasant facial expression; slow-motion films revealed a wave of anger across her face. Ekman, Friesen, and Ellsworth (1982b), while agreeing that micro-momentary expressions may show conflict, repression, or efforts to conceal an emotion, actually find them to be "very rare events" based on extensive analysis of facial movements. However, this does not mean they do not have an impact (possibly a subliminal one) when they occur.

MEASURING THE FACE

Until recently, descriptions of facial movements tended to be impressionistic or idiosyncratic (Ekman, 1982; Rinn, 1984). This changed dramatically with the work of Paul Ekman and Wallace Friesen (1978) and Carroll Izard (1979), teams that independently developed precise systems for describing facial action based on muscle movements. Izard's work has focused on infant expressions, while the Ekman-Friesen system has been applied more generally and appears to be the most widely adopted. In this context, *widely* is relative, however, since learning a system comprehensive enough to describe nearly *any* combination of muscle movements requires a great deal of practice and, consequently, use of the method is limited to dedicated facial researchers.

Ekman and Friesen developed their Facial Action Coding System, or FACS, by painstakingly (and sometimes painfully) learning how to move all their facial muscles and by studying anatomy texts. They studied the faces of other people who had learned how to control specific muscles and considered what movements an observer could reliably distinguish—important since observers would be the data-gatherers. As a consequence, a trained observer can identify which muscles are moving (called "action units"). Sometimes an action unit involves more than one muscle, if those muscles always work in tandem or if an observer cannot see the difference. Figure 9-3 presents the action units identified by Ekman (1979) for the brow/forehead. Altogether, seven different muscles can influence this region of the face.

The FACS allows emotion researchers to categorize a face as expressing a given emotion (through collecting observers' judgments) and then to describe,

Figure 9–3

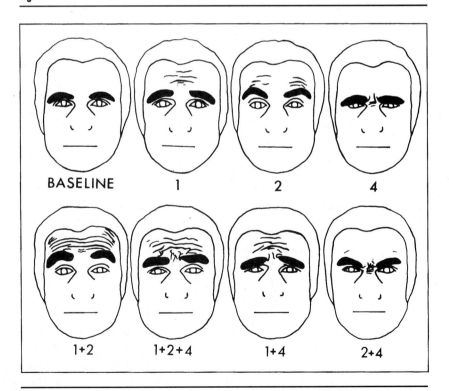

Action units for the brow/forehead. (From P. Ekman, "About Brows: Emotional and Conversational Signals," in M. von Cranach et al. [Eds.] Human Ethology, 1979. Reprinted by permission of Cambridge University Press.)

objectively, what the face did. Ekman and his colleagues (Ekman & Friesen, 1978) have determined, for example, that in the brow/forehead region shown in Figure 9-3, action units 1 or 1 + 4 occur in sadness, along with associated movements across the rest of the face. In surprise, one sees 1 + 2; in fear, 1 + 2 + 4; in anger, 4; and so forth.

Recall that we discussed the role of the face in interaction management. Ekman tells us how the brow/forehead area contributes to these conversational signals as well:

- Accent a word, 1 + 2 (Woody Allen uses 1 + 4 for this, according to Ekman)
- Underline a phrase, 1 + 2 or 4
- Punctuate (like a visual comma), 1 + 2 or 4
- Question mark, 1 + 2 or 4
- Word search, 4
- Listener response (back channel), 1 + 2
- Indicate lack of understanding, 4

We have gone into detail on the brow/forehead just to give a feel for how the system is applied. Although the method is tedious, the results can be very interesting indeed and possibly quite useful in daily life. For example, facial signs can reveal the occurrence of pain and even distinguish among different sources, such as pain from immersion of the hand in cold water, from electric shock, and from surgery or other physical trauma (LeResche, 1982; Patrick, Craig, & Prkachin, 1986). The facial signs of pain, measured in both infants and adults, include a tightening of the muscles surrounding the eye, which narrows the eyes and raises the cheeks; the corrugator and other forehead muscles lower the eyebrows and wrinkle the bridge of the nose; and the levator muscles raise the upper lip and may produce wrinkles at the side of the nose (Prkachin & Craig, 1995). The faces of terminal cancer patients differ according to the stage of disease progression. In the early stages, signs of fear are more prominent ("whole eye tension combined with tension . . . in the lower eyelid") but give way to signs of sadness (in the brow/forehead region) in the late stage (Antonoff & Spilka, 1984–1985).

Some of the most subtle and fascinating work in facial expressions concerns different kinds of smiles. The muscle called the zygomatic major, which stretches out the lips when we smile, is the common denominator. Ekman has shown that the frequency, duration, and intensity of action by the zygomatic major differentiated among facial displays in two happy films and also correlated with how much happiness people said they felt while viewing them (Ekman, Friesen, & Ancoli, 1980). However, other muscles are crucial to understanding what the smile really means. Darwin proposed that in a "felt" or genuinely happy smile, the orbicularis oculi muscle (which gives you crow's feet in the corner of your eye) is also involved but is not involved in a phony or mechanical smile. Research has validated Darwin's observation even, it seems, in infants as young as ten months (Ekman, Davidson, & Friesen, 1990;

Ekman & Friesen, 1982; Fox & Davidson, 1988). Felt smiles are of much less variable duration and have a smoother quality than unfelt smiles, and the two kinds of smiles can be distinguished from one another by naive viewers (Frank, Ekman, & Friesen, 1993). A smile's being felt does not, however, mean that it must occur totally spontaneously. In the study of Olympic medalists described earlier, although most of the medalists' smiles occurred in the interactive-public period, the great majority of those smiles were of the felt variety (showing eye-muscle involvement), suggesting that they were not fake or forced.

Figure 9–4

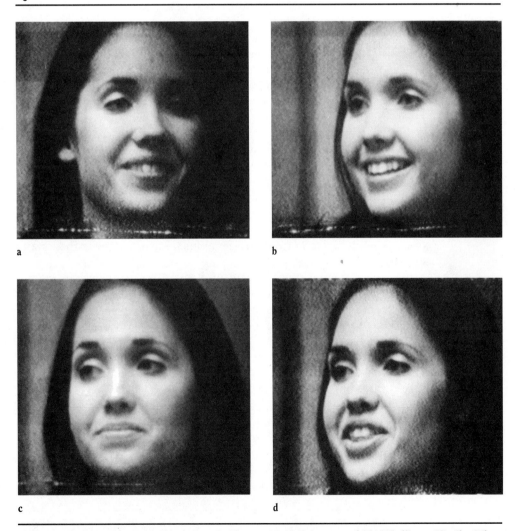

a b

c d

Which is the "felt" happy smile? (From P. Ekman, W. V. Friesen, and M. O'Sullivan, "Smiles When Lying," 1988 Journal of Personality and Social Psychology, pp. 414–20)

In another study, subjects were shown either a pleasant or a stressful film and were asked to act as though the film were pleasant. Those who were watching the stressful film had to lie about their experience. The smiles of those who saw the pleasant film were found to be felt happy smiles (as defined earlier) with no muscular activity associated with any of the negative emotions. Those trying to look pleasant while watching the stressful film showed more "masking" smiles involving the zygomatic major but also the ten or so other muscles associated with fear, disgust, contempt, sadness, or anger (Ekman, Friesen, & O'Sullivan, 1988). Can you tell which of the faces in Figure 9-4 is the felt smile? (See the end of the chapter for the answer.)

The distinction between felt and unfelt smiles, though very important, is still a probabilistic one. This means that in any particular instance, there may be uncertainty about the smile's true meaning. Although it is unlikely that a smile involving only the mouth is a true expression of pleasure or happiness, it is probably possible for a smile involving the eye muscles (i.e., a "felt" smile) to be feigned by someone who is aware that such a smile is more convincing than the mouth-only kind.

Although the face is capable of making a vast number of distinct movements and communicating many emotional states, those discussed by virtually every researcher since 1940 are surprise, fear, disgust, anger, happiness, and sadness. Figures 9-5 to 9-10 show these six basic emotions, with a description of their characteristic facial actions.[1] Facial signs of anxiety include increased blinking, more facial movements associated with fear (such as a horizontal mouth stretch), and more facial movements overall (Harrigan & O'Donnell, in press). Increases in smiling and laughing have also been noted in socially anxious situations. Other emotions, such as interest and shame, are also discussed, but the exact facial muscle movements associated with these states are not well known now.

Although there is much to be gained from the fine-grained anatomical understanding of facial movements reflected in the work of Ekman and others, researchers also employ less highly trained observers for many facial measurement tasks. Observers are asked to count the frequency of facial expressions, rate their intensity, or time their duration. For the measurement of a person's total amount of smiling, for example, these methods are the rule rather than the exception (Briton & Hall, 1995). As long as adequate interobserver agreement is obtained, these approaches have high validity.

Now that we have examined the face itself and explored the characteristics of some basic emotional expressions, we shall now ask the question of whether facial expressions of emotion can be judged accurately.

---

[1]Figures 9-5–9-10 are from P. Ekman and W. V. Friesen, *Unmasking the Face: A Guide to Recognizing Emotions from Facial Clues,* 1975. Reprinted by permission of Prentice-Hall, Inc., Englewood Cliffs, New Jersey.

Figure 9–5

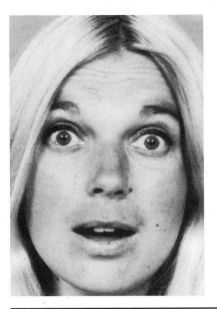 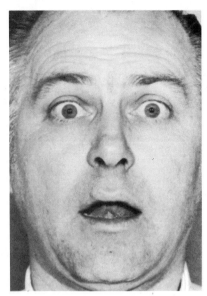

Surprise: *The brows are raised, so that they are curved and high. The skin below the brow is stretched. Horizontal wrinkles go across the forehead. The eyelids are opened; the upper lid is raised and the lower lid drawn down; the white of the eye—the sclera—shows above the iris, and often below as well. The jaw drops open so that the lips and teeth are parted, but there is no tension or stretching of the mouth.*

Figure 9–6

 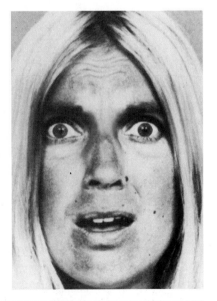

Fear: *The brows are raised and drawn together. The wrinkles in the forehead are in the center, not across the entire forehead. The upper eyelid is raised, exposing the sclera, and the lower eyelid is tensed and drawn up. The mouth is open and the lips are either tensed slightly and drawn back or stretched and drawn back.*

Figure 9-7

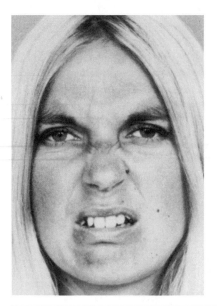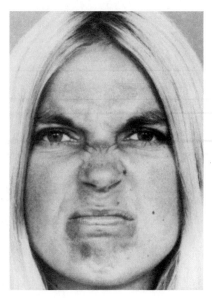

Disgust: The upper lip is raised. The lower lip is also raised and pushed up to the upper lip or is lowered and slightly protruding. The nose is wrinkled. The cheeks are raised. Lines show below the lower lid, and the lid is pushed up but not tense. The brow is lowered, lowering the upper lid.

Figure 9-8

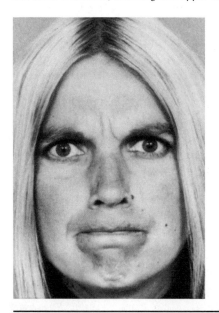

Anger: The brows are lowered and drawn together. Vertical lines appear between the brows. The lower lid is tensed and may or may not be raised. The upper lid is tensed and may or may not be lowered by the action of the brow. The eyes have a hard stare and may have a bulging appearance. The lips are in either of two basic positions: pressed firmly together, with the corners straight or down; or open, tensed in a squarish shape as if shouting. The nostrils may be dilated, but this is not essential to the anger facial expression and may also occur in sadness. There is ambiguity unless anger is registered in all three facial areas.

Figure 9–9

Happiness: Corners of lips are drawn back and up. The mouth may or may not be parted, with teeth exposed or not. A wrinkle (the naso-labial fold) runs down from the nose to the outer edge beyond the lip corners. The cheeks are raised. The lower eyelid shows wrinkles below it and may be raised but not tense. Crow's-feet wrinkles go outward from the outer corners of the eyes (covered by hair in these photographs).

Figure 9–10

 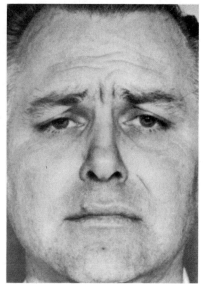

Sadness: The inner corners of the eyebrows are drawn up. The skin below the eyebrows is triangulated, with the inner corner up. The upper eyelid inner corner is raised. The corners of the lips are down or the lip is trembling.

JUDGING FACIAL EXPRESSIONS OF EMOTION

An in-depth analysis of all the important studies of facial expression prompted Ekman, Friesen, and Ellsworth (1982a) to draw the following conclusion:

> Contrary to the impression conveyed by previous reviews of the literature that the evidence in the field is contradictory and confusing, our reanalysis showed consistent evidence of accurate judgment of emotion from facial behavior.

Ekman and his colleagues rightly acknowledge that this conclusion pertains primarily to posed expressions, but an increasing number of studies of spontaneous expressions also show accurate perceptions. Because of the difficulty involved in measuring responses to facial expressions, and because so much of the literature concerns these measurement problems, we will discuss measurement more than we have previously. How we measure responses to facial expressions is central to any statement about accuracy in judging these expressions.

Figure 9–11

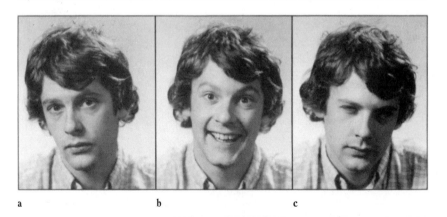

a   b   c

How should these facial expressions be judged?

Examine the three faces shown in Figure 9-11. Then consider the following methods of responding. Would your responses differ depending on the method used? Is one method easier or harder than another? Is one likely to elicit greater accuracy?

1. In the space below, write in the emotion being expressed in each of the faces you observed.

   A. _____ B. _____ C. _____

2. From the choices below, select the one emotion that best describes Face A, Face B, and Face C.

Face A	**Face B**	**Face C**
Rage _____	Happiness _____	Sadness _____
Anger _____	Joy _____	Despair _____
Wrath _____	Delight _____	Solemnity _____
Indignation _____	Amusement _____	Despondency _____
Resentment _____	Pleasure _____	Melancholy _____

3. From this list of emotions, select the one that best describes Face A, Face B, and Face C: Happiness, Sadness, Surprise, Fear, Anger.

This example illustrates one of the many problems involved in testing the accuracy of judgments about facial expressions: the type of response required from the judge. In this case, judging accuracy would depend a great deal on which set of instructions the judge received. In the first testing condition, we have a totally open or free response from the judge. This will provide a wide range of responses, and the researcher will be faced with the problem of deciding whether the judge's label corresponds with his or her label for the emotion. Sometimes the researcher elicits a label that, under other testing conditions, may be perceived as a blend; for example, smugness may contain facial features found in both happiness and anger expressions. The labels used by the experimenter and the responder may be different, but both may respond the same way to the actual emotion in real life. This also raises the problem of the gap between perceiving and naming emotional responses so that others understand. In the second testing condition, the discriminatory task is too difficult—the emotions listed in each category are too much alike. We can predict low accuracy for judges given these instructions. In some cases, the labels all may focus on variants of the same emotion, and the perceiver sees something completely different but is prohibited from adding new categories. For example, photograph "C" seems to be perceived by the researcher as a form of sadness, but a judge might see it as neutral. The last set of instructions is the opposite of the second set—the discriminatory task is easy. Since the emotion categories are discrete, we can predict high accuracy for the third condition.

Studies have used varied ways to elicit these emotions. Some simply describe a situation and tell the actor to react as if he or she were in that situation; others give a list of emotions and tell the actor to portray them; and some use candid photos of people in real situations. One early study (Dunlap, 1927) reached an almost comic extreme. A camera was set up in a laboratory, ready to catch the subject's expressions at the proper moment. To elicit an expression of pain, the experimenter would bend the subject's finger backward forcibly; to produce a startled look, the experimenter fired a pistol behind the subject at an unexpected moment; apprehension was elicited by telling the subject the pistol would be fired again close to his ear on the count of three (at the count of two the photo was taken); amusement was captured when the experimenter told the subject some jokes; disgust resulted from the subject's smelling a test tube containing tissues of a dead rat; and finally—unbelievably—to elicit an expression of grief, a subject was hypnotized and told several members of his family had been killed in a car wreck! "Unfortunately," says the experimenter, "the camera could not catch intense grief because the subject bowed his head and cried," so he had to settle for an expression of mild grief to be used in the study. Another interesting point from this study returns us to our discussion of facial control and display rules. Dunlap found all of his women subjects made facial expressions that approached amusement under what were supposed to be painful conditions. Men did not—nor did they match the women's verbal description of how they felt. It did hurt! When expressors react in a paradoxical manner like this to a stimulus, judges' accuracy is certainly affected.

The idea of presenting subjects with a controlled stimulus and then observing their reactions, though carried to an extreme in Dunlap's study, still underlies research on spontaneous expressions. Subjects are shown slides or films that differ in their content (funny, disgusting, sexy, heartwarming, and so forth) while a videotape camera unobtrusively records their facial reactions. Judges later observe the subjects' faces and try to guess which slide or film each subject had been viewing (Buck, 1979; Zuckerman, Hall, DeFrank, & Rosenthal, 1976). This method can capture completely unpremeditated expressions. However, since subjects are not in a truly communicative situation, their behavior may be no more real or authentic than are expressors' attempts to pose various emotions on the command of the experimenter. Another method, asking subjects to reexperience an emotional event and then talk about it, has been used sometimes as a more natural alternative that blends some elements of deliberate and spontaneous communication (Halberstadt, 1986).

The variety of methods by which the facial stimuli have been presented to judges also adds complexity to interpretation of facial research. Are they "live" faces, photographs, drawings, videotapes, or films? Some research suggests greater accuracy is achieved when filmed expressions are used. Frequently, the length of observation differs from study to study, and there is always the question of advantages and disadvantages of seeing faces that are larger (on the movie screen) or smaller (small photos) than those seen in everyday interactions.

Prior exposure to a face will make a difference in emotional judgment accuracy. If you are familiar with the face and have seen it express other emotions, you are more likely to correctly identify another emotion you have not seen before. If you are familiar with the person, you have a better reference point for making judgments. For instance, a person who smiles frequently and who you then see not smiling may seem very sad. With another person, absence of a smile may simply be part of a normal, neutral expression. Laughery et al. (1971) found that the longer one was exposed to an expression of emotion on a face and the earlier this face appeared in a test series, the greater were the chances of accurate recognition.

Several studies make it clear that additional knowledge concerning the context in which a particular facial expression occurs will affect accuracy in judging the emotion expressed. We can accurately identify facial expressions of emotion without any knowledge of the context in which they occur, but co-occurring perceptions of the social context, the environment, and other people will surely affect our judgments. Although a number of investigators have pursued the question of whether context or expression dominates perceptions, the issue is far from resolved. Perhaps the most often cited study regarding the influence of context in face judging is one by Munn (1940). Facial expressions taken from *Life* and *Look* magazines were shown with and without background context. The background information was very helpful in the identification of these facial expressions. Verbal cues describing the situation also seem to increase accuracy. Munn's study sampled a limited number of faces, emotions, and contexts, but it brings to our attention another important consideration in studying facial expressions. One of our students, as part of a term project assignment, showed two faces to groups of judges with only the background color varied. The facial expressions were previously identified as "neutral." This student found in her limited study that even changing the background color can change interpretation of the facial expression. Warm, bright colors resulted in more positive or "happy" responses; dark or dull tones produced more negative or "not particularly happy" responses.

Cline (1956) used line drawings to test the effect of having another face as part of the total context. He found that the expression on one face influenced interpretation of the other face. For example, when the smiling face in Figure 9-12 was paired with a glum face, it was seen as the dominant face—that of

Figure 9–12

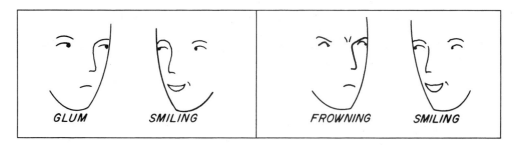

Context effects. (From Marvin G. Cline "The Influence of Social Context on the Perception of Faces," Journal of Personality, *25:2 [December 1956], Figure 1, p.146. Copyright © 1956, Duke University Press. Reprinted by permission of Duke University Press)*

a vicious, gloating, taunting bully. When seen with the frowning face, the smiling face seemed peaceful, friendly, and happy.

Obviously, the context in which a facial expression is embedded can influence our interpretation of the expression; however, the question of whether one matters *more* than the other when we form a total impression of mood or affect has no simple answer. Whether the face or the context overpowers the other, or if they act in a mutually strengthening way, seems to depend on many factors (Ekman, Friesen, & Ellsworth, 1982c).

The list of factors that influence how emotions are judged in the face goes on, but the compelling fact remains that they can be judged, and often with extremely high levels of accuracy. Some emotions are more likely to be confused, but the six basic emotions of happiness, anger, disgust, sadness, surprise, and fear are determined with very high agreement (and accuracy) among observers according to previous studies. This is true not only in the United States but also around the globe. Ekman, Izard, and others have demonstrated in separate research programs that the basic facial expressions of emotion are understood internationally (see Chapters 2 and 3; Ekman, Sorenson, & Friesen, 1969; Izard, 1971). Even in New Guinea, where the people had not been exposed to Western media depictions, photos of U. S. citizens' faces showing the six basic emotions were judged correctly for the most part. Moreover, some New Guineans were photographed while showing how they would react in different situations (such as "you feel sad because your child died"); U. S. respondents later guessed with great accuracy which scenario was being communicated (Ekman & Friesen, 1971).

Most cross-cultural research has dealt with depictions of the face showing very "pure" configurations for the major emotions. However, as noted earlier, facial expressions can be complex blends, with different muscles simultaneously showing elements of different emotions. The question of whether cross-cultural universality also applies to secondary, more subtle, expressions led Ekman and a team of colleagues to introduce a new methodology into the cross-cultural research. These researchers obtained ratings of faces on a variety of emotions from subjects in ten places around the world including Estonia, Sumatra, Scotland, Japan, Italy, and Hong Kong. There was dramatic agreement across cultures not only on the primary emotion being shown by the faces but also on the secondary emotion (Ekman, Friesen, O'Sullivan, Chan, et al., 1987). In this same study yet another emotion, *contempt,* also was found to have a universally recognizable expression—a slight tightening and raising of the corner of the lip on one side. Over all ten countries, 75 percent of the subjects said it indicated contempt (Ekman & Friesen, 1986).

PHYSIOLOGY and the FACE

We all have at least one friend with a face that remains as still as a rock, no matter how much excitement swirls around him or her. We also have friends with faces that seem as sensitive as a butterfly's wings to every shift of the emotional winds. What we may not know is that these differences, aside from being quite real and enduring, also are associated with differences in physiological functioning. The "internalizers" have little overt expression (that is, on the face) but experience high physiological reactivity (on measures such as heart rate and electrodermal responding); the "externalizers" (the expressive ones) show the opposite pattern (Buck, Savin, Miller, & Caul, 1972; Lanzetta & Kleck, 1970; Notarius & Levenson, 1979). Most theorizing about this relationship has pointed to learned factors, for example, the notion that society encourages people to suppress their overt emotional reactions, and that individuals who do so must experience their emotions or arousal in some other way, perhaps through internal activation of the nervous system. The metaphor of discharge can be applied: The emotion is released *either* externally *or* internally (Notarius & Levenson, 1979). However, research on newborns finds a similar negative relationship between expressiveness and physiological responding (heart rate), suggesting that temperamental factors may also be at work (Field, 1982).

Given these differences, it is intriguing to consider a possible connection between expressiveness and one's physical health. Could restraining the outward expression of emotion be damaging to your health? Friedman and his colleagues (1985, 1987) pursued this idea and found that, as predicted, a "repressed" style of expression was related to indications of coronary artery disease and even to the actual occurrence of a heart attack. King and Emmons (1990) found some support for the hypothesis that *ambivalence* over emotional expression would be associated with poorer health. Malatesta, Jonas, and Izard (1987) found that women who showed less expression on their face when talking about an angry experience had more arthritis symptoms, and women who showed less facial expression during a sadness account had more skin problems. Promising evidence for a relation of emotional suppression to health comes from research on *alexithymia,* a term used to describe patients who have a pronounced inability to describe their own emotions. These patients are deficient in facial expressiveness and also seem to suffer from a disproportionate number of psychosomatic ailments (Buck, 1993).

Adding to the complexity and fascination of the relation between the face and physiology is the controversial "facial feedback hypothesis" put forth by Darwin. Darwin believed that an emotion that is freely expressed will be intensified. The facial feedback hypothesis states that expressions on the face can actually *create* emotional experience, via direct neurological connections between facial muscles and emotion centers in the brain.

This hypothesis might appear at first to contradict the internalizing/ externalizing phenomenon. Facial feedback says there is a positive relation of expressiveness to internal physiological reactions (a shown emotion is a more intensely felt one), while the internalizing/externalizing notion says there is a negative relation (more expressive people are less reactive physiologically). Actually, both can be true at the same time if one considers that facial feedback applies to a relation *within* a person—that is, no matter what your overall degree of facial expressiveness is, changes on your face can influence your emotions—whereas internalizing/externalizing refers to differences *among* people (Buck, 1984).

But the question remains: Is the facial feedback hypothesis valid? The idea that emotions can be regulated via facial behavior—that one can create authentic emotional experience from inauthentic outward expressions—has important ramifications for childrearing, psychotherapy, and many other domains (Izard, 1990). The facial feedback hypothesis has been debated at length, for although a majority of studies support it, many are potentially flawed (Matsumoto, 1987). A typical experiment asks subjects to pose their faces in various ways and then measures their emotional state through self-report (Laird, 1974; Tourangeau & Ellsworth, 1979). The flaw in such a study is that subjects may realize that their posed expression is meant to look like fear or happiness. If this happens, it is no surprise that they obediently report feeling those emotions.

Fortunately for the hypothesis, studies exist that do not share this problem. Some studies measure reactions objectively and not in terms of subjects' self-reports. For example, posing strong reaction (versus no reaction) to electric shocks produced relative increases in physiological reaction (via electrodermal measures), suggesting that more pain was experienced; posing a strong reaction also led to subjective reports of more pain (Lanzetta, Cartwright-Smith, & Kleck, 1976).

In a shrewd study, a group of investigators disguised the purpose of the facial posing by telling subjects they were helping to develop ways for persons with disabilities to wield a writing implement; it could be held between the teeth, which naturally expands the lips, or it could be held by the lips, which of course contracts them. Figure 9-13 illustrates these mouth positions. Unknown to the subjects, these two manipulations differ in whether the "smiling" muscles around the mouth are activated. Subjects holding the pen between their teeth (which activates the "smiling" muscles) rated cartoons as funnier than the other subjects did (Strack, Martin, & Stepper, 1988). Thus, the position of the facial muscles can indeed influence one's emotional state.

In another study, these researchers manipulated posture (upright versus slumped) by the use of different seating arrangements and showed that if subjects were upright rather than slumped when hearing they had performed well on an earlier task, they experienced more pride in their performance (Stepper & Strack, 1994)! Apparently, sensory feedback need not be facial in order to influence a person's feelings directly.

Ekman and his colleagues, in a facial feedback experiment, also demonstrated that moving particular facial muscles on command, as well as "reliving" past emotional experiences, produces specific patterns of reaction in the autonomic nervous system (Ekman, Levenson, & Friesen, 1983). Heart rate and finger temperature increased more in anger than in happiness; anger and fear were similar in terms of heart rate increases but differed in finger temperature. Perhaps these results translate into the familiar feelings of being flushed or hot when angry and of having cold hands when afraid.

Figure 9–13

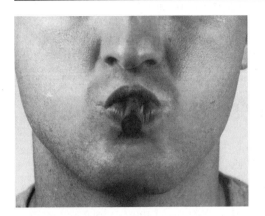 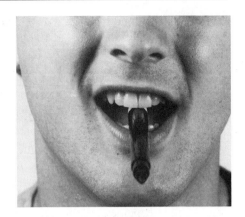

Illustration of the technique used to contract the different facial muscles: left, lips condition; right, teeth condition. (From F. Strack, L. Martin, and S. Stepper, "Inhibiting and Facilitating Conditions of the Human Smile: A Nonobtrusive Test of the Facial Feedback Hypothesis," 1988, Journal of Personality and Social Psychology, 54, p.768–77.)

Researchers studying the face and physiology also have discovered that posed and spontaneous facial expressions are controlled by different pathways within the brain. This has been demonstrated by certain forms of brain injury that result in a person's losing the ability to produce facial expressions deliberately but not losing the capacity to laugh, cry, frown, and so on when genuinely experiencing an emotion; the reverse form of disability also exists (Rinn, 1984). When brain damage occurs, facial expressiveness is especially impaired when the damage is to the right hemisphere of the brain, which is considered the more nonverbal hemisphere (Buck & Duffy, 1980). Several researchers have noted that the left side of a person's face tends to be more expressive and have related this to the fact that the left half of the face is controlled by the right hemisphere. However, consistent with the notion of separate neural pathways, Ekman and his colleagues have shown that this asymmetry is present only for posed expressions; spontaneous (more genuine) ones tend to be symmetrical (Ekman, Hager, & Friesen, 1981). Perhaps now you'll think differently about your friend with the crooked smile!

Finally, physiological researchers have discovered that different emotions produce distinctive facial movements even when the movements are too slight to be seen with the naked eye. Electrodes attached to the face measure electromyographic (EMG) responses. Most consistent are results showing that the zygomatic muscle responds under happy conditions and the corrugator muscle (between the brows) responds under sad, angry, and fearful conditions (Cacioppo, Klein, Berntson, & Hatfield, 1993; Camras, Holland, & Patterson, 1993).

Thus far we have examined the sending and receiving of messages relevant to one's emotional state. But researchers also have asked questions that go beyond the momentary expression of emotion: Does the facial expression of emotion tell us anything about how others will behave or what behavior the sender is likely to engage in following a given expression?

FACIAL EXPRESSIONS and SUBSEQUENT REACTIONS

Ekman and his colleagues were interested in whether facial expressions displayed while watching televised violence would be related to subsequent aggressiveness (Ekman, Liebert, Friesen, Harrison, Zlatchin, Malstrom, & Baron, 1972). They predicted that facial expressions of emotion showing happiness, pleasantness, and interest would predict more subsequent aggressive behavior than unpleasant, sad, painful, and disinterested expressions. Some five- and six-year-old children watched a sports program, while others saw a scene from *The Untouchables,* which included a killing, a chase, the shooting and death of one villain, and an extended fistfight involving a second villain. The segment was only 3.5 minutes long. Then the children were put into a situation where they could help or hurt another child who was supposedly working in the next room. Hurting behavior (making another's task more difficult) was deemed to be a manifestation of aggressiveness. The boys who displayed the pleasant expressions did engage in more aggressive behavior; the girls did not. It remains to be seen whether the portrayal of violence using female role models would evoke similar behavior.

Savitsky et al. (1974) were interested in whether facial expressions of emotion by a "victim" would have any effect on the aggressor's behavior. When individuals thought they were controlling the amount of electric shock that another person (victim) would get, they gave more shocks to victims who responded with expressions of happiness and smiles and fewer to victims who displayed expressions of anger. Expressions of fear and neutrality did not differ from each other in the number of shocks administered, which for both expressions was very low.

In another study, Savitsky and Sim (1974) tried to find out what effect facial expressions had on evaluations of a defendant's account of his crime. Defendants told the story of their crime (petty thefts and vandalism) and varied their emotional expressions. Anger, happiness, sadness, and neutral expressions were used. Sad/distressed and neutral defendants were apparently seen most favorably. Their crimes were rated as less severe; they were perceived as less likely to commit another crime; and they were given the least amount of punishment. Angry (and to a lesser degree, happy) defendants were evaluated the most harshly.

The strong impact of facial expressions takes on special significance because people have a great deal of control over their faces. Most discussions of the face center on emotions—how the face reveals what emotions are being felt. But several times we have mentioned *posed* versus *spontaneous* expressions. By its very nature, a posed expression means that one need not actually feel what one is showing. The face becomes a tool of self-presentation (creating a desirable image for oneself in the eyes of others) and of social influence (producing desirable behaviors in someone else). We may be particularly vulnerable to manipulation by others' faces since we are likely to *assume* that the face is simply (and innocently) revealing a person's true feelings when this might not be the case.

In daily life, posed (deliberate) and spontaneous expressions are intertwined, and it may not be possible to know to what extent a given expression is one or the other. And since even completely spontaneous expressions might influence us in ways we are unaware of, it is useful to review further some of the evidence for the impact of facial expressions in social life. One line of research considers the mass media and finds that different television newscasters seem to prefer different political candidates, as revealed by the pleasantness of their faces when mentioning the candidates' names. Viewers' political preferences could be unconsciously altered in this way (Friedman, DiMatteo, & Mertz, 1980; Mullen, 1986).

The possibility that facial expressions are related to discrimination against women was the topic of Butler and Geis's (1990) study of male and female leaders in groups. Male and female (confederate) leaders in their experimentally composed groups offered the same suggestions and arguments, but the group members, who were the subjects, displayed more pleased responses (smiling, nodding) and fewer displeased responses (furrowed brow, mouth tightening, head shaking) when they were listening to a male leader than when listening to a female leader. Group members were apparently unaware of their gender-biased behavior, or denied it, for they later revealed no gender bias in written evaluations of the different leaders. Butler and Geis argue that nonverbal signals of devaluation of the female leader could convince others, as well as the female leader herself, that her contributions are weak or wrong.

Another connection between the face and sex discrimination was made by Archer's discovery of the "face-ism" or facial prominence phenomenon: In magazine and newspaper pictures of men, proportionately more of the picture is devoted to the face; pictures of women show more of the body. Archer and his colleagues (Archer, Iritani, Kimes & Barrios, 1983) found this pattern in publications from eleven different cultures and in artwork over six centuries, as well as in people's amateur drawings. Both Archer and later researchers (Zuckerman, 1986) have made the case that this "face-ism" is a form of devaluation of women.

Consistent with the view that depicting less of the face devalues the subject, Zuckerman and Kieffer (1994) have demonstrated that face-ism favoring whites over blacks also exists in magazines and art (when the artists are white) and that the higher the status of the subject in magazine photos, the larger the proportional depiction of the subject's face.

Smiling has been discussed a great deal in the context of male/female differences. Women (but not young girls) smile more than their male counterparts (Hall, 1984). Some feminist scholars see this difference as disadvantageous to women—it may make women seem weak or eager to please (Henley, 1977). In this context, it is often assumed that the smile is a badge of submission for a lower-status individual. As yet, however, no firm evidence suggests that women's smiling is due to social weakness.

Another often-cited study found that women tended to smile even when their words did not contain congruently happy messages, but men's smiles were more in accord with their words (Bugental, Love, & Gianetto, 1971). Here is a pattern that could certainly have social impact! However, a subsequent study done under different circumstances found exactly the opposite pattern (Halberstadt, Hayes, & Pike, 1988). Clearly, it is premature to conclude that inconsistent displays are the province of women.

The smile is a profoundly influential social cue that has been studied in many contexts besides male/female differences. People reciprocate smiles quite predictably (Jorgenson, 1978). You can imagine how, after returning someone's smile, facial feedback or attributional processes ("I just smiled at Jim. I must really like him!") could produce real changes in your attitude toward the smiler. Smiles are positive reinforcers that can change behavior just as other, more traditional, reinforcers can; experiments show this, but any parent knows it already. Parents also know, and research shows, that adults' smiles (and other expressions) influence babies' moods and responses to the environment (Cappella, 1981). Smiles certainly influence adults, too: Receiving a smile from one stranger can make you more helpful toward a different stranger (Solomon, Solomon, Arnone, Maur, Reda, & Roth, 1981).

Angry faces are a potent stimulus, too. In a series of experiments, Hansen and Hansen (1988) compared people's ability to pick out an angry face in a crowd of happy faces to their ability to pick out a happy face in a crowd of angry faces. As they predicted, picking out the angry face was faster and more error-free than picking out the happy face. Perhaps our survival as a species has some relation to our sensitivity to threats.

SUMMARY

This discussion of the face and its role in human communication should leave you with several impressions.

First, the face is a multimessage system. It can communicate information regarding personality, interest and responsiveness during interaction, emotional states, and how people want to present themselves to others. Although there is little doubt that people do associate certain personality characteristics with certain expressions and facial features, the research to date does not tell us much. We know the face is used as a conversational regulator that opens and closes communication channels, complements and qualifies other behaviors, and replaces spoken messages.

We learned that facial expressions are very complex entities to deal with. Of all the areas of the body, the face seems to elicit the best external and internal feedback, which makes it easy for us to follow a variety of facial display rules. Not all facial displays represent single emotions; some are blends of several emotions. Sometimes we show aspects of an emotional display when we aren't actually feeling emotional, as with facial emblems that represent commentary on emotions.

We noted some measurement problems involved in the study of facial expressions: the complexity of the decisions observers are asked to make, simulated as opposed to real expressions, the method of presenting the face to the observer (films, photos, and the like), prior exposure to the face, knowledge of the context, and others. Naturally, all these factors may impinge on one's accuracy in identifying facial expressions of emotion.

In spite of these problems, accuracy in judging the face tends to be high. Furthermore, certain basic emotions have been found to be accurately judged in cultures around the world: anger, fear, disgust, sadness, happiness, surprise, and contempt. In order to understand what the face actually does during the expression of emotion, anatomically based coding systems, such as the Facial Action Coding System (FACS), have been developed; these systems can identify which muscles are involved in different kinds of expressions.

A psychophysiological approach has added much to our understanding of facial behavior. People with more expressive faces have less activity in their autonomic nervous systems than less expressive people; this is interesting partly because of its health implications. Under certain circumstances, facial movements can influence the emotions being felt by the expressor; thus, the face may not only "read out" emotions but also may actually produce them. Finally, researchers are finding out more about which activities of the brain and nervous system are associated with different emotions.

We concluded with reports from a few studies suggesting that the identification of facial expressions of emotion may help us predict subsequent behaviors—of the person showing the affect and of people responding to it.

(Answer to Figure 9-4: *b*. All the others have traces of disgust or sadness.)

QUESTIONS for DISCUSSION

1. Facial expressions can show emotions, but they also are used for conversation management. Give examples of each and state which function you consider the most important.
2. Consider men's and women's nonverbal behavior. Does the concept of display rules help you to explain any differences between the sexes?
3. As noted in the chapter, the distinction between a feigned or posed facial display and an authentic or spontaneous one may be hard to make. Discuss the issue of intentionality in facial expressions. Is it important to be able to make such a distinction?

4. The chapter gives examples of how the face is a potent influence on others. Think of some other examples of this, and discuss whether the face is more or less influential than other nonverbal channels in terms of its social impact.

REFERENCES and SELECTED BIBLIOGRAPHY

Abelson, R. P., & Sermat, V. (1962). Multidimensional scaling of facial expressions. *Journal of Experimental Psychology, 63,* 546–51.

Andrew, R. J. (1965). The origins of facial expression. *Scientific American, 213,* 88–94.

Antonoff, S. R., & Spilka, B. (1984–1985). Patterning of facial expressions among terminal cancer patients. *Omega, 15,* 101–8.

Archer, D., Iritani, B., Kimes, D. D., & Barrios, M. (1983). Face-ism: Five studies of sex differences in facial prominence. *Journal of Personality and Social Psychology, 45,* 725–35.

Bavelas, J. B., Black, A., Lemery, C. R., & Mullett, J. (1986). 'I *show* how you feel': Motor mimicry as a communicative act. *Journal of Personality and Social Psychology, 50,* 322–29.

Brannigan, C. R., & Humphries, D. A. (1972). Human non-verbal behavior, a means of communication. In N. Blurton Jones (Ed.), *Ethological studies of child behavior.* New York: Cambridge University Press.

Briton, N. J., & Hall, J. A. (1995). Gender-based expectancies and observer judgments of smiling. *Journal of Nonverbal Behavior, 19,* 49–65.

Brunner, L. J. (1979). Smiles can be back channels. *Journal of Personality and Social Psychology, 37,* 728–34.

Buck, R. (1979). Measuring individual differences in the nonverbal communication of affect: The slide-viewing paradigm. *Human Communication Research, 6,* 47–57.

Buck, R. (1984). *The communication of emotion.* New York: Guilford.

Buck, R. (1988). Nonverbal communication: Spontaneous and symbolic aspects. *American Behavioral Scientist, 31,* 341–54.

Buck, R. (1991). Social factors in facial display and communication: A reply to Chovil and others. *Journal of Nonverbal Behavior, 15,* 155–61.

Buck, R. (1993). Emotional communication, emotional competence, and physical illness: A developmental-interactionist view. In H. C. Traue & J. W. Pennebaker (Eds.), *Emotion, inhibition, and health.* Seattle: Hogrefe & Hubner.

Buck, R. (1994). Social and emotional functions in facial expression and communication: The readout hypothesis. *Biological Psychology, 38,* 95–115.

Buck, R., & Duffy, R. (1980). Nonverbal communication of affect in brain-damaged patients. *Cortex, 16,* 351–62.

Buck, R., Savin, V., Miller, R. E., & Caul, W. F. (1972). Nonverbal communication of affect in humans. *Journal of Personality and Social Psychology, 23,* 362–71.

Bugental, D. E., Love, L. R., & Gianetto, R. M. (1971). Perfidious feminine faces. *Journal of Personality and Social Psychology, 17,* 314–18.

Butler, D., & Geis, F. L. (1990). Nonverbal affect responses to male and female leaders: Implications for leadership evaluations. *Journal of Personality and Social Psychology, 58,* 48–59.

Cacioppo, J. T., Klein, D. J., Berntson, G. G., & Hatfield, E. (1993). The psychophysiology of emotion. In M. Lewis & J. M. Haviland (Eds.), *Handbook of emotions.* New York: Guilford.

Camras, L. A., Holland, E. A., & Patterson, M. J. (1993). Facial expression. In M. Lewis & J. M. Haviland (Eds.), *Handbook of emotions.* New York: Guilford.

Cappella, J. N. (1981). Mutual influence in expressive behavior: Adult-adult and infant-adult dyadic interaction. *Psychological Bulletin, 89,* 101–32.

Chovil, N. (1991). Social determinants of facial displays. *Journal of Nonverbal Behavior, 15,* 141–54.

Chovil, N. (1991/1992). Discourse-oriented facial displays in conversation. *Research on Language and Social Interaction, 25,* 163–94.

Cline, M. (1956). The influence of social context on the perception of faces. *Journal of Personality, 25,* 142–58.

Coleman, J. D. (1949). Facial expressions of emotions. *Psychological Monographs, 63* (1, Whole No. 296).

Darwin, C. R. (1872). *The expression of the emotions in man and animals.* London: John Murray.

Duclos, S. E., Laird, J. D., Schneider, E., Sexter, M., Stern, L., & Van Lighten, O. (1989). Emotion-specific effects of facial expressions and postures on emotional experience. *Journal of Personality and Social Psychology, 57,* 100–108.

Dunlap, K. (1927). The role of eye-muscles and mouth-muscles in the expression of the emotions. *Genetic Psychology Monographs, 2,* 199–233.

Eibl-Eibesfeldt, I. (1974). *Love and hate: The natural history of behavior patterns.* New York: Schocken.

Ekman, P. (Ed.). (1973). *Darwin and facial expression.* New York: Academic Press.

Ekman, P. (1979). About brows: Emotional and conversational signals. In V. von Cranach, K. Foppa, W. Lepenies, & D. Ploog (Eds.), *Human ethology.* Cambridge: Cambridge University Press.

Ekman, P. (1982). Methods for measuring facial action. In K. R. Scherer & P. Ekman (Eds.), *Handbook of methods in nonverbal behavior research.* Cambridge: Cambridge University Press.

Ekman, P., Davidson, R. J., & Friesen, W. V. (1990). The Duchenne smile: Emotional expression and brain physiology II. *Journal of Personality and Social Psychology, 58,* 342–53.

Ekman, P., & Friesen, W. V. (1969). The repertoire of nonverbal behavior: Categories, origins, usage, and coding. *Semiotica, 1,* 49–98.

Ekman, P., & Friesen, W. V. (1971). Constants across cultures in the face and emotion. *Journal of Personality and Social Psychology, 17,* 124–29.

Ekman, P., & Friesen, W. V. (1975). *Unmasking the face.* Englewood Cliffs, NJ: Prentice-Hall.

Ekman, P., & Friesen, W. V. (1978). *The Facial Action Coding System: A technique for the measurement of facial movement.* Palo Alto: Consulting Psychologists Press.

Ekman, P., & Friesen, W. V. (1982). Felt, false, and miserable smiles. *Journal of Nonverbal Behavior, 6,* 238–52.

Ekman, P., & Friesen, W. V. (1986). A new pan-cultural facial expression of emotion. *Motivation and Emotion, 10,* 159–68.

Ekman, P., Friesen, W. V., & Ancoli, S. (1980). Facial signs of emotional experience. *Journal of Personality and Social Psychology, 39,* 1125–34.

Ekman, P., Friesen, W. V., & Ellsworth, P. (1982a). Does the face provide accurate information? In P. Ekman (Ed.), *Emotion in the human face.* (2d ed.). Cambridge: Cambridge University Press.

Ekman, P., Friesen, W. V., & Ellsworth, P. (1982b). Methodological decisions. In P. Ekman (Ed.), *Emotion in the human face.* 2d ed. Cambridge: Cambridge University Press.

Ekman, P., Friesen, W. V., & Ellsworth, P. (1982c). What are the relative contributions of facial behavior and contextual information to the judgment of emotion? In P. Ekman (Ed.), *Emotion in the human face.* (2d ed.). Cambridge: Cambridge University Press.

Ekman, P., Friesen, W. V., & O'Sullivan, M. (1988). Smiles when lying. *Journal of Personality and Social Psychology, 54,* 414–20.

Ekman, P., Friesen, W. V., O'Sullivan, M., Chan, A., Diacoyanni-Tarlatzis, I., et al. (1987). Universals and cultural differences in the judgments of facial expressions of emotion. *Journal of Personality and Social Psychology, 53,* 712–17.

Ekman, P., Hager, J. C., & Friesen, W. V. (1981). The symmetry of emotional and deliberate facial actions. *Psychophysiology, 18,* 101–6.

Ekman, P., Levenson, R. W., & Friesen, W. V. (1983). Autonomic nervous system activity distinguishes among emotions. *Science, 221,* 1208–10.

Ekman, P., Liebert, R. M., Friesen, W. V., Harrison, R., Zlatchin, C., Malstrom, E. J., & Baron, R. A. (1972). Facial expressions of emotion while watching televised violence as predictors of subsequent aggression. In *Television and social behavior: Vol. 5. Television's effects: Further explorations* (Report to the Surgeon General's Scientific Advisory Committee on Television and Social Behavior, Washington: U.S. Printing Office)

Ekman, P., & Oster, H. (1982). Review on research, 1970–1980. In P. Ekman (Ed.), *Emotion in the human face* (2d ed.). Cambridge: Cambridge University Press.

Ekman, P., Sorenson, E. R., & Friesen, W. V. (1969). Pan-cultural elements in facial displays of emotions. *Science, 164,* 86–88.

Ellis, C. (1991). Sociological introspection and emotional experience. *Symbolic Interaction, 14,* 23–50.

Ellis, C., & Weinstein, E. (1986). Jealousy and the social psychology of emotional experience. *Journal of Social and Personal Relationships, 3,* 337–57.

Feleky, A. M. (1914). The expression of emotions. *Psychological Review, 21,* 33–41.

Fernández-Dols, J.-M., & Ruiz-Belda, M.-A. (1995). Are smiles a sign of happiness? Gold medal winners at the Olympic Games. *Journal of Personality and Social Psychology, 69,* 1113–19.

Field, T. (1982). Individual differences in the expressivity of neonates and young infants. In R. S. Feldman (Ed.), *Development of nonverbal behavior in children.* New York: Springer-Verlag.

Fox, N. A., & Davidson, R. J. (1988). Patterns of brain electrical activity during facial signs of emotion in ten-month-old infants. *Developmental Psychology, 14,* 230–36.

Frank, M. G., Ekman, P., & Friesen, W. V. (1993). Behavioral markers and recognizability of the smile of enjoyment. *Journal of Personality and Social Psychology, 64,* 83–93.

Fridlund, A. J. (1991). Sociality of solitary smiling: Potentiation by an implicit audience. *Journal of Personality and Social Psychology, 60,* 229–40.

Fridlund, A. J. (1994). *Human facial expression: An evolutionary view.* San Diego: Academic Press.

Fridlund, A. J., Ekman, P., & Oster, H. (1987). Facial expressions of emotion: Review of literature, 1970–1983. In A. W. Siegman & S. Feldstein (Eds.), *Nonverbal behavior and communication* (2d ed.). Hillsdale, NJ: Erlbaum.

Friedman, H. S., & Booth-Kewley, S. (1987). Personality, Type A behavior, and coronary heart disease: The role of emotional expression. *Journal of Personality and Social Psychology, 53,* 783–92.

Friedman, H. S., DiMatteo, M. R., & Mertz, T. I. (1980). Nonverbal communication on television news: The facial expressions of broadcasters during coverage of a presidential election campaign. *Personality and Social Psychology Bulletin, 6,* 427–35.

Friedman, H. S., Hall, J. A., & Harris, M. J. (1985). Type A behavior, nonverbal expressive style, and health. *Journal of Personality and Social Psychology, 48,* 1299–1315.

Frijda, N. H. (1973). The relation between emotion and expression. In M. von Cranach & I. Vine (Eds.), *Social communication and movement.* New York: Academic Press.

Hager, J. C., & Ekman, P. (1985). The asymmetry of facial actions is inconsistent with models of hemispheric specialization. *Psychophysiology, 22,* 307–18.

Haggard, E. A., & Isaacs, F. S. (1966). Micromomentary facial expressions as indicators of ego mechanisms in psychotherapy. In L. A. Gottschalk & A. H. Auerback (Eds.), *Methods of research in psychotherapy.* New York: Appleton-Century-Crofts.

Halberstadt, A. G. (1986). Family socialization of emotional expression and nonverbal communication styles and skills. *Journal of Personality and Social Psychology, 51,* 827–36.

Halberstadt, A. G., Hayes, C. W., & Pike, K. M. (1988). Gender and gender role differences in smiling and communication consistency. *Sex Roles, 19,* 589–604.

Hall, J. A. (1984). *Nonverbal sex differences: Communication accuracy and expressive style.* Baltimore: Johns Hopkins University Press.

Hansen, C. H., & Hansen, R. D. (1988). Finding the face in the crowd: An anger superiority effect. *Journal of Personality and Social Psychology, 54,* 917–24.

Harrigan, J. A., & O'Donnell, D. M. (in press). How do you look when feeling anxious? Facial displays of anxiety. *Personality and Individual Differences.*

Henley, N. M. (1977). *Body politics: Power, sex, and nonverbal communication.* Englewood Cliffs, NJ: Prentice-Hall.

Hinsz, V. B. (1989). Facial resemblance in engaged and married couples. *Journal of Social and Personal Relationships, 6,* 223–29.

Izard, C. E. (1971). *The face of emotion.* New York: Appleton-Century-Crofts.

Izard, C. E. (1979). *The maximally discriminative facial movement coding system.* Unpublished manuscript, University of Delaware.

Izard, C. E. (1990). Facial expressions and the regulation of emotions. *Journal of Personality and Social Psychology, 58,* 487–98.

Jones, S. S., Collins, K., & Hong, H. (1991). An audience effect on smile production in 10-month-old infants. *Psychological Science, 2,* 45–49.

Jorgenson, D. O. (1978). Nonverbal assessment of attitudinal affect with the smile-return technique. *Journal of Social Psychology, 106,* 173–79.

King, L. A., & Emmons, R. A. (1990). Conflict over emotional expression: Psychological and physical correlates. *Journal of Personality and Social Psychology, 58,* 864–77.

Kraut, R. E., & Johnston, R. E. (1979). Social and emotional messages of smiling: An ethological approach. *Journal of Personality and Social Psychology, 37,* 1539–53.

Laird, J. D. (1974). Self-attribution of emotion: The effects of expressive behavior on the quality of emotional experience. *Journal of Personality and Social Psychology, 24,* 475–86.

Lanzetta, J. T., Cartwright-Smith, J., & Kleck, R. E. (1976). Effects of nonverbal dissimulation of emotional experience and autonomic arousal. *Journal of Personality and Social Psychology, 33,* 354–70.

Lanzetta, J. T., & Kleck, R. E. (1970). Encoding and decoding of nonverbal affect in humans. *Journal of Personality and Social Psychology, 16,* 12–19.

Laughery, K. R., Alexander, J. F., & Lane, A. B. (1971). Recognition of human faces: Effects of target exposure time, target position, pose position, and type of photograph. *Journal of Applied Psychology, 55,* 477–83.

LeResche, L. (1982). Facial expression in pain: A study of candid photographs. *Journal of Nonverbal Behavior, 7,* 46–56.

Malatesta, C. Z., Jonas, R., & Izard, C. E. (1987). The relation between low facial expressibility during emotional arousal and somatic symptoms. *British Journal of Medical Psychology, 60,* 169–80.

Matsumoto, D. (1987). The role of facial response in the experience of emotion: More methodological problems and a meta-analysis. *Journal of Personality and Social Psychology, 52,* 769–74.

Matsumoto, D. (1989). Face, culture, and judgments of anger and fear: Do the eyes have it? *Journal of Nonverbal Behavior, 13,* 171–88.

Mullen, B. (1986). Newscasters' facial expressions and voting behavior of viewers: Can a smile elect a president? *Journal of Personality and Social Psychology, 51,* 291–95.

Munn, N. L. (1940). The effect of knowledge of the situation upon the judgment of emotion from facial expression. *Journal of Abnormal and Social Psychology, 35,* 324–38.

Notarius, C. I., & Levenson, R. W. (1979). Expressive tendencies and physiological response to stress. *Journal of Personality and Social Psychology, 37,* 1204–10.

Osgood, C. E. (1966). Dimensionality of the semantic space for communication via facial expressions. *Scandinavian Journal of Psychology, 7,* 1–30.

Patrick, C. J., Craig, K. D., & Prkachin, K. M. (1986). Observer judgments of acute pain: Facial action determinants. *Journal of Personality and Social Psychology, 50,* 1291–98.

Prkachin, K. M., & Craig, K. D. (1995). Expressing pain: The communication and interpretation of facial pain signals. *Journal of Nonverbal Behavior, 19,* 191–205.

Redican, W. K. (1982). An evolutionary perspective on human facial displays. In P. Ekman (Ed.), *Emotion in the human face* (2d ed.). Cambridge: Cambridge University Press.

Riggio, R. E., & Friedman, H. S. (1986). Impression formation: The role of expressive behavior. *Journal of Personality and Social Psychology, 50,* 421–27.

Rinn, W. E. (1984). The neuropsychology of facial expression: A review of the neurological and psychological mechanisms for producing facial expressions. *Psychological Bulletin, 95,* 52–77.

Rozin, P., Lowery, L., & Ebert, R. (1994). Varieties of disgust faces and the structure of disgust. *Journal of Personality and Social Psychology, 66,* 870–81.

Savitsky, J. C., Izard, C. E., Kotsch, W. E., & Christy, L. (1974). Aggressor's response to the victim's facial expression of emotion. *Journal of Research on Personality, 7,* 346–57.

Savitsky, J. C., & Sim, M. E. (1974). Trading emotions: Equity theory of reward and punishment. *Journal of Communication, 24,* 140–46.

Schlosberg, H. (1954). Three dimensions of emotion. *Psychological Review, 61,* 81–88.

Secord, P. F., Dukes, W. F., & Bevan, W. (1959). Personalities in faces, I: An experiment in social perceiving. *Genetic Psychology Monographs, 49,* 231–79.

Shields, S. A., Mallory, M. E., & Simon, A. (1990). The experience and symptoms of blushing as a function of age and reported frequency of blushing. *Journal of Nonverbal Behavior, 14,* 171–87.

Smith, W. J., Chase, J., & Lieblich, A. K. (1974). Tongue showing: A facial display of humans and other primate species. *Semiotica, 11,* 201–46.

Solomon, H., Solomon, L. Z., Arnone, M. M., Maur, B. J., Reda, R. M., & Roth, E. O. (1981). Anonymity and helping. *Journal of Social Psychology, 113,* 37–43.

Spitz, R. A., & Wolf, K. M. (1946). The smiling response: A contribution to the ontogenesis of social relations. *Genetic Psychology Monographs, 34,* 57–125.

Stepper, S., & Strack, F. (1993). Proprioceptive determinants of emotional and nonemotional feelings. *Journal of Personality and Social Psychology, 64,* 211–20.

Strack, F., Martin, L. L., & Stepper, S. (1988). Inhibiting and facilitating conditions of the human smile: A nonobtrusive test of the facial feedback hypothesis. *Journal of Personality and Social Psychology, 54,* 768–77.

Thompson, D. F., & Meltzer, L. (1964). Communication of emotional intent by facial expression. *Journal of Abnormal and Social Psychology, 68,* 129–35.

Tomkins, S. S. (1962, 1963). *Affect, imagery, consciousness* (Vol. I and II.) New York: Springer.

Tourangeau, R., & Ellsworth, P. C. (1979). The role of facial response in the experience of emotion. *Journal of Personality and Social Psychology, 37,* 1519–31.

Wagner, H. L., & Smith, J. (1991). Facial expressions in the presence of friends and strangers. *Journal of Nonverbal Behavior, 15,* 201–14.

Why is this man smiling? (1989, September 18), *Time,* p. 34.

Zajonc, R. B. (1985). Emotion and facial efference: A theory reclaimed. *Science, 228,* 15–21.

Zuckerman, M. (1986). On the meaning and implications of facial prominence. *Journal of Nonverbal Behavior, 10,* 215–29.

Zuckerman, M., Hall, J. A., DeFrank, R. S., & Rosenthal, R. (1976). Encoding and decoding of spontaneous and posed facial expressions. *Journal of Personality and Social Psychology, 34,* 966–77.

Zuckerman, M., & Kieffer, S. C. (1994). Race differences in face-ism: Does facial prominence imply dominance? *Journal of Personality and Social Psychology, 66,* 86–92.

CHAPTER 10

The Effects of Eye Behavior on Human Communication

He speaketh not; and yet there lies
A conversation in his eyes.

—HENRY WADSWORTH LONGFELLOW

Throughout history, we have been preoccupied with the eye and its effects on human behavior. Do you recall the last time you used one of these phrases?

"She could look right through you."

"It was an icy stare."

"He's got shifty eyes."

"She's all eyes."

"Did you see the gleam in his eye?"

"We're seeing eye to eye now."

"He looked like the original Evil Eye."

"His eyes shot daggers across the room."

"She could kill with a glance."

Greenacre reported that some Bushmen in South Africa believe the glance of a menstruating girl's eye can transfix a man in whatever position he is in at the time and change him into a tree (Greenacre, 1926)! Psychiatric literature reveals numerous cases in which the eye is used as a symbol for either male or female sex organs.

We associate various eye movements with a wide range of human expressions: Downward glances are associated with modesty; wide eyes with frankness, wonder, naïveté, or terror; raised upper eyelids, along with contraction of the orbicularis muscle, with displeasure; generally immobile facial muscles and a rather constant stare with coldness; and eyes rolled upward with fatigue or a suggestion that another's behavior is a bit weird.

Our society has established a number of eye-related norms. For example, we don't look too long at strangers in public places; we are not supposed to look at various body parts except under certain conditions, and so on.

Our fascination with eyes has led to the exploration of almost every conceivable feature of the eyes (size, color, position) and surrounding parts (eyebrows, rings, wrinkles). Eye rings are found mainly in other animals, but some speculate that our eyebrows are residual rings that are raised during surprise or fear and lowered for focus during threat and anger. Eye patches are the colored eyelids sometimes seen in primates. These patches are not a part of the natural human communicative repertoire, although women often

Figure 10–1

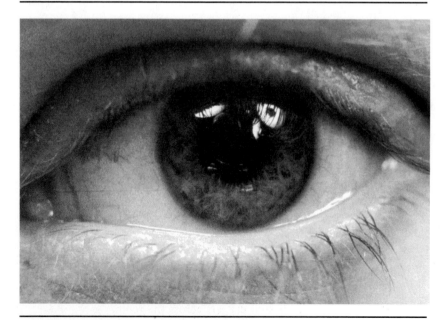

The human eye.

use eyeliner and eyeshadow to achieve a similar effect. Another nonhuman feature that has received scholarly attention is eyespots, eye-shaped images located on other body parts. These can be seen on peacock feathers, butterflies, and fish.

Some researchers have examined the degree to which eyes open as a reflection of various emotional states. Some feel that excessive blinking may be associated with various stages of anxiety—as if attempting to cut off reality. Psychiatrists report some patients who blink up to one hundred times per minute; normal blinking, needed to lubricate and protect the eyeball, occurs about six to ten times per minute in adults. Some evidence shows that when a person is attentive to objects in the environment or during concentrated thought, blinking rate will decrease. Another interesting topic is eye color. Blue eyes appear to be a marker for inhibition and shyness (Rosenberg & Kagan, 1987). An "eye flash" occurs when the eyelids are briefly opened without the accompanying involvement of the eyebrows. This display, which lasts less than a second, is used to emphasize particular words, usually adjectives (Walker & Trimboli, 1983). The "eyebrow flash," used in greetings, was discussed in Chapter 2.

Of the many eye-related topics of inquiry, this chapter focuses on two: The first is known by such terms as *eye contact, mutual glances, visual interaction, gazing,* or *line of regard;* the other concerns *pupil dilation and constriction* under various social conditions.

GAZE and MUTUAL GAZE

We begin by looking at the terminology we have chosen: *gaze* and *mutual gaze* (Argyle & Cook, 1976; Kleinke, 1986; Rutter, 1984). *Gaze* refers to an individual's looking behavior, which may or may not be at the other person; *mutual gaze* refers to a situation in which the two interactants are looking at each other, usually in the region of the face (see Figure 10-2). Eye contact (looking specifically in each other's eyes) does not seem to be reliably distinguished by receivers or observers from gazing at the area surrounding the eyes (von Cranach & Ellgring, 1973). In fact, much of what is considered "looking someone in the eye" is a series of rapid, repeated scans of several parts of the face. In one case, an eye-mark camera recorded eighteen different fixation points for a listener who was apparently maintaining a steady gaze. Indeed, if someone did look fixedly, without moving the eyes, the impression would be one of vacant staring. Gaze and mutual gazing, however, can be reliably assessed. At a distance of three meters, face-directed gazing can be distinguished; shifting the direction of one's gaze by one centimeter can reliably be detected from a distance of one meter.

We know we do not look at the other person during the entire time we are talking to him or her, nor do we avert our gaze 100 percent of the time. So, what would be considered normal gazing patterns? Obviously, the answer

Figure 10–2

Mutual gaze. (Photo credit: Frances M. Cox/Stock Boston)

varies according to the background and personalities of the participants, the topic, the other person's gazing patterns, objects of mutual interest in the environment, and so on. The speaker's fluency also affects gazing patterns. During fluent speech, speakers tend to look at listeners much more than during hesitant speech. Keeping such qualifications in mind, we can get a general idea of normal gazing patterns from two studies of focused interaction between two people shown in Table 10-1. The table shows that on average, people gaze about half the time, that there is a huge range (indicating notable individual differences) in the amount of other-directed gaze, and that people gaze more while listening than while talking.

Table 10–1
AMOUNT OF GAZING IN TWO-PERSON CONVERSATIONS

	(%) Average	(%) Range	(%) Talking	(%) Listening	(%) Mutual Gaze	Average Length of Gaze	Average Length of Mutual Gaze
Nielsen	50*	8–73	38	62	–	–	–
Argyle & Ingham	61	–	41	75	31	2.95 sec.	1.18 sec.

Percentages reflect the amount of time gazing relative to the total interaction time.

FUNCTIONS of GAZING

Kendon (1967) has identified four functions of gazing: (1) *regulatory*—responses may be demanded or suppressed by looking; (2) *monitoring*—people may look at their partner to indicate the conclusions of thought units and to check their partner's attentiveness and reactions; (3) *cognitive*—people tend to look away when having difficulty processing information or deciding what to say; and (4) *expressive*—the degree and nature of involvement or arousal may be signaled through looking.

Our discussion will follow a similar pattern:

1. Regulating the flow of communication
2. Monitoring feedback
3. Reflecting cognitive activity
4. Expressing emotions
5. Communicating the nature of the interpersonal relationship

These functions do not operate independently; that is, visual behavior not only sends information but is also one of the primary methods for collecting it. Looking at the other person as you finish an utterance may not only tell the other it is his or her turn to speak but is also an occasion to monitor feedback regarding the utterance.

REGULATING THE FLOW OF COMMUNICATION

Visual contact occurs when we want to signal that the communication channel is open. In some instances, eye gaze almost establishes an obligation to interact. When you seek visual contact with your waiter, you are essentially indicating the communication channel is open, and you want to say something to him. You may recall instances when an instructor asked the class a question, and you were sure you did not know the answer. Establishing eye contact with the instructor was the last thing you wanted to do. You did not wish to signal the channel was open. We behave the same way when we see someone coming toward us with whom we do not wish to talk. As long as we can avoid eye gaze (in a seemingly natural way), it is much easier to avoid interaction. When confronting unknown others, we typically recognize them with a brief glance, but this initial glance is followed by the avoidance of gaze unless further contact is desired. A length of gaze that exceeds this glance of recognition is likely to signal desire to initiate a conversation (Cary, 1978a). When you want to disavow social contact, your eye gaze will likely diminish. Thus, we see mutual gazing in greeting sequences and greatly diminished gazing when one wishes to bring an encounter to a halt.

In addition to opening and closing the channel of communication, eye behavior also regulates the flow of communication by providing turn-taking signals. Speakers generally look less often than listeners. But speakers do seem to glance during grammatical breaks, at the end of a thought unit or idea, and at the end of the utterance. Although glances at these junctures can signal the other person to assume the speaking role, we also use these glances to obtain feedback, to see how we are being received, and to see if the other will let us continue. This feedback function is addressed in the next section. The speaker/listener pattern is often choreographed as follows: As the speaker comes to the end of an utterance or thought unit, eye gaze toward the listener will continue as the listener assumes the speaking role; the listener will maintain gaze until the speaking role is assumed, when he or she will look away. Research on naturally emerging and appointed leaders in three-person (male) groups has found that the leader controls the flow of conversation using this cue pattern: The leader shows an increased tendency to engage in prolonged gaze at someone at the end of his utterances, as if inviting (possibly instructing) that person to take the floor. Thus, the leader does not necessarily keep the floor for himself but, rather, orchestrates who gets the floor and when (Kalma, 1992).

Gazing by the speaker at the completion of an utterance may help to signal the yielding of a speaking turn, but listener-directed gazes do not always accompany the smooth exchange of speaking turns (Beattie, 1978a; Rutter, Stephenson, & White, 1978). On the other hand, sometimes the speaker glances at the listener when yielding a speaking turn, and the listener delays a response or fails to respond. Further, when a speaker begins an anticipated lengthy response, he or she is likely to delay gazing at the other beyond what would normally be expected. This pattern of adult gazing and looking away during speech seems to have its roots in early childhood development. Observations of the gazing patterns of three- to four-month-old infants and their parents revealed gross temporal similarities between their looking at and looking away sequence and the vocalizing and pausing sequences in adult conversations (Jaffe, Stern, & Peery, 1973).

MONITORING FEEDBACK

When people seek feedback concerning the reactions of others, they gaze at the other person. If the other person is looking at you, it is usually interpreted as a sign of attention to what you are saying. In fact, such a notion seems so firmly held that when people were *told* that their partner looked at them less than normal—regardless of their actual gaze—the partner was rated as "less attentive" (Kleinke, Bustos, Meeker, & Staneski, 1973). Listener facial expressions and gazing suggest not only attention but also whether or not the listener is interested in what is being said. ("Good. Continue.") Being seen is a profound form of social acknowledgment that may be welcome or unwelcome, depending on the circumstances. The power of being seen is well illustrated in the example of a child on a playground who demands to be watched by his or her parent while doing feats on the monkey bars or slide. Being watched adds safety or security but, much more important, it infuses *meaning* into the child's actions. Without a witness, the actions feel pointless to the child—even unreal. People's need to watch and be watched is undoubtedly central to the phenomenon known as *emotional contagion,* whereby one person's mood or emotion is influenced by another's mood or emotion via subtle and mostly unconscious processes (Hatfield, Cacioppo, & Rapson, 1994). When people must communicate without seeing one another, a number of adaptations take place to compensate for this loss of information. For example, they will engage in more verbal back-channel responses (responses such as "uh-huh" that are inserted while another is speaking; Boyle, Anderson, & Newlands, 1994).

Effective monitoring via gaze may have dramatic consequences. In a study of Dutch physicians conducting routine medical visits, those physicians who engaged in more patient-directed gaze were more accurate at recognizing the patients' degree of psychosocial distress (Bensing, Kerssens, & van der Pasch, 1995).

REFLECTING COGNITIVE ACTIVITY

Both listeners and speakers have a tendency to look away when they are trying to process difficult or complex ideas. This averted gaze may reflect a shift in attention from external to internal matters. When we look away during difficult cognitive demands, it is not a random pattern. We seem to look away more on reflective questions than factual ones. Bakan (1971; Bakan & Strayer, 1973) reported studies in which subjects were asked thought-provoking questions while eye movement was measured. It was found that people tended to look preferentially to the left or right while thinking. Typical questions were

- "How many letters are there in the word 'Washington'?"
- "Multiply twelve by thirteen."
- "What is meant by the proverb 'It is better to have a bad peace than a good war'?"

Then, after classifying "right movers" and "left movers," they collected other data to further characterize the two groups. When a person moves his or her eyes in a particular direction, it is thought to reflect activity in the *opposite* hemisphere of the brain: Left-hemisphere activity, often involving intellectual and linguistic tasks, is associated with rightward glances, while right-hemisphere activity, often involving spatial or emotional processing, is associated with leftward glances (Ehrlichman & Weinberger, 1978; Weisz & Adam, 1993; Wilbur & Roberts-Wilbur, 1985). Studies show that electroencephalic activity (EEG) increases in the hemisphere opposite to the direction of the eye movement, and that such activity can actually be stimulated by the movements. Individuals vary in their leftward or rightward eye movement tendencies, with left movers being more susceptible to hypnosis, less scientifically oriented, more involved with feelings and inner experience, more creative, and more prone to psychosomatic symptoms and the psychological defenses of repression and denial.

Expressing Emotions

Rarely is the eye area tested separately from the entire face in judging emotions. Sometimes, however, a glance at the eye area may provide us with a good deal of information about the emotion being expressed. For example, if we see tears we certainly would conclude that the person is emotionally aroused, though without other cues we may not know whether the tears reflect grief, physical pain, joy, anger, or some complex blend of emotions. And as indicated later, downcast or averted eyes are often associated with feelings of sadness, shame, or embarrassment. In one study, fifty-one faces were used as stimuli for judges (Ekman, Friesen, & Tomkins, 1971). The eyes were better than the brows/forehead or lower face for the accurate perception of fear but less accurate for anger and disgust.

The extensive studies of Paul Ekman and Wallace Friesen (1975) have given us valuable insights into facial configurations for six common emotions. The following descriptions pertain to the brow and eye area.

SURPRISE   Brows are raised so they are curved and high. Skin below the brow is stretched. Eyelids are opened; the upper lid is raised, and the lower lid drawn down; and the white of the eye shows above the iris and often below as well.

FEAR   Brows are raised and drawn together. The upper eyelid is raised, exposing the white of the eye, and the lower eyelid is tensed and drawn up.

DISGUST   Disgust is shown primarily in the lower face and in the lower eyelids. Lines show below the lower lid, and the lid is pushed up but not tense. The brow is lowered, lowering the upper lid.

ANGER   The brows are lowered and drawn together. Vertical lines appear between the brows. The lower lid is tensed and may or may not be raised. The upper lid is tense and may or may not be lowered by the action of the brow. The eyes have a hard stare and may have a bulging appearance.

HAPPINESS   Happiness is shown primarily in the lower face and lower eyelids. The lower eyelid shows wrinkles below it and may be raised but is not tense. Crow's-feet wrinkles go outward from the outer corners of the eyes.

SADNESS   The inner corners of the eyebrows are drawn up. The skin below the eyebrow is triangulated, with the inner corner up. The upper-eyelid inner corner is raised.

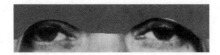

We should also recognize that crucial features of some expressions of emotion are concentrated in the eye area (surprise, fear) and not in others (happiness, disgust). Furthermore, an expression of anger can be ambiguous unless the entire face manifests anger signals. Similarly, in everyday interaction we are likely to see facial blends where the eyes may tell one story and other parts of the face another.

COMMUNICATING the NATURE of the INTERPERSONAL RELATIONSHIP

Gazing and mutual gazing are often indicative of the nature of the relationship between two interactants. Relationships characterized by different status levels may be reflected in the eye patterns. With all other variables held relatively constant, Hearn (1957) found gazing and mutual gazing were moderate with a very high-status addressee, maximized with a moderately high-status addressee, and minimal with a very low-status addressee. Another experiment, with a freshman addressing a senior/freshman pair, adds some support to Hearn's work, since the senior consistently received more eye glances (Efran, 1968). Mehrabian's (1972) work shows less visual contact on the part of both males and females (sitting and standing) with low-status addressees. It may be that if you perceive a low amount of gazing from a higher-status person, it is related to interpersonal needs. The higher-status person may not feel the need to monitor your behavior as closely as you monitor his or hers. (The topic of gaze and dominance is taken up again later in this chapter and also in Chapter 12.)

Consistently related to status or dominance is the *visual dominance ratio*—the ratio of how much a person looks at the other while speaking compared to how much he or she looks at the other while listening. People higher in status or dominance show similar amounts of looking while speaking and listening; people lower in status or dominance do much more looking while listening than while speaking. This pattern can be seen whether status/power is experimentally manipulated or is measured as a trait in the person, for example, a dominant personality (Ellyson, Dovidio & Fehr, 1981; Exline, Ellyson & Long, 1975). Though subtle, the visual dominance ratio does not go unnoticed. When subjects were asked to judge the relative power or potency of individuals engaging in different amounts of eye gaze, they gave higher ratings to individuals engaging in relatively more looking while speaking than to those engaging in relatively more looking while listening.

Several studies testify that we gaze more at people and things perceived as rewarding. Efran and Broughton (1966) found that males gazed more at other males with whom they had participated in a friendly conversation preceding an experiment and who nodded and smiled during the person's presentation. Exline and Eldridge (1967) found that the same verbal communication was decoded as being more favorable when it was associated with more eye gaze than when it was presented with less gazing. Exline and Winters (1965) report that people avoided the eyes of an interviewer and disliked him after he had commented unfavorably on their performance. And mothers of children who have difficult temperaments are reported to look at them less. Generally, we seem to gaze more at people we like, but, as we will see later, we sometimes look long and hard at people we do not like, too. It makes sense to predict that we will look more at those who like us, if for no other reason than to observe signs of approval and friendliness. Mehrabian (1972) asked a group of people to imagine they liked another and to engage this person in conversation. Even in this role-playing situation, increased gazing was associated with increased liking.

The term *making eyes* is frequently used in the context of a courtship relationship. In all likelihood, the maintenance of mutual gaze longer than otherwise expected is a primary way of signaling desire for heightened intimacy. A good example of this occurs in the movie *The Sound of Music,* when Maria and Captain von Trapp are dancing. Their sharing of gaze beyond a purely functional level awakes Maria to the changing nature of their relationship, sparking a crisis and a temporary reversion to her plans to become a nun. Thus, an increased amount of gaze can both signal a wish for more involvement and be an indication that heightened involvement has occurred. Indeed, several sources confirm an increase in eye behavior between two people who are seeking to develop a more intimate relationship. Rubin's (1970) analysis of engaged couples indicated more mutual gaze, and Kleinke et al. (1973) found that longer glances or reciprocated glances were perceived as an indicator of a longer relationship. It may be the amount of gazing increases as relationships become more intimate, but it may also be true that after maintaining an intimate relationship for years, gazing may return to levels below those used during more intense stages of development.

Argyle and Dean (1965) proposed an intimacy equilibrium model. This model suggests that intimacy is a function of the amount of eye gazing, physical proximity, intimacy of topic, and amount of smiling. This model is most applicable to relationships still in the process of establishing themselves. Clearly, there are other variables that might be inserted into the equation, for example, body orientation, the form of address used, tone of voice, facial expression, forward lean, and the like. The central idea behind this proposal is that as one component of the model is changed, one or more of the other components also will change—in the opposite direction. For example, if one person looks too much, the other may look less, move farther away, smile less, talk less about intimate matters, and so on, to reestablish the initial desired level of intimacy. Although this notion has received some support, there are occasions when, rather than compensate for the other's behavior, we seem to imitate it—that is, gazing will elicit gazing. Several scholars have proposed alternatives to the intimacy equilibrium model (Cappella & Greene, 1982; Patterson, 1976). These theories argue that our tendency to exchange the same behavior (reciprocate) or to offset the other's behavior (compensate) is a result of the type and amount of arousal we feel. A general rule suggests that we tend to reciprocate or match the other's nonverbal behavior when their behavior is perceived by us as congruent with our expectations and preferences. When our partner's behavior is not congruent with our expectations and preferences, we are more likely to enact compensatory or offsetting behavior. (See also Chapter 12.)

When the relationship between the two communicators is characterized by negative attitudes, we might see a decrease in gazing and mutual gazing, but not always. In one study, satisfied married couples tended to look at each other less than couples who were dissatisfied with their relationship, but this was particularly true when negative messages were exchanged (Noller, 1980). This increased gazing serves to emphasize the confrontational nature of the relationship while simultaneously providing a way to monitor each other's reactions during critical moments.

As we previously suggested, a hostile or aggressive orientation may trigger the use of staring to produce anxiety in others. A gaze of longer than ten seconds is likely to induce irritation (if not outright discomfort) in many situations. Several studies confirm that mutual gaze is physiologically arousing. We can express our hostility toward another by visually and verbally ignoring him or her, especially when the other person knows we are deliberately doing so. But we can insult another person by looking at that person too much, that is, by not according him or her the public anonymity that each of us requires at times. Sometimes you can elicit aggressive behavior from others just because you happen to look too long at a stranger's behavior. Sometimes threats and aggressive motions can be elicited by human beings who stare too long at monkeys in a zoo! Desmond Morris, in a popular book, *The Naked Ape* (1967), hypothesized that this tendency to produce anxiety in others through staring stems from our biological antecedents as a species—for example, the aggressiveness and hostility signified by the ape's stare. Indeed, a social psychological study found that drivers sped more quickly away from an intersection when stared at by a pedestrian (Ellsworth, Carlsmith, & Henson, 1972).

Thus, if we are looking for a unifying thread to link gazing patterns motivated by positive and negative feelings toward the other, it would seem to be this: *People tend to look at those with whom they are interpersonally involved.* Gazing motivated by hostility or affection *both* suggest an interest and involvement in the interpersonal relationship.

The preceding are several major functions of eye behavior; now we look at a number of conditions that seem to influence the amount of gazing:

1. Distance
2. Physical characteristics
3. Personal and personality characteristics
4. Topics and tasks
5. Cultural background

CONDITIONS INFLUENCING GAZING PATTERNS

DISTANCE

Gazing and mutual gazing seem to increase as the communicating pair increase the distance between themselves. In this case, gazing psychologically reduces the distance between the communicators. There may be less visual contact when the two parties feel too close together, especially if they are not well acquainted. Reducing one's gaze in this situation, then, increases the psychological distance. Several studies by Aiello and colleagues that extended the conversational distances to as much as ten feet found that only for men was there a steady increase in gazing as the distance increased. For women, being beyond six feet from their interactant brought a sharp decline in their gazing (Aiello, 1972, 1977a). Possibly, because women prefer closer interaction distances (see Chapter 5), they may find it difficult to define interactions at relatively great distances as normal and friendly and may react by ceasing their attempts to maintain involvement.

PHYSICAL CHARACTERISTICS

One would think that when interacting with a person who was perceived as disabled or stigmatized in some way (e.g., identified as an epileptic or made to look like an amputee), eye gaze would be less frequent. However, Kleck (1968) found the amount of gazing between normal and disabled interactants did not differ significantly from normal/normal interactions. One possible explanation is that in such situations, the normal person is desperately seeking information that might suggest the proper mode of behavior. This counteracts any tendency to avoid eye gaze. A subsequent study, however, found that when there was a strong possibility that the nondisabled person would have to engage the disabled person in conversation, gaze avoidance increased. When conversation was not expected, people without disabilities tended to stare more at disabled persons than nondisabled (Thompson, 1982).

PERSONAL AND PERSONALITY CHARACTERISTICS

Generally, the relationships between gazing patterns and personality traits are weak. In most cases, the meanings attributed to various gaze patterns seem to reflect the message sender's mood, intent, or disposition. Kleck and Nuessle's (1968) study reflects a number of personality characteristics commonly associated with gaze and averted gaze. A film of people looking at their partners either 15 or 80 percent of the time was shown to observers who were asked to select characteristics that typified the interactants. The 15 percent lookers were labeled as cold, pessimistic, cautious, defensive, immature, evasive, submissive, indifferent, and sensitive; the 80 percent lookers were seen as friendly, self-confident, natural, mature, and sincere. Observers tended to associate anxiety with too little gazing and dominance with too much gazing. Gazing may be associated with efforts to *establish* dominance or to maintain it when someone seems to challenge one's authority. Further, it does seem that dominant persons are more apt to control the other's gazing patterns in situations of reprimand—for example, "You look straight ahead while I'm talking to you, soldier!" or "Look at me when I talk to you!" Dependent individuals, on the other hand, seem to use eye behavior not only to communicate more positive attitudes but also to elicit such attitudes when they are not forthcoming (Exline & Messick, 1967). Dependent males made more eye gaze with a listener who provided them with few, as opposed to many, social reinforcers, whereas dominant males decreased their eye gaze with less reinforcing listeners.

A study of attributions found that interviewees were rated by observers as having increasingly lower self-esteem as their gazing decreased (Droney & Brooks, 1993). Variations in gazing at another person during positive and negative feedback may indeed be related to one's self-esteem. When receiving favorable feedback on their performance, people with high self-esteem tended to gaze more; negative feedback reduced their gazing behavior. But the pattern was reversed for those with low self-esteem. These people gazed more during feedback that criticized their performance than during feedback that compli-mented it (Greene & Frandsen, 1979).

Extraverts seem to gaze more frequently than introverts and for longer periods of time, especially while talking (Mobbs, 1968). A related trait, shyness, is also related to gazing behavior, but the relation can depend on whether the shy person is of a sociable or unsociable type. In a laboratory experiment, Cheek and Buss (1981) classified college students on both a shyness scale and a sociability scale and observed them in a getting-acquainted session. Though shy individuals engaged in less gaze overall (also more self-touching and less talking), this effect was mainly attributable to those who were both shy (e.g., "I am socially somewhat awkward;" "I feel inhibited in social situa-tions") *and* sociable (e.g., "I like to be with people;" "I prefer working with others rather than alone"). Thus, the behavioral deficits associated with shy-ness appear mainly in shy people who crave social interaction; shy people who would just as soon be left alone behaved much like people who were not shy.

Social anxiety, another related concept, is also associated with less gaze; in one study in which socially anxious people were asked to present a viewpoint to two confederates, the socially anxious were especially likely to reduce gaze toward a confederate with opposing views compared to one with agreeing views (Farabee, Holcom, Ramsey, & Cole, 1993).

A number of research studies suggest special gazing patterns (usually less gaze) in depressed, autistic, and schizophrenic persons. For example, depressed patients are characterized by nonspecific gaze patterns and looking-down behaviors which revert to more normal patterns with clinical improve-ment (Schelde & Hertz, 1994). Clinicians and researchers on autism, in particular, cite gaze aversion as a characteristic of these patients (Adrien, Lenoir, Martineau, Perrot, Hameury, Larmande, & Sauvage, 1993; Hutt & Ounsted, 1966; Walters, Barrett, & Feinstein, 1990). And paranoid schizophrenic patients show an interesting deficit in judging another's gaze direction: They seem to be more likely than comparison subjects to perceive another as looking at them when the person is actually looking away (Rosse, Kendrick, Wyatt, Issac, & Deutsch, 1994).

Finally, males and females differ in the amount of gaze shown. Females seem to look more than males on almost all measures of gaze frequency, duration, and reciprocity—and such differences have been observed in infancy and early childhood as well as in adulthood (Hall, 1984). Research also shows that women receive more gaze than males do. This pattern, combined with the greater gazing tendency of females, means that when women interact with each other, the overall level of gaze is much higher than when males interact with each other. Gaze levels between males and females in mixed-sex interaction are intermediate, suggesting that each sex feels free to conform somewhat to the gazing norms of the opposite sex (Hall, 1984).

Interpretations of sex differences in gaze have concentrated on the competing themes of affiliation-warmth versus dominance-power. When one is interpreting overall amounts of gaze, it is indeed difficult to choose between these interpretations since gaze varies with both affiliation-warmth and dominance-power, and the sexes differ on both. However, the visual dominance ratio described earlier is much less ambiguous than overall gazing is; the visual dominance ratio has been linked to differences in status, power, dominance, or expertise in a variety of studies, but to our knowledge no one has suggested that it varies with the warmth or friendliness of the interaction. Dovidio and his colleagues performed two experiments involving mixed-sex pairs of interactants in which the relative status of the interactants was experimentally manipulated. When there was a status difference between the interactants, the party having the higher status (whether male or female) had a higher visual dominance ratio, consistent with research already described. However, when status was *not* manipulated, men behaved in the visually dominant way that high-status communicators display, while women showed the less visually dominant behavior typical of people in low-status roles (Dovidio, Ellyson, Keating, Heltman, & Brown, 1988).

Most of the results of these efforts to link gazing patterns to personality and/or personal characteristics may be accounted for by

1. *The existing need for affiliation, involvement, or inclusion:* Those with high affiliative needs will tend to glance and return glances more often or for longer durations.
2. *Other looking motivations:* Persons who are highly manipulative and/or need much information to control their environment (high Machiavellian types) predictably will look more.
3. *The need to avoid unduly high levels of arousal caused by gazing (especially mutual gazing):* Autistic children, for instance, are thought to have a high level of arousal and will avoid gaze in order to keep arousal down. The reduced gazing of shy/sociable people may also be related to the control of arousal.

4. A feeling of shame or low self-esteem: The lower level of gaze some-times seen in adolescents may reflect the well-known uncertainties about ourselves that most experience during this period.

TOPICS AND TASKS

Common sense suggests that the topic being discussed and/or the task at hand will affect the amount of gazing. We would expect, for instance, more gazing when the topic is a happy rather than sad one for the communicators. And we would expect interactants who have not developed an intimate relation-ship to gaze less when discussing intimate topics, assuming other factors like the need for affiliation or inclusion are controlled. People also may gaze differently during competitive tasks and cooperative tasks. In one study, coop-erators seemed to use longer gazes and mutual gazes to signal trust, liking, and honesty. Gazes also were used to aid coordination. Competitors, however, seemed to use frequent, short gazes to assess their partner's intentions while not giving away their own (Foddy, 1978).

Discussing topics that cause embarrassment, humiliation, shame, guilt, or sorrow might be expected to engender less gazing at the other person. Looking away during such situations may be an effort to insulate oneself against threats, arguments, information, or even affection from the other party. When subjects were caused to fail at an anagram task and were publicly criticized for their work, they not only reported feeling embarrassed, but also the amount of gaze slipped from 30 percent to 18 percent (Modigliani, 1971). When people want to hide some aspect of their inner feelings, they may try to avoid visual contact—for example, in situations where you are trying to deceive your partner. Exline and his colleagues (1970) designed a fascinating (though possibly ethically suspect) experiment. A paid confederate induced subjects to cheat on an experimental task. Later the experimenter interviewed the subjects with the supposed purpose of understanding and evaluating their problem-solving methods. With some subjects, the experimenter grew increasingly suspicious during the interview and finally accused the student subject of cheating and demanded an explanation. Subjects included both those who scored high and low on tests of Machiavellianism. (Machiavellianism is often associated with those who use cunning and shrewdness to achieve a goal without much regard for how unscrupulous the means might be.) Figure 10-3 shows that the high "Machs" seemed to use gazing to present the appearance of innocence after being accused of cheating; low Machs, on the other hand, continued to look away.

The content of discussion may also influence gaze. In the medical study described earlier, physicians' average levels of gaze at patients were much greater when the patients were talking about social and emotional material than when talking about more physiological problems, and also when the physicians were verbally conveying empathy or psychosocial interest; patients

Figure 10-3

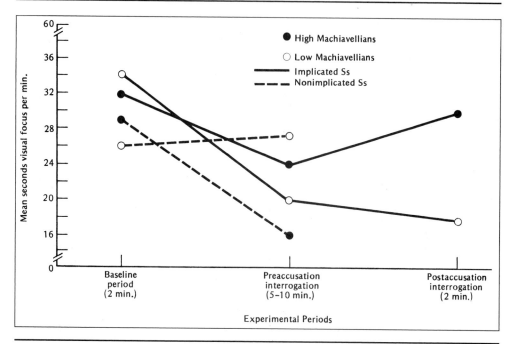

Gazing, Machiavellianism, and deception.

were more satisfied with their visits when the physicians gazed more (Bensing et al., 1995).

Persuasion is another communicative task we often undertake. We know that gazing can add emphasis to a particular point, but Mehrabian and Williams (1969) report that a person trying to be persuasive will generally tend to gaze more. We do not know the actual relationship between attitude change in a listener and speaker gazing, but listeners do seem to judge speakers who gaze more as being more persuasive, truthful, sincere, and credible. Beebe (1974) manipulated the amount of gaze in an informative speech of about seven minutes. Gaze primarily seemed to affect audience ratings on whether the speaker was considered skilled, informed, experienced, honest, friendly, and kind. Similarly, Wills (1961) found that speakers rated as sincere had an average of 63.4 percent eye gaze, while those rated insincere had an average of 20.8 percent.

The application of such findings in a simulated courtroom situation found that witnesses who testified by looking slightly downward rather than directly at their questioner were judged less credible—and the defendant for whom they were testifying was more likely to be judged guilty (Hemsley & Doob, 1978). In another important study, actors reenacted the actual verbal performances of surgery students during oral examinations, using a nonverbal style marked either by direct gaze and a moderate speech rate or by indirect gaze and a slower speech rate. Surgery faculty from forty-six medical institutions who judged the competency of these reenacted oral examinations gave significantly higher scores to the actor who used direct gaze and a moderate rate of speech, even though the answers were the same as in the other conditions (Rowland-Morin, Burchard, Garb, & Coe, 1991). It is clear from these studies that in real-life situations the presence or absence of gaze can have a profound impact, yet an impact that *can* be highly unfair or damaging. One would not want to be the honest witness, the sincere speaker, or the competent medical student who had the misfortune to gaze less than expected.

CULTURAL BACKGROUND

Eye behavior also varies according to the environment in which one learns social norms. Sometimes gazing patterns show differences between "contact" (for example, Arab) and "noncontact" (for example, northern European) cultures. Sometimes the differences may be in duration of gaze rather than frequency (for example, it has been said that Swedes looks less frequently, but for longer periods, than the English). Sometimes *where* we analyze gaze behavior reveals differences among cultures (for example, looking more in public places). Sometimes there are rules regarding *whom* you should or should not look at (for example, a person with a disability). One report says that in Kenya conversations between some men and their mothers-in-law are conducted by each party turning his or her back to the other. We may find different patterns within our own culture. Whites are reported to gaze significantly more at their partners than blacks do, and this difference may be especially pronounced with authority figures—a tendency that could create cross-racial misunderstanding. Some research shows blacks and whites changing gazing patterns in transracial encounters, but the research is not consistent (Fehr & Exline, 1987; Halberstadt, 1985). Such findings underscore the variety of factors that may influence gaze in each encounter, and one's cultural inclinations may be suppressed, neutralized, or emphasized by other forces attendant to the situation. Although cultural experiences may alter gazing patterns, we may also find that perceived extremes in gaze elicit similar meanings in different cultures. For instance, too much gazing may signal anger, threat, or disrespect; too little may signal dishonesty, inattention, or shyness.

PUPIL DILATION and CONSTRICTION

Most of us are aware that the pupils of the eyes constrict in the presence of bright light and dilate in the absence of light. In the early 1960s, however,

Eckhard Hess and his colleagues at the University of Chicago renewed the interest of the scientific community in pupil dilation and constriction as a possible indicator of mental and emotional states. At one point, dozens of universities were conducting pupil dilation research, and advertising agencies were testing magazine ads, package designs, television pilot films, and television commercials using the results of Hess's pupil dilation measures.

In an early experiment, Hess and Polt (1960) presented five pictures to male and female subjects. Males' pupils dilated more than females' pupils in response to pictures of female nudes; females' pupils dilated more than males' to pictures of a partially clothed "muscle man," a woman with a baby, and a baby alone. Thus, it seemed pupil dilation and interest value of the stimulus were related. Hess, Seltzer, and Schlien (1965) found that pupils of male homosexuals dilated more when viewing pictures of males than the pupils of heterosexual males, whose pupils dilated in response to female pictures. Studies since then have had similar results. Barlow (1969) preselected subjects who actively supported either liberal or conservative candidates. He photographed the pupil of the right eye while they watched slides of political figures. There seemed to be a perfect correlation between pupillary response and political attitudes, with dilation occurring for photographs of liked candidates and constriction occurring for disliked candidates.

Several of Hess's studies suggested that pupil response might be an index of attitudes; pupils will dilate for positive attitudes and constrict for negative ones. His oft-cited finding supporting this theory was the constriction of the pupils of subjects who viewed pictures of concentration camp victims, dead soldiers, and a murdered gangster. In Hess's (1975a) words: "The changes in emotions and mental activity revealed by changes in pupil size are clearly associated with changes in attitude." Hess (1975b; Hess & Petrovich, 1987) continued to advocate this position, although he acknowledged the need for more research on the pupil's reaction to negative stimuli. He cited a study that showed photographs like those in Figure 10-4, where the woman's pupils were retouched to appear large in one photo and smaller in the other. Although male subjects did not tend to pick either picture as consistently more friendly or attractive, they tended to associate positive attributes with the woman who had larger pupils and negative attributes with the one with smaller pupils.

Hensley (1990) attempted to replicate Hess's work and obtained the responses of over 500 students to photographs of models with constricted and dilated pupils used by Hess. The students evaluated the photos on twenty-two characteristics, including attractiveness, social skills, persuasiveness, friendliness, and outgoingness. There were no statistically significant differences between photos of constricted and those of dilated pupils on any of the twenty-two characteristics—raising doubts about the strength of Hess's claim.

Woodmansee (1970) tried to improve on Hess's methodology and measuring instruments and found no support for pupil dilation and constriction as an index of attitudes toward blacks. Hays and Plax (1971) found their subjects' pupils dilated when they received supportive statements ("I am very much interested in your speech"), but constriction did not follow from nonsupportive

Figure 10–4

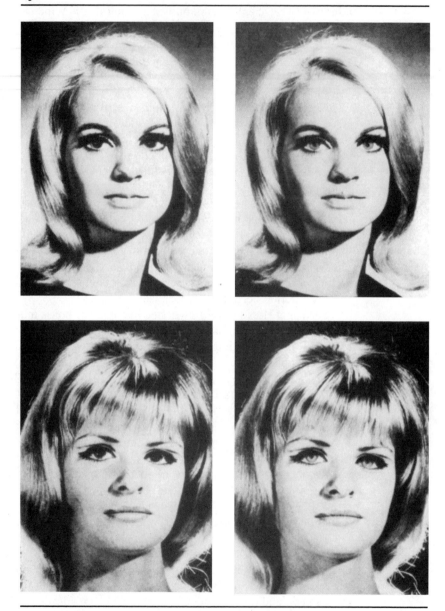

Some of Hess's stimulus photos with pupil dilation varied.

statements ("I disagree completely with the development of your speech"). Some research has found dilation from positive *and* negative feedback (Janisse & Peavler, 1974). Other research has found the reflex dilation reaction of the pupil to be associated with arousal, attentiveness, interest, and perceptual orientation but not to be an attitudinal index. Thus, there is a need for research to resolve the question of whether pupils can be used as a *bi*directional indicator of attitudes.

Even advertising agencies seem to have lost interest in pupils as an involuntary measure of viewer attitudes. Some of the potential problems facing ad testing include

1. The viewer's pupil response may be affected by light and dark colors on the ad itself.
2. It is difficult to know what the viewer is focusing on. In one ad for french fries, viewers' pupils dilated, but subsequent analysis suggested that dilation may have been due to a steak that was also pictured in the ad!
3. One advertising executive, commenting on the viability of a theory of attitudes and pupil dilation for his products, asked: "How excited can a person get about a laundry detergent?"
4. In some experiments it was noted that the pupils did not immediately return to their predilated state after seeing an arousing picture. Hence, the next stimuli were viewed with still partially dilated eyes.
5. Many stimuli can cause variations in pupil dilation. Tightening muscles anywhere on the body, anticipation of a loud noise, drugs, eyelid closure, and mental effort will alter pupil size.

People also have varying absolute pupil sizes. Children, for instance, have larger absolute pupil sizes than adults. With so many sources of variation, it is difficult to state positively that the dilation is exclusively due to an attitudinal orientation.

While pupil dilation reveals emotional arousal, it is still not clear how much people notice it or how close they have to be to see it. However, at least one study suggests that pupil dilation may be influential in selecting interaction partners or even dates. Stass and Willis (1967) dealt with live subjects rather than pictures. Subjects were told they would be in an experiment and they had to choose a partner who was trustworthy, pleasant, and easy to talk to on an intimate basis. They were taken to a room where two other persons waited. These two persons had previously been independently rated as about the same in general attractiveness. Eye gazing and pupil dilation (through use of a drug) were varied. Once the naive subject left the waiting room, the experimenter asked him or her to choose one of the persons and give reasons for the choice. Gazing was an overwhelming factor in choice making, but pupil dilation also was a factor. A few people mentioned visual contact as a reason for their choice, but none mentioned pupil dilation. Thus, for both women and men, pupil dilation seems to be an influential attraction device for interaction. Perhaps this is not a revelation to those many women who, since the Middle Ages, have put belladonna in their eyes to increase attractiveness—or to those expert romancers who suggest a dimly lighted meeting place.

SUMMARY

Although researchers have examined the size, color, and position of the eyes, eye rings, eyebrows, and eyespots, our major concern was with gaze and mutual gaze. We said that gazing serves many interpersonal functions:

1. Regulating the flow of communication—opening the channels of communication and assisting in the turn-taking process
2. Monitoring feedback
3. Expressing emotions
4. Communicating the nature of the interpersonal relationship, for example, variations due to status, liking, and disliking

We also outlined a number of factors that influence the amount and duration of gaze in human relationships, for example, distance, physical characteristics, personal and personality characteristics, topics and tasks, and cultural background. From this review, we would predict *more* gazing when

You are male and are physically distant from your partner.

You are discussing easy, impersonal topics.

There is nothing else to look at.

You are interested in your partner's reactions—interpersonally involved.

You like or love your partner.

You are trying to dominate or influence your partner.

You are from a culture that emphasizes visual contact in interaction.

You are an extravert and are not shy.

You have high affiliative or inclusion needs.

You are dependent on your partner (and the partner has been unresponsive).

You are listening rather than talking.

You are female.

We would predict *less* gazing when

You are physically close to your partner.

You are discussing difficult, intimate topics.

You have other relevant objects, people, or backgrounds to look at.

You are not interested in your partner's reactions.

You are talking rather than listening.

You dislike your partner.

You are from a culture that imposes sanctions on visual contact during interaction.

You are an introvert or shy.

You are low on affiliative or inclusion needs.

You have a mental disorder like autism or schizophrenia.

You are embarrassed, ashamed, sorrowful, sad, submissive, or trying to hide something.

The preceding lists are not exhaustive. Indeed, some of them are dependent on certain important qualifications. For example, you may have less gaze and mutual gaze when you are physically close—*unless* you happen to love your partner and want to get as close, physically and psychologically, as you can! The lists are not intended to replace the qualified principles that appear in the chapter.

The last part of this chapter dealt with pupil dilation and constriction. We reviewed the findings of Eckhard Hess and others who have pursued his ideas. At this time, pupil dilation has been associated with arousal, attentiveness, mental effort, interest, and perceptual orientation. Aside from Hess's own work, however, little support has been found for the idea that pupils reflect attitudinal states. Dilation occurs under conditions that seem to represent positive attitudes, but there is less or no support for the belief that constriction of pupils is associated with negative attitudes toward objects and people. Finally, we examined one study that suggests that pupil dilation may be a factor in our desire to interact with another person.

QUESTIONS for DISCUSSION

1. How do you use gaze in your everyday life? When are you more likely to gaze at someone for a long period of time? for a very short period of time?

2. Watch yourself in a mirror, and try to convey these emotions using only your eyes and eyebrows: fear, anger, disgust, surprise, happiness, sadness. How do your eye positions and movements change? How similar are your expressions to those you see on other people's faces daily?

3. Try to recall a time when you had a conversation with someone with a physical disability—someone on crutches or in a wheelchair, for example. Did your gazing patterns change when interacting with this person, as opposed to an able-bodied person? How?

4. People of higher status are sometimes said to gaze more and for longer periods than people of lower status. What do you think of this? Think of examples that would and would not be supportive.

REFERENCES and SELECTED BIBLIOGRAPHY

Adrien, J. L., Lenoir, P., Martineau, J., Perrot, A., Hameury, L., Larmande, C., & Sauvage, D. (1993). Blind ratings of early symptoms of autism based upon family home movies. *Journal of the American Academy of Child and Adolescent Psychiatry, 32,* 617–26.

Aiello, J. R. (1972). A test of equilibrium theory: Visual interaction in relation to orientation, distance and sex of interaction. *Psychonomic Science, 27,* 335–36.

Aiello, J. R. (1977a). Visual interaction at extended distances. *Personality and Social Psychology Bulletin, 3,* 83–86.

Aiello, J. R. (1977b). A further look at equilibrium theory: Visual interaction as a function of interpersonal distance. *Environmental Psychology and Nonverbal Behavior, 1,* 122–40.

Argyle, M., & Cook, M. (1976). *Gaze and mutual gaze.* Cambridge: Cambridge University Press.

Argyle, M., & Dean, J. (1965). Eye contact, distance and affiliation. *Sociometry, 28,* 289–304.

Argyle, M., & Ingham, R. (1972). Gaze, mutual gaze and proximity. *Semiotica, 6,* 32–49.

Argyle, M., Ingham, R., Alkema, F., & McCallin, M. (1973). The different functions of gaze. *Semiotica, 7,* 19–32.

Argyle, M., Lalljee, M., & Cook, M. (1968). The effects of visibility on interaction in a dyad. *Human Relations, 21,* 3–17.

Argyle, M., Lefebvre, L., & Cook, M. (1974). The meaning of five patterns of gaze. *European Journal of Social Psychology, 4,* 125–36.

Ashear, V., & Snortum, J. R. (1971). Eye contact in children as a function of age, sex, social and intellective variables. *Developmental Psychology, 4,* 479.

Bakan, P. (1971). The eyes have it. *Psychology Today, 4,* 64–67, 96.

Bakan, P., & Strayer, F. F. (1973). On reliability of conjugate lateral eye movements. *Perceptual and Motor Skills, 36,* 429–30.

Barlow, J. D. (1969). Pupillary size as an index of preference in political candidates. *Perceptual and Motor Skills, 28,* 587–90.

Beattie, G. W. (1978a). Sequential temporal patterns of speech and gaze in dialogue. *Semiotica, 23,* 27–52.

Beattie, G. W. (1978b). Floor apportionment and gaze in conversational dyads. *British Journal of Social and Clinical Psychology, 17,* 7–15.

Beebe, S. A. (1974). Eye contact: A nonverbal determinant of speaker credibility. *Speech Teacher, 23,* 21–25.

Bensing, J. M., Kerssens, J. J., & van der Pasch, M. (1995). Patient-directed gaze as a tool for discovering and handling psychosocial problems in general practice. *Journal of Nonverbal Behavior, 19,* 223–42.

Boyle, E. A., Anderson, A. H., & Newlands, A. (1994). The effects of visibility on dialogue and performance in a cooperative problem solving task. *Language and Speech, 37,* 1–20.

Burgoon, J. K., Coker, D. A., & Coker, R. A. (1986). Communicative effects of gaze behavior: A test of two contrasting explanations. *Human Communication Research, 12,* 495–524.

Burgoon, J. K., Manusov, V., Mineo, P., & Hale, J. L. (1985). Effects of gaze on hiring, credibility, attraction and relational message interpretation. *Journal of Nonverbal Behavior, 9,* 133–46.

Burkhardt, J. C., Weider-Hatfield, D., & Hocking, J. E. (1985). Eye contact contrast effects in the employment interview. *Communication Research Reports, 2,* 5–10.

Cappella, J. N., & Greene, J. O. (1982). A discrepancy-arousal explanation of mutual influence in expressive behavior of adult-adult and infant-adult interaction. *Communication Monographs, 49,* 89–114.

Cary, M. S. (1978a). The role of gaze in the initiation of conversation. *Social Psychology, 41,* 269–71.

Cary, M. S. (1978b). Does civil inattention exist in pedestrian passing? *Journal of Personality and Social Psychology, 36,* 1185–93.

Cheek, J. M., & Buss, A. H. (1981). Shyness and sociability. *Journal of Personality and Social Psychology, 41,* 330–39.

Cook, M., & Lalljee, M. G. (1973). Verbal substitutes for visual signals in interaction. *Semiotica, 6,* 212–21.

Cook, M., & Smith, J. M. C. (1975). The role of gaze in impression formation. *British Journal of Social and Clinical Psychology, 14,* 19–25.

Coss, R. G. (1974). Reflections on the evil eye. *Human Behavior, 3,* 16–22.

Davis, L. K. (1978). Camera eye-contact by the candidates in the Presidential debates of 1976. *Journalism Quarterly, 55,* 431–37, 455.

Dovidio, J. F., Ellyson, S. L., Keating, C. F., Heltman, K., & Brown, C. E. (1988). The relationship of social power to visual displays of dominance between men and women. *Journal of Personality and Social Psychology, 54,* 233–42.

Droney, J. M., & Brooks, C. I. (1993). Attributions of self-esteem as a function of duration of eye contact. *Journal of Social Psychology, 133,* 715–22.

Efran, J., & Broughton, A. (1966). Effect of expectancies for social approval on visual behavior. *Journal of Personality and Social Psychology, 4,* 103–7.

Efran, J. S. (1968). Looking for approval: Effects on visual behavior of approbation from persons differing in importance. *Journal of Personality and Social Psychology, 10,* 21–25.

Ehrlichman, H., & Weinberger, A. (1978). Lateral eye movements and hemispheric asymmetry: A critical review. *Psychological Bulletin, 85,* 1080–1101.

Ellsworth, P. C., & Carlsmith, J. M. (1968). Effects of eye contact and verbal content on affective response to a dyadic interaction. *Journal of Personality and Social Psychology, 10,* 15–20.

Ellsworth, P. C., & Carlsmith, J. M. (1973). Eye contact and gaze aversion in an aggressive encounter. *Journal of Personality and Social Psychology, 28,* 280–92.

Ellsworth, P. C., Carlsmith, J. M., & Henson, A. (1972). The stare as a stimulus to flight in human subjects: A series of field experiments. *Journal of Personality and Social Psychology, 21,* 302–11.

Ellsworth, P. C., & Langer, E. J. (1976). Staring and approach: An interpretation of the stare as a nonspecific activator. *Journal of Personality and Social Psychology, 33,* 117–22.

Ellsworth, P. C., & Ludwig, L. M. (1972). Visual behavior in social interaction. *Journal of Communication, 22,* 375–403.

Ellyson, S. L., Dovidio, J. F., & Fehr, B. J. (1981). Visual behavior and dominance in women and men. In C. Mayo & N. M. Henley (Eds.), *Gender and nonverbal behavior.* New York: Springer-Verlag.

Ekman, P., & Friesen, W. V. (1975). *Unmasking the face.* Eaglewood Cliffs, NJ: Prentice-Hall.

Ekman, P., Friesen, W. V., & Tomkins, S. S. (1971). Facial Affect Scoring Technique: A first validity study. *Semiotica, 3,* 37–58.

Exline, R. (1963). Explorations in the process of person perception: Visual interaction in relation to competition, sex and need for affiliation. *Journal of Personality, 31,* 1–20.

Exline, R., & Eldridge, C. (1967). *Effects of two patterns of a speaker's visual behavior upon the perception of the authenticity of his verbal message.* (Paper presented at a meeting of the Eastern Psychological Association, Boston.)

Exline, R., Gray, D., & Schuette, D. (1965). Visual behavior in a dyad as affected by interview content and sex of respondent. *Journal of Personality and Social Psychology, 1,* 201–9.

Exline, R., Thibaut, J., Hickey, C. B., & Gumpert, P. (1970). Visual interaction in relation to Machiavellianism and an unethical act. In P. Christie & F. Geis (Eds.), *Studies in Machiavellianism.* New York: Academic Press.

Exline, R., & Winters, L. (1965). Affective relations and mutual glances in dyads. In S. Tomkins & C. Izard (Eds.), *Affect, cognition and personality.* New York: Springer.

Exline, R. V., Ellyson, S. L., & Long, B. (1975). Visual behavior as an aspect of power role relationships. In P. Pliner, L. Krames, & T. Alloway (Eds.), *Advances in the study of communication and affect* (Vol. 2.) New York: Plenum.

Exline, R. V., & Fehr, B. J. (1978). Applications of semiosis to the study of visual interaction. In A. W. Siegman & S. Feldstein (Eds.), *Nonverbal behavior and communication.* Hillsdale, NJ: Erlbaum.

Exline, R. V., & Fehr, B. J. (1982). The assessment of gaze and mutual gaze. In K. R. Scherer & P. Ekman (Eds.), *Handbook of methods in nonverbal behavior research.* New York: Cambridge University Press.

Exline, R. V., & Messick, D. (1967). The effects of dependency and social reinforcement upon visual behavior during an interview. *British Journal of Social and Clinical Psychology, 6,* 256–66.

Farabee, D. J., Holcom, M. L., Ramsey, S. L., & Cole, S. G. (1993). Social anxiety and speaker gaze in a persuasive atmosphere. *Journal of Research in Personality, 27,* 365–76.

Fehr, B. J., & Exline, R. V. (1987). Social visual interaction: A conceptual and literature review. In A. W. Siegman & S. Feldstein (Eds.), *Nonverbal behavior and communication* (2d ed.). Hillsdale, NJ: Erlbaum.

Foddy, M. (1978). Patterns of gaze in cooperative and competitive negotiation. *Human Relations, 31,* 925–38.

Fugita, S. S. (1974). Effects of anxiety and approval on visual interaction. *Journal of Personality and Social Psychology, 29,* 586–92.

Galin, D., & Ornstein, R. (1974). Individual differences in cognitive style: I. Reflective eye movements. *Neuropsychologia, 12,* 367–76.

Gibson, J. J., & Pick, A. D. (1963). Perception of another person's looking behavior. *American Journal of Psychology, 76,* 386–94.

Goldberg, G. N., Kiesler, C. A., & Collins, B. E. (1969). Visual behavior and face-to-face distance during interaction. *Sociometry, 32,* 43–53.

Goldwater, B. C. (1972). Psychological significance of pupillary movements. *Psychological Bulletin, 77,* 340–55.

Greenacre, P. (1926). The eye motif in delusion and fantasy. *American Journal of Psychiatry, 5,* 553.

Greene, J. O., & Frandsen, K. D. (1979). Need-fulfillment and consistency theory: Relationships between self-esteem and eye contact. *Western Journal of Speech Communication, 43,* 123–33.

Halberstadt, A. G. (1985). Race, socioeconomic status, and nonverbal behavior. In A. W. Siegman & S. Feldstein (Eds.), *Multichannel integrations of nonverbal behavior.* Hillsdale, NJ: Erlbaum.

Hall, J. A. (1984). *Nonverbal sex differences: Communication accuracy and expressive style.* Baltimore: Johns Hopkins University Press.

Harper, R. G., Wiens, A. N., & Matarazzo, J. D. (1978). The eye and visual behavior. In R. G. Harper, A. N. Wiens, & J. N. Matarazzo (Eds.), *Nonverbal communication: The state of the art.* New York: Wiley.

Hart, H. H. (1949). The eye in symbol and symptom. *Psychoanalytic Review, 36,* 1–21.

Hatfield, E., Cacioppo, J. T., & Rapson, R. L. (1994). *Emotional contagion.* New York: Cambridge University Press.

Hays, E. R., & Plax, T. G. (1971). Pupillary response to supportive and aversive verbal messages. *Speech Monographs, 38,* 316–20.

Hearn, G. (1957). Leadership and the spatial factor in small groups. *Journal of Abnormal and Social Psychology, 54,* 269–72.

Hemsley, G. D., & Doob, A. N. (1978). The effect of looking behavior on perceptions of a communicator's credibility. *Journal of Applied Psychology, 8,* 136–44.

Henley, N. M. (1977). *Body politics: Power, sex, and nonverbal communication.* Englewood Cliffs, NJ: Prentice-Hall.

Hensley, W. E. (1990). Pupillary dilation revisited: The constriction of a nonverbal cue. *Journal of Social Behavior and Personality, 5,* 97–104.

Hess, E. H. (1965). Attitudes and pupil size. *Scientific American, 212,* 46–54.

Hess, E. H. (1968). Pupillometric assessment. In J. M. Shlien (Ed.), *Research in psychotherapy.* Washington, DC: American Psychological Association.

Hess, E. H. (1975a). The role of pupil size in communication. *Scientific American, 233,* 110–12, 116–19.

Hess, E. H. (1975b). *The tell-tale eye.* New York: Van Nostrand Reinhold.

Hess, E. H., & Petrovich, S. B. (1987). Pupillary behavior in communication. In A. W.

Siegman & S. Feldstein (Eds.), *Nonverbal behavior and communication* (2d ed.). Hillsdale, NJ: Erlbaum.

Hess, E. H., & Polt, J. M. (1960). Pupil size as related to interest value of visual stimuli. *Science, 132,* 349–50.

Hess, E. H., & Polt, J. M. (1964). Pupil size in relation to mental activity during simple problem solving. *Science, 143,* 1190–92.

Hess, E. H., Seltzer, A. L., & Shlien, J. M. (1965). Pupil response of hetero- and homosexual males to pictures of men and women: A pilot study. *Journal of Abnormal Psychology, 70,* 165–68.

Hindmarch, I. (1973). Eye-spots and pupil dilation in non-verbal communication. In M. von Cranach & I. Vine (Eds.), *Social communication and movement.* New York: Academic Press.

Hobson, G. N., Strongman, K. T., Bull, D., & Craig, G. (1973). Anxiety and gaze aversion in dyadic encounters. *British Journal of Social and Clinical Psychology, 12,* 122–29.

Hutt, C., & Ounsted, C. (1966). The biological significance of gaze aversion with particular reference to the syndrome of infantile autism. *Behavioral Science, 11,* 346–56.

Jaffe, J., Stern, D. N., & Peery, C. (1973). 'Conversational' coupling of gaze behavior in prelinguistic human development. *Journal of Psycholinguistic Research, 2,* 321–29.

Janisse, M. P. (1973). Pupil size and affect: A critical review of the literature since 1960. *Canadian Psychologist, 14,* 311–29.

Janisse, M. P., & Peavler, W. S. (1974). Pupillary research today: Emotion in the eye. *Psychology Today, 7,* 60–63.

Jellison, J. M., & Ickes, W. J. (1974). The power of the glance: Desire to see and be seen in cooperative and competitive situations. *Journal of Experimental Social Psychology, 10,* 444–50.

Kalma, A. (1992). Gazing in triads: A powerful signal in floor apportionment. *British Journal of Social Psychology, 31,* 21–39.

Kanfer, F. H. (1960). Verbal rate, eyeblink, and content in structured psychiatric interviews. *Journal of Abnormal and Social Psychology, 61,* 341–47.

Kendon, A. (1967). Some functions of gaze-direction in social interaction. *Acta Psychologica, 26,* 22–63.

Kendon, A. (1990). *Conducting interaction: Patterns of behavior in focused encounters.* Cambridge, UK: Cambridge University Press.

Kendon, A., & Cook, M. (1969). The consistency of gaze patterns in social interaction. *British Journal of Psychology, 60,* 481–94.

Kleck, R. (1968). Physical stigma and nonverbal cues emitted in face-to-face interaction. *Human Relations, 21,* 19–28.

Kleck, R. E., & Nuessle, W. (1968). Congruence between the indicative and communicative functions of eye-contact in interpersonal relations. *British Journal of Social and Clinical Psychology, 7,* 241–46.

Kleinke, C. L. (1986). Gaze and eye contact: A research review. *Psychological Bulletin, 100,* 78–100.

Kleinke, C. L., Bustos, A. A., Meeker, F. B., & Staneski, R. A. (1973). Effects of self-attributed and other-attributed gaze in interpersonal evaluations between males and females. *Journal of Experimental Social Psychology, 9,* 154–63.

LaFrance, M., & Mayo, C. (1976). Racial differences in gaze behavior during conversations: Two systematic observational studies. *Journal of Personality and Social Psychology, 33,* 547–52.

Lefebvre, L. (1975). Encoding and decoding of ingratiation in modes of smiling and gaze. *British Journal of Social and Clinical Psychology, 14,* 33–42.

Levine, M. H., & Sutton-Smith, B. (1973). Effects of age, sex, and task on visual behavior during dyadic interaction. *Developmental Psychology, 9,* 400–405.

Libby, W. L. (1970). Eye contact and direction of looking as stable individual differences. *Journal of Experimental Research in Personality, 4,* 303–12.

Libby, W. L., & Yaklevich, D. (1973). Personality determinants of eye contact and direction of gaze aversion. *Journal of Personality and Social Psychology, 27,* 197–206.

McAndrew, F. T., & Warner, J. E. (1986). Arousal seeking and the maintenance of mutual gaze in same and mixed sex dyads. *Journal of Nonverbal Behavior, 10,* 168–72.

McCauley, C., Coleman, G., & DeFusco, P. (1978). Commuters' eye contact with strangers in city and suburban train stations: Evidence of short-term adaptation to interpersonal overload in the city. *Environmental Psychology and Nonverbal Behavior, 2,* 215–25.

Mehrabian, A. (1972). *Nonverbal communication.* Chicago: Aldine/Atherton.

Mehrabian, A., & Williams, M. (1969). Nonverbal concomitants of perceived and intended persuasiveness. *Journal of Personality and Social Psychology, 13,* 37–58.

Mobbs, N. (1968). Eye contact in relation to social introversion/extroversion. *British Journal of Social and Clinical Psychology, 7,* 305–6.

Modigliani, A. (1971). Embarrassment, facework and eye-contact: Testing a theory of embarrassment. *Journal of Personality and Social Psychology, 17,* 15–24.

Morris, D. (1967). *The naked ape.* London: Cape.

Mulac, A., Studley, L. B., Wiemann, J. M., & Bradac, J. J. (1987). Male/female gaze in same-sex and mixed-sex dyads: Gender-linked differences and mutual influence. *Human Communication Research, 13,* 323–43.

Nevill, D. (1974). Experimental manipulation of dependency motivation and its effects on eye contact and measures of field dependency. *Journal of Personality and Social Psychology, 29,* 72–79.

Nichols, K. A., & Champness, B. G. (1969). Eye gaze and GSR. *Journal of Experimental Social Psychology, 60,* 481–94.

Nielson, G. (1962). *Studies in self confrontation.* Copenhagen: Monksgaard.

Noller, P. (1980). Gaze in married couples. *Journal of Nonverbal Behavior, 5,* 115–29.

Patterson, M. L. (1976). An arousal model of interpersonal intimacy. *Psychological Review, 83,* 235–45.

Pellegrini, R. J., Hicks, R. A., & Gordon, L. (1970). The effects of an approval-seeking induction on eye-contact in dyads. *British Journal of Social and Clinical Psychology, 9,* 373–74.

Pennington, D. C., & Rutter, D. R. (1981). Information or affiliation? Effects on intimacy on visual interaction. *Semiotica, 35,* 29–39.

Rosenberg, A., & Kagan, J. (1987). Iris pigmentation and behavioral inhibition. *Developmental Psychobiology, 20,* 377–92.

Rosse, R. B., Kendrick, K., Wyatt, R. J., Isaac, A., & Deutsch, S. I. (1994). Gaze discrimination in patients with schizophrenia: Preliminary report. *American Journal of Psychiatry, 151,* 919–21.

Rowland-Morin, P. A., Burchard, K. W., Garb, J. L., & Coe, N. P. (1991). Influence of effective communication by surgery students on their oral examination scores. *Academic Medicine, 66,* 169–71.

Rubin, Z. (1970). The measurement of romantic love. *Journal of Personality and Social Psychology, 16,* 265–73.

Rutter, D. R. (1973). Visual interaction in psychiatric patients: A review. *British Journal of Psychiatry, 123,* 193–202.

Rutter, D. R. (1984). *Looking and seeing: The role of visual communication in social interaction.* New York: Wiley.

Rutter, D. R., Morley, I. E., & Graham, J. C. (1972). Visual interaction in a group of introverts and extroverts. *European Journal of Social Psychology, 2,* 371–84.

Rutter, D. R., Stephenson, G. M., & White, P. A. (1978). The timing of looks in dyadic conversation. *British Journal of Social and Clinical Psychology, 17,* 17–21.

Schelde, T., & Hertz, M. (1994). Ethology and psychotherapy. *Ethology and Sociobiology, 15,* 383–92.

Scherwitz, L., & Helmreich, R. (1973). Interactive effects of eye contact and verbal content on interpersonal attraction in dyads. *Journal of Personality and Social Psychology, 25,* 6–14.

Shuter, R. (1979). Gaze behavior in interracial and intraracial interaction. In N. Jain (Ed.), *International and intercultural communication annual,* (Vol. 5). Falls Church, VA: Speech Communication Association.

Simmel, G. (1921). Sociology of the senses: Visual interaction. In R. E. Park & E. W. Burgess (Eds.), *Introduction to the science of sociology.* Chicago: University of Chicago Press.

Spence, D. P., & Feinberg, C. (1967). Forms of defensive looking: A naturalistic experiment. *Journal of Nervous and Mental Disorders, 145,* 261–71.

Stass, J. W., & Willis, F. N., Jr. (1967). Eye contact, pupil dilation, and personal preference. *Psychonomic Science, 7,* 375–76.

Stephenson, G. M., & Rutter, D. R. (1970). Eye contact, distance and affiliation: A reevaluation. *British Journal of Psychology, 61,* 385–93.

Stephenson, G. M., Rutter, D. R., & Dore, S. R. (1973). Visual interaction and distance. *British Journal of Psychology, 64,* 251–57.

Strongman, K. T., & Champness, B. G. (1968). Dominance hierarchies and conflict in eye contact. *Acta Psychologica, 28,* 376–86.

Thayer, S. (1969). The effect of interpersonal looking duration on dominance judgments. *Journal of Social Psychology, 79,* 285–86.

Thompson, T. L. (1982). Gaze toward and avoidance of the handicapped: A field experiment. *Journal of Nonverbal Behavior, 6,* 188–96.

Vine, I. (1971). Judgment of direction of gaze: An interpretation of discrepant results. *British Journal of Social and Clinical Psychology, 10,* 320–31.

von Cranach, M., & Ellgring, J. H. (1973). Problems in the recognition of gaze direction.

In M. von Cranach & I. Vine (Eds.), *Social communication and movement.* New York: Academic Press.

Walker, M. B., & Trimboli, C. (1983). The expressive function of the eye flash. *Journal of Nonverbal Behavior, 8,* 3–13.

Walters, A. S., Barrett, R. P., & Feinstein, C. (1990). Social relatedness and autism: Current research, issues, directions. *Research in Developmental Disabilities, 11,* 303–26.

Webbink, P. (1986). *The power of the eyes.* New York: Springer.

Weisz, J., & Adam, G. (1993). Hemispheric preference and lateral eye movements evoked by bilateral visual stimuli. *Neuropsychologia, 31,* 1299–1306.

Wilbur, M. P., & Roberts-Wilbur, J. (1985). Lateral eye-movement responses to visual stimuli. *Perceptual and Motor Skills, 61,* 167–77.

Williams, E. (1978). Visual interaction and speech patterns: An extension of previous results. *British Journal of Social and Clinical Psychology, 17,* 101–2.

Wills, J. (1961). *An empirical study of the behavioral characteristics of sincere and insincere speakers.* Unpublished doctoral dissertation, University of Southern California, Los Angeles.

Woodmansee, J. J. (1970). The pupil response as a measure of social attitudes. In G. F. Summers (Ed.), *Attitude measurement.* Chicago: Rand McNally.

CHAPTER 11

The Effects of Vocal Cues That Accompany Spoken Words

I understand a fury in your words
But not the words.

—SHAKESPEARE, *OTHELLO*, ACT 4

Ideally, this chapter would not be in written form. Instead, it should be a recording you can listen to. A recording would give you a greater appreciation for the vocal nuances that are the subject of this chapter—or, as the cliché goes, "*how* something is said rather than *what* is said." But, the dichotomy set up by this cliché is misleading, because *how* something is said is frequently *what* is said.

Some responses to vocal cues are elicited because we deliberately try to manipulate our voice in order to communicate various meanings. Robert J. McCloskey, spokesperson for the State Department during the Nixon administration, reportedly exemplified such behavior:

> McCloskey has three distinct ways of saying, "I would not speculate": spoken without accent, it means the department doesn't know for sure; emphasis on the "I" means "I wouldn't, but you may—and with some assurance"; accent on "speculate" indicates that the questioner's premise is probably wrong. (*Newsweek*, October 5, 1970, p. 106)

Most of us do the same kind of thing when we emphasize a particular part of a message. *Prosody* is the word used to describe all the variations in the voice that accompany speech and help to convey its meaning. Notice how different vocal emphases influence the interpretation of the following message:

1. *He's* giving this money to Herbie. (HE is the one giving the money, nobody else.)
2. He's *giving* this money to Herbie. (He is GIVING, not lending, the money.)
3. He's giving *this* money to Herbie. (The money being exchanged is not from another fund or source; it is THIS money.)
4. He's giving this *money* to Herbie. (MONEY is the unit of exchange, not a check or wampum.)
5. He's giving this money to *Herbie*. (The recipient is HERBIE, not Eric or Bill or Rod.)

We manipulate our pitch to indicate the end of a declarative sentence (by lowering it) or a question (by raising it). Sometimes we consciously manipulate our tone, so that the vocal message contradicts the verbal one, as in sarcasm. For instance, you can say the words "I'm having a wonderful time" so they mean "I'm having a terrible time." If you are perceived as being sarcastic, the vocal cues you have given probably superseded the verbal.

Such an assumption (the predominance of vocal cues in forming attitudes based on contradictory vocal and verbal content) initiated some work of Mehrabian and his colleagues. In one study, he used single words, previously rated as positive, neutral, or negative, and presented them to listeners in positive or negative vocal tones (Mehrabian & Wiener, 1967). From this experiment, it was concluded:

> The variability of inferences about communicator attitude on the basis of information available in content and tone combined is mainly contributed by variations in tone alone. For example, when the attitude communicated in content contradicted the attitude communicated by negative tone, the total message was judged as communicating negative attitude. (p. 109)

A similar study, pitting vocal cues against facial and verbal cues, found the facial more influential (Mehrabian & Ferris, 1967). From these studies, Mehrabian devised a formula that illustrates the differential impact of verbal, vocal, and facial cues:

Perceived attitude = .07 (verbal) + .38 (vocal) + .55 (facial)

Obviously the formula is limited by the design of Mehrabian's experiments. For instance, we do not know how the formula might change if some of the variables were manipulated more vigorously; we do not know whether the formula would apply to verbal materials longer than one word; and we do not know whether these respondents were reacting to the inconsistency itself as a source of attitudinal information. Just the fact that subjects resolved their inconsistency by relying on vocal cues does not mean that evaluative information is conveyed by vocal cues alone.

Questions such as these prompted the work of Hart and Brown (1974). They reasoned, like Markel before them, that the vocal channel probably carries a greater percentage of some classes of information and a lesser percentage of others. Markel's work has suggested support for the idea that evaluative information (like/dislike; good/bad) is most often based on listener perceptions of content, while potency judgments (strong/weak; superior/subordinate) are based primarily on information derived from vocal cues (Markel, Meisels, & Houck, 1964; Markel & Robin, 1965). Hart and Brown tried to use stimuli that more closely approximated natural speech, that is, speech samples representing thought units rather than single words, and natural verbal/vocal interplay rather than exclusively inconsistent patterns. Unfortunately, the scales used for responding to these stimuli did not reflect those commonly used to measure evaluative, potency, and activity dimensions. Thus, we cannot match these results with Markel's. However, the results do show a complex response pattern with several evaluative-type reactions related to verbal content and information on "social attractiveness" apparently conveyed by vocal characteristics.

Studies comparing impressions made by the voice to those made by the face also have found that the voice is especially suited to convey degrees of dominance or potency; the face has a greater impact on judgments of pleasantness or positivity (Zuckerman & Driver, 1989; Zuckerman et al., 1982). Clues to dominance in the voice include speed and loudness; the most obvious clue to pleasantness in the face is the smile. However, each modality can convey through more subtle variations a wealth of other messages. For example, the presence of a smile can be evident in the voice alone; in smiling, the vocal tract is shortened with the effect of raising the resonances (Scherer, 1986).

In spite of relatively little research and the problems associated with these studies, it is significant that vocal cues (manipulated or not) seem to exert a great deal of influence on listener perceptions, particularly with certain classes of information or kinds of responses. Often, these responses are based on stereotypes associated with various vocal qualities, intonations, characteristics, and the like. Some research even suggests we have auditory preferences as we have visual, tactile, and olfactory preferences. Zuckerman and Driver (1989), for example, have documented that listeners generally agree on whether a voice is attractive or not, and that people whose voices are considered more attractive are believed to have personality traits such as dominance, competence, industriousness, sensitivity, and warmth.

Nonverbal vocal cues have emerged as important in many contexts. Psychiatrists tell us of critical insights into patient problems derived from vocal cues; researchers find that vocal cues during the explanation of experimental instructions can affect drastically the results of an experiment; psychologists report a relationship between vocal cues and the ability to identify certain personal characteristics, including some personality characteristics; students of speech communication find important relationships between vocal cues and the effects of various messages on retention and attitude change. The identification of various emotional states from vocal cues has been studied extensively; some have even suggested an important communicative role for nonlanguage vocalizations such as coughs, sneezes, belches, and the like.

THE INGREDIENTS of PARALANGUAGE

Because we must use the written medium to describe vocal phenomena (also called *paralanguage*), the next few paragraphs may seem longer than you would wish. But some methodological detail is necessary for you to understand how research on the voice is done and what has been found.

In one approach to studying the voice, listeners are asked for their impressions or inferences about a voice sample, for example, how anxious or competent it sounds. Using this method, a researcher may gain insight into the social meanings of vocal cues, since listeners' impressions will be based on their store of experience, knowledge, and beliefs; however, a researcher learns little about specific vocal cues that created a given impression.

Another approach is purely descriptive. Here, researchers measure specific vocal characteristics (often called *acoustic properties*) using automated devices or trained coders. Voice research uses fine descriptions like these much more than does research on nonvocal modalities of communication. Some commonly measured acoustic properties are speech rate (words per unit of time); fundamental frequency (F_0), which is the vibration rate of the vocal folds in the throat and the main contributor, along with the harmonics and resonances it produces, to one's perception of pitch; and intensity, which is the energy value for a speech sound and is perceived as loudness. Each of these can be measured as an average value over an utterance or other unit of time or can be described more dynamically in terms of range, variation, and contour (Scherer, 1986).

It is also possible to assess vocal nonverbal behavior at a level *between* these interpretational and purely descriptive extremes. A listener might be asked to characterize a voice as whiny, breathy, or abrupt but not to go to the next level of subjectivity by inferring a trait or mood; for example, from the three adjectives just named one could infer that the speaker is weak, sexy, or rude, respectively. You can see that the last three descriptions are farther removed from the actual vocal cues and are more judgmental than the first three. Scherer (1982) believes it is important to study perceptions at this midway point as a crucial link in understanding the relationship between acoustic features of voices and their social impact.

The fact that the voice has acoustic features that are perceived and interpreted by a listener according to his or her knowledge, stereotypes, and other cognitions is part of what Scherer (1979, 1982) calls the "lens" model of nonverbal judgment. According to this model, a full understanding of vocal (and other nonverbal) phenomena must acknowledge a series of interlocking steps: A person's state or trait (A), is reflected in acoustical behavior (B), which is perceived by a listener (C), and forms the basis of an impression or attribution (D), which may then be the basis for behavioral reaction or change in the listener (E). Studies hardly ever include this whole process. For example, one study will relate a speaker's emotional state to acoustic changes in the voice (A-B), while another will relate acoustic properties of the voice to listeners' impressions of personality (B-D), which would essentially be a study of vocal stereotypes.

Any approach to the measurement of vocal behavior has strengths and weaknesses. The choice often will depend on the questions being asked in a particular study. Hall, Roter, and Rand (1981), for example, were interested in the impact of physicians' and patients' communication of emotion during the medical visit. Accordingly, they obtained ratings of emotions in audiotapes of medical office visits. They found that if the physician sounded angry (or anxious, or contented), so did the patient. In this study, gathering judges' impressions of the emotions being expressed made more sense than measuring fundamental frequency or loudness. Other studies have sought to document the precise behaviors that may be coordinated between two people in conversation. Thus, it has been shown that conversants will converge on their length of utterances, as discussed later in this chapter, as well as on pitch and loudness.

Obviously, finding a rapprochement of the descriptive and interpretational approaches involves uncovering the relationship *between* the descriptive and interpretational levels, that is, finding out what increased fundamental frequency, intensity, and so forth mean in terms of listeners' perceptions of emotions or other messages. For example, it might be found that the more the conversants' vocal behaviors converge or match, the greater rapport they experience. Progress has been made in uncovering the social meanings of acoustic cues (a topic covered later in this chapter).

The voice is capable of a great variety of sounds, which theorists have tried to catalogue. An influential "first approximation" of paralanguage was that of Trager (1958). Those components most closely tied to speech include the three already mentioned (frequency, intensity, and speed) as well as vocal lip control (sharp or smooth transition), articulation control (forceful, relaxed), rhythm control (smooth, jerky), and resonance (resonant, thin). Other nonverbal vocal behaviors are less tied to speech and may even substitute for speech. These include laughing, crying, whispering, snoring, yelling, moaning, yawning, whining, sighing, and belching, along with the common "uh," "um," "mm," "uh-huh," and other such sounds, some of which merge with our definitions of linguistic behavior. Also included as paralanguage are nonsounds: pauses between words or phrases in someone's speech and pauses when a new speaker begins (a switching pause).

Some related phenomena, which Mahl and Schulze (1964) place under the broad heading of *extralinguistic* phenomena, are also relevant to any discussion of communication and vocal behavior. These include reactions to such things as dialect or accent, nonfluencies, speech rate, latency of response, duration of utterance, and interaction rates. There is some overlap, and some paralinguists include these additional aspects within the classification of para-language.

Now that we have a referent for the ingredients of paralanguage, we can ask the next logical question: What reactions do vocal cues elicit, and how are they important in communicating?

VOCAL CUES and SPEAKER RECOGNITION

You may have had this experience: You pick up the phone and say, "Hello." The voice on the other end says, "Hi, how ya doin'?" At this point you realize two things: (1) The greeting suggests an informality found among people who are supposed to know each other, and (2) you don't know who it is! So you try to extend the conversation without admitting your ignorance, hoping some verbal cue will be given or that you eventually will recognize the caller's voice. As a result, you say something like "Fine. What have you been up to?"

Each time you speak, you produce a complex acoustic signal. It is not exactly the same each time you speak (even if it is the same word); nor is the acoustic signal you produce exactly the same as the one produced by other speakers. The knowledge that there are greater differences between the voices of two different speakers than the voice of a single speaker at two different times has led to considerable interest in the process of identifying speakers by their voices alone.

There are three primary methods for identifying speakers:

1. Listening
2. Visual comparison of spectrograms (voiceprints)
3. Recognition accomplished by computers, which compare the acoustic patterns of a standard spoken message to stored versions of the same message previously spoken by the same speaker (Corsi, 1982; Dodding-ton, 1985; Hecker, 1971)

While machines are credited with many accomplishments in today's society, ordinary human listening compares favorably with the other two techniques for accuracy in most speaker recognition tasks. Human beings can recognize speakers with a high degree of accuracy. In one study, a single sentence was enough to identify eight to ten work colleagues at more than 97 percent accuracy (van Lancker, Kreiman, & Emmorey, 1985). In another study, 83 percent accuracy for twenty-nine familiar speakers was achieved (Ladefoged & Ladefoged, 1980). Utterances less than a sentence long and unclear utterances severely decrease accuracy even for familiar speakers. Disguised voices can decrease accuracy by 51 percent to 81 percent depending on the disguise (Reich & Duke, 1979).

People also seem to be better than machines at recognizing when voices are being mimicked. Even though we are able to recognize the voices of unfamiliar speakers, machines are capable of recognizing a greater number and identifying them faster. This capacity has stimulated the use of voice recognition by computers to confirm identity prior to admission to a restricted facility.

Even when listeners accurately pinpoint a speaker's voice, they are not able to explain the perceptual bases for their decision; that is, researchers do not know what features of the voice listeners are reacting to. Of the many characteristics of the voice, listeners probably utilize very few in speaker recognition.

Law enforcement and judicial agencies have had a special concern for identifying speakers objectively from their vocal characteristics. At the famous trial of Bruno Hauptman, the kidnapper of Charles and Anne Morrow Lindbergh's baby, Charles Lindbergh claimed he recognized Hauptman's voice as the voice of the kidnapper even though it had been about three years since he had heard it. While it is not beyond the realm of possibility that such an identification could have been accurate, McGehee (1937) found that accuracy tends to drop off sharply after three weeks, and after five months it dips to about 13 percent. Recent research also has shown that perceived "distinctiveness" of a person's voice (i.e., it stands out in a crowd) shows little correlation with its ability to be recognized.

Many factors affect listening accuracy, but similar problems plague efforts to devise more "objective" methods of speaker recognition—not the least of which is the knowledge that no single set of acoustic cues reliably distinguishes speakers.

One effort to find a more objective method of speaker identification was the *spectrogram,* a visual picture of a person's speech. A spectrogram is a plot of vocal energy in different frequency bands as a function of time. Although some have made strong claims for the accuracy and reliability of spectrographic analysis, it seems to be very fallible (Bolt et al., 1973). Errors in human judgment occur as interpretations of the visual data are made. The interpreter's skill becomes particularly relevant when one looks at Figure 11-1. These two similar spectrograms—admittedly featuring only one word—make it sufficiently clear that our reliance on spectrograms as evidence at trials must be weighed very carefully (Ladefoged & Vanderslice, 1967). Spectrograms are not like fingerprints. True, no two voices are exactly alike, but depending on the voice sample obtained and the equipment used, two different voices may appear very similar. On the other hand, fingerprints, unlike voices, will show little variability from one time to the next, unless, of course, smudges or smears have occurred. One study asked speakers to produce the same sentence using their normal voice and a number of "disguises"—speaking like an old person, using a hypernasal voice, a hoarse voice, a slow rate of speech, and a disguise of one's own choosing. These voice samples were then submitted to spectrographic analysis by experts who were paid fifty dollars if they achieved the highest accuracy of identification. Normal voices were matched with about 57 percent accuracy, but all the disguises significantly interfered with identification. The least accuracy was achieved when speakers chose their own type of disguise (Reich, Moll, & Curtis, 1976).

Figure 11–1

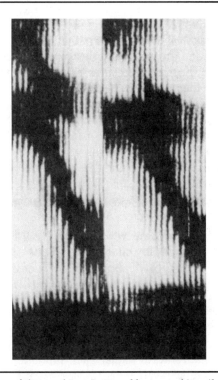

Similar spectrograms of the word "you" uttered by two arbitrarily selected speakers. (Used by permission of Speech Communication Association.)

VOCAL CUES and PERSONALITY

One cultural syndrome that aptly illustrates our association of vocal cues with certain personality characteristics concerns what some speech scientists call our "vocal neurosis" about the low, deep voice in men. Salespeople, radio and television announcers, receptionists, lawyers, and many others try to emulate low vocal tones, which they perceive as being more sophisticated, appealing, sexy, or masculine than higher-pitched voices.

Numerous research efforts have tried to determine whether certain personality traits are expressed in one's voice and whether other people are sensitive to these cues. It is common to find the following:

1. High agreement among judges of the voices regarding the presence of certain personality characteristics
2. Inconsistent agreement between the judges' personality perceptions and the speaker's actual score on personality tests

3. For some voices and some personality traits, a very high correspondence between the judges' perceptions and actual criterion measures

Kramer (1964), in his interpretation of such data, makes several worthwhile observations: First, the criterion measures (personality tests) are also frequently imperfect measures, meaning that there might be a higher correspondence than the data seem to indicate. Second, almost all these studies used a speaker giving a monologue to which the judges responded. Perhaps some personality characteristics associated with vocal cues are only elicited in dialogue form—a possibility that has not been adequately tested. Finally, research has generally ignored differences among listeners with respect to personality, culture, and developmental traits, which may profoundly impact on the listener's accuracy in perceiving personality traits based on vocal cues. Research also suggests that a given personality trait may not be expressed similarly in the voices of people from different cultures.

The finding that listeners cannot always detect personality from vocal cues does not mean that the voice does not contain any cues to personality. There are several lines of positive evidence on this issue. Extraversion/introversion is the trait dimension best documented in vocal cues of American speakers. Cues associated with a speaker's actual (not just perceived) extraversion, when compared to introversion, are more fluency (shorter pauses when the speaking turn switches from one speaker to another, shorter silent pauses within a person's speech, fewer hesitations); faster rate; louder speech; more dynamic contrast; higher pitch (up to a point); and more variable pitch. In addition, extraverted people have been shown to talk more, in both number of words and total speaking time (Siegman, 1987).

Another intriguing set of results has emerged regarding the "Type A" personality, a syndrome of attitudes and behaviors linked to the development of coronary heart disease. Current theory points to hostility or anger as an important feature of this syndrome. Early in the research on these hard-driving, aggressive Type A's, it was found that speech style was very distinctive. In particular, fast or accelerating speech, uneven speech rate, short latencies, interruptions, a loud or explosive voice, and a hard or staccato voice all are more pronounced in Type A individuals. Many of these qualities also have been shown independently to be associated with heart disease, for example, loud, vigorous, and explosive speech (Hall, Friedman, & Harris, 1984).

The trait of dominance also has been documented to have an associated speech style; some of its elements overlap with those found for extraversion and Type A personality. Individuals who speak louder and faster are perceived as more dominant (Harrigan, Gramata, Luck, & Margolis, 1989), a stereotype confirmed in that more dominant individuals do tend to have voices that are louder and faster, as well as less breathy and more low pitched, than less dominant individuals (Siegman 1987; Weaver & Anderson, 1973).

Berry (1991) found that judges' ratings of voices recorded while expressors recited the alphabet were accurate (in terms of the expressors' own ratings of themselves) for male and female expressors' assertiveness, aggression, and social closeness.

As we have mentioned elsewhere in this book, our main concern is not with pathological behavior. It should be noted, however, that a significant body of literature concerns various vocal cues and their relationship to personality adjustment or psychopathology. Depressed voices have been found to be slow and to exhibit long, silent pauses; some schizophrenics have long been noted for their flat voices. One study indicates that schizophrenic and depressed patients sounded sadder than normal controls when asked to tell about a happy, sad, or angry episode in their lives. Also, these patient groups had distinct deficits in their ability to convey these emotions through voice tone. Depressed patients were least able to convey clear cues as to which episode they were describing (Levin, Hall, Knight, & Alpert, 1985). Vocal quality can be tied to psychiatry also by considering the voice as an unobtrusive source of cues to the patient's state—an indicator of whether the patient is improving. Ellgring & Scherer (1996), Ostwald (1961), and others, using acoustic measurements, found evidence that vocal qualities can change following therapy.

How personality is expressed in speech may be complex, but there is no dearth of evidence that people *believe* speech contains clues to personality. Addington (1968) conducted one of the most complete studies in this area. He recognized that stereotyped judgments of vocal cues regularly occur and decided to explore the specific nature of these stereotypes. Male and female speakers simulated nine vocal characteristics, and judges responded to the voices by rating them on forty personality characteristics. Judges were most reliable (i.e., they agreed most with each other) in ratings of masculine/ feminine, young/old, enthusiastic/apathetic, energetic/lazy, and attractive/ ugly. Addington concluded that the male personality generally was perceived in terms of physical and emotional power, while the female personality was apparently perceived in terms of social faculties. Table 11-1 summarizes his results. Addington concluded his study by posing some interesting questions for researchers studying vocal cues and personality. To what extent are these stereotyped impressions of personality maintained in the face of conflicting personality information? And what is the relationship between a given personality impression and vocal cue? For example, Addington's research indicated that increased pitch variety led to more positive personality impressions, but is it not possible that at some point, increasing pitch variety could become so exaggerated as to evoke negative perceptions?

Research on vocal attractiveness also has revealed some personality stereotypes associated with the voice (Berry, 1992; Zuckerman, Hodgins, & Miyake, 1990; Zuckerman & Miyake, 1993). People with more attractive-sounding voices are rated as having better personalities (less neurotic and more extraverted, open, warm, agreeable, powerful, honest, and conscientious) than people with less attractive-sounding voices. Zuckerman also uncovered the particular speech qualities that produced higher ratings on vocal attractiveness. More attractive-rated voices were more resonant, less monotonous, less

Table 11–1

SIMULATED VOCAL CUES AND PERSONALITY STEREOTYPES

Simulated Vocal Cues	Speakers	Stereotyped Perceptions
Breathiness	Males	Younger, more artistic
	Females	More feminine; prettier; more petite, effervescent, high-strung; and shallower
Thinness	Males	Did not alter listener's image of the speaker; no significant correlations
	Females	Increased social, physical, emotional, and mental immaturity; increased sense of humor and sensitivity
Flatness	Males	More masculine, more sluggish, colder, more withdrawn
	Females	More masculine, more sluggish, colder, more withdrawn
Nasality	Males	A wide array of socially undesirable characteristics
	Females	A wide array of socially undesirable characteristics
Tenseness	Males	Older, more unyielding, cantankerous
	Females	Younger; more emotional, feminine, high-strung; less intelligent
Throatiness	Males	Older; more realistic; mature; sophisticated; well adjusted
	Females	Less intelligent; more masculine; lazier; more boorish, unemotional, ugly, sickly, careless, inartistic, naive, humble, neurotic, quiet, uninteresting, apathetic
Orotundity	Males	More energetic, healthy, artistic, sophisticated, proud, interesting, enthusiastic
	Females	Increased liveliness, gregariousness, and esthetic sensitivity
Increased Rate	Males	More animated and extraverted
	Females	More animated and extraverted
Increased Pitch Variety	Males	More dynamic, feminine, esthetically inclined
	Females	More dynamic and extraverted

nasal, and lower in pitch (the latter for male voices only); they also tended to have middling values on pitch, pitch range, shrillness, and squeakiness. In other words, the more attractive voices were *not* extremely low or extremely high, *not* extremely flat or extremely variable in pitch, and so forth.

Personality stereotypes also exist about people with babyish voices. Both adults and young children with more babyish voices are perceived as more warm and honest, but less powerful and competent, than people with more mature-sounding voices; it seems the general qualities attributed to children are attributed to people with younger-sounding voices no matter what their actual age (Berry, 1992; Berry, Hansen, Landry-Pester, & Meier, 1994).

A related line of study involves the association of various personality characteristics with voices representative of large groups of people. These studies deal with judgments of group personality rather than individual personality. For instance, Anisfeld, Bogo, and Lambert (1962) asked Jewish and non-Jewish students to evaluate voices—some speaking standard English, some speaking English with a Yiddish accent. The same students rated both voice samples. Both non-Jews and Jews rated the accented voices as belonging to persons low in height, good looks, and leadership. Non-Jews did not rate the accented voices higher on any trait, while Jews rated accented voices higher on humor, entertainingness, and kindness. Jews perceived many more non-accented voices as being Jewish than did non-Jews. There seemed to be no relationship between a measure of attitudes toward Jews and the personality traits chosen.

Another fascinating group-to-group study centered on the long-standing tension between French- and English-speaking Canadians (Lambert, Frankel, & Tucker, 1966). An initial study, using bilingual speakers, presented judges with the same messages in English-Canadian and French-Canadian. The English-Canadian message was rated significantly better than the French-Canadian message. In fact, the French-Canadian judges rated the English-Canadian speaker higher on such traits as intelligence, likability, dependability, and character. Thus, certain subgroups of college-age French-Canadians seemed to be biased against their own linguistic group.

Closely related to these studies of group personalities and voices are the many efforts to show how people evaluate various dialects and accents. In Shaw's play *Pygmalion* and its musical adaptation, Eliza Doolittle spent considerable time and effort trying to correct her dialect so she could rise in social standing. (Professor Higgins: "Look at her—a pris'ner of the gutters; Condemned by ev'ry syllable she utters." *My Fair Lady*, act 1, scene 1.) Eliza's training, according to one study, was most appropriate. It suggests that if we expect a speaker to reflect a nonstandard and/or "lower class" dialect and the speaker actually presents him- or herself in accord with standard or "upper class" models, the evaluation will be very positive. The reverse also was true; speakers expected to speak "up" but who spoke "down" were evaluated negatively (Aboud, Clement, & Taylor, 1974). Obviously, there is a fine line between adapting to your audience and severely violating expectations based on your own background.

While there are some exceptions, ordinarily we find that dialects other than the one spoken by the listener/evaluator receive less favorable evaluations than those considered standard. Generally, these negative responses occur because the listener associates the speaker's dialect with an ethnic or regional stereotype and then evaluates the voice in accord with the stereotype. Typical of this response are studies (Bradford, Ferror, & Bradford, 1974; Buck, 1968; Giles, Henwood, Coupland, Harriman, & Coupland, 1992; Gill, 1994; Mulac, Hanley, & Prigge, 1974; Williams, 1970; Williams & Shamo, 1972) that found the following:

1. Chicano-English speakers were rated lower on success, ability, and social awareness.
2. Native-born Americans rated Europeans (speaking English) less positively than other native-born speakers.
3. Teachers tended to label a child as culturally disadvantaged if the speech exhibited irregularities in grammar, silent pausing, and pronunciation.
4. Standard dialects were preferred and judged more competent than nonstandard, regardless of who spoke—and standard dialects were more often associated with white speakers than black.

Lawsuits alleging "accent discrimination" have accused employers of denying jobs to individuals with foreign accents; the employers claim that the accent would interfere with effective job performance. Similarly, there have been some efforts to keep teachers with accents from being assigned to teach in the early grades, on the grounds that their accents would interfere with teaching the English language. Attorneys and civil rights activists are concerned that this is ethnic discrimination in disguise, pointing to instances where the foreign-born applicant was denied a job in spite of speaking accurate and perfectly intelligible English.

Do regional varieties of speech in the United States differ in prestige value? Listeners in Maine, Louisiana, New York City, Arkansas, and Michigan rated twelve voice samples of American dialects and one foreign accent (Wilke & Snyder, 1941). The most unfavorably regarded were the foreign accent and "New Yorkese." Although this study is about fifty years old, some dialects and accent stereotypes seem to influence our judgments of a speaker's status today. Many people tested their southern stereotypes as they evaluated the speech patterns of former president Jimmy Carter. Miller's (1975) work appears to be the only effort to go beyond the theory that dialects evoke group stereotypes that influence the judgment of that dialect. In this study, we find some support for the notion that aspects of certain dialects are evaluated independently of the stereotype; that is, some listeners may respond negatively to a French-Canadian speaker because of a negative stereotype *and/or* because of some dislike for the dialect itself.

Several investigators have pursued the question of exactly how we judge the speech and dialects of others. By far the most extensive work in this direction was done by Mulac (1976). Mulac's experiments have used regional and foreign dialects, broadcasters, various speech pathologies, prose and spontaneous speech, and different modes of presentation, such as written, audiotape, videotape, sound film, and so forth.

This work shows we tend to look at samples of speech along three primary dimensions:

1. Socio-intellectual status, that is, high or low social status, blue or white collar, rich or poor, and literate or illiterate
2. Esthetic quality, that is, pleasing or displeasing, nice or awful, sweet or sour, beautiful or ugly

3. Dynamism, that is, aggressive or unaggressive, active or passive, strong or weak, loud or soft

These results confirm studies in many other areas of perception that show we tend to see our world and the things in it according to power, evaluation, and activity dimensions.

VOCAL CUES and JUDGMENTS of PERSONAL CHARACTERISTICS

Over sixty years ago, Pear (1931) did pioneering work on vocal cues and judgments of personal characteristics. Using nine speakers and over four thousand radio listeners, he found a speaker's age could be estimated fairly accurately, the speaker's sex with remarkable accuracy, birthplace with little accuracy, and occasionally vocation with surprising accuracy. The actor and clergy were consistently identified from among the nine professionals represented. Since that time, others have been interested in judgments of such characteristics as body type, height, weight, age, occupation, status or social class, race, sex, education, and dialect region. Three characteristics that are judged accurately with some consistency are sex, age, and social class/status.

SEX   Listeners who heard six recorded vowels of twenty speakers were able to identify the sex of the speaker 96 percent of the time when the tape was not altered in any way. Accuracy decreased to 91 percent for a filtered tape and to 75 percent for a whispered voice sample (Lass et al., 1976). These authors argue that the fundamental frequency is a more important acoustic cue in speaker sex identification tasks than the resonance characteristics of the voices. Sometimes women and men may be identified by their intonation patterns. Some researchers believe, for instance, that women might end a sentence on a higher pitch, relative to where they started the sentence, than men.

It has been said that women speak in an even higher pitch than their anatomy requires. This is notably true in Japan, where women have traditionally spoken with extremely high voices and have been censured for not doing so. Because a high voice is seen as conveying politeness, its extreme is most often heard in women in service occupations, such as elevator operators. Bilinguals of both sexes seem to speak in a higher pitch when speaking Japanese than when speaking English. Recent trends suggest, however, that the voices of Japanese women are steadily deepening as their status becomes more equal to that of men (*New York Times*, Dec. 13, 1995).

Thus, pitch is a likely basis for differentiating male and female voices. Again, the nature of the vocal stimuli will be most influential in determining exactly how well we can discriminate between male and female voices. For instance, males and females *interacting* with each other may manifest different vocal cues than when they present monologues or interact with a member of the same sex (Markel, Prebor, & Brandt, 1972). The topic of discussion also may affect voice production and perceptions. And if there is a gradual narrowing of differences as adaptations to the social community are made, we might speculate that the vocal tones of working women in predominantly male organizations may be harder to distinguish—particularly if the sample is taken in the work milieu. Instead of the phenomenon of children shaping their voices to sound like the adult version of their sex, this may be an instance of adults acquiring some vocal characteristics of the opposite sex (Sachs, Lieberman, & Erickson, 1973).

At the borderline between verbal and nonverbal behavior falls an area of study concerned with speech styles or *speech registers*. A speech register is a total way of communicating through speech, which can include verbal forms, and is believed to vary systematically with social characteristics of the speakers—for example, how socially powerful a person is (Erickson et al., 1978). This research is pertinent to our discussion of speaker sex because it has been suggested that certain verbal forms associated with the powerful-powerless dimension differentiate the sexes (Lakoff, 1975). Examples of less powerful speech that are frequently associated with females include tag questions ("It's a nice day, *isn't it?*"), hedges and qualifiers ("sort of," "maybe"), disclaimers ("I don't know, but"), and intensifiers ("The puppy was *so* cute"). Interruptions, another interactional strategy that can reflect dominance, also have been hypothesized to differentiate between men and women in the direction one might expect based on stereotype. People certainly do have well-developed stereotypes about how the sexes speak, but the evidence supporting the hypothesis of sex differences in language use and interruptions is extremely mixed at this date (Aries, 1987; Dindia, 1987; Hirshman, 1994; Irish & Hall, 1995; Kramer, 1978; Marche & Peterson, 1993; Mulac, Lundell, & Bradac, 1986; Nohara, 1992; Turner, Dindia, & Pearson, 1995). The fact that interruptions can signify enthusiastic, active participation in the conversation rather than efforts to attain or express dominance is probably one reason why studies are mixed as to which sex interrupts more; whereas early studies tended to find that men interrupted more, more recent studies often find no difference, and some find that females interrupt more than males.

Future research will clarify whether, when, and which stereotypes about the sexes' speech are accurate. Until then, Smith's (1979) comment about research on stereotype versus actual behavior is pertinent (and applies to any stereotype and any kind of nonverbal behavior):

> Nevertheless, these sex-associated speech stereotypes merit study in their own right for the insight they give into what is assumed by listeners, and will tend to be expected until disconfirmed. More than idle caricatures, these expectations may define listeners' predispositions towards conversation with women and men, and confirmation of them may be actively sought. (p. 134)

For example, a man's expectations or beliefs about how women speak may shape not only his perceptions and interpretations of women's speech but also his behavior in such a way that it actually elicits the expected behavior; if he expects a woman to speak in a weak or indecisive way, he might treat her in a strong or protective manner that elicits a complementary weak and dependent response.

AGE   As mentioned, studies show age to be fairly accurately assessed from vocal cues, and something is known about how these judgments are made. Several studies have investigated pitch of males during infancy, childhood, adolescence, early adulthood, and middle and advanced age. There seems to be a general lowering of pitch level from infancy through middle age. Then a reversal occurs, and pitch level rises slightly with advancing age. Mysak (1959), for instance, found that males in his eighty- to ninety-two-year-old study group were characterized by higher measures of average fundamental pitch levels than males aged sixty-five to seventy-nine, with age eighty being a sensitive dividing line in terms of pitch change. Pitch changes were explained by physical changes and increasing tension. A similar, but less complete, series of studies has been done on the developing female voice. McClone and Hollien (1963), using research methods similar to Mysak's, found no significant difference in the mean pitch level of two groups (aged sixty-five to seventy-nine and eighty to ninety-four). The data on pitch from the age sixty-five to seventy-nine group were compared with data gathered on young adult women by another investigator. Since again there were no differences, McClone and Hollien conclude that speaking pitch level of women probably varies little throughout adult life, even though data for middle-aged women were not compared. If, as some gerontological studies suggest, our voices change in pitch flexibility, rate, loudness, vocal quality, articulatory control, and the like, the voice may give clues to age that we are largely unaware of. We also quite possibly are responding to other vocal characteristics as yet unreported in these developmental studies—they only give us possible clues.

SOCIAL CLASS/STATUS   Several studies show listeners to be amazingly accurate in judging social class or status on the basis of voice alone. Harms (1961) obtained independent scores from nine speakers on the Hollingshead Two Factor Index of Status Position. The speakers were then categorized as either high, middle, or low status. Each speaker recorded a forty- to sixty-second conversation in which he responded to questions and statements such as "How are you?" "Ask for the time," and so on. Adult listeners rated the speakers according to status and credibility. Results show that these listeners were not only able to identify the speakers' status, but also many of them said they made their decision after only ten to fifteen seconds of listening to the recording. Responses also showed those perceived as high in status were also perceived as most credible. This finding is consistent with other studies of status and vocal cues. Ellis (1967) even conducted a study in which he told speakers to try to fake status and imitate the upper class. Listener judgments still correlated well with independent measures of status for these speakers. It appears that we learn to talk like those around us: in our neighborhoods, our vocational environment, and our educational environment.

TARGET EFFECTS

So far we have been discussing ways in which a speaker's personal characteristics are reflected in his or her nonverbal speech style. But it would be very surprising if a person's speech style did not also reflect characteristics of the *other* person in an interaction. After all, we react to different kinds of people with many emotions and thoughts that may be reflected in our vocal expression, and we also have notions about how one *ought* to talk to different kinds of people.

A well-studied example of such a "target effect" is baby talk (also called *motherese*), which is the high-pitched, sing-song, repetitive, simplified way that parents around the world talk to young children (Grieser & Kuhl, 1988; Snow & Ferguson, 1977). Even young children know how to talk this way to babies or pets. Certain groups of adults who are attributed childlike qualities or who are perceived (often erroneously) as cognitively impaired, such as the institutionalized elderly or the deaf, are also spoken to in a way that resembles baby talk. Psychologists are especially interested in this kind of "secondary" baby talk because of the possibility that it contributes to the stigmatizing of groups perceived as dependent or incompetent (Caporael, 1981).

With this in mind, DePaulo and Coleman (1986, 1987) compared the warmth of speech to children, mentally retarded adults, non-native adult speakers of English, and native adult English speakers, hypothesizing that warmth (one component of baby talk) would decrease across these four groups. The prediction was supported. In addition, when considering the mentally retarded recipients alone, speakers displayed more vocal warmth when speaking to the more-retarded than to the less-retarded recipient. Particular ways of using the language also differed among the groups: Speech to children was clearer, simpler, and more attention maintaining and had longer pauses; speech to the retarded was very similar to this; speech to foreigners, however, was more similar to that addressed to "normal people" except for being more repetitive. Zebrowitz, Brownlow, and Olson (1992) found that adults used baby talk more to children with babyish faces than to same-age children who had more mature-looking faces.

The sex of the person being spoken to also influences how we speak. Men are spoken to more loudly than women are by both men and women (Markel, Prebor, & Brandt, 1972). Similarly, in a study of people's voices on television dramas and talk shows, men were spoken to more dominantly, condescendingly, and unpleasantly than women were by both men and women (Hall & Braunwald, 1981). The judges who made the affect ratings in this study did not know which sex was being addressed in each voice clip, so their stereotypes could not have influenced their judgments. Several other interesting results emerged from this study, too.

First, though men's voices on the television dramas were rated as more stereotypically "macho" (more dominant, unpleasant, condescending, and businesslike) than women's, this rating was greatly reduced on talk shows. Here, many women received the higher ratings on these scales. Thus, actors and their directors incorporated striking male/female stereotypes into the vocal behavior of characters in dramatic programs, but when people interacted more naturally on the talk shows, these stereotyped behaviors were not present.

Second, judges were asked to guess the sex of the person being addressed in each clip. Through an analysis that related these guesses to the judges' ratings and to the actual sex of the target, the researchers concluded that judges (who were college students) held an *incorrect* notion about how women speak to men. The judges were correct in believing that if a man sounded relatively dominant, he was addressing another man. But they were mistaken in believing that if a woman sounded dominant, she was addressing another woman. Both male and female speakers were more dominant when addressing a man. The judges apparently clung to a stereotype that says women are meek when talking to men.

VOCAL CUES and EMOTION

Vocal cues are definitely widespread among many animal species for communication about territory, identity, alarm, physical states, and emotion. Darwin viewed the voice as a primary channel for emotional signals in both humans and animals. In this section we examine what is known about emotional expression in the human voice.

One persistent question is whether people can identify emotions in the voice. Starkweather, in 1961, summarized a series of studies that attempted to specify the relationship between the voice and judgments of emotion. His conclusion reiterates the frequent finding in studies of personality judgments from vocal cues—consistent agreement among the judges.

> Studies of content free speech indicate that the voice alone can carry information about the speaker. Judges agree substantially, both when asked to identify the emotion being expressed and when given the task of estimating the strength of the feeling. Judgments appear to depend on significant changes in pitch, rate, volume and other physical characteristics of the voice, but untrained judges cannot describe these qualities accurately. (p. 69)

Three years later, Davitz (1964, p. 23) seemed to suggest that such judgments are not only reliable but also valid: "Regardless of the technique used, all studies of adults thus far reported in the literature agree that emotional meanings can be communicated accurately by vocal expression." Recent reviews concur. Pittam and Scherer (1993) concluded that the recognition of emotion from the voice is four to five times what would be expected by chance (i.e., if listeners were simply guessing without paying attention).

There is now believed to be a degree of universality of meaning for emotions expressed vocally. American, Polish, and Japanese subjects responded to vocal expressions of anger, sadness, happiness, flirtatiousness, fearfulness, and indifference portrayed by Americans. Accuracy was high but increased as the duration of the stimulus increased (Beier & Zautra, 1972). Better-than-chance accuracy results also are reported by Rosenthal and his colleagues (1979) regarding cross-national administration of their Profile of Nonverbal Sensitivity (PONS) test of decoding nonverbal cues (which includes content-free speech excerpts of twenty affective scenes).

To understand these conclusions, it is necessary to examine the factors that may cause differences in judging emotions accurately from vocal cues. Certainly the authors of the aforementioned conclusions do not intend to imply invariable consistency in judging emotions accurately.

Several *methods* have been used to eliminate or control the verbal information usually accompanying vocal cues. Accuracy may vary depending on the method used. Some studies use "meaningless content," usually having the speaker say numbers or letters while trying to convey various emotional states. Davitz and Davitz (1959) conducted a typical study of this type. Speakers were instructed to express ten different feelings while reciting parts of the alphabet. These expressions were recorded and played before judges who were asked to identify the emotion being expressed from a list of ten emotions. Generally, emotions or feelings were communicated far beyond chance expectation. It is difficult to tell, in this type of study, whether the communicators were using the same tonal or vocal cues they would use in "real life" emotional reactions.

Other studies have attempted to control verbal cues by using "constant content." A speaker reads a standard passage while attempting to simulate different emotional states. The underlying assumption is that the passage selected is neutral in emotional tone. Another approach is to try to ignore content and focus attention on the pauses, breathing rate, and other characteristics that suggest the person's emotional state. This method is frequently used in psychotherapy to identify signs of anxiety.

Finally, some studies have used electronic filtering to eliminate verbal content (Rogers, Scherer, & Rosenthal, 1971). A low-pass filter will hold back the higher frequencies of speech upon which word recognition depends. The finished product sounds much like a mumble heard through a wall. Although this type of speech sample is commonly referred to as "content free," this is, in many respects, a misnomer. Since such voice samples are not literally content free, some prefer to use terms such as *word-free voice* or *vocalic communication*. Certainly a recording that communicates emotional content is not content free—particularly since emotion is the major or most critical content for some messages. One common problem with the electronically filtered technique is that some of the nonverbal vocal cues may be eliminated in the filtering process, creating an artificial stimulus. Though some aspects of vocal quality may be lost in the filtering process, a listener can still adequately perceive pitch, rate, and loudness in order to judge emotional content.

Filtered speech is the most popular method of making words unintelligible and has produced some very intriguing results. In a study of doctors, Milmoe and her colleagues (Milmoe et al., 1967) found that the more *anger* was rated in the filtered voices of doctors talking about their alcoholic patients, the less successful they were in getting those patients into therapy. Later research verified that the tone of voice used when talking *about* patients carries over into the way doctors talk *to* patients (Rosenthal, Vanicelli, & Blanck, 1984). Another study of physicians found that those who provided more medical information to their patients and were more competent according to technical standards (conducting a proper interview, diagnosing correctly, and so forth) were those with the lowest ratings of *boredom* in short, filtered clips of their voices (Hall, Roter, & Katz, 1987). Finally, it has been found that a patient's satisfaction with a medical visit is greatest when the physician's *words* are rated as more *pleasant* but when the physician's *voice tone* is rated as *more angry and anxious*. The combination of pleasant words and not-so-pleasant voice may have conveyed a desirable degree of concern and involvement in the patient's problems (Hall, Roter, & Rand, 1981).

Studies vary in how accurately emotions are judged from voice cues. One reason for this involves the differing methods by which such observations may be made—for example, how long the voice samples are, which content-masking technique is used, or how dissimilar the response alternatives are. Another reason is that speakers (and listeners) vary widely in how accurately they can express (and recognize) different emotions (see Chapter 3). For example, in the Davitz and Davitz (1959) study, one speaker's expressions were identified correctly only 23 percent of the time, while another speaker communicated accurately over 50 percent of the time. In that study, like many others, accuracy was defined in terms of how well listeners could identify the emotion the speaker was asked to express. In the Davitz research, listeners' accuracy in recognizing the intended emotion varied just as widely as the speakers' sending accuracy did. Thus, depending on the skills that individuals bring to a communication situation, they may or may not succeed in sending and receiving vocal emotion cues.

Another qualification to any statement about the voice's overall ability to communicate emotions is that some emotions are easier to communicate than others. For example, one study found anger identified 63 percent of the time, while pride was identified correctly only 20 percent of the time. Another study found that joy and hate were easily recognized, but shame and love were the most difficult to recognize. In general, anger, joy, and sadness are easier to recognize than fear and disgust (Banse & Scherer, 1996; Pittam & Scherer, 1993). The similarity of some feelings may account for some of the difference. For instance, certain errors are consistent in some studies: Fear is mistaken for nervousness, love is mistaken for sadness, and pride is mistaken for satisfaction. It is also possible that as we develop, we rely on context to discriminate emotions with similar characteristics. Thus, when confronted with such cues and no context, we find discriminations difficult.

The most significant work on how emotion actually is reflected in the voice is by Klaus Scherer. One of Scherer's accomplishments has been to bring together knowledge of acoustical features of the voice, theory on how different emotions affect the voice, and results of actual research. One thing is clear: There is no "dictionary" of emotion cues for the voice, any more than there is for any nonverbal channel. You cannot identify key acoustic features and then "look them up" in a book somewhere to see which emotion is being expressed. Many factors enter into the total picture of emotional expression: contextual cues, the words being spoken, other nonverbal behaviors, individual differences in the people, and the fact that there is undoubtedly more than one way to express a given emotion.

The emotion of anxiety well illustrates this complexity. There are wide individual differences in vocal expression by anxious people. Some say anxious people talk slower under experimentally induced anxiety, while those not normally anxious speak faster under such conditions. There is some indication that under stress, dialects become stronger. Silent-pause frequency and duration, raised pitch level, and other factors are associated with anxiety in some studies and not in others.

Anxiety induced in a particular circumstance often is associated with more nonfluencies or speech disruptions (Mahl, 1956; Siegman, 1987). Table 11-2 presents the categories of speech disturbance investigated by Cook (1965).

Table 11–2

SPEECH DISTURBANCE CATEGORIES, FREQUENCY OF OCCURRENCE, AND EXAMPLES

Category	% of total	Example
1. "Er," "Ah," or "Um"	40.5	Well . . . er . . . when I go home
2. Sentence change	25.3	I have a book which . . . the book I need for finals.
3. Repetition	19.2	I often . . . often work at night.
4. Stutter	7.8	It sort of I . . . I . . . leaves me.
5. Omission (leaving out a word or leaving it unfinished)	4.5	I went to the lib . . . the Bod.
6. Sentence incompletion	1.2	He said the reason was . . . anyway I couldn't go.
7. Tongue slip	0.7	I haven't much term (that is, time) these days.
8. Intruding incoherent sound	1.2	I don't really know why . . . dh . . . I went.

"Non-Ah" speech errors (categories 2 through 8) seem to increase with induced anxiety or discomfort, while "Ah" errors (category 1) do not (see "Types of Pauses" later in this chapter). Personality dimensions related to anxiety have also been studied in relation to the production of speech disturbances. Harrigan et al. (1994) obtained anxiety ratings of verbatim transcripts of the speech of individuals who varied in state and trait anxiety as well as in repression (the need to deny negative thoughts, impulses, or behaviors). Repressors' speech was judged to be the most anxious, more so even than the speech of people who were high trait-anxious but not repressive. The authors attributed these effects to differences in the frequency of speech disturbances among groups. Although repressors do not view themselves as high on trait anxiety, their vocal behavior says otherwise.

Acoustic analyses of actors' voices portraying anger, fear, sorrow, and neutral mood were found by Williams and Stevens (1972) to vary in their frequency contours; for example, for sadness the contours were relatively flat. The average frequencies were lowest for sorrow and highest for anger, with neutral and fear in between. These researchers went outside the laboratory also for more evidence; they analyzed recordings of the radio announcer who described, live, the explosion and burning of the hydrogen-filled zeppelin *Hindenburg* at Lakehurst, New Jersey. Comparison of his voice before and immediately after the disaster showed that the fundamental frequency rose considerably after, with much less fluctuation in frequency. Later investigations have confirmed that the voice rises in pitch when the speaker is in a state of stress.

Scherer's work has encompassed a broad range of emotions. In a 1974 study, he used artificial sounds rather than spontaneous speech to approach the question of which vocal features are associated with which emotions. Subjects rated synthesized tones on ten-point scales of pleasantness, potency, activity, and evaluation and indicated whether the stimuli could or could not be an expression of interest, sadness, fear, happiness, disgust, anger, surprise, elation, or boredom. Generally speaking, tempo and pitch variation seem to be very influential factors for a wide range of judgments about emotional expressions. Table 11-3 summarizes the results of several of Scherer's studies.

Scherer (1986) expanded his predictions to include twelve different emotions (such as irritation/cold anger, grief/desperation, elation/joy) and eighteen different acoustic variables (such as average fundamental frequency, variability in loudness, and speech rate). In comparing these theoretical predictions to actual research, Scherer found some impressive consistencies but also considerable variation, partly due to great differences in how the studies were conducted and the number studies conducted. Joy/elation is well studied and is associated with higher average frequency (pitch), greater frequency range, greater frequency variability, higher average intensity (loudness), and faster rate. Anger is conveyed by higher frequency and intensity, and greater frequency range and speech rate, at least for "hot" anger. Fear is shown by higher frequency, especially high-frequency energy, and faster speech rate.

Table 11-3
ACOUSTIC CONCOMITANTS OF EMOTIONAL DIMENSIONS

AMPLITUDE VARIATION	Moderate	Pleasantness, Activity, Happiness
	Extreme	Fear
PITCH VARIATION	Moderate	Anger, Boredom, Disgust, Fear
	Extreme	Pleasantness, Activity, Happiness, Surprise
PITCH CONTOUR	Down	Pleasantness, Boredom, Sadness
	Up	Potency, Anger, Fear, Surprise
PITCH LEVEL	Low	Pleasantness, Boredom, Sadness
	High	Activity, Potency, Anger, Fear, Surprise
TEMPO	Slow	Boredom, Disgust, Sadness
	Fast	Pleasantness, Activity, Potency, Anger, Fear, Happiness, Surprise
DURATION (SHAPE)	Round	Potency, Boredom, Disgust, Fear, Sadness
	Sharp	Pleasantness, Activity, Happiness, Surprise
FILTRATION (LACK OF OVERTONES)	Low	Sadness, Pleasantness, Boredom, Happiness
	Moderate	Potency, Activity
	Extreme	Anger, Disgust, Fear, Surprise
TONALITY	Atonal	Disgust
	Tonal—Minor	Anger
	Tonal—Major	Pleasantness, Happiness
RHYTHM	Not rhythmic	Boredom
	Rhythmic	Activity, Fear, Surprise

Sadness (at least the quiet, resigned sort) involves lower average frequency and intensity and has downward-directed contours (Pittam & Scherer, 1993). Research is progressing on the identification of emotions from acoustic variables, so that someday computers may be able to "recognize" vocal emotions almost as well as human listeners do (Banse & Scherer, 1996).

VOCAL CUES, COMPREHENSION, and PERSUASION

In addition to its role in personality and emotional judgments, the voice also seems to play a part in retention and attitude change, primarily studied in public speaking.

For many years, introductory public speaking textbooks have stressed the importance of the ancient canon of *delivery* to the rhetorical situation. Delivery of the speech (rather than content) was perhaps the first area of rhetoric to receive quantitative examination by speech researchers. Almost every study that isolated delivery as a variable showed that delivery did matter. It had positive effects on the amount of information remembered, the amount of attitude change elicited from the audience, and the amount of credibility audience members attributed to the speaker. Some authors maintain that poor delivery decreases one's chances for accomplishing intended goals, but that good delivery, in itself, does not produce desirable changes—it only allows such effects to take place.

Rather than arguing the merits of good delivery, we are only concerned with one aspect of this larger concept. We want to know whether vocal cues alone (excluding gestures, facial expressions, movements, and other elements of delivery) will significantly affect comprehension, attitude change, and speaker credibility.

Typical prescriptions for use of the voice in delivering a public speech include the following:

1. Use variety in volume, rate, pitch, and articulation. The probability of desirable outcomes is less when one uses a constant rate, volume, pitch, and articulation. Being consistently overprecise may be as ineffective as being overly sloppy in articulation. Although it has not been formally studied, it is quite possible that when vocal variety is perceived as rhythmic or patterned, it is no longer variety, and this decreases the probabilities of desirable outcomes.
2. Decisions concerning loud/soft, fast/slow, precise/sloppy, or high/low should be based on what is appropriate for a given audience in a given situation.
3. Excessive nonfluencies are to be avoided.

How are these prescriptions reflected in the research on vocal cues?

Vocal Cues, Comprehension, and Retention

Several studies tend to support the prescriptions for vocal variety in increasing audience comprehension or retention. Woolbert (1920), in perhaps the earliest study of this type, found that large variations of rate, force, pitch, and quality produced high audience retention when compared with a no-variation condition. Glasgow (1952), using prose and poetry, established two conditions for study: "good intonation" and "mono-pitch." Multiple-choice tests, following exposure to these differing vocal samples, showed that mono-pitch decreased comprehension by more than 10 percent for both prose and poetry. However, Diehl, White, and Satz (1961), using similar methods, found several ways of varying pitch that did not significantly affect comprehension scores. Other research suggests that moderately poor vocal quality, pitch patterns, nonfluencies, mispronunciation, and even stuttering do not interfere significantly with comprehension, although listeners generally find these conditions unpleasant (Kibler & Barker, 1972; Klinger, 1959; Utzinger, 1952). Diehl and McDonald (1956) found that simulated breathy and nasal voice qualities significantly interfered with comprehension, but simulated harsh and hoarse voice qualities did not appear to have a very negative effect. All of these studies indicate that listeners are rather adaptable. It probably takes constant and extreme vocal unpleasantries to affect comprehension, and even then the listener may adapt to the extent that he or she retains important information being communicated. Poor vocal qualities probably contribute more to a listener's perception of the speaker's personality or mood than to a decrease in comprehension.

The study of speaking rate by itself yields additional evidence of listener flexibility and the lack of impact on comprehension of seemingly poor voice-related phenomena. The normal speaking rate is between 125 and 190 words per minute. Some researchers feel comprehension begins to decrease once the rate exceeds 200 words per minute, but other experts in speeded speech place the level of significant decline in comprehension at between 250 and 275 words per minute. King and Behnke (1989) point out that time-compressed speech adversely affects comprehensive listening (understanding a message and remembering it for the future) but does not adversely affect short-term listening (forty seconds or less) or interpretive listening (reading between the lines) until very high levels of compression are reached, that is, 60 percent. Obviously, individual ability to process information at rapid rates differs widely. The inescapable conclusion from studies of speech rate, however, is that we can comprehend information at much more rapid rates than we ordinarily have to cope with. In an experiment in which individual listeners were allowed to vary the rates of presentation at will, the average choice was one and one-half times normal speed (Orr, 1968).

VOCAL CUES AND PERSUASION

What is the role of the voice in persuasive situations? It is clear we can communicate various attitudes with our voice alone, for example, friendliness, hostility, superiority, and submissiveness. Then what contribution, if any, do vocal cues make toward changing people's attitudes?

Mehrabian and Williams (1969) conducted a series of studies on the nonverbal correlates of intended and perceived persuasiveness. The following vocal cues seem to be associated with both "increasing intent to persuade and decoded as enhancing the persuasiveness of a communication": more speech volume, higher speech rate, and less halting speech.

This early study has been followed by many studies on the relation of vocal cues to attitude change. Burgoon and her colleagues (1990) concluded, after reviewing this research, that the following vocal cues are associated with greater perceived persuasiveness, credibility, competence, or actual attitude change. (There are probably upper limits to the effective range on each of these variables, so that extremes would produce less, not more, credibility or persuasion.)

- Fluent, nonhesitant speech
- Shorter response latencies (length of pause when speakers switch turns)
- More pitch variation
- Louder voice
- Faster speech (as measured by words per minute or length of pauses)

Of all these cues, faster speech has received the most attention in its relation to the persuasion process (Miller et al., 1976; Street, Brady, & Lee, 1984). Why is fast speech persuasive? Is it because faster speech seems more credible? Considerable evidence indicates that a speaker's perceived credibility is a potent factor in persuasion (Hass, 1981). While this position is the most widely accepted, other explanations have been offered. When listening to a faster-speaking persuader, we may be kept so busy processing the message that we have little chance to develop counterarguments in our heads. Or we may be simply distracted by noticing the faster speech, and this interferes with our ability to focus on the message and develop counterarguments (Woodall & Burgoon, 1983).

The most recent research suggests that when the topic of persuasion is of high personal relevance, the effect of speech rate is less straightforward (Smith & Shaffer, 1991). College students listened to persuasive messages that were either for or against raising the legal drinking age to twenty-one in their state; the speaker used three different rates of speech. For messages favoring raising the drinking age, faster rate increased persuasion, as one might expect, but for messages against raising the age, the reverse was true. Since the participants' initial position was typically against raising the age, this means that faster speech worked when the arguments went against subjects' initial view, probably because subjects had no time to develop counterarguments, but actually backfired when the arguments agreed with their initial opinion.

Perceptions relating to persuasion also stem from the speech styles mentioned earlier that fall on the borderline between verbal and nonverbal behavior, such as hedges and hesitations. Behaviors such as these constitute a "powerless" speech style and produce the impression of low authoritativeness and competence.

At this point you may legitimately ask, "So what?" What if we know the voice's potential for eliciting various responses related to comprehension, attitude change, and speaker credibility? Obviously in real-life situations, there are visual and verbal cues, prior publicity and experiences with the speaker, and a multitude of other interacting factors that greatly reduce the importance of vocal cues. In short, vocal cues do not operate in isolation in human interaction as they do in the experiments reported here. But we do not know what their role is in context; they may be even more influential. Any textbook that focuses only on nonverbal communication distorts reality by not integrating the role of verbal and nonverbal cues. The study of vocal cues also distorts reality. However, it is necessary to understand the component parts so that when we develop methods for studying more complex phenomena, we will know the nature of the parts we are putting together. Burgoon, Birk, and Pfau (1990) have begun some of this "putting together" in a study of credibility and persuasiveness in which vocal cues were measured along with a host of facial and body-movement behaviors. Controlling for other nonverbal behaviors, vocal fluency remained the strongest predictor of judged competence (a dimension of credibility), and was one of the two strongest predictors of judged persuasiveness.

VOCAL CUES and TURN TAKING in CONVERSATIONS

Thus far we have discussed the role of vocal cues in communicating interpersonal attitudes, emotions, and information about oneself. Vocal cues also play an important role in *managing* the interaction. Vocal cues are part of a system of cues that helps us structure our interactions—that is, who speaks, when, to whom, and for how long. Rules for turn taking, or *floor apportionment,* may have as much to do with how a conversation is perceived as does the actual verbal content of the interaction (Duncan, 1973; Wiemann & Knapp, 1975). Most of us can recall instances where turn-taking rules played a significant role in our responses, for example, when a long-winded speaker would not let you get a word in edgewise, when a passive interactant refused to "take the conversational ball" that you offered, when you were confronted with an "interrupter," or those awkward moments when two people started talking simultaneously. Obviously, vocal cues are only some of the signals we use to manage our turn taking; these can be found in other chapters. Only rarely do we explicitly verbalize this information—for example, "OK, Lillian, I'm finished talking. Now it's your turn to talk."

Our use of these signals is mostly unconscious but conforms to definite rules of usage nonetheless. These have been described extensively by Duncan and Fiske (1977) in their analyses of two-person conversations held in a laboratory setting. They found that certain cues were almost invariably present when smooth turn taking took place, five of which were vocal (verbal or nonverbal). No one of these cues seems to be more important than the others; rather it seems that a smooth switch is best predicted by the sheer number of these cues. In other words, redundancy—sending several equivalent-meaning cues simultaneously—promotes smooth regulation of conversation. These cues included the speaker's pitch or a drawl at the end of a unit of speech, the grammatical completion of a unit of speech, and the use of certain routine verbal phrases. The next sections elaborate on these and other turn-regulating behaviors identified in research (Cappella, 1985; Rosenfeld, 1987).

TURN YIELDING

To yield a turn means to signal that you are finished and the other person can start talking. Sometimes we do this by asking a question—causing the pitch to rise at the end of our comment. Another unwritten rule most of us follow is that questions require (or demand) answers. We also can drop our pitch (sometimes with a drawl on the last syllable) when finishing a declarative statement that concludes our monologue. If the cues are not sufficient for the other person to start talking, we may have to add a *trailer* on the end. The trailer may be silence or a form of a filled pause, for example, "ya know," "so, ah," or "or something." The filled pauses reiterate the fact that you are yielding and fill a silence that might otherwise indicate the other's insensitivity to your signals (or your own inability to make them clear!).

TURN REQUESTING

We can also use vocal cues to show others that we want to say something. Although an audible inspiration of breath alone may not be a sufficient cue, it does help to signal turn requesting. The mere act of interrupting or simultaneous talking may signal an impatience to get the speaking turn. Sometimes you can inject vocalizations during normal pausing of the other speaker. These "stutter starts" may be the beginning of a sentence ("I . . . I . . . I . . .") or just vocal buffers ("Ah . . . Er . . . Ah . . ."). Another method for requesting a turn is to assist the other person in finishing quickly. This can be done by increasing the rapidity of one's responses, much like the increased rapidity of the head nods when one is anxious to leave a situation where another person has the floor. Normally, "back-channel" cues, such as "Uh-huh," "Yeah," and "Mm-hmm," are used to encourage the other to continue speaking and to signal attentiveness. However, when these are used rapidly, the message can be "Get finished so I can talk."

TURN MAINTAINING

Sometimes we want to keep the floor. It may be to show our status or to avoid unpleasant feedback, or perhaps it reflects some exaggerated sense of the importance of our own words and ideas. Common vocal cues in these instances may include

1. Increasing volume and rate when turn-requesting cues are sensed
2. Increasing the frequency of filled pauses

3. Decreasing the frequency and duration of silent pauses (Maclay & Osgood, 1959)

Although Lalljee and Cook's (1969) research does not support the use of pauses for control, Rochester (1973) cites several studies that support the following conclusions:

1. More filled pauses and fewer silent pauses are found more often in dialogue than monologue.
2. More filled pauses and fewer silent pauses are *not* found when people want to break off speaking.
3. More filled pauses and fewer silent pauses are more likely when the speaker lacks visual means of controlling the conversation (as on the telephone).

Turn Denying

In some instances, we may want the other person to keep talking—to deny the turn when offered. The back-channel cues noted earlier may keep the other person talking by giving reinforcement for what is being said. The rate with which these are delivered, however, is probably slower than when we are requesting a turn. And, of course, just remaining silent may dramatically communicate a turn denial. Silence and pauses are the subjects of our next section.

We wish to reiterate that conversational regulation is a delicate matter involving a complex coordination of verbal behavior, vocal behavior, gaze, and body movement. As examples, research finds that even if one would predict a turn switch based on words and voice, a switch is very unlikely if the speaker looks away from the listener during the likely switching point or engages in a hand gesture that is maintained or not returned to a resting state.

HESITATIONS, PAUSES, SILENCE, and SPEECH

Spontaneous speech is actually highly fragmented and discontinuous. Goldman-Eisler (1968) says that even when speech is at its most fluent, two-thirds of spoken language comes in chunks of less than six words—strongly suggesting that the concept of fluency in spontaneous speech is an illusion. Pauses range in length from milliseconds to minutes. Pauses are subject to considerable variation based on individual differences, the kind of verbal task, the amount of spontaneity, and the pressures of the particular social situation.

LOCATION OR PLACEMENT OF PAUSES

Pauses are not evenly distributed throughout the speech stream. Goldman–Eisler (1968, p. 13) outlines places where pauses do occur—at both grammatical and nongrammatical junctures.

Grammatical

1. "Natural" punctuation points, for example, the end of a sentence
2. Immediately preceding a conjunction whether (a) coordinating, such as *and, but, neither, therefore,* or (b) subordinating, such as *if, when, while, as, because*
3. Before relative and interrogative pronouns, for example, *who, which, what, why, whose*
4. When a question is direct or implied, for example, "I don't know whether I will"
5. Before all adverbial clauses of time (when), manner (how), and place (where)
6. When complete parenthetical references are made, for example, "You can tell that the house—the one on the corner—is falling into disrepair"

Nongrammatical

1. Where a gap occurs in the middle or at the end of a phrase, for example, "In each of//the cells of the body// . . ."
2. Where a gap occurs between words and phrases repeated, for example, (a) "The question of the//of the economy" and (b) "This attitude is narrower than that//that of many South Africans"
3. Where a gap occurs in the middle of a verbal compound, for example, "We have//taken issue with them and they are//resolved to oppose us"
4. Where the structure of a sentence is disrupted by a reconsideration or a false start, for example, "I think the problem of France is the// what we have to remember about France is . . ."

Analysis of spontaneous speech shows that only 55 percent of the pauses fall into the grammatical category, whereas oral readers of prepared texts are extremely consistent in pausing at clause and sentence junctures.

TYPES OF PAUSES

The two major types of pauses are the unfilled pause (silent) and the filled pause. A filled pause is simply filled with some type of phonation such as "um" or "uh." A variety of sources associate filled pauses with a range of generally undesirable characteristics. Some people associate filled pauses and repetitions with emotional arousal; some feel filled pauses may reduce anxiety but jam cognitive processes. Goldman-Eisler (1961) found, in four studies, that unfilled pausing time was associated with "superior (more concise) stylistic and less probable linguistic formulations" while higher rates of filled pauses were linked to "inferior stylistic achievement (long-winded statement) of greater predictability." Livant (1963) found the time required to solve addition problems was significantly greater when the subject filled his pauses than when he was silent. Several experimenters reached similar conclusions: When speakers fill pauses they also impair their performance. Thus, in a heated discussion you may maintain control of the conversation by filling the pauses, but you may also decrease the quality of your contribution. Too many filled or too many unfilled pauses may receive negative evaluations from listeners (Christenfeld, 1995). Lalljee (1971) found that too many unfilled pauses by the speaker caused listeners to perceive the speaker as anxious, angry, or contemptuous; too many filled pauses evoked perceptions of the speaker as anxious or bored.

Although these studies suggest that filled pauses are generally to be avoided, research also finds that in lecturers their use is correlated with more complex thought processes and use of a larger vocabulary (Schachter, Christenfeld, Ravina, & Bilous, 1991; Schachter, Rauscher, Christenfeld, & Crone, 1994).

Filled pauses show up, interestingly, much more in the speech of men than of women (Hall, 1984). We might think of men as more assertive in general, but Siegman (1987) observes that more filled pauses are usually associated with "cautious and hesitant speech" (p. 398). Perhaps men are more socially uncomfortable than women are. It may be, however, that filled pauses are serving another function altogether—keeping the speaker's turn from being taken over by the other person, which may be of more concern for men.

REASONS WHY PAUSES OCCUR

During the course of spontaneous speech, we are confronted with situations that require decisions as to what to say and what lexical or structural form to put it in. One school of thought relates hesitancy in speech to the uncertainty of predicting the cognitive and lexical activity while speaking. The speaker may be reflecting on decisions about the immediate message or may even be projecting into the past or future—that is, "I don't think she understood what I said earlier" or "If she says no, what do I say then?" Thus, the assumption is that these hesitation pauses are actually delays due to processes taking place in the brain whenever speech ceased to be the automatic vocalization of learned sequences. Goldman-Eisler indeed found that pause time while "interpreting" cartoons was twice as long as while "describing" them. It also was observed that with each succeeding trial (a reduction in spontaneity), there was a decline in pausing. Recent research continues to support the theory that longer onset latencies and a relatively large number of pauses are sometimes due to the complexity of the message being formulated (Greene & Ravizza, 1995).

Another possible explanation for some pausing behavior involves what is described as *disruption* behavior. Instead of representing time for planning, the pause may indicate a disruption due to an emotional state that may have developed from negative feedback or time pressures. These disruptions may take many forms: fears about the subject matter under discussion; desire to impress the listener with verbal and/or intellectual skills; pressure to perform other tasks simultaneously; pressure to produce verbal output immediately; and so on.

RESPONSE LATENCY AND TALKING TIME

Thus far we have considered hesitations and pauses primarily from the speaker's standpoint. Now we will consider the interaction process and the effect of one person's interpersonal timing on another. For many years, Chapple (1949, 1953; Chapple & Sayles, 1961) explored the rhythms of dialogue, that is, the degree of synchrony found in the give and take of conversations. This involved noting who talks, when, and for how long. He developed a standardized interview in which the interviewer alternates "normal" attentive responding with silences and, later, interruptions. As you might suspect, there are many reactions. Some people respond to a nonresponse, or silence, by speeding up; others match the nonresponse; and most try some combination of the two.

Matarazzo's studies (Matarazzo, Wiens, & Saslow, 1965) of interviewing behavior found most latencies of response were between 1 and 2 seconds, with the mean about 1.7 seconds. The interviewer, however, can have considerable influence on the length of pauses. For example, when the interviewer did not respond to a statement by the interviewee, almost 65 percent of the interviewees began to talk again, but the pause was now closer to 4.5 seconds. In the same manner, Matarazzo demonstrated the impact of *response matching*, showing how the interviewer can also control the length of utterance by increasing the length of his own utterances. Figures 11-2 and 11-3 show the results of several experiments involving three fifteen-minute segments of a forty-five-minute interview with the interviewer varying his responses during different periods. As the interviewer extended the length of his responses, there was a corresponding increase in the length of responses from the interviewee. In the same manner, there must be times when pauses beget pauses. The interviewer also can control response duration by head nodding or saying "Mm-hmm" during the interviewee's response, as shown in Figure 11-3. This demonstrates that back-channel responses do indeed encourage a speaker to continue speaking.

Figure 11–2

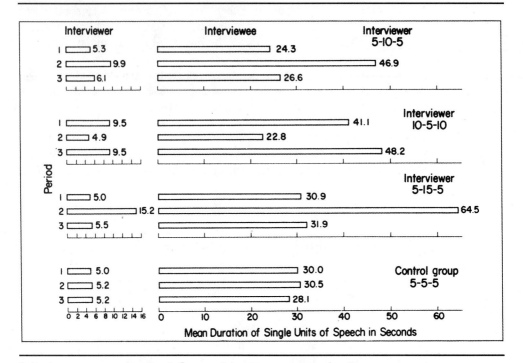

Interviewer response duration influences interviewee response duration.

SILENCE

Most of the hesitations and pauses we have discussed are of relatively short duration. Sometimes silences may be extended. They may be imposed by the nature of the environment, for example, in churches, libraries, courtrooms, or hospitals; they may be imposed for the duration of a given event, for example, at a funeral, during the playing of taps, when praying, or when singing the national anthem; or they may be self-imposed, for example, remaining quiet in the woods to hear other sounds or enjoying with a lover the mutual closeness that silence may bring. Silence can mean virtually anything. Silence is charged with those words that have just been exchanged; words that have been exchanged in the past; words that have not or will not be said but are fantasized; and words that may actually be said in the future. For these reasons, it would be absurd to provide a list of meanings for silence. The meaning of silence, like the meaning of words, can only be deduced after careful analysis of the communicators, subject matter, time, place, culture, and so forth.

Some of the many interpersonal functions served by silence include:

Figure 11–3

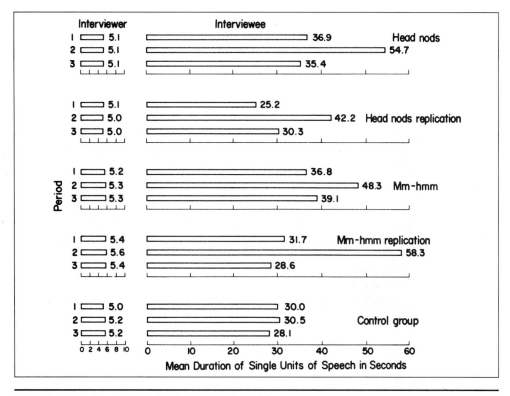

The influence of interviewer head nods and "Mm-hmm" on interviewee response duration.

- Punctuation or accenting, drawing attention to certain words or ideas
- Evaluating, providing judgments of another's behavior, showing favor or disfavor, agreement or disagreement, attacking (for example, not responding to a comment, greeting, or letter)
- Revelation, making something known or hiding something by being silent
- Expression of emotions, the silence of disgust, sadness, fear, anger, or love
- Mental activity, showing thoughtfulness and reflection or ignorance through silence (preceding list from Bruneau, 1973; Jaworski, 1993; Jensen, 1973)

SUMMARY

In the course of reading this chapter, you have been exposed to a considerable number of research studies and a considerable amount of descriptive material.

What do they mean for you as a communicator and as an observer of nonverbal behavior in human interaction?

Generally, this chapter should leave you with the overall impression that vocal cues frequently play a major role in determining responses in human communication situations. You should be quick to challenge the cliché that vocal cues only concern *how* something is said; frequently they are *what* is said. *What* is said might be an attitude ("I like you" or "I'm superior to you"); it might be an emotion; it might be the coordination and management of the conversation; or it might be the presentation of some aspect of your personality, background, or physical features.

As a communicator and observer of the human species, you should also recognize the important role vocal stereotypes play in determining responses. Whether judges are trying to estimate your occupation, sociability, race, degree of introversion, body type, or any of various other qualities about you, they will be very apt to respond to well-learned stereotypes. These stereotypes may not accurately describe you, but they will be influential in the interaction between you and the judge. Almost all the research reviewed in this chapter demonstrated considerable interjudge agreement. So far it is difficult to identify many personality traits that seem to be judged with consistent accuracy. This is partly due, of course, to the imperfect nature of the personality measures. Moreover, a particular person, judging a particular voice, may be very accurate in judging the personality behind that voice. Our judgments of large groups of people are also influential in our judgments of a single person's vocal personality. Although it is not uncommon for a person speaking a dialect other than one's own to be perceived negatively, speakers who try to correct for speech differences and severely violate expectations for their speech may also be perceived negatively.

Accurate judgments (beyond chance) of age, sex, and status from vocal cues alone tend to be fairly consistently reported in the literature. Furthermore, we seem to be able to identify specific speakers from their voice alone; but recently greater attention has been given to spectrographic and electronic means of speaker identification.

Although studies of judgments of emotions from vocal cues have used different methods, different emotions, listeners with differing sensitivity, and speakers with differing abilities for portraying emotions, the results reveal that we can make pretty accurate judgments of emotions and feelings from wordless vocal messages. Obviously, we should consistently remind ourselves that any given individual may vocally express the same emotion differently on different days, in different situations, and with different provoking stimuli.

There is some indication that moderately poor vocal behaviors do not interfere with a listener's comprehension of a message, and that if we use variety in our volume, pitch, and rate we may increase our chances of achieving audience comprehension in public speeches. Unchanging, constant vocal behavior (particularly at the extremes) may be less advantageous in achieving audience comprehension.

Preliminary findings also suggest that the voice may be important in some aspects of persuasion. More fluency, higher rate, more volume, and less halting speech seem related to intent to persuade and perceived persuasiveness. We know that the credibility of the speaker plays an important role in persuasion in some situations. We now know that some decisions concerning credibility (trustworthiness, dynamism, likableness, competency) are made from word-free samples of the voice alone.

Vocal cues also help us manage the give and take of speaking turns. In turn yielding, turn requesting, turn maintaining, and turn denying, we use vocal cues to make our intentions clear.

You should also be more conscious now of the important role of hesitations or pauses in spontaneous speech. Such pauses, ordinarily between one and two seconds long, may be greatly influenced by the other interactant, the topic being discussed, and the nature of the social situation. Pauses may be the overt manifestation of time used to make decisions about what to say and how to say it, or they may represent disruptions in the speech process.

Taken together, these findings show that vocal cues alone can give much information about a speaker, and that our total reaction to another individual is at least somewhat colored by our reactions to these vocal cues. Our *perceptions* of verbal cues combine with other verbal and nonverbal stimuli to mold *conceptions* used as a basis for communicating. Perhaps future study will provide some information on how our responses to our own voices affect self-images and, hence, our communication behavior. First, however, we need to give more attention to voices manifested in naturalistic *interaction*, particularly with partners other than strangers. Some of the preceding results may need modification as we look at spontaneous speech at different stages in relationships.

QUESTIONS for DISCUSSION

1. Consider stereotypes you have about the voice—for example, about high or low voices, fast or slow voices, voices with different accents, and so forth. Discuss what truth you think there is to them, based on as many real examples as you can think of.

2. Analyze the phenomenon of sarcasm in terms of the voice as well as the other cues that might be associated with it. Act out a variety of different comments in a sarcastic manner, and specify the cues that you use.

3. Review the different methods for making voices "content free." Why does the chapter argue that the term *content free* is a misnomer?

4. Theorists argue that some nonverbal channels are easier than others to self-monitor and control. Compare the vocal channel to the face

and body channels. How would you rank these three channels in terms of how easy they are to monitor and control? Why?

REFERENCES and SELECTED BIBLIOGRAPHY

Aboud, F. E., Clement, R., & Taylor, D. M. (1974). Evaluational reactions to discrepancies between social class and language. *Sociometry, 37,* 239–50.

Addington, D. W. (1968). The relationship of selected vocal characteristics to personality perception. *Speech Monographs, 35,* 492–503.

Allport, G., & Cantril, H. (1934). Judging personality from voice. *Journal of Social Psychology, 5,* 37–54.

Anisfeld, M., Bogo, N., & Lambert, W. (1962). Evaluation reactions to accented English speech. *Journal of Abnormal and Social Psychology, 65,* 223–31.

Aries, E. (1987). Gender and communication. In P. Shaver & C. Hendrick (Eds.), *Review of Personality and Social Psychology* (Vol. 7). Newbury Park, CA: Sage.

Banse, R., & Scherer, K. R. (1996). Acoustic profiles in vocal emotion expression. *Journal of Personality and Social Psychology, 70,* 614–36.

Beier, E. G., & Zautra, A. (1972). Identification of vocal communication of emotions across culture. *ERIC,* Ed 056504.

Berry, D. S. (1991). Accuracy in social perception: Contributions of facial and vocal information. *Journal of Personality and Social Psychology, 61,* 298–307.

Berry, D. S. (1992). Vocal types and stereotypes: Joint effects of vocal attractiveness and vocal maturity on person perception. *Journal of Nonverbal Behavior, 16,* 41–54.

Berry, D. S., Hansen, J. S., Landry-Pester, J. C., & Meier, J. A. (1994). Vocal determinants of first impressions of young children. *Journal of Nonverbal Behavior, 18,* 187–97.

Bolt, R., Cooper, F., Davis, E., Jr., Denes, P., Pickett, J., & Stevens, K. (1973). Speaker identification by speech spectrograms. *Journal of the Acoustical Society of America, 54,* 531–37.

Boomer, D. S. (1965). Hesitation and grammatical encoding. *Language and Speech, 8,* 148–58.

Boomer, D. S., & Dittmann, A. T. (1962). Hesitation pauses and juncture pauses in speech. *Language and Speech, 5,* 215–20.

Boomer, D. S., & Dittmann, A. T. (1964). Speech rate, filled pause, and body movements in interviews. *Journal of Nervous and Mental Disease, 139,* 324–27.

Bradford, A., Ferror, D., & Bradford, G. (1974). Evaluation reactions of college students to dialect differences in the English of Mexican-Americans. *Language and Speech, 17,* 255–70.

Bruneau, T. J. (1973). Communicative silences: Forms and functions. *Journal of Communication, 23,* 17–46.

Buck, J. (1968). The effects of Negro and White dialectical variations upon attitudes of college students. *Speech Monographs, 35,* 181–86.

Buller, D. B., & Aune, R. K. (1988). The effects of vocalics and nonverbal sensitivity on compliance: A speech accommodation theory explanation. *Human Communication Research, 14,* 301–32.

Buller, D. B., & Burgoon, J. K. (1986). The effects of vocalics and nonverbal sensitivity on compliance: A replication and extension. *Human Communication Research, 13,* 126–44.

Burgoon, J. K., Birk, T., & Pfau, M. (1990). Nonverbal behaviors, persuasion, and credibility. *Human Communication Research, 17,* 140–69.

Caporael, L. R. (1981). The paralanguage of caregiving: Baby talk to the institutionalized aged. *Journal of Personality and Social Psychology, 40,* 876–84.

Cappella, J. N. (1985). Controlling the floor in conversation. In A. W. Siegman & S. Feldstein (Eds.), *Multichannel integrations of nonverbal behavior.* Hillsdale, NJ: Erlbaum.

Chapple, E. D. (1949). The interaction chronograph: Its evolution and present application. *Personnel, 25,* 295–307.

Chapple, E. D. (1953). The standard experimental (stress) interview as used in interaction chronograph investigations. *Human Organizations, 12,* 23–32.

Chapple, E. D., & Sayles, L. R. (1961). *The measure of management.* New York: Macmillan.

Christenfeld, N. (1995). Does it hurt to say um? *Journal of Nonverbal Behavior, 19,* 171–86.

Cook, M. (1965). Anxiety, speech disturbances, and speech rate. *British Journal of Social and Clinical Psychology, 4,* 1–7.

Corsi, P. (1982). Speaker recognition: A survey. In J. P. Haton (Ed.), *Automatic speech analysis and recognition.* Dordrecht, Holland: Reidel.

Crosby, F., & Nyquist, L. (1977). The female register: An empirical study of Lakoff's hypothesis. *Language in Society, 6,* 313–22.

Davitz, J. R. (1964). *The communication of emotional meaning.* New York: McGraw-Hill.

Davitz, J. R., & Davitz, L. (1959). The communication of feelings by content-free speech. *Journal of Communication, 9,* 6–13.

DePaulo, B. M., & Coleman, L. M. (1986). Talking to children, foreigners, and retarded adults. *Journal of Personality and Social Psychology, 51,* 945–59.

DePaulo, B. M., & Coleman, L. M. (1987). Verbal and nonverbal communication of warmth to children, foreigners, and retarded adults. *Journal of Nonverbal Behavior, 11,* 75–88.

Diehl, C. F., & McDonald, E. T. (1956). Effect of voice quality on communication. *Journal of Speech and Hearing Disorders, 21,* 233–37.

Diehl, C. F., White, R. C., & Satz, P. H. (1961). Pitch change and comprehension. *Speech Monographs, 28,* 65–68.

Dindia, K. (1987). The effects of sex of subject and sex of partner on interruptions. *Human Communication Research, 13,* 345–71.

Dittmann, A. T., & Llewellyn, L. G. (1967). The phonemic clause as a unit of speech decoding. *Journal of Personality and Social Psychology, 6,* 341–49.

Dittmann, A. T., & Llewellyn, L. G. (1969). Body movement and speech rhythm in social conversation. *Journal of Personality and Social Psychology, 11,* 98–106.

Doddington, G. (1985). Speaker recognition: Identifying people by their voices. *Proc. IEEE, 73*, 1651–64.

Duncan, S. (1972). Some signals and rules for taking speaking turns in conversations. *Journal of Personality and Social Psychology, 23*, 283–92.

Duncan, S. (1973). Toward a grammar for dyadic conversation. *Semiotica, 9*, 24–46.

Duncan, S., & Fiske, D. W. (1977). *Face-to-face interaction*. Hillsdale, NJ: Erlbaum.

Ellgring, H., & Scherer, K. R. (1996). Vocal indicators of mood change in depression. *Journal of Nonverbal Behavior, 20*, 83–110.

Ellis, D. S. (1967). Speech and social status in America. *Social Forces, 45*, 431–51.

Erickson, B., Lind, E. A., Johnson, B. C., & O'Barr, W. M. (1978). Speech style and impression-formation in a court setting: The effects of "powerful" and "powerless" speech. *Journal of Experimental Social Psychology, 14*, 266–79.

Fay, P., & Middleton, W. (1940). Judgment of occupation from the voice as transmitted over a public address system. *Sociometry, 3*, 186–91.

Frick, R. W. (1985). Communicating emotion: The role of prosodic features. *Psychological Bulletin, 97*, 412–29.

Gates, G. S. (1927). The role of the auditory element in the interpretation of emotions. *Psychological Bulletin, 24*, 175.

Giles, H. (1971). Ethnocentrism and the evaluation of accented speech. *British Journal of Social and Clinical Psychology, 10*, 187–88.

Giles, H., & Bourhis, R. Y. (1976). Voice and racial categorization in Britain. *Communication Monographs, 43*, 108–14.

Giles, H., Henwood, K., Coupland, N., Harriman, J., & Coupland, J. (1992). Language attitudes and cognitive mediation. *Human Communication Research, 18*, 500–527.

Giles, H., & Powesland, P. F. (1975). *Speech style and social evaluation*. New York: Academic Press.

Gill, M. M. (1994). Accent and stereotypes: Their effect on perceptions of teachers and lecture comprehension. *Journal of Applied Communication Research, 22*, 348–61.

Glasgow, G. M. (1952). A semantic index of vocal pitch. *Speech Monographs, 19*, 64–68.

Goldman-Eisler, F. (1961). A comparative study of two hesitation phenomena. *Language and Speech, 4*, 18–26.

Goldman-Eisler, F. (1968). *Psycholinguistics: Experiments in spontaneous speech*. London & New York: Academic Press.

Greene, J. O., & Ravizza, S. M. (1995). Complexity effects on temporal characteristics of speech. *Human Communication Research, 21*, 390–421.

Grieser, D. L., & Kuhl, P. K. (1988). Maternal speech to infants in a tonal language: Support for universal prosodic features in motherese. *Developmental Psychology, 24*, 14–20.

Hall, J. A. (1980). Voice tone and persuasion. *Journal of Personality and Social Psychology, 38*, 924–34.

Hall, J. A. (1984). *Nonverbal sex differences: Communication accuracy and expressive style*. Baltimore: Johns Hopkins University Press.

Hall, J. A., & Braunwald, K. G. (1981). Gender cues in conversations. *Journal of Personality and Social Psychology, 40*, 99–110.

Hall, J. A., Friedman, H. S., & Harris, M. J. (1984). Nonverbal cues, the Type A behavior pattern, and coronary heart disease. In P. D. Blanck, R. Buck, & R. Rosenthal (Eds.), *Nonverbal communication in the clinical context*. University Park, PA: Pennsylvania State University Press.

Hall, J. A., Roter, D. L., & Katz, N. R. (1987). Task versus socioemotional behaviors in physicians. *Medical Care, 25*, 399–412.

Hall, J. A., Roter, D. L., & Rand, C. S. (1981). Communication of affect between patient and physician. *Journal of Health and Social Behavior, 22*, 18–30.

Harms, L. S. (1961). Listener judgments of status cues in speech. *Quarterly Journal of Speech, 47*, 164–68.

Harrigan, J. A., Gramata, J. F., Luck, K. S., & Margolis, C. (1989). It's how you say it: Physicians' vocal behavior. *Social Science & Medicine, 28*, 87–92.

Harrigan, J. A., Suarez, I., & Hartman, J. S. (1994). Effect of speech errors on observers' judgments of anxious and defensive individuals. *Journal of Research in Personality, 28*, 505–29.

Hart, R. J., & Brown, B. L. (1974). Interpersonal information conveyed by the content and vocal aspects of speech. *Speech Monographs, 41*, 371–80.

Hass, R. G. (1981). Effects of source characteristics on cognitive responses and persuasion. In R. E. Petty, T. M. Ostrom, & T. C. Brock (Eds.), *Cognitive responses in persuasion*. Hillsdale, NJ: Erlbaum.

Hecker, M. H. L. (1971). Speaker recognition: An interpretive survey of the literature. *ASHA Monographs, 16*. Washington: American Speech and Hearing Association.

Hirschman, L. (1994). Female-male differences in conversational interaction. *Language in Society, 23*, 427–42.

Irish, J. T., & Hall, J. A. (1995). Interruptive patterns in medical visits: The effects of role, status, and gender. *Social Science & Medicine, 41*, 873–81.

Japan's feminine falsetto falls right out of favor. *New York Times*. (1995, December 13). pp. A-1, A-4.

Jaworski, A. (1993). *The power of silence: Social and pragmatic perspectives*. Newbury Park, CA: Sage.

Jensen, J. V. (1973). Communicative functions of silence. *ETC, 30*, 249–57.

Kappas, A., Hess, U., & Scherer, K. R. (1991). Voice and emotion. In R. S. Feldman & B. Rimé (Eds.), *Fundamentals of nonverbal behavior*. New York: Cambridge University Press.

Kasl, S. V., & Mahl, G. F. (1965). The relationship of disturbances and hesitations in spontaneous speech to anxiety. *Journal of Personality and Social Psychology, 1*, 425–33.

Kibler, R. J., & Barker, L. L. (1972). Effects of selected levels of misspelling and mispronunciation on comprehension and retention. *Southern Speech Communication Journal, 37*, 361–74.

King, P. E., & Behnke, R. R. (1989). The effect of time-compressed speech on comprehensive, interpretive, and short-term listening. *Human Communication Research, 15*, 428–43.

Klinger, H. N. (1959). The effects of stuttering on audience listening comprehension. Unpublished doctoral dissertation, New York University.

Kramer, C. (1978). Female and male perceptions of female and male speech. *Language and Speech, 20,* 151–61.

Kramer, E. (1963). Judgment of personal characteristics and emotions from nonverbal properties. *Psychological Bulletin, 60,* 408–20.

Kramer, E. (1964). Personality stereotypes in voice: A reconsideration of the data. *Journal of Social Psychology, 62,* 247–51.

Ladefoged, P., & Ladefoged, J. (1980). The ability of listeners to identify voices. *UCLA Working Papers in Phonetics, 49,* 43–51.

Ladefoged, P., & Vanderslice, R. (1967, November). The voiceprint mystique. *Working Papers in Phonetics, 7,* University of California, Los Angeles.

Lakoff, R. (1975). *Language and women's place.* New York: Harper & Row.

Lalljee, M. G. (1971). Disfluencies in normal English speech. Unpublished doctoral dissertation, Oxford University, Oxford.

Lalljee, M. G., & Cook, M. (1969). An experimental investigation of the filled pauses in speech. *Language and Speech, 12,* 24–28.

Lambert, W. E., Frankel, H., & Tucker, G. R. (1966). Judging personality through speech: A French-Canadian example. *Journal of Communication, 16,* 305–21.

Lass, N. J., & Davis, M. (1976). An investigation of speaker height and weight identification. *Journal of the Acoustical Society of America, 60,* 700–3.

Lass, N. J., & Harvey, L. A. (1976). An investigation of speaker photograph identification. *Journal of the Acoustical Society of America, 59,* 1232–36.

Lass, N. J., Hughes, K. R., Bowyer, M. D., Waters, L. T., & Broune, V. T. (1976). Speaker sex identification from voiced, whispered and filtered isolated vowels. *Journal of the Acoustical Society of America, 59,* 675–78.

Levin, S., Hall, J. A., Knight, R. A., & Alpert, M. (1985). Verbal and nonverbal expression of affect in speech of schizophrenic and depressed patients. *Journal of Abnormal Psychology, 94,* 487–97.

Livant, W. P. (1963). Antagonistic functions of verbal pauses: Filled and unfilled pauses in the solution of additions. *Language and Speech, 6,* 1–4.

Maclay, H., & Osgood, C. E. (1959). Hesitation phenomena in spontaneous English speech. *Word, 15,* 19–44.

Mahl, G. F. (1956). Disturbances and silences in the patient's speech in psychotherapy. *Journal of Abnormal and Social Psychology, 53,* 1–15.

Mahl, G. F., & Schulze, G. (1964). Psychological research in the extralinguistic area. In T. Sebeok, A. S. Hayes, & M. C. Bateson (Eds.), *Approaches to semiotics.* The Hague: Mouton.

Marche, T. A., & Peterson, C. (1993). The development and sex-related use of interruption behavior. *Human Communication Research, 19,* 388–408.

Markel, N. N., Meisels, M., & Houck, J. E. (1964). Judging personality from voice quality. *Journal of Abnormal and Social Psychology, 69,* 458–63.

Markel, N. N., Prebor, L. D., & Brandt, J. F. (1972). Biosocial factors in dyadic communication: Sex and speaking intensity. *Journal of Personality and Social Psychology, 23,* 11–13.

Markel, N. N., & Robin, G. L. (1965). The effect of content and sex-of-judge on judgments of personality from voice. *International Journal of Social Psychiatry, 11,* 295–300.

Matarazzo, J. D., Wiens, A. N., & Saslow, G. (1965). Studies in interview speech behavior. In L. Krasner & U. P. Ullman (Eds.), *Research in behavior modification*. New York: Holt, Rinehart & Winston.

McClone, R. E., & Hollien, H. (1963). Vocal pitch characteristics of aged women. *Journal of Speech and Hearing Research, 6*, 164–70.

McGehee, F. (1937). The reliability of the identification of the human voice. *Journal of General Psychology, 17*, 249–71.

Mehrabian, A. (1972a). Nonverbal communication. In J. Cole (Ed.), *Nebraska symposium on motivation 1971*. Lincoln: University of Nebraska Press.

Mehrabian, A. (1972b). *Silent messages*. Belmont, CA: Wadsworth.

Mehrabian, A., & Ferris, S. R. (1967). Inference of attitudes from nonverbal communication in two channels. *Journal of Counseling Psychology, 31*, 248–52.

Mehrabian, A., & Wiener, M. (1967). Decoding of inconsistent communication. *Journal of Personality and Social Psychology, 6*, 109–14.

Mehrabian, A., & Williams, M. (1969). Nonverbal concomitants of perceived and intended persuasiveness. *Journal of Personality and Social Psychology, 13*, 37–58.

Miller, D. T. (1975). The effect of dialect and ethnicity on communicator effectiveness. *Speech Monographs, 42*, 69–74.

Miller, N., Maruyama, G., Beaber, R. J., & Valone, K. (1976). Speed of speech and persuasion. *Journal of Personality and Social Psychology, 34*, 615–24.

Milmoe, S., Rosenthal, R., Blane, H. T., Chafetz, M. E., & Wolf, I. (1967). The doctor's voice: Postdictor of successful referral of alcoholic patients. *Journal of Abnormal Psychology, 72*, 78–84.

Mulac, A. (1976). Assessment and application of the revised speech dialect attitudinal scale. *Communication Monographs, 43*, 238–45.

Mulac, A., Hanley, T. D., & Prigge, D. Y. (1974). Effects of phonological speech foreignness upon three dimensions of attitude of selected American listeners. *Quarterly Journal of Speech, 60*, 411–20.

Mulac, A., Lundell, T. L., & Bradac, J. J. (1986). Male/female language differences and attributional consequences in a public speaking situation: Toward an explanation of the gender-linked language effect. *Communication Monographs, 53*, 115–29.

Mysak, E. D. (1959). Pitch and duration characteristics of older males. *Journal of Speech and Hearing Research, 2*, 46–54.

Newsweek, October 5, 1970, p. 106.

Nohara, M. (1992). Sex differences in interruption: An experimental reevaluation. *Journal of Psycholinguistic Research, 21*, 127–46.

Orr, D. B. (1968). Time compressed speech—A perspective. *Journal of Communication, 18*, 288–92.

Ostwald, P. F. (1961). The sounds of emotional disturbance. *Archives of General Psychiatry, 5*, 587–92.

O'Sullivan, M., Ekman, P., Friesen, W., & Scherer, K. (1985). What you say and how you say it: The contribution of speech content and voice quality to judgments of others. *Journal of Personality and Social Psychology, 48*, 54–62.

Pear, T. H. (1931). *Voice and personality*. London: Chapman & Hall.

Pittam, J. (1994). *Voice in social interaction: An interdisciplinary approach*. Thousand Oaks, CA: Sage.

Pittam, J., & Scherer, K. S. (1993). Vocal expression and communication of emotion. In M. Lewis & J. M. Haviland (Eds.), *Handbook of emotions*. New York: Guilford.

Reich, A., & Duke, J. (1979). Effects of selected vocal disguises upon speaker identification by listening. *Journal of the Acoustical Society of America, 66*, 1023–28.

Reich, A. R., Moll, K. L., & Curtis, J. F. (1976). Effects of selected vocal disguises upon spectrographic speaker identification. *Journal of the Acoustical Society of America, 60*, 919–25.

Rochester, S. R. (1973). The significance of pauses in spontaneous speech. *Journal of Psycholinguistic Research, 2*, 51–81.

Rogers, P. L., Scherer, K. R., & Rosenthal, R. (1971). Content filtering human speech: A simple electronic system. *Behavior Research Methods and Instrumentation, 3*, 16–18.

Rosenfeld, H. M. (1987). Conversational control functions of nonverbal behavior. In A. W. Siegman & S. Feldstein (Eds.), *Nonverbal behavior and communication* (2d ed.). Hillsdale, NJ: Erlbaum.

Rosenthal, R., Hall, J. A., DiMatteo, M. R., Rogers, P. L., & Archer, D. (1979). *Sensitivity to nonverbal communication: The PONS test*. Baltimore: Johns Hopkins University Press.

Rosenthal, R., Vanicelli, M., & Blanck, P. (1984). Speaking to and about patients: Predicting therapists' tone of voice. *Journal of Consulting and Clinical Psychology, 52*, 679–86.

Sachs, J., Lieberman, P., & Erickson, D. (1973). Anatomic and cultural determinants of male and female speech. In R. W. Shuy & R. W. Fasold (Eds.), *Language attitudes: Current trends and prospects*. Washington: Georgetown University Press.

Schachter, S., Christenfeld, N., Ravina, B., & Bilous, F. (1991). Speech disfluency and the structure of knowledge. *Journal of Personality and Social Psychology, 60*, 362–67.

Schachter, S., Rauscher, F., Christenfeld, N., & Crone, K. T. (1994). The vocabularies of academia. *Psychological Science, 5*, 37–41.

Scherer, K. R. (1971). Randomized splicing: A note on a simple technique for masking speech content. *Journal of Experimental Research in Personality, 5*, 155–59.

Scherer, K. R. (1974). Acoustic concomitants of emotional dimensions: Judging affect from synthesized tone sequences. In S. Weitz (Ed.), *Nonverbal communication: Readings with commentary*. New York: Oxford University Press.

Scherer, K. R. (1979). Personality markers in speech. In K. R. Scherer & H. Giles (Eds.), *Social markers in speech*. London: Cambridge University Press.

Scherer, K. R. (1982). Methods of research on vocal communication: Paradigms and parameters. In K. R. Scherer & P. Ekman (Eds.), *Handbook of methods in nonverbal behavior research*. Cambridge, UK: Cambridge University Press.

Scherer, K. R. (1986). Vocal affect expression: A review and a model for future research. *Psychological Bulletin, 99*, 143–65.

Scherer, K. R., Banse, R., Wallbott, H. G., & Goldbeck, T. (1991). Vocal cues in emotion encoding and decoding. *Motivation and Emotion, 15*, 123–48.

Scherer, K. R., Koivumaki, J., & Rosenthal, R. (1972). Minimal cues in the vocal communication of affect: Judging emotions from content-masked speech. *Journal of Psycholinguistic Research, 1*, 269–85.

Siegman, A. W. (1987). The telltale voice: Nonverbal messages of verbal communication. In A. W. Siegman & S. Feldstein (Eds.), *Nonverbal behavior and communication* (2d ed.). Hillsdale, NJ: Erlbaum.

Smith, P. M. (1979). Sex markers in speech. In K. R. Scherer & H. Giles (Eds.), *Social markers in speech*. London: Cambridge University Press.

Smith, S. M., & Shaffer, D. R. (1991). Celerity and cajolery: Rapid speech may promote or inhibit persuasion through its impact on message elaboration. *Personality and Social Psychology Bulletin, 17*, 663–69.

Snow, C. E., & Ferguson, C. A. (Eds.). (1977). *Talking to children*. Cambridge, UK: Cambridge University Press.

Starkweather, J. A. (1961). Vocal communication of personality and human feelings. *Journal of Communication, 11*, 69.

Street, R. L., Jr. (1990). The communicative functions of paralanguage and prosody. In H. Giles & W. P. Robinson (Eds.), *Handbook of language and social psychology*. Chichester, UK: Wiley.

Street, R. L., Jr., Brady, R. M., & Lee, R. (1984). Evaluative responses to communicators: The effects of speech rate, sex, and interaction context. *Western Journal of Speech Communication, 48*, 14–27.

Trager, G. L. (1958). Paralanguage: A first approximation. *Studies in Linguistics, 13*, 1–12.

Turner, L. H., Dindia, K., & Pearson, J. C. (1995). An investigation of female/male verbal behaviors in same-sex and mixed-sex conversations. *Communication Reports, 8*, 86–96.

Utzinger, V. A. (1952). An experimental study of the effects of verbal fluency upon the listener. Unpublished doctoral dissertation, University of Southern California, San Diego.

van Lancker, D., Kreiman, J., & Emmorey, K. (1985). Familiar voice recognition: Patterns and parameters—Recognition of backward voices. *Journal of Phonetics, 13*, 19–38.

Weaver, J. C., & Anderson, R. J. (1973). Voice and personality interrelationships. *Southern Speech Communication Journal, 38*, 262–78.

Weitz, S. (1972). Attitude, voice, and behavior: A repressed affect model of interracial interaction. *Journal of Personality and Social Psychology, 24*, 14–21.

Wiemann, J. M., & Knapp, M. L. (1975). Turn-taking in conversations. *Journal of Communication, 25*, 75–92.

Wilke, W., & Snyder, J. (1941). Attitudes toward American dialects. *Journal of Social Psychology, 14*, 349–62.

Williams, C. E., & Stevens, K. N. (1972). Emotions and speech: Some acoustical correlates. *Journal of the Acoustical Society of America, 52*, 1238–50.

Williams, F. (1970). The psychological correlates of speech characteristics: On sounding 'disadvantaged.' *Journal of Speech and Hearing Research, 13*, 472–88.

Williams, F., & Shamo, G. W. (1972). Regional variations in teacher attitudes toward children's language. *Central States Speech Journal, 23*, 73–77.

Woodall, W. G., & Burgoon, J. K. (1983). Talking fast and changing attitudes: A critique and clarification. *Journal of Nonverbal Behavior, 8*, 126–42.

Woolbert, C. (1920). The effects of various modes of public reading. *Journal of Applied Psychology, 4,* 162–85.

Zebrowitz, L. A., Brownlow, S., & Olson, K. (1992). Baby talk to the babyfaced. *Journal of Nonverbal Behavior, 16,* 143–58.

Zuckerman, M., Amidon, M. D., Biship, S. E., & Pomerantz, S. D. (1982). Face and tone of voice in the communication of deception. *Journal of Personality and Social Psychology, 43,* 347–57.

Zuckerman, M., & Driver, R. E. (1989). What sounds beautiful is good: The vocal attractiveness stereotype. *Journal of Nonverbal Behavior, 13,* 67–82.

Zuckerman, M., Hodgins, H., & Miyake, K. (1990). The vocal attractiveness stereotype: Replication and elaboration. *Journal of Nonverbal Behavior, 14,* 97–112.

Zuckerman, M., & Miyake, K. (1993). The attractive voice: What makes it so? *Journal of Nonverbal Behavior, 17,* 119–35.

Part Five

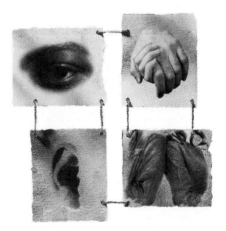

Communicating
Important Messages

Our book concludes with a discussion of how the variety of nonverbal signals discussed earlier in the book combine as communicators pursue critical and familiar outcomes in daily interaction. Specifically, how do nonverbal signals help us effectively communicate intimacy? Power? Involvement? Our identity? Deception?

CHAPTER 12

Putting It All Together: Multisignal Messages

Nothing in nature is isolated; nothing is without connection to the whole.

—Goethe

Try to imagine yourself telling a high-school student how to be a successful college student. Your approach probably would break up the process into its component parts, such as social life (dating, partying); intellectual life (studying, taking notes, relating to teachers); organizational life (what campus and social groups to join); financial life (how to get by with little money); and so on. As informative as your explanations and advice in these separate areas may be, you know it is not enough. You also need to point out how these parts go together to create complex situations; for example, a long-sought date has agreed to go out with you, but it is the night before a big test *and* it's going to cost a lot of money.

In the same way, this book is designed to make you more knowledgeable about human interaction and about nonverbal behavior in particular. The preceding chapters focused on individual parts of the total system: eyes, face, gestures, physical appearance, voice, and so forth. In this chapter, we show how these component parts combine to achieve the various communicative outcomes we seek daily.

To fully understand any process, we continually must look at the isolated parts that make up the system and at how they combine to achieve the system's purpose. Throughout the book, we have made occasional references to multisignal effects—for example, the role of verbal behavior in judgments of physical attractiveness and the close interrelationship of gestures with verbal behavior. Edward T. Hall, who coined the term *proxemics*, which is currently used to identify the study of distance and space, believed one had to consider nineteen different behavioral signals to fully understand proximity in human transactions. In this chapter, we look at how various nonverbal signals help us accomplish the following goals: communicating intimacy; communicating status and power; managing the interaction; communicating our identity; and deceiving others. These outcomes, along with expressing emotion and achieving understanding, seem to cover adequately the most critical interaction goals.[1]

COMMUNICATING INTIMACY

In the late 1960s and early 1970s, Mehrabian (1972) conducted a number of experimental studies of what he called *immediacy*, that is, behaviors that indicate greater closeness or liking. His research identified the following cluster of signals that distinguished a positive evaluation of an interaction partner from a negative one: more forward lean; closer proximity; more eye gaze; more openness of arms and body; more direct body orientation; more touching; more postural relaxation; and more positive facial and vocal expressions. Low frequency of these behaviors, particularly when expected, or the manifestation of opposite behaviors tended to be associated with less intimacy or even disliking.

The work by Mehrabian and others provides a useful perspective for understanding how positive and negative evaluations of interaction partners can be given through clusters of nonverbal signals. In theory, the greater the number of signals activated, the more powerful the message. Immediacy cues can instruct us on what signals to exhibit or look for in our culture during initial interactions with people we do not know very well. They do not tell us much about how people whose relationship has a history (friends, lovers) communicate intimacy. Close relationships to spouses, for example, cannot be accurately judged by the amount of time spent leaning forward with more

---

[1]These goals have been identified in several sources. See the following: Patterson, M. L. (1983). *Nonverbal behavior: A functional perspective*. New York: Springer-Verlag. Siegman, A. W., & Feldstein, S. (Eds.). (1985). *Multichannel integrations of nonverbal behavior*. Hillsdale, NJ: Erlbaum. Burgoon, J. K. (1985). Nonverbal signals. In M. L. Knapp & G. R. Miller (Eds.), *Handbook of interpersonal communication*. Beverly Hills, CA: Sage. The goals of communicating emotion, understanding, and persuasion are not covered in this chapter since it would duplicate too much material in other chapters. The reader is referred especially to Chapters 9 and 11 for the expression of emotion; to Chapters 3 and 7 for achieving understanding; and to Chapter 11 for persuasion cues. A multisignal study of persuasion can be found in Burgoon, J. K., Birk, T., & Pfau, M. (1990). Nonverbal behaviors, persuasion, and credibility. *Human Communication Research, 17*, 140–69.

direct body orientation, in close proximity with more eye gaze, and so on. Because much of this stereotypical immediacy behavior has happened early in the relationship, it needs to be done only on certain occasions once the relationship is mutually agreed to be an intimate one. There are times in established relationships when it is imperative to communicate closeness with utmost clarity, for example, when the relationship has been threatened. At such times, we are likely to see again the cluster of immediacy signals by the partner or partners who wish to offset the threat to the current level of intimacy. Partners in an established close relationship will also use these stereotyped signals of intimacy when they want to communicate their closeness to outsiders. Outsiders will not understand the subtle and sometimes idiosyncratic ways intimates come to communicate their intimacy to one another; they *will* understand close proximity, gazing into one another's eyes, touching, and all the other signals associated with the stereotyped immediacy cluster.

Time is an important limitation of much of the work on nonverbal behavior associated with intimacy, affiliation, or liking. Mehrabian's cluster of immediacy signals is primarily limited to one-time encounters. Ongoing relationships express different levels of intimacy over time, often indicating liking and disliking in quick succession. Clore and his colleagues (1975a, 1975b) realized that the sequencing of immediacy behaviors may have an important influence. They first collected a large number of verbal statements describing nonverbal liking and disliking. These behaviors were limited to a female's actions toward a male. The large number of behavioral descriptions was narrowed by asking people to rate the extent to which the behavior accurately conveyed liking or disliking. Table 12-1 lists (in order) the behaviors rated highest and lowest. An actress then portrayed these behaviors in an interaction with a male, and the interaction was videotaped. To no one's surprise, viewers of the tape felt the warm behaviors would elicit greater liking from the male addressee. The interesting aspect of the studies is what happened when viewers were exposed to a combined tape in which the actress's behavior was initially warm, then turned cold; or when her behavior was initially cold, then turned warm. The reactions to these videotapes were compared with responses to videotapes showing totally warm or totally cold portrayals by the actress. People judged that the man on the videotape would be more attracted to the woman who was cold at first and warm later than he would be to the woman who was warm for the entire interaction. Further, people felt that the woman whose behavior turned from warm to cold was less attractive to the man than the woman who was cold during the entire interaction. Why? It probably has to do with the extent to which the judges felt the male had responsibility for the female's change in behavior. If the man had a part in turning a "cold" female "warm," they felt he could take credit for the change and, thereby, feel better about the interaction.

Whatever nonverbal behavior is used to communicate liking or disliking will inevitably be the result of what *both* interactants do. This perspective prompted Argyle and Dean to propose *equilibrium theory* in 1965. Equilibrium theory maintained that interactants seek an intimacy level that is comfortable

Table 12–1
BEHAVIORS RATED AS WARM AND COLD

Warm Behaviors	Cold Behaviors
Looks into his eyes	Gives a cold stare
Touches his hand	Sneers
Moves toward him	Gives a fake yawn
Smiles frequently	Frowns
Works her eyes from his head to his toes	Moves away from him
Has a happy face	Looks at the ceiling
Smiles with mouth open	Picks her teeth
Grins	Shakes her head negatively
Sits directly facing him	Cleans her fingernails
Nods head affirmatively	Looks away
Puckers her lips	Pouts
Licks her lips	Chain smokes
Raises her eyebrows	Cracks her fingers
Has eyes wide open	Looks around the room
Uses expressive hand gestures while speaking	Picks her hands
Gives fast glances	Plays with her hair's split ends
Stretches	Smells her hair

Adapted from Clore, Wiggins, and Itkin, 1975, Journal of Consulting and Clinical Psychology, 43.

for both of them. Eye gaze, proximity, smiling, and topic intimacy, according to this theory, signal the degree of intimacy. If the nonverbal behavior in one or more of these areas signals an increase or decrease in intimacy, the other interactant will compensate by engaging in behaviors necessary to achieve equilibrium. For example, if a mere acquaintance looked at you too much, stood too close, and talked to you about intimate topics, equilibrium theory would predict that you would increase distance, look away, and try to change the topic to something less intimate. While some attempts to test this theory found support for the predicted compensatory reactions, others found the opposite pattern—reciprocating changes in intimacy rather than offsetting them. This finding led to Patterson's (1976) *arousal model* of interpersonal intimacy, which maintained that gaze, touch, and proximity with another person creates arousal. This arousal state is then labeled either positive or negative. If it is negative (dislike, embarrassment, anxiety), the reaction will be to compensate or offset the behavior. If the arousal state is considered positive (liking, relief, love), the reaction will be matching or reciprocity of behavior. While this theory explained why we sometimes compensate for and sometimes reciprocate the behavior of our partner, it required time-consuming cognitive labeling of another's behavior. In many encounters, these changes are too quick to involve this kind of mental processing. This consideration prompted Cappella and Greene (1982) to posit a *discrepancy arousal theory*. This model suggests that we all have expectations about other people's expressive behavior. Increases and decreases in involvement by one person that violate the other person's expectations will lead to arousal or cognitive activation. Moderate arousal results from moderate discrepancies from expectancies; these are pleasurable and reciprocity ensues. Large discrepancies from what is expected are highly arousing, leading to negative affective response and compensation. Little or no discrepancy from expectations is not arousing, so we would not expect to see any compensatory or reciprocal adjustments made. The bottom line seems to be this:

We tend to reciprocate or match another's nonverbal behavior when it is perceived as generally congruent with our expectations and involvement preferences. We tend to compensate or offset another's nonverbal behavior when it is perceived as a major violation of our expectations and preferences.

Burgoon (1978) and her colleagues proposed and tested a model specifically focused on one element of immediacy—proximity. Since then it has also been used to study and predict involvement in general (Burgoon & Hale, 1988; LePoire & Burgoon, 1994). This model is an important contribution toward our understanding of reciprocal and compensatory reactions, however, because it:

1. Relies on both arousal and cognitive responses
2. Explicates the important role of the communicator's perceived rewardingness

The *violations of expectations model* posits that we all develop expectations for appropriate proximity in conversations from our culture, from our personal experiences, and from our knowledge of specific interactants. When our expectations for proxemic immediacy are met, arousal is not likely to play an important role. When violations occur (too far or too close), arousal is heightened and directs our attention to the nature of the interpersonal relationship. Interpretations then are made that guide one's response. Interpretations vary, according to Burgoon's work, based on the perceptions of the violator's rewardingness. If the person is rewarding (high credibility, high status, positive feedback), the violation of expectations will be perceived more positively than for nonrewarding interactants.

Despite these efforts to identify the processes involved in the exchange of nonverbal intimacy behaviors, some important characteristics of exchange in long-term, established relationships are not accounted for. For example, intimates may engage in matching or reciprocity, but it may not be the exact same kind of behavior, only its equivalent. The extent to which the behavior is equivalent to another is negotiated by the relationship partners. Thus, almost any behavior can communicate intimacy in established relationships if the partners to the relationship agree that it does. Intimates also may respond (either with compensation or reciprocity), but not in the same immediate time frame.

Ironically, intimates in established romantic relationships may exhibit quantitatively less nonverbal behavior typically associated with affection and intimacy than they did in forming the relationship. To establish these relationships usually means a high frequency of hugs, kisses, hand-holding, and so forth; to maintain the relationship, though, it is often the quality of the act, not the frequency, that is important. Perceived sincerity, magnitude of the expression, and perfect timing are examples of qualitative factors. A hand held out to one's partner at just the right moment after a fight may be the equivalent of ten hand-holdings at an earlier point in the relationship. The frequency of nonverbal acts of intimacy becomes important in established relationships when it is necessary to offset a threat to the relationship.

As intimate relationships develop, nonverbal behavior is also likely to change. To communicate a wider range of emotional states, more facial and vocal blends may occur. Sharply defined territories become more permeable. Conventionally performed nonverbal acts gradually give way to performances unique to the couple. The increasing familiarity with auditory, visual, and olfactory signals creates a condition for greater accuracy and efficiency in communicating, but it may also engender an overconfidence leading to decoding problems. More than acquaintances, intimates rely on a variety of nonverbal signals to communicate the same message. Long-term intimates also are subject to the acquisition of one another's facial, postural, and gestural styles, making them look alike. Intimacy brings with it exposure to more personal nonverbal acts and more talk about them. We would also expect more overt evaluations (approval/disapproval) of nonverbal behavior among intimates than among acquaintances (Knapp, 1983).

While the preceding observations focused on interaction partners who are communicating various degrees of intimacy (liking/loving), it also has been noted that we seem to engage in *quasi-courtship behavior* in a variety of settings with a variety of people (Scheflen, 1965). Quasi-courtship behavior has some elements of courting (relating to another for romantic purposes), but these behaviors are qualified by other co-occurring behavior that says, "This is not courtship even though you see some similarities to that behavior." In some cases, quasi-courtship behavior is used to build rapport; in some cases, it is a form of play. The overall message is one of affiliation. Scheflen made sound films of numerous therapeutic encounters, business meetings, and conferences. His content analysis of these films led him to conclude that there were consistent and patterned quasi-courtship behaviors exhibited in these settings. He then developed a set of classifications for such behaviors:

- *Courtship readiness* defines a category of behaviors characterized by constant manifestations of high muscle tone, reduced eye bagginess and jowl sag, lessening of slouch and shoulder hunching, and decreasing belly sag.

Figure 12-1

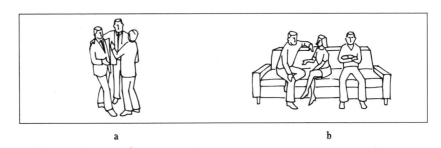

a	b

Positional cues.

- *Preening behavior* is exemplified by such things as stroking of the hair, rearrangement of makeup, glancing in the mirror, rearranging clothes in a sketchy fashion, leaving buttons open, adjusting suit coats, tugging at socks, and readjusting tie knots.
- *Positional cues* were reflected in seating arrangements that suggested, "We're not open to interaction with anyone else." Arms, legs, and torsos were arranged to inhibit others from entering the conversation.
- *Actions of appeal or invitation* included flirtatious glances, gaze holding, rolling of the pelvis, crossing legs to expose a thigh, exhibiting wrist or palm, protruding the breasts, and others.

Others have discussed Scheflen's *positional cues* in terms of who is excluded and who is included. The positioning of arms and legs in Figure 12-1 clearly suggests, "We're not open to others" in *a* and "I'm with you— not him" in *b*.

COMMUNICATING DOMINANCE/STATUS

Tired of feeling weak and unimportant? Want to unlock the secrets of those who have gained authority and power? Want to know how to dominate friends, enemies, and business associates, just about anyone, with a few simple tips?

Sorry, but we can't tell you. You can find this kind of advice in popular books on nonverbal behavior. These books tell you how to arrange your office furniture (put the desk between you and the person you wish to dominate); they tell you to position yourself physically higher than the other, to sit in a relaxed posture (preferably with hands behind head), to take up as much space as possible, and to be sparing with your smiles. One book says it shows dominance to keep your thumbs sticking out when you put your hands in your jacket pockets and to shake hands so that your hand is on top of the other person's hand. The list goes on. We can summarize the research on dominance and nonverbal behavior for you, but there will be no pat answers. The desire for a simple "how to" manual is probably greatest in this area, yet the research is much too complex to warrant any such thing.

Even the basic concepts are complicated. The terms *status, dominance,* and *power* are often used interchangeably, but many authors have noted their ambiguities and have offered many (and sometimes contradictory) definitions (Edinger & Patterson, 1983; Ellyson & Dovido, 1985; Harper, 1985). The concepts are certainly related, but not perfectly: A figurehead leader has status without power, whereas a low-status member of an organization may wield considerable influence by virtue of shrewd insight and social interaction skill. Status often connotes a socially valued quality that a person carries with her or him into different situations, whereas power and dominance are more likely to be situationally defined. But dominance can also be seen as a personality trait (a "dominant" person) in addition to a situational condition. Some researchers would say that any kind of aggressive act is dominant, but for others a behavior is dominant only if it is followed by clear evidence of submission from another individual. In research, many operational definitions have been used to represent these concepts. The following are some illustrations:

- For *status*: attire, occupation, education, military rank, socioeconomic status, role (e.g., professor)
- For *dominance*: initiation of contacts, children's attempts to gain precedence in play, giving orders, boasts, not submitting to others, controlling others' behaviors, attacks
- For *power*: control of resources, expertise, experience, autonomy

Other issues complicate the literature, which we must consider before going further. One is the difference between the *impression* made by a particular nonverbal behavior and the *actual* behavior of people of different degrees of dominance, power, or status. Here are two examples: A nonsmiling face is perceived as dominant (Keating, 1985), and seeing someone touch another raises the viewer's perception of the toucher's dominance (Major & Heslin, 1982). But these findings do not necessarily mean that dominant or high-status people smile less and touch more. The evidence is mixed on this point (Dovidio et al., 1988; Stier & Hall, 1984), and indeed there are situations in which the opposite may be true (Goldstein & Jeffords, 1981; Halberstadt et al., 1988).

This analysis raises the possibility that the nonverbal behaviors used to try to *attain* dominance or status may be different from those used by someone who has already *achieved* this goal (Argyle, 1988; Heslin & Patterson, 1982). Recognition of this possibility may help us sort out contradictory results. For example, research finds that more gazing is perceived as dominant; that people with more dominant personalities, people who initiate speech more in groups, and people who attain higher status in groups are also less likely to be the first to break a mutual glance in face-to-face interaction; and that high-status people gaze more freely at others (Dovidio & Ellyson, 1985; Kleinke, 1986; Lamb, 1981; Rosa & Mazur, 1979; Snyder & Sutker, 1977; Thayer, 1969). Many authors have noted that gaze can carry connotations of threat and coercion, and that high-status individuals (leaders, as one example) enjoy more glances from others (Burroughs, Schulz, & Aubrey, 1973; Exline, 1971).

We might think everything adds up—higher-status people gaze more and receive more gaze—until we also read that dependent people tend to gaze *more*; that people who are gazed at by a confederate feel *less* dominant; that people made to feel dependent gaze *longer* at an experimenter; and that higher-status people gaze *less* at lower-status addressees (Kleinke, 1986; Mehrabian, 1972; Nevill, 1974; Thayer, 1969). These apparent contradictions may be reconciled if we consider that a person of high status or dominance may feel either secure or defensive, and a person of lower status or dominance may be struggling to gain status or may be signaling to more powerful others that he or she is no threat. The nonverbal behaviors, gaze or otherwise, that people use in these different states could differ radically. For example, the person who feels out of control but is striving to gain control might engage in high levels of gaze, while the person who accepts a low-status role might avert his eyes so as to not appear threatening. Gaze, like touch and most other nonverbal behaviors, takes its meanings in a complex way from the situation and other co-occurring nonverbal behaviors.

Fehr and Exline (1987) suggest another intriguing resolution to the contradictory findings on gaze. They suggest that the higher-status person is accorded the privilege of violating norms; in public situations, the norm is not to look much at others, while in more personal, conversational situations, the norm is to look a fair amount at others. Fehr and Exline suggest that the behavior of the higher-status person is to gaze more than the norm in situations involving strangers but to gaze less than the norm in conversations of a more personal nature. This interesting theory has not been fully explored.

Although in this chapter we discuss sex differences in the context of expressing identity, it has often been suggested that the behavior of men and women also might be characterized by dominance and submission (Henley, 1977). Women gaze at others more than men do, and people gaze at women more than they gaze at men (Hall, 1984). In our opinion, these effects defy a simple analogy to status and dominance effects described here, since it is obvious from the results reported previously that one could see the sex difference as suggesting either more or less dominance among women, depending on which result is focused on. Interpretation of sex differences is complicated by the fact that gazing does not connote only degrees of dominance or status; it also connotes degrees of affiliation and openness—traits also associated differently with males and females.

The *visual dominance ratio* (described in the chapter on gaze) is one pattern of nonverbal behavior that has been associated uniquely with status and dominance (Ellyson, Dovidio, & Fehr, 1981; Exline, Ellyson, & Long, 1975). Numerous experiments that defined status, power, and dominance in different ways have found that among white college students, the higher-status person gazes roughly the same amount while listening and while speaking; the lower-status person gazes relatively more while listening than while speaking. When a male and a female interact and one is made to be the expert or accorded higher status, that individual, regardless of sex, will engage in the visual dominance pattern described above. However, if neither is given higher status, the male tends to use the gaze pattern typically used by higher-status people, while the female tends to use the gaze pattern typically used by lower-status people; that is, she will tend to gaze particularly more while listening (Dovidio, Brown, Heltman, Ellyson, & Keating, 1988; Dovidio, Ellyson, Keating, Heltman, & Brown, 1988). This suggests that, other things being equal, females do sometimes portray themselves nonverbally as low in dominance.

Other nonverbal behaviors have been found to be associated with dominance or status. Burgoon et al. (1989) suggest that tension leakage is less likely to occur in a dominant person. More relaxed and expansive postures and a more raised head have been associated with dominance or status; lowered or frowning brows connote dominance; being taller conveys more power, as does physical elevation of one person over another (Keating, 1985; Mehrabian, 1972; Schwartz, Tesser, & Powell, 1982). In a study in which subjects were assigned to teacher and student roles, the teacher pointed and touched the student's possessions more, took more space on the table, talked more, and attempted more interruptions (Leffler, Gillespie, & Conaty, 1982).

Research finds that higher-status people command greater personal space and more territory. People may indeed keep greater distance from their superiors, but it does not necessarily follow that the smallest distances are accorded people lowest in status. Several studies find that people of equal status keep the closest distances, while people accord higher *and* lower status others greater distances (Latta, 1978; Lott & Sommer, 1967).

Touch is often discussed as a status-reflecting and status-attaining variable. Henley (1977) asks us to consider whom we would expect to initiate touching behavior in dyads such as teacher/student, police/accused, doctor/patient, master/slave, supervisor/worker, and so on. Most people tend to see the person of higher status initiating the touch. For a subordinate to initiate (or even reciprocate, sometimes) touching is often perceived as out of line, presumptuous, or an affront. Stier and Hall (1984) summarize evidence that points to these beliefs. However, studies using actual observation of touching in relation to status are quite rare, as seen in the chapter on touch.

In voices, a deep, loud, moderately fast, unaccented, and clearly articulated voice is perceived as more dominant (Burgoon et al., 1989). More talking in groups is a good predictor of status rank (Rosa & Mazur, 1979). Interrupting others in conversation can be a dominance behavior (Henley, 1977; Kollock, Blumstein, & Schwartz, 1985; Leffler et al., 1982; Robinson & Reis, 1989), though this interpretation should not be taken for granted. Interruption is sometimes indicative of a highly involved conversation and is not necessarily a sign of a power struggle in progress (Dindia, 1987; Kennedy & Camden, 1983).

MANAGING the INTERACTION

Most of the time, we do not engage in much conscious thinking about how to greet people, request a speaking turn, show our conversational partner we believe what they were saying, or say goodbye. We do these things to structure the interaction—to regulate the processes of coming together, the back and forth nature of speaking and listening, and departure. As will be noted, however, these acts are also rich in content. When such acts are the subject of conscious reflection, we appreciate the importance of the messages involved.

GREETING BEHAVIOR

Greetings perform a regulatory function by signaling the beginning of interaction. Greetings also convey information about the relationship between the two communicators that helps structure the ensuing dialogue. Verbal and nonverbal behavior during greetings may signal status differences (subordinate/supervisor), degree of intimacy (acquaintance/lover), or a current feeling or attitude (aversiveness/interest). An emotionally charged greeting may reflect one's desired involvement with the other person or it may reflect a long absence of contact. Goffman (1971) proposed an *attenuation rule*, which states that the expansiveness of a greeting with a particular person will gradually subside with continual contact with that person, for example, a coworker at an office. Kendon and Ferber (1973) found the following six stages characterized greetings initiated from a distance.

1. **Sighting, Orientation, and Initiation of the Approach.** A greeting, like any other transaction, requires participation by both interactants. Sometimes both will agree that "acknowledgment" is enough. After mutual recognition, there is an immediate and sustained withdrawal of attention. Goffman (1963) called this common action "civil inattention." When the greeting continues, we move to stage two.
2. **The Distant Salutation.** This is the "official ratification" that a greeting sequence has been initiated and who the participants are. A wave, smile, or call may be used for recognition. Two types of head movements were noted at this point. One, the head toss, is a fairly rapid back and forward tilting motion. Some people tended to lower their head, hold it for a while, and then slowly raise it.
3. **The Head Dip.** Researchers have noted this movement in other contexts as a marker for transitions between activities or shifts in psychological orientation. Interestingly, this movement was not observed by Kendon and Ferber if the greeter did not continue to approach his or her partner.

4. **Approach.** As the greeting parties continued to move toward each other, several behaviors were observed. Gazing behavior probably helped signal that the participants were cleared for talking. An aversion of this gaze was seen just prior to the close salutation stage, however. Grooming behavior and one or both arms moved in front of the body were also observed at this point.

5. **Final Approach.** Now the participants are less than ten feet from each other. Mutual gazing, smiling, and a positioning of the head not seen in the sequence thus far are now seen. The palms of the hands may also be turned toward the other person.

6. **Close Salutation.** As the participants negotiate a standing position, we will hear the more stereotyped, ritualistic verbalizations so characteristic of the greeting ceremony—for example, "Hi, Steve! How ya doin'?" and so on. If the situation calls for body contact (handshakes, embraces, and the like), it will occur at this time. Even though the handshake is very common in the United States, this kind of greeting behavior is not shared in some other cultures.

The specific nature of greetings will vary according to the relationship of the communicators, the setting, and the attendant verbal behavior. Our major concern here is with the nonverbal behavior. The greetings observed by Krivonos and Knapp (1975) were frequently initiated by a vertical or sideways motion of the head accompanied by eye gaze. Smiles, regardless of the degree of acquaintanceship, were also common. Perhaps the smile serves the function of setting a positive, friendly initial mood. The eye gaze signals that the communication channels are open and an obligation to communicate exists. Other eye-related greeting behaviors included winks and the eyebrow flash (discussed in Chapter 2). The hands are often active in the greeting process with salutes, waves, handshakes (Schiffrin, 1974), handslaps, and various emblematic gestures such as the peace sign, the raised fist, or the "thumbs-up" gesture. Hands also may be engaged in grooming, that is, running fingers through one's hair. Touching may take the form of embraces, kisses, or hitting on the hands or arm. The mouth may smile or assume an oval shape, suggesting a possible readiness for talk.

Turn-Taking Behavior

Conversations begin and they are eventually terminated. Between these two points, however, it is necessary to exchange speaking and listening roles, that is, to take turns. Without much awareness of what we are doing, we use body movements, vocalizations, and some verbal behavior that often seem to accomplish this turn taking with surprising efficiency. The act of smoothly exchanging speaking and listening turns is an extension of our discussion of interaction synchrony in Chapter 5. And, since a number of the turn-taking cues are visual, it is understandable that we might have a harder time synchronizing our exchanges during telephone and intercom conversations.

Turn-taking behavior is not just an interesting curiosity of human behavior. We seem to base important judgments about others on how the turns are allocated and how smoothly exchanges are accomplished. Effective turn taking may elicit the perception that you and your partner "really hit it off well" or that your partner is a very competent communicator; ineffective turn taking may prompt evaluations of "rude" (too many interruptions), "dominating" (not enough turn yielding), or "frustrating" (unable to make an important point).

The turn-taking behaviors we are about to outline have generally been derived from analyses of adult, white, and middle- and upper-socioeconomic-class interactants. Some of these behaviors and behavior sequences may not apply to other groups. Blacks, for example, seem to gaze less than whites during interaction (Halberstadt, 1985). Other groups may develop speaking patterns with more unfilled pauses, which may communicate turn yielding to those unfamiliar with the group norm. Children who are learning turn-taking rules engage in behaviors we rarely see in adults, such as tugging at their parent's clothing and hand raising to request a speaking turn.

Speakers engage in two turn-taking behaviors: turn yielding and turn maintaining. *Listeners* also initiate two types of turn-taking behaviors: turn requesting and turn denying. The behaviors associated with these acts are derived from careful analyses of both audio and visual elements enacted at junctures where interactants exchange or maintain the speaking turn (Duncan, 1975; Duncan & Fiske, 1977; Wiemann & Knapp, 1975; Wilson, Wiemann, & Zimmerman, 1984). Any individual behavior associated with speaker or listener intentions will contribute toward a smooth turn exchange, but the greater the number of signals, the greater the chances for a smooth exchange. It should be noted, however, that a familiarity with the rules of interaction is also an important part of effective turn taking. For example, before any specific turn-taking behaviors are observed, most people enter conversations knowing that speaking roles will generally alternate in an ABABAB sequence and that when one person "finishes" an utterance, the other person is generally obligated to "take the conversational ball." Cultures with different conversational rules and specialized systems of communication like sign language will require somewhat different turn-exchange processes.

TURN YIELDING   To "yield" literally means that you are giving up your turn and you expect the other person to start talking. As noted in Figure 7-15, the termination of one's utterance can be communicated with kinesic markers that rise or fall with the speaker's pitch level. Questions are clearly an indication that a speaker yields his or her turn and expects the partner to respond. If it is a rhetorical question that the speaker plans to answer, we probably will see some turn-maintaining cues, but if the listener is eager to get into the conversation, he or she may attempt to answer even the rhetorical question. Vocally, we also can indicate the end of our utterance by a decreased loudness, a slowed tempo, a drawl on the last syllable, or an utterance trailer such as "you know," "or something," or "but, uh." Naturally an extended unfilled pause also is used to signal turn yielding. More often than not, however, the silence becomes awkward, and the speaker adds a trailer onto the utterance. Body movements that have been accompanying the speech may also be terminated; and for example, illustrative gestures come to rest, body tenseness becomes relaxed. Gazing at the other person also will help to signal the end of an utterance. If the listener does not perceive these yielding cues (and gives no turn-denying cues), the speaker may try to convey more explicit cues, such as touching the other, raising and holding the eyebrows in expectation, or saying something like "Well?"

TURN MAINTAINING   If, for some reason, the speaker does not want to yield a speaking turn, several behaviors are likely to be seen. The voice loudness probably will increase as turn-requesting signals are perceived in the listener. Gestures probably will not come to rest at the end of the verbal utterances, creating a gestural equivalent to the filled pause. Filled pauses probably will be increased, while the frequency and duration of silent pauses will be decreased. This minimizes the opportunities for the other person to start speaking without interrupting or speaking simultaneously. Sometimes we see a light touching of the other person by the speaker, which seems to say, "Hold on a little bit longer. I want to make a few more points and then you can talk." This touching is sometimes accompanied by a patting motion as if to soothe the impatient auditor. In some respects, this touch has the effect of the speaker putting his or her hand over the mouth of the auditor—an act not allowed in interpersonal etiquette in this society.

TURN REQUESTING   When we do not have the floor and we want to talk, we may exhibit one or more of the following behaviors. An upraised index finger seems to symbolize an instrument for creating a conversational "hole" in the speaker's stream of words, but it also approximates a familiar, formal turn-requesting signal learned in school—a raised hand. Sometimes this upraised index finger is accompanied by an audible inspiration of breath and a straightening and tightening of posture, signaling the imminence of talk. In some cases, certain self-adaptors classified as "preening" behavior also may signal preparation for a new role. The very act of simultaneous talking (extended interruption) will convey your request for a speaking turn, but to make sure that request is granted, you have to speak louder than your partner, begin gesturing, and look away as if the turn was now yours. When the speaker and listener are well synchronized, the listener will anticipate the speaker's juncture for yielding and will prepare accordingly by getting the rhythm before the other person has stopped talking, much like a musician tapping his or her foot preceding a solo performance. If the requestor's rhythm does not fit the speaker's, we might observe some stutter starts—for example, "I . . . I . . . I wa . . ." Sometimes the turn-requesting mechanism will consist of efforts to speed up the speaker, realizing that the sooner one speaker has his or her say, the sooner the requestor will get his or hers. This same behavior was noted when people were anxious to terminate a conversation (Knapp, Hart, Friedrich, & Shulman, 1973). The most common method for encouraging a speaker to finish quickly is the use of rapid head nods, often accompanied by verbalizations of pseudoagreement such as "yeah," "mm-hmm," and so forth. The requestor hopes the speaker perceives that these comments are being given much too often and do not logically enough follow ideas expressed to be genuine signs of reinforcement.

TURN DENYING   Sometimes we receive turn-yielding cues from the speaker, but we do not want to talk. At such times, we probably will maintain a relaxed listening pose, maintain silence, or gaze intently at something in the surrounding environment. More often, we exhibit behavior that shows our continuing involvement in the content of the speaker's words but denies that we are seeking a turn. This might take the form of smiling, nodding, or shaking the head; completing a sentence started by the speaker; briefly restating what the speaker just said; briefly requesting clarification of the speaker's remarks; or showing approval by appropriately placed "mm-hmm's," "yeah's," or other noises such as the "clicking" sound that suggests "You shouldn't have said that."

The preceding repertoire of turn-taking behaviors, while accurate, may be misleading. The exchange of turns in conversation is a jointly negotiated process and not merely the display of one or more signals associated with yielding, maintaining, requesting or denying. Sometimes it is hard to tell who is playing the speaker role and who is playing the auditor role. For example, before an auditor does any requesting behavior, a speaker may provide signals that essentially project the completion of his or her turn—thereby acknowledging a request before it has occurred. Sometimes an auditor will use gestures that simultaneously signal the desire for a turn, project the type of talk to ensue, and avoid disrupting the speaker's turn.

Many of the actions auditors perform during a speaker's turn are called *back-channel feedback* (Duncan, 1974; Rosenfeld, 1987; Rosenfeld & Hancks, 1980). These listener responses help regulate the flow of information and signal the energy expended in the decoding process. Listener responses can affect the type and amount of information given by the speaker, the length of his or her turn, the clarity of the speaker's content, and the extent to which the speaker communicates in a qualified or specific manner. Back-channel responses by the listener normally occur at the juncture of phonemic clauses by the speaker. The primary nonverbal signals are head nods, but postural changes, smiles, frowns, and eyebrow flashes also occur. Common verbal and vocal back-channel signals include saying "yeah" or "mm-hmm," repeating the speaker's words, asking a clarifying question, or completing a sentence for the speaker. Sometimes the auditor provides these signals prior to the phonemic clause juncture, which may indicate he or she is "ahead" of the speaker. When such signals are "late," it is acknowledgment of what is eing said but may also indicate a lack of full understanding. Once again, though, back-channel cues only affect the speaker if he or she is both motivated to attend to them and motivated to act on the feedback given.

LEAVE-TAKING BEHAVIOR

Having managed our way through the conversation thus far, it is now time to terminate it. Leave-taking seems to serve three valuable functions in daily interaction (Knapp, Hart, Friedrich, & Shulman, 1973). The primary regulatory function is signaling the end of the interaction; that is, immediate physical and/or vocal contact soon will be terminated. Again, specific nonverbal manifestations of these functions will vary with the relationship between the communicators, the preceding dialogue, body position (standing/sitting), the anticipated time of separation, and other factors. Decreasing eye gaze and positioning one's body toward the nearest exit were the two most frequent nonverbal behaviors observed in this study and seem to adequately signal impending absence. Leave-taking rituals also summarize the substance of the discourse sometimes. This is usually accomplished verbally, but a good-night kiss may sufficiently capture the evening's pleasantries to qualify as a summarizer. Finally, departures tend to signal supportiveness. Supportiveness can offset any negativity that might arise from encounter-termination signals, while simultaneously setting a positive mood for the next encounter—that is, our conversation has terminated, but our relationship has not. Nonverbal supportiveness may be found in a smile, a handshake, a touch, head nodding, and forward body lean. Since signaling supportiveness seems so important, we often use the more direct verbal signals—for example, "Thanks for your time. I'm glad we got a chance to talk."

Head nodding and forward lean, of course, serve several simultaneous functions. Rapid head nodding toward the end of a conversation reinforces what the speaker is saying, but it is a rather empty reinforcement since it also signals a desire to terminate the conversation. After all, if there is no apparent disagreement or lack of understanding, the speaker will feel no need to expand on his or her remarks. And, although it is true that people accompany their feelings of liking by sometimes leaning toward another person, it is also necessary to lean forward in order to stand up prior to exiting. So, like words, movements have multiple meanings and serve several functions.

Other nonverbal leave-taking behaviors included looking at one's watch; placing hands on thighs for leverage in getting up (which also signals the other person that the catapult is imminent); gathering one's possessions together in an orderly fashion; and accenting the departure ritual by nonvocal sounds, such as slapping the thighs when rising, stomping the floor with the feet when rising, or tapping a desk or wall with the knuckles or palm. Finally, researchers noticed that nearly all the nonverbal variables studied tended to increase in frequency during the last minute of interaction, with a peak during the fifteen seconds just prior to standing. This increasing activity in at least ten body areas just prior to termination may suggest why we are so frustrated when our partings "fail," that is, when our partner calls us back with "Oh, just one more thing . . ." It means we have to go through the entire process of leave-taking again!

COMMUNICATING OUR IDENTITY

The evening news shows a group of men entering a building. The voice-over tells us that a fugitive sought in several states has been apprehended by the FBI. But did we need to be told? Even without the narrative, we can tell a great deal about the people and what is going on. The bearing and demeanor of some spell out "federal agent." They are likely to be large and burly and to wear their hair conservatively short and keep their faces closely shaved; sunglasses might be worn; and the attire is undistinguished but is likely to be a plain, dark business suit. They do not smile—indeed, they look completely humorless, no-nonsense, erect, and controlling. And what of the suspected criminal? His posture is likely to be slumped, with his head bowed, face wearing a dismal expression, and eyes averted from the camera.

You can imagine variations on this scene. The agents might be seedily dressed undercover agents or uniformed police officers, the suspect might look angry or defiant, and so forth. But the point is the same: Appearance and behavior reveal significant information about people's *identity*—who they are or, in many cases, who they would like to be. Identity includes a person's social attributes, personality, and those attitudes and roles he or she regards as *self-defining*. Thus, being a police officer is a role that is likely to be deeply connected to one's self-definition. Being an arrested suspect is a more fleeting role but could be integral to the self-concept in the case of a career criminal. Sometimes it is hard to tell whether behavior reflects transient emotions and roles or is part of a more enduring identity portrayal. A suspect's slumped or defiant posture could be either one.

People have a great need to convey their identity. In previous chapters, we have talked about ways in which aspects of identity such as age, occupation, culture, and personality are expressed in dress and in nonverbal behaviors. The communication of identity is, in part, self-validating: We confirm for ourselves our sense of who we are. We also show our identities for the benefit of others—both those in our group (to build solidarity and signal belonging) and those not in our group (to emphasize that they are not one of us). Michael Argyle has suggested that people want to know about others' social attributes partly to help maintain the belief that the world is a predictable place. Clues to another's identity also help us decide how to act toward that person. But direct, concrete evidence of others' identities is sometimes hard to come by, so people rely on cues and gestures (Argyle, 1988). In the case of social class, for example, one's way of dressing tells us a great deal, as do other accoutrements, such as cars, pens, briefcases, hairstyles, makeup, and jewelry.

Sometimes people orchestrate these aspects of their material selves to present an "improved version of the self," in the hope of winning acceptance or approval.

One's race and sex are among the most salient aspects of identity, and it is perhaps not surprising that research has turned up nonverbal communication differences associated with these categories. It is, of course, an oversimplification to use these categories as though they are a unitary thing. A woman may express her womanhood differently at home and at the office (let us hope she does!); similarly, a black student in his peer group may send different messages than he would in a predominantly white classroom. We also should be reminded that distinctions such as male/female and black/white are often confounded with other distinctions, such as social status. There can be ambiguity over what factors explain a given nonverbal behavior.

At various places in this book, we have documented differences between the nonverbal behavior of blacks and whites in the United States. Although black/white differences in nonverbal behavior have not been studied extensively, there appear to be differences (at least in the limited populations observed) in style of walking, interpersonal distance, orientation, gaze, and conversational regulators (Burgoon, Buller, & Woodall, 1989; Halberstadt, 1985; Johnson, 1972). Despite anthropologist E. T. Hall's hypothesis (see Chapter 5) that blacks interact more closely than whites, research supports this only among children. Among adults, the distance maintained between interactants is typically greater among blacks, who also exhibit less direct body orientation. As an interesting contradiction to this pattern of reduced sensory involvement, studies have found blacks to touch *more* than whites do. Perhaps the greater amount of touching reestablishes a sense of involvement.

Some research suggests that blacks gaze less than whites during conversation and gaze especially little with authorities (while among whites gaze often increases with authorities). Erickson's analysis of films of conversations pointed to distinct black and white norms for conversational turn taking and signaling attention. Black speakers used less subtle and less frequent cues indicating that a listener should give a "listener response" (a signal that the listener is paying attention). But, as listeners, blacks employed listener responses that were more subtle and likely to be missed by a white speaker. Erickson suggested that these differences could lead to a situation in which a white speaker concludes that a black partner is either not listening or not understanding; the white then repeats himself, which is, in turn, perceived as "talking down" by the black. Although Erickson (1979) found evidence that black subjects displayed bicultural competence (a kind of nonverbal bilingualism), there remained differences in conversational behavior. The potential for serious interracial misunderstanding stemming from these *cultural* differences is obvious and has been noted by educators and others concerned with race relations.

Sex differences in nonverbal behavior also reflect the different identities of males and females. Nonverbal differences appear early in life. "Sex roles" are collections of attitudes, behaviors, and traits deemed desirable for each sex. In our society, the male sex role includes autonomy, assertiveness, dominance, and task orientation; for women, gentleness, empathy, and interpersonal orientation are stereotypical. To a great extent, nonverbal differences correspond to these sex roles. Some nonverbal differences are also quite large, relative to other psychological differences between the sexes. It is as if the *social display* of sexual identity and sex role has special importance. Thus, we may want to show the world not only that we are a man (woman) but also that we behave as a man (woman) is expected to behave. Research (Hall, 1984; Rosenthal & DePaulo, 1979; Vrugt & Kerkstra, 1984) shows that men, compared to women,

- Have less skill in sending and receiving nonverbal cues
- Are less likely to notice (or to be influenced by) people's appearance and nonverbal behavior
- Have less expressive faces and use fewer expressive gestures
- Smile and laugh less
- Look at others less
- Keep greater distances from others

Collectively, women's nonverbal repertoire conveys more openness, sensitivity, and involvement. In some circumstances, these traits may work to women's disadvantage (Henley, 1977). Their smiling may make them appear weak, "too nice," or even insincere; their higher levels of gazing may connote dependency; their nonverbal style may not be distant or threatening enough to win automatic respect in the professional world. On the other hand, it is only because of cultural blinders that we tend to see men's behavior as "normal" and women's behavior as different or in need of correction. Perhaps it makes more sense to focus on *men* as being deficient and handicapped in social relations. "Female" behaviors and skills are a precious commodity in a world that is increasingly violent, competitive, alienated, and mistrustful (Hall, 1987).

As with race and other group differences, it is important to note that male/female nonverbal differences are not invariant. They vary considerably as a function of setting and context, including the affective tone of an interaction (e.g., friendly/unfriendly), other nonverbal behaviors (e.g., interpersonal distance), and the characteristics of the other person involved (Aiello & Aiello, 1977; Hall & Halberstadt, 1986; Putnam & McCallister, 1980). As an example of the latter, people act in the most sex-stereotypic ways when with others of their own sex; in opposite-sex encounters males and females often accommodate to the other's norms. So, for example, gazing is highest between females, lowest between males, and intermediate in male/female interaction (Hall, 1984; Vrugt & Kerkstra, 1984). The fact that nonverbal sex differences vary with these contextual factors demonstrates that we still have a great deal to learn about the origins of male and female behavior.

DECEIVING OTHERS

One of the most common communicative outcomes we seek is to persuade or influence others. In previous chapters, we cited research aimed at identifying the contribution of physical attraction, distance, eye gaze, touch, and vocal cues to perceptions of authoritativeness (expertise) and character (trustworthiness)—the two central factors in the persuasive process. But the area of influence that has captured the attention of the American public and university researchers the most in recent years is the act of lying.

The three major questions driving the research in this area are:

1. What behaviors distinguish liars from truth-tellers?
2. What cognitive/emotional processes are at work during acts of lying?
3. How accurate are we at detecting lies?

The identification of behaviors exhibited by liars has, until recently, focused predominantly on nonverbal signals. It was incorrectly assumed that liars could manipulate their verbal behavior easily but could not or would not control their nonverbal behavior to the same extent, thereby revealing that they were lying. Freud's comment (1959) aptly summarizes this view: "He that has eyes to see and ears to hear may convince himself that no mortal can keep a secret. If his lips are silent, he chatters with his fingertips; betrayal oozes out of him at every pore." Ekman and Friesen (1969) believed it was more likely that clues to deception would be found in the feet/legs area first, the hands next, and the face last. Because the face is more likely to be controlled by the liar, Ekman and Friesen argued that facial clues would be more difficult to detect. Later work by these researchers (1975), however, indicated several ways the face reveals deception, for example, facial morphology, micromomentary expressions, and the timing and location of the expression. For example, smiles made when people were trying to cover up negative feelings with a smile included traces of muscular actions associated with disgust, fear, contempt, or sadness (Ekman, Friesen, & O'Sullivan, 1988).

Attempts to develop a list of behaviors that distinguish liars from truth-tellers always have faced the problem that there are many types of lies (prepared or not, short answer or extended narrative, interrogated or not) and many motivations for lying (protecting oneself or someone else, getting out of an obligation or promise, avoiding conflict). For the lies that comprise most of our daily interaction, people report they are not serious, largely unplanned, and do not make them fearful of being caught (DePaulo, Kashy, Kirkendol, Wyer, & Epstein, 1996). In addition, no behavior occurring during a lie is completely unique to lying (Buck, 1984; Zuckerman, DePaulo, & Rosenthal, 1981). Ekman (1985, p. 90) put it this way: "*There is no sign of deceit itself*—no gesture, facial expression, or muscle twitch that in and of itself means that a person is lying." Still, there have been attempts to examine the behavioral indicators of lying repeatedly found in research regardless of how lying was operationalized (DePaulo, Rosenthal, Rosenkrantz, & Green,

1982; Kraut, 1980; Miller & Stiff, 1993; Zuckerman, DePaulo, & Rosenthal, 1981; Zuckerman & Driver, 1985). When compared with truth-tellers, liars often smile less, have more hesitations during speech, more speech errors, and higher pitch. Verbally, the response length is often shorter; more "allness" terms (all, every, always, none, nobody) are used; and there are fewer specific, verifiable references. More blinking, pupil dilation, and more acts of nervous self-touching are also commonly reported. One behavior that many people expect of liars is a sharp decrease in eye gaze. Although this behavior may occur with some liars in some situations, it has become so stereotypically associated with lying in this culture that liars often consciously seek to control it. Sometimes, of course, the ability to display a normal pattern of gaze is deficient, and the liar ends up staring. And too much gazing signals that something is wrong just as too little gazing does.

If it is difficult to find behaviors that always characterize liars, it is easier to identify behaviors associated with key underlying cognitive and emotional processes that occur during lies (Knapp, Cody, & Reardon, 1987). The two most commonly studied processes are *arousal* and *cognitive difficulty*. Non-pathological liars who know they are lying and who know there will be important consequences if they are caught are likely to experience one or both of these states. Nonverbally, arousal is indicated by pupil dilation, blinking, speech errors, and higher pitch. Verbally, we might see excessive responses (e.g., "WHY DO YOU ALWAYS HAVE TO QUESTION ME?!" in response to a seemingly natural, nonthreatening question), curt replies, or extremes in language usage. Obviously, people experience arousal for reasons other than lying, but aroused truth-tellers and aroused liars do not seem to behave the same. Liars commonly experience cognitive difficulty as well. This may be manifested in speech hesitations, shorter responses, pupil dilation, speech errors, incongruous verbal and nonverbal behavior, and lack of specific references.

Two other processes typical of the lie experience involve attempted control and the display of an affective state. Less spontaneous or what seems to be rehearsed behavior would indicate attempted control. In 1991, military prisoners of war who were forced to make anti-U. S. statements on Iraqi television were reportedly trained prior to their capture to speak and behave in a wooden and mechanical manner to indicate they were lying. Indirect responses to direct questions also may signal an attempt to control one's behavior. The expected affective state is one of anxiety commonly reflected in fidgeting, stammering, and the like. But other emotional states are also relevant to deception. Anger is very common and is reflected in liars' tendencies to be negative and disaffiliative in their responses. Some liars feel enough guilt so that looking away for long periods or covering their eyes with their hands is not uncommon. Duping delight, the pleasure one may experience in deceiving another, occurs sometimes as well and may be reflected in a smile at the wrong time or a sneer of contempt.

The more important the lie is to the deceiver, the easier (paradoxically) it is for others to detect it through nonverbal channels, while, relatively speaking, the reverse is true for the verbal channel. DePaulo and her colleagues (1983, 1988), who have documented this phenomenon repeatedly, propose that this *motivational impairment* is related to the relatively uncontrollable and unconscious nature of the nonverbal channels. Decoders seem to appreciate that some channels are less controllable than others: When they suspect deception, they give more weight to the voice tone than to the face (Zuckerman, Spiegel, DePaulo, & Rosenthal, 1982).

Given what we have said about the nature of liar behavior, it should be no surprise that strangers, without the aid of any mechanical equipment such as a polygraph, are only about 50 to 60 percent accurate in identifying liars. While some may bemoan the fact that our detection rate is not higher, others believe that it would be undesirable to get too accurate at detecting lies. The ability to withhold information and mislead, it is argued, is just as crucial to the well-being of our society as disclosure, openness, and honesty. Overly zealous lie detectors may find lies that are not there and sometimes even elicit lies from people who might not have otherwise intended to lie. It is hoped that these and other issues related to truth and deception will continue to be hotly debated. Only when we stop searching for answers to questions of truth and deception will we be morally bankrupt.

Polygraphs usually have a higher rate of detecting liars (usually reported to be between 80 and 90 percent), but they can be beaten. People whose lies were detected at about 80 percent then received either biofeedback or relaxation training. After they were better able to control their bodily responses, the accuracy of the polygraphs was reduced to about 20 percent (Corcoran, Lewis, & Garver, 1978).

What about people in close relationships? Shouldn't they be more accurate at detecting lies? Since trust is the fundamental reason couples have close relationships, either party is likely to get away with lying quite easily at first. But once suspicion is aroused, those who know a person's behavior best are likely to be the best detectors (Comadena, 1982; McCornack & Parks, 1986). However, it is not uncommon for people in close relationships not to engage in the close monitoring necessary to detect deception. They may not want to confront the lie, or they may be afraid of destroying intimacy if they show distrust by their close monitoring. Effective detectors have been shown to have fewer friends and less satisfying relationships. People can be trained to be better detectors, but, without training, people often use cues for detecting deception that are unrelated to actual liar and truth-teller behavior (deTurck & Miller, 1990; Stiff & Miller, 1986; Zuckerman, Koestner, & Driver, 1981).

A PERSPECTIVE for COMMUNICATORS

Throughout this chapter, we have emphasized the idea that communicators mutually construct their reality. One person's behavior can only be understood as we see how it interacts with the behavior of another interactant. In the abstract, this proposition seems reasonable—one that would not be hard to memorize and recall for a test. But what does the concept of mutual influence mean in practical application to our everyday lives? Two things seem to be particularly important: (1) If the outcome of any transaction is the product of behavior by both interactants, it means we must be very careful in judging and ascribing meaning to the nonverbal behavior of a single person or generalizing a person's behavior with one person to all others. This does not suggest that people do not have a "style" of communicating they may carry from one encounter to another. The parts of that style that are emphasized and deemphasized, however, can change dramatically depending on whom one is interacting with. (2) If the outcome of any transaction is the product of behavior by both interactants, each interactant must share the responsibility for the outcome. This does not mean that in some encounters one person may not take or deserve more of the responsibility than the other. It does mean that we should, perhaps more than we would like to, examine our own verbal and nonverbal behavior to determine how it contributed to the interpersonal outcome. In social life, it is rare indeed for one person to be doing everything "right" and the other to be doing everything "wrong." Unpleasant outcomes are usually constructed mutually.

These notions return us to the self-fulfilling prophecy described in Chapter 1. The most important lessons about social life probably are these: We see what we expect to see, and what we expect of others will likely come true. Through our verbal and nonverbal behavior, we *unconsciously* shape other people into conformance with our expectations, in all areas of life including educational settings (Harris & Rosenthal, 1985), psychological experiments (Rosenthal, 1976), and ordinary interpersonal relationships (Snyder, Tanke, & Berscheid, 1977). Your nonverbal behavior *does* make a difference.

QUESTIONS for DISCUSSION

1. Research tells us men typically smile, laugh, and gaze at their conversational partners far less than women do. Speculate on why and the extent to which it is functional or dysfunctional behavior.
2. What does it mean to collaborate in a lie? Are collaborators and liars subject to similar ethical standards?
3. Identify situations when controlling behavior is likely to be reciprocated and when it is likely to elicit compensatory behavior. Why?
4. Try to imagine a social world in which lies could be detected accurately 99 percent of the time. Describe it.
5. Think of a recent conversation with a friend, lover, or someone you don't know at all—for example, a sales clerk. To what extent are

you willing to take responsibility for your own verbal and nonverbal behavior? For your partner's verbal and nonverbal behavior?

REFERENCES and SELECTED BIBLIOGRAPHY

INTIMACY

Andersen, P. A. (1985). Nonverbal immediacy in interpersonal communication. In A. W. Siegman & S. Feldstein (Eds.), *Multichannel integrations of nonverbal behavior*. Hillsdale, NJ: Erlbaum.

Andersen, P. A., & Andersen, J. F. (1984). The exchange of nonverbal intimacy: A critical review of dyadic models. *Journal of Nonverbal Behavior, 8*, 327–49.

Argyle, M., & Dean, J. (1965). Eye contact, distance and affiliation. *Sociometry, 28*, 289–304.

Burgoon, J. K. (1978). A communication model of personal space violations: Explication and an initial test. *Human Communication Research, 4*, 129–42.

Burgoon, J. K., & Aho, L. (1982). Three field experiments on the effect of violations of conversation distance. *Communication Monographs, 49*, 71–88.

Burgoon, J. K., & Hale, J. L. (1988). Nonverbal expectancy violations: Model elaboration and application to immediacy behaviors. *Communication Monographs, 55*, 58–79.

Burgoon J. K., & Jones, S. B. (1976). Toward a theory of personal space expectations and their violations. *Human Communication Research, 2*, 131–46.

Cappella, J. N. (1981). Mutual influence in expressive behavior: Adult-adult and infant-adult interaction. *Psychological Bulletin, 89*, 101–32.

Cappella, J. N., & Greene, J. O. (1982). A discrepancy-arousal explanation of mutual influence in expressive behavior for adult and infant-adult interaction. *Communication Monographs, 49*, 89–114.

Clore, G. L., Wiggins, N. H., & Itkin, S. (1975a). Gain and loss in attraction: Attributions from nonverbal behavior. *Journal of Personality and Social Psychology, 31*, 706–12.

Clore, G. L., Wiggins, N. H., & Itkin, S. (1975b). Judging attraction from nonverbal behavior: The gain phenomenon. *Journal of Consulting and Clinical Psychology, 43*, 491–97.

DePaulo, B. M., & Coleman, L. M. (1987). Verbal and nonverbal communication of warmth to children, foreigners, and retarded adults. *Journal of Nonverbal Behavior, 11*, 75–88.

Knapp, M. L. (1983). Dyadic relationship development. In J. M. Wiemann & R. P. Harrison (Eds.), *Nonverbal interaction*. Beverly Hills, CA: Sage.

LePoire, B. A. (1991). Orientation and defensive reactions as alternatives to arousal in theories of nonverbal reactions to changes in immediacy. *Southern Communication Journal, 56*, 138–46.

LePoire, B. A., & Burgoon, J. K. (1994). Two contrasting explanations of involvement violations: Expectancy violations theory versus discrepancy arousal theory. *Human Communication Research, 20*, 560–91.

McCormick, N. B., & Jones, A. I. (1989). Gender differences in nonverbal flirtation. *Journal of Sex Education and Therapy, 15*, 271–82.

Mehrabian, A. (1968). Inference of attitude from the posture, orientation, and distance of a communicator. *Journal of Consulting and Clinical Psychology, 32*, 296–308.

Mehrabian, A. (1968). Relationship of attitude to seated posture, orientation, and distance. *Journal of Personality and Social Psychology, 10*, 26–30.

Mehrabian, A. (1968). Significance of posture and position in the communication of attitude and status relationships. *Psychological Bulletin, 71*, 359–72.

Mehrabian, A. (1972). *Nonverbal communication*. Chicago: Aldine.

Noller, P. (1984). *Nonverbal communication and marital interaction*. New York: Pergamon.

Patterson, M. L. (1976). An arousal model of interpersonal intimacy. *Psychological Review, 83*, 235–45.

Patterson, M. L. (1983). *Nonverbal behavior: A functional approach*. New York: Springer-Verlag.

Patterson, M. L. (Ed.). (1985). Nonverbal intimacy and exchange. *Journal of Nonverbal Behavior, 8*, 233–393.

Patterson, M. L., Reidhead, S. M., Gooch, M. V., & Stopka, S. J. (1984). A content-classified bibliography of research on the immediacy behaviors: 1965–82. *Journal of Nonverbal Behavior, 8*, 360–93.

Reece, M., & Whitman, R. (1962). Expressive movements, warmth, and verbal reinforcement. *Journal of Abnormal and Social Psychology, 64*, 234–36.

Rosenfeld, H. M. (1966). Approval-seeking and approval-inducing functions of verbal and nonverbal responses in the dyad. *Journal of Personality and Social Psychology, 4*, 597–605.

Rosenfeld, H. M. (1966). Instrumental affiliative functions of facial and gestural expressions. *Journal of Personality and Social Psychology, 4*, 65–72.

Scheflen, A. E. (1965). Quasi-courtship behavior in psychotherapy. *Psychiatry, 28*, 245–57.

Tickle-Degnen, L., & Rosenthal, R. (1990). The nature of rapport and its nonverbal correlates. *Psychological Inquiry, 1*, 285–93.

DOMINANCE/STATUS

Argyle, M. (1988). *Bodily communication* (2d ed.). London: Methuen.

Berger, J., Rosenholtz, S. J., & Zelditch, M., Jr. (1980). Status organizing processes. *Annual Review of Sociology, 6*, 479–508.

Burgoon, J. K., Buller, D. B., & Woodall, W. G. (1989). *Nonverbal communication: The unspoken dialogue*. New York: Harper & Row.

Burroughs, W., Schulz, W., & Aubrey, S. (1973). Quality of argument, leadership roles and eye contact in three-person leaderless groups. *Journal of Social Psychology, 90*, 89–93.

Dindia, K. (1987). The effects of sex of subject and sex of partner on interruptions. *Human Communication Research, 13,* 345–71.

Dovidio, J. F., Brown, C. E., Heltman, K., Ellyson, S. L., & Keating, C. F. (1988). Power displays between women and men in discussions of gender-linked tasks: A multichannel study. *Journal of Personality and Social Psychology, 55,* 580–87.

Dovidio, J. F., & Ellyson, S. L. (1985). Patterns of visual dominance behavior in humans. In S. L. Ellyson & J. F. Dovidio (Eds.), *Power, dominance, and nonverbal behavior*. New York: Springer-Verlag.

Dovidio, J. F., Ellyson, S. L., Keating, C. F., Heltman, K., & Brown, C. E. (1988). The relationship of social power to visual displays of dominance between men and women. *Journal of Personality and Social Psychology, 54,* 233–42.

Edinger, J. A., & Patterson, M. L. (1983). Nonverbal involvement and social control. *Psychological Bulletin, 93,* 30–56.

Ellyson, S. L., & Dovidio, J. F. (1985). Power, dominance, and nonverbal behavior: Basic concepts and issues. In S. L. Ellyson & J. F. Dovidio (Eds.), *Power, dominance, and nonverbal behavior*. New York: Springer-Verlag.

Ellyson, S. L., Dovidio, J. F., & Fehr, B. J. (1981). Visual behavior and dominance in women and men. In C. Mayo & N. M. Henley (Eds.), *Gender and nonverbal behavior*. New York: Springer-Verlag.

Exline, R. V. (1971). Visual interaction: The glances of power and preference. *Nebraska Symposium on Motivation, 19,* 163–206.

Exline, R. V., Ellyson, S. L., & Long, B. (1975). Visual behavior as an aspect of power relationships. In P. Pliner, L. Kramer, & T. Alloway (Eds.), *Nonverbal communication of aggression*. New York: Plenum.

Fehr, B. J., & Exline, R. V. (1987). Social visual interaction: A conceptual and literature review. In A. W. Siegman & S. Feldstein (Eds.), *Nonverbal behavior and communication* (2d ed.). Hillsdale, NJ: Erlbaum.

Goldstein, A. G., & Jeffords, J. (1981). Status and touching behavior. *Bulletin of the Psychonomic Society, 17,* 79–81.

Halberstadt, A. G., Dovidio, J. F., & Davidson, L. A. (1988, October). Power, gender, and smiling. Paper presented at the meeting of the Society of Experimental Social Psychology.

Halberstadt, A. G., & Saitta, M. B. (1987). Gender, nonverbal behavior, and perceived dominance: A test of the theory. *Journal of Personality and Social Psychology, 53,* 257–72.

Hall, J. A. (1984). *Nonverbal sex differences: Communication accuracy and expressive style*. Baltimore: Johns Hopkins University Press.

Harper, R. G. (1985). Power, dominance, and nonverbal behavior: An overview. In S. L. Ellyson & J. F. Dovidio (Eds.), *Power, dominance, and nonverbal behavior*. New York: Springer-Verlag.

Henley, N. M. (1977). *Body poliltics: Power, sex, and nonverbal communication*. Englewood Cliffs, NJ: Prentice-Hall.

Heslin, R., & Patterson, M. L. (1982). *Nonverbal behavior and social psychology*. New York: Plenum.

Keating, C. F. (1985). Human dominance signals: The primate in us. In S. L. Ellyson & J. F. Dovidio (Eds.), *Power, dominance, and nonverbal behavior*. New York: Springer-Verlag.

Kennedy, C. W., & Camden, C. T. (1983). A new look at interruptions. *Western Journal of Speech Communication, 47,* 45–58.

Kleinke, C. L. (1986). Gaze and eye contact: A research review. *Psychological Bulletin, 100,* 78–100.

Kollock, P., Blumstein, P., & Schwartz, P. (1985). Sex and power in interaction: Conversational privileges and duties. *American Sociological Review, 50,* 34–46.

Lamb, T. A. (1981). Nonverbal and paraverbal control in dyads and triads: Sex or power differences: *Social Psychology Quarterly, 44,* 49–53.

Latta, R. M. (1978). Relation of status incongruence to personal space. *Personality and Social Psychology Bulletin, 4,* 143–46.

Leffler, A., Gillespie, D. L., & Conaty, J. C. (1982). The effects of status differentiation on nonverbal behavior. *Social Psychology Quarterly, 45,* 153–61.

Lott, D. F., & Sommer, R. (1967). Seating arrangements and status. *Journal of Personality and Social Psychology, 7,* 90–95.

Major, B., & Heslin, R. (1982). Perceptions of cross-sex and same-sex nonreciprocal touch: It is better to give than to receive. *Journal of Nonverbal Behavior, 6,* 148–62.

Mehrabian, A. (1972). *Nonverbal communication.* Chicago: Aldine/Atherton.

Nevill, D. (1974). Experimental manipulation of dependency motivation and its effects on eye contact and measures of field dependency. *Journal of Personality and Social Psychology, 29,* 72–79.

Ridgeway, C. L. (1987). Nonverbal behavior, dominance, and the basis of status in task groups. *American Sociological Review, 52,* 683–94.

Ridgeway, C. L., Berger, J., & Smith, L. (1985). Nonverbal cues and status: An expectation states approach. *American Journal of Sociology, 90,* 955–78.

Robinson, L. F., & Reis, H. T. (1989). The effects of interruption, gender, and status on interpersonal perceptions. *Journal of Nonverbal Behavior, 13,* 141–53.

Rosa, E., & Mazur, A. (1979). Incipient status in small groups. *Social Forces, 58,* 18–37.

Schwartz, B., Tesser, A., & Powell, E. (1982). Dominance cues in nonverbal behavior. *Social Psychology Quarterly, 45,* 114–20.

Siegel, S. M., Friedlander, M. L., & Heatherington, L. (1992). Nonverbal relational control in family communication. *Journal of Nonverbal Behavior, 16,* 117–39.

Snyder, R. A., & Sutker, L. W. (1977). The measurement of the construct of dominance and its relation to nonverbal behavior. *Journal of Psychology, 97,* 227–30.

Stier, D. S., & Hall, J. A. (1984). Gender differences in touch: An empirical and theoretical review. *Journal of Personality and Social Psychology, 47,* 440–59.

Thayer, S. (1969). The effect of interpersonal looking duration on dominance judgments. *Journal of Social Psychology, 79,* 285–86.

INTERACTION MANAGEMENT

Ayres, J. (1975). Observers' judgments of audience members' attitudes. *Western Speech, 39,* 40–50.

Baker, C. (1977). Regulators and turn-taking in American sign language discourse.

In L. A. Friedman (Ed.), *On the other hand: New perspectives on American sign language*. New York: Academic Press.

Beattie, G. W. (1980). The skilled art of conversational interaction: Verbal and nonverbal signals in its regulation and management. In W. T. Singleton, P. Spurgeon, & R. B. Stammers (Eds.), *The analysis of social skill*. New York: Plenum.

Beattie, G. W. (1981). The regulation of speaker turns in face-to-face conversation: Some implications for conversation in sound-only communication channels. *Semiotica, 34*, 55–70.

Brunner, L. J. (1979). Smiles can be back channels. *Journal of Personality and Social Psychology, 37*, 728–34.

Cappella, J. N. (1985). Controlling the floor in conversation. In A. W. Siegman & S. Feldstein (Eds.), *Multichannel integrations of nonverbal behavior* (pp. 69–103). Hillsdale, NJ: Erlbaum.

Cegala, D. J., Savage, G. T., Brunner, C. C., & Conrad, A. B. (1982). An elaboration of the meaning of interaction involvement: Toward the development of a theoretical concept. *Communication Monographs, 49*, 229–48.

Coker, D. A., & Burgoon, J. K. (1987). The nature of conversational involvement and nonverbal encoding patterns. *Human Communication Research, 13*, 463–94.

Dickens, M., & Krueger, D. H. (1969). Speakers' accuracy in identifying immediate audience response during a speech. *Speech Teacher, 18*, 303–7.

Duncan, S. D., Jr. (1972). Some signals and rules for taking speaking turns in conversations. *Journal of Personality and Social Psychology, 23*, 283–92.

Duncan, S. D., Jr. (1973). Toward a grammar for dyadic conversation. *Semiotica, 9*, 29–46.

Duncan, S. D., Jr. (1974). On the structure of speaker-auditor interaction during speaking turns. *Language in Society, 2*, 161–80.

Duncan, S. D., Jr. (1975). Interaction units during speaking turns in dyadic face-to-face conversations. In A. Kendon, R. M. Harris, & M. R. Key (Eds.), *Organization of behavior in face-to-face interaction*. Chicago: Aldine.

Duncan, S. D., Jr., & Fiske, D. W. (1977). *Face-to-face interaction: Research, methods, and theory*. Hillsdale, NJ: Erlbaum.

Duncan, S. D., Jr., & Niedereche, G. (1974). On signaling that it's your turn to speak. *Journal of Experimental Social Psychology, 10*, 234–54.

Edinger, J. A., & Patterson, M. L. (1983). Nonverbal involvement and social control. *Psychological Bulletin, 93*, 30–56.

Feldstein, S., & Welkowitz, J. (1987). A chronography of conversation: In defense of an objective approach. In A. W. Siegman & S. Feldstein (Eds.), *Nonverbal behavior and communication* (2d ed.). Hillsdale, NJ: Erlbaum.

Firth, R. W. (1972). Verbal and bodily rituals of greeting and parting. In J. S. Fontaine (Ed.), *Interpretation of ritual*. London: Tavistock.

Gardiner, J. C. (1971). A synthesis of experimental studies of speech communication feedback. *Journal of Communication, 21*, 17–35.

Givens, D. (1978). Greeting a stranger: Some commonly used nonverbal signals of aversiveness. *Semiotica, 22*, 351–67.

Goffman, E. (1963). *Behavior in public places*. New York: Free Press.

Goffman, E. (1971). *Relations in public*. New York: Basic.

Greenbaum, P. E., & Rosenfeld, H. M. (1980). Varieties of touching in greetings: Sequential structure and sex-related differences. *Journal of Nonverbal Behavior, 5*, 13–25.

Halberstadt, A. G. (1985). Race, socioeconomic status, and nonverbal behavior. In A. W. Siegman & S. Feldstein (Eds.), *Multi-channel integrations of nonverbal behavior*. Hillsdale, NJ: Erlbaum.

Karns, C. F. (1969). Speaker behavior to nonverbal aversive stimuli from the audience. *Speech Monographs, 36*, 26–30.

Kendon, A., & Ferber, A. (1973). A description of some human greetings. In R. P. Michael & J. H. Crook (Eds.), *Comparative ecology and behaviour of primates*. London: Academic Press.

Knapp, M. L., Hart, R. P., Friedrich, G. W., & Shulman, G. M. (1973). The rhetoric of goodbye: Verbal and nonverbal correlates of human leave-taking. *Speech Monographs, 40*, 182–98.

Knuf, J. (1990/1991) Greeting and leave-taking: A bibliography of resources for the study of ritualized communication. *Research on Language and Social Interaction, 24*, 405–48.

Kraut, R., & Lewis, S. H. (1984). Some functions of feedback in conversation. In H. E. Sypher & J. L. Applegate (Eds.), *Communication by children and adults*. Beverly Hills, CA: Sage.

Krivonos, P. D., & Knapp, M. L. (1975). Initiating communication: What do you say when you say hello? *Central States Speech Journal, 26*, 115–25.

LaFrance, M., & Mayo, C. (1976). Racial differences in gaze behavior during conversations: Two systematic observational studies. *Journal of Personality and Social Psychology, 33*, 547–52.

Laver, J. (1975). Communication functions of phatic communion. In A. Kendon, R. M. Harris, & M. R. Key (Eds.), *Organization of behavior in face-to-face interaction*. Chicago: Aldine.

Leathers, D. (1979). The informational potential of the nonverbal and verbal components of feedback responses. *Southern Speech Communication Journal, 44*, 331–54.

Norton, R. W., & Pettegrew, L. S. (1979). Attentiveness as a style of communication: A structural analysis. *Communication Monographs, 46*, 13–36.

O'Leary, M. J., & Gallois, C. (1985). The last ten turns: Behavior and sequencing in friends' and strangers' conversational endings. *Journal of Nonverbal Behavior, 9*, 8–27.

Pike, K. (1975). On kinesic triadic relations in turn-taking. *Semiotica, 13*, 389–94.

Rosenfeld, H. M. (1987). Conversational control functions of nonverbal behavior. In A. W. Siegman & S. Feldstein (Eds.), *Nonverbal behavior and communication* (2d ed.). Hillsdale, NJ: Erlbaum.

Rosenfeld, H. M., & Hancks, M. (1980). The nonverbal context of verbal listener responses. In M. R. Key (Ed.), *The relationship of verbal and nonverbal communication*. The Hague: Mouton.

Scheflen, A. E. (1964). Communication and regulation in psychotherapy. *Psychiatry, 27*, 126–36.

Schiffrin, D. (1974). Handwork as ceremony: The case of the handshake. *Semiotica, 12*, 189–202.

Walker, M. B., & Trimboli, C. (1982). Smooth transitions in conversational interactions. *Journal of Social Psychology, 117,* 305–6.

Walker, M. B., & Trimboli, C. (1984). The role of nonverbal signals in co-ordinating speaking turns. *Journal of Language and Social Psychology, 3,* 257–72.

Wiemann, J. M., & Knapp, M. L. (1975). Turn-taking in conversations. *Journal of Communication, 25,* 75–92.

Wilson, T. P., Wiemann, J. M., & Zimmerman, D. H. (1984). Models of turn-taking in conversational interaction. *Journal of Language and Social Psychology, 3,* 159–84.

Yngve, V. H. (1970). On getting a word in edgewise. In M. A. Campbell et al. (Eds.), *Papers from the sixth regional meeting, Chicago Linguistics Society* (pp. 567–78). Chicago: Department of Linguistics, University of Chicago.

IDENTITY

Aiello, J. R., & Aiello, T. D. (1977). Visual interaction at extended distances. *Personality and Social Psychology Bulletin, 3,* 83–86.

Argyle, M. (1988). *Bodily communication* (2d ed.). London: Methuen.

Burgoon, J. K., Buller, D. B., & Woodall, W. G. (1989). *Nonverbal communication: The unspoken dialogue.* New York: Harper & Row.

Dovidio, J. F., Brown, C. E., Heltman, K., Ellyson, S. L., & Keating, C. F. (1988). Power displays between women and men in discussions of gender-linked tasks: A multichannel study. *Journal of Personality and Social Psychology, 55,* 580–87.

Erickson, F. (1979). Talking down: Some cultural sources of miscommunication in interracial interviews. In A. Wolfgang (Ed.), *Nonverbal behavior: Applications and cultural implications.* New York: Academic Press.

Halberstadt, A. G. (1985). Race, socioeconomic status, and nonverbal behavior. In A. W. Siegman & S. Feldstein (Eds.), *Multichannel integrations of nonverbal behavior.* Hillsdale, NJ: Erlbaum.

Hall, J. A. (1984). *Nonverbal sex differences: Communication accuracy and expressive style.* Baltimore: Johns Hopkins University Press.

Hall, J. A. (1987). On explaining gender differences: The case of nonverbal communication. In P. Shaver & C. Hendrick (Eds.), *Review of personality and social psychology* (Vol. 7). Beverly Hills, CA: Sage.

Hall, J. A., & Halberstadt, A. G. (1986). Smiling and gazing. In J. S. Hyde & M. Linn (Eds.), *The psychology of gender: Advances through meta-analysis.* Baltimore: Johns Hopkins University Press.

Henley, N. M. (1977). *Body politics: Power, sex, and nonverbal communication.* Englewood Cliffs, NJ: Prentice-Hall.

Johnson, K. R. (1972). Black kinesics—some nonverbal communication patterns in the black culture. In L. A. Samovar & R. E. Porter (Eds.), *Intercultural communication: A reader.* Belmont, CA: Wadsworth.

Putnam, L. L., & McCallister, L. (1980). Situational effects of task and gender on nonverbal display. In D. Nimmo (Ed.), *Communication yearbook 4.* New Brunswick, NJ: Transaction.

Rosenthal, R., & DePaulo, B. M. (1979). Sex differences in eavesdropping on nonverbal cues. *Journal of Personality and Social Psychology, 37,* 273–85.

Tucker, J. S., & Friedman, H. S. (1993). Sex differences in nonverbal expressiveness: Emotional expression, personality, and impressions. *Journal of Nonverbal Behavior, 17,* 103–17.

Vrugt, A., & Kerkstra, A. (1984). Sex differences in nonverbal communication. *Semiotica, 50,* 1–41.

DECEPTION

Buck, R. (1984). *The communication of emotion.* New York: Guilford.

Comadena, M. E. (1982). Accuracy in detecting deception: Intimate and friendship relationships. In M. Burgoon (Ed.), *Communication yearbook 6.* Newbury Park, CA: Sage.

Corcoran, J. F. T., Lewis, M. D., & Garver, R. B. (1978). Biofeedback—Conditioned galvanic skin response and hypnotic suppression of arousal: A pilot study of their relation to deception. *Journal of Forensic Sciences, 23,* 155–62.

DePaulo, B. M., & Jordan, A. (1982). Age changes in deceiving and detecting deceit. In R. S. Feldman (Ed.), *Development of nonverbal behavior in children* (pp. 149–80). New York: Springer-Verlag.

DePaulo, B. M., Kashy, D. A., Kirkendol, S. E., Wyer, M. M., & Epstein, J. A. (1996). Lying in everyday life. *Journal of Personality and Social Psychology, 70,* 979–95.

DePaulo, B. M., Kirkendol, S. E., Tang, J., & O'Brien, T. P. (1988). The motivational impairment effect in the communication of deception: Replications and extensions. *Journal of Nonverbal Behavior, 12,* 177–202.

DePaulo, B. M., Lanier, K., & Davis, T. (1983). Detecting the deceit of the motivated liar. *Journal of Personality and Social Psychology, 45,* 1096–1103.

DePaulo, B. M., Rosenthal, R., Rosenkrantz, J., & Green, C. R. (1982). Actual and perceived cues to deception: A closer look at speech. *Basic and Applied Social Psychology, 3,* 291–312.

deTurck, M. A., & Miller, G. R. (1990). Training observers to detect deception: Effects of self-monitoring and rehearsal. *Human Communication Research, 16,* 603–20.

Ekman, P. (1985). *Telling lies.* New York: Norton.

Ekman, P., & Friesen, W. V. (1969). Nonverbal leakage and clues to deception. *Psychiatry, 32,* 88–106.

Ekman, P., & Friesen, W. V. (1974). Detecting deception from the body or face. *Journal of Personality and Social Psychology, 29,* 288–98.

Ekman, P., & Friesen, W. V. (1975). *Unmasking the face.* Englewood Cliffs, NJ: Prentice-Hall.

Ekman, P., Friesen, W. V., & O'Sullivan, M. (1988). Smiles when lying. *Journal of Personality and Social Psychology, 54,* 414–20.

Ekman, P., Friesen, W. V., & Scherer, K. R. (1976). Body movement and voice pitch in deceptive interaction. *Semiotica, 16,* 23–27.

Ekman, P., & O'Sullivan, M. (1991). Who can catch a liar? *American Psychologist, 46,* 913–20.

Freud, S. (1959). Fragment of an analysis of a case of hysteria (1905). *Collected papers* (Vol. 3). New York: Basic Books.

Journal of Language and Social Psychology, 13, December, 1994. [Special issue: Interpersonal deception].

Knapp, M. L., Cody, M. J., & Reardon, K. K. (1987). Nonverbal signals. In C. R. Berger & S. H. Chaffee (Eds.), *Handbook of communication science*. Beverly HIlls, CA: Sage.

Knapp, M. L., & Comadena, M. F. (1979). Telling it like it isn't: A review of theory and research on deceptive communications. *Human Communication Research, 5*, 270–85.

Knapp, M. L., Hart, R. P., & Dennis, H. S. (1974). An exploration of deception as a communication construct. *Human Communication Research, 1*, 15–29.

Kraut, R. (1978). Verbal and nonverbal cues in the perception of lying. *Journal of Personality and Social Psychology, 36*, 380–91.

Kraut, R., & Poe, D. (1981). Behavioral roots of person perception: Deception judgments of customs inspectors and laymen. *Journal of Personality and Social Psychology, 39*, 784–98.

Kraut, R. E. (1980). Humans as lie detectors: Some second thoughts. *Journal of Communication, 8*, 209–16.

McCornack, S. A., & Parks, M. R. (1986). Deception detection and relationship development: The other side of trust. In M. L. McLaughlin (Ed.), *Communication yearbook 9*. Newbury Park, CA: Sage.

Miller, G. R., & Stiff, J. B. (1993). *Deceptive Communication*. Newbury Park, CA: Sage.

Stiff, J. B., & Miller, G. R. (1986). Come to think of it . . .: Interrogative probes, deceptive communication, and deception detection. *Human Communication Research, 12*, 339–57.

Zuckerman, M., DePaulo, B. M., & Rosenthal, R. (1981). Verbal and nonverbal communication of deception. In L. Berkowitz (Ed.), *Advances in experimental social psychology* (Vol 14). New York: Academic Press.

Zuckerman, M., & Driver, R. E. (1985). Telling lies: Verbal and nonverbal correlates of deception. In A. W. Siegman & S. Feldstein (Eds.), *Multichannel integrations of nonverbal behavior*. Hillsdale, NJ: Erlbaum.

Zuckerman, M., Koestner, R., & Driver, R. (1981). Beliefs about cues associated with deception. *Journal of Nonverbal Behavior, 6*, 105–14.

Zuckerman, M., Spiegel, N. H., DePaulo, B. M., & Rosenthal, R. (1982). Nonverbal strategies for decoding deception. *Journal of Nonverbal Behavior, 6*, 171–87.

SELF-FULFILLING PROPHECY

Blanck, P. D. (Ed.). (1993). *Interpersonal expectations: Theory, research, and applications*. New York: Cambridge University Press.

Harris, M. J., Milich, R., Johnston, E. M., & Hoover, D. W. (1990). Effects of expectancies on children's social interactions. *Journal of Experimental Social Psychology, 26*, 1–12.

Harris, M. J., & Rosenthal, R. (1985). Mediation of interpersonal expectancy effects: 31 meta-analyses. *Psychological Bulletin, 97,* 363–86.

Rosenthal, R. (1976). *Experimenter effects in behavioral research* (enlarged edition). New York: Irvington.

Snyder, M., Tanke, E. D., & Berscheid, E. (1977). Social perception and interpersonal behavior: On the self-fulfilling nature of social stereotypes. *Journal of Personality and Social Psychology, 35,* 656–66.

Sullins, E. S., Friedman, H. S., & Harris, M. J. (1985). Individual differences in expressive style as a mediator of expectancy communication. *Journal of Nonverbal Behavior, 9,* 229–38.

Word, C. O., Zanna, M. P., & Cooper, J. (1974). The nonverbal mediation of self-fulfilling prophecies in interracial interaction. *Journal of Experimental Social Psychology, 10,* 109–20.

Additional References

CHAPTER 2

Bouchard, T. J., Jr. (1984). Twins reared apart and together: What they tell us about human diversity. In S. W. Fox (Ed.), *Individuality and determinism.* New York: Plenum.

Bouchard, T. J., Jr. (1987). Diversity, development and determinism: A report on identical twins reared apart. In M. Amelang (Ed.), *Proceedings of the meetings of the German Psychological Association—1986,* Heidelberg, Germany.

Boucher, J. D., & Carlson, G. E. (1980). Recognition of facial expression in three cultures. *Journal of Cross-Cultural Psychology, 11,* 263–80.

Ekman, P., & Friesen, W. V. (1969). The repertoire of nonverbal behavior: Categories, origins, usage, and coding. *Semiotica, 1,* 49–98.

Ekman, P., & Friesen, W. V. (1971). Constants across cultures in the face and emotion. *Journal of Personality and Social Psychology, 17,* 124–29.

Field, T. (1982). Individual differences in the expressivity of neonates and young infants. In R. S. Feldman (Ed.). *Development of nonverbal behavior in children.* New York: Springer-Verlag.

Field, T. M., Woodson, R., Greenberg, R., & Cohen, D. (1982). Discrimination and imitation of facial expressions of neonates. *Science, 218,* 179–81.

Fridlund, A. J., Ekman, P., & Oster, H. (1987). Facial expressions of emotion: Review of literature, 1970–1983. In A. W. Siegman & S. Feldstein (Eds.), *Nonverbal behavior and communication.* (2d ed.). Hillsdale, NJ: Erlbaum.

Hahn, M. E., & Simmel, E. C. (Eds.). (1976). *Communicative behavior and evolution.* New York: Academic Press.

Kuhl, P. K., & Meltzoff, A. N. (1982). The bimodal perception of speech in infancy. *Science, 218,* 1138–41.

Lenneberg, E. (1969). *Biological foundations of language.* New York: Wiley.

Miller, E. H. A. (1975). A comparative study of facial expressions of two species of pinnepeds. *Behavior, 53,* 268–84.

Niit, T., & Valsiner, J. (1977). Recognition of facial expressions: An experimental investigation of Ekman's model. *Tartu Riikliku Ulikooli Toimetised: Trudy po Psikhologii, 429,* 85–107.

Pitcairn, T. K., & Eibl-Eibesfeldt, I. (1976). Concerning the evolution of nonverbal communication in man. In M. E. Hahn & E. C. Simmel (Eds.), *Communicative behavior and evolution.* New York: Academic Press.

Plomin, R. (1989). Environment and genes: Determinants of behavior. *American Psychologist, 44,* 105–11.

Thorpe, W. H. (1972). The comparison of vocal communication in animals and man.

In R. Hinde (Ed.), *Non-verbal communication.* Cambridge: Cambridge University Press.

van Hooff, J. A. R. A. M. (1972). A comparitive approach to the phylogeny of laughter and smiling. In R. Hinde (Ed.), *Non-verbal communication.* Cambridge: Cambridge University Press.

van Hooff, J. A. R. A. M. (1973). A structural analysis of the social behaviour of a semi-captive group of chimpanzees. In M. von Cranach & I. Vine (Eds.), *Social communication and movement.* New York: Academic Press.

von Cranach, M., & Vine, I. (Eds.). (1978). *Social communication and movement.* New York: Academic Press.

CHAPTER 6

Frank, M. S., & Gilovich, T. (1988). The dark side of self- and social perception: Black uniforms and aggression in professional sports. *Journal of Personality and Social Psychology, 54,* 74–85.

Lawrence, S. G., & Watson, M. (1991). Getting others to help: The effectiveness of professional uniforms in charitable fund-raising. *Journal of Applied Communication Research, 19,* 170–85.

Sanders, C. (1989). *The body: The art and culture of tattooing.* Philadelphia: Temple University Press.

AUTHOR INDEX

This index refers the reader only to those authors cited in the text itself. Additional references to these authors and others not cited here can be found in the bibliographies at the end of each chapter and the "Additional References" section on page 481.

SUBJECT INDEX